Corrupt Circles

Corrupt Circles

A History of Unbound Graft in Peru

Alfonso W. Quiroz

Woodrow Wilson Center Press
Washington, D.C.

The Johns Hopkins University Press
Baltimore

EDITORIAL OFFICES

Woodrow Wilson Center Press
One Woodrow Wilson Plaza
1300 Pennsylvania Avenue, N.W.
Washington, DC 20004-3027
Telephone 202-691-4029
www.wilsoncenter.org

ORDER FROM

The Johns Hopkins University Press
Hampden Station
P.O. Box 50370
Baltimore, Maryland 21211
Telephone 1-800-537-5487
www.press.jhu.edu/books/

2 4 6 8 9 7 5 3 1

Library of Congress Cataloging-in-Publication Data

Quiroz, Alfonso W.
   Corrupt circles : a history of unbound graft in Peru / Alfonso W. Quiroz. — 1st ed.
    p. cm.
   Includes bibliographical references and index.
   ISBN 978-0-8018-9076-5 (hardback : alk. paper) — ISBN 978-0-8018-9128-1
(pbk. : alk. paper)
    1. Corruption—Peru—History.   2. Political corruption—Peru—History.   I. Title.
JL3429.C6Q57   2008
364.1′3230985—dc22

                                       2008015567

Cover: Vladimiro Montesinos, real chief of the national intelligence service (SIN) under President Alberto Fujimori (1990–2000), counting bribe money in front of a military associate. Detail of a still from a covertly taped video: *Vladivideo* no. 1778–79, November 6, 1999. From *State of Fear,* a Skylight Pictures film, www.skylightpictures.com.

 **Woodrow Wilson
International
Center
for Scholars**

The Woodrow Wilson International Center for Scholars, established by Congress in 1968 and headquartered in Washington, D.C., is a living, national memorial to President Wilson.

The Center is a nonpartisan institution of advanced research, supported by public and private funds, engaged in the study of national and world affairs. The Center establishes and maintains a neutral forum for free, open, and informed dialogue.

The Center's mission is to commemorate the ideals and concerns of Woodrow Wilson by providing a link between the world of ideas and policy, by bringing a broad spectrum of individuals together to discuss important public policy issues, by serving to bridge cultures and viewpoints, and by seeking to find common ground.

Conclusions or opinions expressed in Center publications and programs are those of the authors and speakers and do not necessarily reflect the views of the Center staff, fellows, trustees, advisory groups, or any individuals or organizations that provide financial support to the Center.

The Center is the publisher of *The Wilson Quarterly* and home of Woodrow Wilson Center Press, *dialogue* radio and television, and the monthly newsletter "Centerpoint." For more information about the Center's activities and publications, please visit us on the Web at www.wilsoncenter.org.

For Mónica and my father

In memory of Edith

y la democracia no puede crecer
si la corrupción juega ajedrez

and democracy cannot grow
if corruption plays chess

Juan Luis Guerra
"El costo de la vida," 1992

Contents

Illustrations

Tables and Figure

Tables

Figure

xvii

Preface

A series of rude awakenings triggered the conception and early development of this book. Coming of age in a society where graft is a daily fact of life shaped my ingrained vigilance. Ever since beginning research on a notorious misuse of guano-age public funds more than two decades ago, I have found evidence of multiple corruption scandals that have made a lasting impression in Peruvians' collective memory. Further reflection led me to the realization that graft in Peru was not a sporadic occurrence but a systemic element embedded in the society's core structures. A critical limitation, however, hindered efforts at a comprehensive study of how corruption influenced the historical evolution of a less-developed country. I felt the lack of an adequate analytical framework to evaluate a phenomenon that was widely present but considered by most scholars as anecdotal, intractable, and even useful.

In 1995, I came across new literature on the economic and institutional effects of corruption in developing countries, that was in essence a scholarly and juridical reaction to the rising tide of graft around the world at the time. Almost immediately I was inspired by the new possibilities that it opened to the historical study of corruption. Coincidentally, new scandals uncovered worldwide during the 1990s raised awareness that corruption represented a critical problem for Latin American governments. In Peru, uncontrolled corruption reached an alarming level in the shadow of unchecked presidential power and widespread erosion of democratic institutions. Under such circumstances, specific research for this book started just before the ignominious fall of the Fujimori-Montesinos regime in November 2000, an eye-opening episode that generated abundant historical sources exposing the systemic dimensions of shady schemes and networks of multilayered corruption.

xix

Despite the mounting theoretical advances and empirical evidence, important questions remained largely unanswered. How precisely has corruption affected the historical, political, and economic evolution of less-developed societies? What were its overall costs? Does corruption matter as a historical factor that slows or halts development? Why have some countries curbed corruption, whereas others seem to be inundated by unrestrained and persistent corruption? How to explain the reluctance to conduct a comprehensive, specialized study of the historical impact of corruption in Peru (or, for that matter, in Mexico, Cuba, or other developing countries) in spite of its alleged importance?

These questions are addressed in this book along with pertinent reflections on historical evidence and method. Based on research in multiple archives and libraries, I developed a detailed analysis of key cycles of corruption from the colonial period to the present, each with its own particular characteristics but with certain stubborn similarities. I hope that other studies will continue to improve on the steps taken here toward a better understanding of the causes and consequences of a persistent endemic factor in the life and times of many societies past and present.

Acknowledgments

Without the support and help of generous institutions and individuals, this study could not have been completed. I want to acknowledge first the fellowship and inspirational environment at the Woodrow Wilson International Center for Scholars, Washington, DC (2002–2003); the Fulbright Exchange Program (2003) for funding of research and lecturing in Peru; Baruch College, City University of New York (CUNY), for a sabbatical leave and continuous academic support; and the Professional Staff Congress-CUNY for research awards that allowed preliminary and complementary fieldwork.

The Centro de Investigaciones of the Universidad del Pacífico in Lima proved a true oasis for research and writing. The facilities and services of various archives and libraries are deeply appreciated: the New York Public Library and Newman Library of Baruch College in New York; Library of Congress and U.S. National Archives in Washington, DC, and College Park, Maryland; John Carter Brown Library, Providence, Rhode Island; British Library and National Archives of the United Kingdom in London and Kew; Archives du Ministère des Affaires Étrangères in Paris; Archivo General del Ministerio de Asuntos Exteriores, Archivo Histórico Nacional, Biblioteca Nacional, Biblioteca del Palacio Real, and Real Academia de la Historia in Madrid; Archivo General de Indias in Seville; and Archivo General de la Nación, Archivo del Ministerio de Relaciones Exteriores, Archivo de la Corte Suprema de Justicia, and Biblioteca Nacional in Lima. Various seminars, lectures, and conferences at Columbia University, George Washington University, Harvard University, Johns Hopkins University School of Advanced International Studies, Princeton University, Universidad Católica-Instituto Riva Agüero, and Universidad del Pacífico allowed the presentation of my research and refinement of ideas. My students in the doctoral program in history, CUNY Graduate Center, particularly those who took my colloquium on the history of corruption and institutions in Latin America, as well as my colleagues and students at Baruch College, contributed with their sharp questions and thoughts.

I have also contracted many debts of gratitude with colleagues, friends, family, and professionals who warmly helped and encouraged my research. Felipe Portocarrero Suárez has been a true friend and invaluable supporter in academic endeavors. Peter Klarén, Cynthia McClintock, and Rory Miller read the entire manuscript, provided expert comments that contributed to its overall improvement, and gracefully untangled and corrected mistakes in argument and facts. Likewise, Kenneth Andrien, Kendall Brown, Herbert Klein, and Kris Lane made helpful suggestions pertinent to colonial history. I assume sole responsibility for the end result. In New York, Stanley Buder and Margaret Crahan provided ready advice, and my daughter Daniela, understanding. In Lima, Francesca Denegri, Antonio and Luis González Norris, Scarlett O'Phelan, Patricio Ricketts, José de la Puente Brunke, and Antonio Zapata made things so much easier. Conversations with Julio Castro, Gustavo Gorriti, Luis Paredes Stagnaro, and Héctor Vargas Haya aided in my orientation. For dedicated and priceless research assistance in Peru, I thank Juan Fuentes, and, for her bright and gracious aid as a Woodrow Wilson Center intern, Molly Marie Hueller. My deep gratitude is also extended to several people who allowed access to key documents and sources but preferred to remain anonymous.

With loving company and spirit-lifting enthusiasm, Mónica Ricketts contributed immensely to bringing this project to port. She wholeheartedly read and commented on the entire manuscript and offered key insights from her own research. My father, Alfonso Quiroz Muñoz, continued to inspire with his example and kind words. I remain truly grateful to him and to the happy memories my mother passed on.

Corrupt Circles

Introduction

Corruption, History, and Development

Countless people have raised their voices in the past against the abuse and corruption of power for the benefit of a few at the expense of the greater public interest. Historians have struggled to interpret those distant pleas and thorny issues. In the history of the less-developed parts of the world, the ubiquitous corruption of public administrations has been commonly disregarded as a cultural constant or inevitable institutional legacy. Neglect and skepticism have shrouded historical evidence central to the reinterpretation of often lonely reformist battles against damaging corrupt practices.

This study analyzes the historical significance of corruption in a country, Peru, paradigmatically exposed to corruption's deleterious spell. The efforts, writings, and careers of those who opposed successive waves of unrestricted, systematic corruption provide the guiding threads to detect cycles and unravel causes and consequences of corrupted governance since colonial times. Many generations of corrupt networks, endemic violation of ineffective rules, and international interconnections emerge as factors linking corrupt practices in the public and private spheres. Economic and institutional costs of corruption are evaluated over time and against the backdrop of an impoverished population. The most recent and profusely documented cycle of corruption in Peru, ending in the year 2000, is compared to previous phases of unchecked corruption.

This multifaceted and long-term analysis aims primarily to determine the most salient connections between key cycles of corruption and frustrated development. This approach is based on the notion that corruption matters in explaining underdevelopment, and that controlling the systemic or institutional roots of corruption enhances the possibilities for overall development. Since corruption is enmeshed in complex and broad development

1

processes, it is useful for the sake of analytical clarity to focus on the political and economic dimensions of corruption. Thus, for the purposes of this work, corruption is understood as the misuse of political-bureaucratic power by cliques of public officials, colluding with other self-seeking interests, to obtain economic or political gain inimical to societal development objectives, through the misappropriation of public resources and the distortion of policies and institutions.[1]

Corruption is truly a wide and varied phenomenon, engulfing public and private activities. It is not just the coarse plunder of public funds by corrupt officials as is commonly assumed. It involves bribe giving and taking, misappropriation and misallocation of public funds and procurement expenditures, interested misguidance of policies, financial and political scandals, electoral fraud, and other administrative transgressions (such as the illegal favor-seeking financing of political parties) that arouse reactive public perceptions. Throughout the text the reader will sense the wide spectrum of cases and modes of corruption always in reference to the systemic, antidevelopment core of corrupt activities: abuse of public resources for the benefit of a few individuals or groups at the cost of general public and institutional progress.

Less-developed systems cope with the interrelated quandaries of how to allow and promote growth, devise and enforce constitutions favoring sta-

---

1. A vibrant debate over the definition of the term "corruption" continues, although earlier, dated notions—expressed in the compilations by Arnold Heidenheimer, ed., *Political Corruption: Readings in Comparative Analysis* (New York: Holt, Rinehart, and Winston, 1970), followed most recently by Heidenheimer and Michael Johnston, eds., *Political Corruption: Concepts and Contexts* (New Brunswick, NJ: Transaction Publishers, 2002), and notably those articulated by Jacob van Klaveren, Nathaniel Leff, David Bayley, Samuel Huntington, and J. S. Nye—have been superseded. For theoretical and conceptual treatments of corruption, refer to Susan Rose-Ackerman, *Corruption and Government: Causes, Consequences, and Reform* (New York: Cambridge University Press, 1999); and Donatella della Porta and Alberto Vannucci, *Corrupt Exchanges: Actors, Resources, and Mechanisms of Political Corruption* (Hawthorne, NY: Aldine de Gruyter, 1999). On key connections between corruption and development, see Michael Johnston, "Corruption and Democratic Consolidation," in *Corrupt Histories*, ed. Emmanuel Krieke and William Chester Jordan (Rochester, NY: University of Rochester Press, 2004), 138–64, esp. 139; and, on the conceptual evolution of and distinction between "venal" and "systematic" corruption, with emphasis on the antigrowth effects of politically motivated factions in power, see John Joseph Wallis, "The Concept of Systematic Corruption in American History," in *Corruption and Reform: Lessons from America's Economic History*, ed. Edward Glaeser and Claudia Goldin (Chicago: University of Chicago Press, 2006), 23–62.

bility and progress, distribute income more equitably, democratize and balance political power, establish the rule of law, and educate citizens within a strong civil society overseeing efficient state administration. Corrupt agents undermine these efforts at times with devastating consequences and costs. In the case of Peru this pattern is clearly discernible at least since the first structural efforts at administrative overhaul and reform in the late eighteenth century. The analysis of the particular inroads of corruption in the long run, as well as the goals of previous efforts at containing its corrosive effects, underscore the need for collaboration and reinforcement of diverse reform agendas in all key areas of underdevelopment. In this sense, the limited outcomes of successive phases of economic reform adopted in Latin America in the 1990s, under the advice of the "Washington consensus," might be explained, among other key causes, as the consequence of unrestrained and persistent corruption.

The phenomenon of corruption has exhibited both continuity and variation in human affairs since the earliest states and civilizations. Corrupt manipulations of power and justice have had a long history and a universal presence in all cultures.[2] Some societies have had more success than others in curbing corruption, but none has been able to stamp out completely this ingrained aspect of human affairs. As recent global and corporate scandals have shown, corruption can resurface amid the most advanced and efficient public administrations and private sectors, causing incalculable losses for the general public. Constant global vigilance in the control and punishment of corruption has been emphasized by a growing number of anticorruption watchdogs.[3] Yet the study of the historical evolution of corruption in developing societies and institutions is still in its infancy.

This historical study benefits from the recent transformation in the analysis of corruption brought about by persuasive new studies by economists and other social scientists centering on current manifestations of corrupt practices. Only recently has there been a consistent effort at factoring in cor-

---

2. John T. Noonan, Jr., *Bribes: The Intellectual History of a Moral Idea* (Berkeley: University of California Press, 1984), xx, 9–13; Robert Payne, *The Corrupt Society: From Ancient Greece to Present-Day America* (New York: Praeger, 1975); David Loth, *Public Plunder: A History of Graft in America* (New York: Carrick and Evans, 1938); Syed Hussein Alatas, *Corruption: Its Nature, Causes, and Functions* (Aldershot, Hampshire, England: Avebury, 1990).

3. Peter Eigen, *Las redes de la corrupción: la sociedad civil contra los abusos del poder* (Barcelona: Editorial Planeta, 2004); George Moody-Stuart, *Grand Corruption: How Business Bribes Damage Developing Countries* (Oxford: Worldview, 1997).

ruption so as to render more realistic accounts of present and past social, political, and economic systems.[4] In the last ten years, a significant consensus has emerged concerning the institutional causes of corruption and its negative consequences for economic development, investment, democracy, and civil society.[5] The old view on the supposedly positive effects of corruption as "grease" for the lubrication of stringent bureaucracies in developing societies has been thoroughly superseded.[6] However, the few historians who have ventured to study corruption in specific detail continue to disagree widely over a series of issues related to the feasibility of documenting corruption and its significance in the past. Several of these assumptions continue to rest on outdated arguments that have precluded or advised against engaging in the historical study of corruption.

One such a priori argument holds that because corruption is by definition a clandestine activity, records documenting it are either difficult to find or unreliable if they proceed from politically motivated whistle-blowers.[7] Contrary to the opinion of skeptics, sundry historical sources for the study of corruption are generally abundant and, treated with necessary methodological

4. For early calls for the integration of corruption as a factor in social scientific analysis, see James C. Scott, *Comparative Political Corruption* (Englewood Cliffs, NJ: Prentice-Hall, 1972), 3, 10; and Neil Jacoby, Peter Nehemkis, and Richard Eells, *Bribery and Extortion in World Business: A Study of Corporate Political Payments Abroad* (New York: Macmillan, 1977).

5. Paolo Mauro, "Corruption and Growth," *Quarterly Journal of Economics* 110, no. 3 (1995): 681–712, and "The Effects of Corruption on Growth, Investment, and Government Expenditures: A Cross-Country Analysis," in *Corruption and the Global Economy*, ed. Kimberly Ann Elliot (Washington, DC: Institute for International Economics, 1997), 83–107; Robert Klitgaard, *Controlling Corruption* (Berkeley: University of California Press, 1988); Rick Stapenhurst and Sahr Kpundeh, *Curbing Corruption: Toward a Model for Building National Integrity* (Washington, DC: World Bank, 1999). For an ambivalent perspective, see Andrei Shleifer and Robert Vishny, "Corruption," in *The Grabbing Hand: Government Pathologies and Their Cures* (Cambridge: Cambridge University Press, 1998), 91–108.

6. See Nathaniel Leff, "Economic Development through Bureaucratic Corruption," David Bayley, "The Effects of Corruption in a Developing Nation," and J. S. Nye, "Corruption and Political Development: A Cost Benefit Analysis," all in *Political Corruption*, ed. Heidenheimer, 510–20, 521–33, and 564–78, respectively; and Jean-Claude Waquet, *Corrruption: Ethics and Power in Florence, 1600–1700* (Cambridge, MA: Polity Press, 1991), 20, 62.

7. Jean-Claude Waquet, "Some Considerations on Corruption, Politics, and Society in Sixteenth- and Seventeenth-Century Italy," in *Political Corruption in Europe and Latin America*, ed. Walter Little and Eduardo Posada-Carbó (London: Macmillan, 1996), 21–40, esp. 21–22; Scott, *Comparative Corruption*, ix.

caution, usually quite reliable in providing useful information. Complaints, reactions, and informed comments concerning abusive corruption abound in administrative, legislative, judiciary, and diplomatic documents. In the case of Peru and other Latin American countries, there is a long trail of archived colonial-era manuscripts and printed sources (*pesquisas* or legal inquiries, *juicios de residencia* or post-tenure trials, *memoriales,* and *proyectos*) and postindependence records (published and unpublished reports on public sector revenue and spending, congressional investigations, judicial trials, notary records, official and private correspondence, memoirs, diaries, pamphlets, and newspaper and magazine reports) documenting key cases of corruption in a context of institutional failures and frustrated reform. Diplomatic sources help triangulate and cross-check information. Foreign informants can confirm or deny allegations of corruption and provide valuable insights into the political and economic ramifications of domestic corruption schemes. Although not all of these foreign diplomatic and business observers are sufficiently detached or produce the same quality of information, the best among them and their reports should be carefully considered.[8]

Another argument emphasizes that corruption can be studied only through the detection of public perceptions, rather than on the basis of hardcore evidence. The study of perceptions of corruption is a useful yet indirect tool.[9] It is profusely used in the elaboration of current international indices and economic studies of comparative corruption levels in hundreds of countries. Economic historians have also quantified imaginatively the frequency of use of words such as "corruption" and "fraud" over time using new digital collections of historic newspapers.[10] Perceptions, however, are

8. Based on research experience, bad or mediocre diplomatic informants generally are too lazy to write reports, and when they do their lack of preparation and shallow analysis are obvious. In contrast, competent, highly educated foreign observers write lengthy, well-informed, and researched communications. In this work, my confidence is placed in the latter after the careful cross-checking of other evidence.

9. For careful methodological reflections on available historical evidence of changing administrative state systems and individual officers for evaluating whether a particular historical period is more corrupt than another, see Joel Hurstfield, *Freedom, Corruption, and Government in Elizabethan England* (London: Jonathan Cape, 1973), chapter 5. An indirect approach that analyzes public perceptions and official "discourse" on corruption can be found in Linda Levy Peck, *Court Patronage and Corruption in Early Stuart England* (Boston: Unwin Hyman, 1990), 5–11.

10. Edward Glaeser and Claudia Goldin, "Corruption and Reform: Introduction," in *Corruption and Reform: Lessons from America's Economic History,* ed. E. Glaeser and C. Goldin (Chicago: University of Chicago Press, 2006), 3–22, esp. 12–18.

highly impressionable and often manipulated. Despite the dearth of standard, long-term statistical series on the costs of corruption, historians do not have to rely exclusively on perceptions to gauge or estimate real, historic levels of corruption in different epochs. Although there continues to be a debate over the methods and even the possibility of quantifying corruption, the use of samples and informed estimates can offer reliable approximations of actual levels.[11]

Extremely cautious historians also contend that corruption is subject to historical relativism. They argue that what is defined and perceived as corruption in one epoch or culture does not have the same definition and connotation in another. These arguments are similar to the casuistic arguments used by early modern judges to neutralize or evade corruption charges.[12] However, acts of corruption and their punishment have been defined and legislated since ancient and premodern times. In the Spanish world, the words *corruptela* (illegal abuse), *cohecho* (bribe), and *prevaricato* (perversion of justice) had clear definitions in entries of early language dictionaries and legal codes.[13] Moreover, even if certain types of corruption have been only recently included in legal definitions, the impact of those corrupt practices has been recorded in allegations, judicial processes, complaints, and accusations. In the historical analysis of corruption, it is important not to assume the role of anachronistic judges of the past. Judicial proof of guilt is of a different nature than historical proof, the latter pertaining more to the realm of probability than absolute certainty. Lack of condemnatory sentences does not imply that corruption did not take place or leave lasting legacies, or that nonjudicial sources cannot inform about the occurrence and implications of corrupt activities.[14]

---

11. Charles Sampford, et al., eds., *Measuring Corruption* (Aldershot, Hampshire, England: Ashgate, 2006); Rafael Di Tella and William Savedoff, "Shining Light in Dark Corners," in *Diagnosis Corruption: Fraud in Latin America's Public Hospitals,* ed. R. Di Tella and W. Savedoff (Washington, DC: Inter-American Development Bank, 2001), 1–26, esp. 9–12.

12. Noonan, *Bribes,* 117, 149, 175; Waquet, "Some Considerations," 27–31; Tamar Herzog, *Upholding Justice: Society, State, and the Penal System in Quito (1650–1750)* (Ann Arbor: Michigan University Press, 2004), 10–21, 160.

13. *Diccionario de la Real Academia Española* (Madrid: Imprenta de Francisco del Hierro, 1729), 623, 401; and (Madrid: Herederos de Francisco del Hierro, 1737), 373.

14. Alejandro Nieto, *Corrupción en la España democrática* (Barcelona: Ariel, 1997), 85; José Manuel Urquiza, *Corrupción municipal: por qué se produce y cómo evitarla* (Córdoba: Editorial Almuzara, 2005), 9–15; Carlo Ginzburg, *El juez y el historiador: acotaciones al margen del caso Sofri* (Madrid: Anaya, 1993), 23–24.

Historical and anthropological relativists often assume that particular cultural constants make corruption a common and accepted fact in developing societies. According to this view, premodern political systems actually need corruption as a lubricant in order to function and provide a degree of stability and accommodation of emerging groups. Hence "patronage" and "clientelism" would better define the exchanges of favors and misappropriation of public funds and resources that support caudillos and other political leaders in Latin American past and present structures of power.[15] In this sense, corruption could actually facilitate the workings of patronage networks to provide social and political gains. Such a scenario would apply, according to some historians, in explaining the access to power through corrupt practices by formerly marginalized groups, such as the colonial Creole elite who bought influential posts of authority and engaged in contraband, thus reducing potential conflicts.[16]

A corollary to cultural approaches is the view that corruption is culturally determined and that culture alone explains the difference in levels of corruption around the world. Thus, southern Catholic regions are noted for higher levels of perceived corruption, compared to the Protestant north, despite the fact that not all Catholic regions have high levels of perceived corruption. The solution proposed, embarking on "cultural change," is more intractable and controversial than engaging in urgent institutional reform.[17] These new versions of cultural determinism are unable to explain the interest-driven and institutional factors at the heart of the causes and consequences of corruption.

Political scientists and foreign affairs policymakers in the 1960s through the 1980s also considered corruption a lesser evil, an inevitable fact of "real

15. Alvaro Vargas Llosa, *Liberty for Latin America: How to Undo Five Hundred Years of State Oppression* (New York: Farrar, Straus and Giroux, 2005), 194; Luis Roniger and Ayşe Güneş-Ayata, eds., *Democracy, Clientelism, and Civil Society* (Boulder, CO: Lynne Rienner, 1994), chapter 1. For a more nuanced discussion on the structural connections between clientelism and corruption, see Junichi Kawata, ed., *Comparing Political Corruption and Clientelism* (Aldershot, Hampshire, England: Ashgate, 2006), chapters 1 and 8.

16. Waquet, *Corruption*, 191; Kenneth Andrien, *Crisis and Decline: The Viceroyalty of Peru in the Seventeenth Century* (Albuquerque: University of New Mexico Press, 1985), 128; and Mark Burkholder and Lyman Johnson, *Colonial Latin America*, 5th ed. (New York: Oxford University Press, 2004), 92.

17. Seymour Martin Lipset and Gabriel Salman Lenz, "Corruption, Culture, and Markets," in *Culture Matters: How Values Shape Human Progress*, ed. Lawrence Harrison and Samuel Huntington (New York: Basic Books, 2000), 112–124; Vargas Llosa, *Liberty*, 193–196.

politics" or "politics as usual" in Latin America during the Cold War. Together with confused notions on possible income distribution benefits of
corruption, its persistence was condescendingly accepted as connatural to
less-developed political systems.[18]

Those who look at history from a Marxist perspective tend to associate
capitalism with corruption, unjust expropriation, and foreign dependence.
For them, the elite or oligarchies in power have based their supremacy on
one sort or another of corrupt or criminal practice and proimperialist sell-
out.[19] This perspective provides crude generalizations and unproven assumptions, useful as political and ideological weapons, but often unable to
explain the antigrowth factors of corruption, especially under revolutionary
socialist regimes.[20]

This study adopts an alternative institutional framework of analysis to
evaluate and explain causes and consequences of corruption. According to
this theoretical approach, large-scale or "systematic" corruption occurs
when formal and informal, pro-growth, and constitutional rules—protecting
property rights, reducing transaction costs, discouraging rent seeking, and
guaranteeing political checks and balances—are nonexistent, distorted, or
uncertain. Consequently, adequate disincentives fail to contain greedy "free-
rider" and despotic behavior, preferential rent-seeking or monopolistic gain
and influence among those with access to political power, public administration, and economic privilege. This results in increased transaction costs,
hindered growth, and faltering rule of law arising from an overall lack of
open economic and political competition.[21] Corruption is thus considered

18. On Cold War realpolitik policies condoning corruption of allied dictatorships, as
well as criticism of the idea that corruption "softens rigidities," see Laurence Whitehead,
"On Presidential Graft: The Latin American Evidence," in *Corruption: Causes, Consequences, and Control*, ed. Michael Clarke (New York: St. Martin's Press, 1983), 146–62,
esp. 159. On shifting views on alleged income distribution benefits of corruption, see
Peter Ward, ed., *Corruption, Development, and Inequality: Soft Touch or Hard Graft?*
(London: Routledge, 1989), introduction, 1–12.

19. Carlos Malpica, *Petróleo y corrupción: la ley Kuczynski* (Lima: Escena Contemporánea, 1985), 13–23; *Los dueños del Perú*, 5th ed. (Lima: Peisa, 1973; 1st ed. 1964),
15–16, 277–78; Alfredo Schulte-Bockholt, *The Politics of Organized Crime and the Organized Crime of Politics* (Lanham, MD: Lexington Books, 2006), 21, 25–26, 30, 35.

20. For a fresh analysis of corruption in socialist Cuba, see Sergio Díaz-Briquets and
Jorge Pérez-López, *Corruption in Cuba: Castro and Beyond* (Austin: University of
Texas Press, 2006).

21. Douglass North, *Institutions, Institutional Change, and Economic Performance*
(Cambridge: Cambridge University Press, 1990); *Structure and Change in Economic
History* (New York: Norton, 1981); *Understanding the Process of Economic Change*

here both an independent variable, causing the deterioration of institutions, and a dependent variable, a by-product of weakened institutions.

There are, however, some cultural elements and historical legacies ("path dependence") in all established institutions, whether they manifest pro-growth and democratic strengths or antigrowth and undemocratic flaws.[22] Additionally, theories on pressure or interest groups help explain concerted activities of vested interest networks that push for preferential treatment, institutional stagnation, and the stalling of reform: corrupt interests, coalescing in networks of corruption, vie to capture or influence the state and its different branches to continue benefiting from existing corruption and monopoly gains.[23]

The treatment of corruption in history merits careful consideration of the issue of continuity and change. Obviously, corruption is not immutable and does not have the same effects in every temporal or spatial context. The historical continuity of corruption is based on institutional flaws and failed reforms that facilitate a legacy of systemic corruption. Change arises from efforts at curbing corruption and effectively overhauling institutions. Further change derives from evolving political needs of implicit or explicit rewards for loyalty and support. Partial modernization also intensifies or demands improved efficiency of institutions, thus providing incentives to curb corruption. Technical, judicial, and institutional changes bring about periodic loopholes that may provide new opportunities for unrestrained or revived corruption.

The costs of corruption can be direct, indirect, and institutional depending on the predominant modes of corruption that adapt and evolve over

---

(Princeton, NJ: Princeton University Press, 2005), 68. Luis Felipe Zegarra, *Causas y consecuencias de la corrupción: un análisis teórico y empírico* (Lima: Centro de Investigación de la Universidad del Pacífico, 2000), 9–14; Wallis, "Concept of Systematic Corruption," 24–25; Johann Graf Lambsdorff, "Corruption and Rent-Seeking," *Public Choice* 113 (2002): 97–125.

22. Robert D. Putnam, Robert Leonardi, and Raffaella Y. Nanetti, *Making Democracy Work: Civic Traditions in Modern Italy* (Princeton, NJ: Princeton University Press, 1993), 131–35.

23. Donatella della Porta and Alberto Vannucci, "A Typology of Corrupt Networks," in *Comparing Political Corruption and Clientelism,* ed. J. Kawata (Aldershot, Hampshire, England: Ashgate, 2006), 23–44; Luis Moreno Ocampo, "Corruption and Democracy: The Peruvian Case of Montesinos," *Revista: Harvard Review of Latin America* 2, no. 1 (2002): 26–29; Alfonso W. Quiroz, "Redes de alta corrupción en el Perú: poder y venalidad desde el virrey Amat a Montesinos," *Revista de Indias* 66 (2006): 237–48; Jeremy J. Richardson, ed., *Pressure Groups* (Oxford: Oxford University Press, 1993), 3; Graham K. Wilson, *Interest Groups* (Oxford: Basil Blackwell, 1990), 2–3.

time. Certain time-tested modes of corruption tend to endure as networks of corruption inherit general and specific practices and savvy from previous cliques, especially in a context of weak civil societies. For the case of Peru, and many other parts of Spanish America, a prevalent mode and associated direct cost of corruption has been attached to the executive: the illegal gains and spoils of patronage of viceroys, caudillos, presidents, and dictators. A second enduring yet fluctuating mode and cost of corruption has been military graft, often linked to procurement contracts for arms and equipment. The irregular handling of public foreign and domestic debts to benefit a few, particularly after independence, has been a third pervasive mode and cost of corruption. Bribery in the approval and implementation of public contracts, procurement, and construction works, and the delivery of public administrative services, has consistently caused damage to the general citizenry. Bribe-giving contractors and businesspeople, eager to obtain monopoly and windfall gains, simply pass on the cost of bribes to the general costs of the projects involved. Bribe-taking ministers, congresspersons, and judges allow and foment this rise in overall transaction costs and undermine the efficiency and prestige of key regulating and corrective institutions.

Indirect costs of corruption include those derived from contraband, a mechanism that since colonial times has reduced tax revenue and contributed to dishonesty among civil servants. More recently, since the 1940s—and dramatically since the 1980s—similar indirect costs are caused by drug trafficking that engulf, through bribery and other illegal activities, mainly law enforcement and judicial institutions as well as politicians. With reduced institutional stability and efficiency, and rising transaction costs due, in part, to bribery and corruption, one important indirect cost also to take into account is the associated loss of investment, mainly foreign but also domestic.

All of the above factors contribute to the formation of what is referred to here as cycles of corruption. They are analyzed in detail in the following chapters taking into account the particular institutional framework and characteristic modes of corruption in each period. One important clarification concerns, however, the distinction between cycles of systemic corruption and cycles of perceived corruption. They are not the same as they vary in their peaks and troughs, although at certain points they might coincide. The former can be pictured as more organic and linked to the evolution of institutions, the state, legal frameworks, available economic and public resources, export booms, and adapted networks of corruption. The latter can be more volatile and dependent on the exposure of scandals through the media, civil society, and the contentious political system, as well as the moral and ethical reaction to those scandals. In this study we consider both types of cycles as evidence is collected from all available reliable sources, although the main analytical thrust relies more on evidence of systemic corruption.

It is not sufficient, although initially necessary, for the historian to describe the details of corrupt affairs. He or she must at the same time assess the effects of corruption and corrupt interests on the evolution of the state and general welfare of the population.[24] From the historian's perspective it is important to contribute to the historical record as well as deeply analyze the phenomenon. Recent historical analysis has focused on the differences between the patrimonial absolutist state, which allows private sinecures and other corrupt practices, and the modern constitutional state, which underwent transformative reforms between the seventeenth and nineteenth centuries. With its Weberian undertones, this literature is pertinent for the identification of key bureaucratic and political determinants of persistent corruption in some cases and reduced or curbed corruption in others. Likewise, various political processes and their effects on development can be scrutinized through evidence of the impact of corruption in political decisions.

During the Old Regime in France, the sale of royal offices or posts in the administration and the army was widely considered venal yet justifiable as a necessary evil. This practice was most difficult to eradicate owing to the fiscal and financial compromises it had accrued over time. Voltaire's father, for example, purchased and farmed one such official post while Voltaire himself, a critic of venality, obtained a profitable court office through favor. Montesquieu, a holder of an inherited post, opined that the venal system was useful as it enhanced opportunities for ennoblement and encouraged wealth creation. Diderot saw it as an obstacle to despotism.[25] The venal system was not replaced by the more efficient bureaucratic order based on talent and merit until serious inefficiencies, such as unsustainable financial burdens and military losses, became unbearable on the eve of the French

---

24. Hurstfield, *Freedom, Corruption,* 141–42; William Doyle, "Changing Notions of Public Corruption, c. 1700–c. 1850," in *Corrupt Histories,* ed. Emmanuel Krieke and William Chester Jordan (Rochester, NY: University of Rochester Press, 2004), 83–95, esp. 84–85; Waquet, *Corruption,* 19.

25. Roger Pearson, *Voltaire Almighty: A Life in Pursuit of Freedom* (New York: Bloomsbury, 2005), 13; William Doyle, *Venality: The Sale of Offices in Eighteenth-Century France* (Oxford: Clarendon Press, 1996), 76–77, 250–51.

Revolution. The venal sale of offices was finally abolished in 1789.[26] But even under the Reign of Terror, and soon thereafter under Napoleon, old venality was replaced by modified forms of corruption such as the bribing of "incorruptible" legislators deciding key matters of war, and the misappropriation of war loot and other public funds.[27]

There has been a long Western tradition of grappling intellectually and legally with the issue of the contamination of public affairs by private wealth and greed opposed to civic virtue and common interests in government. Only in the late eighteenth century did the determination to eviscerate patrimonial corruption from governance coalesce more firmly among British and North American thinkers and legislators.[28] The U.S. Constitution was clearly designed, in intention as well as wording, to preclude and disallow the damaging influence of corruption in government.[29] Major political transformations, reinforcing parliamentary checks on patrimonial absolutism in Britain in the 1680s, gave way to reformed administrative, fiscal, and market-based public financial systems under the spur of war and domestic dissent.[30]

These reforms gradually shed "Olde Corruption" in the form of royal influence in boroughs and Parliament acquired through corrupt private privileges, the scourge of an empire exposed to periodic corruption scandals as in the cases of the South Sea Company and the East India Company.[31] This

26. Doyle, "Changing Notions," 85–87, quoting *De l'ésprit des lois,* book 5, chapter 9.

27. Olivier Blanc, *La corruption sous la Terreur (1792–1794)* (Paris: Éditions Robert Laffont, 1992), 11–13; Frank McLynn, *Napoleon: A Biography* (New York: Arcade Publishing, 2002), 96, 146–48.

28. Bernard Bailyn, *The Ideological Origins of the American Revolution* (Cambridge, MA: Harvard University Press, 1992 [1967]), 130–35; J. G. A. Pocock, *The Machiavellian Moment: Florentine Political Thought and the Atlantic Republican Tradition* (Princeton, NJ: Princeton University Press, 1975), ix, 462, 468–69, 507–8; Wallis, "Systematic Corruption," 23–25; Thomas Ertman, *The Birth of the Leviathan: Building States and Regimes in Medieval and Early Modern Europe* (Cambridge: Cambridge University Press, 1997), 156–58, 187.

29. James D. Savage, "Corruption and Virtue at the Constitutional Convention," *Journal of Politics* 56 (1994): 174–86; James Alt and David Dreyer Lassen, "Political and Judicial Checks on Corruption: Evidence from American State Government," EPRU Working Paper Series (University of Copenhagen, 2005).

30. Ertman, *Birth of Leviathan,* 187, 218–23; John Brewer, *The Sinews of Power: War, Money, and the English State, 1688–1783* (London: Unwin and Hyman, 1989), chapters 3, 4; Doyle, "Changing Notions," 87.

31. Nicholas Dirks, *The Scandal of Empire: India and the Creation of Imperial Britain* (Cambridge, MA: Harvard University Press, 2006), chapter 2.

tendency was reinforced by the politics of Economical Reform, from the 1780s through the mid-nineteenth century, laying siege to surviving private sinecures, persecuting malfeasance, and sanitizing an expanded bureaucracy to preclude radical protest over old-style corruption.[32] British public officials, diplomats, and imperial administrators, schooled in the ethics of disinterested public service, then spread their reconstituted liberal and anticorruption stances around the world.[33] Corrupt practices in British elections were gradually eradicated by the second half of the nineteenth century.[34] (However diminished, obviously corruption has not been stamped out completely in Britain and it remains a recurrent problem, as in the rest of the developed world, especially at the local and public sector construction and procurement levels.)[35]

By contrast, Spain and its former colonies continued to struggle with patrimonial governments and persistent, systematic corruption. By the early nineteenth century, failure to reform had contributed instead to a transition from traditional corruption of the royal and viceregal courts to the patronage or clan-like corruption enveloping caciquism and caudillismo.[36] Important elements of the patrimonial state survived to preclude modernization and reform in the administration of power and public resources. In Cuba during the nineteenth century, a loyalist clique within the colonial bureaucracy expected allowance of corrupt rewards for their violent opposition to reform and abolition of slavery.[37] In this Spanish American context,

32. Philip Harling, *The Waning of "Old Corruption": The Politics of Economical Reform in Britain, 1779–1846* (Oxford: Clarendon Press, 1996), 6–7; and "Rethinking 'Old Corruption,'" *Past and Present* 147 (1995): 127–58. W. D. Rubinstein, "The End of 'Old Corruption' in Britain, 1780–1860," *Past and Present* 101 (1983): 5–86.

33. Harling, "Rethinking," 145; Niall Ferguson, *Empire: The Rise and Demise of British World Order and the Lessons for Global Power* (New York: Basic Books, 2003), 307–8.

34. Cornelius O'Leary, *The Elimination of Corrupt Practices in British Elections, 1868–1911* (Oxford: Clarendon Press, 1962), 2–4.

35. I thank Rory Miller for pointing this out to me. See Alan Doig, "Politics and Public Sector Ethics: The Impact of Change in the United Kingdom," in *Political Corruption,* ed. Little and Posada-Carbó, 173–92.

36. Ertman, *Birth of Leviathan,* 90–91, 111; Antonio Robles Egea, ed., *Política en penumbra: patronazgo y clientelismo políticos en la España contemporánea* (Madrid: Siglo Veintiuno, 1996), 7; Luis Arrillaga Aldama, *Clientelismo, caciquismo, corporativismo: ensayo sobre algunas formas de particularismo social* (Pamplona: Zubillaga, 1994); Manuel González Jiménez, et al., *Instituciones y corrupción en la historia* (Valladolid: Universidad de Valladolid, 1998), 9–30.

37. Alfonso W. Quiroz, "Implicit Costs of Empire: Bureaucratic Corruption in Nineteenth-Century Cuba," *Journal of Latin American Studies* 35 (2003): 473–511.

patronage and clientelism are inextricably tied to corruption, as most political appointee clients tend to abuse and misuse public office and funds.

By the mid and late nineteenth century, political and business cronyism and caciquism had consolidated in Latin America and Spain, relying on arrangements of privileged economic gains and unchecked executive and presidential power at the expense of open markets, economic efficiency, and better distribution of income, democracy, and overall development.[38] Dictators Francisco Franco, Fulgencio Batista, Rafael Trujillo, and Marcos Pérez Jiménez during the twentieth century adapted corruption to authoritarian molds.[39] Mexico's single-party system likewise buttressed centralization through corrupt cooptation and patronage.[40]

Since the 1980s, return to democracy, more successful in Spain than in most Latin American countries, shifted the modes of corruption exercised by executive branches overpowering legislatures and judiciaries. The world has seen efforts to consolidate undue political gain and reward close collaborators (through ad hoc party "enterprises" and illegal electoral slush funds) made by fund-thirsty parties and party leaders. This is the case of the Spanish Socialist Party in the 1980s, the administrations of Fernando Collor de Mello in Brazil, Carlos Andrés Pérez in Venezuela, Carlos Saúl Menem in Argentina, Carlos Salinas in Mexico, Arnoldo Alemán in Nicaragua, Alan García Pérez and Alberto Fujimori in Peru, and the more recently publicized cases of Hugo Chávez's regime in Venezuela and Luis Inácio Lula da Silva's Workers' Party in Brazil.[41] Personal graft among

38. Stephen Haber, ed., *Crony Capitalism and Economic Growth in Latin America: Theory and Evidence* (Stanford, CA: Hoover Institution Press, 2002), xv–xviii.

39. Mariano Sánchez Soler, *Negocios privados con dinero público: el vademécum de la corrupción de los políticos españoles* (Madrid: Foca, 2003), 14, and *Villaverde: fortuna y caída de la Casa Franco* (Barcelona: Planeta, 1990); Fernando Jiménez Sánchez, *Detrás del escándalo político: opinión, dinero y poder en la España del siglo XX* (Barcelona: Tusquets Editores, 1995); José Díaz Herrera and Isabel Durán, *Los secretos del poder: del legado franquista al ocaso del felipismo, episodios inconfesables* (Madrid: Ediciones Temas de Hoy, 1994); Asociación Venezolana de Derecho Tributario, *La corrupción en Venezuela* (Valencia, Venezuela: Vadell Hermanos, 1985), 39–40; Stephen Niblo, *Mexico in the 1940s: Modernity, Politics, and Corruption* (Wilmington, DE: Scholarly Resources, 1999), 253–55; Joaquín Soler Serrano, *Pérez Jiménez se confiesa* (Barcelona: Ediciones Dronte, 1983), 95–98; Whitehead, "On Presidential Graft," 151–53.

40. Stephen Morris, *Corruption and Politics in Contemporary Mexico* (Tuscaloosa: University of Alabama Press, 1991), 24–25, 41, 66.

41. Nieto, *Corrupción*, 17–38; José Díaz Herrera and Ramón Tijeras, *El dinero del poder: la trama económica en la España socialista* (Madrid: Cambio 16, 1991), 37–39;

high-level office holders is only the most visible and sometimes spectacular part of the problem. Corruption in a context of economic liberalization and democratization is not a transitory phenomenon; it is another historical example of the adaptive capabilities of a persistent, structural feature under new institutional infringements that tend to swing the balance back to old unchecked presidential power.[42]

In summary, pertinent theoretical and empirical studies of past and present corruption point at key issues to look for in analyzing the historical evidence. In the first place, special attention should be given to how effectively legislative and judicial measures embodied in constitutions and legal codes achieve reform or fail to curb corruption. Second, evidence on the effects of corruption on economic, fiscal, and financial policies adopted in the past can highlight the potential costs of decisions taken under the influence of corrupt vested interests interacting in the public and private sectors. Third, variations in the structure of incentives and disincentives for corruption can be correlated to changing institutional and technological conditions arising from economic and investment booms, international war and conflict, and domestic political instability. Fourth, focusing on specific institutions, such as the armed forces, might reveal the penetration of self-serving and political corruption at the expense of democracy and overall national interests. Fifth, the participation of foreign companies, investors, and

---

José Díaz Herrera and Isabel Durán, *Pacto de silencio: (el saqueo de España II: la herencia socialista que Aznar oculta)* (Madrid: Temas de Hoy, 1996), 61–65, 72; Andrés Torres, *La financiación irregular del PSOE: seguido de las armas del poder* (Barcelona: Ediciones de la Tempestad, 1993), 10; Eduardo Martín de Pozuelo, Jordi Bordas, and Santiago Tarín, *Guía de la corrupción* (Barcelona: Plaza y Janés, 1994), 42–48; Andrés Oppenheimer, *Ojos vendados: Estados Unidos y el negocio de la corrupción en América Latina* (Buenos Aires: Editorial Sudamericana, 2001); Keith Rosenn and Richard Downes, *Corruption and Political Reform in Brazil: The Impact of Collor's Impeachment* (Coral Gables, FL: North-South Center Press / University of Miami, 1999); Conrado Pérez Briceño, *La corrupción revolucionaria: informe sobre los principales casos de corrupción de Hugo Chávez* (Caracas: Editorial CEC, 2004); Larry Rohter, "As Brazil Prepares to Vote, Scandal's Taint Seems to Fade," *New York Times,* September 25, 2006, http://www.nytimes.com.

42. Laurence Whitehead, "High-Level Political Corruption in Latin America: A 'Transitional' Phenomenon?" in *Combating Corruption in Latin America,* ed. Joseph Tulchin and Ralph Espach (Washington, DC: Woodrow Wilson Center Press and Johns Hopkins University Press, 2000), 107–29; Mitchell Seligson, "The Impact of Corruption on Regime Legitimacy: A Comparative Study of Four Latin American Countries" *Journal of Politics* 64, no. 2 (2002): 408–33; Kurt Weyland, "The Politics of Corruption in Latin America," *Journal of Democracy* 9 (1998): 108–21.

agents in adapting to, enticing, or reinforcing domestic trends of persistent corruption should be carefully assessed as foreign interests are often targeted by the left as major culprits. Sixth, the search for venal support by political forces and their leaders, organized in political parties since the mid-nineteenth century, illuminates systematic corruption in government and the obstacles it poses to structural progress. And seventh, particular vigilance should be placed on the role of the press and other means of communication in either reinforcing corrupt structures or serving as instruments of civil society's interest in limiting corruption.

The history of corruption in Latin America matters. Over time corruption has had crucial economic, institutional, and policymaking costs (as an independent variable), and has been determined (as a dependent variable) in large measure by formal and informal rules of the economic and social game. Latin American economies and societies have born costly burdens resulting from public and private corruption. The endemic and cyclical "path dependence" of corruption in Latin American countries demands a historical comparative approach.

Peru represents a textbook case of a country deeply affected in the distant and recent past by administrative, political, and systematic corruption. Despite recurrent and cyclical effects of corruption, surprisingly little is known about the specific causes of corruption and its long-term economic and institutional costs. In part, this paucity in the analysis of corruption is due to nationalistic and idealistic imperatives among historians and social scientists who have downplayed the role or importance of corruption in the country's history. International experts, either conceding to national sensibilities or adopting condescending perspectives on corruption, have also contributed to an inadequate historical perspective. At the same time, excessive historical pessimism fails to detect past anticorruption battles and present possibilities for curbing administrative venality, undoing systematic corruption, and restructuring the modern state.[43]

A specific, well-informed history of corruption in Peru can contribute to a more realistic interpretation of Peruvian general history. The study of Latin American and other developing societies can also benefit from fresh

---

43. Alfonso W. Quiroz, "Historia de la corrupción en el Perú: ¿es factible su estudio?" in *Homenaje a Félix Denegri Luna,* ed. Guillermo Lohmann et al. (Lima: Fondo Editorial Universidad Católica, 2000), 684–90; and "Basadre y su análisis de la corrupción en el Perú," in *Homenaje a Jorge Basadre: el hombre, su obra y su tiempo,* ed. Scarlett O'Phelan and Mónica Ricketts (Lima: Instituto Riva Agüero, 2004), 145–86.

views on an in-depth history of corruption's local and international linkages. In seeking to contribute toward a more informed comparative international perspective, this study aims to reinterpret Peruvian history based on new evidence and a new emphasis on the impact of corruption in public governance, policies, and development.

This volume's narrative strategy follows a descriptive, third-person account of how corruption cases were initially investigated and exposed to public scrutiny in various time periods and political, institutional, and economic contexts. Along its pages the study documents the struggle of successive anticorruption advocates in their uphill attempts to revamp institutions, starting with enlightened reformist Antonio de Ulloa's efforts and ordeals in mid–eighteenth-century Peru. Ulloa was followed by other would-be reformists in the republican period such as Domingo Elías, Francisco García Calderón Landa, Manuel González Prada, Jorge Basadre, Héctor Vargas Haya, and Mario Vargas Llosa, among several others. Following this initial exposition of revelations by anticorruption reformers, throughout the text and in the Appendix, the study analyzes cumulative evidence from varied other sources to evaluate the cyclical and long-term costs of corruption. At particular points, the historical role of key civilian and military authorities—such as Manuel Amat y Junyent, Agustín Gamarra, Antonio Gutiérrez de la Fuente, Juan Crisóstomo Torrico, José Rufino Echenique, Nicolás de Piérola, Augusto B. Leguía, Manuel Prado, Víctor Raúl Haya de la Torre, Manuel Odría, Juan Velasco Alvarado, Alan García Pérez, and Alberto Fujimori—are reevaluated on the basis of new and revised evidence of detected corruption mechanisms and networks.

Each of the book's seven chapters corresponds to major eras and cycles of corruption witnessed by key anticorruption whistle-blowers. The first chapter analyzes the colonial roots of systematic administrative corruption under patrimonial viceregal courts, supported by a patronage entourage benefiting from monopolies, privileges, and proprietary official posts. Corrupt colonial practices buttressed the abuse and exploitation of the indigenous population, neglect in the administration of mines, widespread contraband, and the failure of colonial reform, a first major but frustrated effort at administrative modernization in the eighteenth century.

The second chapter explains the legacy of colonial corruption under new postindependence institutional conditions. Caudillo dominance through corrupt patronage networks allowed private dispossession and expropriation, "patriotic" plundering, distorted and wasteful foreign and domestic credit and trade policies, venal diplomacy, and ingrained contraband, all of which undermined the foundations of the new republic. In a changing legal context that maintained at its center the patrimonial brokerage of the executive, the third chapter evaluates the impact of corruption on faulty financial and trade policies wasteful of the mature guano age's economic opportunities. Corrupt linkages between governing cliques and a few foreign interests contributed to widespread corrosion that, in the frenzy of misappropriation of public resources, bred oblivion to the dangers of a looming, disastrous war.

Analyzing a period of partial modernization crucial to Peruvian history, the fourth chapter centers on the crooked revival of the Peruvian state and military after the War of the Pacific, as well as the rise of Leguía, a civilian modernizer bent on remaining in despotic control through multiple corrupt means in politics, business, and media. The fifth chapter focuses on the murky political and economic situation arising from the crises of the early 1930s that encumbered venal military dictators, populist (demagogic, interventionist) leaders, and limited electoral democracy through hidden pacts adverse to public interest. Chapter 6 concentrates on the failures of weak democratic governments in the 1960s and 1980s that were beset by grave corruption scandals and unable to contain the rising power of politically motivated military leaders, accusers as well as beneficiaries of corruption. Chapter 7 analyzes the complex corrupt conspiracy of the Fujimori-Montesinos regime, which squandered the opportunities of liberal reforms and privatization of the 1990s and contributed to a major shift in the way Peruvians view corruption and its legacy. Finally, the Epilogue points out continuities and changes that threaten the few anticorruption advances of the first years of the century.

This study does not claim to break new theoretical ground in the study of corruption. Such effort should build upon more comparative studies and statistical reconstructions that are still in their infancy. This inquiry does apply recent methodological advances to historical analysis by carefully considering and reinterpreting available and newly discovered evidence obtained through painstaking research. One outcome of this procedure is tentatively offered in the Appendix, which aims to estimate the historical costs of corruption in Peru. These calculations are preliminary estimates, obviously subject to revision and mistakes of over or underestimation. They do not intend to settle the ongoing methodological debate over the different ways of measuring the costs of corruption; they do provide, however, a necessary initial overview based on new quantitative evidence unearthed through piecemeal research combined with qualitative evidence laid out in the book.

Comparisons with other Latin American cases, while important to place the Peruvian case in its hemispheric context and calibrate similarities and crucial differences among national histories, are attempted here only sporadically. Specific historical research on corruption is not yet adequate to sustain systematic regional and international comparisons. Also, in analyzing the negative long-term impact of corruption in the history of a developing state and society, the tone adopted in this work is not intended to be particularly pessimistic or accusative. By tracking often-forgotten reformist quests to curb corruption, emphasis is placed in highlighting the possibility and promise of reform as well as the partial advances in the struggle against corruption over time.

Chapter 1

The Failure of Colonial Reforms, 1750–1820

In 1757 naval captain Antonio de Ulloa was appointed to a strategic post in the Andean mining town of Huancavelica, 12,000 feet above sea level. With some reluctance Ulloa took charge of the province's local government and the supervision of the legendary mercury mine of Santa Barbara. These were daunting tasks of the highest responsibility, even for the distinguished officer and enlightened man of science. Under royal monopoly, Huancavelica was the only major American source of the liquid metal, a main input in the amalgamation process for refining silver. In Huancavelica, Ulloa found a critical situation upon his arrival in November 1758: endemic mismanagement and fraud in the collection and accounting of royal revenues, dangerous technical neglect in exploitation of the mines, shady administrative schemes, and justice swayed by bribes (*cohechos*). Mineral wealth in the famed Peru had attracted several generations of ambitious and unruly fortune seekers. Ulloa denounced corrupt collusions among greedy authorities, treasury officers, miners, and merchants that caused incalculable damage to the Spanish Crown and its subjects. The Peruvian mercury and silver mining system, a main pillar of the imperial economy and revenues, faced continued and irreversible decadence.[1] Ulloa confronted powerful vested interests that posed

1. Antonio de Ulloa, "Relación de Gobierno del Capitán de Navío de la Real Armada dn. Antonio de Ulloa; en la Villa de Huancavelica; su Real Mina, Gremio de Mineros; Cajas Reales de Guancavelica, y demás del reino donde se hace expendio de azogues; Gobierno Civil y Político de la villa, y de la Provincia de Angaraes, desde el día 4 de noviembre de 1758 que tomó el mando, hasta 10 de febrero de 1763," signed by Antonio de Ulloa in Huancavelica (last entry May 15, 1763), 206 ff., ms. II/2453, Biblioteca del Palacio Real, Madrid (hereafter BPR), f. 3v, 88, 91, 101v. This is a duplicate, apparently in Ulloa's own handwriting, of the "Relación de Gobierno" (exact

insurmountable difficulties to his tenacious reformist efforts at correcting and punishing the bureaucratic transgressions he uncovered.

It was not the first time that Antonio de Ulloa (1716–1795) had denounced widespread corrupt practices in the Peruvian colonial administration. Nine years before starting his governorship in Huancavelica, he had written the bulk of a confidential report on colonial bureaucratic dysfunctions and abuses, partially coauthored by Jorge Juan (1713–1773). The scathing report, written in 1748–1749 following orders from the Crown's first secretary, the Marqués de la Ensenada, was based on earlier direct observations, mainly in Lima and Quito, but also in Cartagena, Panama, and Chilean ports. The manuscript, "Discurso y reflexiones políticas sobre el estado presente . . . de los reinos del Perú" (Discourse and Political Reflections on the Kingdoms of Peru), submitted for the confidential use of King Ferdinand VI's ministers, remained unpublished and read only by top imperial bureaucrats.[2]

---

same title, no folio numbering) signed by Ulloa in Huancavelica and sent to the king and Council of the Indies with the letter, Ulloa to S.M. el Rey, Huancavelica, June 20, 1763, reiterating previous requests to be exonerated from his governorship and allowed to return to Spain, in "Correspondencia y nombramientos de gobernadores de Huancavelica 1763–1795," Gobierno, Lima, leg. 777, Archivo General de Indias, Seville (hereafter AGI). There is a third copy, not signed by Ulloa, under the title "Relación circunstanciada del Gobierno y Superintendencia de la Real Mina de Asogues de la villa de Huancavelica desde el 4 de noviembre de 1758 hasta 11 de mayo de 1763," last entry dated in Huancavelica, May 15, 1763, in Mapas y Planos: Libros Manuscritos, leg. 67 (microfilm, no. 42/ C-11162), AGI (Kendall Brown is working on a first edition of the manuscript's latter copy). Details of Ulloa's original appointment and traveling arrangements in "Licencia a Dn. Antonio de Ulloa para jurar en la Real Audiencia de la Contratación de Cádiz el empleo de Gobernador de Huancavelica," Buen Retiro, September 6, 1757, Contratación, leg. 5500, n. 3, r. 26, AGI.

2. "Discurso y reflexiones políticas sobre el estado presente de la marina de los reynos del Perú, su gobierno, arsenales, maestranzas, viajes, armamentos, plana mayor de sus oficiales, sus sueldos, de los navíos, marchantes, gobierno, reximen particular de aquellos avitadores, y abusos que se han introducido en un y otro. Dase individual noticia de las causales de su origen, y se proponen algunos medios para evitarlas. Escritas de orden del Rey, Nro. Sor. por Don Jorge Juan, Comendador de Águila en el Orden de San Juan, y Don Antonio de Ulloa, miembros de la Real Sociedad de Londres, socios correspondientes de la Academia Real de las Ciencias de París, y Capitanes de Navío de la Real Armada. Año de 1749. Del uso del Sr. Dr. D. José Antonio de Areche de la distinguida Rl. Orn. Española de Carlos III del Consejo de S.M. en el Supremo de Indias y Visitador General de los reinos del Perú," Manuscript II/1468, BPR. There are at least five other manuscript versions of this document; the one cited here belonged to reformist councilor and visitador Areche. See Arthur Whitaker, "Antonio de Ulloa," *Hispanic American Historical Review* 15 (1935): 155–94, esp. 158–59, 166, and 174.

Not until 1826 was the Spanish text unofficially published in London under the sensational title *Noticias secretas de América*. The published text had a new prologue written by the traveling editor and collector David Barry, a British merchant formerly stationed in Cádiz. After returning from a failed business trip to Peru, Barry published the revealing manuscript to warn about the adverse investment and political conditions inherited in Spanish America just after independence.[3] The published Spanish version was later abridged and translated, with anti-Spanish and anti-Catholic bias, as the *Secret Expedition to Peru*.[4] The text became a classic source for de-

3. Jorge Juan and Antonio de Ulloa, *Noticias secretas de América sobre el estado naval, militar y político de los reinos del Perú y provincias de Quito, costas de Nueva Granada y Chile; gobierno y régimen particular de los pueblos de indios; cruel opresión y extorsiones de sus corregidores y curas; abusos escandalosos introducidos entre estos habitantes por los misioneros; causas de su origen y motivos de su continuación por el espacio de tres siglos. Escritas fielmente según las instrucciones del excelentísimo señor marqués de la Ensenada, primer secretario de Estado, y presentadas en informe secreto a S.M.C., el señor Fernando VI . . . sacadas a la luz para el verdadero conocimiento del gobierno de los españoles en la América meridional por David Barry* (London: R. Taylor, 1826), 2 vols. The Spanish government was immediately concerned with the repercussions of the published *Noticias secretas;* in April 1827, the Crown's first secretary (de Estado y del Despacho) sent letters to the Spanish ministries in London and Paris asking them to inform Madrid about their inquiries concerning "los efectos que dicha obra produzca en la opinión pública," and informing them that "existen sospechas de que el original se extrajo de los archivos del Soberano el año de 1823," in "Papeles de los comisionados de Costa Firme José Sartorio y Juan Barry," Indiferente General, leg. 1571, AGI. In 1821, David Barry had traveled to Peru, where he collected detailed and accurate extracts of statistical and other curious documents. In 1824, Barry met former viceroy of Peru, Joaquín de la Pezuela, in Madrid, and obtained from him key information and documents (Pezuela may have had access to "Discurso y reflexiones"), according to Barry's own notes in "Colección de notas, extractos, itinerarios, derroteros y papeles varios, para formar idea del Perú: sacados, la mayor parte, de la *Guía política, eclesiástica y militar del virreynato del Perú* por don Joseph Hipólito Unánue en Lima por el año 1796 y 7: colectados por David Barry" (latest note entry dated Cádiz, 1832), ff. 37, 53, 54v, 111, and 113, Rare Books and Special Collections, Library of Congress (hereafter LOC).

4. The first abridged English translation misidentified the authors as George and Anthony Ulloa, a mistake reiterated in a later edition of the same translation, with an anti-Catholic new title. See Juan and Ulloa, *Secret Expedition to Peru, or, the Practical Influence of the Spanish Colonial System upon the Character and Habits of the Colonists, Exhibited in a Private Report Read to the Secretaries of His Majesty, Ferdinand VI, King of Spain, by George J. and Anthony Ulloa* (Boston: Crocker and Brewster, 1851); *Popery Judged by Its Fruits: As Brought to View in the Diary of Two Distinguished Scholars and Philanthropists, John and Anthony Ulloa, during a Sojourn of Several Years in the States of Colombia and Peru. Tr. from the Spanish by a Member of the Principia Club*, ed. I. W. Wheelwright (Boston: Albert J. Wright, 1878).

nouncing the legacy of Spanish corrupt administration in the Americas. It can also be considered a foundational text of the anticorruption tradition in Hispanic and Peruvian letters.

During his extended official career in Spanish America, Ulloa contributed invaluably to our understanding of the mechanisms of colonial bureaucratic corruption. He was not the first or the last reformer to attack systemic imperial and colonial corruption. Ulloa in fact based his informed criticisms partly on earlier authors and petitioners bent on describing and advising action against corrupt agents. Arguably, however, he was the most informed and articulate among the group of anticorruption reformers of the time. Despite corroboration by countless other sources, Ulloa's critical observations and reformist intentions have been ignored, misinterpreted, or dismissed by several generations of historians.[5] Consequently, some have opted to avoid acknowledging the central role of systematic corruption at the core of colonial administration, or even justify it as favorable.

Ulloa's anticorruption stance was imbedded in the early phase of the most comprehensive process of late-colonial institutional and policy reform, known as the Bourbon reforms, which aimed at improved administrative efficiency in Peru and other Spanish American colonies. More productive and efficient colonies implied greater revenues for the Spanish Crown engaged in strategic competition with other European powers. These imperial imperatives, however, did not necessarily result in improved con-

---

5. Among early doubters of the authenticity of *Noticias secretas* and critics of the accuracy of its authors, several Spanish historians can be cited, such as Rafael Altamira and Antonio Ballesteros, as well as Lesley Byrd Simpson (see his review of *Indian Labor in the Spanish Colonies* by Ruth Kerns Barber, *Hispanic American Historical Review* 13 (1933): 363–64). See also Luis Merino, Augustine priest and scholar, *Estudio crítico sobre las "Noticias secretas de América" y el clero colonial* (Madrid: Consejo Superior de Investigaciones Científicas, Instituto Santo Toribio de Mogrovejo, 1956), 196–99, 210–11; John Leddy Phelan, *The Kingdom of Quito in the Seventeenth Century: Bureaucratic Politics in the Spanish Empire* (Madison: University of Wisconsin Press, 1967), 157; Luis J. Ramos Gómez's introduction to his edition of Ulloa and Juan, *Noticias secretas de América* (Madrid: Historia 16, 1990), 14; Francisco de Solano Pérez-Lila, *La pasión por reformar: Antonio de Ulloa, marino y científico, 1716–1795* (Sevilla: Escuela de Estudios Hispano-Americanos/Universidad de Cádiz, 1999), 74, 125–27; and Kenneth Andrien, "The *Noticias Secretas de América* and the Construction of a Governing Ideology for the Spanish American Empire," *Colonial Latin American Review* 7, no. 2 (1998): 175–92. For an opposite perspective, see Lewis Hanke, "Dos palabras on Antonio de Ulloa and the *Noticias Secretas*," *Hispanic American Historical Review* 16 (1936): 479–514, esp. 485, and the works by Arthur Whitaker, John TePaske, and Scarlett O'Phelan cited in subsequent notes.

ditions for the colonial elites and subjects as they drained resources (especially at times of war with Great Britain and France) and clashed with customary pacts and allowances of the old Hapsburg order. Instead of contributing to a political evolution toward a more balanced constitutional monarchy, as was expected and hoped for by some Spanish reformists, these reforms reinforced enlightened absolutism, itself still a nest for corrupt administration. Perhaps only in Cuba were the Bourbon reforms mostly successful in this transitional period, as the economic and political benefits of public works, freer trade, and moderate taxation were shared more with the rising Creole elite.[6]

The ideological biases, policy limitations, political failures, and ultimately frustrated or misguided reformist efforts of Ulloa's time—including his own alleged mistakes and character flaws—should not impede a balanced and critical analysis of Ulloa's and other reformers' contributions to the study of the legacies of colonial corruption. This long story of corrupt governance in Peru begins therefore with Ulloa's personal ordeal in discovering, exposing, and trying to solve the problems associated with administrative corruption of the late colonial period.

Uncovering Abuses

In 1735, nineteen-year-old Antonio de Ulloa and his fellow naval lieutenant, the promising mathematician and astronomer Jorge Juan, were commissioned by the Spanish king Philip V and his chief minister José Patiño for a special task. They were to join an expedition of six members of the Parisian Academy of Sciences led by naturalist Charles-Marie de La Condamine. Among other scientific observations, Ulloa and Juan were to assist in measuring the length of an arc of the Earth's meridian, intersected by the span of one degree of latitude, near the Equator in the environs of the Andean city of Quito.[7] Ulloa and Juan were also ordered to collect and deliver

6. Stanley Stein, "Bureaucracy and Business in Spanish America, 1759–1804: Failure of a Bourbon Reform in Mexico and Peru," *Hispanic American Historical Review* 61 (1981): 2–28; Allan Kuethe, "Guns, Subsidies, and Commercial Privilege: Some Historical Factors in the Emergence of the Cuban National Character, 1763–1815," *Cuban Studies* 16 (1986): 123–39.

7. The measurements were intended to settle the issue of whether, according to Isaac Newton's calculations, the Earth bulged at the Equator because of gravity. For a detailed critical view of Ulloa's scientific mission and enlightened ideology, allegedly adverse to

strategic information on the colonies and their inhabitants according to a separate set of instructions.[8] At the onset of their scientific activities in 1737, the young lieutenants clashed with the self-seeking president of the Quito Audiencia, the Lima-born José de Araujo, over a matter of formal address, rank, and honor.[9]

Creoles and Indians (in line with allegations by exiled Peruvian Jesuit Juan Pablo Viscardo y Guzmán), see David A. Brading, *The First America: The Spanish Monarchy, Creole Patriots, and the Liberal State, 1492–1867* (Cambridge: Cambridge University Press, 1991), 423–28, 536. On the official licenses for the expedition and appointment of Juan and Ulloa, see Patiño to Francisco de Varas y Valdés (minister of the Council of the Indies), El Pardo, January 4, 1735, in "Peru: Registro de Partes," Gobierno, Lima, leg. 590(1), AGI.

8. Scholars have questioned the complex double nature of the royal commission given to Ulloa and Juan in 1735, arguing that the authors had insincere and interested motives for writing "Discurso y reflexiones," a.k.a. *Noticias secretas de América* in 1748–1749. See Ramos Gómez's introduction to his edition of Juan and Ulloa, *Noticias secretas de América*, 85, 89; comp. 120. However, no convincing evidence is provided to doubt Ulloa's interpretation of the original, and subsequent comprehensive orders cited in the original manuscript's prologue. The official confirmation of the commission, a royal decree signed by the king and Patiño in El Pardo, January 4, 1735, stated: "He resuelto nombrar a los tenientes de navío de mi Real Armada dn. Jorge Juan y dn. Antonio de Ulloa para que pasen con los referidos astronómicos asistir con ellos a todas las observaciones y mapas que hicieren para perfeccionar la navegación a Indias y que *apunten separadamente* todas las que se fueren ejecutando según la instrucción que se les dará para su gobierno," in "Registro de partes: América Meridional," Lima, leg. 590(1), AGI [my emphasis]. In a separate ten-point instruction (drafted by Varas and signed by Patiño in Aranjuez, April 22, 1735), they were to—independently from their work with the French scientists—make "planos de las ciudades y puertos . . . y se informaran del término de su *provincia y gobernación de los pueblos o lugares que contiene* y lo fértil o estéril de sus campos, como también de la inclinación, industria y habilidad de sus naturales" [my emphasis]. They also were to send this information directly to the king through local authorities: See "Instrucción que han de observar los tenientes de navío de la Real Armada dn. Jorge Juan y dn. Antonio de Ulloa," ibid. Ulloa later declared that his instructions included "adquirir con exactitud, y la más posible prolixidad, y atención todo lo que pareciese digno de ella a cerca del Govierno, Administración de Justicia, costumbres, y estados de aquellos Reynos, con todo lo tocante a su civil economía militar y política," in Arthur Whitaker, "Documents: Jorge Juan and Antonio de Ulloa's Prologue to Their Secret Report of 1749," *Hispanic American Historical Review* 18 (1938): 507–13, esp. 512.

9. Whitaker, "Ulloa," 161–64, based on judicial documents exposing Araujo's corrupt administration of justice and trade with contraband goods in Gobierno, Quito, legs. 104, 105, and 133, AGI. For a different, distorted version of the incident, based on secondary sources, see Solano, *Pasión de reformar*, 75–76. Merino, *Estudio crítico*, 139–40, cites Araujo's self-seeking judicial role; his dubious expropriatory measures in Ramos Gómez, "Los intentos del virrey Eslava y del presidente Araujo en 1740 para obtener

Fortunately for the endangered Ulloa and Juan, Viceroy José Antonio de Mendoza, Marqués de Villagarcía (1736–1745), intervened from Lima on their behalf. Two years later, in the middle of the War of Jenkins's Ear, the viceroy requested their naval services to better defend the Peruvian ports and coast from attacks such as those carried out by British Vice Admiral George Anson. While performing these official duties and during their several trips in the region of Quito, Lima, and Chilean ports between 1736 and 1744, Ulloa and Juan gathered important confidential information and evidence on all matters of dysfunctional colonial administration, from smuggling activities to the customary bribing of colonial officials.[10] In October 1744, Ulloa and Juan returned separately to Spain in an effort to avoid a potential loss of their precious scientific and confidential information in case of misfortune at sea. Juan arrived in Spain without major problems. However, the British captured the French ship in which Ulloa traveled. Before being apprehended, Ulloa threw overboard the confidential papers produced during his mission. After exhibiting his scientific credentials, Ulloa was in fact well treated in Boston and London by navy authorities and made a member of the Royal Society. He returned safely to Spain in July 1746.[11]

The 1749 confidential report titled, "Discourse and Political Reflections on the Kingdoms of Peru," was unrelenting in exposing malfunctions in practically every aspect of colonial administration as well as proposing reformist solutions.[12] The treatise detailed many forms of corruption in an

préstamos del comercio del Perú desplazado a Quito y la requisa de 100,000 pesos en 1741," *Revista de Indias* 63 (2003): 649–74, esp. 651, 669.

10. John TePaske does not doubt the intention of the manuscript's authors and their firsthand, reliable, and sincere observations on site: Juan and Ulloa, *Discourse and Political Reflections on the Kingdoms of Peru. Their Government, Special Regimen of Their Inhabitants, and Abuses Which Have Been Introduced into One and Another, with Special Information on Why They Grew Up and Some Means to Avoid Them,* ed. and prologue by John TePaske, trans. with Besse Clement (Norman: University of Oklahoma Press, 1978), 24–25.

11. Whitaker, "Ulloa," 165–66; *Enciclopedia Universal Ilustrada* (Madrid: Espasa Calpe, 1929), 65:920–22. The British system of improved military and administrative efficiency, as witnessed in Boston and London, left a lasting impression on Ulloa, as did Admiral George Anson's naval feats in the 1740s and major overhaul of the British navy in the 1750s; see Brading, *First America,* 426.

12. "[G]overned by people who often neglect the public interest for their own, those areas [of Peru] are now in a bad state because of the longevity and deep-rooted character of these ills. Justice does not have sufficient weight or reason enough power to counteract disorder and vice. Consequently, it is not surprising that abuses have been introduced into all affairs of the republic: the harm done from disobedience of the law or

overall explanation of their linkages. Specific new measures were recommended to solve particular and general problems. It proposed a major reform program to avoid bad government, injustice, and religious apathy—all of which weakened the loyalty of colonial subjects and caused dangerous indigenous rebellion. Ulloa and Juan produced a remarkable blueprint of the colonial system's main problems and most urgently needed reforms. Individual chapters of the report dealt with specific issues that had obvious interconnections, from maritime trade and defense to Indian mistreatment and corrupt administration.

The authors' first topic of concern was colonial naval reform to confront recent British challenges in the Pacific. The report detected customary fraud in the administration of port garrisons by its authorities and troops who mishandled the royal allocation of supplies, wages, and construction funds, particularly in Callao, Valdivia, and Concepción. Improved supply of arms and munitions, as well as the reorganization of troops, were recommended.[13] The widespread and irrepressible contraband of goods from Europe and China was the next issue of concern. The report emphasized the loss of sorely needed royal revenues due to smuggling, especially during times of war, and the serious damage to legal trade resulting from this commercial fraud in which colonial authorities were deeply involved through bribery and extreme permissiveness. The authors' strikingly innovative suggestions ran against established monopoly interests. Yet they insisted that the Lima market be well supplied with frequent "loose" shipments (*navíos de registro*) outside the cumbersome fleet cycle to reduce the incentives for contraband. They concluded that the cheaper Cape Horn interoceanic route was better than the corrupted route through Panama or Cartagena.[14]

The next major issue reported by Ulloa and Juan in their "Discourse" was the extensive abuse and dispossession suffered by Indians under the rule of

---

introduction of unjust procedures; excesses on the part of ministers and people in power, seriously detrimental to the weak and the helpless; scandals in the licentious behavior of all; and an almost continuous general drift away from what is right, desirable, and necessary for well-ordered societies. With no good examples to follow and with the senseless spread of evil, it is not surprising that, with few exceptions, everyone is corrupted and powerless to re-establish conditions as they should be," Juan and Ulloa, *Discourse* (1978), 38–39.

13. Juan and Ulloa, "Discurso y reflexiones" (1749), sessions 1–2; *Noticias secretas* (1990), 135–38.

14. Juan and Ulloa, "Discurso y reflexiones" (1749), session 3; *Discourse* (1978), 45–68; *Noticias secretas* (1990), 201–29.

district authorities and first instance judges (*corregidores*), priests, and landowners seeking private enrichment.[15] In a rational description, informed with plenty of examples and direct observations of corrupt practices in public administration, starting at the lowest rungs of colonial society, Ulloa and Juan proceeded to explain in detail unfair abuses of authority that made victims of the poorest and weakest subjects, the Indians. Indigenous people, according to these enlightened informers, were subjected to tyranny and suffered more than slaves for no apparent reasons other than their simplicity and "humble ignorance."[16]

Abuses started with the collection of tribute from Indians by the corregidores. The inflow of income from Indian tribute into the hands of corregidores allowed ample opportunities for misappropriation and abuse. Adult male Indians had to pay an annual head tax or tribute ranging between four and nine pesos. According to Spanish law, several groups of Indians were exempt from this tribute due to age (under eighteen or over fifty-five years of age), physical disability, or privilege (chieftains or *caciques*, altar boys). Corregidores disregarded these rules and collected tribute from as many Indians as possible regardless of exemption status. Extortion and force were used to squeeze payments out of those who could not pay. To supplement and increase their income, the corregidores practiced double accounting. With the complicity of caciques and priests, corregidores officially reported lower numbers of taxable Indians and pocketed the difference between the actual amount collected and the official amount declared. This illegal undercounting of Indian tributaries was revealed by a new official poll (*revisita*) conducted during the administration of the Marqués de Castelfuerte, viceroy in the late 1720s. Corregidores used the illegally diverted tribute funds for purposes of their own, such as investing in private commercial deals, and delayed payment due to the royal treasury for years.[17]

15. Juan and Ulloa, "Discurso y reflexiones" (1749), sessions 4–8.

16. Juan and Ulloa, *Discourse* (1978), 69; *Noticias Secretas* (1990), 231. (Unless otherwise noted, all translations have been made by the author.) Based mainly on textual content analysis, a school of historians contends that Juan and Ulloa "appropriated" previous Andean and metropolitan reformist "discourses" to elaborate a politically biased project with doubtful firsthand information; see Andrien, "The *Noticias Secretas*," 177, 185–87. Corroborated and directly obtained information evident in the confidential report and other sources authored by Ulloa, especially his "Relación de Gobierno," contradicts this view.

17. Juan and Ulloa, "Discurso y reflexiones" (1749), session 4, ff. 434–98; Scarlett O'Phelan, "Orden y control en el siglo XVIII: la política borbónica frente a la corrupción fiscal, comercial y administrativa," in *El pacto infame: estudios sobre la corrup-*

Illegal abuse of Indians by greedy corregidores was capped by the forced sale (*reparto*) of overpriced, sometimes useless, goods and mules, which Ulloa and Juan intensely criticized and blamed for the 1742 indigenous insurrection of Juan Santos Atahualpa. Similar independent complaints against corrupt corregidores had been recorded since the time of the first corregidores in the 1560s in trials and judicial correspondence. However, a notable deterioration of most corregidores' administrative behavior had reached an alarming level in the first half of the seventeenth century with a concomitant weakening of effective checks. As evidenced from sources beyond the revelations of Ulloa and Juan, by the mid-eighteenth century the corruption of corregidores was a well-entrenched element of the colonial system.[18]

According to the "Discourse," at the end of their tenure corregidores and other local authorities simply bribed the judge in charge of the customary official review to avoid punishment.[19] These post-tenure residency trials (*juicios de residencia*), including those imposed on viceroys, were traditional administrative devices prominently inefficacious for the prosecution and sanction of officials guilty of corruption. The officially designated judges were favorable to the individual officer on trial or were part of the same circle of patronage and interests. The accused was often absolved or mildly reprimanded by residency judges through procedural technicalities, statutes of limitations, or arbitrary dismissal of the evidence. The residency inquiry trials remain, however, important historical sources in the study of colonial corruption, as they encompass original accusations and demands by different private and public parties.[20]

Widespread corrupt abuse by Spanish authorities also undermined Indians' ability to raise communal capital to ensure themselves against unfore-

---

ción en el Perú, ed. Felipe Portocarrero S. (Lima: Red de Ciencias Sociales, 2005), 13–33, esp. 14–17; Alfredo Moreno Cebrián, *El virreinato del marqués de Castelfuerte, 1724–1736: el primer intento borbónico por reformar el Perú* (Madrid: Editorial Catriel, 2000), 166–70.

18. Noble David Cook, "The Corregidores of the Colca Valley, Peru: Imperial Administration in an Andean Region," *Anuario de Estudios Hispanoamericanos* 60, no. 2 (2003): 413–39, esp. 428, 431–32, 435–36.

19. Juan and Ulloa, *Discourse* (1978), 71–73, 86–87; *Noticias secretas* (1990), 233–36, 250.

20. These same conclusions apply to other Spanish American cases: Teresa Albornoz de López, *La visita de Joaquín Mosquera y Figueroa a la Real Audiencia de Caracas (1804–1809): conflictos internos y corrupción en la administración de justicia* (Caracas: Academia Nacional de Historia, 1987), 53; Aída R. Caro Costas, *El juicio de residencia a los gobernadores de Puerto Rico en el siglo XVIII* (San Juan, Puerto Rico: Instituto de Cultura Puertorriqueña, 1978), 18, 188–91.

seen needs, according to sources other than the confidential report of Ulloa and Juan. The Cajas de Censos de Indios were community funds accruing from legally established liens on and loans granted to rural properties and public institutions, including the royal treasury. This rent income assigned to Indian communities had been secured by Spanish legislation in part to compensate for early expropriations of communal lands, as well as to guarantee the payment of Indian tribute and defray the costs of religious activities in times of trouble when Indians could not afford such payments. The funds of individual communities were consolidated in three general funds in Lima, Cusco, and Charcas, and administered by colonial authorities in charge of collecting the payments and debts owed to Indian communities. Collusion between collectors and debtors, interested neglect of proper accounting, and other transgressions of the Laws of the Indies that protected and regulated these funds had thoroughly depleted Indian communal capital by the mid-eighteenth century. Royal interests were also injured by the loss of income from Indian tribute not paid because of the depletion of the Indian censo funds.[21]

Ulloa and Juan proposed changing basic principles of the system to prevent abuse of Indians. They advocated banning repartos, forbidding corregidores to engage in private deals and trade (while promising promotion for competent service and permitting terms of office of more than five years), imposing strict punishments on transgressors, and paying Indians as free workers rather than subjecting them to forced labor (*mita*). Ulloa and Juan had no illusions, however. "Everyone in Peru would rail against a measure of this type," they added.[22] It was not sufficient to appoint a few honest authorities since corrupt or permissive authorities would always prevail. The systemic rules needed to change to truly transform the administrative hierarchy.[23]

According to Ulloa and Juan, the quality of public administration had seriously deteriorated. Under the venal system of sale of public offices intro-

---

21. Alfonso W. Quiroz, *Deudas olvidadas: instrumentos de crédito en la economía colonial peruana, 1750–1820* (Lima: Fondo Editorial Universidad Católica, 1993), 58–67; and "Reassessing the Role of Credit in Late Colonial Peru: *Censos, Escrituras,* and *Imposiciones*," *Hispanic American Historical Review* 74 (1994): 193–230, esp. 206–9, based on Audiencia de Lima, Caja de Censos, leg. 39, Archivo General de la Nación, Lima (hereafter AGN), and Gobierno, Lima, legs. 817, 833, AGI.

22. Juan and Ulloa, *Discourse* (1978), 149. See also *Noticias secretas* (1990), 320: "[T]odo el mundo gritaría en el Perú contra una determinación de esta calidad, y con ponderaciones no cortas harían presente que se arruinaban aquellos reinos enteramente libertando a los indios de mita."

23. Juan and Ulloa, *Discourse* (1978), 94–101; *Noticias secretas* (1990), 257–64.

duced in the Peruvian viceroyalty in 1633, the posts of treasury officials (*oficiales de cajas reales*) were sold to the highest bidders. The venal sale of official posts was extended to include corregidores in 1678 and high-court audiencia judges (*oidores*) in 1687. These important posts were mostly sold to wealthy, interested Creoles. During the seventeenth century, the sale of offices, tax farming, long-term loans (*juros*), and forced donations to the Crown had two main purposes: to defray the pressing costs of wars in Europe and to avoid charging higher taxes to local elites through the brokerage of venal treasury officials. These administrative customs, buttressed by local interests, contributed to a steady deterioration in the quality of colonial government, administrative honesty, and colonial finances.[24] Favoritism in the local appointment of corregidores and other officials was also deeply rooted, as was the practice of illegal presents and bribes paid to the highest colonial authorities responsible for interim appointments.[25]

Many of the fee-earning and salaried posts for sale were hereditary and could be transferred by the original purchaser (*oficios vendibles y renunciables*). In the 1690s, at least two cases were revealed in which viceroys in Peru and Mexico purchased their high positions of authority through a private contract with the Crown.[26] The sale of other nonhereditary or transferable higher posts, including that of oidores of the Lima Audiencia, increased substantially in two periods of financial strain for the Spanish Crown, 1701–1711 and 1740–1750.[27] Thus, during Ulloa's first sojourn in

24. Kenneth Andrien, "The Sale of Fiscal Offices and the Decline of Royal Authority in the Viceroyalty of Peru, 1633–1700," *Hispanic American Historical Review* 62 (1982): 49–71; "The Sale of Juros and the Politics of Reform in the Viceroyalty of Peru, 1608–1695," *Journal of Latin American Studies* 13 (1981): 1–19; and *Crisis and Decline: The Viceroyalty of Peru in the Seventeenth Century* (Albuquerque: University of New Mexico Press, 1985), 74–75, 128–29. For a still valid evaluation of the overwhelming financial and institutional costs of the sale of offices, see J. H. Parry, *The Sale of Public Office in the Spanish Indies under the Hapsburgs* (Berkeley: University of California Press, 1953), 73.

25. Alfredo Moreno Cebrián, *El corregidor de indios y la economía peruana en el siglo XVIII (Los repartos forzosos de mercancías)* (Madrid: Consejo Superior de Investigaciones Científicas, Instituto G. Fernández de Oviedo 1977), 737–41.

26. The merchant Francisco de Villavicencio, Conde de Cañete, purchased the post of viceroy of Peru for 250,000 pesos but died before reaching Lima to exploit it. Antonio Domínguez Ortiz, "Un virreinato en venta," *Mercurio Peruano* 49, no. 453 (1965): 43–51, cited in M. A. Burkholder and D. S. Chandler, "Creole Appointments and the Sale of Audiencia Positions in the Spanish Empire under the Early Bourbons, 1701–1750," *Journal of Latin American Studies* 4, no. 2 (1972): 187–206, esp. 188.

27. Burkholder and Chandler, "Creole Appointments," 191–92.

Peru the sale of offices was still the prevailing system of public appointment.[28] According to Ulloa and Juan, the principle of merit and royal reward in colonial administration continued being distorted and, consequently, the quality of colonial service debased.[29] The Spanish Crown began replacing venal offices with salaried appointments, accompanied with increasing royal warnings against the "pernicious abuse" of fraud by royal officers, only in the 1750s.[30] The generic sale of offices was not abolished until 1812.

Toward the end of their long treatise, Ulloa and Juan touch the core of colonial corruption: "In Peru abuse starts with those who ought to correct it."[31] They were referring to the interested collusion of the highest authority, the viceroy, with corrupting local interest groups. The viceroy had the centralizing authority for brokering access to local power, thus reinforcing his networks of patronage for political advantage and corrupt gain. To govern without major internal opposition, viceroys actively or passively supported abuses and excesses in conjunction with the audiencia's oidores and other local authorities.[32] Several viceroys received open or covert bribes and illegal presents for granting vacant official posts and enforcing and deciding fraudulent court rulings.[33] This essential truth at the center of the

28. Juan and Ulloa, *Discourse* (1978), 94–95; *Noticias secretas* (1990), 258.

29. "[S]ólo consiguen ser provistos en los corregimientos vacantes los que tienen el auxilio de la introducción adquiridos con regalos de valor y de ninguna manera a aquellos en quienes puramente hay mérito por el servicio. . . Así quedan los que sirven al rey defraudados de los premios que el mismo monarca les destina," Juan and Ulloa, "Discurso y reflexiones" (1749), f. 834.

30. Pedro Ureta (secretary of the viceroy) to Oficiales de las Cajas Reales, Lima, May 12, 1777, box 15, no. 157, Andean Collection, Yale University.

31. Juan and Ulloa, "Discurso y reflexiones" (1749), f. 830: "Empieza el abuso del Perú desde aquellos que debieran corregirlo."

32. This corrupt accommodation between viceroys and other colonial authorities and elite groups is similar to that which emerged after independence from Spain between military caudillos, trying to consolidate their power under highly unstable institutional conditions, and the domestic and foreign interest groups that advanced loans on import and export taxes. See Chapter 2.

33. "Virreyes ha conocido el Perú tan poco cautos en este particular que hacían fuese público el cohecho, otros que lo han admitido con tono, o disfraz de regalo, y otros más cautos aún que lo han permitido a su propio beneficio, ha sido con tal industria que han dejado dudar del hecho, para que unos lo atribuyan a intereses de sus criados y confidentes, y otros a utilidad de los mismos virreyes partiéndolo con los que intervienen en la negociación. Pero también ha habido otros tan apartados de intereses y tan arreglados a justicia que ni han querido admitir nada por estas mercedes, ni han consentido que lo hiciesen sus familiares," Juan and Ulloa, "Discurso y reflexiones" (1749), ff. 834–35.

colonial administration's workings was to personally affect Ulloa when he engaged in bitter disputes during his 1758–1764 tenure as Huancavelica's provincial governor and superintendent of mines in the years. Ulloa was not the first author to expose the corruption ills of the Peruvian colony and viceregal court. Ulloa actually formed part of an important group of anticorruption colonial reformers of varied provenance. Some were influenced by the style of reform projects proposing new empirewide and local measures (*arbitrios*) initiated by the so-called *arbitristas* in the seventeenth century and continued by the *proyectistas* in the eighteenth century.[34] In April 1747, a Lima-born contemporary of Ulloa submitted to the king in Madrid a treaty entitled "Estado político del Reino del Perú: gobierno sin leyes, ministros relajados . . ." (Political State of the Kingdom of Peru: Government without Laws, Dissolute Ministers . . .).[35] From the out-

---

See also ff. 837–39, and John Fisher, *Government and Society in Colonial Peru: The Intendant System, 1784–1814* (London: Athlone Press, 1970), 9.

34. For a discussion of the works and influence of the proyectistas around the mid-eighteenth century in Spanish America and Peru, see José Muñoz Pérez, "Los proyectos sobre España y las Indias en el siglo XVIII: el proyectismo como género," *Revista de Estudios Políticos,* no. 81 (1955): 169–95; and Quiroz, *Deudas olvidadas,* 82–90. The proyectistas were not simply limited to a "theoretical" model as has been argued to explain their supposed imperial ideology. The most important among them had a real effect on the economy and understanding of local realities, especially the economic, financial, and administrative thought of the time. Postmodern criticism considers them followers of a "discourse" with little impact, or a distorted one, on reality, and Ulloa and other reformists like him have been favorite targets. However, these critics do not consider in detail the incorporation of experience in the elaboration of such projects and their practical impact. See Andrien, "The *Noticias secretas,*" 177; Ramos, "Estudio histórico"; and Solano Pérez, *Pasión por reformar,* 125–26.

35. [Mariano Machado de Chaves], "Estado político del Reino del Perú: gobierno sin leyes, ministros relajados, tesoros con pobreza, fertilidad sin cultivo, sabiduría desestimada, milicia sin honor, ciudades sin amor patricio; la justicia sin templo, hurtos por comercios, integridad tenida por locura; Rey, el mayor de ricos dominios, pobre de tesoros. Estos atributos constituyen en grave detrimento de este Reyno; y para su remedio se proponen dos arbitrios a S.M. por un leal vasallo que solo los escribe inflamado del verdadero amor a su Príncipe y señor natural, y por el mayor bien del Reyno del Perú y de su Patria Lima. Al Exmo. Señor Dn Jossef de Carvajal y Lancaster, Ministro de Estado y decano de este Consejo, gobernador del Supremo de Indias, presidente de la Junta de Comercio, y moneda, y superintendente general de las postas y estafetas de dentro y fuera de España," Madrid, April 30, 1747, in Real Academia de la Historia (hereafter RAH), Colección Benito Mata Linares, vol. 67 (9-9-3/1722). This anonymous document was published with several obvious mistakes, including its alleged earlier date (1742), in *Revista Peruana* 4 (1880): 147–90, 351–69, and 497–504. Its authorship was hesitantly yet mistakenly ascribed to Vitorino Montero (mayor of Lima in 1747) by histori-

set, this author professed a genuine desire to serve the king in restoring Peru to its former splendor as well as his commitment to the public good, exhibition of the plain truth, and love of his country (*patria*). He dedicated the manuscript to the head of the Council of the Indies, the reformer anglophile Josef de Carvajal y Lancaster. The author preferred to remain anonymous to avowedly better inform Carvajal y Lancaster. He noted, however, that he was of trustworthy and noble origin. Many key observations of this earlier text coincided with central points of Ulloa's confidential report. There is evidence that Ulloa might have read this well-thought-out report before writing "Discurso" or shortly after.[36] Other reformist bureaucrats also had access to the nameless author's treatise centered on colonial administrative graft. The same basic text with a new title was resubmitted to the king in 1759, at a time of heightened concern over contraband. This time the author clearly stated his full name, Mariano Machado de Chaves, a man of certain means and a long-term resident at the court in Madrid, where he apparently pursued a royal post.[37]

---

ans Rubén Vargas Ugarte and Philip Means, the latter repeating the mistaken date of 1742. There is a copy of the same manuscript (same title, date, text, and dedication to Carvajal y Lancaster) at the Rare Book/Special Collections Reading Room, LOC, although it is still cataloged (with some suspicion according to a librarian's note) as authored by Montero (name originally attributed by the French book dealer Leclerc in his 1878 catalog; the LOC bought the manuscript from Librairie Ch. Chadenat of Paris). Two other copies, one annotated, in the Latin American-Peru manuscript collection, Lilly Library, Indiana University, are also assigned to Montero.

36. In 1763, Ulloa referred to this 1747 manuscript as "cierto proyecto que años hace tuve noticia haberse presentado a Su Majestad por un sujeto de Lima y ciertamente si su autor hubiese estado instruido de los términos a que esto ha llegado en los tiempos presentes pudiera haberlo amplificado con algunos fundamentos más convincentes de los que entonces había." Ulloa, "Relación de Gobierno," part 5, no. 23, Lima, leg. 777, AGI (refer also to copy in BPR). See also Arthur Whitaker, *The Huancavelica Mercury Mine: A Contribution to the History of the Bourbon Renaissance in the Spanish Empire* (Cambridge, MA: Harvard University Press, 1941), 139–40, note on misidentified "anonymous" 1747 manuscript attributed to Montero by other authors.

37. Mariano Machado de Chaves, "Estado político y de justicia de el Reino del Perú con demostraciones de las causas de su ruina, medios para su reforma y arbitrios para su mayor aumento por Dn. Mariano Machado de Chaves quien los dirige y ofrece como su más fiel y celoso vasallo a su Majestad Católica. Al Rey nuestro señor Carlos Tercero de España y de las Indias," Madrid, December 8, 1759, ms. II/930, BPR. We know little about Machado de Chaves except that he was from Los Reyes (Lima), had perhaps resided in Santiago de Chile, lived permanently in Madrid in the 1740s and 1750s, owned several houses in Seville (incidentally sequestered—owing to a sizable, unpaid private debt transferred to an official dependency—despite Machado de Chaves's legal allegations and a suspension of the seizure signed by Carvajal y Lancaster himself), and

In the 1747 version of his text, Machado de Chaves attributed the perceived decadence of Peru to the aging and decline of colonial institutions since "time, a malign traitor of all establishments, deteriorates everything." Passage of time, and the immense distance ("that other kind of time") separating the monarch from his colonial subjects, made it imperative to reinforce with new laws the strict observance of already established laws. Legal dissipation had resulted in "the reprieve of mischief, disregard of the authority of precept and, in such confidence, ambition has carved usurious disloyalty [and] iniquity has grown from bad to worst."[38]

According to Machado de Chaves, in the two hundred and more years of colonial dominance in Peru leading to 1747, there had been three different generations of viceroys. The first generation had imposed the pacification of the realm after the Conquest, establishing adequate rewards of *encomiendas* and government posts bestowed to the few armed and obedient Spaniards who faced millions of defeated Indians. The second generation was more assured of its dominance with the increased number of Spaniards and declining number of Indians. Ambition then started to reign over merit and honor of arms, and viceroys fed their avarice for private gain by granting favors to miners and merchants. The third generation of viceroys contributed especially to the decadence of Peru and reached the pinnacle of dissolution aided by local oidores. Viceroys now enforced the law as if they were absolute princes with the expectation of pecuniary gratuities (*indultos pecunarios*) for deciding against justice, right, and truth: "[V]iceroys and oidores in agreement is the same as if wolves and dogs united to devour a flock of sheep when the main shepherd is far away." Moreover, as viceroys and oidores were the key components of colonial government and court, Machado de Chaves thought it necessary to focus his observations on the harm they caused since other subaltern officials "not only imitate the

---

filed a statement of his accomplishments and services in November 1760. See José Toribio Medina, *Biblioteca Hispano-Americana* (Santiago de Chile: Imprenta casa del autor, 1901), 5: 550: "Relación de los méritos y servicios de Don Mariano Machado de Chaves y Osorio, natural de la ciudad de los Reyes . . . Madrid 4 noviembre 1760." No such "relación" was found in the AGI, although relevant information exists in the 1749–1751 trial, "Mariano Machado de Chaves con el Fiscal de la Superintendencia de Azogues [de Sevilla] sobre paga de [42,138 reales de vellón]," in "Pleitos del ramo de azogue," Escribanía, leg. 1005B, ff. 3–4, 31–32, AGI.

38. Machado de Chaves, "Estado político" (1747), f. 2: "[E]l tiempo traidor maligno de los establecimientos que lo relaja todo. . . [O]tra especie de tiempo . . . se ha hecho indulto de la malicia, desconocer al dueño del precepto, y de la misma confianza ha labrado la ambición una infidelidad de usuras, creciendo de lo inicuo a lo pésimo."

example of their elders but precisely as subjects they obey all the arbitrary excesses," believing perhaps that the authority has two sets of laws.[39] Machado de Chaves's revelations multiply the number of faults by viceroys and judges reported by Ulloa.

Upon arrival at the viceroyalty, starting in fact with the last 230-league stretch of their trip from Paita to Lima, viceroys and their families and sizable entourage were fed, kept, and regaled by corregidores and other local officials. For their private gain, viceroys imposed an improper, mandatory excise fee on those already appointed as corregidores by the king. The amount of that fee varied according to the size of the viceroy's family and relatives. Viceroys granted pardons on the day of their saint or birth for a going rate of up to four thousand pesos. They also exploited to their advantage private contracts for the supply of gunpowder and wages of garrisons, and allowed illicit trade to certain merchants and shipmasters. From these illegal activities, the viceroys and their relatives obtained most of their private benefits. Viceroys also found advantage in immersing officials in permanent litigation and residence trials. Consequently, every high or low official, including the clergy, was obliged to provide gifts to gain the viceroy's favor. Abuses of subaltern officials were therefore sheltered and multiplied everywhere. Oidores engaged in excessive, interested litigation, received illegal tribute from other officials, and protected ecclesiastical abuses, or *corruptelas*.[40] Treasury officials were interested parties in delaying the collection of debts owed to the royal treasury, thus causing fiscal losses of approximately 10 million pesos in five decades. The clergy bribed authorities to enhance their property and cover up their faults.

If urgent remedies were not applied to all these abuses, Machado de Chaves warned, popular unrest in the name of "libertad de la patria" could

---

39. Machado de Chaves, "Estado político" (1759), ff. 3v–4v: "[M]utuados a un dictamen virreyes y oidores, es lo mismo que unirse los lobos y los canes a devorar un rebaño porque el principal pastor se halla lejos. . . [Los demás jueces y ministros] no solo imitan el ejemplo de los mayores, sino que precisamente como súbditos obedecen todas las libertades de el arbitrio, creyendo que los que mandan tendrán unos libros de leyes para los gobernados y otros de derechos civiles para lo judicial."

40. Machado de Chaves, "Estado político" (1747), f. 21. The author makes literal use of the word *corruptela*, which was defined in the 1729 edition of the Spanish *Diccionario de la Real Academia* as follows: "Por alusión vale mala costumbre, o abuso, introducido contra la ley que no debe alterarse. Lat. *Abusus, Corruptela.* RECOP. Lib.7 tit.10 l 11. Como dicen que se acostumbra en algunos de los lugares: pues es injusta esta extorsión y *corruptela.* SOLORZ. Polit.lib.5.cap.2. Pero no por ello puedo aprobar la costumbre, o mejor decir, *corruptela* de algunos Corregidores."

result—unrest like that experienced since 1730 in Paraguay, Cochabamba, and Oruro—"a true ghost to be frightened of among all people and even more so in Peru where everything smells of slavery as laws are turned into tyranny."[41]

Before Machado de Chaves and Ulloa, other critics had considered corruption of the principles of government and justice by greedy colonial officers to be a serious problem in Peru since the late sixteenth and early seventeenth centuries. These critics argued that the king's stake in public order and justice as well as general Christian principles were gravely undermined by illegal yet common practices. Such critics included Andean indigenous writers of memorials and chronicles documenting abuses against Indians and arguing for reform.[42] As early as 1615, the chronicler Felipe Guamán Poma de Ayala produced a unique indigenous account with original and critical drawings. Although Guamán Poma's powerful denunciation was disregarded and shelved by royal authorities, it can be considered the first known anticorruption statement against the mistreatment of Indians by colonial authorities and the clergy. The author considered his work useful for correcting the abuses of corregidores, *encomenderos* (early holders of Indian labor grants), clergy, and miners, as well as in conducting fair official reviews (*residencias* and *visitas*) of Indians. Guamán Poma, an interpreter and artist disciple of Spanish chronicler Fray Martín de Murúa, criticized the legacy of Viceroy Francisco de Toledo as part of a personal quest to justify his claims as Indian provincial authority (*cacique principal*) of Huamanga against other caciques of Incan *mitimaq* (colonizer) background. He opposed *mestizaje* (people of mixed ancestry, or mestizos), and was committed to a premodern utopian and deeply religious alternative to the observed corruption, advocating strict Christianization of the Indians.[43]

---

41. Machado de Chaves, "Estado político" (1759), f. 22v: ". . . digno fantasma a temerse en todos los pueblos, y mucho más en el Perú, donde todo respira esclavitudes y se hacen tiranía las leyes."

42. Andrien, "The *Noticias Secretas*," 180–82, cites the cacique and procurator Vicente Morachimo (1732) and Fray Calixto Túpac Inca (1750).

43. Rolena Adorno, *Guamán Poma: Writing and Resistance in Colonial Peru,* 2nd ed. (Austin: University of Texas Press, 2000), xxvii, xlii. See Guamán Poma's unique graphical representations and text, especially the images and passages referring to the Audiencia Real, corregidores and encomenderos, priests, Spaniards, Creoles, mestizos, and blacks, in Felipe Guamán Poma de Ayala, *Nueva corónica y buen gobierno* (1615), ed. Franklin Pease (Caracas: Biblioteca Ayacucho, 1980), 1:359–61, 364, 370, 373, 387, 391, 396–97, 401, 411, 427; 2:10–11, 16–17, 38–39, 78–79, 80–81, and 118–21, reproduced from a 1936 facsimile version produced in Paris. Also reproduced in *Nueva*

Following a different tradition, Sergeant Juan de Aponte wrote one of the first reformist arbitrista projects aiming at correcting corruption in 1622.[44] Aponte was born in Granada but resided in the Andean city of Huamanga, where he signed his "representación" or "memorial" addressed to the king. Aponte initially justified his work as an example of the responsibility of true royal subjects to truthfully inform their king of the "notable perdition" of Peru and the need of a "great reformation" (*gran reformación*). Toward the end of his text, he said that he had served ten years in a royal ship on duty in the Pacific (Mar del Sur) and retired without reward (*premio*). He realized how poorly honest and steadfast service was compensated in Peru because "everything is based on interest and those who have can and the poor die."[45]

Aponte's early negative views on the viceroys coincide with those Machado de Chaves expressed later about the second generation of viceregal rulers. Although administrative reform was sorely necessary, viceroys were not interested in pursuing reform owing to their own private interest and what they hoped to take back with them to Spain.[46] The principal interest of many oidores was also in enriching themselves. Treasury officers took advantage of the royal treasury in deals with private parties: They

---

crónica y buen gobierno (1615), ed. John Murra, Rolena Adorno, and Jorge Urioste (Mexico: Siglo XXI, 1980), 2 vols., reissued (Madrid: Historia 16, 1987), 3 vols. For a more realistic view of the original manuscript, see the electronic edition of "El primer nueva coronica y buen gobierno," 1615, ms. GkS 2232 4, at the Royal Library, Copenhagen, Denmark, http://www.kb.dk/permalink/2006/poma/1/en/text/.

44. Juan de Aponte, "Representación que en el año 1622 hizo a Su Majestad el sargento Juan de Aponte Figueroa, natural de Granada y vecino de la ciudad de Guamanga sobre las cosas del reino del Perú y los daños que padecía por la codicia de los que lo gobernaban y medios que debían aplicarse para su reforma," Guamanga, April 24, 1622, BPR, ms. II/2839, ff. 144–82. Aponte's text was published under the title, "Memorial que trata de la reformación del reino del Pirú. . ." in *Colección de documentos inéditos para la historia de España* (Madrid: Real Academia de la Historia, 1867), 51:521–62.

45. "No son señor buenos deseos solos, sino también obras que en su Real Servicio he tenido, habiéndolo servido diez años últimamente en aquella mar del sur de oficial de Guerra en la Real Capitana Jesús María, donde me retiré sin ningún premio, viendo la poca remuneración de que gozan los que sirven a V.C.M., que en aquel Reyno premianse mal buenos servicios, porque todo corre fundado en interés, y los que tienen pueden y los pobres mueren," Aponte, "Representación," ff. 181v–82, cf. f. 145.

46. "[E]l interés de lo que [los virreyes] llevan a España no les da lugar a ninguna reformación porque resultará de ella muy poco aprovechamiento para sí, y de esta manera atienden al bien propio que al servicio de Dios N.S. y al de V[uestra] R[eal] M[ajestad] y ansí no se reforma nada y todo corre de una manera y forma digna de muy gran remedio," Aponte, "Representación," f. 146.

should have been closely supervised and forbidden to engage in private deals. Corregidores were like locusts, Aponte continued, acting more like merchants and dealers than judges: they illegally introduced quantities of wine for sale at high prices to Indians in their districts, although they forbade others from doing the same. They also harbored forbidden card games in their own homes.

Among the many ills identified by Aponte in 1622, the most damaging for the colonial economy was the corrupt administration of the Huancavelica mercury mines. Its administration under conditions of royal monopoly was dismal: "[I]t is a weight and ballast in this kingdom of Peru, a matter Your Majesty requests every year to be looked after and about which the least active steps are taken for its improvement."[47] The mine had been carelessly worked since its early exploitation. The abutments and arches supporting the mine's ceilings had been damaged or destroyed when minerals were extracted from them, with little or no attention paid to restoration. As a result, frequent collapses killed many Indian miners. Authorities did not punish this abusive and costly practice. Moreover, authorities kept for their own gain much of the mercury produced instead of distributing it among silver miners. Moreover, royal officers did not implement necessary technical improvements such as a ventilation and drain shaft (*socavón*), which Aponte believed was absolutely necessary. Indians were also overexploited. Many of them died of exhaustion and disease, because tributary Indian recruits through the mita system were scarce. Impoverished Indian communities and their *curacas* or caciques paid for exonerating Indians from labor service in the mines. With the connivance of judges and corregidores, miners took advantage of these illegal payments, abused the Indians working for them, and jeopardized mine productivity.[48]

Aponte's insights into the mining situation in Huancavelica were corroborated by official correspondence during the second half of the seventeenth century and after. In 1645, the Marqués de Mancera, viceroy from 1639 to 1648, stated that when he assumed the post, Huancavelica mercury mining was in "a notorious miserable condition due to large ruinous collapses that had occurred shortly before and . . . thereafter continue[d] its

47. Aponte, "Representación," ff. 150v–51: "el peso y lastre de este reino del Perú, y la cosa que V.M. más encarga todos los años y en la que menos diligencias se hacen de su aumento."
48. Aponte, "Representación," ff. 152–53v.

deterioration to such a degree that hardly any quicksilver could be extracted."[49] The matter was urgent because preservation of the Peruvian kingdoms and, consequently, of the monarchy itself depended on restoration of the mine. The completion of a shaft that had remained unfinished since the early 1600s was considered. Mancera assigned a talented specialist of "notable integrity and lack of interest," Constantino de Vasconcelos, to visit the mine and propose technical solutions. Vasconcelos, who was trained in mathematics, geometry, architecture, and drawing, concluded that the disorganized and careless method of exploitation—that is, exclusive focus on extraction while ignoring the mine's infrastructure—was the main cause of its ruinous state. Based on his detailed mapping of the site, Vasconcelos recommended a rationalization of the mining works. His sound technical advice was opposed by "private persons who vied to obscure the truth of useful changes and return to the bad ways of the past."

A lay associate (*familiar*) of the Inquisition and member of the viceroy's inner circle, Luis de Sotomayor Pimentel, was then appointed governor of Huancavelica, a post customarily reserved for the oidores of Lima. Sotomayor thoroughly rejected Vasconcelos's prudent and well-argued innovations, and insisted that the best way to proceed was to go after the rich mineral veins, repairing the mine where necessary using Indian labor and following longtime practices.[50]

A few years later, it was clear that Huancavelica's situation had not improved. On the contrary, a new visit and inspection of the mine in 1649 verified abundant high-risk damage in arches and bridges caused by plundering and mistakes. In such a state, the inspectors avowed, the Huancavelica operation did not deserve the label of "mine."[51] Further problems such as

49. "Copia del asiento que el marqués de Mancera [Pedro Álvarez de Toledo y Leiva, primer marqués de Mancera] mi Sor. Virrey del Perú celebró con los mineros de la mina de azogue de la villa de Huancavelica," Huancavelica, September 6, 1645, in "Visitas de las minas de Huancavelica, 1572–1686," Gobierno, Lima, leg. 271, AGI.

50. Ibid., ff. 6–11v, and report by Luis de Sotomayor Pimentel listing the "inconveniencias" of Vasconcelos's report, Huancavelica, May 23, 1645, and detailed response by Vasconcelos, Huancavelica, July 4, 1645, in "1649: Autos y diligencias fechas por los señores doctores Juan González de Peñafiel y don Melchor de Omonte caballero de la orden de Calatrava, oidor y alcalde del crimen de la Real Audiencia de Los Reyes sobre la visita y vista de la mina del cerro de Huancavelica," ff. 12–36, Gobierno, Lima, leg. 279, AGI.

51. Acuerdo, Viceroy García Sarmiento Conde de Salvatierra, Lima, January 22, 1649, in "1649: Autos y diligencias," ff. 1–3, Gobierno, Lima, leg. 279, AGI.

continued decline in production and fund mismanagement by Huancavelica officials were reported in the 1660s.[52] Almost a hundred years later, the enlightened, technical reformer Antonio de Ulloa had to confront similar problems during his tenure as governor of Huancavelica.

The Purgatory of Mining Administration

After submitting in 1749 his confidential report on misgovernment in Spanish America and Peru, Ulloa served as a secret informer and agent of the Spanish Crown in France, the Netherlands, Denmark, and Sweden through the early 1750s.[53] Under the guise of a mathematics scholar, he provided the Spanish government sensitive information on ports, canals, roads, factories, mines, and labor in those countries. Through his travels and studies, Ulloa had reached the pinnacle of an enlightened, reformist modernizer. His scientific contributions—including his early report on a yet-to-be named metal he encountered in his first American voyage, platinum—were widely recognized in Europe. He then settled in Cadiz and continued working as a naval officer until he accepted the more remunerative appointment in Huancavelica. Previous attempts at reforming mining misadministration, malfeasance, and contraband had been seriously limited and were eventually defeated by interested local opposition during the administration of reformist viceroys, the Duque de la Palata (1681–1689) and the Marqués de Castelfuerte (1724–1736).[54] Ulloa was aware of the degree of difficulty of his new

52. Juan del Solar to the Viceroy Conde de Lemos, Madrid, January 16, 1669; Reina Gobernadora to Conde de Lemos, Madrid, June 15, 1668; and "Año 1661: Relación de la causa de visita que de orden de Su Mgd. a sustanciado Alvaro de Ibarra presidente de la Rl. Audiencia de Quito contra el Dor. Don Tomás Verzón de Caviedes oidor de la de Lima y demás culpados en la distribución de 232 mil pesos que por fines del año 1661 mandó remitir a Huancavelica siendo virrey del Perú el conde de Santisteban para en parte de pago de azogues que entraron en los Rls. Almacenes dicho año de 1661 los mineros y buscones de dicho asiento," in Gobierno, Lima, leg. 271, AGI.

53. Jorge Juan also spied for the Spanish Crown in England, where he observed shipbuilding techniques, and as ambassador in Morocco. TePaske, "Introduction," in Juan and Ulloa, *Discourse,* 6, 9.

54. Jeffrey Cole, "Viceregal Persistence versus Indian Mobility: The Impact of Duque de la Palata's Reform Program on Alto Peru, 1681–1692," *Latin American Research Review* 19 (1984): 37–56; Kendall Brown, "La crisis financiera peruana al comienzo del siglo XVIII, la minería de plata y la mina de azogues de Huancavelica," *Revista de Indias* 48 (1988): 349–81; Moreno Cebrián, *Virreinato de Castelfuerte,* 621–26.

job but could not foresee the depth of troubles that awaited him in what he later dubbed his Peruvian "purgatory."[55]

Ulloa's earlier reports on colonial administrative corruption had been delivered from the point of view of a confidential direct observer. As governor of Huancavelica since November 1758, however, his insights into serious administrative flaws originated from the innermost entrails of the colonial bureaucracy.[56] In the lengthy and important account of his administration in Huancavelica, the "Relación de gobierno" (1763), the picture he painted was even grimmer than that of the previous "Discourse."[57] He subsequently wrote another major official report based on his Andean administrative experience, penned countless official letters, and got embroiled in several trials and legal proceedings in which he stood maliciously accused of the same crimes he was actually trying to stamp out.[58] Essentially he clashed with a bulwark of corrupt interests in collusion with top colonial authorities, and he lost. The honest and enlightened administrator had to leave Peru in 1764, unable to change the networks that continued to under-

55. Whitaker, "Ulloa," 178, 183, citing letters of Ulloa to Julián Arriaga, Cádiz, July 27, 1757, in Gobierno, Lima, leg. 775, and Huancavelica, August 20, 1763, in Gobierno, Lima, leg. 777, AGI. See also Ulloa to S.M. el Rey, Huancavelica, June 20, 1763, complaining about "la horrible tempestad de persecuciones" he had suffered in almost five years at his post "constituyéndose mi vida en un purgatorio de continuos desabrimientos," Gobierno, Lima, leg. 777, AGI.

56. "[L]o que puedo asegurar a V.E. es que habiendo conocido estos parajes desde el año de [17]36 hasta el de [17]44, los he hallado tan distintos de lo que eran que enteramente está todo trastornado," Ulloa to Arriaga, Huancavelica, June 20, 1763, Gobierno, Lima 777, AGI.

57. The seldom-quoted and -analyzed "Relación de gobierno" consists of five parts or points, each signed by Ulloa and methodically completed in successive dates in Huancavelica: part 1, royal mercury mine, containing 133 subtitles, dated February 10, 1763; part 2, miners' guild, 30 subtitles, February 28, 1763; part 3, treasury (caja real) and azogue distribution, 26 subtitles, March 7, 1763; part 4, civil and political government, 55 subtitles, April 15, 1763; and part 5, Angaraes province, 34 subtitles, May 15, 1763. Quotations from this source, provided below, are based on the original in Gobierno, Lima, leg. 777, AGI, and duplicate copy, signed also by Ulloa, BPR.

58. "Informes de D. Antonio de Ulloa dirigidos a Carlos III . . . sobre las inteligencias que se hacen con el azogue en perjuicio de las labores de las minas de plata del Perú. . . ," signed by Ulloa, Real Isla de León (Cádiz), September 14, 1771, 36 ff., ms. 19568, Manuscritos, Biblioteca Nacional de Madrid (hereafter BNM). Unable to dispute that these reports confirm the core of "Discurso y reflexiones políticas" and refute the claim that Ulloa had exaggerated or lacked direct observation, the modern critics of Ulloa now present him as a rigid governor with an "exaggerated sense of command," unable to "convince" those who opposed his reforms. Solano, *Pasión por reformar*, 183, among others.

mine the Peruvian colonial economy through corrupt administration, twisted private benefit, and appalling public loss.

The Spanish imperial leadership in Madrid understood clearly the importance of the Huancavelica mines for the silver-based imperial economy: With their demise the empire would suffer devastating strategic losses. During the first two decades of the eighteenth century, crisis conditions at the mines continued in the midst of an overall economic and administrative decline in the viceroyalty. Since the 1720s, top Bourbon bureaucrats had endeavored to reform the decadent situation of the local administration and government in Huancavelica, as described by Aponte, Mancera, and Vasconcelos. These efforts netted mixed results. Miners of mercury and silver were chronically short of working capital, heavily indebted to the Crown, and at the mercy of private merchant creditors and corrupt local governors who also extended usurious credit to miners. An important step toward ameliorating the mining crisis was the introduction of royal treasury cash advances to mercury miners to help maintain official monopoly prices of mercury legally supplied to and purchased by silver miners. The management of these royal credit funds was transferred from the hands of viceroys and treasury officials in Lima to the supervision of more honest, newly appointed governors of Huancavelica. The royal treasury also began to supply mercury on credit to silver miners all over the viceroyalty. Mercury miners stopped selling to private purchasers eager to obtain quicksilver (mercury) illegally to refine untaxed, unregistered silver destined for contraband trade. All these measures brought a much-needed boost to the Andean silver economy by the early 1750s.[59]

However, at the time Ulloa took over Huancavelica's local government, the old corruption was in a vengeful resurgence. The preceding interim governor of Huancavelica, greedy Pablo de la Vega y Bárcena (1755–1758), had completely dismantled the order and restorative work of his two predecessors, Jerónimo de Sola and Gaspar de la Cerda y Leiva. According to what Ulloa deemed Vega's own confession, the mine was exploited without concern over its future collapse, the royal treasury was left to the onslaught of fraud by officers and private individuals (*inteligencias particulares*), the monopoly of purchasing and distributing mercury made it the object of private profit, tyranny had replaced good government, and bribery

59. Adrian J. Pearce, "Huancavelica, 1700–1759: Administrative Reform of the Mercury Industry in Early Bourbon Peru," *Hispanic American Historical Review* 79 (1999): 669–702.

dominated the administration of justice. When Ulloa took office Vega did not deliver customary accounting reports of the three most important branches (treasury, miners' guild, and mercury). Instead, Vega left behind monumental disorder that hid countless abuses and frauds against royal interests. Through illicit means, Vega had gained more than 30,000 pesos per year during his tenure (an extravagant figure if we consider that a Lima oidor's legal annual salary at the time was between 4,000 and 5,000 pesos, a low-ranking treasury officer earned 400 pesos a year, and a free mining worker was paid 4 pesos a week or around 200 pesos annually). Most revealingly, the highest authorities in Lima allowed these illegal actions to occur because they received part of the ill-gotten gains as "presents" in the form of silver bars for their saint's day or whenever there was a difficulty to be resolved. Failure to comply with this illegal custom and accept cohechos and *sobornos* brought Ulloa many bitter problems.[60]

Ulloa had expected to apply his reformist scientific and technical knowledge to improve mercury exploitation and mine organization. However, complicit miners and official supervisors (*veedores*) systematically disregarded or maliciously lied about complying with Ulloa's administrative orders and technical regulations. Not trusting the supervisors, Ulloa had to personally verify the physical condition of the mines on a periodic basis. He demonstrated that urgent maintenance tasks—such as repairs of mine walls, ceilings, and abutments, as well as the clearing, fortification, and paving of the San Javier and San Nicolás draining shafts—were critically delayed. Miners resisted these duties; they obtained instead falsified permissions to work in forbidden sites inside the mine, extracted the mineral from key abutments (*estribos*), and later covered up the illegal work with loose debris that should have been cleared from the mine. Dangerous and ruinous collapses ensued, thanks to the careless illegal works of several miners including Francisco Gómez and Baltasar de Cañas, son-in-law and brother-in-law (*concuñado*), respectively, of veedor José Campuzano. Other supervisors such as Fernando Anthesana, Juan Afino, and Francisco San Martín were also guilty of either fraud or complicity with unscrupulous miners and merchants.[61] As he had in the "Discourse" of 1749, Ulloa also

60. Ulloa, "Relación de gobierno," part 1, introd., ff. 3–4v, BPR (see also copy in AGI).

61. Ulloa, "Relación de gobierno," part 1, nos. 1–10, 27, 35, 44–46, and 51. Other destructive and corrupt agents included the powerful merchant Francisco Ocharán (illicit purchase of mercury, abusive reparto de mercancías among Indians), Miguel Guisaburuaga (embezzlement), assistant veedor José Gordillo, and Joachim Ramery, a ser-

denounced the excesses of repartos and the fraud in counting Indian tributaries and using Indian labor.[62]

Regarding the declining quality of the mine's ore, Ulloa confirmed that deeper layers of the mineral had a lower metal content. He blamed the miners' guild for not implementing the necessary investment in its furnaces and inputs to enhance productivity. Ulloa even experimented with a publicly financed mine operation, the Minería del Rey, much opposed by the miners who feared eventual state control of the Huancavelica mining activities. Ulloa realized that it was impossible to reconcile the interests of the miners' guild with those of the Crown. Miners were there only for their own interest and profit. Ulloa was of the opinion that the worst "monstrosities" committed by men were common within the miners' guild of Huancavelica, and considered leadership of the guild tantamount to punishment. Miners were accustomed to providing the Huancavelica governor with gifts and rewarding him with monies raised in card games played at his house, a custom Ulloa made it his business to curtail. More important, despite official cash advances provided to finance mercury production, miners engaged in the forbidden sale of quicksilver to private parties instead of repaying debts and depositing the mercury in royal stores.[63] Royal officers also made illegal profit by granting mercury advances to unscrupulous, undercapitalized miners who resold the mercury at higher prices and then shared the difference with the granting officers. There had been years of neglect in collecting debts owed by miners to government sources. The royal treasury thus lost precious funds that it needed to continue and enhance its credit operations for miners.[64]

In October 1760, fed up with technical incompetence and corrupt insubordination and abuse, Ulloa exiled several miners, and imprisoned top supervising officials Campuzano and Afino and their assistant José Gordillo, charging them with allowing illegal exploitation that risked the collapse of the mine works.[65] The local supporters of the imprisoned officials included

vant of Vega. On mine collapses, "1760: carta de Ulloa acusando recibo de un informe acerca del estado de una mina," Huancavelica, May 18, 1760, Colección Santa María, doc. 110, AGN.

62. Ulloa, "Relación de gobierno," part 5, nos. 12–17.

63. Ibid., part 1, nos. 22 and 43; part 2, introd., nos. 1, 7, 13–15, and 29; and part 4, no. 4. See also Ulloa to Arriaga, Huancavelica, August 20, 1763, Gobierno, Lima, leg. 777, AGI.

64. Ulloa, "Informes a Carlos III," ff. 6–8v, BNM.

65. Ulloa, "Relación de gobierno," part 1, no. 92, ff. 43–43v, BPR (also copy AGI);

the royal accountant Juan Sierra and the priest Juan José de Aguirre. (Ulloa had previously crossed the paths of three secular parish priests in Huancavelica in separate incidents. In 1759, the governor had blamed priest Manuel Joseph de Villata for speculating with flour and contributing to a dangerous scarcity of bread, charged the philanderer priest Antonio Segura with abducting a young woman, and rejected Aguirre's pretensions of becoming Ulloa's adviser. The viceroy and ministers in Lima, as well as the bishop of Huamanga, did little to correct these priests' transgressions. Ulloa excoriated the behavior and lack of respect of Huancavelica's ecclesiastics, whom he accused of taking advantage of Indians and publicly beating Indian chieftains.) According to Ulloa, Aguirre had benefited under the previous Vega administration by overcharging for burial fees. Aguirre pressed for Ulloa's removal from office and the return of Vega as governor and Campuzano as supervisor. Facing this conspiracy, Ulloa managed to secure an order to remove Vega from Huancavelica.[66]

Aguirre then organized a local extralegal, almost subversive campaign to disqualify and denigrate Ulloa's actions against the imprisoned mining officials who had confessed their guilt. In addition, Aguirre mobilized, through illegal gifts and mendacious letters, corrupt contacts at the court of the viceroy, the Conde de Superunda (1745–1761), in Lima, and that of his successor Manuel Amat y Junyent (1761–1776). Aguirre's complaints prompted a first official inquiry in late 1761. Cristóbal de Mesia, oidor of Lima, with Corregidor Carlos Platsaert as witness, carried out an official visita of Huancavelica. This intervention freed the incarcerated officials without proceeding with their prosecution.[67] Ulloa soon learned that several members of the Lima Audiencia and even Amat had sided with his local enemies at the behest of Amat's legal adviser, the shadowy and thoroughly corrupt José Perfecto de Salas.[68]

Miguel Molina Martínez, *Antonio de Ulloa en Huancavelica* (Granada: Universidad de Granada, 1995), 69.

66. Ulloa, "Relación de gobierno," part 4, nos. 40–47.

67. Ibid., part 1, no. 92, and part 4, no. 44; see also "Expediente del juicio de Ignacio de Elizalde, minero de Huancavelica" against the "maliciosas imputaciones del cura Aguirre," Huancavelica, October 10 and 15, 1761, signed by Ulloa and Juan de Alasta as witness.

68. Vicente Rodríguez Casado, "Estudio preliminar," in Manuel Amat y Junyent, *Memoria de gobierno,* ed. and introd. Rodríguez Casado and Florentino Pérez Embid (Seville: Escuela de Estudios Hispano-Americanos, 1947), xcvii, citing Gobierno, Lima, leg. 846B, AGI. The priest Aguirre eventually fled Huancavelica to organize the power-

Redoubled efforts against Ulloa led to a second official inquiry carried out by the Lima Audiencia's prosecutor Diego de Holgado, who opened a residency trial against Ulloa. Despite initial judicial decisions favorable to Ulloa, Amat and Holgado proceeded with new inquiries thoroughly undermining Ulloa's authority, and charged Ulloa with the same crimes of corruption he had previously filed against guilty officers and miners. In his turn, Ulloa reported to his superiors in Spain that Amat was a corrupt viceroy who got angry because Ulloa had refused to give him the customary bribe of 10,000 pesos with which the governorship of Huancavelica was unofficially earmarked for the private benefit of the viceroy.[69] In his "Relación de Gobierno" Ulloa took the opportunity to lash out against the scandalous sale of corregidor posts and other corrupt transgressions by viceroys Superunda and Amat.[70] Likewise, the former contractor (*asentista*) for the mule transport of mercury, Gaspar Alejo de Mendiolaza, later accused Holgado of abusing his post and endangering the strategic supply and public good in favor of an undercapitalized, scheming new bidder of the transport contract.[71]

Ulloa's reformist efforts toward technical improvements in mine operations and Huancavelica's urban infrastructure were undercut by the legal

---

ful opposition to Ulloa in Lima, led by José Perfecto Salas (1714–1778), Amat's adviser. Salas, born in Corrientes and with a law degree from the University of San Marcos (1737), "spent 1761 to 1775 in Lima as the legal advisor of Viceroy Manuel Amat and earned hatred for his arbitrary actions and corruption. He may have written Amat's *Memoria*. . .[,] was a dominant political figure, an illegal landowner and smuggler, an opponent of reform, and a major beneficiary of corruption in government. When he left Lima for Chile, opponents believe he took 2 to 3 million pesos," Mark Burkholder and D. S. Chandler, *Biographical Dictionary of Audiencia Ministers in the Americas, 1687–1821* (Westport, CT: Greenwood Press, 1982), 307–308, based on archival sources of Archivo General de Simancas and AGI.

69. Whitaker, "Ulloa," 181, citing several letters of Ulloa dated 1761–1765 in Gobierno, Lima, legs. 842–43, AGI.

70. Ulloa, "Relación de gobierno," part 5, nos. 22–30.

71. The rich mule driver and former *asentista del trajín de azogues* Gaspar de Mendiolaza accused *fiscal* Holgado, in the proceedings of Holgado's *juicio de residencia,* of favoring bidder Bernabé de Olano. Mendiolaza claimed a 50,000-peso investment loss, charging that Olano did not have sufficient mules, tack and equipment, and funds for the mercury transport business, which entailed delivering a total of four or five thousand *quintales* of mercury to many distant places and the use of up to four thousand mules. This favoritism endangered the public good: "[S]e expone enteramente la Real Hacienda y el público a una ruina irreparable," in "Autos de querella y demanda de Dn. Gaspar Alexo de Mendiolaza al Sor. Dn. Diego de Holgado ante el Sr. Juez de su residencia, año 1769, quaderno primero," Consejos, leg. 20331, exp. 1, doc. 1, f. 2v, AHN.

mess he was sucked into.[72] Nevertheless, during Ulloa's administration levels of mercury and silver production improved, although they fell again after his departure. Other subsequent Bourbon attempts to reform the administration of the Huancavelica mines and overcome technical problems also failed. Huancavelica's production continued to decline—except for very short interludes—until 1813, when it produced a small fraction of what it had under Ulloa, and its ultimate ruin at the time of independence.[73] Peruvian mining thus suffered a historical setback owing in no small part to persistent corrupt practices. Colonial systematic corruption consequently had three negative effects for the local and imperial economy: the technical and operational neglect of the mercury mines, the worsening of labor conditions for Indians working in the mines, and increased costs of financing and producing both mercury and silver.

Deeply entrenched corrupt interests defeated Ulloa, as well as other reformers after him, as has often happened in the course of many crucial historical efforts to introduce administrative and technical reform in Peru. Ulloa's repeated pleas to be relieved of his increasingly painful duties in Huancavelica were finally heard in Spain. In July 1764, he was replaced as governor of Huancavelica and ordered to travel to Cuba and later assume the governorship of Louisiana.[74] Viceroy Amat was ordered not to interfere with Ulloa's departure from Peru. From Panama, Ulloa wrote a scathing last letter to Amat listing the illegal actions he had allowed to go unpunished,

72. Molina, *Ulloa en Huancavelica,* 75–78. This author develops the hypothesis that Ulloa failed in his reforming quest in Huancavelica because he was not a practical governor in an environment where the practice of justice and honesty were not sufficient to succeed. By not engaging or negotiating with corrupt parties, Ulloa actually unleashed destabilizing local opposition, ibid., 186. A similar argument is used by Anthony McFarlane, "Political Corruption and Reform in Bourbon Spanish America," in *Political Corruption,* ed. Little and Posada-Carbó, 41–63, esp. 57–60. For these students of colonial administration, corruption was a necessary and even positive factor for the smooth working of Spanish colonies and their interested antireform Creole elites.

73. Whitaker, *Huancavelica Mine,* 81–84; see also John Fisher, *Silver Mines and Silver Miners in Colonial Peru, 1776–1824* (Liverpool: Centre for Latin American Studies, University of Liverpool, 1977), 77, 109, 120–22, who finds a temporary increase in silver production in 1776–1800 due to the supply of Spanish and Idrian mercury and despite Huancavelica's irreversible decline and overall mining technical failure; and Fisher, "Silver Production in the Viceroyalty of Peru, 1776–1824," *Hispanic American Historical Review* 55 (1975): 25–43.

74. Ulloa was not well received in formerly French Louisiana and faced hurricane losses and a local uprising. He later moved to Cadiz and resumed his navy career.

including those of Ulloa's replacement, Carlos Beranger, Amat's own "dependent."[75] One casualty of the conflict with Amat was Ulloa's supporter and guarantor, Juan de Alasta, who was linked to the wealthy Mendiolaza family. Alasta suffered imprisonment and showed signs of insanity as a result of Amat's vengeful actions.[76]

What were the deeper systemic roots underlying the corrupt opposition to Ulloa's reformist efforts in Huancavelica? To answer this question one must go back in time, at least to the early eighteenth century, and focus on the connection between political authority and vested interests behind silver mining, trading and financing, taxation, and contraband. This linkage favored private gain at the expense of increased economic output and good administration. One also needs to consider once again Ulloa's view on this issue in his last and mostly forgotten treatise on colonial affairs, his "Informes" to Charles III written in Cadiz in 1771, some years after his Peruvian nightmare as governor of Huancavelica.

Silver and Contraband

Linked to declining mercury mining, the ultimate economic basis of the Spanish empire in the Americas was silver production.[77] The Spanish monarchy subsidized often-undercapitalized silver miners by providing them with

75. Copy of Ulloa to Amat, Panama, December 5, 1764, enclosed in Amat to Consejo, Lima, March 3, 1765, underscoring "la mala conducta de Ulloa y la necesidad que hay de que un hecho igual no quede sin castigo," in Gobierno, Lima, leg. 775, AGI.

76. In "The Curious Insanity of Juan de Alasta and Antonio de Ulloa's Governorship of Huancavelica," *Colonial Latin American Review* 13 (2004): 199–211, esp. 204, and the forthcoming "Antonio de Ulloa's Troubled Governorship of Huancavelica," Kendall Brown places Ulloa's legal and political measures as governor of Huancavelica in an unfavorable light, based on his alleged "reformist zeal, rigid morality, and political inexperience," as reported in details and charges found in local trial procedures against Ulloa. I thank Professor Brown for generously sharing these views that help place in detailed documentary context Ulloa's anticorruption stance. See also Ulloa to Arriaga, Havana, December 3, 1765, copy of Joseph de Jussieu to Ulloa, Lima, May 22, 1765, and Callao's priest Francisco Javier Villata y Núñez to Ulloa, Lima, June 12, 1765, Gobierno, Lima 775, AGI.

77. "Es principio asentado, que el objeto más importante de las Indias, está cifrado en las minas de plata y oro, por ser tesoro más seguro de la monarquía de V. Mgd. . . . Y así siendo el nervio y espíritu más activo de la monarquía es el objeto contra [el] que tiran cuantos pueden introducir sus facultades en él para reducirlo en provecho propio," Ulloa, "Informes" (1771), ff. 4–5.

mercury on credit. Corrupt colonial officials in charge of provincial treasuries (*cajas*) imposed self-interested conditions for the distribution of mercury on credit to miners. By speculating with the official price of mercury—in complicity with miners who received mercury on privileged credit terms and then resold it at higher prices—colonial officials and their business backers (traders and financiers) secured undetectable, illicit profits for themselves. These treasury officers also demanded repayment of mercury loans with "unofficial" (untaxed, unsealed) silver (*plata piña*). A 20-percent tax (*quinto real*) was required on "official" silver, that is, silver that was melted, sealed, and barred (*plata sellada*). Because of delays in collecting debt owed to the Crown and in the presentation of formal accounts cultivated by corrupt treasury officials, the Crown lost enormous amounts of money without achieving the avowed goal of improving mining productivity.[78]

Moreover, unsealed silver was the preferred means of payment for contraband imports. In this way as well, the colonial government lost substantial tax income. Lima merchants were the main beneficiaries of these illegal contraband transactions. They bribed customs officials and manipulated and bribed the trade court judges of the merchant guild (Consulado) in Lima. The enormous drain of revenue through contraband was one of the most serious causes of concern among Spanish bureaucrats and reformers. Earlier Spanish intellectual formulations on the costs of contraband (literally, contravening a *bando* or decree) emphasized its illicit character because it involved trading with the enemies of the king. Fighting contraband was therefore a necessary effort for protecting the kingdom.[79]

Since the early eighteenth century, the Spanish Crown had centered its attention on foreign-backed contraband, especially British and Dutch goods from Jamaica and Curaçao (transported into Panama, Cartagena, and Cuba), Portuguese goods from the colony of Sacramento, Asian-Pacific goods transported into Mexico, and French goods transported into Buenos Aires

78. Ulloa, "Informes," ff. 6–11; Alfonso Rodríguez Ovalle, "Estado general de la Real Hacienda en el reino del Perú," Lima, June 20, 1776, ff. 122–169v, ms. II/2855, BPR.

79. Pedro González de Salcedo, *Tratado jurídico político del contra-bando compuesto por el licenciado Pedro González Salcedo, alcalde que fue de las guardas de Castilla y juez de contra-bando de esta corte: en esta tercera y última impresión sale corregida de muchos yerros que en la segunda se había introducido, y se han añadido muchas reales cédulas que después han salido concernientes a la materia de contrabando y también los sumarios a los capítulos de toda la obra. Con privilegio* (Madrid: Por Juan Muñoz, 1729), 18–20 (1st. ed., Madrid: Diego Diaz de la Carrera, 1654).

and Peru. The Crown, through its Council of the Indies, implemented a series of orders, inquiries, and measures to check the spread of "such damaging traffic" and the participation of its own subjects in such infractions. The Council received alarming information from Lima concerning the notorious increase in smuggling in the South Pacific, partly the consequence of naval defense reliance on French allies against English and Dutch interlopers.[80] Foreign interests were linked to corrupt merchants and officials through contraband. This was one of the earliest contributions by foreigners to Spanish American local corruption, an action justified by commercial interests and commercial warfare against the Spanish enemy.[81]

The royal reformist thrust against contraband in the Spanish Empire coincided with the ascent of the Bourbon dynasty in Spain under Philip V, grandson of Louis XIV, and the War of the Spanish Succession (1701–1714), which pitted France and Spain against the coalition of the Hapsburg Austrian Empire, England, and the Dutch Republic. Paradoxically, the first viceroy appointed by the Bourbons to govern Peru, the Catalan Manuel de Oms y de Santapau, Marqués de Castelldosrius (1707–1710), participated conspicuously in scandalous cases of French contraband in Peru. Castelldosrius's staunch support of the Bourbon cause, acting as Spanish ambassador in the court of Louis XIV, had earned him the post of viceroy as a reward by 1702. Because of naval warfare, however, he could not embark for Peru until 1706. As a result of the war, he lost his property in Barcelona when the city fell under the control of the pro-Austrian party. He was heavily indebted and had made many promises to return favors. It was difficult to ignore his intentions to recoup his wealth and enrich himself in Peru.

80. "Reales órdenes de Su Majestad para impedir el trato ilícito con extranjeros en las Indias Occidentales," 1749–1761, ms. II/61, BPR; "Expediente para evitar el comercio ilícito en el distrito de aquella Audiencia [de Lima]: años 1705 a 1715," Gobierno, Lima, leg. 480, AGI; "El Consulado de Lima dando cuenta de las grandes introducciones de ropas que franceses hacen en todos aquellos puertos," Lima, July 31, 1702, in Estado, leg. 74, no. 70/1, AGI; and "Acuerdo que celebró el comercio de Sevilla en 8 de junio de 1707 . . . sobre comercios ilícitos en el Perú, Tierra Firme y Buenos Aires," Colección Mata Linares, vol. 67, part 2, RAH.

81. Admittedly the economic effects of contraband can be the subject of a cost-benefit analysis, as illegally imported goods reduce costs and taxes for importers and consumers. These "benefits" should then be compared to the "costs" of forgone tax revenue, administrative corruption, and institutional (laws and rules) and policy distortions. For the purpose of this study, the links between contraband and costs of corruption are emphasized. I thank Herbert Klein and Kris Lane for calling attention to this debate among colonial historians.

Castelldosrius applied for the customary travel license for an unusually large group of relatives, servants, and dependents—his inner entourage, comprised of many French people, and the basis of the court he envisioned establishing in Lima.[82]

From the moment he arrived in the Peruvian viceregal capital in 1707, Castelldosrius endeavored to enhance his private wealth and establish alliances with the local elite to gain political support for his activities. Emulating Louis XIV, Castelldosrius patronized literary contests, musical events, and a literary academy comprised of the best local intellects. At the same time, Castelldosrius established notorious partnerships with high-ranking Peninsular merchants—Francisco de Lártiga, Bernardo de Solís Bango, Pedro Pérez de Hircio, and Alonso Panizo, among others—who conducted sizable contraband transactions with French captains of vessels docking in the southern port of Pisco with the connivance of local authorities. Castelldosrius obtained a 25-percent cut from the illegal introduction of approximately 3 million pesos worth of contraband from three French vessels. The illegal sums were collected, in the name of the viceroy, by his trusted adviser and representative Antonio Marí Ginovés, aided by the viceroy's nephew Ramón de Tamaris. Marí also managed other illegal sources of income for the viceroy such as the appointment of interim corregidores, most notably the strategic corregidor of Pisco and Ica, Phelipe Betancur, who acted as *corregidor* instead of the officially designated Francisco Espinosa de los Monteros. Espinosa and a sizable group of Basque merchants, in dispute over the Consulado leadership and opposed to what they perceived as damaging "corrupt" contraband that diverted millions in piña silver and bars, denounced Castelldosrius to the Council of the Indies. The chief prosecutor in Madrid calculated that in ten years the French had diverted 100 million silver pesos through illegal trade on which the royal treasury did not collect approximately a fifth in taxes. He also opined that the viceregal palace had been converted into a "brothel," and that exemplary punishments should be delivered to implicated governors, royal officers, and judges. In 1709, Castelldosrius was separated from his post, a sanction with few precedents. He died in Lima in 1710 while waiting for the results of his appeal.

82. Núria Sala i Vila, "La escenificación del poder: el marqués de Castelldosrius, primer virrey Borbón del Perú (1707–1710)," *Anuario de Estudios Americanos* 61, no. 1 (2004): 31–68, esp. 34–39; and Alfredo Moreno Cebrián and Núria Sala i Vila, *El "premio" de ser virrey: los intereses públicos y privados del gobierno virreinal en el Perú de Felipe V* (Madrid: Consejo Superior de Investigaciones Científicas, 2004), 23–26.

Predictably, his belated residence inquiry in 1717 did not yield any serious penalties for his heirs.[83] The death of Castelldosrius did not stop the well-established contraband network. His successor, Diego Ladrón de Guevara (1710–1716), former bishop of Quito, was also accused by the Consulado of aiding French contraband in the Pacific. The viceroy's ecclesiastical judge and adviser, Andrés Munive, contributed to the illegal amassing of wealth through several cases of well-documented contraband. An officer of the Consulado caught Munive red-handed as he and other individuals close to the viceroy illegally delivered 80,000 pesos in silver aboard a French vessel. Through direct viceregal orders, prompted by Munive and the viceroy's secretary Luis Navarro, the bothersome Consulado officer was removed from his position in Lima to allow the unfettered arrival of subsequent French contraband shipments. Additional complaints concerning Ladrón de Guevara's "greediness" and his sale of official posts in "public auction," resulted in his removal from office.[84] In the meantime, the Huancavelica mine continued to deteriorate, prompting the misled, desperate attempt of the Italian aristocrat, Viceroy Príncipe de Santo Buono (1716–1720), to close the mine.

It was not until the arrival of a stern military man, Viceroy José de Armendariz, the Marqués de Castelfuerte (1724–1736), that some measures

83. Representaciones by Marcos y Pedro Ulaortúa et al., n.d., and January 2, 1708; responses by fiscal del Real Consejo de Indias Agustín Joseph de los Ríos, Madrid, March 12, 1710; petición by 26 merchants, Lima, March 10, 1708; Castelldosrius to S.M. and Consejo, Lima, July 31, 1708; certification by fiscal Bautista de Orueta, Lima, November 13, 1717; and printed memoriales by Catalina and Antonio Samanat, 1709–1710, in "Expediente sobre quejas contra el virrey marqués de Castelldosrius años de 1709 y 1710," Gobierno, Lima, leg. 482, AGI. See also Alfredo Sáenz-Rico, "Las acusaciones contra el virrey del Perú, marqués de Castelldosrius, y sus 'noticias reservadas' (febrero 1709)," *Boletín Americanista,* no. 28 (1978): 119–35; Geoffey Walker, *Spanish Politics and Imperial Trade, 1700–1789* (Bloomington: Indiana University Press, 1979); Carlos Malamud, *Cádiz y Saint Malo en el comercio colonial peruano, 1698–1725* (Cádiz: Diputación Provincial de Cádiz, 1986). For the identification of Peninsular merchants dominating the leadership of the Consulado, see Jesús Turiso, *Comerciantes españoles en la Lima borbónica: anatomía de una elite de poder (1701–1761)* (Valladolid: Universidad de Valladolid, 2002), 86–88, 96–100, and 289–335, and Paul Rizo-Patrón, *Linaje, dote y poder: la nobleza de Lima de 1700 a 1850* (Lima: Fondo Editorial Universidad Católica, 2000), passim.

84. Consulta, Consejo de Indias to S.M., Madrid, February 6, 1712, Gobierno, Lima, leg. 480, AGI; Turiso, *Comerciantes españoles,* 114–15, citing a revealing report by Lima's Consulado officer Bartolomé de la Torre, May 10, 1711, in Gobierno, Lima, leg. 427, AGI, and Ladrón's residency inquiry in Consejos, leg. 21.308, AHN.

were taken to curb contraband at least temporarily. He issued a special order to limit the outflow of silver into foreign hands and the inflow of smuggled textiles from China and Europe. The traditional fleet system's trade fairs in Portobelo and Panama had declined as a consequence of this contraband. Castelfuerte especially attacked the previous administration of the viceroy and archbishop, Diego Morcillo (1720–1724), under whose administration contraband had achieved high levels. With some positive results, Castelfuerte implemented naval surveillance, inspections, punishments, confiscations of smuggled goods, and rewarded whistle-blowers with a third of the seized contraband value, among other measures. Moreover, Castelfuerte imprisoned the Creole José de Santa Cruz y Gallardo, Conde de San Juan de Lurigancho and holder of the inherited post of Lima's mint treasurer, because of irregularities in the weight and content of local coins. Castelfuerte also uncovered serious transgressions by corregidores, priests, and caciques in the accounting and use of mita Indians. Not surprisingly, Castelfuerte was attacked by affected interests who denounced his private gains from confiscations of smuggled articles and funds. Like his predecessors, the evidently less corrupt Viceroy Castelfuerte took advantage of his position of power to engage in covert private deals that enriched him personally.[85]

The effectiveness of measures against contraband was challenged during the transitional period in which loose shipments (*navíos de permiso* and *navíos de registro* that allowed more frequency and flexibility of commercial exchange) eventually replaced the old fleet system that was plagued by rigidity, monopoly, and high risk of foreign attack and looting. Between 1700 and 1750, several royal exemptions to foreign traders (slave supply *asiento* contracts granted to the French and, after 1713, to the English) and other measures attempted to introduce trade relaxations so as to refurbish the failing monopoly trade policy embodied in the fleet systems of the Pacific and the Atlantic. The traditional Portobelo trade fair on the Caribbean coast of the Panamanian Isthmus, where Peruvian silver arriving from the Pacific coast was exchanged for imported goods from Spain, was not held during the years 1707 to 1720. It also faltered in 1721, 1723, 1730, and, finally, 1739–1740. The monopoly system was doomed, as naval warfare be-

85. Moreno Cebrián, *Virreinato de Castelfuerte,* 208–227; Moreno Cebrián and Sala i Vila, *"Premio" de ser virrey,* 23, 155–56, 201–2, 235–46, 274–75 (based on painstakingly traced income and expenses, "laundered" remittances, trials, testament, and opaque personal wealth of Castelfuerte); Rizo-Patrón, *Linaje,* 53.

came more widespread and the costs of financing the fleet in the Pacific (the Armada del Sur) rose. Expensive sundry taxes paid by merchants in Lima, many already suffering from competing contraband, drove relative costs up further. In addition, merchants from Lima were subjected to the rapacity of Panama, Santa Fe, and Quito authorities who confiscated part of their silver while in transit under the excuse of local defense expenses.[86]

Despite the erosion of their monopoly privileges by the transition toward a freer trade system and direct shipments through Cape Horn, merchants in Lima adapted well by diversifying, concentrating in their captive profitable markets of Chile and Quito, and exploiting the opportunities of contraband. In fact, the merchant elite in Lima was thriving economically and socially, increasing its commercial credit operations and networks of correspondents, and purchasing titles of nobility and important official posts. These merchants were principal beneficiaries of widespread contraband, now an integral part of the Peruvian economy, arising through the complicity of corrupt authorities. The wealthiest merchants and their heirs engaged in notorious instances of contraband, as in the case of northern Peninsular (*montañés*) José Bernardo de Tagle Bracho, Marqués de Torre Tagle, habitually connected with French contraband merchants from whom he also purchased costly vessels. Additional documentation singled out other prominent Spanish merchants as participants in contraband operations, including Pedro Gómez de Balbuena and Bernardo de Quirós. Antonio Hermenejildo de Querejazu, the Creole son of a Basque merchant enriched in Lima, acquired special permissions to exercise authority and marry while conducting trade activities and holding property locally. This flagrant conflict of interests was prohibited by Spanish law. Likewise, the merchant elite incorporated in the merchant guild increased its leverage with imperial authorities by granting donations and loans to the Crown.[87]

The Lima merchant guild acted as a front for corrupt trade deals while simultaneously filing complaints about contraband competition and the loosening of monopoly restrictions. The deputy of the Lima Consulado in Madrid, Dionisio de Alsedo y Herrera, voiced this double strategy, de-

86. Turiso, *Comerciantes españoles,* 102–104, 107; Quiroz, *Deudas olvidadas,* 72, 95; Ramos, "Intentos del virrey Eslava," 650–51; Lance Grahn, "An Irresoluble Dilemma: Smuggling in New Granada, 1713–1763," in *Reform and Insurrection in Bourbon New Granada and Peru,* ed. J. Fisher, A. Kuethe, and A. McFarlane (Baton Rouge: Louisiana State University Press, 1990), 123–46.

87. Turiso, *Comerciantes españoles,* 102, 116, 239–40, 256–57, based on notarial and judicial records from AGN and AHN; Quiroz, *Deudas olvidadas,* 124, 141–43.

manding restitution of tax collecting and monopoly privileges, as part of his complaints against French "illicit introductions" protected by local authorities, while at the same time praising trade with other nations through Panama and defending trade secrecy as a mercantile right.[88]

In 1759, Machado de Chaves, in a revealing recycling of his 1747 reformist proposal, this time encompassing a continental view of the Spanish South American colonies, proposed the convenience of the alternative and cheaper route via Buenos Aires and Cape Horn rather than Cartagena and Panama-Portobelo.[89] This proposal was visionary in terms of tackling the inadequate trade policy underpinning systematic corruption. However, establishment of the Viceroyalty of La Plata (1776), through which competitive direct trade with Europe now supplied the market of Alto Perú (formerly part of the Viceroyalty of Peru), and the enactment of the Reglamento de Comercio Libre (1778), opening more ports for official trade, did not stop smuggling activities from Brazil and Buenos Aires.[90] They were too ingrained in the Peruvian colonial establishment.

Contraband activities contributed significantly to making public and pri-

---

88. Dionisio de Alsedo y Herrera, *Memorial informativo, que pusieron en las reales manos del rey nuestro señor (que Dios guarde) el Tribunal de Consulado de la ciudad de los Reyes, y la Junta General del comercio de las provincias del Perú sobre diferentes puntos tocantes al estado de la Real hazienda, y del Comercio, justificando las causas de su descaecimiento, y pidiendo todas las providencias que conviene para restablecer en su mayor aumento el Real Patrimonio, y en su antigua comunicación, y prosperidad los comercios de España y de las Indias* ([Madrid]: N.p., [1726]), 2–3, 4, 11–12; Víctor Peralta Ruiz, "Un indiano en la corte de Madrid: Dionisio de Alsedo y Herrera y el *Memorial* informativo del Consulado de Lima (1725)," *Histórica* 27, no. 2 (2003): 319–55, esp. 342–43.

89. Mariano Machado de Chaves, "Memorial arbitrativo, político, legal, sobre el estado decadente de los reinos del Perú, Tierra Firme, Chile, y provincias del Río de la Plata en la América, sus causas y remedios y como el más importante se propone la inversión de la actual carrera de Galeones, entre otros medios y arbitrios de la mayor importancia para el aumento de la Real Hacienda y comercios hizo Mariano Machado de Chaves y Osorio quien lo ofrece a la Católica Majestad del Rey Nro. Sor. El Señor Dn. Carlos 3o. de Borbón y Farnesio," Madrid, October 1, 1759, ms. II/2817, BPR. See also his "Estado político" (1747; 1759).

90. Carmen Parrón Salas, *De las reformas borbónicas a la República: el Consulado y el comercio marítimo de Lima, 1778–1821* (San Javier, Murcia: Academia General del Aire, 1995), 488–89; Cristina A. Mazzeo, *El comercio libre en el Perú: las estrategias de un comerciante criollo, José de Lavalle y Cortés conde de Premio Real, 1777–1815* (Lima Fondo Editorial Universidad Católica, 1994), 166–67; John Fisher, *The Economic Aspects of Spanish Imperialism in America, 1492–1810* (Liverpool: Liverpool University Press, 1997); Quiroz, *Deudas olvidadas,* 111, 115–16.

vate corruption an integral part of the economic and political leadership in the Peruvian colony starting in the latter part of the seventeenth century, if not earlier.[91] As in the case of Rio de la Plata, the origins and formation of the colonial mercantile and bureaucratic elite were enmeshed with corrupt practices and smuggling.[92] These and other corrupt interests formed the bases of colonial networks of patronage, which at the top were controlled by political authorities seeking private gain at the expense of the public good.

Viceregal Patronage Circles

A primary political problem faced by the first leaders of the Spanish conquest, royal envoys, and viceroys was how to conciliate a diversity of ambitions for fast and easy enrichment attracting successive waves of rank-and-file conquistadors and colonizers. These rough and fractious incoming groups were not easy to control in the absence of a regular, disciplined army that was not organized until the eighteenth century. As verified by the differing experiences of Christopher Columbus, Hernán Cortés, and the Pizarro brothers, the use of force was combined with skillful patronage and bribes to establish any semblance of stable governance acceptable to sometimes interested royal ministers in Spain.[93] Among the first viceroys of

91. For earlier cases of corruption linked to contraband, see Margarita Suárez, *Comercio y fraude en el Perú colonial: las estrategias mercantiles de un banquero* (Lima: Instituto de Estudios Peruanos, 1995), 30–32, and *Desafíos transatlánticos: mercaderes, banqueros y Estado en el Perú virreinal, 1600–1700* (Lima: Fondo Editorial Universidad Católica, 2001), 64–66, 303–5.

92. Zacarías Moutoukias, "Power, Corruption, and Commerce: The Making of the Local Administrative Structure in Seventeenth-Century Buenos Aires," *Hispanic American Historical Review* 68 (1988): 771–801; Eduardo Saguier, "La corrupción administrativa como mecanismo de acumulación y engendrador de una burguesía comercial local," *Anuario de Estudios Americanos* 46 (1989): 261–303; Susan Socolow, *The Bureaucrats of Buenos Aires, 1769–1810: Amor al Real Servicio* (Durham: Duke University Press, 1987), chapter 8.

93. For a new interpretation of Columbus's failed government in Santo Domingo, a result of unmanageable internal conflict according to a newly discovered, devastating judicial investigation (*pequisa*) by Francisco de Bobadilla, see Consuelo Varela, *La caída de Cristóbal Colón,* ed. and transcr. Isabel Aguirre (Madrid: Marcial Pons, 2006), 23–24, 27, 71–73, 86–87; Hernán Cortes, *Letters from Mexico,* ed., trans., and introduction, Anthony Pagden, introductory essay by J. H. Elliot (New Haven, CT: Yale Nota Bene, 2001); Rafael Varón, *La ilusión del poder: apogeo y decadencia de los Pizarro en la conquista del Perú* (Lima: Instituto de Estudios Peruanos / Instituto Francés de

Peru, Blasco Núñez de Vela and the Marqués de Cañete initially failed to enforce new royal rules and centralization without major conflicts. Rebellion and discontent among former conquistadors and encomenderos dispossessed of indigenous labor grants, and respective clients, were common, particularly in strategic mining centers. The adroit negotiations of "pacificator" Pedro de la Gasca, and the corruption of Viceroy Conde de Nieva, however, produced an accommodation of interests. This type of accommodation served as the basis for viceregal stability that lasted nearly two and a half centuries, albeit occasionally interrupted by flare-ups of factional conflict and indigenous rebellion.[94]

Viceregal stability through patronage implied high costs over time. Patronage was accompanied by corruption that could sometimes assuage immediate frictions but ultimately facilitated unremitting benefits for a few at the expense of laws and institutions guaranteeing the common good.[95] This venal solution to political conflict remained an antique yet significant obstruction to institutional development in postcolonial Peru.

Through sometimes sophisticated corrupt means, the consolidation of the viceroy's executive power prevailed in the midst of structural conflicts of jurisdiction posed by judicial and ecclesiastical authorities. Corrupt viceroys patronized factions that could support them in power and neutralize other groups. They were initially surrounded by the numerous family

---

Estudios Andinos, 1996), 176–77, 364–65. For the earliest corrupt liaisons of conquistadors and governors in America with ministers of the Council of the Indies, discovered in a visita ordered by Charles V in the early 1540s, see Antonio Acosta, "Estado, clases y Real Hacienda en los inicios de la conquista del Perú," *Revista de Indias* 66, no. 236 (2006): 57–86, esp. 82–83.

94. Ana María Lorandi, *Ni ley, ni rey, ni hombre virtuoso: guerra y sociedad en el virreinato del Perú, siglos XVI y XVII* (Barcelona: Editorial Gedisa, 2002), 86, 106, 124, and citing Guillermo Lohmann Villena, *Las ideas jurídico-políticas en la rebelión de Gonzalo Pizarro: la tramoya doctrinal del levantamiento contra las Leyes Nuevas en el Perú* (Valladolid: Universidad de Valladolid, 1977); José de la Puente, *Encomienda y encomenderos en el Perú: estudio social y político de una institución colonial* (Sevilla: Diputación Provincial, 1992), 20–30.

95. For a different, relativistic interpretation of the alleged meaning of colonial laws, "common good," and "corruption," see Herzog, *Upholding Justice*, 159–60; and Horst Pietschmann, "Corrupción en las Indias españoles: revisión de un debate en la historiografía sobre Hispanoamérica colonial," in *Instituciones y corrupción en el historia*, ed. Manuel González Jiménez et al. (Valladolid: Universidad de Valladolid, 1998), 33–52, esp. 45–46, in debate with opposite views held by Saguier, "Corrupción administrativa," and backed by Robert Patch, "Imperial Politics and Local Economy in Colonial Central America 1670–1770," *Past and Present*, no. 143 (1994): 77–107.

members, relatives, clients, and servants (*criados*) who traveled with them all the way from Spain. This immediate entourage was instrumental for obtaining illegal benefits in representing the viceroy. The viceregal network then expanded through various illegal means to attract local interests eager to court the new viceroy. This pattern repeated itself throughout the governments of successive viceroys from early colonial times on.

There are several well-documented examples of corrupt viceregal patron —client networks that had significant impact on colonial affairs. The household members of Viceroy Fernando de Torres y Portugal, Conde del Villar (1584–1589), were accused of corrupt influence peddling by disgruntled subjects. Among the charges, later officially investigated and recorded in a general visita, Villar was blamed of having been paid bribes through the intermediation of close relatives (mainly his son Jerónimo de Torres and nephew Diego de Portugal) and clients (such as Villar's scapegoat secretary Juan Bello), to distribute unfair official appointments and other grants. Villar's patronage had infiltrated and dominated Lima's audiencia and the city council (*cabildo*) that invariably upheld the viceroy's abusive and highhanded decisions. His unprecedented downfall was triggered by an excommunication decree of the indomitable Holy Office of Inquisition against him. The inquisitorial blow followed mutual accusations of abuse of power, unlawful activities, and bitter disputes over issues of preeminence and jurisdiction, including the right to hold corrupt witness Bello in prison.[96]

In a long residencia trial, former viceroy Pedro Álvarez de Toledo, Marqués de Mancera (1639–1648), was accused by reliable witnesses of transgressions similar to those perpetrated by Villar. Mancera had assigned large salaries, amounting to an estimated 343,000 pesos, to many of his criados and ministers. He employed them as corregidores, treasury officers, and judges, and assigned them the delicate judicial tasks of conducting visitas to preside over the sale of public lands and arrangement of estate boundaries (*composición de tierras*) in several provinces. An Indian representative of communal lands near the city of Cajamarca, Lázaro Julca Guamán, bitterly complained that an envoy of Mancera, Pedro Meneses, in collaboration with the local lieutenant corregidor Matheo Bravo de Lagunas and the cacique, had dispossessed local Indians of their land in favor of Span-

96. Miguel Costa, "Patronage and Bribery in Sixteenth-Century Peru: The Government of Viceroy Conde del Villar and the Visita of Licentiate Alonso Fernández de Bonilla" (Ph.D. diss, Florida International University, 2005), chapter 5, 323–26; see also Oswaldo Holguín Callo, *Poder, corrupción y tortura en el Perú de Felipe II: el doctor Diego de Salinas (1558–1595)* (Lima: Fondo Editorial del Congreso, 2002), 120–25.

ish and mestizo private interests. Similar abuses involving Indian communal lands were practiced in the provinces of Jauja and Cusco. Likewise, another member of the Creole Bravo de Lagunas clan, Don Fernando, a royal treasury accountant of the Tribunal de Cuentas, obtained privileged additional payments.[97]

A detailed and lengthy anonymous letter from Lima, reporting flagrant irregularities in the viceregal treasury, reached King Philip IV in 1662 through the intermediation of a "person of credit and very good zeal" at his service. The king ordered the governor of the Council of the Indies to investigate the matter.[98] The anonymous report complained that letters, written to inform the king about bad administrators, did not reach their destiny because they were handed to the same authorities being denounced. These high officers, "corrupted by gifts [*dádivas*], falter in loyalty and public faith on which exchanges among people are based."[99] Moreover, according to the revealing letter, the ignorance and incompetence of treasury officers and accountants, and the utter accounting confusion they introduced, reflected the damage caused by the sale of official posts because "he who buys also sells."[100] These posts should have been assigned to experienced and deserving persons. Embezzlement, lack of periodic reports, increasing deficits, and uncollected debts were common in the important treasuries of Potosí, Cusco, Huancavelica, and all the other provincial cajas. Additional fiscal frauds included mismanagement in the collection of the royal fifth on silver

97. "Memorial del maestre de campo Lázaro Julca Guamán," Los Reyes, November 20, 1649; Memorial of parish priest licenciado Alonso de Quesada Salazar, Lima, April 8, 1650; and "Relación que hace a S.M. y su Real Consejo de Indias el Dr. don Pedro Vázquez de Velasco fiscal de la R. Audiencia de Lima y Juez de Residencia del marqués de Mancera," Lima, March 15, 1650, in "Expedientes respectivos a la residencia tomada al marqués de Mancera que sirvió en el virreinato del Perú: año de 1641 a 1653," Gobierno, Lima, leg. 278, AGI. For the patronage and corruption of viceroys Príncipe de Esquilache (1615–1621) and Conde de Chinchón, see Eduardo Torres Arancivia, *Corte de virreyes: el entorno del poder en el Perú del siglo XVII* (Lima: Fondo Editorial Universidad Católica, 2006), chapter 3.

98. Royal decree, February 4, 1662, cited in Gobernador del Consejo de Indias, Antonio Monsalve, and Gil de Castejón to His Majesty, Madrid, July 26, 1662, in "Visita de la Audiencia y demás tribunales de Lima, 1654–1672," Gobierno, Lima, leg. 280, AGI.

99. Anonymous, "Avisos tocantes a los grandes fraudes que hay en el Reyno del Perú contra la Real Hacienda de Su Magd. y otras cosas que se deben remediar," Lima, November 12, 1660, point 1 of 28, f. 1 of 18, in "Visita de la Audiencia," Gobierno, Lima, leg. 280, AGI.

100. Ibid., points 3 and 4, ff. 2v–4v.

and the *avería* tax on shipped commercial goods.[101] The informer asserted that good or bad treasury administration depended on the main movers of the bureaucracy: the viceroys. Since officers, like chameleons, adopted the colors of viceroys seemingly more "absolute" than the king himself, an autonomous fiscal administrator was indispensable to improve treasury management. Furthermore, viceroys should not arrive to assume their posts in the company of their sons, as there appeared to be as many viceroys governing as the number of their sons plus the viceroys themselves, all tending their own ends.[102]

Spurred no doubt by royal mandate, the reaction of the Council of the Indies to such serious charges was swift. The governor and two commissioned ministers recognized that the alarming report on the treasury of Peru was authored by someone of great knowledge, intelligence, and experience. Most of the points on the quality of viceroys, the damage caused by their sons, and the need to solve cases of fraud and obtain regular reports (but not the issue of sale of offices, which was mostly ignored) were accepted as true by Council ministers. They even pointed to similar cases in New Spain that led to a visita of the Mexican treasury. They added a point on the conduct of judges of the Lima Audiencia, several of them Creoles of that city or married to local women, thus compromising unbiased administration of justice. The ministers also stated that specific royal orders (*cédulas*) against such practices had already been issued without the desired results. Consequently, after joint consideration about the need for a "universal remedy," the Council ministers advised the king to order a visita of the Lima Audiencia, including in the visita the viceroy or viceroys acting during the review and the accounting tribunal and royal treasuries.[103]

Judge Juan Cornejo, former president of the Santa Fé de Bogotá Audiencia, was appointed for the complex task of carrying out the general visita in Peru. An official review of the Lima Audiencia had not been conducted since 1622. Cornejo soon revealed, among many faults in Lima attributed to chief accountant Francisco Antonio Mansolo, an unexplained subtraction of 35,285 pesos in the funds remitted by royal officer Diego Ruiz de Atriaca from the mining town and province of Cailloma in 1664. Ruiz had been previously condemned by royal decree in 1661, resulting in the loss of his

101. Ibid., points 10, 12, and 13, ff. 8–8v, 10v–12.

102. Ibid., point 2, ff. 2–2v.

103. Gobernador, Monsalve, and Castejón to His Majesty, Madrid, July 26, 1622, in "Visita de la Audiencia," Gobierno, Lima, leg. 280, AGI.

official rank, confiscation of property, and ten-year banishment from the kingdoms of Peru. He appealed to the Tribunal de Cuentas in Lima, and the viceroy, Conde de Santisteban (1661–1666), allowed Ruiz to continue in his post until questioned by Cornejo.[104]

From the mining town of Laicacota (La Ycacota, Puno), not far from Cailloma, Cornejo received alarming information about an incident that he considered the most serious during the period of his official review. In 1665, the growing quarrels between two factions of miners, the "Creole Andalusians" and the "Bascongados" (Basques), had unleashed violence that left many dead. Thousands of mestizos and Indians had sided with one or the other side. According to Cornejo, the local corregidor, Andrés Flores, initially tried to contain the situation by unleashing punishment and banishment against the Basques' aggressive moves. Viceroy Santisteban, pressed by his clients and family members, decided to replace Flores with the pro-Basque Angel Peredo, who allowed the Basques to return to Laicacota. This time, in the midst of major destruction and pillage, the Creole Andalusians were driven out of the town. Some went to Lima to demand justice. The viceroy, influenced by interests that pushed him to pervert justice (*prevaricar*), arrested the Creole Andalusian leaders against the opinion of Cornejo and other judges. Santisteban's decision had exacerbated the situation. Moreover, whereas Cornejo advised the ousting of Peredo, the viceroy, under the advice of oidor Francisco Sarmiento, answered that he would keep Peredo in his post even if the kingdom was lost. A few days later, in March 1666, Santisteban died in Lima. The tide now turned once more against the Basques. Before the conflict could be settled, the new royal administration in Madrid (following the death of Philip IV in September 1665) ordered Cornejo to cease the official review. Consequently, the visita accomplished little except recording for posterity the corrupt underpinnings of an incompetent administration dealing with the reawakened conflicts of a rough colonial society.[105]

In the new Bourbon century, the patronage circles of viceroys Castelldosrius and Ladrón de Guevara—discussed above in connection with the

---

104. Juan Cornejo, Visitador General de Lima, to S. M., Lima, November 29, 1664; and Reina Gobernadora to Francisco Antonio Mansolo, Contaduría Mayor de Cuentas de los Reyes, Madrid, March 23, 1668, in "Visita de la Audiencia," Gobierno, Lima, leg. 280, AGI.

105. Cornejo to S. M., Panama, April 20, 1667, including "Informe que hace a Su Magd. el doctor Juan Cornejo visitador de la Real Audiencia de Lima sobre lo sucedido en el asiento de minas de la Ycacota," dated Lima, May 31, 1666, in "Visita de la Audiencia," Gobierno, Lima, leg. 280, AGI.

contraband frenzy of the early eighteenth century—did not seem to differ much from those of Hapsburg viceroys. But one possible difference can be pointed out: the increasing role played by close viceregal advisers or trusted sidekicks outside the immediate family of viceroys. Such were the cases of Marí, who conducted a network of illegal activities under the protection of corrupt Castelldosrius, and Munive, who aided the illegal enrichment of Ladrón de Guevara. In the case of military Viceroy Castelfuerte, there seems to have been a temporary decline of overall corrupt patronage. During the government of another military viceroy, the Conde de Superunda (1741–1761), however, there seems to have been a gradual recrudescence of such patronage. Evidence of suspected widespread corruption just after the devastating earthquake of 1746,[106] and the deterioration of Huancavelica's administration witnessed by Ulloa, appear to indicate this. Moreover, Superunda's expanding patronage network, according to recent research in private archives, allowed him to remit unofficial private funds from Peru to Spain through trusted clients such as Juan Bautista Casabone, and especially his right-hand man Martín Sáenz de Tejada.[107] If the unfortunate Superunda—who suffered unfair punishment just after he left Peru for his accidental role in the 1762 defense of Havana[108]—enriched himself during his tenure (as it was widely expected after a long military and viceregal career), his successor Amat y Junyent elevated patronage and systematic corruption for personal gain to new levels.

Viceroy Amat was a model of corrupt high authority despite his distinguished military service in Europe.[109] His residency trial was one of the longest and most complicated among those housed in Spanish archives.[110]

106. Francisco Quiroz Chueca, "Movimiento de tierra y de piso: el terremoto de 1746, la corrupción en el Callao y los cambios borbónicos," *Investigaciones Sociales* 3, no. 4 (1999): 37–50, esp. 43–45.

107. Pilar Latasa, "Negociar en red: familia, amistad y paisanaje; el virrey Superunda y sus agentes en Lima y Cádiz (1745–1761)," *Anuario de Estudios Americanos* 60, no. 2 (2003): 463–92, esp. 472–75.

108. Alfredo Moreno Cebrián, *Relación y documentos de gobierno del virrey del Perú, José A. Manso de Velasco, conde de Superunda (1745–1761)* (Madrid: Consejo Superior de Investigaciones Científicas, Instituto Gonzalo Fernández de Oviedo, 1983), 23–26.

109. Fisher, *Government and Society,* 11. See also the praise-prone biography by Alfredo Sáenz-Rico, *El virrey Amat: precisiones sobre la vida y la obra de don Manuel de Amat y de Junyent* (Barcelona: Museo de Historia de la Ciudad, 1967), vol. 1, chapter 2.

110. Residencia a Manuel Amat y Junyent por Melchor Jacot Ortiz Rojano regente de la Audiencia de Lima, año 1777, 121 piezas, Consejos, legs. 20332–20343; 20348–20349, AHN.

The many accusations against his administration ranged from high-level fraud and corruption charges to petty ones, such as illegal appropriation of jewels and other property. His private lifestyle involved scandal and moral controversy. He carried on a public affair with beautiful Creole actress Micaela Villegas, nicknamed the Perricholi (mongrel-bitch), a young woman of modest means who amassed a fortune thanks to the viceroy's favors.[111] Like many officials guilty of engaging in or allowing administrative corruption, Amat blamed instead Creole elite members and the colonial setting for the widespread venality he acknowledged existed among the local audiencia judges and treasury officials during his administration.[112]

In fact, an important Creole member of the audiencia, Dean Pedro Bravo del Rivero, was suspended from his duties in 1764 by orders of the Council of the Indies for engaging in illegal business affairs. Amat also accused retired judge José de Tagle Bracho, Marqués de Torre Tagle, for defrauding the soldiers of the Real Felipe garrison in Callao and conspiring with other Lima judges. In addition, the feisty Catalan viceroy opened proceedings against several officers in Callao and Lima for contraband through several ports in the Pacific, imprisoned the Creole Antonio Navia Bolaño, Conde del Valle de Oselle (grandson of the Asturian contraband merchant Bernardo Solís Bango) for serious failings as Callao's military administrator, and supported accusations against the departed viceroy, the Conde de Superunda. The key to this apparent lashing out against corrupt officials was that most of the accused contradicted directly the interests of Amat's inner entourage.[113] Amat was careful, however, not to unleash a wider cleansing campaign that might have alienated his own supporters.

111. Ilana Lucía Aragón, "El teatro, los negocios y los amores: Micaela Villegas, 'La Perricholi,' " in *El virrey Amat y su tiempo,* eds. Carlos Pardo-Figueroa and Joseph Dager (Lima: Instituto Riva Agüero PUC, 2004), 353–404, esp. 368, 381.

112. Amat y Junyent, *Memoria de gobierno:* "Estos [oficiales reales de Hacienda] han aspirado y aspiran a enrriquezer con semejantes empleos," 351; "considerando que siendo los corregidores las manos y conductos para la administración y buen gobierno del reino . . . con el desconsuelo de saber que todas las líneas que tiran únicamente se dirigen al punto céntrico del interés y propia utilidad," 191. See also "El virrey del Perú, Manuel de Amat, informa al Rey del estado de las audiencias del virreinato y en especial de la de Lima, compuestas por magistrados ignorantes y venales; propone algunas medidas para atenuar esos males," Lima, January 13, 1762, ms. 1995, Sección Manuscritos, Biblioteca Nacional, Buenos Aires, published in *Revista de la Biblioteca Nacional* 24 (1942): 345–50.

113. Leon G. Campbell, "A Colonial Establishment: Creole Domination of the Audiencia of Lima during the Late Eighteenth Century," *Hispanic American Historical*

Amat's court clique and patronage network, headed by his corrupt legal adviser José Perfecto Salas, satisfied only narrow interests. Salas was directly implicated in several lawsuits filed against Amat and his ministers during the viceroy's voluminous residency trial.[114] Amat, a proud and self-serving military man, had to govern a vast territory during a long and difficult period. He activated colonial militias following royal orders prompted by adverse military results during the Seven Years' War (1756–1763). However, there are indications that he inflated the number of troops he commanded so as to misappropriate royal funds destined for new troops, according to later military assessments and reviews.[115] Amat was also in charge of carrying out the drastic expulsion of the Jesuits in 1767. He handled that complex matter with cunning dexterity, although the subsequent public sale of expropriated Jesuit estates opened ample opportunities for mismanagement, waste, and corrupt favoritism.[116]

By the end of his tenure, Amat had alienated an important sector in Lima. Before his departure he was required to find guarantors who could vow for the unprecedented sum of 100,000 pesos. According to the files of his res-

---

Review 52 (1972): 1–25, esp. 6–7; Quiroz Chueca, "Movimiento de tierra," 41–42, quoting the 1764 *pesquisa* procedures against Oselle in Consejos, leg. 20328, exp. 1, pieza 9, AHN; Moreno Cebrián, *Relación del virrey Superunda*, 26. On the enmity between Amat and Bravo del Rivero's scheming clique, including scholar and satirist Francisco Ruiz Cano, Marqués de Sotoflorido, see Guillermo Lohmann Villena, "Estudio preliminar," in *Un tríptico del Perú virreinal: el virrey Amat, el marqués de Soto Florido y la Perricholi: el drama de dos palanganas y su circunstancia,* ed. Lohmann Villena (Chapel Hill: University of North Carolina Department of Modern Languages, 1976), 36.

114. "Demandas particulares: Colegiales del Real Colegio de San Felipe y San Marcos sobre paga de pesos" and "José Muñoz Bernardo de Quirós marqués de Bellavista con Manuel de Amat, sobre paga de pesos procedentes del remate de unas haciendas," Consejos, legs. 20342–20343, exp. 1, caja 1, piezas 145, 152, 154–155, 157 (years 1778–1803), AHN; "Herederos del oidor Pedro Bravo del Rivero contra los del virrey Amat y los de José Perfecto Salas, asesor que fue del anterior, sobre pago de daños y perjuicios," Consejos, leg. 21269, AHN; also Consejos, leg. 20297, exp. 4, and leg. 20298, exp. 1, AHN. On the "escandalosos sobornos" received by Salas, see Ricardo Donoso, *Un letrado del siglo XVII, el doctor José Perfecto Salas* (Buenos Aires: Universidad de Buenos Aires, 1963), 1: 12, 215.

115. See Mónica Ricketts, "Pens, Politics, and Swords: The Struggle for Power during the Breakdown of the Spanish Empire in Peru and Spain, 1760–1830" (Ph.D. diss., Harvard University, 2007), chapter 3, citing correspondence by Areche and Guirior complaining about unexplained troop numbers and costs just after Amat's government, Secretaria de Guerra, leg. 7128, exps. 11, 18, 20, and 22, Archivo General de Simancas.

116. Amat, *Memoria,* chapter 25; Cristóbal Aljovín, "Los compradores de Temporalidades a fines de la colonia," *Histórica* 14 (1990): 183–233.

idency trial, there were multiple complaints from important Creole and local interests, including those of the wealthy merchant and former oidor José
de Tagle Bracho, Marqués de Torre Tagle, and his brother Pedro de Tagle,
as well as the Conde del Valle de Oselle and the Marqués de Bellavista.[117]
These private individuals and others sued Amat for more than 750,000 pesos. The picture one forms from these demands is that of a vindictive, corrupt, and ruthless Amat, an image similar to that which Ulloa had depicted
some years before.

In the 1770s, viceroys were under increasing attack by metropolitan reformers headed by José de Gálvez in the Council of the Indies. The view
that the excessive power exerted by viceroys had to be curtailed and
checked, as a means for making colonial administration more efficient and
less corrupt, grew stronger in Madrid. Other imperial advisers were opposed to this reformist stance, convinced that a strong viceregal hold was
necessary to manage distant colonies. Diminished power of the viceroy entailed a radical shift affecting the role of corrupt patronage.

Amat's successor, the aristocratic and weak Manuel Guirior (1776–
1780), courted ample local elite interests. Guirior was the quintessential
ruler relying on favors and patronage. Local elites seeking viceregal protection opposed Galvez's impending reforms entailing an increase in taxes
and the dismantling of the old system based on linkages among corregidores, repartos, and the mita. Guirior relied on prominent Creole advisers,
including the Conde de Sierrabella, Antonio de Boza, Marqués de Casa
Boza, the Marqués de Sotoflorido, Oidor Antonio Hermenejildo de Querejazu, and the rehabilitated Pedro Bravo del Rivero.[118] One elite member
benefiting from Guirior's favor was the ambitious Creole nobleman José
Baquíjano y Carrillo, a notorious gambler suspected of having obtained,
through bribery, a cherished seat in the audiencia.[119] Baquíjano followed
the steps of another notable Peruvian patrician, Pablo de Olavide, the

117. Residencia a Manuel Amat, Consejos, leg. 20341, exp. 1, docs. 1, 7; leg. 20338,
exp. 1, doc. 19; leg. 20342, exp. 1, doc. 10, AHN.

118. Campbell, "Colonial Establishment," 8, n. 30; Mark Burkholder, "From Creole to Peninsular: The Transformation of the Audiencia of Lima," *Hispanic American
Historical Review* 52 (1972): 395–415, esp. 403–404; Guillermo Lohmann Villena, *Los
ministros de la Audiencia de Lima en el reinado de los Borbones (1700–1821): esquema
de un estudio sobre un núcleo dirigente* (Seville: EEHA, 1974), xlviii; and "Estudio preliminar" in *Un tríptico del Perú virreinal,* 37–39.

119. Mark A. Burkholder, *Politics of a Colonial Career: José Baquíjano and the Audiencia of Lima* (Wilmington, DE: Scholarly Resources, 1990), 41–42, 52, 115–116.

youngest purchaser of the Lima oidor post. Olavide left Lima for Spain in disgrace, accused and found guilty of (private) fraud—he had falsified a credit instrument (*escritura*) for a substantial sum with the intention of illegal appropriation.[120]

In blatant support of Lima's landowners and aristocrats, Guirior and his entourage, headed by his young wife—Bogotá-born María Ventura—opposed reform and tax increases. In 1778, Guirior even proposed moderation of the tax burden on local trade and agricultural products.[121] This opposition came at the time when Gálvez was launching a blatant campaign to reform the Peruvian colony, starting with the decisions to incorporate Upper Peru and the Potosí mines into the newly created Viceroyalty of La Plata (1776), and dismantling the monopoly trade system (1778).[122] Gálvez envoy, Visitador José Antonio de Areche, was armed with competing powers to control the colony's finances, investigate irregularities, and decide necessary changes in Peru's colonial administration. Areche, guided by a personal copy of the confidential "Discurso y reflexiones políticas" by Ulloa and Juan, informed Madrid in detail about the widespread corruption and

120. "Expediente de Olavide y Casa Calderón sobre falsedad de escritura," 1761, and "Operaciones y procedimientos de Dn. Pablo Olavide y Jáuregui, oidor de la Real Audiencia de Lima, a raiz de la causa que sigue el marqués de Negreiros, apoderado de Dn. Domingo de Jáuregui, presidente actual de la Real Audiencia de Charcas, sobre intereses," Gobierno, Lima, leg. 813, AGI; "Cádiz, año 1755: autos hechos en virtud de Real Orden de S.M. sobre embargar los caudales pertenecientes a Dn. Pablo Olavide," Consejos, leg. 20212, AHN. Olavide illegally altered a loan instrument, where he originally appeared as debtor to the Marqués de Casa Calderón for 42,651 pesos, to appear as creditor of the same amount so as to proceed to fraudulently lend the sum to a third person at 5 percent interest. See also Quiroz, *Deudas olvidadas*, 108–9. In Spain, he joined the enlightened group and was appointed intendant of Andalucia, where he endeavored to colonize the Sierra Morena; this and other ambitious reformist efforts brought him trouble with the Inquisition, according to his own confession, "embebido en estas vehemencias habló sin reflexión, con temeridad, con imprudencia . . . y de todo quanto a su parecer podía impedir o dejar de fomentar estos proyectos." He was sentenced as a formal heretic by the Inquisition in 1778: "Sentencia de don Pablo de Olavide" and "Relación del auto de fe de don Pablo de Olavide, 24 de noviembre de 1778," in Barry, "Colección de notas," ff. 258–60, 283–89.

121. "Representación que el Excmo. Sr. D. Manuel Guirior, virrey del Perú, hizo al Ministerio de las Indias en 5 de noviembre de 1778 sobre el estado actual de aquel reino," ff. 300–308v, ms. II/2853, BPR.

122. Eunice Joiner Gates, "Don José Antonio de Areche: His Own Defense," *Hispanic American Historical Review* 8 (1928): 14–42, esp. 23–26; Fisher, *Government and Society*, 19.

hypocrisy he encountered in Lima, as well as the local interests pressing Guirior to hinder the visitador's reforming mission. Areche considered the Peruvian Creole nobility, magistracy, and officials to be corrupt and involved in patent conflicts of interest. Despite his enmity with the visitador, the Spanish-born Melchor Jacot, newly appointed presiding judge (*regente*) of the Lima Audiencia, corroborated Areche's view of the venality and wealthy connections of Creole judges. Areche demanded that Guirior dismiss his Creole advisers. Guirior refused to do so. Consequently, Areche and Guirior clashed in epic fashion.[123]

In the proceedings of Guirior's residency trial Jacot and others filed confidential complaints, among several other private grievances. Regente Jacot denounced Guirior's opposition to his regulations and the insubordination of audiencia judges led by Oidor Bravo del Rivero, who boasted of Guirior's protection.[124] Areche added that under Guirior, confidential administrative matters did not benefit from confidentiality as they were widely talked about in public cafés, a chaotic situation that jeopardized Areche's reformist mandate. He blamed all of this on Guirior's "tired age," lax career and education, and the "harmful lessons of freedom" given to Americans devoid of rectitude, unselfishness, and sense of duty in paying the king what he is owed. Areche felt that the Creole advisers' support of Guirior undermined the authority of his visita. Since the failure of his mission could result in despotic and freewheeling procedures, Areche asked to be removed from his post or else provided with all necessary power.[125]

These and other arguments convinced Gálvez to remove Guirior from office. To his surprise, Guirior got the news of his replacement from his successor, Lieutenant General Agustín de Jáuregui, upon the latter's arrival in Callao in July 1780. Guirior obeyed Madrid's decision, but pointed out that

123. Campbell, "Colonial Establishment," 7–9; Burkholder, "From Creole," 401–3; Vicente Palacio Atard, *Areche y Guirior: observaciones sobre el fracaso de una visita al Perú* (Sevilla: EEHA, 1946).

124. "Índice de los expedientes que se hallan en esta vía reservada de quejas dadas contra el virrey Manuel Guirior por varios particulares," in "Expedientes sobre competencias entre el visitador del Perú, José Antonio de Areche y el virrey Manuel de Guirior en el desempeño de la visita de aquel, y sobre la residencia de dicho virrey que le toma Fernando Marquez de la Plata, alcalde del crimen de la Audiencia de Lima," Gobierno, Lima, leg. 780, AGI.

125. Carta reservada, no. 145, Areche to Gálvez, Lima, October 29, 1779, in "Expedientes sobre competencias," Gobierno, Lima, leg. 780, AGI.

the most important and wealthy subjects of Peru were the main witnesses of his "incorruptibility" and had willingly volunteered to act as his guarantors just prior to his departure to Chile.[126] Areche complained later that the judge in charge of Guirior's residency trials, Fernando Marquez de la Plata, was a close friend of the agents of the former viceroy and that his biased proceedings were mistaken in concluding that Guirior had been a good viceroy.[127] The disputes over jurisdictional authority between visitador and viceroy did not cease with Jáuregui's arrival.

While these bureaucratic issues were being played out, a great rebellion started in 1780 led by José Gabriel Condorcanqui, who claimed Inca heritage and had assumed the name Túpac Amaru II. Condorcanqui was an Indian cacique who had a solid transport business and owned a large pack of mules in the province of Tinta, bishopric of Cusco. Educated in the city of Cusco in the Jesuit-run school of Indian nobles, he imbibed the literature of another indigenous nobleman, mestizo writer Inca Garcilaso de la Vega (1539–1616), who glorified the Inca past.[128] Another indigenous critic, Guamán Poma, had also denounced bad colonial government, injustice, and the abuse of Indians by corregidores, priests, and Creoles in the early seventeenth century.[129]

In this tradition, Condorcanqui was another reformer who criticized corruption among colonial officials, particularly the corregidores, and endeavored to upset the traditional order of the Cusco Inca nobility.[130] Condorcanqui had a thoroughly negative experience trying to redress abuses against Indians through legal means. He had also failed, after long-term lit-

---

126. Guirior to the king [and Gálvez], Lima, August 24, 1780, in "Expedientes sobre competencias," Gobierno, Lima, leg. 780, AGI.

127. Areche to Gálvez, reserved, no. 3, Lima, October 31, 1783, and Madrid, March 17, 1787, in "Expedientes sobre competencias," Gobierno, Lima, leg. 780, AGI.

128. Inca Garcilaso de la Vega, *Comentarios reales,* ed. César Pacheco Vélez, Alberto Tauro, and Aurelio Miró Quesada (Lima: Banco de Crédito, 1985). See also edition and selection of this work by Mercedes Serna (Madrid: Editorial Castalia, 2000).

129. Guamán Poma, like Condorcanqui 175 years later, proposed the abolition of the post of corregidor: "[E]s muy justo y conveniente que los dichos corregidores de los indios se quite, y el salario que se aplique a la defensa de la corona real," Guamán Poma, *Nueva corónica* (1980), 2: 345, among other reforms in favor of the Indians, and their work in the mines and demographic recovery.

130. Fisher, *Government and Society,* 22; David Garrett, *Shadows of Empire: The Indian Nobility of Cusco, 1750–1825* (New York: Cambridge University Press, 2005), 197–210.

igation, to secure his personal claims to inheritance of a noble Inca title (mayorazgo of Ñusta Beatriz).[131] All his formal attempts ended in frustration, and in particular his appeals submitted in person to Lima's corrupt court. In institutional terms, Condorcanqui's reformist stand against bad government and bad administration called for the abolition of corregidores, repartos, tributes, and the mita. He also demanded the creation of a high court or audiencia in Cusco. Urban Creole and Inca nobles in Cusco sternly opposed Condorcanqui's provincial movement backed mainly by rural Indians who were tired of the corrupt abuses described earlier by Guamán Poma and Ulloa. After Condorcanqui's apprehension and execution, the radical rebellion spread into Upper Peru before ending in bloodbath, repression, and the ultimate demise of privileges held by Indian nobles and caciques.[132]

However, Condorcanqui's reformist legacy had an important impact in the southern highlands of Peru, along the Cusco-Puno-Arequipa axis. Areche and General Jerónimo de Avilés, in charge of repressing the rebellion, agreed with Ulloa and, paradoxically, also with Condorcanqui, on the general causes of indigenous rebellions. Areche, Avilés, and their chief, Gálvez in Madrid, concluded that the posts of corregidores, as well as the repartos and mita, had to be abolished. They also agreed that it would be wise to create an audiencia in Cusco. But before any reform could be implemented in the southern highlands, the rebellion had to be ruthlessly quelled. Institutional reform to curtail corruption was thus once again delayed. The sizable military deployment, and the quarrels between Viceroy Jáuregui (based in Lima) and Areche and Avilés (based in Cusco)—over what the latter pair considered a premature and ill-advised amnesty offered by Jáuregui to relatives of the rebels—continued to block the reformist agenda.[133] Only after the departure of the unpopular Areche, a distinct administrative history in each of the two most important regions of colonial Peru—Lima and the central highlands on the one hand, and the southern highlands on the other—began to unfold.

131. Garret, *Shadows of Empire,* 202–4.

132. Scarlett O'Phelan Godoy, *Un siglo de rebeliones anticoloniales: Perú y Bolivia 1700–1783* (Cusco: Centro Bartolomé de las Casas, 1988), chapter 5; and *La gran rebelión en los Andes: de Túpac Amaru a Túpac Catari* (Cusco: Centro Bartolomé de las Casas / Petroperú, 1995), chapter 6.

133. Fisher, *Government and Society,* 55–61; and *Bourbon Peru 1760–1824* (Liverpool: Liverpool University Press, 2003), 34, 39–40.

Dwindling Reformist Zeal

The eventual pacification of the Túpac Amaru rebellion made administrative reform more viable in the southern highlands than in Lima's central region. At least in the short term, no region benefited more than the southern highlands with the abolition of the corregimientos and repartos, as well as the implementation in 1784 of a decentralizing intendant administrative system. The Cusco Audiencia was also established in 1787. These momentous changes took place under the command of a new visitador and superintendant, Jorge Escobedo (1781–1787), who replaced Areche.

Escobedo was the main architect of important, more felicitous reforms. The detailed and meticulous implementation of the intendant system was his great achievement. In particular, the autonomous (from viceregal control) collection and administration of royal revenues was significantly improved under the new intendant system as it somewhat reduced corruption. The intendants of each newly created intendancy or province were put in charge of the provincial royal treasuries. Consequently, revenue collection increased in the 1785–1795 period. Mining output in the central and northern mining areas also experienced a noticeable improvement in the same period. Even Huancavelica experienced short periods of improvement, even if the overall result was further mine and technological depletion, according to one deposed official.[134] Law enforcement and policing among the more than 40,000 inhabitants of the dangerous and chaotic city of Lima improved.[135] However, these initial reformist successes were limited and temporary. Local interests offered formidable resistance to reform as illustrated by antireform advocates.

134. In the years 1777–1780, Areche failed to reform Huancavelica and circumvent corrupt local interests when he appointed mining contractor Nicolás González Saravia y Mollinedo to deliver the promised production levels of mercury at low prices. This prompted the indignant complaint by displaced governor of Huancavelica, José Fernández de Palazuelos, who had been separated from his post and accused of illegal practices. Palazuelos lashed out against "Galvez, Areche, Guirior y compañía" for the disastrous public damage he believed they had caused in Peru. "Peru, 1782 y 1784: informes dados por D. José Fernández de Palazuelos sobre el gobierno y estado de dicho virreinato," Ministerio de Guerra, Caja, no. 5590, subcarpeta 5-B-9, Servicio Histórico Militar, Madrid. See also Fisher, *Silver Mining,* 20–21.

135. "Informe sobre el mal estado de policía, costumbres y administración de la ciudad de Lima y conveniencia de establecer en ella el Tribunal de la Acordada, a semejanza del de México," Escobedo to Croix, ca. 1786, Manuscritos de America, ms. 19262, BNM.

An articulate voice for traditional Creole and Peninsular interests in Lima, Alonso Carrió de la Vandera, expressed the nuances of the opposition to reform. Carrió was a picaresque writer, merchant, and medium-rank royal officer. Although born in Gijón, Asturias, and having spent a decade in Mexico, Carrió was a long-time resident of Lima married to a Creole woman with influential family connections. In 1776, on the eve of the institutional reform launched by Gálvez, Carrió's classic work, *El lazarillo de ciegos caminantes,* was published. It not only made witty fun of southern highland Indians, whom he held in low esteem, it also defended the Spanish historical legacy in Peru and rejected accusations of abuse against Creoles and Peninsulars.[136]

In another work, an untitled and unfinished manuscript of 1781 published only in 1966 under the editorially assigned title *Reforma del Perú,* Carrió advocated the continuation of corregidores and repartos even after the Túpac Amaru rebellion. In the same manuscript, however, he proposed an alternative reform not contemplated by Escobedo. Carrió envisioned a direct poll tax applicable to all subjects in Peru with the sole distinction between *españoles originarios* (Indians), who were to pay 16 pesos annually, and *españoles* (Peninsulars, Creoles, and mestizos), who were to pay 20 pesos per year.[137] This universal direct tax, allegedly designed to unify Peruvian colonial subjects, regardless of ethnicity or race, would have been rejected thoroughly by Creoles and mestizos alike. These interests had traditionally opposed the payment of direct taxes and would continue to do so after independence. They favored indirect taxes on silver production and trade, while continuing to lend to the needy state since new interest-bearing colonial loans and an embryonic public credit system were not established until 1777.[138] They also upheld that the direct tax burden continue to be assigned to the Indian population, the majority of whom lived in the southern highlands.

136. Alonso Carrió de la Vandera (a.k.a. Concolorcorvo), *El Lazarillo de ciegos caminantes,* ed. and introd. Antonio Lorente Medina (Caracas: Biblioteca Ayacucho, 1985) [1st ed., Lima, 1776; the original imprint (Gijón, 1773) is apocryphal according to recent bibliographic studies]. Translated as *El Lazarillo: A Guide for Inexperienced Travelers between Buenos Aires and Lima,* ed. and trans. Walter D. Kline (Bloomington: Indiana University Press, 1965).

137. Carrió, *Reforma del Perú,* ed. and prolog. Pablo Macera (Lima: Universidad Nacional Mayor de San Marcos, 1966), 67, 100.

138. Quiroz, *Deudas olvidadas,* 142–49.

Opposition to reform expressed itself in several other ways. Soon after the implementation of the new intendant system, serious jurisdictional problems arose especially in the intendancy of Lima. The super-intendant in Lima and intendants under him were empowered to exercise local executive powers including matters of royal patronage over the Church, as well as the local administration of royal funds, revenues, and accounts. Consequently, frictions rose between intendants and bishops. However, the most serious conflict occurred in the intendancy of Lima, where the prerogatives of the viceroy overlapped with those of the super-intendant. Viceroy Teodoro de Croix (1784–1790) initially collaborated with super-intendant Escobedo. But Croix increasingly disregarded and ignored Escobedo's measures and authority, especially over matters of the royal treasury, traditionally under the jurisdiction of the viceroy. In 1787, a change of imperial policy gave back full political-military and fiscal authority to viceroys: Escobedo was recalled to Madrid, surrendering the fiscal administrative autonomy of his super-intendancy to Croix.[139]

The forceful architect of colonial reform, José de Gálvez, had died in 1787. A divided Council of the Indies subsequently reversed the reformist drive. Traditional metropolitan views began relying more on viceroys than on intendants. This conservative tendency was reaffirmed and consolidated after the death of the reformist monarch Charles III in 1788. His weak son Charles IV, advised by Manuel Godoy, the corrupt, *preferido* (favorite) minister, led Spain and its empire in a downward spiral of wars and crises. In this context, the viceroy of Peru, Croix, became the main advocate for the suppression of the intendant system. His position was rejected by the Council of the Indies in 1801–1802, however, thanks to the advice of none other than Escobedo, who acted as a member of the Council until his death in 1805. But this was a pyrrhic victory for the reformers. Colonial politics as usual had devolved into customary unchecked, almost absolute power to viceroys, widely reopening the opportunities for corrupt colonial administration. The Spanish monarchy thus faltered in its institutional reformist zeal. Thereafter, colonial administrative corruption, mining misadministration, contraband, and nepotism resurged once again.

At the provincial level, the posts of subdelegates or district authorities under the supervision of the intendant were much coveted among the Creoles displaced from other colonial administrative jobs. In practice, the in-

---

139. John Fisher, "Redes de poder en el virreinato del Perú, 1776–1824: los burócratas," *Revista de Indias* 66, no. 236 (2006): 149–64, esp. 156.

tendants and subdelegates began assuming the same despotic authority as that of corregidores, left behind deficits and debts, and increasingly engaged in repartos and the same irregularities and abuses as their predecessors.[140] There were serious complaints against intendants who "sold" the post of subdelegate in their jurisdictions for personal gain. Proposals and demands multiplied for the revival of repartos, under other names and implemented by either the merchant guild or the colonial state.[141]

In effect, forced sale of merchandise among Indians continued. Likewise, the reformed and growing tax burden on Indians opened opportunities for corrupt officials engaged in fraudulent and purposely delayed collection of the Indian tribute. By the early years of the nineteenth century, these local authorities were combining tax collection with revived reparto deals abhorred by Indian communities. The same interests that benefited from the corrupt collection of the Indian tribute defeated any possibility of establishing a unified tax structure that would include other colonial subjects besides the Indians.[142] Contraband of British and North American merchandise also increased, especially through ports in Arequipa, despite the efforts of reformist intendant Bartolomé Salamanca to curb the activities of smugglers such as Santiago Aguirre, supported by Arequipa's city council.[143] All these factors testify to the accommodation of corrupt interests pressing for the ultimate derailment of reform.

140. Carmen Arellano Hoffmann, "El intendente de Tarma Juan Ma. de Gálvez y su juicio de residencia (1791): aspectos de la corrupción en una administración serrana del Perú," *Histórica* 20, no. 1 (1996): 29–57, based on Intendente Galvez' juicio de residencia, Consejos, leg. 20347, AHN; Antonio de Villa Urrutia to Intendant Tomás Samper, Plata, September 24, 1798, concerning "el ingente descubierto que resultó contra el subdelegado don Carlos Rogers y ministros de Rl. Hacienda de la caja foránea que residía en el partido de Carabaya," Colección R.P. Julián Heras, no. 19, Archivo Histórico Militar del Perú.

141. Josef de Lagos, "Proyecto económico a fabor de los Indios y habitantes del Reyno del Peru," Cádiz, October 13, 1786, and "Reflexiones a fabor de los Reynos del Perú," Madrid July 10, 1787, in Gobierno, Lima, leg. 1029, AGI; Quiroz, *Deudas olvidadas,* 87–89.

142. Núria Sala i Vila, *Y se armó la tole tole: tributo indígena y movimientos sociales en el virreinato del Perú, 1790–1814* (Huamanga: Instituto de Estudios Rurales José María Arguedas, 1996), 56–60.

143. J. R. Fisher, ed., *Arequipa, 1796–1811: la Relación de Gobierno del intendente Salamanca* (Lima: Seminario de Historia Rural Andina, Universidad Mayor de San Marcos,1968), xx, xiv; "Relación de gobierno que forma Bartolomé María de Salamanca," Arequipa, January 31, 1812, *Boletín de la Sociedad Geográfica de Lima* 10 (1900): 207–36, 312–37, esp. 210, 236, 312–13. See also Kendall Brown, *Bourbons and Brandy: Im-*

Huancavelica continued to decline despite major organizational changes as officials experimented with private, guild, and state administration of the mines. Since the late 1780s, the intendants of Huancavelica and judges had been investigating suspicious mine collapses and "defraudación de Real Hacienda," as well as putting corrupt contractors and mine officials in prison.[144] Viceroy Gabriel de Avilés (1801–1806) suspended the sale of mercury on credit to miners in 1804 owing to emergency fiscal needs caused in part by the enormous accumulation of unpaid debts owed by miners. These debts had grown and defaulted with the collusion of corrupt collectors and officials.[145] Avilés lamented the thwarting of forceful, universal reform due to systemic local opposition. He advised his successor, José de Abascal (1806–1816), to apply instead "slow and calm operations" in deal-

---

perial Reform in Eighteenth-Century Arequipa (Albuquerque: University of New Mexico Press, 1986), 92.

144. Intendant Marquez de la Plata discovered "el fraude y mala versación en las substracciones en que incurrió el director de labores dn. Francisco Marroquín, dn. Francisco Sánchez Tagel como sobre estante de la Rl. Quilca, y dn. Antonio García sobre estante de la mina, inmediatamente los puso presos, les confiscó sus bienes . . . formándoles la correspondiente causa criminal," in "Demanda seguida por dn. Gregorio Delgado en la residencia del Señor dn. Fernando Marquez de la Plata en Huancavelica a 9 de marzo de 1791," Consejos, leg. 20347, exp. 1, doc. 1, f. 80v, AHN. On the collapse of the Santa Barbara mine in 1786 and the issue of Marquez's responsibility in it, an old miner averred that "desde la entrega [de la mina] del señor [Antonio de] Ulloa, aseguraban todos debía caerse o sentarse aquella parte de la mina . . . lo que también se afirma con lo que públicamente dijo el señor visitador Areche las tres veces que reconoció con prácticos el citado paraje antes de la ruina [de 1786]," in "Demanda," f. 126v–27. See also Fisher, *Silver Mines,* 75, 78.

145. Avilés stood accused by silver miners of forbidding "la venta de azogues al fiado con el plazo que estaba en costumbre . . . en todo lo cual han recibido los mineros conocido perjuicio y agravio y también la causa pública . . . la prohibición de azogues al fiado imposibilita a la mayor parte de los mineros que carecen de fondos para comprarlos inmediatamente y los obligó a haberlos de segundas manos y a mayor precio del establecido por punto general y aun a recurrir a esos cohechos o gratificaciones [imputadas al comisionado de las ventas de azogue Felipe del Risco]" in "Cuaderno 1o. del Juicio Secreto de la Residencia del Exmo. Sor. marqués de Avilés del tiempo que fue virrey governador y capitán general de estos reinos del Perú. Año de 1807," Consejos, leg. 20350, exp. 1, doc. 1, 224v–225, AHN; "[M]uchos mineros . . . han hecho banca rota de las habilitaciones recibidas tanto que fue preciso mandarlas suspender por decreto de quinze de abril de [1795] . . . que los mineros deben imputar a su mala correspondencia y desperdicios su poca prosperidad y no a las providencias del gobierno," in "Cuaderno," f. 244. The total debt outstanding for mercury on credit to miners was 550,000 pesos in 1806. Fisher, *Silver Mines,* 82.

ing with the "decadence" of Peru.[146] By 1812, the Huancavelica mines had been closed and mercury was instead imported from Almadén, Spain.

By 1809, there were clear signs that the old corruption had become widespread again. The political uncertainty created by Napoleon's invasion of Spain and the impotent liberal legislation of the Cortes de Cádiz, created a confusion of institutional rules and emergency war financing that allowed renewed opportunities for corrupt colonial administration. Rising military expenditures since the late eighteenth century, within the colony itself and at the imperial level, drained domestic fiscal resources collected from trade taxes and the regressive Indian tribute.[147] Viceroy Abascal had imposed military dictatorial power and was busy confronting successive insurrections. He was able to tap badly needed funds and revenues from a supportive commercial and landed elite upholding an embryonic domestic public credit and fiscal system introduced in 1777 and restructured in 1815.[148] Abusive financial measures and policies remained a prominent legacy in postindependence Peru.

Despite his personal honesty, Abascal was forced to condone administrative corruption and accommodate distinct conflicts of interest among high-level colonial authorities. Judges, treasury officials, and city council members "profited from their posts with injustices and damage to the poor . . . all due to the bribing or connections of the officials since most of them

146. "[U]na relación de providencias públicas, que por su general ramificación abrazan los sólidos fundamentos de una universal reforma. Expuesta ésta a las decepciones del celo y al orgullo de los sistemas, suele producir multiplicados males de difícil remedio y peligrosa curación: aún en la práctica de las mejoras no se encuentran las más veces las ventajas proclamadas por la teoría; y el pueblo amante de la novedad pero esclavo de la costumbre, no examinando con reposo lo que se aparta de sus envejecidos abusos, presenta con irreflexión a las innovaciones más útiles el temible obstáculo del disgusto y la censura. Por operaciones tranquilas y lentas ha de restablecerse la decadencia del Perú, pues en los cuerpos políticos como en los físicos, los suaves paliativos son, en ocasiones, más a propósito que las grandes medicinas," *Memoria del virrey del Perú marqués de Avilés,* ed. Carlos Alberto Romero (Lima: Imprenta del Estado, 1901), 4.

147. Herbert Klein, *The American Finances of the Spanish Empire: Royal Income and Expenditures in Colonial Mexico, Peru, and Bolivia, 1680–1809* (Albuquerque: University of New Mexico Press, 1998), 53.

148. Quiroz, *Deudas olvidadas,* 134–36, 145–46; Víctor Peralta, *En defensa de la autoridad: política y cultura bajo el gobierno del virrey Abascal, Perú, 1806–1816* (Madrid: Consejo Superior de Investigaciones Científicas, 2002), chapter 3, and "El virrey Abascal y el espacio de poder en el Perú (1806–1816): un balance historiográfico," *Revista de Indias* 66, no. 236 (2006): 165–94.

are embroiled in their vices and occupied in their own estates and business as it is public knowledge."[149]

Another key accommodation under military viceroys such as Abascal involved ominous changes within the military establishment. Among military officers of the regular army, Creoles comprised approximately 50 percent in the early nineteenth century despite the military reform of the 1780s that trimmed down the Creole-dominated militias. Corrupt resource management in army units had been denounced by Ulloa several decades before and became notorious under Amat, reinvigorated by expanded corps privileges and judicial jurisdiction (*fuero militar*) since 1768. The colonial military represented a bastion of privilege and graft that became more evident on the eve of the wars for independence.[150]

Under the government of the penultimate Spanish viceroy, Joaquín de la Pezuela (1816–1821), military graft and favoritism reached new heights. Pezuela, a tyrannical and conservative viceroy, gratified through patronage royal officers faithful to him and his inner entourage.[151] Pezuela was bribed to grant irregular commercial speculation between Peru and Chile. He squandered vital resources, painfully squeezed from colonial subjects, in failed military expeditions intended to quell the rising tide of independence in Chile and elsewhere. Guided by private interest despite an increasingly desperate military situation, he relied heavily on his son-in-law Brigadier Mariano Osorio, who demonstrated military incompetence as well as a high

149. Andrés Vega Salazar to M.P.S., Lima, January 10, 1809, Junta Central Gubernativa del Reino y del Consejo de Regencia, Estado, leg. 54, no. 45, f. 1v–2, AHN. This critic of corrupt Creole and Peninsular administrators deeply immersed in conflict of interest (since, contrary to established rules, they owned local property and had family connections with the local elite), named the following officials: Manuel García [de la Plata], Domingo Arnaiz, José Pareja, Manuel María del Valle, Juan del Pino Manrique, and Tadeo Bravo. The latter, resident in Spain, was accused of bribing Chief Minister Manuel Godoy to obtain posts for Lima city council members (*cabildantes*).

150. Leon Campbell, "The Army of Peru and the Tupac Amaru Revolt, 1780–1783," *Hispanic American Historical Review* 56 (1976): 31–57; and *The Military and Society in Colonial Peru, 1750–1810* (Philadelphia: American Philosophical Society, 1978); Juan Marchena Fernández, "The Social World of the Military in Peru and New Granada, 1784–1810," in *Reform and Insurrection in Bourbon New Granada and Peru*, ed. J. Fisher, A. Kuethe, and A. McFarlane (Baton Rouge: Louisiana State University Press, 1990), 54–95.

151. Pezuela to Secretario de Estado (Hacienda), Lima, November 30, 1818, no. 333, urging to concede to "los militares algunas recompensas en la carrera de Hacienda," Gobierno, Lima, leg. 761, AGI; and Pezuela to Juan de la Madrid Dávila (Secretario del Supremo Concejo de Estado), Lima, November 2, 1820, Gobierno, Lima, leg. 762, AGI.

level of corrupt ambition.[152] For his military failings and corruption, Pezuela was ousted in what can be termed the first military coup led by the Spanish liberal general José de la Serna (1821–1824), commander of the last stand against invading pro-independence forces in the midst of war conditions favorable to contraband and double-faced corruption.[153]

Cycles of Colonial Graft

Cycles of colonial corruption are difficult to ascertain, given the centrality of corruption in most key aspects of colonial affairs. However, based on the evidence provided by Ulloa and other relevant sources discussed in this chapter, it is possible to suggest the following sequence: a very high level of corruption since at least the second half of the seventeenth century into the early eighteenth century, a temporary albeit slight decline in the 1720s through the 1740s, a marked increase in the 1750s through the 1770s, a short but significant fall in the 1780s and 1790s, a slight increase during the early 1800s, and a sharp hike in the decade before independence.

In the following, this sketch of successive cycles is the subject of a more detailed comparative analysis that takes into account available figures and quantitative estimates on the main modes of colonial administrative corruption and their associated costs over time. As shown in Table 1.1, it is pos-

---

152. Manuel González (married to Condesa de Villar de Fuentes) to former viceroy Abascal, Lima, December 12, 1818, Archivo Abascal, Diversos, leg. 5, ramo 1, doc. 46: "Hay cosas que no se dicen, como se siente, así no puedo explicar a V.E. el anhelo de este déspota [Pezuela] en proporcionar a Osorio cuanto ha pedido para el logro de su empresa. Las contribuciones casi forzadas, los desaires a los hombres de bien, los recursos para sacar plata y la mala política con que se maneja son otros tantos absurdos que vienen asombrando todo el reino. Por que le diesen 300 mil pesos unos comerciantes emigrados de Chile, unidos con varios de este comercio le ha concedido el permiso de poder llevar en los buques de la expedición 50 mil arrobas de azúcar y 500 mil mazos de tabaco saña libres de todo derecho, y puestos de cuenta de la Rl. Hacienda en el Reino de Chile; donde no podrá el rey ni particular alguno introducir estos artículos hasta después de un año de pacificado el reino." See also González to Abascal, Lima, December 10, 1817 and April 10, 1818, ibid.

153. La Serna to Secretario de Estado (Hacienda), Cusco, September 16, 1822, September 20, 1822, and November 1, 1822, Gobierno, Lima, leg. 762, docs. 12, 15, and 18, AGI. For the mercantile rivalries and political conundrums of this complex final period of Spanish control in Peru, see Patricia Marks, "Power and Authority in Late Colonial Peru: Viceroys, Merchants, and the Military, 1775–1821" (Ph.D. diss., Princeton University, 2003), 2 vols.; Parrón Salas, *De las reformas borbónicas,* 130–37; Ricketts, "Pens, Politics, and Swords," chapter 6.

sible to conservatively quantify and provisionally estimate four main costs of corruption, underscored by the reformist literature and residencia and visita trial records of the time, during key viceregal administrations. These categories or modes of graft were (1) the viceroy's illegal and improper gains or premio obtained through unfair and interested granting of official posts, other commissions charged, and private deals or *granjerías,* initially customary but progressively banned by royal decrees since the late seventeenth century[154]; (2) irregular and abusive profits derived from the milking of venal royal posts such as those of governors, corregidores, and judges (the sale of offices was particularly intense in the seventeenth and early eighteenth centuries) and interim positions assigned by the viceroys to their clients and patronage circles; (3) administrative inefficiencies linked to graft such as the interested delay in the collection of debts and neglect in mining supervision and maintenance; (4) forgone revenues (quinto real and alcabala taxes) lost to contraband trade of imported foreign goods exchanged for untaxed piña silver, a cost that can be classified as indirect. All these were funds diverted from their intended or expected public purposes for private or group gain. Until more specific quantitative research and statistical reconstruction are carried out, this working definition of diverted (direct and indirect) cost is useful for the provisional estimates of the costs of corruption continued for the postindependence period in the Appendix.

From the figures of Table 1.1, it can be observed that the viceroys who amassed most illegal gains were Castelldosrius, Amat y Junyent, and Pezuela. Despite the scandalous allowance of graft and contraband-related commissions charged by family members and his secretary, at the time of his death Villar left only a moderate amount of wealth to his heirs. Personally less corrupt viceroys included Monclova, Castelfuerte, and Gil de Taboada. However, other categories of administrative corruption, including other officials' graft and inefficiency, as well as contraband indirect costs, were more prominent under Villar, Mancera, Monclova, and Castelldosrius, mainly in the seventeenth and early eighteenth centuries. In the 1740s

154. Apart from the classic works of Juan and Ulloa, Ulloa, Machado de Chaves, and Aponte quoted previously, recent detailed research on viceroys' income, remittances, and private correspondence, modeled after the important work by Moreno Cebrián and Sala i Vila, *"Premio" de ser virrey,* is transforming the notions and quantification of colonial graft. See also Costa, "Patronage and Bribery"; Holguín, *Poder, corrupción y tortura;* Torres-Arancivia, *Corte de virreyes;* Margaret Crahan, "The Administration of Don Melchor de Navarra y Rocafull, Duque de la Palata: Viceroy of Peru, 1681–1689," *The Americas* 27, no. 4 (1971): 389–412; Latasa, "Negociar en red"; Sáenz-Rico, *El virrey Amat;* and other detailed studies of specific viceregal administrations.

Table 1.1 Estimated costs of corruption by direct and indirect categories, selected viceregal administrations, Peru, 1584–1821 (annual averages in millions of current pesos[a])

Administration (years)	I Viceroy's illegal gains (premio)	II Other officials' irregularities	III Graft-related inefficiency	IV Indirect revenue lost to contraband	Total
Conde del Villar (1584–1589)	0.1	2.0	0.3	0.1	2.5
Marqués de Mancera (1639–1648)	0.2	1.2	0.5	0.2	2.1
Conde de Monclova (1689–1705)	0.1	1.3	0.5	0.4	2.3
Marqués de Castelldosrius (1707–1710)	0.4	1.0	0.5	0.4	2.3
Marqués de Castelfuerte (1724–1736)	0.1	0.8	0.3	0.3	1.5
Amat y Junyent (1761–1776)	0.3	1.2	0.5	0.3	2.3
Gil de Taboada (1790–1796)	0.1	0.6	0.3	0.3	1.3
Pezuela (1816–1821)	0.3	0.8	0.5	0.4	2.0

Note: I: Based on viceroy's documented total wealth. II: Based on total administrative costs. III: Based on estimated uncollected debts. IV: Based on estimated value of contraband.
[a] Peso de ocho reales = 272 maravedíes.
Sources: Juan and Ulloa, "Discurso y reflexiones" (1749), ff. 830–35; Ulloa, "Relación de gobierno" (1763), ff. 3–4v; Machado de Chaves, "Estado político" (1747), ff. 21–22v; Fiscal Ríos (1710), Gobierno, Lima, leg. 482, AGI; Aponte, "Representación" (1622), ff. 146–51; Moreno Cebrián and Sala i Vila, *"Premio" de ser virrey,* 45, 110–11, 269–70; Klein, *American Finances,* 51, 69; Malamud, *Cádiz y Saint Malo,* 30; Costa, "Patronage and Bribery," 311–12; Holguín, *Poder,* 69–70.

through the 1770s, under Superunda and Amat y Junyent, these additional costs were also prominent. The period of intendancy reform under Escobedo and Gil de Taboada in the late eighteenth century exhibited the lowest costs of corruption, whereas there is a noticeable increase in graft related to military expenditures under Pezuela.

To gauge the impact of corruption costs on the colonial economy over time, Table 1.2 uses estimates of gross domestic product (GDP) (based on silver output value),[155] as well as reliable total fiscal expenditures,[156] to es-

155. John TePaske and Richard Garner, "Annual Silver Data: Colonial Lower and Upper Peru, 1559–1821," https://home.comcast.net/~richardgarner05/TPfiles/PeruS .xls; see also Richard Garner, "Long-Term Silver Mining Trends in Spanish America," *American Historical Review* 93 (1988): 898–935.

156. Klein, *American Finances,* tables 3.9 and 4.7, complemented with figures for the period 1810–1819 from John TePaske and Herbert Klein, with Kendall Brown, *The*

Table 1.2 Estimated costs and levels of corruption, viceroyalty of Peru,
1680–1819 (annual averages per decade in millions of current pesos
and percentages)

Decades	I Silver output	II GDP estimate[a] (I/0.1 or 0.07)	III Fiscal expenditures	IV Cost of corruption estimate	V Level of expenditures (IV/III %)	VI Level of GDP (IV/II %)
1680–1689	5.1	51	5.3	2.1	40	4
1690–1699	4.5	45	4.6	2.3	50	5
1700–1709	2.7	27	3.8	2.3	61	9
1710–1719	2.9	29	2.4	2.1	88	7
1720–1729	3	30	2.6	1.5	58	5
1730–1739	3.5	35	2.6	1.7	65	5
1740–1749	4.3	43	2.6	2	77	5
1750–1759	4.8	48	3.4	2	59	4
1760–1769	5.7	57	4.2	2.3	55	4
1770–1779	6.8	68	5.3	2.3	43	3
1780–1789[b]	2.7	39	5.3	2	38	5
1790–1799	4.4	63	4.7	1.3	28	2
1800–1809	4.2	60	5.2	1.7	33	3
1810–1819	3.3	47	4.9	2	41	4

[a] Assuming silver output = 10 percent of GDP (following Garner's method of GDP estimates), except for Lower Peru (1777–1819), an economy relying more on trade; thus, silver output = 7 percent of GDP.
[b] Viceroyalty of Peru (Lower Peru) without Audiencia of Charcas, ca. 1777 to 1819.
Sources: TePaske and Klein, *Royal Treasuries* (1982), vol. 1; TePaske and Garner, "Annual silver data, 1559–1821"; Klein, *American Finances,* 49, 67; same as in Table 1.1.

tablish the relative level of corruption costs (on the basis of the totals from Table 1.1) by decade from 1690 to 1819. The highest corruption level as a percentage of expenditures occurred in 1700–1709 and 1710–1719 (61 and 88 percent, respectively), coinciding with higher administrative corruption inherited from the late seventeenth century and a marked decline in silver production and royal revenues and expenditures, a crisis that started to be surmounted gradually only since the 1750s. Between 1690 and 1719, the average level of corruption as a percentage of expenditures reached a staggering 66 percent, whereas the level of corruption as a percentage of GDP also reached its highest point at 7 percent. Other decades of high corruption levels were the 1730s through the 1770s (especially the 1740s), averaging 60 percent of expenditures but only 4.2 percent of GDP. The decades from

Royal Treasuries of the Spanish Empire in America, vol. 1: Peru (Durham, NC: Duke University Press, 1982).

the 1780s through 1809 represented the lowest levels (especially 1790–1809), with an average of only 30 percent of expenditures and 3.3 percent of GDP. Toward the last decade of colonial rule, corruption levels were rising to 41 percent of expenditures and 4 percent of GDP. Overall these were serious long-term costs that undermined any small gains in growth of the colonial economy. The costs of corruption comprised a heavy burden and legacy that compounded the economic and financial collapse during the wars of independence and early postcolonial years.

Colonial historians skeptical of the importance of corruption in the Viceroyalty of Peru or other Spanish American colonial societies have doubted or disregarded the precious information and analysis provided by Ulloa and other colonial reformers discussed in this chapter. Additional detailed evidence from judicial, administrative, and quantitative sources corroborate the main finding that corruption was central to the colonial system and the basis for future systemic corruption. Despite serious attempts at reform, deeply rooted corruption prevailed. An overall assessment must conclude that late colonial reforms in Peru came short of achieving the long-term goals necessary to overhaul colonial administrative efficiency and curb corruption.[157] Reform was undermined and ultimately derailed by shifting imperial leadership in Spain beginning in the 1790s and, consistently throughout the eighteenth century, by local interests who colluded with corrupt authorities. Transgressions in fiscal and trade policy, military expenditures, war finance, and provincial and mining administration facilitated graft. Peninsular and Creole corrupt interests remained unchecked, while the majority of subjects in the viceroyalty bore the costs. Consequently, colonial institutions were based partly on traditional or reformed Spanish laws and authority and partly, sometimes even crucially, on corrupt interests and practices inherent to patrimonial governance. The study of corruption is thus essential to understanding the real and practical systemic workings of colonial institutions that set the groundwork for unbounded corruption in postindependence Peru.

---

157. Comparative assessments of the degree of success of the Bourbon reforms vary from more positive results achieved in Cuba and Mexico, mixed results in Peru, and largely failure in New Granada, see Stein, "Bureaucracy and Business in Spanish America, 1759–1804," and critique by Jacques Barbier and Mark Burkholder; Allan Kuethe and G. Douglas Inglis, "Absolutism and Enlightened Reform: Charles III, the Establishment of the *Alcabala,* and the Commercial Reorganization in Cuba," *Past and Present,* no. 109 (1985): 118–43; Brown, *Bourbons and Brandy,* 214–15; Quiroz, "Implicit Costs of Empire"; and Fisher, Kuethe, and McFarlane, eds., *Reform and Insurrection.*

Significant continuities and legacies of corruption in the transition from colonial to republican institutions in Peru were rooted in the centralist, patrimonial power of military viceroys supported by corrupt patronage circles. Abuse of fiscal financial policies and institutions remained an important feature of the colonial "path dependence." Lacking significant traditions of constitutional checks and balances and division of power, the new power structures arising in the 1820s relied on well-rooted patronage networks dominated by military *caudillos,* the heirs of privileged and ever more influential military officers of the late colonial establishment.

Chapter 2

Early Republic's Institutions Undermined, 1821–1859

> In Peru the upper class is profoundly corrupted. . . . [S]elfishness moves her to the most antisocial attempts at satisfying her lust for gain, love for power, and other passions.
>
> —Flora Tristán (1836)[1]

In 1818, young Domingo Elías (1805–1867) traveled to study in Spain and France as did several other Creole sons of landowners and merchants in late colonial Peru. At the time of his departure just prior to the final phase of the wars of independence, economic woes and corruption had overwhelmed the declining Peruvian viceroyalty. With the failure of late colonial reforms, conservative elite groups were accommodated to a decaying colonial order that condoned corruption as a means to gather local support against impending independence. Fraud and contraband were rampant and uncontrollable.[2] Increasing military expenses led authorities to extract voluntary or forced public loans from Lima's rich merchants and nobility who expected to preserve their privileges. As fiscal resources collapsed, scarcity and warfare pushed colonial military morale and honesty overboard.

---

1. *Peregrinaciones de una paria, 1833–1834,* ed. Fernando Rosas (Arequipa: Ediciones El Lector, 2003), 11.

2. José de la Serna, "En el expediente para esterminar el ilícito comercio y venta de plata piña y barra a los extranjeros en los puertos intermedios, he dictado la providencia asesorada siguiente," edict printed in Cusco, March 9, 1824: "[C]on la mira de precaver fraudulentas extracciones de las platas en pasta que los mineros necesitados venden a los mercaderes y rescatadores de este metal en manifiesta contravención de las leyes que prohiben el comercio de ellos antes de estar quintados."

Having acquired liberal economic and political ideas in Europe of the post-Napoleon era, Elías returned to Peru in 1825 after political independence had been achieved at enormous costs.[3] During his absence, what modes of graft prevailed and what interests were behind them? What effects did they have on the new economic, institutional, and political bases brought about by independence? How did the young entrepreneur adapt to these changes and continuities? Tracing the economic, commercial, and political activities of the polemical civilian reformer Domingo Elías is revealing of the old and new bases of corrupt administration in a fledgling Spanish American republic.

Patriotic Plunder

Lacking financial resources, the pro-independence leaders and military *caudillos* combined graft, expropriation, and fraudulent foreign and domestic debts in the name of patriotic causes. In 1821–1822, Liberator José de San Martín and his chief minister, Bernardo Monteagudo, thoroughly expropriated and depleted Lima's economic elite without securing independence for Peru. Monteagudo held Peruvians' level of civilization and democratic possibilities in very low esteem. He contributed to the prime objective of eradicating the Spanish threat to an independent La Plata and Chile at any cost, including the economic ruin of Peru.[4] He confiscated currency and other resources to organize local spy networks and undercover activities that damaged the local population's trust of San Martín and other

3. Juan Rolf Engelsen, "Social Aspects of Agricultural Expansion in Coastal Peru, 1825–1878" (PhD diss., University of California-Los Angeles, 1977), 424–25, cited by Juan Luis Orrego, "Domingo Elías y el Club Progresista: los civiles y el poder hacia 1850," *Histórica* 14, no. 2 (1990): 317–49.

4. Bernardo Monteagudo, *Memoria sobre los principios políticos que seguí en la administración del Perú y acontecimientos posteriores a mi separación* (Quito: Imprenta de Quito, 1823), 3–4, 5–6, and (Guatemala: Beteta, 1824), 5, 7–9; Timothy Anna, "Economic Causes of San Martín's Failure in Lima," *Hispanic American Historical Review* 54 (1974): 657–81, and "Peruvian Declaration of Independence: Freedom by Coercion," *Journal of Latin American Studies* 7 (1975): 221–48. Favoring a monarchical framework for independent Peru, Monteagudo was expelled from Lima in 1822. During his exile in Guayaquil, he met Simón Bolívar who enlisted him as a political supporter of the Liberator's designs for Peru. In 1825, Monteagudo was assassinated in Lima, probably on order of his political enemies who included José Faustino Sánchez Carrión. Jorge Basadre, *Historia de la República del Perú*, 6th ed., 16 vols. (Lima: Editorial Universitaria, 1968), 1:101–5.

rebel leaders and support for the independence cause. Outraged Peruvians protested Monteagudo's "unlimited ambition" that targeted private wealth and stripped the city's churches of their treasures, not to save the *patria,* but to pay for spies and useless public works. Such radicalism and depredations led to his removal from Peru.[5]

Monteagudo's confiscatory practices (*secuestros*) further undermined a weak tradition of property rights, and laid the foundations of postindependence expropriations motivated by political reasons.[6] The confiscated property of loyalist Spaniards and Creoles, mainly in the central coastal region, was valued at approximately 2 million pesos. This policy caused additional economic upheaval (and hence scarce investment). Under these conditions, confiscated properties were difficult to sell as a means of raising public revenues. Like the previous sale of expropriated Jesuit estates in 1767–1780, the long process of selling and reallocating the property confiscated during the struggle for independence was rife with graft, favoritism, and patronage. Eventually the lion's share of these expropriated assets was awarded to military officers demanding compensation and rewards for their patriotic feats. High-ranking military officers who received such "patriotic" rewards included Antonio José de Sucre, Bernardo O'Higgins, José Rufino Echenique, Juan Francisco Reyes, Blas Cerdeña, and José María Plaza, among others.[7]

5. Municipalidad de Lima, *Lima justificada en el suceso del 25 de julio: impreso por orden de la ilustrísima Municipalidad* (Lima: Manuel del Río, 1822), 7–8; Rattier de Sauvignan, "Rapport sur la situation de la République du Pérou et de son Gouvernement au mois de décembre 1823," Lima, December 1823, Correspondance Politique (hereafter CP), Pérou, vol. 2, ff. 27, 34, Archives du Ministère des Affaires Étrangères, Paris (hereafter AMAE). See also Scarlett O'Phelan, "Sucre en el Perú: entre Riva Agüero y Torre Tagle," and Paul Rizo Patrón, "Las emigraciones de los súbditos realistas del Perú a España durante la crisis de la independencia," in *La independencia en el Perú: de los Borbones a Bolívar,* ed. S. O'Phelan (Lima: Instituto Riva-Agüero, Pontificia Universidad Católica, 2001), 379–406, and 407–28, esp. 381–88 and 412–19.

6. A typical case of politically motivated expropriation in 1838 is that of Miguel Otero, the richest miner in Cerro de Pasco, for up to two million pesos by order of the caudillo Gamarra as part of his revenge against supporters of Santa Cruz and the Peru-Bolivia Confederation. See Basadre, *Historia* 2:197, citing General Francisco Vidal, "Memoria escrita en 1855, después de la Batalla de La Palma," *Fénix: Revista de la Biblioteca Nacional* 6 (1949): 595–640, esp. 628.

7. Alberto Flores Galindo, *Aristocracia y plebe: Lima, 1760–1830* (Lima: Mosca Azul, 1984), 222–24, 256–57: appendices 8–9, based on Juzgado de Secuestros records, AGN; Alfonso W. Quiroz, "Estructura económica y desarrollos regionales de la clase dominante, 1821–1850" in *Independencia y revolución (1780–1840),* ed. A. Flores Galindo (Lima: Instituto Nacional de Cultura, 1987), 2:201–67, esp. 222–24; and *La*

At the provincial level, local officials replicated the abuse of power and despoliation in the name of patriotic causes. In October 1821, Captain Juan Delgado, the military commander and lieutenant governor of Sayán, province of Chancay, was accused of oppression and unlawful extractions used to enrich himself at the expense of local inhabitants and the state. Despite his efforts to manipulate the ensuing investigation (*juicio de pesquisa*), fifty-eight witnesses confirmed the charges.[8] Corruption of provincial authorities, an expression of the ultimate collapse of the old intendancy reform, remained a persistent fixture after independence.

To make matters worse, the mercenary Admiral Thomas Cochrane, whose naval services and expenses had remained unpaid, seized the bullion reserves painfully extracted in Lima during San Martín's administration. Cochrane was the commander of the Chilean "liberating" fleet that had also benefited from the war appropriation of loyalist Peruvian merchant vessels.[9] A French diplomat informed his headquarters in Paris that the lack of popular enthusiasm for "freedom" and independence was explained by the corruption of the new separatist authorities and their internecine struggles. Another envoy attributed the weakness of these governments to their reliance on protection and intrigue rather than merit in the distribution of official posts.[10] These weak organizational foundations allowed fertile conditions for graft and abuse of power.

Even General Simón Bolívar, who led the final campaign to defeat the Spanish army in Peru, engaged in damaging practices of local expropriation and abuse of authority. Bolívar and his devoted minister José Faustino Sánchez Carrión decreed in 1824–1825 the appropriation of rents and the subsequent expropriation of those who had taken refuge in Callao's fortress of San Felipe, the last desperate stand of diehard Spaniards and Creole loy-

---

deuda defraudada: consolidación de 1850 y dominio económico en el Perú (Lima: Instituto Nacional de Cultura, 1987), 30–36.

8. "Expediente sumario promovido por don Jerónimo Pareja . . . [contra] don Juan Delgado . . . sobre injurias y atropellos," Lima, 1821–1822, f. 2, Juicios de Pesquisa, Corte Superior de Justicia de Lima (hereafter CSJL), leg. 431, AGN. The official in charge of the investigation, Francisco Zárate of Huacho, concluded that witnesses in this case "presentan el cuadro más criminal del abuso que se ha hecho del empleo, por la opresión, violencias, gravámenes, multas, exacciones, y bárbaro despotismo," ibid., ff. 51v–52.

9. Flores Galindo, *Aristocracia y plebe,* 211, 228; Peter Klarén, *Peru: Society and Nationhood in the Andes* (New York: Oxford University Press, 2000), 131–32.

10. Edmond de Boislecomte, "Notice historique sur la révolution du Pérou," attached to note, no. 83, Aranjuez, May 10, 1825, CP, Pérou, vol. 1, ff. 41–41v; Rattier de Sauvignan, "Rapport," Lima, December 1823, CP, Pérou, vol. 2, f. 34, AMAE.

alists. Sánchez Carrión received several properties rewarding his faithful services. Under conditions of extreme fiscal penury and indebtedness, a servile Congress in 1826 rewarded Bolívar himself more than 1 million pesos.[11] Underpaid government officials ransacked provincial revenues and seized private property. Such was the documented case of the governor of Chincha Baja, Lieutenant Colonel Juan Pablo Santa Cruz, a protégé of Bolivarian caudillo General Antonio Gutiérrez de la Fuente: Twenty-nine neighbors verified Santa Cruz's illegal appropriation of livestock and goods "not for the service of la patria" but for his private gain, a form of despotism believed to have been worse than that of the Spaniards.[12]

Despite Bolívar's persecution of corrupt enemies, he actually ordered his own officers to engage in plunder, including the stripping of silver ornaments from churches, as means of financing the army.[13] In flattering gratitude, which he promised would last "until the grave," the *prefecto* (prefect or provincial governor) of Cusco, General Agustín Gamarra, presented Bolívar with 80 gold and 500 silver medals freshly minted locally in his honor, and reported having complied with his decrees to dispossess and tax ecclesiastical property.[14] Bolívar's finance minister, Hipólito Unánue, and

11. Basadre, *Historia* 1:101, 136, 221, 228–29. Information on expensive parties in Bolívar's honor paid by local magnates, and "accounts settled by some of the chief persons in power . . . sufficient for their dread of a Congress that would make any investigation," in William Tudor (U.S. Consul in Lima) to Henry Clay (U.S. Secretary of State), confidential, Lima, May 17, 1826, in *Diplomatic Correspondence of the United States Concerning the Independence of the Latin American Nations,* ed. William R. Manning (New York: Oxford University Press, 1925), 3:1794–1895. Other close collaborators of Bolívar, including the aging Hipólito Unánue and Bernardo O'Higgins, were also suspected of enriching themselves in the midst of public penury or due to past venal connections, Tudor to Clay, confidential, Lima, April 9, 1826, and May 17, 1826, *Diplomatic Correspondence,* 1787, 1795.

12. "Causa de residencia promovida por los vecinos de Chincha Baja contra el ex gobernador don Juan Pablo Santa Cruz a quien acusaban de insultos y atropellamientos, año 1825," Juicios de Residencia, CSJL, leg. 430, AGN. A similar case of proven corruption and abuse involved a protégé of Bolivarian caudillo General Andrés de Santa Cruz, "Expediente sobre juicio de residencia seguida al señor coronel don Carlos Zabalburú, ex intendente y comandante general de la provincia de Chachapoyas, años 1824–1825," Juicios de Residencia, CSJL, leg. 430, AGN.

13. Carlos Marichal, *A Century of Debt Crises in Latin America: From Independence to the Great Depression, 1820–1930* (Princeton, NJ: Princeton University Press, 1989), 30–31, citing Bolívar's correspondence.

14. Gamarra to Bolívar, Cusco, September 12, 1825, in Agustín Gamarra, *Epistolario del Gran Mariscal Agustín Gamarra,* ed. Alberto Tauro (Lima: Universidad Nacional Mayor de San Marcos / P. L. Villanueva, 1952), 29–30.

his successor, José de Larrea y Loredo, expressed concerns about the excesses and fiscal chaos of Gamarra and other provincial authorities.[15] In practical and political terms, Bolívar and his faithful partner José Antonio de Sucre trained the first generation of Andean military caudillos in the art of abusive army finance practices under the banner of patriotic heroism. Bolívar crushed liberal-minded leaders and usurped constitutional power.[16] He was forced to leave the reins of Peruvian dictatorial power in 1826 due to Colombian, Peruvian, and Bolivian opposition to his grandiose scheme of an imperial confederation under his leadership.[17]

"Unfortunately for Peru," wrote the U.S. consul in Lima, William Tudor, to Secretary of State John Quincy Adams in May 1824, "the invaders who came to proclaim liberty and independence were cruel, rapacious, unprincipled and incapable. Their mismanagement, their profligacy, and their thirst of plunder soon alienated the affections of the inhabitants."[18] Tudor did not limit his criticisms to foreign liberators; the people of Peru, he observed, were mild, effeminate, and ignorant of the rest of the world due to their seclusion under Spanish rule. The consul also complained about the prohibitively high customs duties as well as the seizure of U.S. ships and property with no apparent aim other than to "pillage neutrals." Plunder and abuse of private and public assets by military leaders seeking personal gain remained common and caused recurrent diplomatic problems during the early republican period. These corrupt practices consistently derailed and delayed urgent commercial reform and foreign trade treaties necessary to rebuild the country's economy.

15. Note at the margin, Gamarra to Ministro de Hacienda, Cusco, January 23, 1825, and Cusco, June 27, 1825, in Gamarra, *Epistolario,* 17, 27; José Larrea y Loredo, *Principios que siguió el ciudadano José de Larrea y Loredo en el Ministerio de Hacienda y Sección de Negocios Eclesiásticos de que estuvo encargado* (Lima: Imprenta J. M. Concha, 1827), 3.

16. Bolívar displaced, imprisoned or exiled "several individuals of fine talents and pure character, and popular in the country, who would have been adequate to its administration. Marshal La Mar, the Canon Luna Pizarro, the Conde de Vista Florida, Generals Necochea, Alvarado and others were of this class. These individuals are all of irreproachable character, and their probity is proved by their poverty: it is indeed a grateful reflection, that the purest and most enlightened men in Peru are all republicans," Tudor to Clay, Lima, August 24, 1826, *Diplomatic Correspondence* 3:1808.

17. See Tudor's diplomatic correspondence pregnant with confidential details and backed by personal conversations with the major actors of the time, including Bolívar, La Mar, Santa Cruz, and others, especially Tudor to Clay, Lima, May 17, 1826, *Diplomatic Correspondence* 3:1792–1795.

18. William Tudor to John Quincy Adams, Callao, May 3, 1824, *Diplomatic Correspondence* 3:1751.

The abusive and inept handling of domestic credit through compulsory, unserviced loans imposed mainly on local and foreign merchants, as well as the issue of inadequately backed debt scrip (*billetes*), resulted in the early loss of the new Peruvian state's domestic credit lines.[19] A Peruvian congressman declared that "it was too evident and well-known that the credit [borrowing capacity] of the State was entirely lost due to the lack of compliance in all celebrated [loan] agreements."[20] The domestic internal debt at the time included unpaid salaries of government employees, sundry claims of local suppliers and dispossessed property owners, and unfulfilled payments originally backed by foreign debt, all adding approximately 7 million pesos on top of more than 14 million pesos of legitimate debt owed to private lenders inherited from the late colonial period.[21] This initial and growing domestic debt, a casualty of abusive emergency finance, was the first instance of a recurring tendency in republican Peru of camouflaging the spoils of corruption and mismanagement with public debt obligations that, in effect, common citizens had to eventually pay at greater costs.

Shady Foreign Loans

Dwindling possibilities for further ransacking diminished private resources and ruined domestic credit led corrupt government officials and others to actively intervene in the creation of costly foreign public debt. The careless and corrupt contracting of the first foreign loans in London's capital market in 1822–1825 ended in almost immediate default. Peru was not alone in this financial failure as New Granada under Bolívar established this pattern in 1820, and Chile and Mexico later followed suit. Under the onerous terms of the loans, financial strain, and mounting legal and public opinion problems abroad, the new republican authorities and their usurious contractors were unable to pay amortization and interest after using the loan funds on military and other unproductive expenditures and rewards. Also, the mon-

19. See for example "Razón rectificada de las personas acotadas en el empréstito de los 100,000 pesos," Lima, November 23, 1837, Manuscritos, 1837-D10367, Biblioteca Nacional del Perú, Lima (hereafter BNP).

20. Estevan Llosa, Deputy for Moquegua, in Peruvian Congress session of August 4, 1827, in *Mercurio Peruano,* no. 8 (August 8, 1827): 2.

21. Basadre, *Historia* 1:222–223. See also multiple claims by private individuals against the state addressed to the Peruvian Congress, "Indice General del Archivo de la H. Cámara de Diputados, 1827 a 1885," in Archivo General del Congreso de la República del Perú, Lima (hereafter AGCP).

etary expansion and speculative boom in London, of which the Latin American loan issues were a part, led to a spectacular stock market collapse at the end of 1825. Thereafter, international markets remained effectively closed to the needy Peruvian state until the late 1840s.[22]

From the very first efforts to raise foreign loans, a pattern of abuse emerged among Peruvian officers and diplomats and their foreign financial agents who thus contributed to the ruin of the new state's public credit abroad. Thereafter, diplomatic agents, armed with ample discretionary powers yet privately interested in negotiating abroad matters of grave national importance, remained a serious problem. As the Peruvian state was consistently unable to satisfactorily pay salaries and operating costs abroad, diplomatic officers sought to exploit the situation to their personal advantage.

The first foreign loan amounting to £1.2 million at 6 percent annual interest was negotiated in the buoyant London market of the early 1820s by two shady envoys and friends of General San Martín, the Colombian Juan García del Río and the British doctor James Paroissien.[23] The latter, already well rewarded by the San Martín administration with the military rank of general and part of a confiscated estate, established improper business connections incompatible with his mission in London. Paroissien engaged in private deals with the London merchant banker Thomas Kinder, enterprising contractor of the Peruvian loan issue, while at the same time agreeing to unfavorable terms for the public sector loan.[24] In the opinion of Lon-

22. W. M. Mathew, "The First Anglo-Peruvian Debt and Its Settlement, 1822–49," *Journal of Latin American Studies* 2 (1970): 81–98; José Arnaldo Márquez, *La orjía financiera del Perú: el guano y el salitre, artículos publicados en La Libertad Electoral* (Santiago de Chile: Imprenta de La Libertad Electoral, 1888), 2. For the overall speculative atmosphere in London see Frank Griffith Dawson, *The First Latin American Debt Crisis: The City of London and the 1822–25 Loan Bubble* (New Haven, CT: Yale University Press, 1990), 23–26, 70–71.

23. "La exceziva abundancia de fondos que hay en este país fuera de circulación, ha inducido ya a varios especuladores a solicitarnos para facilitar la realización de un empréstito," García del Río and Paroissien to Ministro de Relaciones Exteriores (hereafter M.R.E.), London, September 7, 1822, no. 26, 5-17/1822, file 1; see also García del Río and Paroissien to M.R.E., London, November 6, 1822, no. 59, 5-17/1822, file 3, Archivo General y Documentación, Ministerio de Relaciones Exteriores del Perú, Lima (hereafter AMRE).

24. Carlos Palacios Moreyra, *La deuda anglo peruana 1822–1890* (Lima: Studium, 1983), 13, 32–33, citing R. A. Humphreys, *Liberation in South America 1806–1827: The Career of James Paroissien* (London: Athlone Press, 1952). According to Márquez, *Orjía financiera,* 2: "Ha sido opinión mui válida en el Perú que el comisionado para celebrar en Londres el primer empréstito peruano, derivó de esta operación una riqueza mui

don's solicitor general, the loan contract was virtually void on the ground of usury.[25]

The first foreign loan contract was signed in October 1822, and the first Peruvian Constituent Congress approved it in 1823 during the short administration of the first Peruvian president, José de la Riva Agüero. The earliest patronage networks of republican militarism had imposed Riva Agüero's presidency just after San Martín's departure from Lima and before the arrival of Bolívar. Marshal Riva Agüero was a Creole aristocrat who gained notoriety thanks to his activities as pro-independence spymaster. As he recalled in a letter to British Foreign Secretary George Canning in 1823, Riva Agüero had provided the British with secret information on Napoleon's designs for Spain and Spanish America in 1808.[26] In Peru, Riva Agüero had been awarded its highest military rank despite never having participated in battle. While acting as president, he was accused of pressing Congress to pass a law that earmarked 100,000 pesos of foreign loan funds and valuable state land grants for his personal compensation as well as that of several contractors associated with him.[27]

---

superior a la moderada holgura de su posición anterior. Quedó poseyendo 100,000 pesos i llegó a ser uno de los principales capitalistas de su tiempo. Esa fortuna se aumentó más tarde (de 1853 a 1854); de modo que a su muerte legó a su hijo una herencia como de un millón de pesos." According to official documents, San Martín and his foreign minister granted del Río and Paroissien 40,000 pesos, through a financial arrangement with John Begg & Co. and his correspondent in Liverpool James Brotherston, to pay the annual income of both commissioners and installation expenses of the first Peruvian unofficial legation in London: Del Río and Paroissien to M.R.E., London, October 6, 1822, no. 32, 5-17/1822, file 2, AMRE.

25. "Peruvian Loan: Copy of Mr. Solicitor General's opinion," *Lincoln's Sun,* February 20, 1823, in 5-17/1823, AMRE, on the basis that it was a loan to be repaid in thirty years, at 6-percent annual interest, advancing only £75 out of £100 contracted. The loan contract and the contract between Kinder and the subscribers or purchasers of the issued bonds were thus legally void and potentially not enforceable by the parts.

26. Riva Agüero to Canning, Lima, June 1, 1823, FO 61/1, ff. 95–96, National Archives of the United Kingdom, Kew (incorporating the former Public Record Office, hereafter NAUK).

27. Márquez, *Orjía financiera,* 2; Antonio Gutiérrez de La Fuente, *Manifiesto que di en Trujillo en 1824 sobre los motivos que me obligaron a deponer a D. José de la Riva Agüero y conducta que observé en ese acontecimiento* (Lima: José M. Masías, 1829), 24–25: General La Fuente, a corrupt officer himself, denounced "la increíble y espantosa dilapidación de los caudales públicos, inmensas sumas desaparecieron en el corto periodo de la administración de Riva Agüero, sin que jamás se hayan sabido los objetos de su inversión; pues ni el ejército ni los empleados fueron pagados de sus sueldos. La nación quedó enormemente gravada por el resultado de contratas absurdas y ruinosas,

A second loan for £616,000, also at 6 percent interest, was contracted in January 1825 between a new agent of the Peruvian government, merchant speculator John Parish Robertson, who charged a hefty commission of 2 percent, and the ubiquitous Kinder. Bolívar was by then in power and eagerly expecting the loan funds, £40,000 of which were used to purchase and ship 25,000 rifles. Robertson had obtained his commission from the Peruvian government thanks to his connections with Robert Proctor, an agent for Kinder in Lima. A small clique of London-based merchant bankers with political and financial connections dominated the business of Latin American loan issues as they also engaged in other speculative mining and business schemes and partnerships.[28]

The serious irregularities in loan contracting brought legal problems and public opinion debates that in turn led to difficulties in placing Peruvian bonds in London. Finally, lack of compliance by both Kinder, who failed to advance the contracted amounts, and the Peruvian government, which was unable to pay interest, resulted in the loan's default. Of the total sum raised on paper by the two loans, £1,816,000, the Peruvian government received only 50 percent after deductions of high commissions, transaction costs, and advance interest payments. Moreover, these heavily discounted loan funds were squandered further in improper payments to officers in the victorious Bolivarian army.[29]

Newly appointed diplomatic agents José J. Olmedo and José Gregorio Paredes witnessed the disaster of the Peruvian loan defaults of 1826 due to the speculative transactions of agents Kinder and Robertson compounded by the sudden contraction of the London capital market. As Olmedo and Paredes were consequently deprived of funds for their salaries and expenses, they insistently complained of how they had to pay official expenses with their own private resources and credit.[30] This situation reached absurd lev-

---

y con la responsabilidad de las exacciones escandalosas permitidas para dividir con los suyos la subsistencia del Estado." Riva Agüero justified his actions citing lack of funds, and interested Congressional, Bolivarian, and foreign factional opposition: *Exposición de don José de la Riva Agüero acerca de su conducta política en el tiempo que ejerció la presidencia de la República del Perú* (London: C. Wood, 1824), 11, 52, 58–60.

28. Palacios, *Deuda anglo-peruana*, 15, citing official correspondence and Robert Proctor, *Narrative of a Journey Across the Cordillera of the Andes, and of Residence in Lima and Other Parts of Peru, in the Years 1823 and 1824* (London: Thomas Davison, 1824); see also Marichal, *Century of Debt*, 19, citing John P. and William P. Robertson, *Letters on South America* (London: J. Murray, 1843).

29. Mathew, "First Anglo-Peruvian Debt," 83, citing Samuel Haigh, *Sketches of Buenos Ayres, Chile, and Peru* (London: Efingham Wilson, 1831), 369.

30. "Continúa el estado calamitoso de esta plaza, la misma desconfianza y la para-

els in the late 1820s and 1830s when Peruvian diplomatic agents in London customarily became "creditors" of the state due to salaries owed to them. It was, however, the duty of these irregularly paid Peruvian diplomats to conduct the affairs, deals, and contracts essential to the international standing, finances, and trade of the fledgling nation.

Lacking sufficient legitimate income, Peruvian diplomats found the means of securing illegal commissions and deals to enrich themselves. Juan Manuel Iturregui continued a trend established by the first diplomatic envoys in the 1820s of engaging in dubious negotiations with foreign financiers and providers of weapons and other equipment.[31] When he first took charge of the Peruvian legation in London in 1827, he complained about the meager income assigned to him. In his official correspondence, Iturregui initially proposed the unorthodox and unethical project of secretly buying the depreciated Peruvian bonds to cope with debt default and interest payment problems.[32] He continued, with several breaks in service, as Peru's representative in London until 1838.

---

lización de los negocios. . . Por lo tanto no nos es dado mover nada en materia del nuevo empréstito: y nuestra atención está en la actualidad repartida entre el examen de cuentas, procurar que el contratista D. Tomás Kinder realize la suma necesaria para el pago de dividendos que se cumple en el próximo abril, cuya falta acabaría por postrar el abatido crédito que se hallan los fondos del Perú que algún día han descendido a 30, y tratar por último con el mismo de que proporcione los medios de nuestra subsistencia y de los ocho jóvenes que nos están encomendados," Olmedo and Paredes to M.R.E., London, March 2, 1826, no. 19, 5-17/1826, AMRE. Costs included support of eight (later fifteen) young Peruvians (among them Juan Gutiérrez de la Fuente and Francisco Rivero) sent by the state to study in London and Paris. Urged to return the unsold portion of the issued bonds, Kinder refused "por haber dispuesto [de los *bonds*] indebidamente. El único remedio de este mal es entrar en un litis que debe reputarse como un mal mayor siendo como son sumamente dilatorios y extremadamente costosos los pleitos en este país, en donde poca o ninguna protección deben esperar los extranjeros especialmente los que no pertenecen a estados reconocidos," Olmedo and Paredes to M.R.E., London, May 15, 1826, no. 31, 5-17/1826, AMRE. Regarding their precarious personal financial situation, see also Olmedo and Paredes to M.R.E., London, April 12, 1826, no. 24, September 5, 1826, no. 49, and November 20, 1826, no. 60, 5-17/1826, AMRE.

31. Colonel and later General Juan Manuel Iturregui (1795–1871), a patriot involved in supplying arms for the separatist army, lived in Liverpool tending his private mercantile affairs in 1827 when he accepted the difficult diplomatic mission of heading the Peruvian legation in London: "Imposible vivir en Londres en el grado más inferior a la publicidad, sin un gasto de £ dos mil cuando menos; y la asignación que se me hace es de ochocientos." Iturregui to Conde de Vista Florida, London, October 12, 1827, 5-17/1827, AMRE. See also Iturregui to M.R.E., London, December 20, 1827, no. 1, ibid.

32. "Sería de la mayor importancia descargarnos de nuestra presente deuda y exorbitantes intereses. El mejor expediente para esto sería pagar con nuevos *bonds* los intereses vencidos; comprar enseguida nuestra deuda privadamente hasta la cantidad que

The business of loan issues in London was fueled by hopes that the new Spanish American countries would soon recover from the late colonial mining slump and the disruption and destruction of the wars for independence. After years of neglect and decay, mining activities needed massive capital investment to produce enough silver and gold to balance the rising trade deficit. Despite some highly speculative mining enterprises that raised funds in London, necessary investment in Peruvian mining did not materialize.

However, the illegal exportation of silver bullion (plata piña) and silver coins, sometimes carried in British and other foreign warships, as well as contraband of imported goods, continued and even grew after independence. Foreign merchants and diplomats active in major Peruvian ports and cities described these activities as if they were customary and part of their everyday tasks.[33] Similar illegal exchanges were also common on the west coast of Mexico and persisted until the late 1850s.[34]

---

pudiéramos; y finalmente hacerlo en público. . . Con lo que debemos de intereses podríamos comprar hoy casi toda nuestra deuda." Iturregui to Vista Florida, London, October 12, 1827, 5-17/1827, AMRE. "[E]l Perú en lugar de remitir dinero para pagar los intereses que adeuda, lo haga, consultando el mayor secreto, para comprar sus propias obligaciones." Iturregui to M.R.E., London, December 20, 1827, no. 2, 5-17/1827, AMRE.

33. Heinrich Witt, *Diario 1824–1890: un testimonio personal sobre el Perú del siglo XIX,* trans. Gladys Flórez-Estrada Garland, 2 vols. (Lima: Banco Mercantil, 1992), 1:82–83. (This publication includes only the periods 1824-1842 [vol. 1] and 1843-1847 [vol. 2] of Witt's multivolume manuscript diary that ends in 1890. This is an uniquely important source by a German merchant resident in Peru, originally written mostly in English and recently transcribed into typewritten form by its private owners. For information on later periods, this study uses an earlier printed compilation of extracts from the diary [1987] as well as parts of the typewritten version of the original text in English cited in subsequent notes.) In the diary's entry corresponding to July 4, 1825, Witt wrote: "supervisé el despacho de $60,000 [para Antony Gibbs & Sons] en el 'Mersey.' También conversé un poco con el arriero que había transportado la plata piña desde Arequipa y con Turner, el piloto que se había comprometido a contrabandearla a bordo del buque de guerra, y estuvimos de acuerdo en que ello debía de hacerse esa noche, lo que se llevó a cabo sin contratiempos." Also, Charles Ricketts, British consul in Lima, reported that between 1819 and 1825, British warships had taken $27 million in silver and gold from Peru: *British Consular Reports on the Trade and Politics of Latin America, 1824–1826,* ed. R. A. Humphreys (London: Royal Historical Society, 1940), 195, cited in Marichal, *Century of Debt,* 21. In 1836, the Peruvian minister of foreign relations complained over the custom of receiving "barras de plata y oro" by foreign warships without paying official dues, Mariano de Sierra to Samuel Larned, Lima, June 11, 1836, Despatches from United States Ministers to Peru, 1826–1906, microcopy T-52 (hereafter Despatches 1826–1906), roll 4, U.S. National Archives and Records Administration (hereafter USNA).

34. Barry M. Gough, "Specie Conveyance from the West Coast of Mexico in British Ships, c. 1820–1870: An Aspect of the Pax Britannica," *Mariner's Mirror* 69 (1983):

The Peruvian liberal congressman, Francisco Javier de Luna Pizarro, wished for increased customs collections to contribute to the "moralization" of customs officials and thus to eradicate the "immense contraband."[35] The prefect of Arequipa in the late 1820s, General Antonio Gutiérrez de la Fuente, protected smuggling operations and diverted public funds to amass a fortune of at least 200,000 pesos.[36] The inadequate set of trade prohibitions and barriers to free trade inherited from the colonial regime was considered the germ of corruption, according to a contemporary liberal thinker.[37] Illegal silver extraction and contraband linked private and official interests in webs of corruption that caused a serious drain of capital and currency in the depressed domestic market. Provincial prefects and subprefects, often military officers, were customarily involved in these networks, compounding their local abuse, patronage, and corruption in administration and military procurement contracts.[38] Throughout the century, the corruption of local authorities remained mostly unchecked.

There were some early but feeble attempts at moralizing public administration with a few anticorruption rules and measures. Historian Jorge Basadre, searching for roots of the elusive ideal of an efficient and honest

419–33, and John Mayo, "Consuls and Silver Contraband on Mexico's West Coast in the Era of Santa Anna," *Journal of Latin American Studies* 19 (1987): 389–411, quoted in the important comparative contribution by Rory Miller, "Foreign Capital, the State, and Political Corruption in Latin America between Independence and the Depression," in *Political Corruption,* ed. Little and Posada-Carbó, 65–95, esp. 68–69, 89.

35. Peruvian Congress, July 30, 1827 session, in *Mercurio Peruano,* no. 6 (August 7, 1827): 2–3.

36. Barrère to Ministre des Affaires Étrangères (hereafter M.A.E.), Lima, April 4, 1831, CP, Pérou, vol. 4, f. 167v, AMAE.

37. S. T., *Informe [sobre el contrabando]* (Lima: Imprenta de José M. Masías, 1832): "[E]l contrabando fomentado y sostenido [por la corrupción y venalidad de los empleados] . . . se propaga su contajio de los empleados del fisco y de los comerciantes a todas las clases de la sociedad . . . nace necesariamente de los estancos, de las leyes prohibitivas, de los impuestos excesivos. No hay contra él otro preservativo que la libertad y moderación de los impuestos," 1–2; "cuya fatal consecuencia se estiende y contamina a los magistrados y a toda la sociedad," 6; "Acabada [la administración colonial], cuando el tiempo había arraigado profundamente estas costumbres, nada fue más impolítico que conservar el aliciente del crimen, manteniendo prohibiciones parciales, imponiendo derechos excesivos sobre artículos de primera necesidad. La prosperidad de la nación demandaba suspenderlos y moderarlos para destruir ese jermen de corrupción," 8.

38. Thomas Krüggeler, "El doble desafío: los artesanos del Cusco ante la crisis regional y la constitución del regimen republicano, 1824–1869," *Allpanchis,* no. 38 (1988): 13–65, cited in Miller, "Foreign Capital," 71, 90.

national state, has documented these moralizing legislative and administrative efforts—mainly by Luna Pizarro, President Manuel Menéndez (1844–1845), and other liberals—against various *corruptelas* and frauds among the military and other public servants. In the 1820s, legislators were forbidden to solicit favors from executive authorities or hold jobs that would present conflicts of interest.[39]

In theory, as in colonial times, government officers were also subject to trials of accountability and administrative inquiries (*juicio de residencia* and *pesquisa,* respectively) explicitly searching evidence on fraud and bribery (*cohecho*).[40] Customs officers could face the death penalty if found guilty of aiding contraband. These measures were rarely enforced: The officials being investigated generally managed to emasculate the inquiries through bribes and falsified statements of witnesses. Many of these accused enjoyed protection or received only mild punishments, if any, according to the few remaining records of incomplete and vitiated trials.[41] The surviving legal evidence is, however, symptomatic of the serious corruption problems plaguing the early republican state. According to a pessimistic observer at the time, "corruption is too inveterate and of too strong a growth in Peru to be speedily eradicated by any means however judicious or however severe."[42]

Caudillo Patronage Circles

The first and subsequent generations of republican military caudillos can be explained as the apexes of patronage networks emerging as old institutions

39. Basadre, *Historia* 1:18, 20, 196; and 3:66, 69, citing Menéndez's 1845 message to Congress, deemed a fleeting yet "admirable" denunciation against spying, secret expenditures, favoritism in public employment, and pension fraud. Regarding the moral circumstances of the country Luna Pizarro stated "adolecemos de estas faltas . . . nuestras malas habitudes que con el ser nos transmitieron nuestros padres . . . el defecto de espíritu público," *Mercurio Peruano,* no. 6 (August 7, 1827): 1.

40. See, for example, "Expediente sobre el juicio de residencia seguida contra el señor coronel don Manuel Francisco Osores, ex subprefecto de Chota, años 1835–1836," especially questions 6 and 8 to witnesses in the secret inquiry questionnaire, Juicios de Residencia, CSJL, leg. 430, f. 2v, AGN: "[D]igan así mismo si [el residenciado] . . . admitió cohecho o soborno a alguno y se dejó seducir de empeños o miras particulares . . . si ha impuesto multas en su beneficio."

41. See Juicios de Residencia and Juicios de Pesquisa, CSJL, legs. 430–32, AGN.

42. Thomas Willimott to Earl of Dudley, Lima, March 20, 1828, no. 1, FO 61/14, f. 61v, NAUK.

collapsed or new institutions were stunted or weakened at birth. Military officers such as Andrés de Santa Cruz, Agustín Gamarra, Antonio Gutiérrez de la Fuente, Ramón Castilla, and José Rufino Echenique had been initially formed in the Spanish army before they served in the separatist army. To a large extent, they reproduced in disjointed miniatures the patronage networks previously headed by the colonial viceroy and other bureaucratic officers. Patronage circles were either cemented by corruption or provided ample opportunities for it. The influx of Argentinean, Chilean, Colombian, and European military officers and soldiers also contributed to the rising importance of military cliques after independence.[43] Considering the regional, provincial, rural, and even socioeconomic bases of these caudillos is not sufficient to explain their motivations and means of support. It is necessary to also consider corrupt interests and their networks as major explanatory factors of caudillo power bases and misguided policies.

The connections established among military caudillos, state administration, and private cronies defined postindependence patronage circles. An early example is the network headed by Gamarra and his ally and sidekick Gutiérrez de La Fuente. Early in their quest for power, together with other separatist officers they staged the first military *pronunciamiento* (coup) that made Riva Agüero president in 1823. Thereafter, the political and pecuniary destinies of Gamarra and La Fuente were linked. Gamarra consistently relied on La Fuente to provide arms and funds to put his political designs into practice.[44] During the upheaval caused by the forced departure of Bolívar in 1826, Gamarra and La Fuente made their move to extend their power and influence. They had been placed by Bolívar as prefects (governors) of the southern provinces (*departamentos*) of, respectively, Cusco and Arequipa. Prefects Gamarra and La Fuente conspired with the governor of Puno, Benito Laso (also a Bolívar supporter and collaborator), to form a separate southern federation. La Fuente even withheld the remittance to Lima of public revenue collected in Arequipa.[45] The prefects' maneuver did not progress due to the decisive action of General Santa Cruz, Gamarra's nemesis and head of an opposing patronage group.

The insubordination of Colombian troops stationed in Lima against Bolívar's continental plans led to the peaceful withdrawal of these foreign forces

43. Celia Wu, *Generals and Diplomats: Great Britain and Peru 1820–40* (Cambridge: Centre of Latin American Studies, University of Cambridge, 1991), 11–18.

44. Gamarra to La Fuente, Cusco, February 21, March 25, and April 25, 1827, in Gamarra, *Epistolario,* 64–67.

45. Basadre, *Historia* 1:23, 25, 190.

from Peru. The liberal patriot Luna Pizarro, Bolívar's moralizing opponent and head of a new Peruvian Congress, could now call for true presidential elections among congressional representatives on June 9, 1827. The contenders were generals Santa Cruz and José de la Mar. Judge Manuel Lorenzo Vidaurre, Bolívar's intimate collaborator and former minister, backed Santa Cruz. Citing informed sources, James Cooley, the U.S. chargé d'affaires, wrote that Santa Cruz and Vidaurre had "a bad reputation for little talent and less honesty."[46] Moreover, French diplomat Chaumette des Fossés considered Vidaurre wholly unfit to occupy the post of Supreme Court president: "[N]o person sacrifices more easily the rights of justice to his [own] interests or the influence of his relatives and friends. . . [Vidaurre] is, according to almost all reports, the last man one should choose, among the dissolute inhabitants of Lima, to make . . . the top magistrate of Peruvian justice."[47]

La Mar won the elections and Santa Cruz was sent to a diplomatic post in Chile from where he later went to Bolivia to become its president. La Mar, one of the few honest high-ranking military officers at the time, was said to have been an admirer of the United States and its institutions. He was strongly supported by Luna Pizarro, leader of the liberal party.[48] However, the opportunistic Gamarra and La Fuente conspired against La Mar and Luna Pizarro. A successful military campaign against Bolivia's president, Marshal José Antonio de Sucre, was led from Cusco by maverick Gamarra acting autonomously and in defiance of Lima's government. Immediately after, another war with Colombia (1829) over territorial, political, diplomatic, and debt issues, gave Gamarra and La Fuente the opportunity for seizing supreme power. The war was fought in Ecuadorian territory and ended with the withdrawal of the Peruvian invading army commanded

46. James Cooley to U.S. Secretary of State Henry Clay, Lima, May 22, 1827, Despatches 1826–1906, roll 1, USNA.

47. Chaumette des Fossés to Baron de Damas, Lima, January 2, 1828, CP, Pérou, vol. 3, f. 344, AMAE.

48. For his military services, La Mar was rewarded a valuable coastal estate, Ocucaje; however, he soon returned it to its rightful owner, a proper action ignored by other republican leaders. Basadre, *Historia* 1:232, 278, 281. Foreigners recognized his high moral standing, but added that such stance had little backing in public opinion and translated rather in political weakness. Letter signed by W. Tudor, May 12, 1830, Epistolario, Archivo Paz Soldán (hereafter Epistolario APS), vol. 7, BNP. According to Cooley, Luna Pizarro, although "a priest, . . . is liberal, intelligent" and his party "very favorably inclined towards the United States." Cooley to Clay, Lima, June 14, 1827, Despatches 1826–1906, roll 1, USNA.

by La Mar himself. Meanwhile, in Lima La Fuente staged a coup that ousted Vice President Manuel Salazar and congressional leader Luna Pizarro. In the north, Gamarra, in coordination with La Fuente, arrested and exiled La Mar, ending in this way the only honest, liberal parliamentary government Peru had in the early years of republican government.

Despite a weak popular basis, the warring and xenophobic Gamarra was elected president under armed pressure. While Gamarra was still absent in the interior, as vice president, La Fuente controlled Lima's government with an iron fist. According to local observers, Gamarra and La Fuente received support from a "party" that acted as a "mere instrument" of Bolívar's authoritarian designs. More importantly, Gamarra bolstered his uncommonly enduring military despotism by appointing faithful high-ranking officers as departmental governors, repaying favors with salary increases and jobs, and manipulating military promotions and retirements.[49] In early 1830, La Fuente traveled to the southern provinces to collect by all means possible badly needed funds for Gamarra's cause. A foreign diplomat insinuated that La Fuente's imminent trip had a purpose of a "more personal nature."[50]

The graft-laden collaboration between Gamarra and La Fuente was documented in their correspondence with each other during that scavenging "fund-raising" campaign. La Fuente was in charge of milking as much revenue as possible from prefects and subprefects of those provinces despite the dire economic situation of the southern region. Domestic interests now despised La Fuente and Gamarra for the heavy extortion. Officers had to be promised favors and other enticements, or they were simply threatened, to surrender hundreds of thousands of pesos that maintained Gamarra in power until 1833.[51]

49. Wu, *Generals and Diplomats*, 60; Basadre, *Historia* 2:46; Charles Walker, *Smoldering Ashes: Cuzco and the Creation of Republican Peru, 1780–1840* (Durham, NC: Duke University Press, 1999), chapter 5, 136–37.

50. Samuel Larned to Secretary of State Martin Van Buren, Lima, December 19, 1829, Despatches 1826–1906, roll 1, USNA.

51. La Fuente unsuccessfully tried to obtain from Lima's Congress 1 million pesos for Gamarra's military campaigns. La Fuente to Gamarra, October 8, 1829, Epistolario APS, vol. 6, BNP. He informed Gamarra of a 60,000-peso remittance from Puno (49,000 pesos) and Arequipa (11,000 pesos): La Fuente to Gamarra, Arequipa, January 12, 1830, ibid., vol. 7. Several other letters refer to deals with prefects Juan Pardo de Zela (Arequipa), Juan Angel Bujanda (Cusco), and Juan Francisco Reyes (Puno), and the remittance to Gamarra of a total of approximately 300,000 pesos from the southern provinces including Moquegua, Arica, and Tarapacá. Gamarra did not cease to ask La Fuente for funds: "Mándeme U. plata porque aquí estamos arañando la cubierta," Gamarra to La

La Fuente informed Gamarra about the prefects' resistance to surrender painfully scraped-together taxes and compulsory donations from local landowners, merchants, clergy, and indigenous peasants. La Fuente also intervened in local policies concerning contraband, gold mines, irrigation projects, and foreign merchants and entrepreneurs. He admitted that contraband and illegal extraction of silver by natives and foreigners were major activities in the southern ports of Islay, Arica, and Iquique in the mining province of Tarapacá. However, he was in favor of allowing illegal silver extraction due to its local trade value and until the state was able to impose export duties. In this regard, he supported the claims of local businesspeople and miners and most probably continued to engage in protecting contraband. He also managed to place, with the aid of Gamarra, several employees in the customs administration. Moreover, he insisted on splitting with Gamarra shares of the Empresa Vincocaya, an irrigation project aimed at diverting a river to bring water to uncultivated lands lying to the east and west of the Misti volcano in Arequipa. La Fuente thanked him for the official decree establishing this project that, according to La Fuente, would increase the affection toward Gamarra in Arequipa.[52] La Fuente also requested increased salary allowances, while unflinchingly complaining that an article in a Chilean publication accused him of administrative dishonesty.[53]

Corruption within the military loomed over private sector activities and depleted public funds and credit lines. Crippling compulsory loans and levies imposed on domestic and foreign businesspeople and property owners became endemic with almost every military insurrection and counterinsurgency. Such is the case of the insurrection of January 1834 that was vividly and humorously described by Flora Tristán who witnessing its ef-

---

Fuente, Piura, June 17, 1829. See also Piura, July 3, 1929, and Lima, April 5, 1830, in Gamarra, *Epistolario,* 165, 172.

52. Letters from La Fuente to Gamarra: Arequipa, February 19, 1830: "No es menos el interés que tomo en la resolución sobre Vincocaya, que U. conoce lo interesante de esta empresa. Ella es de U. tanto como mía, pues de mis dos acciones, una es de U. desde el año pasado, quiera o no quiera," February 4, 1830, and March 19, 1830, Epistolario APS, vol. 7, BNP. See also *El Republicano,* no. 20 (April 8, 1826) in *El Republicano (Arequipa): Noviembre 1825–Febrero 1827,* facsimile ed. (Caracas: Gobierno de Venezuela, 1975), 90–91. In 1871, the Peruvian state ceded twenty-two worthless shares to a private consortium since the irrigation works had been abandoned for thirty years, Francisco García Calderón, *Diccionario de la legislación peruana,* 2nd ed., 2 vols. (Paris: Librería de Laroque, 1879), 2:1836.

53. La Fuente to Gamarra, March 5, 1830: "[Q]ue he sido muy honrado y que no tengo con qué vivir si me falta mi triste sueldo," Epistolario APS, vol. 7, BNP.

fects in Arequipa.[54] A large portion of the extorted sums were handled dishonestly and incompetently in the name of shady political and military causes. Illegal seizures, condemnations, and confiscation of foreigners' property since the wars for independence soured relationships with foreign powers during the first thirty or so years of the young republic.[55] Diplomatic correspondence with Peruvian authorities was plagued with petitions and requests concerning claims by private individuals and companies as well as frustrated negotiations over bilateral treaties of friendship and commerce aimed at regulating against abuses and unfavorable treatment of foreign subjects in Peru. These claims and negotiations revealed to foreign diplomats that local corrupt interests were bent on stalling fair treaties and settlements.

In Lima, Gamarra had a revealing conversation with an American citizen who then relayed the content of it to U.S. diplomat Samuel Larned. Gamarra disclosed a key intention that explained the patronage interests behind his antiforeigner policies. After demanding, mostly unsuccessfully, cash advances from foreign merchants in exchange for tariff concessions, Gamarra wanted to favor the creation of domestic capitalists on the basis of native merchant groups. He calculated that after being favored with advantageous commercial and custom legislation protecting national production and commercial activities, native businesspeople would respond favorably when asked for financial support or else suffer the consequences. Gamarra, on the other hand, believed foreign merchants would not agree to that.[56]

---

54. Tristán, *Peregrinaciones,* 239–57.

55. See, for example, U.S. claims handled by successive U.S. diplomats in Lima amounting to more than $750,000 (or $1.2 million if forgone interest was taken into account), including seizures of ships and cargo (1829) and claims by merchants Henry Tracy (1827), Samuel Tracy (claiming an additional $104,559 for arbitrary expropriation and imprisonment for political reasons by xenophobic Gamarra in 1839–1840), and Alsop & Co. (1835), all unpaid until 1842. "Memoranda" signed by Samuel Larned, Lima, December 24, 1836; J. B. Thorton to M.R.E., Lima, April 23, 1837; J. C. Pickett to Forsyth, Lima, November 21, 1839 and May 25, 1840, Despatches 1826–1906, roll 5, USNA.

56. "The reason for all these vexations and unfriendly persecution [of foreigners], as given by the President, Gamarra himself, to one of our countrymen, who waited on him respecting the shutting up of the auctions, are the 'duty of promoting the prosperity of the native merchants'; 'the necessity of creating capitalists amongst them, in order to facilitate, thereby, the operations of government; and the alleviation of the natural wants.' 'For,' said his Excellency—'when we have raised up a set of native capitalists, we can say to them "the government is in need, you must each contribute for its relief the amount specified; or in case of refusal will take measures to compel you": whereas to the foreign capitalist we cannot say so.'!" Larned to Van Buren, Lima, March 8 and 31, 1830, Despatches 1826–1906, roll 1, USNA.

Protectionist commercial legislation thus had shady underpinnings in addition to commercial vested interests in the traditional trade of Chilean wheat for Peruvian sugar and raw cotton.[57] Gamarra thus intended the creation of a local base of support for his administration and personal power among private interests that was indistinguishable from cronyism.

To complement this political economic strategy and realize his grandiose scheme of making Peru the "American France,"[58] Gamarra strove to create an army "entirely devoted to his person, who owing everything to him would be more likely to support his ambitious projects" and "cement his military despotism." According to the British consul in Lima, Belford Hinton Wilson, this "military mania" was one of the main causes of the unsound financial conditions of the country that supported 1,000 officers in an army of barely 4,000 men.[59] However, the constant dangers of foreign wars did little to enhance the efficiency of the Peruvian state as might have been expected. An inefficient state and institutional disorder provided favorable conditions for corrupt transactions.

In reality, the small groups of Peruvian capitalists formed part of patronage networks of private cronies benefiting from official favors exchanged for political and financial support to caudillos. One important such mechanism of favoritism during Gamarra's administration was the supply of sums to the state in advance payment (*abono*) of extremely high customs duties (average of 90 percent), but at a considerable discount and paying in part with depreciated domestic debt scrip (billetes). This system of abonos benefited a small group of native merchants who became privileged creditors of the state. This sort of biased commercial "nationalism" defeated in practice ill-conceived protectionist goals since effective protection declined below 50 percent thanks to this abono jobbery. Notwithstanding these inherent flaws, Gamarra's entourage of vested interests aggressively defended protectionist measures against free trade reform and foreigners associated

57. Larned to Van Buren, Lima, March 5, 1830, Despatches 1826–1906, roll 1, USNA. High tariffs had been imposed in 1826 and early 1827 by Santa Cruz. See also Paul Gootenberg, *Between Silver and Guano: Commercial Policy and the State in Postindependence Peru* (Princeton, NJ: Princeton University Press, 1989), chapter 3; and "North-South: Trade Policy, Regionalism, and *Caudillismo* in Post-Independence Peru," *Journal of Latin American Studies* 23 (1991): 1–36.

58. After Bolívar's death, according to Gamarra, Peru projected itself as "un 'coloso' entre los demás estados americanos. Si marchamos con juicio y unión haremos del Perú la Francia Americana," Gamarra to La Fuente, Cusco, March 12, 1832, in Gamarra, *Epistolario,* 222.

59. Wilson to Palmerston, Lima, June 12, 1834, FO 61/27, ff. 149–157v, NAUK.

with it. Corrupt interests benefiting from the abono finance system were at the basis of these protectionist policies that obstructed and delayed the urgently needed commercial reform in Peru.[60]

Searching for reliable commercial statistics for Peru, Consul Wilson and other diplomats found that it could only be privately "purchased" from public officials. In 1834, Wilson thus remarked that "bribery is the main spring of action of all public and private relations of life."[61] Moreover, in Peru there was no system or fixed principles of government among aspirants to power except "personal aggrandizement as a means of enriching themselves."[62] The legacy of relying on authoritarian, patrimonial power and corruption as the means to maintaining political power thus extended from colonial times into the early republican period and beyond.

In analyzing La Fuente's vice-presidential administration a few years earlier, French minister Barrère had concluded that "depredations, corruption, and theft were the three great spheres of the Peruvian body politic."[63] A masterful witness of the time observed about La Fuente's moral integrity that "not many good things could be said. . . He is an inveterate gambler, extravagant when he has money and, with respect of how to obtain it, he has never been particularly worried about the selection of the means."[64]

Gamarra's feisty wife, Francisca Zubiaga de Gamarra, and her own entourage of flour monopolists and protectionist landowners (including flour

60. "Mr. Belford Wilson's Report upon the Peruvian trade 1837," FO 61/53, ff. 161–212, esp. 184v–185, NAUK. See also Gootenberg, "Paying for Caudillos: The Politics of Emergency Finance in Peru, 1820–1845," in *Liberals, Politics, and Power: State Formation in Nineteenth-Century Latin America,* ed. Vincent Peloso and Barbara Tenenbaum (Athens: University of Georgia Press, 1996), 134–65, esp. 143–44, where corruption and patronage are considered tangential in the discussion of abono jobbery to emphasize instead broader social bases.

61. Wilson to Palmerston, Lima, November 4, 1834, FO 61/28, ff. 302–303, NAUK, quoted also in Wu, *Generals and Diplomats,* 61. A few years earlier the Foreign Office had disapproved an expense of $260 paid to customs officers by the British consul in Arequipa for information on export and import trade of Quilca and Islay since consular instructions did not authorize incurring "any expense on the part of the publick to procure such information." Bidwell to Passmore, London, February 18, 1829, FO 61/16, ff. 11–11v, NAUK.

62. Wilson to Palmerston, Lima, December 5, 1834, FO 61/28, f. 362v, NAUK.

63. Bernard Barrère to M.A.E, Lima, April 4, 1831, CP, Pérou, vol. 4, f. 167v, AMAE: "les dilapidations, la corruption et les vols sont trois grandes plans du corps politique péruvien."

64. Heinrich Witt, *Diario y observaciones sobre el Perú (1824–1890),* trans. Kika Garland de Montero, prolog. Pablo Macera (Lima: Cofide, 1987), 253. This first printed version of Witt's diaries contains only selected excerpts.

merchant Frederick Pfeiffer and Lima's Prefect Juan Bautista Eléspuru who was prosecuted for corrupt administration), provided the caudillo with another important base of crony support.[65] In fact, Doña Francisca, also known as Pancha the Mariscala or Presidenta, sensing a growing dissent between Gamarra and La Fuente over the Peruvian presidency, forced Vice President La Fuente out of office in April 1831 after accusing him of conspiracy and peculation (embezzlement).[66] Gamarra and la Presidenta were themselves driven out of office and exiled by liberal forces led by General Luis José Orbegoso in 1833–1834. After Doña Pancha's death, Gamarra's interrupted partnership with La Fuente was resumed during the struggles of both against Santa Cruz that led to Gamarra's second presidency (1839–1841).[67]

Felipe Santiago Salaverry (a young officer of "violent and reckless temper, and of insatiable ambition") initiated his regime with a garrison mutiny on February 23, 1835, against Orbegoso. Salaverry, allied to Gamarra's crony Bujanda, returned administrative matters to typical caudillo plundering and xenophobia: "Heavy contributions, enforced by the bayonet and imprisonment in the common jail . . . have been levied . . . to the amount of [150,000] dollars . . . [and the seizure of] men, horses, and other beasts of burden." Foreigners were compelled to grant forced loans under the threat of imprisonment and "shooting a couple of consuls." A special repressive and

65. Basadre, *Historia* 2:27–32; Juan Evangelista Montes de Oca (Rafael Valdés?), *Carta de un particular al Jeneral El-es-burro prefecto de Lima* (Guayaquil: J. Rodríguez, 1832), 4, 13, accusing General Eléspuru, of illegal appropriations and enrichment. Eléspuru was subjected to an unfinished juicio de residencia in which his lawyer argued that the secretive character of such trial was a colonial antique incompatible with republican constitutions. "Expediente sobre el juicio de residencia abierta al señor general Juan Bautista Eléspuru, ex prefecto del departamento de Lima, años 1833–1834," Juicios de Residencia, CSJL, leg. 430, AGN. See also Larned to Van Buren, Lima, April 18 and May 17, 1831, Despatches 1826–1906, roll 1, USNA.

66. Willimott to Earl of Aberdeen, Lima, December 8, 1829, FO 61/16, f. 195v, NAUK.

67. Gamarra's wife died during exile in Chile in 1835. Seriously ill, doña Pancha sent for La Fuente who was also in Chile at the time. La Fuente "immediately waited on her, and continued to do, with great assiduity and kindness, until her last moments, when, in the presence of several witnesses, she confessed having been the sole cause of the revolution [of 1831 against La Fuente with orders to shoot him], and of the ruin of his fortunes, and entreated his forgiveness, which being forthwith granted she expired in his arms. The charges of her last sickness, and her funeral, were defrayed by General La Fuente. . . These occurrences will, doubtless reunite those once arbiters of the fate of Peru, Gamarra and La Fuente," Larned to Forsyth, Lima, June 26, 1835, Despatches 1826–1906, roll 3, USNA.

confiscating tribunal (Acordada) was restored. Neither the "Constitution nor laws afford[ed] the slightest guarantee against his encroachments[,] . . . [n]or restraint upon the exercise of his power."[68]

Francisco Quirós—a merchant with mining and political interests in Cerro de Pasco originally forged by his Galician father as deputy of the colonial Tribunal de Minería—had relied on foreign partners since the 1820s to obtain official concessions and monopolies. He was instrumental in the formation of the first mixed mining company, the Pasco Peruana Co., and was involved in the first railway schemes.[69] Initially linked to Riva Agüero, Quirós was appointed prefect of Junín by his friend Gamarra in 1833. In return, Quirós supported Gamarra and even granted him personal credit guarantees.[70] Another patronage–crony link in Gamarra's network was military officer José Rufino Echenique's business connections in Arequipa: Echenique was married to the eldest daughter of the southern local boss Pío Tristán.[71]

Was Domingo Elías, like many of the local capitalists of the time, a crony to one of the caudillo power networks? Under the precarious institutional conditions of early republican Peru, Elías must have had enormous diffi-

68. Larned to Forsyth, March 17, 1835, no. 128, and April 7, 1835, no. 131, Despatches 1826–1906, roll 3, USNA. See also Salaverry's confiscation decrees published in *Gaceta del Gobierno,* no. 2 (extraordinaria), March 2, 1835, and, no. 10, March 28, 1835. In his manifesto, "El Jefe Supremo de la República a sus conciudadanos," February 25, 1825, Salaverry justified his coup as a reaction to "mi patria destrozada por un club de hombres sin moral. . . He visto enriquecerse a una facción en medio de la indijencia general."

69. In London in 1822–1825, Quirós associated with notorious investors Thomas Kinder, John Parish Robertson, and others, and was one of the directors of the Pasco Peruana Co., and later the Empresa Anglo-Peruana de Minas together with William Cockran, Joseph Fletcher, and T. Holland. Rafael Quirós Salinas, *Los Quirós: una familia criolla en la historia del Perú,* 2 vols. (Lima: Propaceb, 2000), 1:127, citing Emilio Dancuart, *Anales de la Hacienda Pública* (Lima: Guillermo Stolte, 1902).

70. Quirós, *Los Quirós* 1:158, citing BNL and private family documents. Francisco Quirós was also appointed to important posts by presidents Orbegoso, Salaverry, and Castilla.

71. Regarding Colonel Echenique's political activities in 1834, a critic wrote: "Cuando los encargados del interés público traicionan la virtud y providad de su carácter; entonces la máquina social carece de ornato, están dislocadas sus bases y pronta a sucumbir en la nulidad. El bien común, los dulces vínculos de la sangre y la más hacendrada reputación se prostituyen, se hollan y se sacrifican al bien estar individual," Simón García, *Pequeñas observaciones que Simón García hace a parte del manifiesto del Sr. Coronel D. Rufino Echenique publicado en el Cuzco en 23 de julio de 1834* (Arequipa: Imprenta de Francisco Valdés, 1834), 1.

culties or, conversely, exceptional opportunities in the process of building his business emporium. He initially expanded his property in the Ica valley by buying land from bankrupt aristocratic owners through family connections. Land prices had collapsed after independence and the average annual return on agricultural production was as low as 3 percent. The supply of long-term mortgage loans was extremely scarce, while the annual interest for commercial loans—practically the only type of credit available for farmers and ranchers—was prohibitively high at 12 to 24 percent. Very few businessmen were interested in investing in agriculture.

Elías saw the opportunity for developing commercial production of cotton and wine using the slave labor force on his estates, supplementing it with clandestine purchases of slaves and the nominally free children of slaves from New Granada.[72] At the time, cotton and wine had sheltered local markets due to official customs protection, especially for coarse cotton manufactures produced locally. Elías followed a combined strategy of acquiring cheap productive coastal land in the province of Ica with the fierce elimination of possible competitors in the establishment of monopoly niches. Although his strategy was risky, it allowed Elías to accumulate capital, mostly fixed to landed property that served as a basis for his political ambitions. According to one of his creditors, the ambitious Elías was an honest person or otherwise he would not have been able to obtain commercial credit. He was not a gambler, although he sometimes did bet handsomely; he did not drink excessively but ate too much. It was difficult to tell if money for him was a means to obtain power or an end of his political efforts.[73]

Elías complemented his real estate strategy with active lobbying to obtain from the state very profitable official monopolies. In this process, he continued to use aggressive tactics against business competitors as well as obtaining doubtful political favors that entailed glaring conflicts of interest. One of his early caudillo mentors and business partners was Marshal Santa Cruz who appointed Elías to an official post.[74] During the regime of the

---

72. In June 1847, Elías and two other estate owners bought 87 New Granadan slaves and 116 *manumisos* or *libertos* delivered to Pisco for 39,500 pesos, according to John W. Kitchens, "The New-Granadan-Peruvian Slave Trade," *Journal of Negro History* 64 (1979): 205–14, esp. 210; or 54,888 pesos according to Peter Blanchard, "The 'Transitional Man' in Nineteenth-Century Latin America: The Case of Domingo Elías of Peru," *Bulletin of Latin American Research* 15 (1996): 157–76, esp. 165–67, 171.

73. Witt, *Diario* (1987), 245.

74. Rolf Engelsen, "Social Aspects of Agricultural Expansion," 433–40, cited in

Peru-Bolivia Confederation (1836–1839), inspired and led by Santa Cruz (after the defeat and execution of protectionist dictator Salaverry), Elías bought from the state two valuable haciendas with depreciated billetes at face value.[75]

Santa Cruz was considered at the time more honest than other military caudillos: "Despite the fact that [Santa Cruz] knew how to take care of his own interests he was never accused of illegal enrichment and, even less so, to allow any of his subalterns to do so."[76] Santa Cruz's main power base was, however, a group of faithful foreign generals active in the Peruvian army since the independence campaigns as well as foreign merchants and diplomats interested in free trade agreements and customs policy reform.[77] In 1836, generous official gifts of high salaries and rewards in cash and real estate benefited Santa Cruz, his ally General Orbegoso, and their military high command. When Gamarra returned to power in 1839, his administration outdid the previous profligate excesses in the troubled impoverished nation. Gamarra granted the main agents of Santa Cruz's defeat—the Chilean "Restaurador" army and navy and his own military staff—1 million pesos.[78] In his campaign against the Confederation, Gamarra received initial support of long-time ally General Juan Crisóstomo Torrico, one of the most corrupt and scheming figures of nineteenth-century Peru.[79]

Diana Balmori, Stuart Voss, and Miles Wortman, *Notable Family Networks in Latin America* (Chicago: University of Chicago Press, 1984), 213–14.

75. Orrego, "Domingo Elías," 320, citing Echenique, *Memorias,* 1:104.

76. Witt, *Diario* (1992), 1:329–30. Witt also compared the moral character of key military presidents: "Santa Cruz . . . era sin duda un hombre de gran capacidad; en su ámbito cotideano era un buen esposo y un buen padre, no era un libertino como Echenique, ni borrachín como Orbegoso, ni jugador como Castilla," 328.

77. Wu, *Generals and Diplomats,* 27, 75.

78. Basadre, *Historia* 2:135–36, 170.

79. After Gamarra's deportation of Torrico for his role in a failed rebellion in December 1840, an observer wrote: Torrico "has proven that he is not the man either to make a revolution or to give direction to one. . . [H]e is deficient both in courage and in discretion. This officer's treachery is an example of the baseness of which the military men of Peru are capable. He owes almost everything to Gen. Gamarra—rank, distinction and fortune—the last acquired by plundering and oppressing the people and he repays it all with the vilest ingratitude. He is . . . the greatest ruffian in Peru, where ruffians are by no means scarce; and the impunity extended to him in his career of violence and wrong is not among the least of Gen. Gamarra's errors or rather his delinquencies. . . In the Peruvian army there are many not much better than [Torrico]. And in Peru, public opinion (if there is such thing here) imposes very few restraints." Pickett to Forsyth, Lima, January 8, 1841, no. 31, Despatches 1826–1906, USNA. Additional devastating facts concerning Torrico's corruption are recorded in Manuel de Mendiburu, *Biografías*

Obviously Elías's association with Santa Cruz meant enmity with the Gamarra—La Fuente—Torrico patronage network. The final defeat of Santa Cruz in 1839 brought down painfully negotiated liberal commercial codes and trade and friendship treaties with foreign powers, especially the British. A slightly earlier, elaborate report by the British consul general reflected on the interests behind the formidable opposition to "radical reform of ancient abuses" and resistance to order and method in Peru. According to the report, no strong public support for the extirpation of such abuses could be expected. In reality, increased abuses were favored by the executive, as well as the subordinate legislative and judicial authorities, because it afforded "the richest harvest for the realization of their own fortunes." Corruption in Peru was comparable to that in Mexico except for the sanguinary character of the latter, Consul Wilson wrote. However, Peruvian administrative morality was lower than that of any other Spanish American nation: "The Peruvians may truly be looked upon as the Neapolitans, and the Mexicans as the Russians of America."[80]

Enmity toward foreigners guided the actions of Generals Gamarra, La Fuente, and Torrico, who were once again in power.[81] Evidence of threats and plots against the life of Consul Wilson surfaced in 1841. A judicial investigation was opened and a diplomatic scandal ensued. Based on the declaration of witnesses (including one who had rejected an offer to join the plotters), anonymous warning notes, and other journalistic and circumstantial evidence, Wilson charged that General La Fuente and his henchmen, Major Isidro Pavón, and journalist Colonel José Félix Iguaín, were the main conspirators in an attempt to assassinate him. Moreover, Wilson accused Supreme Court judges Francisco Javier Mariátegui and Manuel Antonio Colmenares of being La Fuente's creatures who turned the investigation into a trial against Wilson himself.[82]

---

de los generales republicanos, ed. Félix Denegri Luna (Lima: Academia Nacional de la Historia, 1963), 388–436, esp. 399, 420–21, 428.

80. "Mr. Belford Wilson's report upon the Peruvian trade in 1837," FO 61/53, ff. 191–192, NAUK.

81. Vice Consul Crompton to Wilson, Islay, April 20, 1839, FO 61/62, ff. 99–100; Wilson to Palmerston, Lima, July 29, 1839, FO 61/62, ff. 111–112v, NAUK.

82. Wilson to Palmerston, Callao, November 17, 1841, FO 61/80, ff. 211–215, NAUK, and attachments on legal proceedings, ff. 234–327v. Fearing for his life, Wilson took refuge aboard a French ship. Foreign Minister Agustín Guillermo Charún protested Wilson's lack of confidence in Peruvian law enforcement and judicial authorities in a publication containing relevant correspondence and documents: Protesta que hace el gobierno del Perú contra la conducta del Encargado de Negocios de Su Majes-

The death of Gamarra in battle (1841) and the downfall of his constitutional successor Manuel Menéndez in 1842 opened yet another crisis of political instability, anarchy, and plunder that prompted foreign powers to intervene to protect their nationals in Peru.[83] La Fuente continued his depredations in 1843. Serving as finance minister in the short-lived administration of General Francisco Vidal, La Fuente was suspected of absconding with $23,000 after a failed attempt to hire French agents to destroy a vessel connected to caudillo Manuel Ignacio Vivanco.[84]

In this context Elías initially collaborated politically and economically with the self-proclaimed Supreme Director Vivanco. However, in June 1844, as prefect of Lima, Elías seized "supreme authority" for himself and issued a proclamation against Vivanco's alleged selfishness, incompetence, dishonesty, cruelty, and cowardice.[85] A profound enmity between Echenique and Elías also dates to these days of confused power struggles that momentarily positioned Elías, the leader of Lima's urban militias, as head of the Peruvian government in defiance of Echenique's military authority in the highlands of Lima and Junín.

---

tad Británica D. Belford Hinton Wilson y su inmotivada separación del territorio peruano, acompañada de los documentos principales sobre los motivos de queja alegados por ese funcionario (Lima: Imprenta del Estado por Eusebio Aranda, 1842).

83. Blockades and embargoes since 1842 had vexed neutral commerce, and "[s]o low has the military character fallen here, that the commanders of blockading vessels of war . . . have engaged in smuggling, using their ships as receptacles for smuggled merchandise and participating, without doubt, in the profits." Pickett to Secretary of State (hereafter S.S.), Lima, July 3, 1844, no. 96, Despatches 1826–1906, roll 6, USNA. In 1843, the intendant of the police, Manuel Suárez, was publicly accused of administrative abuses, including imposing fines but not remitting them to the public treasury, and fraud in public works: "Manuel Suárez . . . contra Antonio Baeza," Abuso de Libertad de Imprenta, CSJL, leg. 714, AGN.

84. Witt, *Diario* (1992), 2:66–67.

85. "It is rather difficult to account for Elías's defection. . . He is wealthy and respectable and influential . . . but after having supported Vivanco through thick and thin, with money and service, for fifteen months, making himself the instrument to carry into effect, his harsh, illegal and arbitrary measures . . . certainly gives some room to doubt [Elías's] desinterestedness. . . [However, he] is said by those who know him well to be honest about money matters and he would not plunder and peculate as almost all do here that can." Pickett to S.S., Lima, July 3, 1844, no. 96, Despatches 1826–1906, roll 6, USNA. Later, however, Elías was accused of "having peculated enormously," as "whilst in power he paid off" all of his previous debts. "If this be true he has played his game skillfully, and his well-timed abandonment of Vivanco was not only politic, but has been also profitable. At the time he united with the Director, however, he was considered to be rich, though much in debt." Pickett to John C. Calhoun, Lima, October 31, 1844, no. 103, Despatches 1826–1906, roll 6, USNA.

In 1844–1845, anarchy in Peru gave rise to support, including that of Elías and Echenique, for military caudillo Ramón Castilla who, after defeating Vivanco, was elected president.[86] Castilla was a brave and able general, Gamarra's former finance minister, and a good friend of La Fuente early in his career. Castilla was also an intimate friend of Pedro Gonzales Candamo, an important merchant and money-lender who obtained important favors during Castilla's two administrations. Castilla, a pragmatic yet xenophobic leader, initiated basic administrative reforms and political deals that brought a degree of stability for several years. However, Castilla was accused, as were several other military caudillos, of administrative dishonesty. During his tenure as subprefect of Tarapacá in 1829, he was charged with complicity in smuggling liquor through the port of Arica.[87] In November 1845, the U.S. chargé d'affaires in Lima, Albert Jewett, reported that in contending with the Peruvian government's reluctance to make previously agreed restitution payments to U.S. citizens, he dealt with a "most extraordinary, faithless, corrupt, and insolent government." According to Jewett, General Castilla was a "very ignorant man" and his cabinet composed of "unprincipled and bold robbers of the public treasury who will not permit one dollar of the public money to be diverted from the use of themselves and friends, except what it may be necessary for the purpose of bribery."[88]

In 1848, Castilla wrote: "They call me a dissipated gambler and thief of the Treasury when I have always gone after the gamblers and thieves."[89]

---

86. In 1844, interim civilian president Meléndez revealed the existence of several costly *corruptelas* in granting official posts and pensions, and the failure to prosecute corrupt officials due to malfunctions and purposeful delays in the judicial system, leading to impunity. Basadre, *Historia* 3:69.

87. Basadre, *Historia* 3:77–78. See also Castilla's correspondence with Antonio Gutiérrez de la Fuente (1823–1840) in *Archivo Castilla* 3 (Lima: Instituto "Libertador Ramón Castilla," 1961): Epistolario.

88. Jewett to Buchanan, Lima, November 27, 1845, Despatches 1826–1906, roll 7, USNA. Jewett added that the unpopular minister of finance, Manuel del Río (who had occupied the post several times since 1832 and was later questioned publicly by Congress), asked the Ecuadorian chargé for a bribe of $30,000 to settle Ecuadorian restitution claims: "[T]he men that compose this administration . . . are little better than a Junta of land robbers, who came into power by bloodshed, rapine, fraud, treachery, and bribery of secondary officers."

89. Castilla to General Pedro Cisneros, November 11, 1848, cited in Basadre, *Historia* 3:107. However, Jewett reported in 1846 that guano income was misused: "The present public plunderers are not satisfied with using all the public money and leaving many of the current debts, soldiers etc. unpaid; they get an advance to divide before going out of power—or as a gambling fund, in which business I am informed the president

Indeed, he curbed the actions of some dishonest officials in his first administration, albeit too benevolently, in a case involving Minister of Foreign Affairs José Gregorio Paz Soldán, a shrewd and feared lawyer with whom Castilla had serious differences.[90] Castilla stubbornly retained other high-ranking officials, such as Minister of Finance Manuel del Río, despite incessant rumors and charges of fraud and squander of national revenues in the press and by judges and members of congress. Del Río had collaborated closely with Castilla in enacting the domestic debt consolidation law and in promoting hundreds of officers in the army.[91] Despite his leniency toward these corrupt men, Castilla did contribute to important reorganizations of the state administration and implanted the practice of national budgets for the first time. A keen observer and admirer remarked that Castilla was an honest and sensible man, a true patriot who made efforts for the well-being of the country, although he was hardly educated and coarse, rather obstinate, and a friend of cards and dice games.[92]

As a means to remain in power, Castilla acted as a referee among several people with competing political ambitions, especially those of Elías and Echenique. During Castilla's first administration, Echenique headed the ministry of war and later was appointed prime minister. Meanwhile, Elías had a critical role as member, together with Quirós and Manuel de Mendiburu, of an official commission investigating the budget for 1846–1847. In 1849, Castilla's government also granted Elías two crucial monopoly concessions under the umbrella of the "General Law of Immigration." The first allowed payments of 30 pesos per indentured Chinese coolie contracted and shipped by Elías and his partners for use in coastal agriculture; and the sec-

---

is engaged most of the time when he is not engaged in a still more fashionable vice." Jewett to Buchanan, Lima, February 28, 1846, no. 7, Despatches 1826–1906, roll 7, USNA.

90. Castilla sought to limit the abuses of favor-seeking José Gregorio Paz Soldán, minister of foreign affairs until 1847, and his brother Mateo. With political calculation, Castilla pursued the recovery of 20,000 pesos owed to the treasury by the Paz Soldáns. Later Castilla reminded the former minister that placing him as director of the treasury at Paz Soldán's own request was nothing other than a "commission" awarded to him. Castilla to Pedro Cisneros, Lima, November 13–14, 1847, in *Archivo Castilla* 8 (1974): 22–23; Castilla to Dr. José G. Paz Soldán, Lima, August 18, 1850, in *Archivo Castilla* 3 (1961): 229–31. See also Basadre, *Historia* 3:107–8.

91. William Pitt Adams to Palmerston, Lima, March 12, April 13, and November 13, 1848, FO 61/118, ff. 128–30, 153–54v, and 270–72, NAUK. Del Río was finally forced to resign by congressional pressure in July 1849. Basadre, *Historia* 3:96–97.

92. Witt, *Diario* (1987), 250–51.

ond was the exclusive contract for the loading of guano for which Elías used a labor force comprised of indentured workers, slaves, and convicts.[93] Conversely, Castilla favored Echenique, a wealthy and well-connected presidential candidate, during the violent and corrupted electoral process of 1850. Echenique was elected by a majority of delegates in the final electoral contest with Elías, the runner-up, and General Vivanco.[94] Once in office, President Echenique soon revoked both of the official contracts previously granted to Elías.

Due to shady deals between caudillos and crony capitalists, opportunities for honest and competitive entrepreneurs were scant. One such marginal investor, Manuel Argumaniz Muñoz, left a revealing, unpublished record denouncing top businessmen's collusion with corrupt authorities. Argumaniz was a self-made entrepreneur from Lima who accumulated his initial capital as a merchant in Valparaíso. Already as a young merchant marine officer, he quarreled with his employer, a despotic Peruvian ship owner prone to smuggling activities. In 1835, Argumaniz had organized a sizable shipment destined for Lima but he was forced to sell his merchandise in Ica province due to the struggles engulfing the Peruvian capital at the time. Despite disruptive military campaigns and extortion, Argumaniz became a large-scale supplier of consumer goods such as flour, rice, and brandy (*aguardiente*) in the southern localities of Ica, Pisco, and Chincha. However, those were territories zealously guarded by the domineering Domingo Elías who pressed municipal authorities and local landowners to harass Argumaniz's competitive activities. Despite Argumaniz's efforts to strengthen his local business position by forming a partnership with foreign capitalist Miguel Montané, the monopolist maneuvers of Elías prevailed. In 1841, Argumaniz had to relocate to Lima.[95]

93. W. M. Mathew, "A Primitive Export Sector: Guano Production in Mid-Nineteenth-Century Peru," *Journal of Latin American Studies* 9 (1977): 35–57, esp. 35–37; Orrego, "Domingo Elías," 322–24; Watt Stewart, *Chinese Bondage in Peru: A History of the Chinese Coolie in Peru, 1849–1874* (Westport, CT: Greenwood Press, 1951), 12–13.

94. Armed followers of Vivanco and Echenique's *mazorqueros* engaged in "riot and bloodshed" in the preliminary parochial elections of February 17, 1850: The echeniquistas "got possession of the ballot boxes . . . as the friends of Vivanco knew that the possession of them, at a Peruvian election, is tantamount to a victory, they attacked the polls—held in the Church of the Merced in the centre of Lima—and after a hard struggle were defeated." Clay to John Clayton, Lima, March 12, 1850, Despatches 1826–1906, roll 8, USNA. See also Marquez, *Orjía,* 18; Basadre, *Historia* 3:289–91.

95. María Luisa Palacios McBride, "Un empresario peruano del siglo XIX: Manuel de Argumaniz" (Lima: B.A. thesis, Universidad Católica, 1989), 7–12, based on the un-

Moreover, among several other business projects, Argumaniz established a partnership with usury-prone Gonzales Candamo between 1842 and 1844 for the speculative purchase of plata piña in Cerro de Pasco. Problems between the two led to the unfriendly dissolution of their partnership. Argumaniz also considered General Castilla his enemy. During Castilla's first presidency, Argumaniz's proposals for coveted railway construction contracts were rejected and, predictably, were granted instead to Gonzales Candamo and his partners. Disillusioned with the business atmosphere in Peru, Argumaniz lived mainly in Paris since 1848, acting as a partner of guano contractor Julián Zaracondegui. When he returned to Peru years later, he continued to be ostracized and disliked by Lima's capitalist clique.[96]

Although guided by self-interest, Elías eventually denounced corruption among military caudillos at the peril of his wealth, freedom, and life.[97] He espoused liberal civil reforms that clashed with corrupt and authoritarian traditions and interests. In this sense, his participation as the candidate of the first civilian-based party, the Club Progresista, in the 1851 presidential elections was an important departure from caudillo politics as usual. Elías, together with Francisco Quirós, another reconstructed liberal proposing democratic reform after years of collaborating with military caudillos, aimed at an institutional change to avoid abuse and political corruption.[98] The formation of civilian political parties directly confronted and competed with old patronage networks and, at least theoretically, narrowed the opportunities for corruption and favoritism in the political culture of the time. Unfor-

---

published manuscript "Memorias" by Manuel Argumaniz Muñoz (1876), a unique source consisting of six volumes in the private collection of Eduardo D'Argent (Lima) of which there is a typewritten copy with notes by Carlos Moreyra Palacios.

96. Palacios, "Un empresario peruano," 14–18; Witt, *Diario* (1992), 2:140.

97. Domingo Elías, ed., *Documentos que prueban el hecho del asesinato contra la persona del Consejero de Estado Domingo Elías en la noche del 12 de abril del corriente año de 1849* (Lima: Imprenta del Correo, 1849).

98. Other important liberal, civilian leaders of the Club Progresista included Quirós, its president in 1851, Pedro Gálvez, and José Sevilla. Quirós was detained and exiled by Echenique in 1854. In his *Manifiesto* of 1851, Quirós, in reference to military power, stated: "Rodeado de la gloria inmarcesible que en Junín y Ayacucho conquistara, no ha limitado su prestigio a mantener ilesas y en vigor esas instituciones que brotaron a la sombra de sus frescos laureles, sino que reservó para sí sólo todas las posiciones importantes; colocó a los individuos de su seno en cuantas esferas reconoce la jerarquía administrativa; y desconociendo que el Gobierno, para llenar su fin, debe ser esencialmente civil, como lo es la sociedad que representa; falseó desde su nacimiento la verdadera democracia, y tendió a la oligarquía centralizando la autoridad en unos pocos." Cited in Quirós, *Los Quirós* 1:235.

tunately, these civilian reformers and those who followed in their footsteps were defeated or blocked from achieving their general goals by recalcitrant vested interests firmly attached to the budding state bureaucracy, military despotism, and the corrupt administration of guano revenues.

The Curse of Guano Administration

In 1841, foreign diplomats informed their governments of the discovery of a new source of Peruvian wealth. One such report read "*huano* is generally supposed to be the excrement of marine birds. . . It is found in great abundance, in some small islands, a few degrees south of Lima, and has been used in agriculture, for manure, from time immemorial. . . [It] sells in England at ten dollars a ton giving a net profit of at least fifty [percent]."[99] Soon the guano islands became the object of ambition among officials, businessmen, and creditors. As collateral for paying multiple claims and debts owed by the depleted Peruvian exchequer, the islands also were the subject of continuous threats and schemes to seize them as a coercive measure by foreign powers to force Peru to pay its obligations.[100]

In November—December 1840, Gamarra and his finance minister, Castilla, granted native capitalist Francisco Quirós and his French partners (Aquiles Allier, Barroilhet, and Dutey) the first, extremely profitable guano monopoly contract. The native and foreign consortium of Quirós, Allier & Co. paid only 90,000 pesos (£18,000) in cash installments and depreciated debt scrip for nine years of unlimited guano extraction and sale in Europe. The Peruvian state, in dire need of cash advances as war with Bolivia approached, had traditionally granted those monopolies. The onerous contract was rescinded in 1841 and replaced by other contracts with a new consortium of wider local and foreign participation.

Independent sources attest to the payment of bribes to high authorities toward securing these contracts. Foreign merchant competitors complained about these bribe schemes.[101] In addition, General Francisco de Vidal said

99. Pickett to Webster, Lima, November 27, 1841, Despatches 1826–1906, roll 6, USNA.

100. Consul Stanhope Prevost to Minister Albert G. Jewett, Lima, October 25, 1845, and Jewett to Captain N. M. Howison, Lima, October 23, 1845, Despatches 1826–1906, roll 7, USNA.

101. W. M. Mathew, "Foreign Contractors and the Peruvian government at the Outset of the Guano Trade," *Hispanic American Historical Review* 52 (1972): 598–620,

in his memoirs that if he had accepted the generous cash offers of Lucas Fonseca, an agent of Quirós and Allier, Vidal would have become the "greatest millionaire of the Republic."[102] Likewise, under Gamarra, judicial institutions, the ultimate guarantors of fair business deals and contracts, could not be trusted: "Certainly, in no country in Christendom, is judicial purity less above suspicion than in Peru, and in none, can less confidence be reposed in the integrity of the magistrates. . . . [S]ome of the Peruvian Judiciary are neither incorruptible nor uncorrupted" due in part to "the endless and demoralizing civil wars, the official profligacy of the times, the poverty of some judges, their dependence on the Executive . . . and finally, their salaries are paid with very little regularity."[103] At the time, several inquiries exposed bribery schemes between prominent judges and private interests.[104]

Unsound institutional arrangements in the contracting of guano extraction and commercialization contributed crucially to the frustration of socioeconomic and political progress in mid-nineteenth-century Peru. The first generation of guano contracts in the 1840s and 1850s paved the way for future financial problems experienced by the Peruvian state. These contracts mainly granted monopoly concessions to merchant houses with avowedly solid financial backing for the sale of guano shipments in Europe, the United States, and other foreign markets. The Peruvian state remained the sole

citing correspondence of Antony Gibbs & Sons (Guildhall Library, London), and letters of British chargé d'affaires Belford Hinton Wilson.

102. Francisco de Vidal, "Memoria," 629.

103. J. C. Pickett's comments on fallacies in Gamarra's address to Congress, Pickett to Forsyth, Lima, July 15, 1840, no. 16, Despatches 1826–1906, roll 5, USNA.

104. An inquiry set against Pascual Francisco Suero, Lima's district judge (juez de primera instancia), in 1830 found evidence of *cohecho* to favor flour merchant Frederick Pfeiffer, Juicios de Pesquisa, leg. 432, AGN. Other cases against judges charged with cohecho and *prevaricato* included those of Mariano Santos de Quiroz (vocal, Corte Superior de Lima) 1830, José Lisa (Ica) 1834–1835, and Juan Manuel Campoblanco (Jauja) 1836. See also Fernando López Aldana, Felipe Santiago Estenós, Justo Figuerola, and Lorenzo Soria, *Refutación documentada de las principales falsedades y errores de hecho y de derecho que contiene el manifiesto publicado por el S. D. D. Mariano Santos Quirós contra los magistrados de la Suprema Corte de Justicia que sentenciaron en primera instancia el juicio de su pesquisa* (Lima: Imp. José Masías, 1831), 39–40: "Ser incorruptible y parecerlo . . . es administrar justicia imparcial y desinteresadamente . . . que no le ocurra a nadie la tentación de irlo a provocar con dádivas. . . Pero si en vez de esto se juega, se dan banquetes, no se paga la casa en que se vive, y se anda a la caza de los litigantes y se pignoran hasta las alhajas de la mujer ¿qué juicio se formará del magistrado?"

owner of guano deposits while paying a commission to guano contractors, after all trading costs had been covered on the state's account. Moreover, contracts were generally granted to enterprises willing to advance badly needed funds at onerously high interest rates of up to 1 percent a month, as well as pay bribes, to successive governments and officials. All this meant that many guano contractors had few incentives to reduce intermediary costs or to be honest with guano accounts. Cash advances and loans to governments, partly in depreciated debt paper, and chronic budgetary shortcomings also induced state officials to perpetuate these flawed contracts.[105]

Two sorts of interests pressed for the continuation of this basic model for guano contracts: those of corrupt government officials and those of merchant houses seeking monopoly gain. A British diplomat with vast experience in Peru explained that attempts to establish sound trading policies and contracts in the 1840s were hindered by "the personal and pecuniary interests of the then corrupt administration of Peru and of the wealthy foreigners who desired to obtain the monopoly."[106] Unscrupulous and dishonest guano contracting houses in this early period included Montané & Co., supplier of the French guano market, Cristóbal de Murrieta & Co., supplier to Spain, Quirós, Allier & Co. and Puymerol, Poumarroux & Co., suppliers to other European markets, and Federico Barreda y Hno., supplier to the United States.

Antony Gibbs & Sons and its subsidiaries in Peru emerged in the 1842–1861 period as the most important guano contractors. President Castilla trusted Gibbs's managerial and financial services. However, the conservative British house's financial stability, and its willingness to advance large sums to the government, counted as more important factors in being granted guano monopolies. Like other guano contractors, Gibbs was involved in du-

105. W. M. Mathew, "Foreign Contractors," 598, 604–7, 619–20; Basadre, *Historia* 3:151–65; Compañía Quirós y Allier, *Exposición que Quirós y Allier hacen a los señores diputados que componen la Comisión de Hacienda* (Lima: Imprenta de J. Masías, 1849). On a loan of $850,000 of "onerous conditions" negotiated with Gibbs and Montané in exchange for exclusive rights to export guano, under the pressing need to pay six months of unpaid salaries to government officials: "The terms of this contract are so extraordinary that one may be equally surprised that any individuals should offer such proposals. . . . The most remarkable feature is that the Peruvian government agrees to accept its depreciated paper, which is now at a discount of about 80 percent, at par, in payment of one fourth of the sum produced by the sale of the Huano." See John Randolph Clay to Buchanan, Lima, January 11, 1848, Despatches 1826–1906, roll 8, USNA.

106. Belford Wilson to Stanley, June 9, 1852, FO 61/137, cited by Mathew, "Foreign Contractors," 614.

bious and self-interested manipulations. In 1846, the Peruvian government ordered its representative in London to inquire about the commissions charged by Gibbs and other guano contractors suspected of being unduly high and fraudulent.[107]

As soon as General Echenique took office in 1851, it was remarked that he had personally spent far more in securing his election than what he could earn as president. According to U.S. diplomat J. Randolph Clay, guano contractors would take advantage of those circumstances to "secure the influence of the new president by personal loans" as had occurred with his predecessors.[108] In 1853, Gibbs negotiated in Lima an extension (*prórroga*) to its guano contract with the corrupt Echenique administration. This extension was shrouded in secrecy, its clauses and conditions never published. A large advance and probably the bribery of officials were involved. A special commission investigating the affair in 1856 during the second Castilla administration left Gibbs unpunished.[109] Moreover, Gibbs also engaged in additional commissions buried in shipping costs and over-debiting government accounts.

Under this institutional setting bolstered by bribery, unfair privileges, and shady deals, guano revenues were used by Peruvian governments mainly for unproductive expenditures. The problem was compounded by lack of education and experience among state officials faced with a sudden source of national wealth.[110] Harmful and specious mechanisms such as consolidation of the domestic debt and owners' compensation for the manumission of slaves were devised to benefit narrow interests via guano revenues.

107. José Gregorio Paz Soldán (M.R.E.) to Juan Manuel Iturregui (Peruvian representative in London), Lima, September 14, 1846, 5-17/1846, AMRE.

108. J. R. Clay to Daniel Webster, Lima, February 8, 1851, Despatches 1826–1906, roll 8, USNA. Clay also complained about the mismanagement of the consignment of guano to the United States held by Barreda y Hno. Clay strove to convince successive Peruvian finance ministers of the convenience of abandoning the corrupting system of consignment in favor of a system of direct sales at the guano islands. However, the guano income was already mortgaged to foreign creditors, especially Gibbs & Co. and British bondholders. Clay to William Marcy, Lima, April 20, 1855, Despatches 1826–1906, roll. 11, USNA.

109. W. M. Mathew, *The House of Gibbs and the Peruvian Guano Monopoly* (London: Royal Historical Society, 1981), 106–108, 230–31.

110. "Como para el manejo y adelantamiento de un gran caudal es necesario talento e instrucción, y como para no abusar del poder que presta, es necesario probidad, nada más precario y peligroso que la riqueza repentina." Santiago Távara, *Administración del huano escrita con motivo de la moción del H. Diputado por Parinacochas* (Lima: Imprenta de El Comercio, 1856), 5.

Debt Consolidation Scandals

One of the best-documented corruption scandals in the early republican history of Peru is connected with "consolidation" of the domestic debt in the
1850s. Parallel to efforts at regaining access to foreign loans by restructuring the foreign debt, the avowed goal of consolidating sundry domestic
debts was to revamp confidence in domestic public credit. Finally, after
decades of neglect and abuse, it was clearly and publicly recognized that a
well-serviced public debt was the foundation on which financial and economic development could ensue. Important steps were consequently taken
toward reforming the bases of Peruvian foreign and domestic credit during
the first administration of Castilla. The domestic debt consolidation measure was a major foundation of modern public credit in Peru.

In fact, two distinct types of domestic debt had evolved since the 1820s.
The debt incurred from expropriations and forced loans was mostly unrecognized or guaranteed with extremely depreciated government scrip. To this
first and by far largest type of debt belonged bona fide credits owed to private lenders of the old colonial state. On the other hand, a group of merchant creditors who supplied emergency loans in the 1830s and 1840s had
managed to obtain, through cronyism and negotiations with successive
caudillos, privileged recognition and service of their high-interest loans to
the state. To this second type of favored debt belonged the funds serviced
by taxes on imports or *arbitrios,* which by 1850 amounted to 1 million pesos at a monthly interest rate of between 1 and 2 percent. Moreover, big
merchants were the principal beneficiaries of paying import taxes with billetes or other public debt certificates.

However, since the late 1840s and culminating in the law of March 16,
1850, the unrecognized credits dating since the war of independence were
gradually guaranteed by *cédulas* and *vales* or consolidation bonds. The law
of 1850 that officially opened the domestic debt consolidation was itself a
faulty piece of legislation on two counts. First, it did not establish firm standards for the recognition of insufficiently proven debt claims, and second,
it did not clarify proper endorsing qualifications. These legal pitfalls allowed the perversion of long-term debt bonds into values of short-term
commercial exchange.[111] The law of 1850, together with complementary

---

111. Ley de la consolidación, *El Peruano* 23, no. 23, March 16, 1850; Felipe Barriga
Alvarez (Timoleón), *El Perú y los gobiernos del general Echenique y de la revolución*
(Lima: J. M. Monterola., 1855), 22; Anonymous, *Al gobierno, a la Convención Nacional*

legislation between 1851 and 1853, opened up ample opportunities for speculation and fraudulent recognition procedures that eventually defeated the strategically important financial goals of the consolidation.

Interest group lobbying pushed for exaggerated and fraudulent recognition of neglected domestic debts. Almost worthless claims before 1850 now became the subject of speculative interests aware of the consolidation's Midas touch. The most important capitalists, including Elías and Gonzales Candamo, engaged in patronizing the recognition of large claims or *expedientes* with the expectation of hefty commissions. Speculators bought claims on the cheap and negotiated their recognition at a value many times higher than what they had originally paid. Government officials also patronized such claims with the promise of privileged recognition in exchange for illegal stakes and commissions. Consequently, the consolidated domestic debt ballooned from 5 million pesos in 1851 to 24 million in 1852. A final rush of debt recognition took place in the few months prior to the deadlines of June and October 1852 during which most of the fraudulent expedientes were processed. The new governing clique led by President Echenique excelled in the corrupt handling of domestic debt administration.

The business of negotiating claims brought about conflicts and public denunciations that exposed lurid details of illegal and fraudulent procedures. Documents were forged, signatures falsified, government clerks bribed. Some notorious cases involved debts being recognized for hundreds of thousands of pesos and distributed among different intermediary agents with much reduced sums actually obtained by original claimants. One such case, the claim of Doña Ignacia Novoa de Arredondo, resulted in a dispute between Elías and Echenique's minister of war, General Juan Crisóstomo Torrico. Novoa had legitimate business arrangements with Elías who negotiated some of her financial matters for a commission. In 1852, Elías tried to get the government's approval of Novoa's debt claim for 500,000 to 600,000 pesos, the estimated value of an expropriated hacienda with 500 slaves and its forgone income during the ensuing thirty-two years. Elías expected to receive 200,000 pesos for his agency in this business. This was not the only debt claim in which Elías was involved as an intermediary. Echenique personally told Elías that the Novoa claim had not met the official deadline for its approval. However, a few days later the claim was ap-

y a la opinión pública (Lima: Imprenta Libre, 1856), 9, 20, 70–71; Manuel Amunátegui et al., *Señor, los abajo firmados propietarios y comerciantes de esta ciudad y tenedores de vales de consolidación* (Lima: N.p., 1862), 4, 10, 20.

proved for the startling sum of 948,500 pesos in bonds thanks to the direct involvement of Torrico who assured Novoa that her claim could only be approved through his intervention.[112] Novoa probably received around 180,000 pesos in consolidation bonds.[113]

Conflict with Echenique and Torrico led Elías to denounce the corrupt nature of the consolidation process in two letters addressed to Echenique and published in a local newspaper in August 1853. Elías caused a great stir with these letters. He warned against the disorderly management of public finances, the finite nature of the guano deposits and revenues, and the scandalous administration of the domestic public debt and its shady conversion into foreign debt. The debt consolidation had been "turned into an obstacle to the course of industrial, mercantile, and investment (*rentística*) matters of the country, into a gangrene of all the springs of public morality of citizens"; it did not benefit the original claimants but rather speculative usurers (*agiotistas*).[114]

Moreover, he denounced the corrupt handling of several notorious expedientes: the donation of 1 million pesos to Bolívar's heirs, handled through bribes by the Venezuelan minister in Lima, Leocadio Guzmán (helped, according to others by Manuel María Cotes, a Venezuelan merchant and agent and Echenique's cousin in-law); the unfair claim of Count Montemar y Monteblanco, Fernando Carrillo de Albornoz y Zavala, and his mother Petronila Zavala (helped by her in-law relative José Gregorio Paz Soldán, a Supreme Court prosecuting attorney and minister of foreign affairs under Echenique and married to Grimanesa Zavala); and the indebted landowner Manuel Aparicio's claim protected by his conservative nephew Bartolomé Herrera, another minister (of justice) under Echenique. Corrupt speculators included the Chilean Juan José Concha, several military officers, and Echenique's relatives. Despite the obvious evidence, Echenique's government did nothing to prosecute those involved in the corruption of the consolidation measure.[115] Not surprisingly, Elías was imprisoned shortly

112. Second letter of Elías to Echenique, Lima, August 16, 1853, in *El Comercio,* reprinted in *El señor don Domingo Elías a la faz de sus compatriotas* (Valparaíso: Imprenta del Mercurio, 1853), 31–33, 76.

113. Quiroz, *Deuda defraudada,* 170–72.

114. First letter of Elías to Echenique, Lima, August 12, 1853, in *El Comercio,* reprinted in *El señor don Domingo Elías,* 9–10.

115. *El señor don Domingo Elías,* 22, 30, 32, 37. Several of these cases are analyzed in detail in Quiroz, *Deuda defraudada,* chapter 6. Witt includes in the Echenique's corrupt inner circle his brother Nicasio, sister Benita, and Cotes. Witt, *Diario* (1987), 238.

after the publication of his letters. After his release, Elías led a revolutionary movement to topple Echenique.

Independent study of the official *consolidación* records and subsequent inquiries confirm the core of Elías's denouncements. The ill-conceived consolidation bonds or vales contributed little to the domestic capital market as they were subject to short-term speculation mainly due to their corrupt origins. Of the total consolidation debt amounting to 24 million pesos, highly concentrated among few individuals, approximately 16 percent went directly to venal officials and their cronies; more than 30 percent went indirectly to corrupt interests through illegal commissions; and around 50 percent was converted to foreign debt through shady conversion deals and contracts.[116] Moreover, after a few years the remaining debt certificates were almost entirely concentrated among few merchants and speculators. Most of the original claimants and legal debtors, and the small investors, were radically excluded from this debt mechanism. This fact frontally contradicts Echenique's cynical claim that, despite inevitable speculation, thousands of families benefited from the consolidation measures. He had, in fact, followed corrupt patronage strategies for gaining private and military support similar to those used previously by Gamarra. Echenique justified such strategies by arguing that the consolidation funds had created a national capitalist class. (Likewise, the military in the 1970s claimed that their interventionist policies favored *capitalistas nacionales*.) Some influential historians have echoed Echenique's interested justification of blatant corruption.[117] In fact, under Echenique's administration of the public credit, domestic capitalism lost a crucial opportunity to develop solid financial bases and broader social roots in Peru.

Instead, notorious networks of venal authorities and cronies demonstrated their ability to use the consolidation of the domestic debt to further their narrow interests. Furthermore, from this point on a pattern of corruption reproduced and regenerated itself through successive generations of

116. See Quiroz, *Deuda defraudada*, chapter 4.

117. José Rufino Echenique, *El general Echenique, presidente despojado del Perú, en su vindicación* (New York: N.p., 1855), 101. This argument repeated in his *Memorias para la historia del Perú*, ed. Jorge Basadre and Félix Denegri Luna (Lima: Editorial Huascarán, 1952), 2:200–1. See the same argument repeated in Basadre, *Historia* 4:15, 25–30, 70–71. For an analysis of Basadre's views on corruption, see Alfonso Quiroz, "Basadre y su análisis de la corrupción en el Perú," in *Homenaje a Jorge Basadre: el hombre, su obra y su tiempo*, eds. Scarlett O'Phelan and Mónica Ricketts (Lima: Instituto Riva-Agüero, Pontificia Universidad Católica, 2004), 145–70.

corrupt networks undermining key domestic institutions. Thanks to increasing guano revenues, the first military caudillo networks of patronage, dependent on costly war and emergency finance, now evolved to more sophisticated networks that boldly abused public financial devices at a previously unknown scale and coordination. The links between the main leaders and figures of these networks, and their generational liaisons, are revealing historical evidence of the dark side of Peruvian history and its legacy of organic, systematic corruption.

The network of corruption that grew during the years of debt consolidation connected several dozens of individuals as *mazorqueros* or underground clique members.[118] Collectively, they also became known as the *consolidados,* a term used extensively at the time to denote corrupt persons or political thieves.[119] The highest authorities, including Echenique and most of his ministers (Torrico, La Fuente, Paz Soldán, Piérola, Herrera, and others), also headed shadow interests set to gain or allow illicit political and pecuniary benefits from vulnerable financial mechanisms and other institutions. A corrupt military leadership was the main core. General Echenique relied excessively on one of the most corrupt generals ever, Juan Crisóstomo Torrico, first as chief minister and then as head of the strategic Ministry of War. Torrico pretended to be Echenique's successor in the presidency despite the stern opposition of Castilla. Torrico accumulated a large war chest from illegal consolidation proceeds and commissions in the purchase of military materiel.[120] Likewise, our old friend Marshal Antonio Gutiérrez de la Fuente, at one point also minister of war under Echenique, had a proven participation in illegal consolidation proceeds and official favors with the help of his henchman Colonel Felipe Rivas.[121]

118. The word *mazorquero* derives from la Mazorca (the Corncob), the secret police during the dictatorship of Argentinian Juan Manuel de Rosas.

119. Pedro Paz Soldán y Unánue (pseud. Juan de Arona), *Diccionario de peruanismos* (Lima: Ediciones Peisa, 1974), 1:140–43.

120. Torrico officially received 23,100 pesos in consolidation vales but had major illegal participation in the recognition of the most important *expedientes.* Quiroz, *Deuda defraudada,* 84, 97; and Manuel de Mendiburu, "Noticias biográficas de los generales que ha tenido la República desde 1821," *Revista Histórica* 25 (1960–1961): 160.

121. La Fuente was granted the considerable sum of 82,500 pesos in vales, but also participated in the favored recognition of expedientes that he patronized. La Fuente wrote to the then minister of finance, Manuel de Mendiburu: "Tiene U. a la firma unos vales de consolidación valor de 98,000 pesos que pertenecen a Don Juan de Dios Carrión y d. Maximiliano Albertini. Me haría U. un distinguido servicio si U. me los firmara de preferencia. . . [El coronel] Rivas está encargado de recoger o sacar cien de mi parte."

Under the influence and command of Echenique, La Fuente, and especially Torrico, several army colonels intervened as in-between satellite figures in consolidation deals: Felipe Rivas, Felipe Coz, and Pascual Saco among many others.[122] Saco also favored his uncle Pío Tristán, Echenique's wealthy father-in-law. Tristán suddenly got involved in illegal consolidation deals that netted him 124,000 pesos in consolidation bonds; together with his daughter Victoria, Tristán was also the largest arbitrios creditor in 1852–1855.[123] As the co-owner of an estate in Camaná (Arequipa), Saco was also a partner of another *arequipeño* bonded to Tristán, Don Nicolás (Fernández) de Piérola y Flórez, one of Echenique's key finance ministers (1852–1853).[124] As seen in the next chapter, Piérola's son, Nicolás de Piérola y Villena, would head the next generation of corrupt public administrators. (Despite her reputed poverty, Piérola y Flórez's widow, Teresa Villena de Piérola, listed among her possessions in her last will, dated May 14, 1857, "one consolidation *vale* for the amount of fifty thousand pesos and the amount of its interests that have not been paid, of which value my executor has knowledge."[125]) Echenique and several of his direct relatives and

La Fuente to Mendiburu, Lima, January 7, 1852. "Completó U. la obra haciendo que se me reconozca los 40 mil y pico resto de este espediente y que giró bajó la firma de D. Juan de Dios Carrión. . . Estos 40 mil y pico de pesos me pertenecen a mi exclusivamente como se lo haré ver a U. luego que lo vea." La Fuente to Mendiburu, Lima, June 3, 1852. Letters in Colección Mendiburu: Epistolario, MEN 54, nos. 27 and 28, Archivo Histórico Riva Agüero (hereafter AHRA).

122. According to the consolidation records, Colonel Coz received 731,200 pesos worth of consolidation bonds, Sargent Major Domingo Solar, 250,000, Colonel Pérez Vargas, 198,700, Sargent Major Viviano Gómez Silva, 146,100, Colonel Saco, 78,800, and Colonel Rivas, 77,500. Respectively, they were listed as numbers 5, 13, 15, 27, 50, and 53 among those who received the largest consolidation values. See Quiroz, *Deuda defraudada,* table 4; Fernando Casós, *Para la historia del Perú:Revolución de 1854* (Cusco: Imprenta Republicana, 1854); and "Lista de la principales personas consolidadas por la corruptora administración del ex-General Echenique," in *Manifiesto de D. Domingo Elías a la Nación* (Arequipa: Imprenta Libre de Mariano Madueño, 1855), 14–15. Witt identified General Felipe Rivas and Juan José Concha as principal agents of Torrico. Rivas had been subjected to a juicio de residencia for his role as subprefect and governor of the port of Callao and for illegally influencing elections there in 1847. Juicios de Residencia, CSJL, leg. 430, AGN.

123. Quiroz, *Deuda defraudada,* 46–47, 84, 169–70.

124. Correspondence between Pío Tristán and Pascual Saco; inventory of Saco's property in 1868, Colección Plácido Jiménez, nos. 123, 147, AHRA.

125. "Testamento de la Sra. Da. Teresa Villena de Piérola," Lima, May 14, 1857, in "Papeles de la familia Piérola," Archivo Piérola (hereafter AP), vol. 1, Manuscritos, BNP. Her son Nicolás de Piérola y Villena was among the three executors of the will.

in-laws also benefited directly and indirectly through the consolidation measures.[126]

A second tier of agents facilitating illegal benefits to the 1850s network were civilian government employees, linked to attorney, and later minister of foreign affairs, José Gregorio Paz Soldán, and Supreme Court judge Manuel del Carpio. These facilitators included official judicial appraiser Nicanor González and clerk Fernando Casós.[127] Also several commercial speculators were involved, including, among many others, José Manuel Piedra (Echenique's cousin and delegate of the Cerro de Pasco miners), Martín Daniel de la Torre, Manuel and Camilo González, the Chileans Gregorio Videla and Juan José Concha, and the Venezuelan merchant and guano contractor Manuel María Cotes, Echenique's cousin in-law and official agent of the Venezuelan government for receiving, in 1853, the sizable Bolívar payment owed by Peru.[128] According to a long-term resident in Peru, Cotes and Torrico were among the few corrupt agents during the consolidación years who were able to bequest their ill-gotten wealth to their respective widows.[129]

The last crucial tier of corrupt linkages involved agents acting as money launderers abroad. These covert actions implied coordination among Peruvian diplomats, special commissioners and agents, and interested foreign merchants and financiers. The latitude allowed to underpaid Peruvian diplomats in important matters had a well-established tradition since the 1820s.

126. Although Echenique swore in his writings that he did not benefit personally in the consolidation affair, he was officially awarded 13,800 pesos in vales. Quiroz, *Deuda defraudada,* 84. Echenique was also suspected of receiving up to 2 million pesos indirectly. Casós, *Para la historia.* See also Elías, *Manifiesto,* 14.

127. See Junta de Examen Fiscal, *Informes de la Junta de Examen Fiscal creada por resolución suprema de febrero de 1855 para revisar los expedientes relativos al reconocimiento de la deuda interna consolidada de 20 de abril de 1851, publicación oficial* (Lima: Imprenta del Estado, 1857), expedientes nos. 5666, 5742, 5771, 5848, 5958, 6013; Quiroz, *Deuda defraudada,* 98–103. Allegations against the administrative integrity of Casós appear in "Fernando Casós contra Manuel Jesús Vivanco, año 1851," Abuso de la Libertad de Imprenta, CSJL, leg. 716, AGN.

128. In 1853, Cotes, as agent of the Venezuelan government, received in London four *libranzas* for a total of 555,000 pesos from Gibbs & Co., according to an inquiry on a suspicious overpayment of 150,000 pesos to another Venezuelan agent, Lucio Pulido, by Barreda y Hno. of Baltimore and Murrieta of London: Francisco de Rivero to M.R.E., London, December 13, 1856, no. 347, 5-14/1856 (Gran Bretaña y Francia), AMRE. On Cotes's consolidation and guano deals, see Quiroz, *Deuda defrauda,* 104, n. 22.

129. Witt, *Diario* (1987), 238, 248.

In the late 1840s and early 1850s Peruvian envoys who were suspected of shady deals in contracting purchases and financial agreements abroad included Juan Manuel Iturregui, José Joaquín de Osma, Felipe Barreda (of Barreda y Hno.), Francisco de Rivero, and Manuel de Mendiburu. The foreign houses suspected of collusion were the most important: Murrieta, Uribarren, Montané, and Gibbs.

In 1845, during Castilla's first administration, Iturregui had returned to Europe as plenipotentiary minister in the courts of London, Paris, Madrid, and Rome. Among the many supply orders from Peru, Iturregui was in charge of arms purchases for the Peruvian army. He and his immediate successors in London also arranged the construction of one of the first steamships for the Peruvian Navy.[130] In 1847, Iturregui negotiated with guano contractors in Europe a loan worth 900,000 pesos of which 350,000 were to be sent to Joaquín José de Osma for other purchases on the government's account. As the main diplomatic representative in Washington at the time, Osma was also engaged in contracting the building of a ship, the *Vapor Rímac,* and arms shipments from the United States.[131] The arms race and the frenzy for raising loans were prompted by the threat of an invading expedition organized in Europe by the former conservative president of Ecuador, General Juan José Flores.[132]

Iturregui deemed necessary the publication in Peruvian newspapers of a defense of his financial arrangements abroad.[133] In 1848, Osma headed to London as plenipotentiary minister, leaving his brother, Juan Ignacio de Osma, in charge of the Peruvian legation in Washington. The younger Osma also complained about what he considered an insufficient salary that lim-

130. "Relación de las armas, municiones y demás artículos de artillería que deben encargarse a Inglaterra." M.R.E. José G. Paz Soldán to Iturregui, Lima, September 10, 1845; October 14, 1845, 5-17/1845; Francisco de Rivero to M.R.E., London, January 15, 1851, no. 57, 5-17/1851, AMRE.

131. Joaquín José de Osma y Ramírez de Arellano had represented Peru in Madrid in 1843 and in Washington in 1846–1848. 5–13/1843 (Legación del Perú en España) and 5–3/1846 (Legación del Perú en Estados Unidos), AMRE. On Osma's shipbuilding arrangements: Osma to M.R.E., Washington, February 12, 1847, no. 150, and José Rufino Echenique (Minister of War and Navy) to M.R.E., Lima, June 10, 1847. On shipment of 600 U.S. carbines by merchant Samuel Tracy on Osma's orders: Osma to M.R.E., New York, January 6, 1848, no. 98, 5–3/1847–1848, AMRE.

132. Casa de Supremo Gobierno to M.R.E., Lima, December 11, 1846, 5-17/1846, AMRE.

133. Juan Manuel Iturregui, *Reimpresión de los artículos con que se vindica Juan Manuel Iturregui en el empréstito que celebró por orden del Supremo Gobierno* (Trujillo: N.p., 1847).

ited the fulfillment of his important official duties.[134] In December 1848, President Castilla named Joaquín José de Osma and Felipe Barreda (Osma's relative and future guano contractor for the U.S. market) agents in charge of restructuring the old debt with British bondholders in London.[135] The Peruvian agents, aided by diplomat Francisco de Rivero, initially approached the guano contractors Antony Gibbs & Sons, soliciting an illegal personal commission of up to 0.5 percent of the total debt settlement amount, in exchange for granting Gibbs the sole management of the old debt conversion into new bonds. Gibbs would not agree to pay the commission charge; Gibbs would only cede them a commission if it was plainly justified and accounted for to the Peruvian government.[136]

In January 1849, the Peruvian diplomatic agents, however, preferred to appoint instead Cristóbal de Murrieta & Co., a London-based Spanish house of dubious prestige and guano contractor for the Spanish market, as Peru's debt-conversion agent. The old bonds of 1822 and 1825 were converted to new foreign debt bonds duly served at 4-percent annual interest; the old unpaid interests were recalculated at 65 percent of their value. Castilla approved Osma's contract with the British bondholder representative George Richard Robinson as well as that with Murrieta, which included an undisclosed reward (*premio*) for the Peruvian commissioners.[137] These contracts were later criticized under the growing suspicion that Osma, Barreda, and Rivero had personally benefited from them. These diplomats were interested parties in the debt settlement since they received a commission in new bonds that in the short term netted them profits of more than 300 percent.[138]

134. "Con los tres mil pesos que tengo de sueldo, no me es posible atender los gastos de mi persona de una manera decorosa al Gobierno que represento y cubrir los de correo y secretaría de la legación. Los asuntos que me obligan a permanecer en esta, ocasionándome gastos superiores a mis recursos, y no me dejan por consiguiente la libertad que tendría en otro caso, de presentar mi renuncia por la insuficiencia del sueldo que se me da." J. I. de Osma to M.R.E., Washington, D.C., December 10, 1850, no. 67, 5–3/1850, AMRE.

135. Files 1 and 2, 5-17/1849, AMRE.

136. Mathew, *House of Gibbs,* 102–3. On other types of corruption of the time, see also Mathew, "First Anglo-Peruvian Debt," 96–98.

137. M.R.E. Felipe Pardo to Osma, Lima, July 13, 1849, no. 50, 5-17/1849, AMRE.

138. Márquez, *Orjía financiera,* 13–16. In 1871, Manuel de Mendiburu wrote a draft letter addressed to Echenique where he affirmed that in 1849 Osma and Rivero received a commission "en bonos por que éstos la tomaron posesionándoselos a 33 y los vendieron a 108 con más por vía de apéndice 45 cupones gratis de diferidos en cada bono [deleted: ambos tenían su caudal]." Colección Mendiburu, Epistolario, MEN 441, no. 10, AHRA.

In 1853, President Echenique sent Manuel de Mendiburu as plenipotentiary minister to London with a letter of reference to Murrieta & Co.[139] Mendiburu had as main tasks renegotiation of the previous debt settlement of 1849, and arrangement of a dubious "conversion" of an important part of the consolidated domestic debt into fresh foreign debt. Mendiburu argued that parts of Osma's prior debt arrangement were detrimental to Peruvian interests and, most importantly, that owners of the 1849 bonds were not subject to a limit in bond amortization at par even if the bonds' market price was above par.[140] Osma, at the time also Echenique's envoy to Madrid, protested Mendiburu's statements and argued that the 1849 debt contract did not have such alleged omissions and obscurities.[141] This was written after the 1849 contract had offered Osma the opportunity of cashing his own dubiously obtained bonds at above par. Mendiburu, on the other hand, always justified his actions as disinterested and beneficial to Peruvian finances, although he was also awarded a "legal" commission albeit far "inferior" to that of Osma and friends.[142]

However, the most controversial of Mendiburu's financial deals in London was the scandalous conversion of domestic debt into new foreign debt. The operation consisted of exchanging domestic vales earning 6 percent in-

139. Echenique to Sres. Murrieta, Lima, September 10, 1852, in Colección Mendiburu, Epistolario, MEN 441, no. 2, AHRA. A handwritten note at the margin of this letter of recommendation reads: "Echenique me recomienda a los Murrieta—no resa esto en las memorias."

140. Manuel de Mendiburu, *Consideraciones sobre el empréstito de 1853* (London: T. F. Newell, 1853), 2–3.

141. In his official correspondence, Osma rejected Mendiburu's claim that "la oscuridad u omisiones que a su entender había en el convenio para el arreglo de nuestra deuda [en 1849] . . . pretendiendo hacer creer que por ese convenio tenían derecho los acreedores a que se amortizasen sus Bonos a cualquier precio sobre la par, y que por consiguiente sus operaciones salvaron al Estado de un grave quebranto." Osma demanded the publication of all the pertinent documents that raised the Peruvian credit abroad "a un grado que yo desearía que conservase en la actualidad." They were approved by Castilla in 1849: Osma to M.R.E. Paz Soldán, Madrid, February 25, 1854, 5–13/1854, AMRE. Just after Echenique's ouster, Osma wrote that Echenique and Mendiburu had tried to deceive the public "por motivos que yo no debo calificar ahora." Osma to M.R.E., Madrid, May 26, 1855, 5–13/1855, AMRE.

142. In a draft letter to Echenique in 1871, Mendiburu protested that he was "un hombre honrado que no supo nunca lucrar y que en las ventajosas operaciones de Londres [of 1853] sólo tuvo una comisión legal, diré inferior a la dada antes a Osma y Rivero. . . [O]jalá todas las operaciones posteriores se hubiesen parecido en algo a las mías, que otra fuera la suerte de la hacienda." Colección Mendiburu, Epistolario, MEN 441, no. 10, AHRA.

terest into newly issued foreign debt bonds at 4.5 percent interest. Approximately 50 percent of all the consolidated domestic debt was quietly converted through official contracts with guano dealers Uribarren et Cie. of Paris (signed in London by Mendiburu and ultimately amounting to 6 million pesos in vales) and Montané & Company (signed in Lima and amounting to 3 million pesos in vales). These companies had hoarded vales before the actual signing of their contracts, and consequently benefited with the sudden rise in the quotations of the converted debt; they had established a shady lobby through private operations with interested vales holders. Another conversion of 2 million pesos in domestic vales had been contracted earlier, in August 1852, with investor Joseph Hegan who financed the railway Tacna-Arica with this highly profitable speculation.[143] In essence, these conversion schemes were designed to "launder" financial instruments tainted with corrupt origins. By compromising Peruvian foreign credit to honor a debt created through administrative dishonesty, these conversions benefited unscrupulous speculators in vales while simultaneously preventing future official inquiries and efforts to invalidate such corrupt arrangements.

Rigged Manumission Compensation

Through a strategic alliance with Marshal Castilla, Elías succeeded in forcing Echenique out of power after a bloody civil war fought in almost every corner of the country. Elías raised at the center of his campaign against Echenique the banner of fighting a "gang of false patriots, devious dealers," and a "prostituted justice" that had led the country to a stinking swamp of corruption capped by the unforgettable consolidation of the internal debt. Elías linked the failure of the Peruvian Republic, after 34 years of "premature" independence, to despotism, militarism, privilege, and corruption. In his 1855 manifesto, Elías stated his historical diagnosis: "Corruption,

143. The Peruvian government advanced Hegan 2 million pesos in foreign debt bonds at 4.5 percent interest, in London, while he deposited in Lima initially only 500,000 in *vales* and the rest over a period of two years. Despite the interest reduction from 6 to 4.5 percent, the new bonds soon acquired a market value of almost par while the discredited *vales* only reached around 40 percent of their face value. Quiroz, *Deuda defraudada,* 59, 181; Manuel de Mendiburu, "Memorias" (unpublished, typed version in Félix Denegri Luna's private library), 589–91. Even so, before even starting the construction of the railway, José Hegan & Co. entertained the idea of selling his construction rights; such intention and conduct "al gobierno le ha sido muy desagradable." Piérola to Mendiburu, Lima, June 12, 1853, no. 64, 5-17/1853, AMRE.

spreading like burning lava throughout the corners of our immense territory, has wounded the Republic in everything it held as great, noble, and generous: its morals, religion, and laws."[144] However, once in power, the new government led by Castilla and his finance minister, Elías himself, engaged in a scheme of compensation to owners of emancipated slaves that repeated in several ways the type of favors bestowed on a small clique evident in the consolidation business.

In the midst of the civil war, Castilla had decreed the emancipation of slaves in 1854 as a measure to win popular support and recruit soldiers. Starting in 1855, manumission bonds (*vales de manumisión*) bearing 6 percent interest were distributed to former slave owners who had applied for compensation. The compensation value for each slave was established at 300 pesos. Former slave owners received approximately 2.8 million pesos in cash and 5.2 million pesos in bonds for a total of nearly 8 million pesos. The third most important compensated owner, Minister of Finance Domingo Elías, received 111,000 pesos in vales for 370 emancipated slaves; other major compensated owners included several monasteries and hacendados such as Fernando Carrillo de Albornoz, Antonio Fernández Prada, and Mariano Osma. Manumission bonds were promptly serviced and paid at almost par by 1860–1861. Due to their rapidly rising value, merchants, many of whom were creditors of the generously compensated landowners, soon acquired bonds and cornered the exclusive manumission bonds market.[145]

The manumission compensation process was riddled with inaccuracies, speculation, and exaggerated and outright fraudulent claims. Some former slave owners included dead slaves or otherwise artificially increased the number of slaves they claimed to have had prior to the manumission decree.[146] Castilla and Elías carried out with unusual celerity the compensation process that was rife with favoritism. They were paying back political favors to consolidate elite support to the new regime at the expense of national finances. By the late 1850s, a new phase of inflated contracts and compensations had initiated in a climate of revived financial expansion. In the meantime, the much-hailed fight against corrupt abuses of public finances and credit had collapsed. In 1855–1858, another historical opportunity to introduce effective anticorruption reforms and controls was missed.

144. Elías, *Manifiesto*, 4, 5–15.
145. Quiroz, *Deuda defraudada*, 159–65, based on *El Peruano*, October 11, 1856 and May 31, 1857. Manumission accounting records H-4-2032, 2029, 2055, 2030, Libros Manuscritos Republicanos, AGN.
146. Márquez, *Orjía financiera*, 39–40.

Unchecked Venality

As soon as Echenique was ousted, an official investigative board com-
menced an in-depth inquiry into the abuses and illegalities of the consolidation and conversion affairs and other issues involving corruption. Thanks
to the efforts of the Junta de Examen Fiscal, detailed information of guilty
individuals and their networks has been preserved. The investigation was
thorough and it had initially the support of the executive and legislative
branches.[147] According to a law passed on December 29, 1856, domestic
debt bonds that had originated from fraudulent, illegal, and exaggerated
claims were suspended from debt service. In addition, conversions of domestic into foreign debt were halted. Some individuals were brought to trial,
although many had already fled the country, including Torrico, Echenique,
and Mendiburu.[148]

Executive officials and legislators were subjected to strong pressure, however, to reverse the anticorruption measures adopted in 1855–1856. One argument was that the debt securities were issued in a way similar to that of a
bill subject to endorsement and, consequently, innocent holders of bonds
should not be subject to the penalty of losing their investment just because
corrupt authorities had issued such securities. The opposite argument, used
by legal investigators of the Junta de Examen Fiscal and the newly created
Dirección de Crédito Nacional, was that domestic debt bonds, although endorsed widely in commercial operations, did not lose their original condition
of state debentures and as such were subject to legal recalls due to fraud or
corruption.[149] This legal conflict brought about several lawsuits and peti-

147. The Junta de Examen was in charge of "revisar los expedientes sobre que han
recaído los decretos para emisión de vales de la deuda interna, y examinar las disposi-
ciones fiscales de la última administración, en que puedan haberse defraudado los intereses del Estado." *El Peruano,* February 7, 1855. See also the official compilation of
reports, Junta de Examen Fiscal, *Informes.* The Junta detected 12.2 million pesos (almost half of all the consolidated domestic debt) in 141 irregular or illegal claim files (*expedientes*) and four stolen expedientes.

148. Manuel Toribio Ureta to Rivero, Lima, August 25, 1855, no. 53 reservada, regarding the restriction of converted debt or its reduction to half its value, according to
National Convention guidelines, due to "la naturaleza de la deuda trasladada . . . de
anatema público y estado de nuestra Hacienda," 5-17/1855, AMRE; *El Peruano,* June
18, and August 5, 1856.

149. Comisión Especial del Crédito Público, *Informe de la Comisión Especial del
Crédito Público sobre los vales consolidados y tachados* (Lima: Imprenta Félix Moreno,
1856), 6.

tions headed by the most powerful foreign and domestic merchants as well as the diplomatic envoys of Great Britain and France.[150]

A crucial retraction in the position of the highest-level officials brought the reversal and defeat of anticorruption efforts to redress the tremendous injury to state finances inflicted by the corrupt consolidation and conversion deals. In the middle of yet another civil war waged by "regenerator" General Manuel Ignacio de Vivanco, official government control over the guano islands was threatened by Vivanco's ships as well as by British and French warships ready to intervene in defense of their subjects' claims, including outraged investors holding excluded conversion bonds. Echenique also conspired to organize an expedition of mercenaries hired in the United States.[151]

Castilla moved to obtain support from the most important foreign diplomats and creditors in Lima. Foreign representatives Albert Huet and Stephen Henry Sulivan refused to aid Castilla if he did not acknowledge the validity and interest arrears of all converted consolidation bonds issued under the Echenique administration. This arrangement was probably the only

150. Petition (*representación*) to the government by the commission of "tenedores de bonos de la deuda trasladada" headed by José Hegan, Angel Richon, and José Vicente Oyague, January 29, 1857, published in *El Peruano,* February 19, 1857. J. Randolph Clay to William Marcy, Lima, September 25, 1855, Despatches 1926–1906, roll 12, USNA. See also Diego López Aliaga, *Breve exposición que el apoderado de la casa Thomas Lachambre y Cia. presenta a la ilustrísima Corte Superior de Justicia sobre el pleito que su parte sigue con el Sr. Dr. D. José Gregorio Paz-Soldán* (Lima: Imprenta Calle de la Rifa, 1863). In 1859, the ubiquitous lawyer Paz Soldán, the corrupt former minister under Echenique, claimed to be the owner of four consolidation vales worth a total of 90,000 pesos issued during Echenique's administration. Paz Soldán had used those vales as collateral to obtain a 35,000-peso loan from Juan Antonio Menéndez in 1857. The latter proceeded to use those vales as guarantee to obtain a loan for 45,000 pesos in cash from the merchant house of Lachambre. A long lawsuit ensued in which Paz Soldán argued that those vales, being pledged values (*prendas*), could not be transferred. Lachambre's lawyers argued that the vales had the widely used market condition of securities with blank endorsement (*endoso en blanco*). Clearly Paz Soldán had benefited immensely from the 1857 restitution of the illegal part of the consolidated debt.

151. "Juicio seguido contra el ciudadano de Estados Unidos Luis [Lewis] Lomer, quien por contrato con D. José Rufino Echenique y aprobado por Manuel Vivanco se disponía a invadir el país y levantar a los pueblos en perjuicio del General Ramón Castilla. Año 1857." Invasión, CSJL, leg. 719, AGN. See also J. R. Clay to Lewis Cass, Lima, December 27, 1857, Despatches 1826–1906, roll 13, and Lima, January 11, 1858, and attachments, roll 14, USNA. Echenique established a contract with Lomer for $200,000 to recruit 500 men in the United States and purchase a steamship for an expedition to restore Echenique as president.

one that Castilla could expect to keep him in power.[152] A scandal also erupted over Castilla's signature of orders to proceed with the servicing of converted debt instruments in Europe.[153] Under domestic and foreign pressure, Castilla and the legislature under his influence enacted the law of March 11, 1857 that in effect restored all suspended bonds and conversion agreements. This "clean slate" law in effect absolved speculators and officers involved in corrupt consolidation and conversion. Vivanco was eventually defeated and Castilla was able to enjoy undisputed power for the next few years.

In August 1857, a group of three or four gunmen invaded the home of British Consul General Sulivan and assassinated him. It was speculated that Sulivan's assassination was an act of political vengeance "by persons of a certain standing in society" for having supported first Vivanco and Echenique and then switching sides to support Castilla: "[T]he assassins may not be discovered, as through the negligence of the police and the maladministration of the law in Peru, the most atrocious criminals often escape justice."[154]

The most notorious corruption scandal during the "Liberator" Castilla's administration involved his minister of foreign affairs, Manuel Ortiz de Zevallos, the main force behind the restitution of the questioned consolidation and conversion debts. An agent of the French company Société Générale

---

152. See Quiroz, *Deuda defraudada,* 63–64, based on Jorge Basadre, *Introducción a las bases documentales para la historia de la República del Perú,* 2 vols. (Lima: P.L. Villanueva, 1971), 1:307–8; Anonymous, *El tratado de 21 de mayo, o el protectorado anglo-francés* (Lima: J. Sánchez Silva, 1856), 15; *El Peruano,* February 19, 1857, 173; Sulivan to Clarendon, Lima, January 26, 1857, confidential, on talks between the governments of Great Britain and France over measures to force General Castilla to pay French claims and press the conversion debt issue, FO 61/172, ff. 171–76; Sulivan to Clarendon, Lima, June 12, 1857, informing on the convention signed on May 21, 1857 by Minister of Foreign Affairs Manuel Ortiz de Zevallos and the chargés de affairs Stephen Sulivan (Great Britain) and Albert Huet (France) for the "integrity of Peruvian huano deposits," FO 61/174, ff. 1–4, NAUK. See also J. R. Clay to William Marcy, Lima, December 11, 1856, Despatches 1826–1906, roll 12, and Lima, March 11, 1857, roll 13, USNA.

153. Juan Gualberto Valdivia, *Memorias sobre las revoluciones de Arequipa desde 1834 hasta 1866* (Lima: Imprenta de La Opinión Nacional, 1874), 335–36.

154. J. R. Clay to Lewis Cass, Lima, August 24, 1857, Despatches 1826–1906, roll 13, USNA; Sulivan, a nephew of Lord Palmerston, had been reprimanded by his superior Earl Claredon for being "partisan in Peruvian politics." Sulivan to Clarendon, Lima, June 25, 1855, FO 61/154, f. 282, NAUK. See also John Barton to Clarendon, Lima, August 12, 1857, FO 61/174, NAUK; and Clay to Cass, Lima, August 12, 1857, Despatches 1826–1906, roll 13, USNA.

Maritime, Juan B. Colombier, declared that in order to secure from the Peruvian government a contract of guano consignment to France and Spain in May 1858, he had bribed Ortiz de Zevallos with a gift of 50,000 pesos. Colombier informed his company that he had in fact unsuccessfully spent 70,000 pesos in secret expenses. Although indignantly reacting against these allegations in his correspondence and the press, Ortiz de Zevallos had continued negotiating with the French agent. Most shocking, however, was the minister's official revelation that the bribe of 70,000 pesos had been actually distributed among members of Congress who were in charge of approving the contract in question.[155] In fact, the legislative body at the time enjoyed little public confidence. The only congressman with experience was Buenaventura Seoane but he was considered "time serving and venal."[156]

The bribing of key public officials by foreign companies and investors eager to obtain a monopoly advantage over their competitors was a clearly established practice, in public works and guano consignment contracts of ever increasing amounts, in the 1860s and 1870s, as discussed in the next chapter. The restitution of fraudulent debt instruments in 1857 had enhanced this onerous tendency.

Elías had been initially opposed to the restitution of impeached bonds despite contradictory decisions regarding conversions abroad. In response to growing pressure, Elías was forced to abandon Castilla's cabinet to serve as Peruvian chargé d'affaires in France. Many other hard-core anticorruption fighters were also diminished by the new political circumstances. In Europe, Elías accomplished little, as his health deteriorated and he had to return to Peru. After a failed comeback as a presidential candidate in 1858, he retired from politics until his death in 1867.[157] And so the political career of the first civilian chieftain ended. Elías had desired reform but benefited from deals arising from glaring conflicts of interests and links with corrupt authorities.

155. "Expediente sobre el caso de J. B. Colombier," 5-14A/1858, AMRE.

156. Clay to Cass, Lima, September 27, 1858, Despatches 1826–1906, roll 15, USNA.

157. Ministro de Hacienda Domingo Elías to Rivero, Lima, July 11, 1855, reservada, ordering investigation on the serious issues of Murrieta's handling or guano consignments to Spain and to withdraw all funds deposited in that house, 5-17/1855, AMRE. Elías left his post in Paris due to illness in March 1857, shortly after presenting his credentials to the French Emperor Louis Napoleon, and before the news of the restitution of the questioned consolidation and conversion bonds reached Paris. Elías to M.R.E., Paris, March 11, 1857, and Lima, September 10, 1857, 5-14/1857, AMRE.

In conclusion, the early republican period inherited old patrimonial structures of corruption adapted to military caudillo patronage. These caudillo networks bore important similarities to viceregal court patronage and engaged in comparable war-related transgressions in public finance and abusive expropriations. The prominence of caudillo "patriotic" plunder and graft in military procurement emulated the old viceroy's "premio" and drain of military resources. Contraband in silver and the concomitant loss of revenues continued and even increased during the first decade after independence, and then continued albeit in gradual decline until the 1850s. Bribery in public contracts, particularly guano exports, spiraled in the 1840s and 1850s as guano public revenues increased and cliques sought rent-seeking monopoly gains (see Table A.3 in the Appendix). Extensive abuses and unchecked corruption of provincial authorities underscored the total failure of former administrative reforms. These were not only Peruvian phenomena as they also appeared in newly independent Mexico, New Granada, and the United Provinces of the Río de la Plata. This legacy or path dependence interacted with the crumbling of old institutions, and the deformation of new ones, in an enduring context of political and economic instability.

Public debt legislation, early guano trade contracts, and economic and trade policies were purposefully turned away from their common-good objectives by corrupt civil servants, legislators, and domestic and foreign lobbyists. The composite legal result was an unnecessarily complex, opaque, and contradictory set of rules that significantly inflated the transaction costs for ordinary creditors and investors.

Colluding state officials, diplomatic envoys abroad, and foreign and domestic businessmen manipulated to their advantage the rules and goals of public credit. Instead of laying a secure basis for badly needed capital markets, fraudulent instruments of the primitive public credit seriously undermined Peruvian financial development. Instead, these corrupt financial manipulations served the narrow interests of venal officials and speculative traders who sought rent-seeking privileges. This mode of financial corruption was a costly "innovation" in Spanish America after independence as public debt mechanisms were used to "hide" or launder bribes and other corrupt gains. This detour and misallocation of funds weighed heavily on future generations and resulted in the sizable indirect losses (due to undermined credit standing and financial instability) of domestic and foreign portfolio and direct investment. In Peru these losses were particularly heavy in the 1820s and 1850s and later during 1860s and 1870s (see Table A.3).

In combination, the various modes of corruption characteristic of the

early republican administrations inflicted heavy costs and gross misallocation of public resources with negative consequences for economic recovery, development, and welfare. According to the estimates explained and
calculated in Table A.4 of the Appendix, the highest comparative levels of
corruption (6.1 percent of estimated GDP and 135 percent of official government expenses), compounded by warfare and fiscal penury, occurred in
the 1820s. However, the 1830s and 1840s continued to have high levels
(hovering around 4.2 and 4.3 percent of GDP, and 79 and 42 percent of government expenses, respectively). A spike in the total estimated costs of corruption, amounting to an annual average of 5 million pesos, occurred in the
1850s (doubling total costs of the 1840s), and continued increasing to 8.3
million pesos/soles in the 1860s. Apart from the 1820s, the highest levels,
as a percentage of expenditures (63 percent) and GDP (4.3 percent), were
achieved in the 1850s. Consequently, and with the qualitative evidence shown
in this chapter, the administrations of Echenique—Torrico (1851–1855) and
Gamarra—La Fuente (1829–1833) can be considered the most corrupt of
the early republican period (surpassed later, however, by the administrations of the late 1860s and early and late 1870s), according to the summa-
rized estimates of Table A.7.

Public tolerance of incremental corruption nevertheless had certain limits imposed by obvious depredations, exposed scandals, journalistic campaigns, and political opposition. Elías and Castilla bid for power riding several waves of heightened perception of corruption. Like other political
leaders of the time they protested, stimulated uprisings and civil strife, and
ousted corrupt authorities. However, the most promising structural efforts
by liberal civilian reformists, although relevant in exposing serious administrative flaws and corruption, were feeble and not devoid of self-interest.

Despite legislative and judicial attempts to cleanse polluted public credit
and contracts of corrupt practices in the mid-1850s, well-established pressure groups forced a radical back-pedaling. (Thereafter, the notorious
bribery of senators and deputies to obtain congressional approval of public
contracts by privileged parties and moguls seeking monopoly gains continued.) The persistence of anticorruption efforts might have triggered the fall
of a government supporting honest public credit reform. The pragmatic
Castilla, and his entourage that included at one point civilian reformist
Domingo Elías, adapted to the inherently tainted public credit administration. Indomitable corruption had established the conditions for further
abuse of guano revenues, public credit, and public works contracts during
the next cycle of depredations at the public's expense.

Chapter 3

The Crooked Path to Disaster, 1860–1883

> Ever since the declaration of Peruvian independence, venality, corruption, and bribery had not been entirely strange in the offices of the Ministers and their dependents neither in the saloons of the President himself, nor in the apartments of his near relations. Under Echenique's administration at the time of the Consolidacion they, it was believed, had reached the highest pitch, but greatly did they deceive themselves who had thought so; never had those crimes stalked about with more unblushing effrontery than at the present period.
>
> —Heinrich Witt (November 20, 1871)[1]

Amid unrestrained corruption, the city of Lima enjoyed a peculiar prosperity in the 1860s. The poorly administered guano boom was inescapably transforming the old viceregal capital. New fortunes established banks and other financial ventures, built railways, and were spent on lavish lifestyles. The wealthy consumed imported luxuries, spruced up the city center, and erected elegant ranches in the summer gambling resort of Chorrillos. The new rich and powerful flaunted their wealth at society balls where men and women adorned themselves extravagantly with gold and precious jewels. A mirage of economic bonanza and feverish ambition dispelled serious concerns about the financial dangers lying ahead. Inherited administrative dishonesty clouded the fortieth anniversary of independence. What did it all matter, a pamphleteer asked with shame and scorn, ". . . isn't there a ball in the presidential palace tonight?"[2]

---

1. Heinrich Witt, "Diary" (typescript of original manuscript in English owned by Kika Garland de Montero, private collection), vol. 7, 292–93.
2. Manuel María del Maso (Ibrahim Clarete), *Aniversario* (Lima: A. Alfaro y Cia.,

The country's burgeoning business, printing, and intellectual life was concentrated in Lima. The city attracted ambitious and adventurous men from abroad and the provinces. A twenty-five-year-old lawyer from Arequipa, Francisco García Calderón Landa, arrived in Lima in 1859, armed with letters recommending him to influential *arequipeños* in Lima and a manuscript he had authored while teaching in his native city, the *Diccionario de la legislación peruana.* The two volumes of this monumental work were published between 1860 and 1862 with the financial support of the Castilla administration. It soon became required reading for Peruvian legal experts, and the work gained government support, recognition and honors.[3] At last a major enlightened effort, based on human natural rights and positive legislation, contributed to the national systematization of new and old laws on civil, business, penal, and administrative affairs.[4]

García Calderón's career accomplishments swiftly increased both as a functionary at the Ministry of Finance and leading lawyer for the most important domestic and foreign firms. At times bordering on conflicts of interest in his dual role as private lawyer and public official, García Calderón contributed to the revamping of administrative and contractual rules. He also witnessed these same rules consistently violated during the crucial years preceding fiscal bankruptcy and the ensuing and disastrous War of the Pacific (1879–1883).

According to García Calderón's legal dictionary, *corrupción* was succinctly defined as a crime committed by those with any degree of authority who "succumb to seduction" as well as by those who endeavor to corrupt

---

1861), 11–13: "¿no bailan, no cantan, no comen, no beben, no se refocilan, no se ríen, no se pavonean satisfechos y orgullosos vuestros despiadados, ignorantes e insolentes mandones? . . . ¿no juegan los ladrones vuestro oro a manos llenas? ¿No ostentan, inocentes, sus mujeres y sus hijas en su vanidosa y erguida frente, en este nuevo festín de Baltazar, las perlas, los diamantes y las joyas compradas con el oro robado al tesoro nacional en la infame y funesta feria de la Consolidación? Siempre la mano mugrienta, fatídica de la Consolidación metida en todo! Oh, vergüenza!!!"

3. José Luis Bustamante y Rivero, *La ideología de don Francisco García Calderón* (Paris: Desclée de Brouwer, 1946), 12–13; Basadre, *Historia* 5:37–41; Carlos Ramos Núñez, *Historia del derecho civil peruano, siglos XIX y XX: los jurisconsultos El Murciélago y Francisco García Calderón* (Lima: Fondo Editorial Universidad Católica, 2002), 3:239–40.

4. Bustamante y Rivero, *Ideología de García Calderón,* 14–17; Fernando de Trazegnies, *La idea del derecho en el Perú republicano del siglo XIX* (Lima: Fondo Editorial Universidad Católica, 1992), 110–15; Ramos, *Historia del Derecho* 3:323.

them. Likewise, *corruptela* was defined as the bad custom or abuse established against law and justice. Other more formal and detailed definitions of bribery and the interested sale and distortion of justice were included in entries on *cohecho, concusión, prevaricato,* and *soborno* that legally defined corruption among public officials according to already existing laws that, admittedly, were rarely enforced.[5]

Establishing and enforcing the rule of law in the young republic was a major challenge that overwhelmed individual efforts. The early constitutions of 1823, 1826, 1836, and 1839, alternating between liberal and authoritarian in character, had been discarded or ignored in the course of coups d'etat and executive decrees of military chieftains. New commercial and civil codes were enacted in 1852 to establish basic, moderate liberal principles in trade and civil and property rights that conflicted nevertheless with traditional customs. This clash accentuated the litigious nature of Peruvian business and social practices. Moreover, the laws regulating public administration were either incomplete or faulty. A law establishing mandatory public budgets was enacted only in 1849, almost simultaneously with the flawed legislation regulating public domestic and foreign credit. Other key parts of the public administrative apparatus, including the judicial system, were left unreformed.[6]

Between 1856 and 1860, a major constitutional debate highlighted the need for a more efficient legal framework under the pressure of economic modernization. These were years of political instability due to a series of military uprisings against President Castilla. Under domestic and foreign pressures, Castilla and his supporters in Congress continued in power by repealing anticorruption legislation that interfered with foreign creditors' demands. They also modified the liberal constitution of 1856; the resulting

5. Francisco García Calderón, *Diccionario de la legislación peruana: segunda edición corregida y aumentada con las leyes y decretos dictados hasta 1877,* 2 vols. (Paris: Librería de Laroque, 1879), 1:626, 420, 511–12, and 2:1585, 1727. See also this work's first edition, *Diccionario de la legislación peruana,* 2 vols. and suppl. (Lima: Imprenta del Estado por Eusebio Aranda, 1860-1862), and its indexes reproduced in Ramos, *Historia del Derecho,* appendix 2, 3:415–555.

6. Trazegnies, *Idea del derecho,* 151–52, 185, 201; Carlos Ramos Núñez, *Historia del derecho civil peruano, siglos XIX y XX: la codificación del siglo XIX, los códigos de la Confederación y el Código Civil de 1852* (Lima: Fondo Editorial Universidad Católica, 2001), 2:273–80. See also Ramón Gutiérrez Paredes, *Abusos y reformas del Poder Judicial en todos sus grados* (Lima: Imprenta del Universo, 1889) (reprinted articles originally published by the *Gaceta Judicial* in 1861), 4–5, 7–8.

moderate constitution of 1860 continued in force with some interruptions until 1919.[7] This constitutional transformation contributed to limiting the customary rule of force in favor of the rule of law.

However, the revamped legal framework had a major flaw carried over from the colonial past. The constitution of 1860 continued to sanction a centralized patrimonial state that concentrated property rights over the main sources of national wealth. Consequently, the state administration acted as the main economic and business broker. Domestic and foreign businessmen had to court political administrators in order to obtain official favors and monopolies. This flaw was at the center of the institutional causes or incentives for corruption and the vested interests that benefited from it.

Heinrich Witt was an exceptional witness to and participant in the business and institutional transformations of the 1860s and 1870s. As a prominent member of the Lima business elite, he built his fortune closely tied to commercial lending and guano exports consigned to monopoly companies. Witt participated in the profits of Witt, Schutte & Company, guano contractors for Germany. By the late 1860s, he held shares in new and initially promising banks and insurance, railway, water, and gas companies. All of these ventures depended in one way or another on the soundness of public finances due to their particular financial or monopoly arrangements with the government. When public finances faltered, these enterprises immediately felt the pinch. Witt was also enmeshed in protracted litigation over urban properties, tenants, neighbors, and amounts owed to him.

In his revealing diary, kept over the decades of his long life in Peru, Witt's German Protestant upbringing allowed him to keenly observe the moral and ethic behavior of fellow businessmen and local politicians and officials. This diary was useful as memory aid to identify character and family traits essential for his own business deals with sundry clients and partners. He recognized the moral and intellectual value of key figures such as Manuel Pardo and Francisco García Calderón despite occasional friction with them. Conversely, Witt suspected or feared José Gregorio Paz Soldán, Manuel Ortiz de Zevallos, Juan Manuel Iturregui, and many others for their corruption, misuse of power, gambling/drinking habits, and/or fraudulent practices. He was also repulsed by the corrupt schemes of the Echenique clan, Nicolás de Piérola, and Henry Meiggs. Witt's observations and examples of bribery and administrative venality closely coincided with those of other

7. Basadre, *Historia* 5:126–27.

major critics of corruption such as José Arnaldo Márquez and Manuel González Prada, and those cited by historian Watt Stewart.

From these sources, it is possible to retrace how state officials and military chieftains, in connivance with business agents, continued to form corrupt networks interested in circumventing, cheating, and violating legal measures. These actions undermined the efficiency of the three branches of the state: the executive, legislature, and judiciary. Corrupt networks linked ministers, legislators, judges, and businessmen as well as lawyers who acted as crucial intermediaries. Under these circumstances, private property rights and contractual arrangements remained insecure and subject to unpredictable litigation. Bribes and political favors crowded out open competition in the bidding of official contracts and injected serious bias in decision making crucial for the country's economic and institutional development. All of this raised financial risks and transaction costs to undermine the overall efficiency of the economy. Despite the existence of formal legal restrictions, widespread abuse of the system led to an ascending scale of corrupt gains. These corrupt practices were justified by economic developmental and common good promises associated with huge public projects that climaxed in the early 1870s.

Monopoly Guano Deals

One important legal modification in 1860 was the mandatory congressional approval of all major public contracts.[8] This was an initially welcomed innovation after decades of public contracting mainly through executive decisions and decrees. However, this new rule also proved difficult to enforce, as exemplified by the complicated manipulations of guano contracts, or it became seriously distorted. In fact, with larger numbers of officials to bribe, congressional sanction of all state contracts might have increased the use and extent of bribery aimed at rent-seeking objectives.

The quasimonopoly guano contract held by Antony Gibbs & Sons was criticized due to its shady extension approved by the Echenique administration, among other alleged abuses. Accusations against Gibbs implicated Peruvian diplomatic agents in London and Paris. In 1860, Francisco de Rivero, Peruvian chargé d'affaires in London, defended himself against the

8. Law of August 27, 1860, article 2, published in *El Peruano,* September 5, 1860.

public attacks of fellow diplomat Luis Mesones and former guano contractor Carlos Barroilhet. Rivero was accused of serious conflicts of interest in siding with Gibbs's guano price policies, charging improper fees for his diplomatic services tied to Peruvian financial transactions in Europe, and speculating in Peruvian bonds to enhance his own private fortune. Instead of denying the charges, Rivero affirmed his right to charge a commission of 2 percent in his handling of official financial transactions abroad as well as to speculate with Peruvian bonds. He based his claims on similar allowances to former envoys Osma and Mendiburu. Rivero also approved Gibbs's lower guano prices despite higher prices set elsewhere.[9] Obviously the lack of strict administrative regulation permitted these appalling conflicts of interest bordering on corruption.

When Gibbs shady contract ended in January 1862, a new contract for the supply of guano to Great Britain and its colonies was signed with a group of native capitalists (Clemente Ortiz de Villate, Felipe S. Gordillo, José Canevaro, Manuel Pardo, Carlos Delgado, and Felipe Barreda) forming the Compañía Nacional. Despite the law of 1860, the new contract was not submitted to congressional confirmation but approved instead by Castilla's minister of finance, José Fabio Melgar. Strident voices of protest were raised by businessman and demagogic politician Guillermo Bogardus who charged that the contract was illegal and that Congress should void it and prosecute the new contractors for abuses against the state's interests. Moreover, Bogardus argued that these "national" contractors formed a "greedy circle" that had betrayed the spirit of an 1849 legal principle granting preference to Peruvian nationals in cases of matching bids for public contracts. According to Bogardus, the Compañía Nacional lacked sufficient capital and had combined with the British house Thomson, Bonar & Company in financial "corruptelas" damaging to the state.[10] Bogardus haunted the national guano capitalists for more than a decade culminating in an 1878

9. Carlos Barroilhet, *Examen crítico de un opúsculo sobre el huano* (Paris: Imprenta Tipográfica de G. Kugelmann, 1860), 9–11, and *Examen crítico de dos publicaciones del señor don Francisco Rivero* (Paris: Imprenta Tipográfica de G. Kugelmann, 1861), 5; Francisco Rivero, *Reflexiones sobre una carta del doctor Luis Mesones publicada el 13 de diciembre de 1860 en el no. 6693 del periódico Comercio de Lima* (Paris: Imprenta Tipográfica de G. Kugelmann, 1861), 16–25.

10. Guillermo Bogardus, *La Compañía Nacional y Thomson Bonar y Ca., consignatarios del guano en Inglaterra y agentes financieros del Perú en Londres: dedicado al público y muy especialmente a los diputados del Congreso de la Restauración* (Lima: Imprenta Liberal, 1866), 6, 20.

settlement with Thomson, Bonar & Company, after a lawsuit carried by Peruvian fiscal agents in London over irregular charges dating back to the 1860s. The sum settled was relatively small, Bogardus got a part of it as reward for serving as a whistle-blower, but the national capitalists bore no guilt and in fact acted as co-plaintiffs against the British firm.[11]

Several domestic and foreign factors conspired against the fulfillment of new constitutional and legal requirements notwithstanding the occasional congressional veto of some of Castilla's ministers. In October 1862, Castilla managed once again to arrange a peaceful transition of power under the new constitution in the midst of a deteriorating fiscal situation arising from increased military and naval expenses, public works, and a short war with Ecuador.[12] General Miguel de San Román, an old supporter of Castilla, was elected president, General Juan Antonio Pezet became first vice president, and General Pedro Diez Canseco (Castilla's brother-in-law) acted as second vice president. However, San Román died barely five months into his administration. Pezet took the helm of the Peruvian government after returning from Europe where he had been at the time of San Román's death. President Pezet soon confronted the most serious foreign crisis of the young republic since independence.

The governments of Peru and Spain had tried to regularize their diplomatic relations since the 1850s. Important obstacles complicated this diplomatic rapprochement, including Spanish claims for unpaid colonial private debts, a seized commercial vessel bearing the Spanish flag, and abuses against Spanish subjects in Peru.[13] Bad press in Paris and Madrid on Peruvian corrupt affairs and alleged abuses against foreigners contributed to an adverse international public opinion that played into the hands of specula-

---

11. Basadre, *Historia* 7:38–42, 284–88. See also Joaquín Torrico, *Manifestación documentada que eleva al soberano Congreso de 1876 el Coronel Joaquín Torrico, en su carácter de la Comisión de Delegados Fiscales del Perú en Londres* (Lima: Imprenta de La Patria, 1877).

12. Márquez, *Orjía financiera*, 46–47; Salvador Tavira to Secretario de Estado (S.E.), Lima, October 11, 1959, no. 10, Correspondencia, H-1676, Archivo General del Ministerio de Asuntos Exteriores, Madrid (hereafter AGMAE): "[L]as rentas públicas están agotadas con los inmensos gastos que exige un ejército numeroso (doce mil hombres) y una escuadra considerable."

13. Tavira to S.E., Lima, October 27, 1859, and Ramón Merino Ballesteros to S. E., Paris, January 5, 1861, H-1676, AGMAE; "Apresamiento de la barca española 'María y Julia' por un crucero peruano en la isla de Puná," "Reclamación del súbdito español Cayetano Garvizo," Lima, October 14, 1861, Política-Perú, H-2578, AGMAE.

tors on Peruvian debt instruments abroad.[14] Diplomatic agents José Barrenechea and José Gálvez tried to counteract this publicity problem. They
requested government funds to pay journalists and editors of French and
Spanish publications in Paris to write favorably about Peru. This was a common practice by other Latin American diplomatic missions in that city.[15]

In 1863, a Spanish fleet with a combined diplomatic and scientific mission arrived in Callao to press Spanish claims before the Peruvian government. The exaggerated sense of honor of Spanish envoys Luis Hernández
de Pinzón and Eusebio Salazar y Mazarredo, and the lack of tact of the Pezet
administration, led to a serious diplomatic incident complicated by new
claims of abuses against Basque immigrants in the northern estate of Ta-
lambo. In April 1864, the Spanish fleet seized the Chincha islands, the main
source of guano revenues used as public debt collateral. The Pezet government was consequently placed in a dire financial situation. Guano contractors would advance short-term funds only at very high interest (up to 30 percent in some cases). In London, a duly authorized fiscal commission
composed of two prominent businessmen, José Sevilla and Manuel Pardo,
had difficulties raising loans and purchasing warships as Peruvian credit
abroad deteriorated due to Spanish actions.[16] Under duress, Pezet negotiated a treaty with Spain that essentially granted a payment of 3 million pesos to satisfy Spanish claims.[17]

14. Márquez, *Orjía financiera,* 50–55; Luis Mesones to Ministro R.E., Paris, December 31, 1858, no. 127, 5-14/1858, AMRE, who reported that in French newspapers,
especially *L'Univers* (November 10, 1858), "se hicieron graves e inmerecidas ofensas a
Su Ex. el Libertador presidente constitucional de la República y a la misma nación peruana con los innobles epítetos de cobardía, venalidad, corrupción, etca."

15. José Barrenechea to Ministro de R.E., Paris, October 29, 1859, no. 25, 5-14/1959,
AMRE, on hiring writer José María Torres Caicedo to write favorably on Peru in the
Correo de Ultramar; José Gálvez to M.R.E., Paris, November 15, 1860, nos. 6, 7, and 8;
November 30, 1860, no. 15; and December 15, 1860, no. 21, 5-14/1860, AMRE.

16. Comisión Fiscal (Sevilla and Pardo) to Ministro de Hacienda, London, August
17 and 29, 1864; Pardo to Ministro de Hacienda, London, September 30, 1864, Colección Manuel Pardo (hereafter Colección Pardo), D2-51/3352, AGN.

17. Settling the old colonial debt was also considered. M.R.E. Juan Antonio Ribeyro
to Ministro de Hacienda, Lima, May 19, 1864: "No creo necesario detenerme en mani-
festar a U.S. que es de mayor importancia conocer el monto de los bienes secuestrados
a los que emigraron al ejército español en la época de la guerra de la independencia . . .
[y contribución impuesta por españoles de] auxilio patriótico," and requesting the formation de una fiscal commission to review these accounts, in "Expediente relativo al aco-
pio y organización de la deuda española antigua y secuestros," 1865-D2811, Manuscritos, BNL.

Old generals Castilla and Echenique, respectively, the heads of the Senate and Chamber of Deputies in Congress, commanded initially an outraged political opposition to Pezet's appeasing policy. The deportation of Castilla in 1865 was followed by a series of military insurrections led by Colonels Mariano Ignacio Prado and José Balta, supported by General Diez Canseco. This movement managed to oust Pezet and establish a patriotic dictatorship under the leadership of Colonel Prado. In alliance with Chile, Peru then declared war against Spain. Pezet was accused of tyranny, treason, and stealing public funds. He answered that the huge expenses and high-interest loans were urgently necessary for the national defense; those who staged the coup against him in violation of the law had committed the real damage.[18] Years later, however, Pezet flaunted a considerable fortune that allowed him to build a "palace" at the summer resort of Chorrillos.[19] During his presidency, Pezet also allowed the return to Peru of the notoriously corrupt General Juan Crisóstomo Torrico, an old crony of Pezet. Torrico had been spending his ill-begotten wealth in Paris since his shameful exile in 1855. In 1865, Pezet scandalously rewarded Torrico with the plenipotentiary ministry before Napoleon III's court in Paris where Torrico remained undisturbed, still engaged in shady deals related to Peru, until his death.[20]

Under the guidance of the Prado administration's minister of finance, Manuel Pardo, several administrative and tax reforms were introduced such as the abolition of burdensome hereditary pensions and the reorganization of public finance civil servants to enhance professionalism. Some of these reforms unleashed opposition such as the Indian uprisings in Huancané, Puno, in 1866 against the reintroduction of the Indian head tax (*contribución indígena*). Pardo also ordered inquiries into the administration of the customs houses of Arica, Pisagua, and Iquique. The latter proved to be utterly disorganized and plagued with fraudulent debts that caused damage to

18. Juan Antonio Pezet, "Exposición del General don Juan Antonio Pezet ex-presidente del Perú," in *La administración del General don Juan Antonio Pezet en la República del Perú* (Paris: Imprenta Parisiense Guyot y Scribe, 1867), 117–31. See also the harsh official accusations leveled against Pezet by former crony Joaquín Torrico, *Informe del fiscal de la Corte Central Sr. Coronel Joaquín Torrico en la vista de la causa Tratado Vivanco-Pareja de 27 de enero de 1865* (Lima: Imprenta del Estado por J. E. del Campo, 1867), 17, 37, 43.

19. Witt, "Diary," February 4, 1872, vol. 7, 312. Pezet's elegant and comfortable "ranch" was valued in 160,000 pesos. Márquez, *Orjía financiera,* 56.

20. Mendiburu, *Biografías de generales,* 424, 436; Alberto Tauro del Pino, *Enciclopedia ilustrada del Perú,* 6 vols. (Lima: Peisa, 1987), 6:2100–2101.

the national treasury and private commerce.[21] Moreover, during Pardo's tenure several serious cases of corruption were unveiled. One involved the Pezet administration's former minister of finance, José García Urrutia. With the complicity of the ministry's treasurer and other officials, García Urrutia illegally appropriated 200,000 pesos from fiscal revenues.[22] Another case implicated former interim treasurer Manuel Lombard accused of embezzling 50,000 pesos through fraudulent salary payments.[23]

Manuel Pardo's critics used rumors and scandals about his business and family members (he was the son of conservative writer and politician Felipe Pardo y Aliaga and Petronila Lavalle, and was married to Mariana Barreda y Osma) against him.[24] Some of his in-laws were not particularly honest, such as his brother-in-law Mariano Osma who falsified loan agreements and was incarcerated for attacking a representative of his creditors in the street.[25] Moreover, Pardo was attacked on several other grounds: his connections with the Compañía Nacional, the usurious loans contracted with Thomson, Bonar & Company in 1865 and Thomas Lachambre & Com-

21. Manuel Figuerola to Pardo, Reservada, Iquique, June 30, 1866, Colección Pardo, D2-51/3363. See also D2-51/3367 and 3368, AGN.

22. Gil Antonio Toledo (Dirección de Contabilidad Nacional) to Pardo, Lima, April 3, 1866, Colección Pardo, D2-52/3398, AGN: "Un crimen de tamaña magnitud merece ser perseguido y castigado con la mayor actividad y energía, y al ponerlo en conocimiento de V.S. me es honroso contribuir a uno de los tantos fines que invocaron los pueblos al iniciar la gloriosa revolución que terminó el 6 de noviembre." Pardo denounced the guilty parties (García Urrutia, treasury administrator José Félix García, and cashier José Manuel García y García) to the proper executive and judicial authorities.

23. Carmen McEvoy, *Un proyecto nacional en el siglo XIX: Manuel Pardo y su visión del Perú* (Lima: Fondo Editorial Universidad Católica, 1994), 222–23, citing a document of the Tribunal Mayor de Cuentas O.L. 478-230, Hacienda, AGN.

24. Pardo's early business career included wholesale trade, army supplies procurement (1853), administration of the Villa sugar estate (1854–1856), guano trader and contractor (Cía. Canevaro, Pardo y Barrón since 1861, contract for Holland), partner in the Compañía Nacional's guano contract with father-in-law Felipe Barreda and other fellow merchants (1862), financier and banker (Banco del Perú, 1863), and shareholder (31,078 pesos) of an enterprise formed with José F. Canevaro, José Sevilla (64,864 pesos), and Carlos Delgado (43,245 pesos) to import Chinese goods and coolies (1863–1864). "Liquidación de la testamentería de nuestro finado padre D. Felipe Pardo y Aliaga," Lima, January 14, 1869, Colección Pardo, D2-52/3399, AGN; partnership documents signed by Canevaro and Pardo "para negociaciones sobre China de colonos o mercaderías," Lima, May 2, 1863 and July 6, 1864, with attached original coolie contracts; "Contrata de emigración china para el Perú" (Macao, May 26, 1868 and May 21, 1872), Colección Pardo, D2-52/3347, AGN. See also D2-52/3390 and 3391; and Mc Evoy, *Proyecto nacional*, 38, 46–48.

25. Witt, "Diary," October 16, 1868 and January 30, 1869, vol. 7, 40, 63.

pany in 1866, and the purchase in the United States of two very expensive warships (the *Oneoto* and *Catawba* renamed *Manco Cápac* and *Atahualpa,* respectively) from a suspicious American builder, under the exigencies of the war with Spain and its aftermath.[26] Pardo and his supporters answered publicly that the loans and the purchases were justified and that Pardo's main accuser, Bogardus, was calumnious and a shady person himself.[27] High-interest advances during times of war did not seem to be a basis for credible accusations of Pardo's corruption. In fact, Pardo conducted his official affairs then and thereafter with uncommon transparency and honesty despite the failings of some of his business associates.

The conflict with Spain, internal political dissent, and huge expenses to arm the Peruvian military and navy had undermined both the constitutional order and shaky national finances. The Spanish fleet withdrew from the Peruvian coast after suffering casualties in its useless punitive attack of Callao on May 2, 1866. Thereafter, Colonel Prado's dictatorship attempted to legitimize itself by sponsoring a constitutional assembly to write yet another constitution to replace the 1860 version. Liberal legislators, including the radical José María Quimper, untrustworthy Fernando Casós, and moderate Francisco García Calderón, developed the liberal constitution of 1867. It placed particular emphasis on reforming the judicial system. However, like its 1856 predecessor, the 1867 charter faced harsh opposition by Catholic clergy and conservative zealots.[28]

26. U.S. Congress (translation), *Investigación acerca de la venta hecha por el gobierno de los Estados Unidos de los monitores Oneoto y Catawba hoy Manco-Cápac y Atahualpa* (Lima: Imprenta El Nacional, 1869), 3, and appendix B. In October 1867, the Peruvian minister of war and navy, Mariano Pío Cornejo, signed two contracts with the Cincinnati ship builder Alexander Swift & Co. to purchase and equip the two warships for more than twice their original value. This sale was deemed "fraudulent" in the Congressional investigation (House, 40th Congress, 2nd session, June 19, 1868), as the ships were the property of the U.S. government, as per prior contract with Swift.

27. Manuel Pardo, *Los consignatarios del guano: contestación de Manuel Pardo a la denuncia de Guillermo Bogardus precedida de un estudio histórico por Evaristo San Cristóbal* (Lima: Imprenta Gloria, 1922); Anonymous, *La acusación de D. G. Bogardus contra D. Manuel Pardo ministro de Hacienda y D. Federico Barreda ex-ministro plenipotenciario del Perú en Francia* (Paris: Imprenta Parisiense Guyot y Scribe, 1867): "Diariamente luchamos por demostrar al mundo que no estamos tan atrasados ni somos tan corrompidos como nos suponen, y en medio de esa lucha salta de un lodazal un Bogardus a dar razón y material a nuestros difamadores," 22. See also the defense of guano contractor and creditor Witt & Schutte against the "vulgarity" of the accusations against their firm in the pamphlet, *Consignatarios del guano* (Lima: N.p., 1867), 4–5.

28. Basadre, *Historia* 6:56–59.

Within the constitutional assembly itself, opposition to Prado was brewing. Once again García Calderón, as president of the assembly, distinguished himself in defending the rule of law and constitutional principles. Arguing that the new 1867 constitution had been flagrantly violated by the Prado regime, García Calderón proclaimed the presidency vacant and petitioned Prado's resignation for the common good. García Calderón expressed these views precisely when Prado had left Lima to lead the military repression of an armed uprising led by General Diez Canseco in García Calderón's native Arequipa.[29] Almost simultaneously another military rebellion commanded by Colonel Balta in the north sealed Prado's ultimate downfall.

Provisionally back in power in 1868, Diez Canseco restored the 1860 constitution. He remained long enough in power to sanction public contracts, which "are said to have enriched him."[30] During his short administration, Diez Canseco inaugurated a new phase in the contracting of public works with the building of a railway connecting the city of Arequipa with the port of Mollendo.[31] The arequipeños Diez Canseco and his prime minister, Manuel Polar, invited the North American railway contractor Henry Meiggs to build the Arequipa railroad with the avowed intention of benefiting that province. They insisted that Meiggs had a well-deserved reputation after building the profitable Valparaíso-Santiago railway in Chile. No other guarantees were demanded from the contractor who was to be paid in cash per mile of railway built in a very advantageous arrangement for Meiggs. Public opinion suspected the payment of bribes to Diez Canseco, his ministers, and close aides (among them Diego Masías and Domingo Gamio). There is also evidence that Meiggs offered Diez Canseco and Polar gifts of 100,000 pesos each, which were supposedly returned to Meiggs.[32]

29. Basadre, *Historia* 6:80–83.

30. Alvin P. Hovey to Hamilton Fish, August 22, 1870, subject: "Resume of his proceedings as Envoy Extraordinary and Minister Plenipotentiary of the U.S. to Peru from November 1865: Observations on the Past, Present, and Future of Peru," in Despatches 1826–1906, roll 24, USNA.

31. Previous railway contracts for short distances involved personal connections (Gonzales Candamo and Castilla), and financial speculation with domestic and foreign credit to finance them (Joseph Hegan, Tacna-Arica railway). The Lima-Callao and Lima-Chorrillos railways owned by Pedro Gonzales Candamo and partner José Vicente Oyague, for example, were soon profitable. In the mid-1860s, they were sold with capital gains for £600,000 to Antony Gibbs & Sons who, in turn, sold them to the Peruvian government for £800,000 in 1871. Witt, "Diary," January 15, 1871, vol. 7, 223–24; Basadre, *Historia* 5:129.

32. Watt Stewart, *Henry Meiggs: Yankee Pizarro* (Durham, NC: Duke University

This was just the beginning of the amazing business Meiggs conducted in Peru while taking advantage of the evident venality of the highest authorities. In December 1868, shortly after leaving the presidency, Diez Canseco faced a congressional investigation into several of his momentous yet irregular measures, including his deals with Meiggs. Predictably, the investigation did not prosper.[33]

Colonel Balta was elected president and assumed power in August 1868. He became known for choleric and authoritarian outbursts, and his administration, for uncontrolled military spending. For his first cabinet, Balta appointed Francisco García Calderón as minister of finance. García Calderón attempted to curb corruption by introducing administrative reforms to reward expertise and merit. Early during his ministerial administration, a law was passed holding public officials responsible for misconduct; however, this law was mostly disregarded thereafter. García Calderón also planned to reorganize the customs service to limit contraband, control public expenditures, and reduce the growing fiscal deficit. To finance the deficit he proposed to continue relying on advances by guano contractors. Although he supported a new system of open guano sales at its source to replace the old guano consignment system, he understood that until the fiscal crisis was solved, changes in guano contracting had to be gradual. He opposed the increase of foreign indebtedness because it was reaching dangerous levels.[34]

Serious disagreements with Balta over the issue of foreign debt, and congressional opposition to the honest finance minister's proposed measures,

---

Press, 1946), 47, 51–52, citing documents published by Jesús Antonio Diez Canseco, son of the former president, in the pamphlet, *Para la historia de la patria: el ferrocarril de Arequipa y el Gral. Don Pedro Diez Canseco* (Arequipa: N.p., 1921). Of the Diez Canseco administration, Witt wrote the following in his "Diary" in April 1868: "[T]here was much dissatisfaction with the present administration whose members it was well known only cared for their own pockets. Domingo Gamio and Diego Masías, the President's right and left hand were named respectively administrator of the Aduana del Callao, and Director de la Moneda de Lima, two of the most lucrative situations in the Republic at the disposal of the Executive"; and on May 18, 1868: "The rumour went and probably not without foundation that Meiggs had spent in bribes near a million of soles in order to obtain this contract . . . to each of the five ministers he had probably paid S/.100,000 and Diego Masías made no secret of the fact that for his services he had been remunerated with $100,000 dollars [for his influence over Diez Canseco]." Witt, "Diary," vol. 7, 6, 8–9, 122.

33. Basadre, *Historia* 6:116–17.

34. Ramos, *Historia del derecho* 3:240–43, citing Bustamante y Rivero, *Ideología de Francisco García Calderón,* 25, and Luis Humberto Delgado, *La obra de Francisco García Calderón* (Lima: American Express, 1934), 51–81. See also Basadre, *Historia* 6:224–26.

resulted in the resignation of García Calderón on December 22, 1868. A seemingly unstoppable yet corrupt strategy was being hatched in the Chamber of Deputies for granting ample executive powers to contract foreign loans in order to "resolve" the deficit.[35] García Calderón's successor, Nicolás de Piérola, led the country into financial disaster through the corrupt signing and implementation of many new contracts for guano sales, foreign loans, and railway construction, among other public works.

The Infamous Dreyfus Contract

Immediately after the resignation of García Calderón as minister of finance, former President José Rufino Echenique strongly recommended young Nicolás de Piérola for the vacant post. Echenique had returned to Lima in 1862 after a long exile imposed by President Castilla. While abroad, Echenique had not ceased to organize several unsuccessful insurrections against Castilla. In 1860, allegedly under financial strain despite help received from his wealthy father-in-law Pío Tristán, General Echenique tried to influence old friends in Congress to legislate in favor of his back salary claims and property compensation.[36] After his return, Echenique reorganized his network of corruption and patronage helped by his sons (Juan Martín, Rufino, and Pío), in-laws, relatives, and political followers. Echenique also succeeded in being elected congressman and to obtain restitution for his lost property and salary. In 1868–1872, Echenique sought to influence President Balta, formerly his subaltern in military rank, as a means to bolster his own presidential ambitions.

Piérola was Echenique's distant relative and political ally, an ambitious merchant, conservative Catholic, and son of a controversial former minister of finance (1852–1853) during Echenique's corrupt administration. In his memoirs, Echenique minimized his role as the direct sponsor of Piérola before Balta. Echenique wrote that his recommendation came through a third person, despite admitting having had several confidential meetings with Balta at the time. Other sources placed Echenique directly in Balta's presence to forcefully support Piérola as minister of finance.[37] There is no

35. Witt, "Diary," December 24, 1868, vol. 7, 51–52; Basadre, *Historia* 6:120–25.

36. Echenique to Mendiburu, Caracato (Chile), August 26, 1860, MEN 441, no. 5, Colección Mendiburu, AHRA. Echenique counted among his friends in Congress Mendiburu, Bartolomé Herrera, and Dr. Juan Miguel del Carpio.

37. Echenique, *Memorias* 2:294–95; Philippe de Rougemont, *Una pájina de la dic-*

doubt, however, that Piérola was a close associate of Echenique. Piérola eventually headed a new generation of corrupt officials and politicians that inherited old corrupt know-how from Echenique's generation. The "inexperienced" Minister Piérola soon surprised everyone. Piérola swiftly became a leading force of dubious strategies to deal with the alarming fiscal deficit. His approach was utterly different from that of García Calderón and reinforced the move by corrupt congressmen, among them Juan Martín Echenique, and President Balta to rely heavily on foreign indebtedness. Lawyer Fernando Palacios had conceived the idea of raising a loan to cover the deficit through open bidding (*licitación*) previously authorized by Congress. Between December 1868 and January 1869, Palacios had several meetings with Balta and Piérola in which he revealed to them the details of this project. To Palacios's original plan, Balta and Piérola added a shrewd twist of their own: they first obtained on January 25, 1869 broad congressional authorization, although there had been ongoing contacts, since December 1868, between the Parisian house Dreyfus Frères et Cie. and the administration. While the "open" bidding was proceeding with at least four proposals on the table, Piérola had all but approved Dreyfus's offer to advance funds to the state against 2 million tons of guano, which the state would sell to Dreyfus at a fixed price over a period of time.[38]

---

tadura de D. Nicolás de Piérola (Paris: Imprenta Cosmopolita, 1883), 11; Basadre, *Introducción a las bases* 2:539, no. 7037; and Basadre, *Historia* 6:129–30.

38. Fernando Palacios to José María González, Lima, June 16, 1870, in *Carta dirigida por el Sr. D. José María González diputado a Congreso al Sr. D. Fernando Palacios y su respuesta, en la que se revelan hechos de gran importancia en el negociado Dreyfus* (Lima: Imprenta de La Libertad, 1870), 4–5. The four proposals were (1) Fernando Casós (Lima, July 20, 1869) proposed to transfer £7.2 million worth of domestic debt as collateral for a loan in London; (2) Compañía de Guano de Gran Bretaña (José Canevaro, Schutte y Cia., Thomas Lachambre, Valdeavellano y Cia., Lima, August 10, 1869) offered a loan of 20 million pesos at 95 percent of face value and 5 percent interest; (3) Carlos G. de Candamo and Manuel G. Chávez, representing Cia. General Sud Americana of London (Lima, August 17, 1869), offered a loan of 100 million francs at 95 percent face value and 2.5 percent commission; and (4) Guillermo Scheel manager of Dreyfus Hermanos of Lima, representing Dreyfus Frères of Paris (probably in coordination with Luis Benjamín Cisneros, Peruvian consul in Havre), proposed the purchase of 2 million tons of guano at a price of 36.5 soles per ton (Lima, May 26, 1869). Scheel to Piérola, Lima, May 5, 1869; and Cisneros to Piérola, Paris, May 7, 1869, in Archivo Piérola, vol. 3, Manuscritos, BNP. See also Cisneros to Piérola, Paris, March 7, 1869, reporting on Cisneros's project for the sale of guano for three years that he submitted with success to a Parisian "casa de banco," in Luis B. Cisneros, *Obras completas de Luis Benjamín Cisneros: mandadas publicar por el gobierno del Perú,* 3 vols. (Lima: Librería e Imprenta Gil, 1939), 3:106–107. Rougemont affirms that as early as

Dreyfus was already advancing money to the Peruvian government since May 1869 prior to the formal presentation of the other three proposals. Moreover, Juan Martín Echenique had already been sent to Paris as official commissioner with precise instructions to sign, with Toribio Sanz, a formal treaty with Dreyfus. The contract was signed together with a complementary secret pact on July 5, 1869. The secret contract established that the Peruvian government's financial agent in London, Thomson, Bonar & Company, was to be replaced with another British house to be selected by Dreyfus later; his choice was Henry Schroder & Company, a London banking company that played a key role in subsequent financial deals between Dreyfus and the Balta administration.[39]

With the additional financial partnership of the giants Société Générale and Leiden Premsel et Cie. of Paris, Dreyfus was set to exert quasi monopolistic control over the core of Peruvian finances as creditor, financial agent, and guano merchant. Before the ad referendum contract was ratified in Peru, Dreyfus had distributed shares for 60 million francs among his partners in Paris: the Société Générale took shares for 22.5 million francs, Leiden Premsel for 22.5 million, and Dreyfus retained 15 million. Shortly afterwards each major partner branched out to other subscribers. Dreyfus obtained the participation of Peruvians with strategic interests in defending the contract's ultimate ratification: the former guano-loading contractor Andrés Alvarez Calderón "took" shares for 600,000 francs; the controversial diplomat Francisco de Rivero, 500,000; Luis Benjamín Cisneros, the Peruvian consul at Havre and liaison between Dreyfus and the Balta administration, 190,000; the old *consolidado* Nicanor González, 156,750; legislator and lawyer Fernando Casós, 95,000; future fiscal agent Colonel Joaquín Torrico, the sidekick brother of corrupt General Juan Crisóstomo Torrico,

---

December 1868, Cisneros was already acting as liason between Dreyfus's original design and a corrupt ring within the Balta administration and Congress (Manuel Ortiz de Zevallos, Juan Martín Echenique, Dionisio Derteano, among others). Rougemont, *Una pájina,* 12–13. On the congressional intrigues that pressured Minister García Calderón to resign on December 22, 1868, see Basadre, *Historia* 6:121–25.

39. "Contrato secreto ajustado entre los comisionados fiscales Toribio Sanz y D. Juan Martín Echenique relativo al contrato principal sobre venta de guano con anticipación de fondos," Paris, July 5, 1869, in Archivo Piérola, vol. 3, Manuscritos, BNP. Piérola had accepted monthly loans in soles from Dreyfus as early as May 1869. See Piérola's note attached to letter Scheel to Piérola, Lima, 26 May 1869, with the original proposal by Dreyfus Hermanos, ibid. Also, see Palacios to González, June 16, 1870, in *Carta dirigida,* 17.

47,500; Guillermo Bogardus, 4,750; and even the official negotiator Juan Martín Echenique, 100,000, among many others.[40]

According to the final public contract ratified in Lima on August 17, 1869, Dreyfus would substitute existing guano consignees in all of Europe at the expiration of their contracts. Dreyfus promised to advance the government 700,000 soles every month, for a total of 2.4 million soles, and service Peru's 1865 foreign loan and debts owed to former guano contractors. These monopolistic conditions and the outrageous handling of a supposedly open contest prompted demands for rescinding the Dreyfus contract. However, Piérola had the deal practically secured because a cancellation of the contract would entail refunding Dreyfus in cash for the sums already advanced to the government, which was impossible for the cash-strapped national treasury.[41]

A major public debate between contending interests ensued. Those searching for means to dislodge the native guano consignees' influence over fiscal matters, and deny the extension of their contracts arguing excessive profits and alleged abuses, supported or justified the Dreyfus contract.[42] The official inquiries by Toribio Sanz in Europe since 1867 had revealed irregularities that preceded legal accusations against the contractors for Germany (Schutte) and France (Lachambre) in 1869.[43] Devious Luis Benjamín

40. Heraclio Bonilla, *Guano y burguesía en el Perú* (Lima: Instituto de Estudios Peruanos, 1974), 95–98, citing documents from the Fonds Dreyfus, Frères, et Cie., 28AQ 7, Archives Nationales de la France (formerly kept in Paris, currently in Roubaix). See also Bertrand Gille, *État sommaire des archives d'entreprises conserves aux Archives Nationales (série AQ)* (Paris: Imprimerie Nationale, 1957), 1:84–85. On Echenique's participation, Basadre, *Historia* 7:30, cites a study of Pablo Macera based on the Dreyfus papers.

41. Dreyfus Frères & Cie., *Texto del contrato celebrado por el Supremo Gobierno del Perú con la casa Dreyfus Hermanos y Ca.: aclaraciones presentadas por los contratistas* (Lima: Tipografía Aurelio Alfaro, 1869), 5, 12, 16–17.

42. El Nacional, *La Excma. Corte Suprema en el juicio sobre el contrato celebrado por el supremo poder ejecutivo con la casa de Dreyfus HH. y Ca.* (Lima: Imprenta de El Nacional, 1869), x, 24–26; these are editorial positions favorable to the Dreyfus Contract. Daniel Ruzo, *Los consignatarios del huano y muy especialmente los titulados nacionales según su propia confesión en los contratos de préstamos y prórrogas: documentos oficiales para la historia financiera del Perú recogidos y publicados por el Dr. D. Daniel Ruzo* (Lima: Imprenta de la Sociedad, 1870), 36–38; Luis B. Cisneros, "El negociado Dreyfus" (first published in Havre, 1870), in *Obras completas* 3:187–357, esp. 192–93.

43. Toribio Sanz, *Guano: comunicaciones importantes del Señor Toribio Sanz, Inspector General de las consignaciones de guano con el despacho de Hacienda y Comercio, públicadas por acuerdo de la H. Cámara de Diputados* (Lima: Imprenta de El Comercio, 1868), 9, 30.

Cisneros and his brother, lawyer and legislator Luciano B. Cisneros, formerly staunch supporters of Echenique and deeply involved in deals with Dreyfus, distinguished themselves for their oratorical and legal defense of the Dreyfus contract and their attacks against the national capitalists. They shrewdly alleged connections between older guano contractors' usurious practices and abuses of the newer *nacionales*.[44] In this climate, the French chargé in Lima observed that the guano consignees were considered very unpopular.[45] Conversely, those who opposed the Dreyfus contract argued that it was illegal since its signature had not complied with specific legislative authorization and procedures of open bidding. The native contractors made public their counteroffer to the Dreyfus deal. They demanded compliance with the legislative resolutions of 1849 and 1860 that granted preference to Peruvian citizens in public biddings in which natives and foreigners made equal offerings.[46]

The political and legal struggle turned nasty and dominated Peruvian politics for months. When the national capitalists offered to match Dreyfus's financial provisions with support of the local Banco del Perú, a bank established in 1863 by ten native partners and guano contractors, the executive retaliated by decreeing that the bank's paper money would not be accepted in government offices. Opponents to the Dreyfus contract were arrested, among them Emilio Althaus, the manager of the Banco del Perú. Between October and November 1869, the Supreme Court reasserted its jurisdiction to declare that the nacionales had been stripped of their rights by the Dreyfus contract and, in consequence, it should be rescinded. Approximately at the same time, a congressional commission voted by a majority of 8 to 6 that the contract was illegal because it was unconstitutional. These temporary reversals brought about a conflict between Balta and Piérola from which Piérola and Dreyfus emerged the winners. The executive redoubled its campaign in favor of the contract and simply overruled the ju-

44. Luciano B. Cisneros, minister of justice under Balta, was considered "a clever man but whose moral character did not stand high in general estimation." Witt, "Diary," August 4, 1868, vol. 7, 25; Carlos Ramos Núñez, *Toribio Pacheco: jurista peruano del siglo XIX* (Lima: Fondo Editorial Universidad Católica, 1993), 40.

45. Gaceldrée Boilleau to Ministre des Affaires Étrangères (M.A.E.), Lima, August 20, 1869, C.P., Pérou, Suplément vol. 2 (1869–1880: Guanos), ff. 9–14, AMAE.

46. Dreyfus Frères et Cie., *Refutación de las acciones interpuestas judicialmente por "Los Nacionales" con motivo del contrato Dreyfus; precedido de algunas consideraciones económicas, fiscales y políticas sobre dicho contrato por un antiguo contradictor de las consignaciones y los consignatarios* (Lima: Tipografía A. Alfaro, 1869).

diciary by placing the ultimate decision in the hands of the legislature.[47] By November 1870, Dreyfus's legal and public campaigns and bribing of legislators had swayed conditions in favor of the approval of the contract by a vote of 63 against 33 in the Chamber of Deputies, a decision shortly after ratified by the Senate.[48]

Although Manuel Angulo replaced Piérola temporarily as minister of finance, Piérola remained influential in defending the Dreyfus contract behind the scenes. Angulo was considered a mere puppet of Piérola between November 1869 and February 1870. During these months, and when Piérola returned as minister of finance between February 1870 and July 1871, the financial future of the country was sealed with the implementation of two devastating financial schemes: the first with railway contractor and speculator Henry Meiggs for the construction of two gargantuan railways; and the second with no other than Dreyfus in Paris on May 19, 1870 for a mammoth foreign loan of £12 million (pounds sterling) (59.6 million soles) that was naturally followed by another refinancing loan again by Dreyfus for £36.8 million on December 31, 1871. Moreover, as early as the first half of 1870 Dreyfus charged commissions of up to £357,000 in handling interest payments of foreign railway bonds. Piérola was attacked in the press for these irregularities. Despite Piérola's claims of rectitude and

---

47. Boilleau to M.A.E., Lima, October 21, 1869, and February 19, 1870, CP, Pérou, Suplément vol. 2, ff. 45–48, esp. 46–46v, and 113–16v, esp. 116v, AMAE; Witt, "Diary," October 4, 1869, October 19, 1869, and December 27, 1869, vol. 7, 115, 117, and 132; Basadre, *Historia* 6:133–44.

48. Perú, Cámara de Diputados, *Informe de la Comisiones de Hacienda y Justicia de la H. Cámara de Diputados sobre el contrato celebrado por el Supremo Gobierno con la casa de Dreyfus Hermanos y Compañía de París, en 17 de agosto de 1869* (Lima: N.p., 1870), 3, 24, signed among others by Luciano B. Cisneros and Modesto Basadre, recommended approval of the Dreyfus Contract by Congress. In a private conversation, Balta's minister of government, Rafael Velarde, agreed with Witt that the national consignees had lost to Dreyfus "mainly to them not having come forward with sufficient heavy bribes." Witt, "Diary," August 19, 1869, vol. 7, 100. Charges by the French chargé d'affaires pointed to members of the Supreme Court succumbing to bribery of Dreyfus or his opponents. Boilleau to M.A.E., Lima, September 21, 1869, CP, Pérou, Suplément vol. 2, ff. 29–34, esp. f. 30v, AMAE. A flyer titled, "Partija del negociado con Dreyfus y Ca.," circulating at the time listed twelve persons allegedly guilty of receiving illegal shares for up to 1.6 million soles, including President Balta (500,000 soles), his wife Doña Melchora (200,000), Nicolás de Piérola (200,000), Juan F. Balta (150,000), Juan Martín Echenique (100,000), Rafael Velarde (100,000), José Rufino Echenique (40,000), and Pedro Balta (40,000), among other high-level officials. Attachment to report by Boilleau to M.A.E., Lima, August 27, 1869, ibid., ff. 17–21; Basadre, *Historia* 6:143–44.

defense of his official actions by respected historian Jorge Basadre, the young finance minister's penchant for power and personal gain contributed decisively to causing the disastrous default and bankruptcy in Peru a few years later.[49]

The core of the business community in Lima had to adapt to the new financial dynamic adopted and imposed by the government and heavily influenced by the de facto alliance between Dreyfus and Meiggs. The engine of the economy was heading in the wrong direction of unprofitable public works financed by fiscal deficit and unmanageable foreign debt. Several local and foreign entrepreneurs were aware of this reality but opted for seeking marginal advantages before the collapse.[50] Former business and financial enemies of Dreyfus and Meiggs now gingerly participated with them in joint ventures. Lima's banks offered their current account services and commercial credit to Dreyfus and Meiggs while supporting overdue loans owed by the state. Private projects to develop productive railways such as the Cerro de Pasco Mineral Railway Company risked insolvency and looked toward the government for support. At this point of financial uncertainty, Juan Martín Echenique and Emilio de Piérola, brother of Nicolás, erupted onto the business scene. With ill-gotten funds, surreptitious government support, and working on behalf of their corrupt political clique, Echenique and Piérola bought or invested in ailing or new private stock companies and eventually took control of them. These included the Cerro de Pasco Mineral Railway, the real estate and building company La Constructora, and the Lima-Huacho Railway Company.[51]

49. Compare Witt, "Diary," December 8, 1869 and February 26, 1870, vol. 7, 128, 147, with Basadre, *Historia* 6:176–78, 189, 195–203, esp. 200–201. Basadre argued that the Dreyfus contract was Piérola's achievement in liberating national finances from the clutches of the native financial oligarchy. However, at the end of Piérola's ministerial tenure, it was believed at the time that while in office "his financial operations had invariably two objectives, firstly, his own private advantage, and secondly, the interest of the state." Witt, "Diary," July 21, 1871, vol. 7, 269. Gootenberg minimizes the role of corruption in the developing financial troubles of the time. See Gootenberg, *Imagining Development: Economic Ideas in Peru's "Fictitious Prosperity" of Guano, 1840–1880* (Berkeley: University of California Press, 1993), 109.

50. "In Peru, notwithstanding the apparent material progress of the Republic the present government is in my opinion hurrying the country into an abuse of the most frightful financial embarrassment, from which it will finally only be saved by a bankruptcy and the repudiation of all its debts. Loans are to be raised until no European capitalist will be inclined to invest his funds in Peruvian bonds, and then what is to be done? Pay nobody." Witt, "Diary," January 1, 1871, vol. 7, 218–19.

51. Witt, "Diary," December 11, 1869 (Frederic Ford, manager of the Bank of Lon-

In effect, under the Balta administration the Echenique-Piérola network advanced considerably in gaining strategic positions of power and wealth. Its members crowded out the managerial staff of companies under its control: General Echenique's sons Juan Martín, Rufino, and Pío, nephew-in-law Augusto Althaus, brother-in-law Santiago Lanfranco, César Saco y Flores, Simón Paredes, and Emilio de Piérola, were all *gerentes* of La Constructora. This company was favored with several public construction projects. After leaving his ministerial post, Nicolás de Piérola was elected as the *echeniquista* deputy for Lima in the congressional elections of November 1871. Piérola supported the so-called Catholic party that dovetailed with the conservative politics of General Echenique. For the presidential elections of 1872, General Echenique was initially President Balta's favorite official candidate. The general's ambition, however, backfired after an executive decree granted Juan Martín Echenique the exclusive privilege of exporting and importing all government materials. Facing generalized outrage and scandal, Balta decided to annul this decree of absurd favoritism. As a result, the relations between Balta and General Echenique chilled to the extent that Balta decided to support instead Antonio Arenas, a civilian lawyer, as the official presidential candidate.[52] Arenas faced the opposition's candidate Manuel Pardo, the increasingly popular former mayor of Lima and head of a broad-based Partido Civil formed in 1871. This political organization was Peru's first modern civilian party, poised to supersede caudillo-led political groups that were based mainly on electoral patronage, violence, and corruption.[53]

---

don & Mexico in Lima, assists Dreyfus's current account needs), February 19, 1870 (Banco de Lima, presided by Manuel Argumaniz, grants short-term loan to Meiggs), March 28, 1870 (Witt and his son Juan buy Dreyfus's guano contract shares), September 17, 1870 (Cerro de Pasco Mineral Railway Co. at the brink of insolvency), October 1, 1870 (government debt payment to Banco de Lima for $130,000 long overdue), May 2, 1871 (Dreyfus transfers his current account to Banco del Perú and holds shares in Banco de Lima), February 8 and 15 and April 28, 1871 (Juan Martín Echenique and Emilio Piérola, shareholders and directors of La Constructora; Echenique clique controls the company), June 12, 1871 (J. M. Echenique takes control of Cerro de Pasco Railway Co. using internal debt bonds approved and signed by N. de Piérola), December 23, 1871 (Emilio de Piérola, director of Lima-Huacho Railway Co.), vol. 7, 129, 146, 153, 192, 196, 250, 251, 236–37, 259, 302.

52. Witt, "Diary," April 28, 1871, June 8, 1872, vol. 7, 250, 340; Jerningham to Granville, Lima, June 13, 1872, FO 61/272, ff. 117–18v, esp. 117, NAUK.

53. For the early political and organizational history of the Partido Civil, see Carmen Mc Evoy, "Estampillas y votos: el rol del correo político en una campaña electoral decimonónica," *Histórica* 18, no. 1 (1994): 95-134, and *Proyecto Nacional,* chapter 4;

The complex and corrupt bidding and legal questioning of official contracts undermined efforts at establishing orderly rule of law in business and public affairs. According to a foreign diplomat, the constitution and the laws did not have control; instead, "the will of a few families alone is the law."[54] In such circumstances, lawyers such as Francisco García Calderón were in high demand to negotiate legal matters between the government and private interests. García Calderón had a well-deserved reputation as an honest legislative reformer as well as a scrupulous private sector lawyer and civil servant. But in the context of his time, not even García Calderón was exempt of embarrassing conflicts of interest. His clients looked for a legal advisor who could navigate the cumbersome bureaucratic maze and at the same time offer a position of influence or favor among decision makers in control of the government.

With these ambiguous assumptions, García Calderón secured the legal representation of important private clients such as U.S. claimants, guano contractor Schutte & Company, and even Henry Meiggs, among others. Some of his clients were willing to bribe authorities to obtain favorable resolution to their claims and contracts. U.S. chargé Alvin Hovey recognized that several U.S. claimants represented by García Calderón against the Peruvian state were blackmailers who had bribed or lied to obtain legal justification for their reparation claims. Not surprisingly, García Calderón also became involved in bitter and public disputes with his clients over his legal fees, which were invariably considered disproportionately high at the end of legal proceedings. These disputes arose from García Calderón's own lack of clarity in establishing previous payment agreements concerning his clients' dubious claims.[55] Moreover, it is surprising that García Calderón performed

---

and Ulrich Mücke, "Elections and Political Participation in Nineteenth-Century Peru: The 1871-72 Presidential Campaign," *Journal of Latin American Studies* 33 (2001): 311–46, and *Political Culture in Nineteenth-Century Peru: The Rise of the Partido Civil* (Pittsburgh: University of Pittsburgh Press, 2004).

54. Hovey to Fish, "Resume of his proceedings," Lima, August 22, 1870, Despatches 1826–1906, roll 24, USNA.

55. Hovey to Fish, "Resume of his proceedings," Lima, August 22, 1870; H. M. Brent to Fish, Lima, September 27, 1870, and note attached by John P. Polk, Washington, DC, November 1870, citing earlier diplomatic correspondence on García Calderón's "exorbitant" charges of 33,188 soles, a percentage of the total claimed since 1863, against the flat fee of 10,000 soles that was reportedly agreed to with U.S. diplomats in Lima. According to Polk, García Calderón had suggested "that through his intimacy with the Peruvian commissioners [to settle the claims]," he would "ensure to each claimant an award in no case less than six eights of amount claimed." It later became

as the legal representative of the railway mogul and speculator Henry Meiggs, notorious in the early 1870s for bribery schemes and other illegal exploits that contributed to Peruvian institutional and financial collapse.

A Deluge of Public Works

The Dreyfus contract and the financial arrangements that followed did not solve the deficit problems that had alarmed responsible Peruvian citizens and businessmen in 1868. On the contrary, these financially irresponsible measures were designed to allow opportunities for corrupt gain. The financial deals with Dreyfus covered the illegal expenses of huge public works projects by increasing the foreign debt; these deals attracted ambitious speculators smelling quick profits at the expense of an entire nation. On January 15, 1869, Congress authorized the executive to grant contracts for the construction of railways and to finance those works with bonds bearing 6 percent interest. This financial arrangement was also flawed because it favored risky speculation, as contractors who were paid with bonds sought to place them in foreign markets. Thereafter, a frenzy of public works contracting was unleashed for the building of railways, irrigation projects, bridges, piers and docks, public buildings, and urban improvements, without sound estimates of their profitability and viability. Most of these projects were not completed or even started. However, these public works were announced to ordinary citizens as the magic wand that would lead to wealth and development.

Some Peruvians earnestly believed in the benefits of railway construction and other public projects brokered by the state. Manuel Pardo himself had contributed decisively to implanting the idea that railways meant progress.[56] But this was clearly not the case under circumstances of widespread corruption. Businessman and capitalist Manuel Argumaniz Muñoz participated in the official bidding to build a trans-Andean railway line uniting the central highland town of Jauja with the capital Lima. Argumaniz's

---

evident that he did not possess the influence he pretended to. Despatches 1826–1906, roll 24, USNA. Despite these disagreements, García Calderón continued to work with U.S. clients in subsequent decades. See also *F. García Calderón y la casa de Schutte y Compañía: contestación al Sr. D. Gerardo Garland* (Lima: Imprenta de "El Nacional," 1875), 5; and Witt, "Diary," March 29, 1872, vol. 7, 323.

56. Manuel Pardo, *Estudios sobre la provincia de Jauja* (Lima: La Época, 1862).

proposal had the support of native and foreign financial institutions, but unfortunately faced Meiggs, a master corrupter, in the bidding process. Argumaniz wrote in his memoirs that Meiggs was favored by officialdom due to "spilling over gold even to the doormen of the ministry . . . knowing perfectly well the nature of the country." Furthermore, Argumaniz recalled that a lady in Lima with connections in the Chamber of Deputies and government visited him to propose making an illegal payment for approval of his railway bid. To his polite refusal to engage a lady in a matter of bribery in which he, moreover, did not want to participate, she answered with regret that it was a well-established custom of the land and that nothing could be achieved without recourse to same.[57]

To secure the approval of his bids to build the trans-Andean Lima-La Oroya and Arequipa-Puno railways, Meiggs followed the same procedure he had used when negotiating the Arequipa-Mollendo railway. Meiggs confided to a representative of British creditors that his secret in dealing with various administrations consisted of allowing the highest authorities in power to sell themselves at their own price. Thereafter, Meiggs simply added the bribery amounts to the contract's total cost. These common practices "made Peruvian bribery and corruption a by-word even in South America."[58] It is estimated that Meiggs distributed more than 11 million soles in bribes (approximately 8 to 10 percent of the total railway building costs of 120 to 140 million) among Peruvian authorities, the record of which he kept in legendary green or red notebooks.[59]

Following Meiggs's example, other local entrepreneurs vied to build at very high costs to obtain high profits. Such was the case of the Chimbote-Huaraz Railway Company promoted by Benito Valdeavellano and Dreyfus's most conspicuous "silent" partner, Dionisio Derteano, and formed by

57. Manuel de Argumaniz, "Memorias," 6 vols., unpublished manuscript, 1876, vol. 5, 40–41v, cited in Palacios McBride, "Empresario peruano," 83.

58. William Clarke, *Peru and Its Creditors* (London: Ranken & Co., 1877), 118–19, cited in Stewart, *Henry Meiggs,* 47–48. See also Alexander James Duffield, *Peru in the Guano Age: Being a Short Account of a Recent Visit to the Guano Deposits with Some Reflections on the Money They Have Produced and the Uses to Which It Has Been Applied* (London: Richard Bentley & Son, 1877), 16; and Fernando Casós, *Romances históricos: Los hombres de bien; Los amigos de Elena* (Paris: Renée Schmitz, 1874).

59. On the existence of a red or green notebook with amounts of bribes and secret payments by Meiggs to Peruvian authorities, see Ernest W. Middendorf, *Perú* (Lima: Universidad Mayor de San Marcos, 1973), 2:152, 159–60, cited by Palacios, "Un empresario peruano," 78–80, and Márquez, *Orjía financiera,* 66–67, cited by Stewart, *Henry Meiggs,* 45, note 7; Basadre, *Historia* 6:181–82.

ten other shareholders. Their proposed total cost was 21 million soles. Meiggs took over this deal by siding with Valdeavellano and Derteano, buying out several of the original partners for up to 600,000 soles each, and paying bribes to key relatives of top authorities. As a consequence, the total cost asked by Meiggs and approved by the government rose to 24 million soles.[60]

To celebrate the laying of the first stone of the Lima-Oroya railway on January 1, 1870, Meiggs and the government hosted elaborate events, parades, and a fancy lunch for 800 guests that cost around 47,500 soles.[61] Likewise, for the opening of the completed Arequipa-Mollendo railway in January 1871, approximately one thousand guests were carried from Lima in three warships and a steamer, which also transported large quantities of food, beverages, fireworks, and a team of equestrian performers for the public entertainment and dances that Meiggs, Balta, and local magnates offered over several days of celebrations.[62] Meiggs was known as the "most generous man in Peru." Between April 1868 and December 1871, Meiggs was awarded or took over contracts for the construction of seven lines totaling 700 miles and 120 million soles. However, Meiggs was paid mostly in government bonds issued since 1869 at 6 percent interest and 2 percent cumulative amortization to start ten years after the date of issue. This placed Meiggs at risk of bankruptcy if the market for Peruvian railway bonds abroad collapsed. As early as August 1870, the financial future of Peru looked worrisome based on its large and ballooning foreign debt and fiscal deficit. The U.S. attaché in Lima recommended that U.S. capitalists should not invest in Peruvian railway bonds. The frenzy of trans-Andean railways fueled by overblown expectations of corrupt gain had conveniently neglected the limited market conditions for freight and passengers in Peru that precluded profitable railways when built at such high costs.[63]

While railway construction was by far the biggest speculative business of the times, it was by no means the only source of corrupt gain in the concession of public works. Meiggs was also involved in real estate specula-

60. According to Witt, who was initially interested in this speculative railway deal but decided not to participate due to suspicion of corruption, one of the original partners, Gerardo Garland, received 600,000 pesos, and doña Melchora de Balta 700,000 soles. Witt, "Diary," November 20, 1871, vol. 7, 293–94.

61. Stewart, *Henry Meiggs*, 65–66.

62. Witt, "Diary," December 19–31, 1870, and January 10, 1871, vol. 7, 216, 222.

63. Alvin Hovey to Fish, Lima, August 22, 1870, Despatches 1826–1906, roll 24, USNA; Stewart, *Henry Meiggs*, 85–86.

tion opened up by the demolition of the old colonial walls encircling Lima, and the construction and pavement of streets, pedestrian walkways, and public and private buildings, as well as mineral concessions and irrigation works. Meiggs even risked supplying U.S.-made firearms and ammunition to Bolivia under the interested watch of Peruvian authorities and U.S. diplomat General Hovey, a privileged witness. In 1874, Meiggs also organized the financial and construction concern Compañía de Obras Públicas y Fomento to buy and sell urban and rural real estate through its intermediation between private investors and public entities. García Calderón acted as this company's vice president in handling delicate legal negotiations with the state. The specialized lawyer and negotiator remained as legal advisor to Meiggs until the latter's death in 1877. García Calderón continued to advise Meiggs's heirs on subsequent bankruptcy proceedings and debt settlements with the state.[64]

Other large public projects also left traces of corruption for posterity. One involved the public contracting for the building and administration of dock facilities and customs in the port of Callao, the Muelle y Dársena, initially for a period of sixty years, and an exclusive privilege of ten years in the loading and unloading of vessels. The Chamber of Deputies granted the contract to the firm Templeman, Bergman & Company in August 1869, despite the company's limited capital resources and strong public opposition to the deal that was expected to increase port costs for import-export merchants. The heads of the company, brothers Charles and Frederick Bergman, who were brothers-in-law of Auguste Dreyfus, had bribed, among others, a minister to secure the contract with the clear intention of transferring the concession to a big European concern a soon as possible. In 1874, the Bergmans and Dreyfus completed their speculation by selling their rights to the Société Générale. The Parisian company took control of Callao's pier and dock works, resulting in delays causing high costs to commerce and the public, and proceeded to charge high fees that were opposed by users of the port facilities.[65]

---

64. Stewart, *Henry Meiggs,* 236, 238–40; Ramos, *Historia del Derecho* 3:273–74.

65. Reporting on a courtesy visit of the then former minister of government, Rafael Velarde, to Frederick Bergman, Witt noted that "in order to secure [Velarde's] good will in the Muelle Dársena question [when Velarde was still minister, Bergman] had named a *pagaré* in his favor for a pretty large amount." Witt, "Diary," March 9, 1870, vol. 7, 149. See also July 20, 1869, January 6 and November 6, 1871, vol. 7, 93–94, 220, 291. Dreyfus was married to Sofía Bergman who died in Lima in 1871. Basadre, *Historia* 6:230. Márquez, *Orjía financiera,* 80–81. E. J. Casanave, *El contrato Galup-Dársena*

Another onerous project, the protracted construction of a government building, the Palacio de la Exposición, and surrounding park and zoo, triggered another scandal in Lima due to the unexpected high cost of approximately two million soles between 1869 and 1872. In an attempt to emulate fashionable European exhibitions, this extravagant project was under the supervision of the old caudillo Vivanco and lawyer Manuel Atanasio Fuentes who was suspected of pocketing part of the project's funds. This affair, as well as the purchase of warships in the United States supervised by Judge Mariano Alvarez (who was accused of personally profiting from the transaction), brought about serious friction between Balta and Piérola.[66] A few years later, a parliamentarian of liberal ideology wrote the ultimate epitaph for the period: "Peru ceased being a nation of citizens to become a society of dealers: corruption infiltrated all its pores."[67]

Moving toward Default

The 1872 presidential elections were clearly won by Manuel Pardo, the highly popular leader sustained by his modern Partido Civil. Just before the transfer of power, a military coup led by the corrupt and ruthless Gutiérrez brothers—Colonels Silvestre, Marceliano, Tomás, and Marcelino Gutiérrez —ousted and assassinated their former patron President Balta. In response, people in the streets butchered three of the coup's ringleaders. Pardo was subsequently inaugurated as the constitutionally elected president. In his first public message to Congress in September 1872, Pardo was blunt: The guano bonanza would turn into a nightmare if drastic measures were not adopted. Revenues from guano sales were entirely committed to servicing

---

en sus relaciones con los intereses fiscales (Lima: Tipografía Industrial, 1886), 9–10, 75. "Note sur l'affaire du Muelle Darsena," in file "Travaux publis. Môle Darsena 1881–1890," Affaires Diverses Politiques (ADP), Pérou, vol. 2, AMAE.

66. Witt, "Diary," March 24, 1871, June 27, 1871, and July 1, 1872, vol. 7, 244, 263, 343. Earlier public accusations of dishonesty against Fuentes (a.k.a. El Murciélago after his satiric publication) were countered by a libel suit. "Manuel Atanasio Fuentes contra José Toribio Polo por el artículo 'Murciegalografía'," 1863, Abuso de Libertad de Imprenta, Corte Superior de Justicia, leg. 716, AGN. See also Basadre, *Historia* 6:231–34; Ramos, *Historia del Derecho* 3:83; Márquez, *Orjía financiera,* 56.

67. José María Quimper, *Manifiesto del ex-Ministro de Hacienda y Comercio: J. M. Quimper, a la Nación* (Lima: Imprenta F. Masías e Hijo, 1881), cited by Alberto Tauro del Pino in his introduction to Quimper's *El principio de libertad* (Lima: Ediciones Hora del Hombre, 1948), 11.

the foreign debt. The fiscal deficit had to be financed by new export and other indirect taxes. Pardo also proposed fiscal savings through reform and decentralizing measures.[68]

All this echoed the lamentations of a prominent businessman, "What good use has been given to those millions and millions of dollars provided by guano? Almost none for the country itself! Private concerns have been enriched and much money has been spent in gunpowder, bullets, cannons, rifles, swords, and ironclad warships."[69] To well-informed foreign observers, the lavish expenditures under the Balta administration had left the national treasury in a most lamentable state notwithstanding guano and customs revenues. Questionable public works of all sorts had been granted "to maintain [the government's] popularity"; the costly railways were "premature, to say the least."[70] Under the weight of excessive public debt, chronic fiscal deficits amounted to more than 20 million soles annually.[71] According to a critical yet revealing journalistic assessment, the *dreyfuistas* had pledged the nation's credit for an entire generation, sold the last speck of guano, built railways "to the moon" among other monumental works, and distributed public works contracts among themselves through the farce of public tender, leaving practically nothing for succeeding governments. The transition from the government of Balta-Dreyfus to Pardo's was the transition from the scandal of "pestilent corruption to notable purity."[72]

Pardo was considered a "real reformist" in line with his earlier policy as minister of finance in the 1860s. He spearheaded an earnest effort at reforming public financial and state administration in order to build institutional stability.[73] As early as November 1872, Pardo engaged in a thorough

68. "President Pardo and the Nation, Financial Conditions of Peru: Inaugural Message Delivered to Congress," *South Pacific Times*, September 28, 1872, in Despatches 1826–1906, roll 25, USNA. Thomas Francis to Fish, Lima, October 21, 1872, in U.S. Department of State, *Papers Relating to the Foreign Relations of the United States* (Washington, DC: Government Printing Office, 1873), 2:745–46. See also Basadre, *Historia*, 7:7–13; Mc Evoy, *Proyecto nacional*, chapter 3.

69. Witt, *Diario* (1992), 2:140, comment written in 1871 and inserted in an earlier diary entry.

70. Jerningham to Granville, Lima, September 24, 1872, FO 61/272, ff. 187–89v, esp. 187, NAUK.

71. Henry Bellemois to M.A.E. Duc de Broglie, Lima, September 15, 1873, CP, Pérou, Supplément vol. 2, ff. 122–27, esp. 125v, AMAE.

72. La Opinión Nacional, *Lo que se ve y lo que no se ve: ojeado sobre los principales actos del gobierno civil (editoriales de "La Opinión Nacional")* (Lima: Imprenta La Opinión Nacional, 1874), 5–8, 10.

73. Jerningham to Granville, Lima, December 11, 1872, FO 61/272, ff. 226–27; Lima, May 10, 1873, FO 61/277, ff. 120–22v, NAUK.

reorganization of the army, reducing its size and military expenses while expanding professional instruction through the establishment of military and naval schools. Many officers were separated from active duty, while a new national guard recruited civilians to ensure public order. Likewise, the overall bureaucracy, the nest of corrupt patronage, was downsized, especially the venal customs administration where personnel numbers were reduced and salaries increased to minimize corruption and smuggling. Pardo's fiscal decentralization and administrative reform raised the banner of the struggle against public corruption through constitutional means. During Pardo's administration, corrupt practices were uncovered in the national treasury. Congress held hearings and debates on constitutional charges against several of Balta's former ministers. However, this anticorruption drive in Congress was unable to muster a majority that could impose punitive actions. Pardo's reform platform for his "practical republic" included increased public investment in primary education, reaffirming the conviction that human capacities could be enhanced through instruction and the practice of local self-rule.[74]

These reformist efforts were opposed by those seeking a return to conditions favorable to corrupt wealth accumulation and power. Disaffected army officers separated from active service brewed deep resentment against Pardo and were at the center of plots against his life. Religious zealots joined the opposition in defense of traditions that they felt Pardo was attacking, especially concerning public education. On August 22, 1874, a failed assassination attempt against Pardo in Lima's central square involved disgruntled Captain Juan Boza and other army officers. The refrain, "Long live religion, and death to Pardo," was heard at the scene. Conspiracies multiplied during Pardo's regime that was, however, remarkably resilient thanks to popular support in Lima and faithful leadership in the regular army, navy, and national guard.[75]

Among Pardo's most outspoken and violent foes was Nicolás de Piérola, now a civilian caudillo who benefited from conservative and corrupt opposition to Pardo. In 1872, Piérola defended his actions as minister before a legislature unable to prove forcefully his administrative corruption. Thereafter, Piérola was involved in armed conspiracies raising the banner of a necessary war against the establishment. In December 1872, Bogardus, Piérola's faithful supporter and Pardo's archenemy, devised a plot to blow

74. Basadre, *Historia* 6:381–82; 7:81, 99, 112; Márquez, *Orjía financiera*, 82–84.

75. Thomas to Fish, Lima, August 27, 1874, in U. S. Department of State, *Papers Relating to Foreign Relations of the United States* (1875), 2:991–93.

up the train in which Pardo was traveling to Chorrillos. In 1874, Bogardus invested about 60,000 soles in Liverpool to purchase the ship *Talisman* and 2,000 rifles. Commanded by Piérola himself, the *Talisman* expedition created havoc in the north and south of Peru, spilling over to Arequipa in 1875 before being defeated by Pardo and his naval and military forces. A permanent conspirator, Piérola cultivated the art of political uprisings and military adventures. His financial and political backers included Dionisio Derteano, Juan Martín Echenique, Guillermo Billinghurst, the Chilean Barahona, and of course, Dreyfus, who expected handsome paybacks once Piérola succeeded in capturing power.[76]

Pardo initially confronted Dreyfus and Meiggs over contractual legal matters and illegal fees charged, but was unable to immediately free the Peruvian treasury from their hold. The country's foreign debt had to be serviced, the state urgently needed revenues, local business was starved for bills of exchange, and the railway works had to be continued or otherwise risk domestic upheaval with the discharge of approximately twenty thousand railway workers. Continued financial arrangements with both Dreyfus and Meiggs were inevitable during the first years of monetary and financial crisis endured by the Pardo administration. Two new accords with Dreyfus guaranteed a fixed monthly income and service of the public debt. In April 1874, Pardo secured the bases for the ultimate liquidation of the Dreyfus contract.[77]

However, Dreyfus fought back with tenacity. As a matter of fact, Dreyfus now counted on the political favor of his former lawyer Jules Grévy, president of the French National Assembly (and later president of the French Republic from 1879 to 1887), who made a special recommendation on behalf of Dreyfus to the French mission in Lima. In September 1873, the French attaché feared that the Peruvian government's "campagne contre la maison Dreyfus" could have disastrous consequences to French interests in Peru, and that the French government might have to intervene.[78] In March

76. Thomas to Fish, Lima, October 27 and November 13, 1874, U.S. Department of State, *Papers Relating to Foreign Relations of the United States* (1875), 2:993–94; Basadre, *Historia* 6:401–7.

77. Evidence of Dreyfus's public relations campaign against the Pardo administration appears in *Exposición que la Casa Dreyfus Hermanos y Compañía hace ante la sana opinión pública del Perú sobre su manejo de los negocios fiscales del Perú* (Lima: Imprenta La Patria, 1873). See also Basadre, *Historia* 7:13, 23.

78. Bellemois to M.A.E. Duc de Broglie, Lima, September 20, 1873, CP, Pérou, Supplément vol. 2, 168–73v, esp. 168v, AMAE: "je rappellerai en passant que M. Dreyfus a été spécialement recommandé aux bons offices de la légation de France sur la demande de M. Grévy alors Président de l' Assemblée Nationale (D. Com. No. 9.118bre

1876, the Peruvian envoy to London, General Mariano Ignacio Prado, signed a new guano sales contract with the merchant bank Raphael & Sons and Peruvian capitalists Carlos Gonzales Candamo and Arturo Heeren, who formed the Peruvian Guano Company. Dreyfus resisted the moves to dislodge him from the guano monopoly, and declared open war on the Peruvian government that entailed costly litigation in London and Paris. As a consequence, this conflict with Dreyfus accentuated Lima's inability to service the foreign debt, a de facto default that affected the country's credit abroad and intensified the monetary and economic crisis in Peru in the midst of an international economic recession.[79]

The combined internal pressure exerted by Piérola, along with foreign financial and political pressure stirred by Dreyfus, limited the actions that President Pardo could take to disentangle the state's financial quandary. Under such circumstances, and under pressure from Congress, Pardo pursued a policy of increased taxation and eventual expropriation of the nitrate fields in Tarapacá as a means to resolving fiscal problems. This proved Pardo's one major mistake, since this nitrate strategy netted less income than expected and failed to halt the competition between guano and nitrate prices. The official assessments for expropriation and speculation with nitrate certificates issued as compensation to owners opened new avenues for corruption.[80] Moreover, higher nitrate taxes and expropriation triggered the militant opposition of Peruvian (Guillermo Billinghurst), Chilean, and British (Gibbs & Company) interests linked to the nitrate business.

In order to finance such nitrate measures and the increasing deficit, Pardo also made the mistake of relying on the weakened and unethical Peruvian banks. Public perception considered the local banks as the offspring of the guano age's excesses. The monetary crisis of 1872–1873 and increasing fiscal needs inclined the government to decree that banks had to guarantee their issues of paper money with public debt. Thereafter, the state increased its intervention in the banking system, a tendency that García Calderón criticized.[81] In August and September 1875, the perilous fates of the banks and

1872)." On Grévy's undue influence as Dreyfus's lawyer in the legal suits between the Peruvian government and Dreyfus Frères et Cie. in Paris, see also Márquez, *Orjía financiera,* 95.

79. Basadre, *Historia* 7:23, 28–29; Márquez, *Orjía financiera,* 86–87.

80. Basadre, *Historia* 7:290; Márquez, *Orjía financiera,* 103–20.

81. Francisco García Calderón, "Legislación en materia de bancos," in *El Comercio,* December 30–31, 1873, cited in Basadre, *Introducción a las bases documentales* 1:450. See also Francisco García Calderón, *Estudios sobre el Banco de Crédito Hipote-*

the state were linked together: the banks offered loans to the government and the depreciating bank notes were declared obligatory currency. This and previous banking measures contributed to mismanagement by leading banks, including internal borrowing for their own private concerns (Banco del Perú), clandestine or illegal issues of paper money (Dreyfus's Banco Nacional, Banco Garantizador), and outright fraud and embezzlement (Banco de la Providencia managed by Domingo Porras).[82] The bankers' collaboration with the government in the commercialization of nitrates and other credit and monetary arrangements obstructed the necessary bankruptcy of the least efficient banks that in turn undermined the entire banking and credit system at the eve of the War of the Pacific.

Ignominy in War

During General Mariano Ignacio Prado's elected government (1876–1879), former president Pardo, acting then as head of the Senate, was assassinated as he was being greeted by a military detachment at the entrance of the congressional building. A member of the saluting group, Sergeant Melchor Montoya, used his rifle to shoot Pardo at short range. The *civilista* leader had been targeted by military conspirators in retaliation for military promotions reform being discussed in Congress. Angry opponents had finally succeeded in killing Pardo after several previous attempts staged by *pierolistas* and their military and conservative allies. Pardo was expected to return to power at the end of Prado's presidency. Thus was the career of a true reformer cut short by forces resisting necessary restructuring of institutional conditions that nurture corruption.

Piérola continued to conspire against Prado with the staunch support of Juan Martín Echenique, Bogardus, and Colonel Federico Larrañaga. They were behind the serious insubordination aboard the warship *Huáscar* that

---

cario y las leyes de hipotecas (Lima: Imprenta J. M. Noriega, 1868); Carlos Camprubí, *Historia de los bancos en el Perú (1860–1879)* (Lima: Editorial Lumen, 1959), 177; Márquez, *Orjía financiera,* 59.

82. Camprubí, *Historia de los Bancos,* 300–301, 393–94; Banco de la Providencia, *Exposición que hacen al público, a los tribunales, al supremo gobierno, el directorio y accionistas* (Lima: Imprenta de El Comercio, 1868), 2–6; Márquez, *Orjía financiera,* 90. See also Alfonso Quiroz, *Domestic and Foreign Finance in Modern Peru, 1850–1950: Financing Visions of Development* (Pittsburgh, PA: Macmillan and University of Pittsburgh Press, 1993), 28–30.

shook the regime in 1877 and caused considerable monetary expense just prior to the war with Chile. Dreyfus continued to compete with the Peruvian Guano Company and disputed in court the financial settlement demanded by the Peruvian government. In this complicated financial international scenario, four major interests were at play: the Peruvian government (represented by fiscal commissioners José Araníbar and Emilio Althaus), the foreign debt bondholders, Dreyfus, and the Peruvian Guano Company. The latter ceased to service the foreign debt in January 1879, the second de facto default in three years. During the war, the Peruvian Guano Company also stopped payments to the Peruvian government and, together with a committee of British holders of Peruvian debt bonds, preferred to deal directly with Chile.

Strained diplomatic relations with Chile over Bolivian taxation policies in the nitrate region of Atacama, and a secret defensive alliance between Peru and Bolivia, were the main alleged factors that unleashed the War of the Pacific (1879–1883). The Peruvian government's foreign debt default increased its isolation from sources of international credit and diplomatic support. Obtaining funds and credit for national defense grew ever more difficult.[83] Only a few interested merchant houses risked aiding the beleaguered Peruvian government in purchasing badly needed arms abroad. Most prominent among them was Grace Brothers & Company, a medium-sized firm with a strategic international organization backed by an initial capitalization in Peru since the 1850s during the early guano bonanza. Their very profitable business evolved from ship chandlers, based in the Chincha guano islands and the port of Callao, to wholesale importers servicing prominent clients (including Dreyfus), brokers for Peruvian navy ordnance materiel (as early as 1869 during Balta's administration), suppliers of pine lumber for Meiggs's railway projects, creditors of sugar estate owners, and guano and nitrate consignees and speculators supported financially by Baring Brothers & Company of London. The head of the company, William R. Grace, married an American woman and eventually moved to New York where he became the first Irish Catholic mayor (1881–1882) supported by the Democratic Party machine. A younger brother, Michael P. Grace, left in

---

83. Heraclio Bonilla, *Un siglo a la deriva: ensayos sobre el Perú, Bolivia y la guerra* (Lima: Instituto de Estudios Peruanos, 1980), chapters 4 and 5; Alfonso Quiroz, "Las actividades comerciales y financieras de la casa Grace y la Guerra del Pacífico," *Histórica* 7 (1983): 214–54 (based on "Trade and Financial Aspects of the War of the Pacific, 1879–1890," master's thesis, Columbia University, 1981).

charge of the Peruvian business, later developed his own emporium based in London.[84]

The Graces and their associates had endeavored to develop friendly relationships with the highest Peruvian authorities over the years. They had personal correspondence with President Prado concerning, among other private and official business prospects, the purchase of purebred horses, and guano and nitrate deals. Grace Brothers & Company also acted as Prado's private commercial creditors in 1879. In turn, Prado granted Grace guano and nitrate consignment contracts for U.S. and British markets, and permission to act as Peru's financial agent in New York and San Francisco. Upon these personal and official bases, Grace also profited handsomely from the trade of U.S.-manufactured rifles, carbines, cartridges, torpedoes, and torpedo boats supplied to the Peruvian armed forces during the war.[85] Business and financial interests placed the Grace network squarely on the side of Peru throughout its war with Chile. The company also used its important financial, print media, and political influence in the United States to lobby for a U.S. diplomatic policy favorable to their guano and nitrate interests at stake in the War of the Pacific.[86]

From the start of the war, Peru's naval and military defeat was almost guaranteed due to Chile's superior naval and army forces and well-developed international network of support. After the first lost battles, President Prado decided to leave the country in the middle of the war to avowedly purchase badly needed war equipment abroad. This was a serious mistake thoroughly criticized for generations to come and, according to some witnesses, perhaps induced by illness or fear for his life under the growing threat of Piérola's insurrectionary movement.[87] The opportunistic Piérola

---

84. "Incoming letters and documents to W. R. Grace, New York," box 9, letter binder, no. 51, and box 10, no. 52, W. R. Grace & Co. Papers, Rare Books and Manuscript Library, Columbia University (hereafter WRGP). Detailed institutional evolution appears in Lawrence A. Clayton, *Grace: W. R. Grace & Co.: The Formative Years 1850–1930* (Ottawa, IL: Jameson Books, 1985), esp. chapters 3–4, and Marquis James, *Merchant Adventurer: The Story of W. R. Grace* (Wilmington, DE: SR Books, 1993).

85. Six letters from Prado to W. R. Grace, May 19 to December 22, 1876, "Catalogued correspondence," WRGP. See Quiroz, "Actividades comerciales," 232–33; and C. Alexander G. de Secada, "Arms, Guano, and Shipping: The W. R. Grace Interests in Peru, 1865–1885," *Business History Review* 59 (1985): 597–621.

86. For a few of many examples of the Grace company "lobbying," see M. P. Grace to Grace Bros. & Co. (Lima), New York, December 1, 1881, relating conversations on Grace's imperiled nitrate claims with Assistant Secretary of State and President Chester Arthur in Washington, box 57, no. 152, ff. 175–177, WRGP.

87. Spenser St. John to Salisbury, Lima, December 22, 1879, no. 175, FO 61/319,

staged a coup and took control of the government. He denigrated Prado as a coward and thief of national funds. Piérola's dictatorial government, however, continued to purchase very expensive and sometimes defective weapons and munitions from Grace Brothers & Company and other providers.[88] As a result of these business connections, Piérola became a good friend of M. P. Grace, with whom he participated in a regular and surprisingly candid correspondence.[89]

Piérola's dictatorship imposed damaging financial decisions that accelerated the inevitable military defeat. Of course, one of his administration's first measures was to restore Dreyfus as Peru's main financial agent and creditor abroad, which violated existing financial arrangements with other companies. A decree signed by Piérola and his finance minister Manuel Antonio Barinaga in November 1880, also recognized all past accounting claims of the French house against Peru. Despite a previous 1878 resolution establishing that Dreyfus in fact owed 657,387 soles, the sweeping total debt to Dreyfus that Piérola recognized amounted to almost 17 million soles (£3.2 million).[90] With these actions, Piérola was clearly rewarding Dreyfus's political support and financial backing. The legal suits triggered by this highly controversial decree lasted for decades.

Piérola also canceled the Rosas-Goyeneche contract with Dreyfus's competitor, the Crédit Industriel, representing French, Belgian, and Dutch bondholders that promised resources to wage the war. Piérola lashed out against the negotiators of that and other arrangement abroad by confiscating the properties of Francisco Rosas and Juan M. Goyeneche in Peru. Many other persons critical of Piérola's financial policies were also imprisoned and threatened.[91] Moreover, Piérola devised the cancellation of for-

---

ff. 315–16v, NAUK: "I have ever thought General Prado to be totally unworthy of his position: on every great occasion he has shewn a lamentable want of personal courage . . . [His] financial reputation . . . is on par with that of his courage: he is accused by all parties of the worst system of spoliation."

88. W. R. Grace to Piérola's minister of war, April 29, 1880, box 56, no. 148, f. 400, WRGP.

89. Quiroz, "Actividades comerciales," 234, based on M. P. Grace, private correspondence, boxes 57–59, WRGP.

90. J. A. Miró Quesada, "Exposición . . . sobre los antecedentes de las reclamaciones de la casa de Dreyfus Hermano & Cia," Lima, September 22, 1890, vol. 3, Archivo Piérola, BNP.

91. Expropriating Rosas and Goyeneche, a "mesure violente et arbitraire cause ici une grande excitation et il est à craindre qu'elle n'achève de ruiner le crédit du Pérou en Europe. Mais Mr. Pierola qui a, dit-on, des intérêts personnels dans la maison Dreyfus,

eign debts with a bold transfer of national railway properties to foreign debt bondholders, who rejected the offer and dealt directly with Chile. Piérola's monetary policy exacerbated the financial crisis and inflation.[92] All these measures were "marked by ignorance or dishonesty," and the new contracts with Dreyfus were seen as disastrous and corrupt since most observers believed that Piérola participated in the profits.[93]

Piérola's strategy to defend Lima from Chilean invading forces was thoroughly inept, led by politically appointed officers of the reserve army such as Juan Martín Echenique. In their escape from the Chilean army advancing on Lima, Piérola's incompetent officers neglected to destroy sensitive and confidential information that fell into Chilean hands. Such information revealed, among other things, Piérola's foreign policy and his strained relationship with the British minister in Peru.[94]

In the middle of extreme crisis, Piérola found excellent opportunities to misappropriate and loot funds destined to the national defense.[95] No official accounts and records were ever submitted to justify withdrawals and expenses of between 95 and 130 million soles under Piérola's year-long dictatorship: An official investigation carried out a few years later found that there were extreme irregularities under Piérola's administration of public funds and expenses during the war but no sanction was ever imposed.[96] This careless and corrupt use of public funds in the middle of the war was justified as im-

ne veut entendre parler d'aucun arrangement que ne soit avec cette maison": Des Vorges a M.A.E. Freycinet, Lima, February 25, 1880, no. 6, CP, Pérou, Supplément vol. 2 (1869–1880: Guanos), ff. 327–28, AMAE.

92. Juan M. de Goyeneche y Gamio, *Los arreglos del dictador y el contrato Rosas-de Goyeneche* (Paris: A. Chaix et Cie., 1880), 8; Francisco Rosas, *La verdad sobre el contrato Rosas-Goyeneche y sobre los contratos Piérola-Dreyfus* (Paris: Imprenta Hispano-Americana, 1881); Rougemont, *Una pájina,* 28–29.

93. Spenser St. John to Marquis of Salisbury, Lima, January 21, 1880, and February 25, 1880, FO 61/235, ff. 37–40, and ff. 65–68v, NAUK.

94. Vallés to M.E., Lima, February 12, 1881, no. 30, H-1676, AGMAE.

95. The most graphic indictment of Piérola's corruption and military ineptitude during his dictatorship is Rougemont, *Una pájina,* a source bluntly dismissed as calumnious by Basadre (*Introducción a las bases documentales* 2:539), despite the French author's unique information as a former member of Piérola's inner circle. Rougemont points out the contradiction between Piérola's self-proclamation of protector of religion, morals, and family, and his administrative and moral corruption involving concubine Madame Garreaud née LeBlanc: "Nunca, en ninguna época después de la independencia han imperado en más vasta escala el prevaricato y el cohecho. Hasta la querida misma instaló una oficina en la calle del Tigre en que puso a remate los favores de S.E.," 49.

96. Report dated June 30, 1884, by "comisión investigadora y calificadora" led by

perative actions to "save" and "defend" the motherland. The practical results of Piérola's deeds were quite the opposite of salvation and successful defense.

Fleeing to the interior of the country, Piérola continued to subject various villages and towns to expropriations that served mainly his own dwindling political fortunes. He appointed three major regional political chiefs to head his movement: Pedro A. del Solar (south), Juan Martín Echenique (center), and Lizardo Montero (north). Soon political dissent among many Peruvian warring factions created conditions of civil and class warfare under conditions of foreign occupation and oppression.[97] After a "private and confidential" understanding reached with Chilean occupation authorities, and with their consent, Piérola finally left the country in March 1882. He went directly to exile in Paris, where his friend Dreyfus's purse and hospitality supported him in yet another campaign to recapture power when conditions permitted.[98] At the time, Michael P. Grace also wrote to an associate that Piérola "has always proved himself a valuable friend, and will probably [be] in a position to do so again."[99] Moreover, at Piérola's request Grace furnished him "loans" in recognition of past "services" and with the interested expectation that the former dictator would become president again.[100] (Grace had already developed "evident Chilean propensities" and opened a company branch in Valparaíso.[101]) This pattern of corrupt means

---

Joaquín Torrico, cited in Basadre, *Historia* 9:36. Torrico tried to divert blame onto Quimper and Prado. See also J. M. Quimper, *Exposición a los hombres de bien* (Lima: N.p., 1880), and Basadre, *Historia* 8:252–53.

97. Vallés to M.E., Lima, October 4, 1881, no. 150, H-1676, AGMAE; J. P. Christiancy to W. M. Evarts, Lima, January 22, 1881, no. 230, Despatches 1826–1906, roll 35, USNA: "The Chileans, I feel quite sure would have treated [Piérola] kindly, and recognized him as the only government with which they could treat for peace." See also Christiancy to Evarts, Lima, February 2, 1881, no. 237, and March 16, 1881, no. 256, Despatches 1826–1906, roll 35, USNA.

98. Rougemont, *Una pájina,* 22, 26. Vallés to M.E., Lima, November 22, 1881, no. 175, H-1676, AGMAE: "Llegada de Piérola al Departamento de Lima . . . tiene entendimientos con autoridades chilenas de carácter privado y confidencial." A. de Pont to M.A.E, Lima, April 5, 1882, no. 16, CP, Pérou, vol. 54, ff. 92–92v, AMAE: "En abandonnant Lima dans un moment aussi critique . . . n'a-t-il pas préféré venir en Europe, intéresser peut-être a son propre sort, et attendre que les événements se dénouement?"

99. M. P. Grace to Edward Eyre, November 10, 1882, box 58, no. 153, f. 176, WRGP.

100. M. P. Grace to E. Eyre, New York, August 27, 1884, box 58, no. 155, f. 292, WRGP.

101. Stephen A. Hurlbut to S.S. James Blaine, New York, June 30, 1881, unofficial, Despatches 1826–1906, roll 36, USNA, reporting a meeting with Michael P. Grace just before Hurlbut's trip to Peru.

to obtain political power at any cost, including illegal subsidies by foreign interests, became a lasting tradition in Peruvian politics.

Compounded Losses

In 1882, Lima was a "ville complètement ruinée," with commerce at a standstill, and its population and business and property owners exposed to cruel abuses and destructive reprisals and levies by the Chilean occupiers.[102] As a means to press their annexationist territorial demands, the Chilean army destroyed properties and exacted compulsory contributions in much the same way as the earlier military caudillos in the turbulent past. In the ashes of defeat, the Peruvian elite coalesced around Francisco García Calderón, who was appointed provisional president of Peru under the Chilean occupation. Chilean authorities thought that the captive government of Magdalena, named for the town just outside Lima where García Calderón conducted his official business, would satisfy their demands. Instead, García Calderón's token administration defended Peruvian property owners against Chilean despoliation, reestablished the constitution of 1860, consulted a nominal legislature, and criticized Piérola's dictatorial ambitions.[103] García Calderón used his precarious position to develop an intelligent strategy for rejecting territorial concessions to Chile, unite Peruvian political leaders, and gain diplomatic support from the United States. If someone could have pulled off such feats, it would have been the experienced and deft lawyer and negotiator who had contributed in the past to legal and constitutional reform in Peru.

To the alarm of Chilean authorities and Spanish diplomats acting as mediators, the U.S. envoy extraordinary and plenipotentiary minister to Peru, Civil War general and Republican diplomat Stephen A. Hurlbut, engaged in detailed negotiations with García Calderón to press for accepting payment of a financial indemnity to Chile rather than ceding territory. Hurlbut developed this "firm and temperate" strategy following general instructions from U.S. Secretary of State James Blaine, who approved this interventionist approach toward the conflict, based on the Monroe Doctrine and Amer-

102. Tallenay to M.A.E., Lima, September 19, 1882, no. 24, CP Pérou, vol. 54, f. 272, AMAE; Vallés to M.E., Lima, January 30, 1881, no. 19, and June 14, 1881, no. 94, H-1676, AGMAE.

103. *Mensaje de S. E. el Presidente Provisorio de la República Dr. D. Francisco García Calderón al Congreso Extraordinario de 1881* (Lima: Edición Oficial, 1881), 5–6.

ican interests on the west coast of South America, to counteract the British-backed power of Chile in the Pacific.[104] Urging union among Peruvian factions, Hurlbut and Blaine openly rejected any deal with former dictator Piérola, who had led Peru to defeat and was trying desperately to undermine García Calderón's government.[105] Several European powers with interests in the region, most notably Spain due to its stakes in colonial Cuba, endeavored to curb U.S. intervention in the tense international situation.

On September 20, 1881, Hurlbut obtained an important concession signed by García Calderón: According to a four-point protocol, Peru would grant the United States the indefinite right (subject to cancellation with a one-year notice) to establish a coal-fueling and naval station in the port and harbor of Chimbote. Hurlbut wrote to Blaine that he regretted not getting more out of the agreement, but remarked that the Chimbote concession was a valuable foothold that could later become more exclusive in a jurisdictional sense.[106]

The Chilean authorities and press, alerted by the British and Spanish ministers in Lima who were opposed to the Chimbote protocol, exaggerated the ramifications of this protocol, calling it a "secret treaty" and spreading biased news of U.S. intentions of annexation or establishment of a pro-

104. Hurlbut to Blaine, Lima, August 10, 1881, no. 2, Despatches 1826–1906, roll 36, USNA: "The forcible annexation of territory ought not to be allowed. By such action on the part of our government, we would gain the highest influence in South America, we should subserve the purpose of a true civilization, and inaugurate a higher style of national and international law on this continent." See also Hurlbut to Blaine, Lima, August 24, 1881, no. 6, and October 26, 1881, no. 23, Despatches 1826–1906, rolls 36 and 37, USNA. Hurlbut also consulted and obtained important information from José María Quimper, "one of the strongest intellects" in Peru and supporter of the García Calderón government. Hurlbut to Blaine, Lima, September 14, 1881, enclosing letter of Quimper to Blaine, Lima, September 14, 1881, Despatches 1826–1906, roll 36, USNA. The American strategy was also contemplated by Hurlbut's predecessor who believed that a peace settlement could "only be secured by active intervention in some form, against the will of the Chilean government." Christiancy to Blaine, Lima, March 21, 1881, no. 262, confidential, and May 4, 1881, personal and confidential, Despatches 1826–1906, rolls 35 and 36, USNA.

105. Hurlbut to Aurelio García y García (Piérola's chief of staff), Lima, September 12, 1881, attached to dispatch of Vallés to M.E., Lima, September 19, 1881, no. 141; and Lima, November 22, 1881, no. 176, H-1676, AGMAE. See also Hurlbut to Blaine, Lima, September 13, 1881, no. 11, enclosing original letter to García y García (enclosure no. 2), Despatches 1826–1906, roll 36, USNA.

106. Hurlbut's dispatch published in Washington and translated into Spanish, in Vallés to M.E., Lima, March 2, 1882, no. 48, H-1677, AGMAE. The original "Protocol for cession of naval station and coaling station at Chimbote" enclosed in handwritten dispatch Hurlbut to Blaine, Lima, October 5, 1881, no. 19, Despatches 1826–1906, roll 37, USNA.

tectorate.[107] Blaine and Hurlbut were also allegedly linked to colossal speculation on the basis of doubtful Franco-American claims (Cochet, Landreau) against Peru, in alleged coordination with the Crédit Industriel. This
syndicate claimed the right to exploit the guano and nitrate deposits of the
occupied Peruvian province of Tarapacá to pay the Chilean government a
financial indemnity.[108] Even French President Grévy was allegedly involved in this plan according to press reports in New York and Chile.[109] Although partly based on facts, such reports were largely triggered by unfounded allegations fueled in part by the campaign of New York lawyer
Jacob Shipherd, head of the "Peruvian Company" syndicate, who was lobbying for a U.S. protectorate over Peru to enforce a multimillion settlement
of the Cochet and Landreau speculative claims.[110]

The protocol signed by Hurlbut and García Calderón contained a major
flaw that prompted its rejection in the United States: Hurlbut had been assigned as the temporary legal holder of the concession, which raised suspicions of conflicts of interest with his official duties. Hurlbut received an en-
crypted telegram from Blaine himself warning about possible improper
actions.[111] The protocol was subsequently rejected by the U.S. government.
While preparing for his imminent departure from Lima to face a congres-

107. Vallés to M.E., Lima, December 13, 1881, no. 191, and November 30, 1881,
no. 179, H-1676, AGMAE. On the "singularly and indecorously" unacceptable behavior of British Minister Spenser St. John, see Hurlbut to Blaine, Lima, December 7, 1881,
no. 32, and December 11, 1881, no. 33, Despatches 1826–1906, roll 37, USNA.

108. Vallés to M.E., Lima, December 6, 1881, no. 185, and Lima, December 29, 1881,
no. 206, H-1676, AGMAE; "Affaire Landreau (Jean Théophile)," ADP, Pérou 1836–1895,
vol. 2, AMAE; José G. Rivadeneyra, *Breves observaciones sobre los derechos de Cochet
y Landreau a propósito de la gran compañía Americana destinada a explotar el Perú* (Valparaíso: N.p., 1882). Blaine was accused of having personal interests in a syndicate negotiated in Paris through Levi P. Morton, Blaine's envoy, who had direct business interests in the deal being worked out with Crédit Industriel. These charges were not proven.

109. "Exterior: Dreyfus i el Crédito Industrial," *El Comercio* (Santiago de Chile),
article translated from *The Sun* (New York), March 20, 1882, attached to dispatch A. de
Pont to M.A.E., Lima, May 14, 1882, no. 26, CP, Pérou, vol. 54, ff. 133–34, AMAE:
"fait intervenir la haute personnalité de Mr. Grévy." Vallés to M.E., March 18, 1882, no.
61, AGMAE: Accepting as true President Grévy's intervention and criticizing the
"política mercenaria e interesada de Mr. Blaine queriendo quitarle a Chile sus derechos
de conquista, no en beneficio del Perú sino para apropiárselos, una política invasora . . .
de dominación en el Pacífico."

110. Hurlbut to Blaine, Lima, November 2, 1881, no. 25, and December 28, 1881,
no. 39, Despatches 1826–1906, roll 37, USNA, enclosing copious and revealing letters
penned by Shipherd, author of "infinite mischief" and charges of conspiracy against U.S.
diplomats.

111. "Influence of your position must not be used in aid of Credit Industriel or any

sional inquiry in Washington, D.C., Hurlbut suffered what appeared to be a heart attack (angina pectoris) and died in late March 1882.[112]

Blaine's interventionist strategy radically changed following the death of Republican President James Garfield (leader of the more liberal Republican "half-breed" faction). The new president, Chester Arthur (a Republican "stalwart") appointed conservative F. T. Frelinghuysen to replace Blaine as secretary of state in late December 1881. U.S. envoys were now instructed to press for the acceptance of Peruvian territorial concessions as a requirement for a peace treaty between Peru and Chile.[113] Consequently, the prestige of U.S. policy in the region suffered, according to a Spanish envoy, due to its vacillations, mistakes, "ineptitude and highly questionable honorableness" of its diplomatic agents.[114]

Michael P. Grace, who had similarly criticized Washington's erratic diplomatic policy,[115] now recognized the need for territorial concession and so he wrote in his letters to the exiled former dictator Piérola.[116] One of Piérola's close political associate and former ministers, General Miguel Iglesias, took heed of the opportunity offered by Chilean authorities and foreign diplomats and businessmen to sign the peace treaty of Ancón that surrendered a huge part of Peruvian territory to Chile.

Despite the ultimate failure of García Calderón's negotiations, doomed and tainted by the influence of foreign interests and enormous pressures, his efforts laid the bases of constitutional reconstruction at the end of the war. He offered an alternative to that of self-serving caudillo Piérola and more in line with the reformist civilian options opened by Manuel Pardo since the late 1860s. After García Calderón's return from exile, imposed by Chilean authorities, the ultimate conciliating negotiator of public and private inter-

---

other financial or speculating association," quoted in Hurlbut to Blaine, Lima, November 2, 1881, no. 25, roll 37, USNA.

112. W. K. Schofield and L. B. Baldwin (surgeons U.S. Navy) to U.S.N. Rear Admiral George Balch, Lima, March 28, 1882, Despatches 1826–1906, roll 37, reporting postmortem results.

113. M. P. Grace to E. Eyre, January 31, 1882, box 57, no. 152, ff. 282–83, WRGP.

114. Emilio de Ojeda to M.E., Lima, May 29, 1886, no. 52, H-1677, AGMAE.

115. "The United States will be thoroughly hated in the West Coast and will be jeered and laughed at by the foreign legations." M. P. Grace to E. Eyre, January 31, 1882, box 57, no. 152, ff. 282–283, WRGP.

116. Francisco García Calderón, *Mediación de los Estados Unidos de Norte América en la Guerra del Pacífico. El Señor Cornelius A. Logan y el Dr. D. Francisco García Calderón* (Buenos Aires: Imprenta y Librería de Mayo, 1884); *Memorias del cautiverio* (Lima: Librería Internacional, 1949). Quiroz, "Actividades comerciales," 234, based on WRGP; Basadre, *Historia* 8:342–46.

ests contributed to rebuilding the business and legal foundations that launched Peru into a new era of modernization, which was, unfortunately, also associated with unbridled corruption.

At odds with historical views that have downplayed the role of graft during this crucial period of the guano age bonanza, evidence shows that corruption had a crucial bearing in defeating urgent legal and administrative reforms, reducing economic development potential, and ultimately contributing to the worst economic and political disaster of Peruvian history.

This cycle of corruption, already on the increase since the 1850s in parallel with larger guano resources, reached its peak in the late 1860s and early 1870s with the highest overall costs of the century, amounting to an estimate of 10.8 million soles for the 1870s (see Table A.3). Likewise, the comparative level of corruption measured as a percentage of GDP reached its highest level since the 1820s: a staggering estimated 4.6 percent (see Table A.4). Specifically, the administration of Balta-Piérola (1869–1872), and the dictatorship of Piérola (1879–1881) during the war with Chile, proved the most corrupt of the period (Table A.7).

Total direct costs of corruption rose when purposely mismanaged public debt and bribery in guano and public works contracts, already well established by the 1850s, became the principal vehicles of corruption. Congressmen and judges, together with executive authorities, now participated more broadly in graft within a more complex government apparatus and circumvented improved laws and regulations. Military graft, a constant throughout the century, although temporarily restrained in the mid-1870s, expanded considerably with the war buildup through arms and equipment procurement in which an unduly favored foreign company intervened. Peru's international reputation as a nest of corrupt politicians and businesspeople exacerbated the situation of debt default, low credit standing, and isolation on the eve of war.

Exposure of these corrupt transgressions reached a paroxysm in the 1870s as journalistic and pamphleteering campaigns multiplied, often financed by interested parties blaming each other. A misguided trip of the president in the middle of the war was used to justify an insurrection that resulted in even worse instances of graft despite pending military defeat. During the Chilean occupation, the efforts of a few Peruvian leaders at curtailing compounded losses floundered. The road toward reconstruction and recovery remained encumbered by corruption. Generations of Peruvians have been marked by this ignominious build-up to war, defeat in war, and loss of national patrimony, all of which has been difficult to forget or disguise.

Fig 1. Private hoarding among viceregal authorities: "Corregidor and encomendero quarrel over coins of *reales*, who should take more." Early critical portrayal of the damaging collusion of private and public interests in colonial administration.

Fig 2. Abuse of indigenous people via diverse corrupt practices: "Poor Indians: about six animals [provincial officer, master, storekeeper, notary, priest, and chieftain] that eat and are feared by the Indians of this kingdom." A main source of colonial corruption targeted by reformist critics of the seventeenth and eighteenth centuries.

Felipe Guamán Poma de Ayala, "Nueva corónica y buen gobierno" (1615), 495, 708. Courtesy of the Royal Library, Copenhagen, Denmark.

The visual representation of corruption is not an easy task because corrupt transactions are generally clandestine and complex. Historical illustrations of corruption include symbolic exchanges of coins or cash, milch cows as depleted national treasuries, entangling tentacles, masked robbers, card games, and imprisoned culprits. All depict the costly impact of bribery and corruption on public perceptions.

Fig 3. Viceroy José Manso de Velasco, Conde de Superunda, 1745–61. The head of the colonial court relied on venal patronage networks. Customarily, viceroys hoarded an informal "reward" (*premio*) for holding the royal commission (symbolized by the document held in the left hand and baton of authority in the right hand). Portrait by José Joaquín Bermejo (ca. 1760). Courtesy of Museo Nacional de Arqueología, Antropología e Historia del Perú, Lima.

Fig 4. Viceroy Manuel Amat y Junyent, 1761–76. A military viceroy who epitomized the abuse of power and private gain of corrupt colonial administration. Aided by advisor Juan Perfecto Salas and a circle of clients, Amat lashed against the reformist governor Antonio de Ulloa. Many illegal transgressions were recorded in Amat's postresidency trial. Portrait by Cristóbal Aguilar (1769). Courtesy of Monasterio de Nazarenas Carmelitas, Lima.

GRATITUD DE LOS GALLINAZOS.

Fig 5. Minister Juan Crisóstomo Torrico, 1851–54. A ringleader surrounded and hauled by vultures, smoking an expensive cigar that represents millions of pesos squandered by the corrupt handling of domestic public debt during the administration of General José Rufino Echenique: "The gratitude of the buzzards." Cándido, *Adefesios* (Lima: L. Williez, 1855), print no. 2.

Fig 6. Advances on guano exports. Graft-laden and costly fiscal dependence on fund advances by foreign contractors (Gibbs, Montané) of the guano trade during the second administration of General Ramón Castilla (1855–62): "Let's see mister . . . three million now." *La Zamacueca Política* no. 44 (1859), n. p.

Fig 7. Milking the national milch cow. Military and civilian extractions of perceived fiscal abundance (while imposing austerity among famished citizens) during the administration of President General Manuel Ignacio Prado (holding the cow) and Vice-President General Pedro Diez Canseco (milking). "Peruvian dairy" by J. J. Rasoir. *La Campana* no. 3 (1867), 4.

Fig 8. Draining of national income by corrupt economic and political elite: "In this land of guano, a great feeding bottle!" *El Cascabel* no. 16 (1873), 3.

Fig 9. Auguste Dreyfus: Foreign mogul and close associate of Minister of Finance Nicolás de Piérola, around the time of the signing of the infamous Dreyfus Contract in 1869.

Courtesy of Biblioteca Nacional del Perú, Lima.

Fig 10. President Nicolás de Piérola, an admirer of Napoleon III, in 1897. A controversial politician, former dictator, and perennial threat to political stability, Piérola was blamed by even his closest followers for his dishonesty and political corruption.

Photographic collection of Humberto Currarino, Callao.

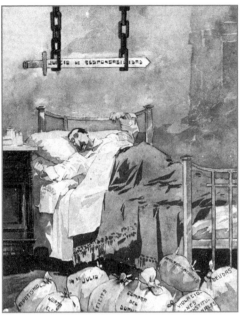

Fig 11. Minister of Finance Augusto B. Leguía, entangled by controversial and suspected measures, trying to sell his catch to President José Pardo: "Leguía's octopuses" by Chambon. *Fray K Bezón* no. 29 (1907), 4.

Courtesy of Biblioteca Central, Universidad Católica, Lima.

Fig 12. President Augusto B. Leguía, untroubled by judicial sanctions. Perceptions of impunity increased toward the end of Leguía's first administration: "Pleasant sleep" by González Gamarra. *Variedades* vol. 8, no. 240 (1912), 1.

Courtesy of Biblioteca Nacional del Perú, Lima.

Fig 13. President Augusto B. Leguía with ministers, exiting the Cathedral of Lima during his long, dictatorial, and pervasively corrupt second administration, 1919–30. Photo by José L. Avilés, ca. 1921.

Photographic collection of Humberto Currarino, Callao.

Chapter 4

Crony-Style Modernization, 1884–1930

Manuel González Prada (1844–1918), who witnessed the fall of Lima to the Chilean army, built on those painful memories a powerful literary indictment of the political and social leadership deemed responsible for the disaster. From one of the last-ditch defensive garrisons a mile south of the city, the rebel heir of an old landowning family observed the desertion of makeshift Peruvian troops under the merciless attack of better-trained Chilean forces. Amid the improvised last-minute preparations, several of his fellow reserve officers had abandoned their posts at night to carouse and drink in seedy neighborhoods. Local vandals and unruly soldiers looted and burned Chinese stores and houses following the ignominious military defeat. Unharmed in combat, a demoralized González Prada returned to his home. He remained indoors during the two and a half years of military occupation that ended after the signature of the onerous peace treaty of Ancón on October 20, 1883.[1]

González Prada presented his indictment in several speeches, newspaper articles, books, and unpublished manuscripts written during the postwar years. He stands as one of the fiercest fighters and critics of corruption in modern Peruvian history. Vowing to break an "infamous pact" of silence and rumor, he exposed the legacy and historical roots of corrupt, inept, and irresponsible leadership. In striking similarity to the stand taken against corruption by his maternal ancestor Antonio de Ulloa, González Prada charged

---

1. Manuel González Prada, "Impresiones de un reservista," article published in 1915 and reprinted in *El tonel de Diógenes* (first edition, 1945, by son Alfredo González Prada), in *Obras* (Lima: Ediciones Copé, 1985), vol. 1, part 2, 37–44. On events following Lima's military defeat, see J. P. Christiancy to S.S. W. M. Evarts, Lima, February 2, 1881, no. 237, Despatches 1826–1906, roll 35, USNA.

that politicians had sold their conscience and writers their pens to the high-est bidders. As if by inherited right, entire families had lived off the national treasury without implementing necessary and truly patriotic social change and reform. This type of livelihood bred mediocrity and moral cowardice, he argued. Everyone pretended to be what he or she was not, like actors in a colossal farce. Recurrent struggles for power yielded unmerited rewards to political supporters through illicit favors and abuse of the government's finances. Political parties were mere electoral clubs of unwholesome mercantile ambitions. "What was the judiciary," he asserted, but "a public auction." Congress was a debased group formed by the president's relatives, friends, and servants.[2] Peru was a sick organism—"[W]herever one probed, pus erupted."[3]

In his impotence and rage over the calamitous state of the country after the war with Chile, González Prada launched a radical attack on almost all Peruvian institutions and individuals. Accordingly, he believed that there was not a single honest person living in Peru. A grim historical interpretation buttressed his criticism. Since the 1840s, native finance "experts," *hacendistas criollos,* had balanced chronic budget deficits with high-interest loans granted by the consignees of guano fiscal wealth. The country benefited nothing or very little from the income of guano and nitrate exports: He calculated that only about 2 or 3 percent of such exports' total value had been invested in genuine public works. Peru's "political merchants" had plundered national assets, and "wealth served as a corrupting element, not for material progress." Scandalous pilfering took place during the implementation of public sector loans, railway construction, paper money issues,

2. González Prada, "En el año 2200," *El tonel de Diógenes,* in *Obras,* vol. 1, part 2, 169–71. On the family lineage linking González Prada's mother, Josefa Alvarez de Ulloa y Rodríguez (1820–1887), to the colonial reformist Antonio de Ulloa, see Luis Alberto Sánchez, *Mito y realidad de González Prada* (Lima: P. L. Villanueva, 1976), 12, n. 3.

3. González Prada, "Propaganda y ataque" (speech delivered in 1888), in *Pájinas libres; Horas de lucha* (Caracas: Biblioteca Ayacucho, 1976 [1894]), 107–8. His historical summary is devastating: "En la orgía independiente, nuestros antepasados bebieron el vino y dejaron las heces . . . bochornoso epitafio de una generación que se va marcada con la guerra civil de medio siglo, con la quiebra fraudulenta y con la mutilación del territorio nacional . . . prefirió atrofiar su cerebro en las cuadras de los cuarteles y apergaminar la piel en las oficinas del Estado. . . [B]uscaron el manjar del festín de los gobiernos, ejercieron una insaciable succión en los jugos del erario nacional y sobrepusieron el caudillo que daba pan y los honores a la patria que exijía oro y sus sacrificios." "Discurso en el Politeama" (1888), in *Pájinas libres,* 43–45. See also "Los partidos y la Unión Nacional" (speech delivered in 1898) in *Horas de lucha,* 202.

and the expropriation of nitrate fields. The Dreyfus, Meiggs, and Grace contracts represented great fairs in which the press, public employees, diplomats, courts of justice, chambers of Congress, ministers, and presidents were placed on sale. All classes sought fast and shady enrichment, infected by a "metallic neurosis" that drove husbands to sell their wives, parents their sons and daughters, and brothers their sisters. Catering to Meiggs's philandering in Lima, leading "decent" families participated in the overall climate of moral prostitution. Moreover, in the middle of a hopeless war, military commanders—described as "eternal suckers of the national juices"—had embezzled monies destined for troops, gambled, drank, and cavorted with lowly women instead of fighting.[4]

These pessimistic views had a powerful effect on several generations of Peruvians. As a political avenging angel, however, González Prada envisaged only vague alternatives of social revolution. His anarchist ideas, reinforced during a sojourn in Europe between 1891 and 1898, fertilized Peruvian radical leftist movements that developed thereafter. Not even the evident economic recovery experienced since the 1890s dissuaded González Prada from his dismal perspective. For him economic progress only meant the enrichment of the elite in the midst of widespread poverty. These ideas adapted well to a growing attitude in Peru: either one profited from the mess or else endeavored to destroy it all. A consequence of this logic was the development of political ambitions geared toward demolishing institutions whether they worked or not.[5] Despite the nihilistic ideas of González Prada, the reality of recovery and modernization imposed itself. After reaching a nadir, the country's situation improved. Yet notorious elements of the old corruption that had weakened institutions and growth in the past persisted.

Military for Hire

War, economic disaster, and a substantial loss of territory would not serve as lessons to mend inherited ills, González Prada claimed. The civilian elite

4. González Prada, "Mercaderes políticos," July 1915, galley proofs reprinted in *Propaganda y ataque* (first ed., 1939), in *Obras,* vol. 2, part 4, 171–73.

5. Sánchez, *Mito y realidad,* 34; Eugenio Chang-Rodríguez, *La literatura política de González Prada, Mariátegui y Haya de la Torre* (Mexico: Ediciones de Andrea, 1957), 124–25; Bruno Podestá, introduction to his anthology of Manuel González Prada's writings, *Sobre el militarismo (antología). Bajo el oprobio* (Lima: Editorial Horizonte, 1978), 7–11.

had been thoroughly weakened by heavy levies, expropriation, bankruptcy, and economic disruption during the war and the Chilean military occupation. Sharp political divisions continued to undermine national unity and stability. The road toward recovery inevitably started with the rebirth of domestic military fiefdoms paid and supported by an entourage of patron, foreign and domestic, interest groups or networks. To a certain degree, the War of the Pacific had contributed to an institutional and political devolution reminiscent of the darker days of postindependence caudillismo. Similar to the early days of the republic, military chieftains struggled against each other for power, public finances were chaotic, foreign credit did not exist, and the collection of public revenue resembled illegal plunder under the guise of a national cause.

General Miguel Iglesias's government (1882–1885) was depicted as a puppet of Chilean interests.[6] Repudiated by most Peruvians, it was in fact sustained by Chilean troops. Iglesias's regime was hastily recognized by foreign governments eager to inject stability in that volatile region of the Pacific, to support Chilean "rights of conquest," and to oppose any type of U.S. intervention.[7] With Chilean acquiescence, Grace Brothers & Company, the main arms supplier of Peru during the war, now sold U.S.-manufactured carbines and munitions to Iglesias as part of its new ambitious strategy to obtain concessions and leverage for its business plans in the region.[8] Iglesias also received the support of key Pierolista leaders (Manuel

6. Emilio de Ojeda to Ministro de Estado, Lima, November 18, 1884, no. 183, leg. H-1677, AGMAE: Chile "ha convertido al Gobierno de Iglesias en instrumento humilde de sus designios." Charles E. Mansfield to Marquis of Salisbury, Lima, October 24, 1887, no. 65, Confidential, FO 61/369, ff. 270–275v, NAUK: "Iglesias had been a puppet of the Chilean government."

7. Enrique Vallés to M.E., Lima, March 20, 1883, no. 55, no. 135, leg. H-1677, AGMAE: "Indicaciones hechas por los representantes de Francia, Italia e Inglaterra de acuerdo con los Estados Unidos para gestionar a favor de la paz entre las república beligerantes del Pacífico." See also Vallés to M.E., Lima, February 9, 1884, no. 135, leg. H-1677, AGMAE.

8. Alfonso Quiroz, "Las actividades comerciales y financieras de la casa Grace y la Guerra del Pacífico," *Histórica* 7 (1983): 233, based on M. P. Grace to E. Eyre, July 1883, box 58, no. 154, p. 88, WRGP: "I doubt very much the General [Iglesias] will be able to sustain himself, consequently it will be very undesirable to make shipments of arms unless the Chilean Government guarantee them." See also Miguel Pajares (Jefe del Parque General del Ejército) to Oficial Mayor del Ministerio de Guerra y Marina, Lima, April 15, 1884, and Lima, November 6, 1884, Correspondencia General, 0.1884.4 and 0.1884.5, Archivo Histórico Militar, Lima (hereafter AHM), on some problems Grace Brothers encountered in supplying ammunition and rifles to the army of Iglesias.

Antonio Barinaga, Juan Martín Echenique, Joaquín and Rufino Torrico), who served as his first cabinet ministers and high-level officials, and just a handful of Partido Civil maverick members (Civilistas), such as Ignacio de Osma (brother of Pedro de Osma, a stalwart follower of Piérola).[9]

The Treaty of Ancón would have meant political suicide for any leader who had agreed to sign it. The Iglesias movement, aided by the remains of Piérola's corrupt following, was a convenient scapegoat that signed off on the loss of the provinces of Iquique and Tarapacá as well as the temporary bondage of Tacna and Arica. The Iglesias government was a new type of militarism born out of defeat and surrender that had no political future, although it did not fail to extract a steep price for its services, including fees and taxes bordering on extortion, as well as bribes and sinecures paid by foreign and domestic interests committed to economic and financial remedies essential for economic recovery. An old political opponent, General Manuel de la Cotera, characterized Iglesias as an obscure conspirator, servile instrument of former dictator Piérola, and his government one of "terror, violence, and embezzlement, attracting to it the most corrupted elements of the country."[10]

While the Chilean troops were being evacuated from Peruvian territory in August 1884, a bitter political and armed conflict raged between Iglesias and General Andrés A. Cáceres, a resilient hero of the resistance against Chilean occupation. This internal struggle paralyzed the scant "vital forces" of the country. Piérola's growing influence, through his party, renamed the Partido Demócrata, and followers among Lima's lower classes, provided noticeable support to the beleaguered Iglesias as did Chilean mercenary officers who enlisted in his army.[11] Neither Cáceres nor Piérola intended to undo the treaty of Ancón; they actually expressed their acceptance of it as a fait accompli. Instead, their ambitions were mundanely practical: to oc-

9. Vallés to M.E., Lima, July 30, 1883, no. 150, and October 2, 1883, no. 189, leg. H-1677, AGMAE: "Progresos del General Iglesias en la consolidación de su gobierno... El partido pierolista que ahora se titula Nacional ha decidido adherirse a Iglesias y sostenerlo en su empresa para la paz," and "Progresos rápidos del General Iglesias. Apoyo y facilidades dadas por [Chilean Foreign Minister] Aldunate." On Piérola's "very close relations with Iglesias" and the role of the Pierolista paper, *El Bien Público,* see S. L. Phelps to F. T. Frelinghuysen, Lima, March 11, 1884, no. 72, Despatches 1826–1906, roll. 39, USNA.

10. "El General Manuel G. de la Cotera a sus compatriotas," *El Comercio,* June 16, 1884.

11. Phelps to Frelinghuysen, Lima, August 30, 1884, no. 129, September 2, 1884, no. 132, and March 4, 1885, no. 213, Despatches 1826–1906, rolls 40 and 41, USNA.

cupy the presidency and replace Iglesias who was rapidly losing ground.[12] Cáceres followed what González Prada considered the goal of high-ranking military officers at the time: to achieve the presidency as the ultimate promotion in the military career path.[13]

Pressed by Chilean authorities and aided by the corrupt minister of war Juan Martín Echenique, Iglesias unleashed a cruel political and military repression against Cáceres's followers and supporters. Many died or were deported, especially during the repression of the Cacerista uprising of Trujillo in October 1884. A decade later, a letter signed by more than 400 neighbors of Trujillo who vehemently opposed the promotion of Echenique, one of Piérola's oldest and closest cronies, to the rank of general. They still recalled the "sacking, burning, devastation," and the extortion carried out by the punitive expedition led by Echenique against the northern city. He was described as a "dishonest son of Peru" (*hijo ímprobo del Perú*) and terrible officer with a notoriously inept and irregular military career based on political favors. During the attack on Trujillo, Echenique even helped himself to luxury items seized as "war booty" from the home of the then provincial governor (prefecto), José María de la Puente. "In this country there is no moral sanction," the signers of the letter affirmed.[14]

In November 1884, a Spanish diplomat lamented Iglesias's "barbarous" actions against his own countrymen.[15] Fearing growing opposition in his rear guard and mounting pressure from the Chilean government, in September 1885, Iglesias also unleashed deportations and imprisonment of Partido Civil leaders José María Quimper and Manuel Candamo, and, under Chilean pressure, even of Piérola and some of his followers.[16] Moreover, British businessmen complained that the "administration of justice . . . has become unworthy of the name," and that heavy fines were extorted from

12. Vallés to M.E., Lima, February 9, 1884, no. 135, and Ojeda to M.E., February 13, 1885, no. 25, leg. H-1677, AGMAE.

13. González Prada, "Los partidos y la Unión Nacional" in *Horas de lucha,* 202.

14. "Hijos y vecinos the Trujillo" to Nicolás de Piérola, Trujillo, September 27, 1897, in file "1895–1899. Correspondencia oficial y particular," Archivo Piérola, vol. 7, BNP. Among the more than 400 signatories are Agustín and Juan J. Ganoza, Ramón and Luis Barúa, Pedro Rivadeneyra, and Pablo Uceda.

15. Ojeda to M.E., Lima, November 18, 1884, no. 183, leg. H-1677, AGMAE: "Da cuenta de la manifestación que ha tenido lugar con motivo del entierro de [jefe cacerista] Miró Quesada."

16. Ojeda to M.E., Lima, September 6, 1885, no. 136, "Muy Reservado," leg. H-1677, AGMAE; Charles E. Buck to S.S., Lima, September 5, 1885, no. 28, and September 12, 1885, no. 30, Despatches 1826–1906, roll 42, USNA.

foreign companies.[17] The U.S. envoy in Lima reported the arbitrary behavior of the Iglesias government toward American railroad contractors who suffered exactions, requisitions, and lack of compensation for transportation rendered under the threat of seizure of railway properties. Iglesias had come to power with little wealth, and his government collected scant revenues and had no credit.[18]

In the midst of this penury, the Iglesias administration granted several important concessions to foreign concerns by executive decrees signed "in the darkness of the night" in violation of existing legislation. The beneficiaries included several U.S. citizens, such as Edward Du Bois (Trujillo R.R.) and his associate Michael P. Grace "of New York," thus settling temporarily their "long continued difficulties" with Peruvian authorities.[19] In February 1885, Grace Brothers & Company, holding the strategic rights over the trans-Andean railway line Lima-Chicla (purchased by M. P. Grace from the Meiggs family and related security holders), was granted the right to build its extension to the mining sites of Oroya and Cerro de Pasco as well as the latter's draining works. This concession provided Grace with a strategic leverage that was used to the company's fullest advantage in complex and graft-laden financial negotiations leading to the signing of the so-called Grace Contract.

Grace had supplied small loans and handouts to the cash-starved Iglesias government to obtain coveted concessions and other paybacks, as explained by M. P. Grace himself in reference to an earlier financial negotiation with the government: "Our authorization . . . to advance £5,000 to the Government in exchange for the proper powers to force a settlement from the Peruvian Guano Company [a debtor of the state] was given because we feel convinced that with such power we will eventually force a settlement, which . . . will . . . place us in funds so as to oblige the government to cancel any indebtedness to [Grace Brothers & Company, especially the large one for $66,023] of the Trujillo railroad."[20] Unwilling to place all his eggs

17. A. M. Saunder (Pacific Steam Navigation Co.) to Marquis of Salisbury, Liverpool, July 28, 1885, FO 61/305, ff. 1–2v, NAUK, citing complaints by George Sharpe, the company's manager in Callao.

18. S. L. Phelps to S.S. Frelinghuysen, Lima, February 11, 1884, no. 58, Despatches 1826–1906, roll 39, USNA.

19. Phelps to Frelinghuysen, Lima, March 13, 1885, no. 216, Despatches 1826–1906, roll 41, USNA.

20. M. P. Grace to E. Eyre, New York, August 27, 1884, box 58, no. 155, p. 292, WRGP. See also Ojeda to M.E., Lima, February 28, 1885, no. 31: "Concesión a Grace Brothers," leg. H-1677, AGMAE; Lawrence A. Clayton, *Grace: W. R. Grace & Co.: The Formative Years, 1850–1930* (Ottawa, IL: Jameson Books, 1985), 143–44.

in a single basket, Grace also explained in the same letter that "the advance of a thousand pounds to Monocle [code name for Piérola][,] which we authorized[,] . . . we did in view of the many services which we have received heretofore at his hands, and we did not consider on the whole that it would be at all policy to refuse him this amount, he being the leader of a large political party, and may at any future time come to the front again."[21]

Likewise, a "twisted and vicious" procedure led to a contract signed by Iglesias's minister of finance, Manuel Galup, granting the Société Générale of Paris a fifty-year extension of the costly and unfavorable monopoly administration of the Callao port's pier and docks (Muelle y Dársena). (The initial exclusive privilege to load and unload ships had been set in 1877.) The government obtained in return from the Société Générale a badly needed loan for half a million soles guaranteed by customs revenues. In the meantime, the French company charged high fees, unfairly reduced only for Chilean and British shipping companies.[22] These agreements were questioned and renegotiated after Iglesias's fall of power, but they continued to represent flawed strategic cornerstones for Peru's economic and financial recovery. Given the shady origins of these contracts, it is not surprising that Iglesias and his entourage benefited personally from these official deals. It also seems to indicate the improper friendship between Michael P. Grace and Iglesias despite Grace's parallel courting of the two other contenders for power, Piérola and Cáceres. Barely a year and a half after his forced withdrawal from the political scene, Iglesias was seen enjoying Grace's hospitality in Paris.[23]

During peace negotiations, Iglesias had tried to bribe Cáceres with the promise of amnesty and a diplomatic post to Europe if he laid down his arms against the government. The "Wizard of the Andes," as Cáceres was known for his military exploits against the Chileans, indignantly rejected the offer and broke off negotiations.[24] As the armed conflict between the two gener-

21. Grace to Eyre, New York, August 27, 1884, box 58, no. 155, p. 292, WRGP. The word "monocle" stood for Piérola according to his own encryption codes in "Relación de claves en archivo: clave telegráfica enero 1883," Archivo Piérola, vol. 6, BNP.

22. E. J. Casanave, *El contrato Galup-Dársena en sus relaciones con los intereses fiscales* (Lima: Tipografía Industrial, 1886), 10–15; Basadre, *Historia* 9:53–56.

23. Carlos Gonzales Candamo to Manuel Candamo, Paris, June 1, 1887: "En casa de [Grace] encontré al general Iglesias que no conocía y me sorprendió agradablemente pues yo creía encontrar en él un indio feroz en vez de un hombre de cara simpática y maneras afables." In *Epistolario de Manuel Candamo* (forthcoming edition by José A. de la Puente Candamo and José de la Puente Brunke).

24. Andrés Avelino Cáceres, *Memorias del Mariscal Andrés A. Cáceres*, 2 vols. (Lima: Editorial Milla Batres, 1986), 2:157.

als intensified, Cáceres outwitted the army commanders sent against his forces in the central highlands. Cáceres then took control of the practically defenseless Lima and exacted the resignation of Iglesias in December 1885. An interim council of ministers, with support of the business community and foreign diplomatic corps, reintroduced the constitution of 1860 and called elections that were held in June 1886. In this transition, the Spanish minister, Emilio de Ojeda, played a key role as mediator, becoming also a confidant with unique access to Cáceres and exceptional information of internal political affairs. Piérola had returned from exile in January but abstained from proffering his candidacy; he publicly rejected the mishandling of electoral rules while he covertly prepared his next insurrectionary action.[25]

The transitional council led by the elderly civilian Antonio Arenas was able to guarantee a modicum of order despite a multitude of disbanded soldiers and the continued abuses of local military authorities, described as "men who have so long been accustomed to military process and the disregard of legal methods."[26] Apprehension subsisted, however, concerning the influence exerted over Cáceres by those demanding benefits and rewards for their loyalty. Cáceres was believed to be "too yielding to his friends."[27] Unopposed, General Cáceres won the indirect elections backed by his newly formed party, the Partido Constitucional, in alliance with the Partido Civil, which was too weak to field its own candidate.

Once in power, Cáceres did not differentiate himself much from other previous military caudillos. González Prada was of the idea that there were two personifications of Cáceres: one was the hero of the resistance against Chile, and the other surfaced during his two presidential tenures (1886–1890, 1894–1895). President Cáceres engaged in "domestic pillage" (*rapiña casera*) and tyranny. He violated individual rights, was involved in at least two political assassination scandals, interfered with judicial investigations, and misappropriated public funds. Just as Piérola represented the interests of Dreyfus, so Cáceres represented the interests of Grace.[28]

25. Ojeda to M.E., Lima, January 22, 1886, no. 11, and April 6, 1886, no. 36, leg. H-1677, AGMAE, on Piérola's political and insurrectionary maneuvers. See also Basadre, *Historia* 9:89.
26. Charles Buck to T. F. Bayard, Lima, February 27, 1886, no. 81, Despatches 1826–1906, roll 42, USNA.
27. Buck to Bayard, Lima, February 27, 1886, no. 81, and April 24, 1886, no. 95, Despatches 1826–1906, rolls 42 and 43, USNA.
28. González Prada, "Los partidos y la Unión Nacional" in *Horas de lucha,* 204–5; *Sobre el militarismo,* 84–85; "El momento político" (1903), *Propaganda y ataque,* in

Foreign and domestic observers verified some of González Prada's assertions. Initially, the scarcity of financial resources compelled the Cáceres administration to exact loans from the business community through "every subterfuge in their power to obtain money from whomsoever[, and] . . . in many instances unjustly."[29] A note delivered through the intermediation of two Spanish diplomats revealed an attempt by the Chilean government to bribe Cáceres, offering him money to derail foreign financial deals being officially negotiated at the time and deemed contrary to Chile's interests. Cáceres rightly perceived this as a trap. However, the British diplomat who revealed this confidential information sincerely doubted an outright refusal of the Chilean offer by Cáceres since "the want of money is so urgent, and [the] 'camarillas' are so greedy, that I should be indisposed to embark upon any definite prognostications."[30] In order to remain in power, Cáceres had to feed a clique of hungry cronies.

Who comprised such a *camarilla* or clique? Mainly members of the military entourage who aided Cáceres in capturing power after legendary campaigns against the Chileans and Iglesias. Among the closest and most faithful collaborators who were rewarded with high government posts or congressional seats were Justiniano Borgoño, Remigio Morales Bermúdez, Hildebrando Fuentes, Luis Ibarra, Mariano Alcázar, Manuel Patiño Zamudio, Francisco Mendizábal, Daniel de los Heros, Teodomiro Gadea, and Manuel E. Lecca. Several of these military officers were also members of the board of the new Centro Militar del Perú, an influential military social club, which together with several military publications, were sponsored by the Cáceres government. Civilians Pedro A. del Solar, Aurelio Denegri, Isaac

---

Obras, vol. 2, part 4, 165–68. In the latter, on p. 166, González Prada compares the political strategy of both Piérola and Cáceres as the product of their ambition and greed: "Piérola y Cáceres nos legan a dos insaciables tiburones de la riqueza nacional, a Dreyfus y Grace."

29. Octavus Stokes to Marquis of Salisbury, Lima, March 28, 1887, no. 18, FO 61/369, ff. 162–164v, NAUK.

30. Charles Mansfield to Salisbury, Lima, October 24, 1887, no. 65, Confidential, FO 61/369, ff. 270–75v. The information in this dispatch was obtained from "secret and trustworthy sources" revealing secret and confidential correspondence between two Spanish diplomats, Vallés (Santiago de Chile), and Ojeda (Lima). No copy of this irregular correspondence was found in the AGMAE. However, Mansfield certainly had reliable means to spy on Ojeda, as evidenced by other corroborating official records found in the Spanish and British diplomatic archives. Following an official Spanish foreign policy at the time, both Vallés and Ojeda opposed U.S. involvement in the Andean region.

Alzamora, Antero Aspíllaga, and Elías Mujica, leading ministers appointed after 1886, had also collaborated mainly as political figures with military rank in the campaigns led by Cáceres.[31] In particular, Solar was Cáceres's most faithful and close political advisor despite his Pierolista origins.

During the first years of the Cáceres presidency, a serious rift between the executive and the legislative branches existed. In the legislature, influential Civilistas regretted the selection of Solar as first minister because of his former close connections with Piérola and proclerical stances. Moreover, the legislative body lacked either internal discipline or competence: Most of its young members owed their elections to favors for past services to Cáceres. Cacerista deputies also resented the influential position held by Solar and claimed that he had joined Cáceres at the last moment of his struggle against Iglesias. In October 1886, Solar was criticized in Congress and had to resign, but subsequently Cáceres reappointed him as cabinet chief in two other crucial moments. At one point, Solar and Cáceres considered closing the legislature, but a pact with former president García Calderón—at the time leader of a Civilista congressional faction amenable to collaboration with Cáceres—prevented the crisis. Deeper fissures arose from the executive's favoritism of certain businessmen in official contracts and lack of compliance with rules of the public budget in matters of expenses and appointments. Frictions also surfaced among Cáceres's ministers themselves: His finance minister and prime minister, José Araníbar, resigned in November 1886 allegedly because "the President urged him to satisfy the pressing demands of the military camarilla that surrounds him."[32]

After Cáceres's guerrillas and Iglesias's troops were disbanded, the remaining outmoded military establishment led by Cáceres in power had gigantic tasks to accomplish. It was necessary to strengthen, modernize, professionalize, and arm the Peruvian military forces to prevent more defeats in foreign wars and "impose respect" on Chile. The Cáceres administration contributed modestly to reorganizing the army with a basic restructuring of the chaotic military rank system and the reopening of the military school created in 1872.[33] This limited reshuffling benefited mainly the officers

31. Cáceres, *Memorias,* vol. 2, figures 74–76; Comisión Permanente de Historia del Ejército del Perú, *Cáceres: conductor nacional* (Lima: Ministerio de Guerra, 1984), 135.

32. Ojeda to M.E., Lima, November 23, 1886, no. 127; and for well-informed political insights, see Ojeda to M.E., Lima, June 7, 1886, no. 58; September 3, 1886, no. 95; and October 26, 1886, no. 114, leg. H-1677, AGMAE. See also similar observations in Buck to Bayard, Lima, October 8, 1886, no. 163, Despatches 1826–1906, roll 43, USNA.

33. Comisión Permanente, *Cáceres,* 135, 158–59: Escalafón General (1886), re-

comprising those "loyal and dedicated men who had been part of the campaigns . . . against the Chileans and, later, the government imposed by the latter."[34] Cáceres himself had been formed in the old tradition of military caudillos Castilla and Prado. Lack of funds limited the size of the regular armed forces to no more than 3,300 men, including 3 division generals, 8 brigade generals, 32 colonels, 217 major colonels, and other lesser officials adding to an inflated total of 2,131 officers; and three small ships (only one of which was purchased during the Cáceres administration).[35] Regular military salaries were very low. Additionally, the military also had police functions that complicated matters since, according to a British witness, "the police in Peru [are] . . . perhaps the worst among so-called civilized communities; that in Lima forms an integral part of the regular army."[36] Under this scarcity and overstretching of resources, military reform was at risk.

Systematic diversion of public funds for private gain was at the root of obstinate resistance to military reform and modernization. In November 1887, Cáceres's prime minister, Aurelio Denegri, asserted to a local newspaper that national funds had been illegally diverted by his immediate predecessors in the cabinet, mentioning especially the minister of war, who had refused to implement necessary army reforms to overcome "mess and disorder."[37] Extortion by military officers was justified as hard-won rewards for past patriotic actions. Under Cáceres, opportunities expanded for military officers to obtain income beyond their salaries. In response to González Prada and similar critics, Cáceres defended his reputation as follows: "I cannot allow being insulted by doubts of my patriotism and good intentions . . . to restore the [country's] credit, attract capital, [and] provide jobs for the poor."[38]

Cáceres's popularity as president started to decline by April 1887 as a consequence of several factors, including the mysterious disappearance of Colonel Romero Flores, suspected of having been shot and secretly buried

---

vamping of National Guard (1888), and Ordenanzas del Ejército and reopening of military school (1889).

34. Cáceres, *Memorias* 2:175.

35. Comisión Permanente, *Cáceres*, 161; Inés Cárdenas Sánchez, *Andrés A. Cáceres: biografía y campañas* (Lima: Editora Lima, 1979), 72; Basadre, *Historia* 9:187–88.

36. Mansfield to Salisbury, Lima, July 16, 1889, no. 47, FO 61/381, ff. 115–16, NAUK.

37. Ojeda to M.E., Lima, November 21, 1887, no. 116, leg. H-1678, AGMAE: "Da cuenta de la irritación producida . . . especialmente entre los militares por las declaraciones hechas a un redactor de *El Nacional* por [Aurelio Denegri]."

38. Quoted from an internal memo (circular) in Cárdenas Sánchez, *Cáceres*, 74.

under direct orders by the president.[39] Discontent also stemmed from a pro-longed economic depression, unemployment, and extended poverty, all of which were considered worse than under Iglesias.[40] In January1891, the prestige of Cáceres had crumbled further after four years of a government full of "peculations and abuses," among which the most flagrant and un-justified was Cáceres's obvious private fortune despite having come to the presidency with no more wealth than his "unblemished" name.[41] Two and a half years later, the British minister affirmed that the Peruvian treasury was unusually empty due to waste, embezzlement, and misappropriation, and that "General Cáceres is utterly discredited through the exposure of his corruption during his presidency and the unscrupulous illegalities etc. of his present [political] canvass."[42] To complete the picture, French representa-tives later remarked that Cáceres's administration had been marked by depredations that characterized it as a "[g]ouvernement de bandits."[43]

Under extreme revenue shortfalls and no foreign credit to abuse, how-ever, where did the military and state bureaucrats find their expected cor-rupt rewards?

Despite frustrated military and state reform, businessmen and financiers lobbied intensely to lay the legal foundations of economic recovery. During the first Cáceres administration, those bases included the repudiation of de-preciated paper money (harmful to workers and others with modest savings in paper currency who rose in protest), implementation of gold and silver currency, establishment and reorganization of commercial banks and insur-ance agencies and, especially, the creation of the first real estate registry (1888). This registry solved a major bottleneck for the establishment of clear property rights in urban real estate, which contributed to the development of mortgage credit based on an innovative mortgage bank law in 1889.[44]

---

39. Ojeda to M.E., Lima, April 11, 1887, no. 24, leg. H-1678, AGMAE.
40. Buck to Bayard, Lima, March 21, 1887, no. 217, Despatches 1826–1906, roll 44, USNA.
41. Ojeda to M.E., Lima, January 10, 1891, no. 1, leg. H-1678, AGMAE.
42. Mansfield to Earl of Rosebery, Lima, August 14, 1893, no. 29, FO 61/398, ff. 130–33, esp. 132, NAUK.
43. Eognes to M.A.E. Delcasse, Lima, April 10, 1903, no. 8; Merlou to M.A.E. Pi-chon, Lima, April 28, 1908, no. 51 (citing opinion of businessman M. Saint-Seine), Cor-respondance Politique et Commerciale, Nouvelle Série (hereafter CPC-NS), Pérou, vol. 1, ff. 45–46v, and f. 70, respectively, AMAE.
44. Ismael Acevedo y Criado, "La institución del Registro de la Propiedad Inmue-ble en el Perú, sus antecedentes legales y formas más urgentes," *Revista de la Facultad de Derecho y Ciencias Políticas* (1959): 95–182, esp. 96–97; Basadre, *Historia* 9:170.

Foreign and domestic capitalists and their political and journalistic networks were eager to patronize Cáceres's camarilla in exchange for the official approval and implementation of these economic and financial measures. Moreover, foreign interests also required the favorable disposition of Cáceres and his executive and legislative entourage to settle key contracts for public works, railways, and foreign debt arrangements. Previous measures by Piérola and Iglesias were voided by the Cáceres regime in October 1886 because constitutional rules and approval by Congress were ignored. Several foreign interests were injured by this move. The U.S. minister, considering approaching conflicts involving American interests, asserted that a firm stand was necessary against this challenge to "international rights and principles."[45] After a serious diplomatic incident with France, the Muelle y Dársena contract with the Société Générale was renegotiated to limit the monopoly's duration to only twenty-five years (instead of fifty), regulate the fees charged, and obtain future loans.[46] However, the real prize for corrupt officials came with the protracted and complex negotiations of the Grace Contract.

The Grace Contract

Michael P. Grace, the kingpin negotiator of the strategic arrangement with Peru's foreign creditors known to posterity as the Grace Contract, was a true and improved disciple of mogul Henry Meiggs. In the 1870s, Grace had lavishly partied and shared profitable business deals with Meiggs in Lima.[47] Grace developed a similar but more economical strategy to that of Meiggs in official relations with various governments in Peru. As explained in a letter by a long-time associate and cousin, "[D]uring the many years of his residence in Peru, [M. P. Grace] maintained our house on the most friendly and

45. Buck to Bayard, Lima, October 28, 1886, no. 171, Despatches 1826–1906, roll 43, USNA.

46. The new contract was signed by Minister of Finance Manuel Irigoyen and F. Berthold for the Société Générale, and later approved by Congress: Basadre, *Historia* 9:162–63. See also Ojeda to M.E., Lima, May 11, 1887, no. 35, leg. H-1678, AGMAE; and Buck to Bayard, Lima, May 12, 1887, no. 238, Despatches 1826–1906, roll 44, USNA.

47. In July 1872, Michael Grace and his wife threw a dancing party at their Lima residence for a hundred guests, including Meiggs, where they "had a good time but it is too much work and too costly to repeat daily." Clayton, *Grace,* 67, quoting Grace's correspondence in Grace Papers.

closest relations with each and every Government as it came along." Admonishing the inexperienced successors of Grace at the helm of the Lima office, the writer added,

We do not propose that you shall incur any unreasonable expense in bringing about such friendly relations, and we dwell on this point because we know from experience that unless overtures are made cautiously, you will frequently be met with unreasonable demands for financial accommodation, and your ability will consist in steering clear of such demands without giving offence.[48]

This strategy accomplished substantial results in Grace's uphill battle toward finally obtaining the official approval of the Grace Contract by the Peruvian executive and legislative authorities. The negotiation of the Grace Contract went through various phases in 1886 to 1890; at several moments it came very close to failing completely. At stake was the difficult issue of the defaulted Peruvian debts of 1869, 1870, and 1872 for approximately £32 million owed mostly to investors represented by the Committee of Foreign Bondholders based in London. Under the circumstances of defeat and economic depression, Peru was utterly unable to repay such debt. Moreover, the British bondholders were in the midst of a very bad relationship with the Peruvian government because they had tried to negotiate this debt payment directly with Chile. Grace offered the Committee his services as broker citing his railway interests and the good relations he kept with Peruvian authorities.[49] This international financial agreement promised sorely needed inflows of foreign capital to exploit and enhance the costly railway system that sat mostly as a gigantic monument to prewar corruption. Functioning railway connections and further construction to principal mining centers could contribute to realizing the nation's core economic potential.

Grace's ability in brokering and selling the agreement as a link between a practical solution of debt problems and Peru's much-desired economic recovery contributed to gaining local support for his scheme. In reality, however, Grace's business strategy in Peru was highly skeptical of the country's possibilities for capital investment. Threatened by huge losses of the mag-

48. Edward Eyre to Lima House, February 27, 1899, box 72, no. 13, pp. 391–92, WRGP.

49. M. P. Grace to Sir Henry Tyler (M.P. and Chairman of the Committee of Peruvian Bondholders), New York, May 18, 1885, box 58, no. 156, pp. 57–62, WRGP.

nitude of $200,000 due to bad Peruvian private and public debt, as well as by periodic international financial contractions in the early 1880s, Grace sought to obtain cash payments to develop business elsewhere, including Chile, where Grace opened a new branch.[50] Since his early endeavors to acquire the control of official railway contracts, Grace had recognized in private correspondence that his legal commitment to build railway extensions and mining drainage works was nothing more than a bargaining chip to secure future speculative gains.[51] His negotiations toward the signing of the Grace Contract using railway contractual rights as his main participation in the deal were part of a grand speculative scheme that in the end paid him handsomely.

Nationalist and other local interests stubbornly opposed the signing of the contract. They argued that Peru would pay an exorbitant price for a debt that had become the sole responsibility of Chile, the occupier of formerly Peruvian territories with guano and nitrate deposits mortgaged to Peru's foreign creditors. Moreover, they warned that the proposed control of the railway system by foreign capitalists would mean the ruin of Peru under domination similar to that suffered by India at the hands of the East India Company. Miners and landowners of the central highlands with influence in Congress filed lawsuits against Grace as part of their opposition to railway and mining monopolies exerted by foreign interests that, they feared, would result in financial losses and dispossession of valuable mining resources.[52]

Grace recognized as his project's main enemies Senator Manuel Candamo and his Civilista majority faction in both houses of the congress.[53] Candamo and his followers represented the national elite of businessmen, landowners, and miners; they opposed U.S. business and geopolitical penetration in accordance with the Spanish diplomatic principle of "avoiding at all costs even the minimum possibility of the United States' interference in these countries."[54] Candamo publicly criticized Grace, describing him

50. M. P. Grace to E. Eyre, New York, July 19, 1883, box 58, no. 154, p. 87; Grace to A. Leslie, April 17, 1884, box 58, no. 156, WRGP: "[T]he condition in Peru is such that it does not offer sufficient inducement for mineral enterprise, or in fact for any other enterprise where capital is to be invested."
51. Grace to Eyre, February 1883, box 58, no. 153, p. 274, WRGP: "I do not flatter myself that I will ever attempt to raise the necessary funds to finish the road to Oroya, continue it to Cerro de Pasco, and cut the necessary tunnel under the Cerro de Pasco mines."
52. E. Eyre to M. P. Grace, Lima, June 12, 1886, box 59, no. 159, pp. 114–17, WRGP.
53. Box 59, no. 159, pp. 146–48, WRGP.
54. Ojeda to M. E., Lima, October 20, 1887, no. 99; and May 2, 1888, no. 46, Reser-

as a shrewd speculator of railway concessions harmful to the country and the Yauli mining sector.[55] Several other congressmen led by José María Quimper opposed the contract until the bitter end. Denigrating comparisons were made with past corrupt contracts negotiated by Dreyfus and Meiggs. Grace was accused of being motivated by the prospect of a "grandiose" and "monstrous" business scheme sure to yield him tremendous gains. He nevertheless continued to try to convince the opposition inside and outside Peru of the benefits of his project. He even used friends as intermediaries to try and sway the main opposition figures.[56] He also used unscrupulous methods of persuasion.

With the support of the Candamo Civilistas, the Cacerista prime minister, Aurelio Denegri, pressed energetically for nationalization of the entire railway system, moved by "jingoism" and desires of "spoliation" according to U.S. minister Charles Buck.[57] This nationalistic thrust was initially confronted by moves for a decided U.S. diplomatic intervention pressed by W. R. Grace's interests in Washington, D.C., including plans to display U.S. naval power in defense of "American" interests in Peru.[58] However, M. P. Grace's ultimate "special" scheme associated with British interests forced an embarrassing back-pedaling by U.S. diplomats. As part of his efforts to

---

vado (informing about a confidential conversation between Ojeda and Manuel Candamo regarding serious frictions with U.S. representative Charles Buck over the Peruvian government's decision to seize railway properties contracted to U.S. citizens), leg. H-1678, AGMAE. This report was secretly intercepted by the British chargé in Lima, Charles E. Mansfield, and a copy of its translation (misdated May 1, same, no. 46) passed to the U.S. diplomat Charles Buck. See Mansfield to Marquis of Salisbury, Lima, July 16, 1888, no. 63, FO 61/375, ff. 289–90v, NAUK; and Buck to Bayard, Lima, July 31, 1888, no. 407, and August 1, 1888, no. 408, Despatches 1826–1906, roll 47, USNA.

55. Peru, Cámara de Senadores, *Diario de los debates,* 1889 (Lima: Imprenta de El Comercio, 1889), 237–38.

56. José María Quimper, *Las propuestas de los tenedores de bonos por J.M.Q.* (Lima: Imprenta de La Época, 1886), 4–5, 11, 50–52; Manuel Velarde, *El General Velarde ex-ministro de Gobierno y el contrato Grace* (Lima: Imprenta de La Época, 1886), 3, 5: "[E]l señor Grace se valió de un amigo mío, para que le permitiera seguir discutiendo con la creencia de que llegaría a convencerme de las ventajas que para mi patria tenía su proyecto."

57. Buck to Bayard, Lima, May 22, 1888, no. 375; February 20, 1888, no. 349; and telegram, Buck to Bayard, Lima, April 24, 1888, Despatches 1826–1906, roll 46, USNA.

58. "Mr. W. R. Grace talked this whole situation over with President Cleveland, Secretary Bayard and other members of the Cabinet, and we are convinced that the government will not allow the interests of their citizens to be made a play toy." W. R. Grace & Co. to E. Eyre, New York, February 20, 1888, box 59, no. 160, p. 24, WRGP.

obtain approval of the Grace Contract in Peru, M. P. Grace attempted to prevent the fall of the Denegri cabinet due to U.S. pressure. A casualty of this fiasco was Buck, who had implemented the initial tough U.S. policy in Lima. Recognizing Grace's political clout in the United States, Buck complained directly to the secretary of state, Democrat Thomas F. Bayard. Buck blamed Bayard for failing to support him and for his unprincipled inconsistency, which he described as damaging to "the dignity of the U.S. Government." Buck decried that the "influence and official action [of the U.S. government] should be played with 'fast and loose' to suit the convenience or interests of a speculative venture or a commercial enterprise, and that too not an American one." He further remarked that the Grace Contract scheme was regarded in Lima "with great suspicion, and . . . great opposition, as it had . . . involved much foul reflection as to the influences that actuated the members of the [Peruvian] Government and Congress."[59]

A fierce public debate raged among supporters and opponents of the Grace Contract. Convinced by principle or mercenary greed, important newspapers and journalists either opposed (*La Época, El Amigo del Pueblo*) or supported (*La Opinión Nacional, El Bien Público*)[60] the Grace project. In November 1886, a first favorable report by special commissioners Francisco García Calderón, Francisco Rosas, and Aurelio Denegri had signified a reputable endorsement of a settlement that promised opportunities for foreign investment.[61] However, Cáceres himself was initially reluctant to endorse the signing of the contract, although he later wholeheartedly supported it. In November 1888, the Chamber of Deputies initially rejected a final version of the Grace Contract. At this low ebb of hope for the contract's success, an important British partner wrote to W. R. Grace:

> The business to you is a purely mercantile venture. If it had gone through, well and good; you would have recouped all outlay, you would have made a considerable profit or commission, you would have dominated the whole of the contracts for railway extension and would have controlled the trade and enterprise of Peru.[62]

59. Buck to Bayard, Lima, February 27, 1889, no. 473, Despatches 1826–1906, roll 48, USNA.
60. For an example of a hired pen, see *El señor J.M.Q. y el contrato Grace* (Lima: Imprenta Bacigalupi, 1887).
61. Basadre, *Historia* 9:112–16.
62. G. A. Ollard to W. R. Grace, London, February 19, 1889, box 60, no. 161, WRGP.

However, by April 1889 opinion shifted in favor of Grace. What had transpired to allow this change that led to the final approval of the Grace Contract? Grace modified his initial proposal by lowering the portion of the debt to be repaid with the temporary alienation of national assets, mostly railway concessions, and allowing shorter periods for such monopoly concessions. Moreover, key agents who had influence over others were recruited as "friends" of Grace's cause, including Pedro del Solar, Cáceres's close political collaborator and recipient of personal loans by Grace's manager in Lima, congressional leader Alejandro Arenas, and cabinet minister and prosecuting attorney (fiscal) José Araníbar.[63] Grace's friends were found in the highest spheres of the executive and legislative power, as well as the middle ranks of public and private decision makers, especially people charged with preparing "technical" reports for government ministries such as Simón Irigoyen and Narciso Alayza, congressmen Martín Álvarez Delgado (Cusco) and Wenceslao Venegas (Callao), journalists Rafael Galván and E. J. Casanave, and the mining entrepreneur Antenor Rizo Patrón. These men received from Grace expensive gold watches ordered from New York as rewards for their "assistance to our cause," although one of them also received a "cartita de atención" (warning memo) reprimanding his more ambitious pretensions.[64]

The ultimate measure that guaranteed the approval of the Grace Contract in Congress was the executive decree of April 8, 1889, signed by Prime Minister Solar and President Cáceres, calling for special elections to replace congressional deputies, led by Quimper, who were consistently opposed to the contract's approval. This constitutional transgression consolidated the forces within Congress favorable to the Grace Contract, a process in which bribe money was involved (*corrió dinero*).[65]

63. Box 59, no. 159, pp. 117, 146–48, WRGP.
64. E. Eyre to M. P. Grace, Lima, June 10, 1890, box 81, "E.E. 1890," p. 25, WRGP: "GOLD WATCHES. I have ordered a lot of watches from N.Y. to present to the following friends that lent their assistance to our cause: A. Arigoni, Narciso Alayza, Santiago Pacheco, Antenor Rizo Patrón, three brothers Estremadoyro, José A. Medina, David Torres Aguirre [despite his "high pretensions"], Rafael Galván, Brando Zúñiga, E. J. Casanave, Salomón Rodríguez, Pascual del Castillo, M. Alvarez Mercado, Martín Alvarez, Wenceslao Venegas, señores Venegas, Simón Yrigoyen." On the multiple reports of directors and chiefs of sections of the ministries of finance, government, justice, and public works, presented to prosecuting attorneys (*fiscales*) José Araníbar and M. A. Fuentes in 1887, see Basadre, *Historia* 9:115–16.
65. Basadre, *Historia* 9:123.

Regardless of the unscrupulous and unethical methods used to approve the Grace Contract, it did play an important role in the financial and economic recovery of Peru by removing major obstacles to the inflow of foreign direct and portfolio investment. It was by far a better deal than the Dreyfus Contract, and its elaboration and discussion were at least made public. The Dreyfus Contract had ruined Peruvian finances for several decades. To some extent, the Grace Contract was the logical and inevitable corollary of the corrupt Dreyfus affair and the disastrous war with Chile. Despite Peru's defeat and loss of territory, the country was still responsible for a substantial part of its old debt. However, the signing of the Grace Contract also involved corruption of Peruvian officials that ultimately added to the high cost Peru paid to regain its international credit rating. Additionally, the positive effects of the contract took too long to become evident as economic depression and mismanagement continued to plague the Cacerista regime until its demise.[66]

Soon after the final approval of the Grace Contract in October 1889 and the settlement of Chilean objections, the Peruvian Corporation was formed in 1890 to replace the Committee of Foreign Bondholders. Representing its shareholders, the Peruvian Corporation obtained the right to manage the major railways and conduct other financial and business services and monopolies in Peru for sixty-six years. Peru's defaulted debt was cancelled in exchange for the rights granted to its former creditors by the Grace Contract. Grace surrendered his railway rights to the Peruvian Corporation in exchange for a third of the new corporation's Oroya railway shares. Grace also received brokerage fees and a 3-percent commission on the shares distributed to the former bondholders.[67] Corruption of Peruvian authorities had translated in a windfall profit for Grace and his interests in Peru but, in contrast, very modest or practically no gains for the rest of the shareholders of the Peruvian Corporation.

To guarantee ready access to power as well as cover up illegal bribes and misappropriations, Cáceres followed the custom of choosing a successor

66. John Hicks to Walter D. Gresham, Lima, April 17, 1893, Despatches 1826–1906, roll 52, USNA: "Business is depressed. The national treasury is depleted. Money is scarce and every Peruvian looks forward to the future with feelings of serious apprehension. . . The South American conception of self-government is not a government by the people but the government of the strongest."
67. Rory Miller, "The Making of the Grace Contract: British Bondholders and the Peruvian Government, 1885–1890," *Journal of Latin American Studies* 8 (1976): 73–100, esp. 90, 99–100.

who could guarantee him impunity from prosecution after his term as president. Despite formally accepting the Constitution of 1860 and agreeing to step down, Cáceres strove to manipulate loopholes and gray areas in electoral legislation and practice to the advantage of his designated successor, Colonel (and later General) Remigio Morales Bermúdez.[68] The Morales Bermúdez administration was deemed "normal and tolerably honest." This despite accusations of misappropriation of funds against the minister of foreign affairs, Federico Elmore, corruption and abuse in municipal elections, and the bribing of dissenting congressmen in a campaign termed *propaganda del cohecho.*[69]

The untimely death of Morales Bermúdez before the end of his presidential term and just prior to the 1894 elections, led Cáceres to impose himself as president through blatant illegalities aided by docile interim president Justiniano Borgoño, who had displaced first vice president Solar following the death of Morales Bermúdez.[70] During Borgoño's short administration, in Chamber of Deputies his finance minister, Horacio Ferreccio, was accused of up to ten corruption-related charges, to which the minister responded by fleeing the country.[71] In addition, the illegal use of municipal bonds to finance the purchase of the steamer *Coya* and its artillery fittings (for which Grace Brothers & Company charged up to £15,000 in cash), among other weapons supply deals at the time, were denounced in Congress in December 1894.[72] Grace continued to provide loans to Cáceres to "sustain his government."[73] In particular, the Cacerista recourse to electoral corruption contributed to further undermine the battered institution of democratic elections, a major problem that continued to beset Peruvian politics during most of the following century.

Cáceres's ill-advised and illegal decision to occupy the presidency again added to his already blemished reputation. His political and ethical mistakes

68. Hicks to Gresham, Lima, April 17, 1893, no. 488, Despatches 1826–1906, roll 52, USNA.

69. Ojeda to M.E., Lima, June 15, 1891, no. 39; September 25, 1891, no. 66; March 2, 1893, no. 17; and July 16, 1893, no. 42, leg. H-1678, AGMAE.

70. James H. McKenzie to S.S., Lima, April 3, 1894, no. 110, Despatches 1826–1906, roll 54, USNA.

71. Basadre, *Historia* 10:100–1.

72. W. R. Grace & Co. to M.P. Grace, New York, July 28, 1894, box 71, no. 10, p. 425, WRGP; Alfred St. John to Earl of Kimberley, Lima, September 17, 1894, FO 61/408, NAUK; Basadre, *Historia* 10:106.

73. Telegram, M. P. Grace to W. R. Grace Co., December 4, 1894, box 72, no. 11, pp. 197–98, WRGP.

brought him in direct conflict with his political nemesis, Nicolás de Piérola, known by his followers as "the caliph." Together with associate Echenique, Piérola had been tirelessly organizing uprisings from their exile in Chile. Since 1889, Piérola's insurrections had failed, leading to the caliph's imprisonment in April 1890 followed by his escape six months later. In 1895, however, Cáceres suffered political defeat at the hands of the popular former dictator who led this time a successful insurrection in Lima.

Even after his forced retirement, Cáceres retained his political-military influence during the first two decades of the twentieth century, obtaining prized diplomatic posts abroad from civilian presidents Romaña, Pardo, and Leguía. Cáceres was essentially paid with public and private funds to deter him from destabilizing the constitutional-civilian order inaugurated after 1895. This type of political sinecure became a tradition in dealing with politically ambitious high-ranking military officers throughout the twentieth century.

The Legacy of the Caliph

The historical role of civilian caudillo Nicolás de Piérola and his political movement continues to be debated among historians. One view is represented by Jorge Basadre's monumental *Historia de la República del Perú* in which he passionately argues that President Piérola (1895–1899) was the true popular hero of the reconstruction period. Basadre believed that Piérola rectified past mistakes and reinvented himself to deal with a government deemed disorganized and improvised ("Estado empírico").[74] Economic historians have also praised Piérola's financial and economic policies that were supposedly favorable—along with exchange rate depreciation—for developing exports and domestic manufacturing in the 1890s.[75] Perhaps impressed by obvious economic and financial improvements, the U.S. chargé d'affaires in Lima at the time concluded that Piérola's administration "appears to be efficient, conservative and honest, and to commend itself to the business interests of the people of Peru generally."[76]

74. "Efigie de Piérola," in Basadre, *Historia* 10:128–43.
75. Rosemary Thorp and Geoffrey Bertram, *Peru 1890–1977: Growth and Policy in an Open Economy* (New York: Columbia University, 1978), chapter 3, esp. 26–29.
76. Dudley to William R. Day, Lima, August 22, 1898, no. 166, Despatches 1826–1906, roll 59, USNA.

A radically opposite perspective derives from the arguments and evidence presented by Manuel González Prada who singles Piérola as one of the worst political leaders ever, as he was unable and unwilling to change his corrupt ways throughout his life. According to González Prada, Piérola was one of those politicians born for the "ruin and shame of the people among whom they live: where he places one hand he leaves stains of blood; where he applies the other he leaves traces of mud."[77]

González Prada followed Piérola's career closely. Almost contemporaries, they had studied in the same seminary school but they later adopted starkly opposing ideas. González Prada was an atheist, freethinker, and democrat. Piérola was conservative, proclerical, dictatorial, fond of his theocratic nickname "the caliph," and admirer of Napoleon III after whom he modeled his stylized goatee and whiskers.[78] González Prada had few followers, Piérola led a large-scale movement; one was sincere and honest, the other deceitful and corrupt. For González Prada, the former dictator was a prehistoric barbarian in the middle of modern civilization, representing all that was bent and wrong in Peruvian history.[79]

Piérola's "legal" presidency, the product of nonstop insurrectionary conspiracies and violence, was also plagued by authoritarian attacks against press freedoms, political and electoral rights, and civil service honesty.[80] Governing from the business sector's "purulent nucleus" of Lima, Piérola cultivated a new strategic alliance with the Civilistas, his former enemies, betraying his most radical followers and catering instead the economic elite and its remodeled arrangements with the government. Piérola's second government was also an "economic dictatorship" that lacked respect for fiscal regulations and transparent public sector accounts.[81]

The logic of postwar economic recovery, based on pragmatic arrangements with new foreign and domestic interests, had transformed the role of

77. González Prada, "De bajo imperio" (originally published in *Los Parias,* no. 48, June 1909), *Prosa menuda,* in *Obras,* vol. 2, part 4, 384.

78. Alberto Ulloa Sotomayor, *Don Nicolás de Piérola: una época en la historia del Perú* (Lima: Minerva, 1981), 360–61, 389; Sánchez, *Mito y realidad,* 20–22.

79. González Prada, "Piérola" (written in 1898–1899), *Figuras y figurones* (first published in 1938), in *Obras,* vol. 1, part 2, 338, 341–42, 346, 362–63, and 373.

80. González Prada, "Cuidado con la bolsa" (originally in *Germinal,* February 18, 1899), and "Las autoridades y la Unión Nacional" (February 28, 1899), *Propaganda y ataque,* in *Obras,* vol. 2, part 4, 115–16, 121–24.

81. González Prada, "La retirada de Billinghurst" (originally in *Germinal,* January 14, 1899); "El momento político" (1903), *Propaganda y ataque,* in *Obras,* vol. 2, part 4, 106–7, 167.

the state as economic agent prior to Piérola's second administration. Private sector groups were granted contracts for government revenue collection, public works, and other services. There were now fewer opportunities for political leaders to manipulate foreign indebtedness to cover up corrupt administration. Piérola had to change his previous reliance on foreign interests who would profit from speculation with the Peruvian public debt. The new economic and financial arrangements had shifted the influence of political lobbying in favor of a few monopolistic interests based mainly on direct investment and local bank credit lines rather than foreign portfolio investment. Under these circumstances Piérola's old strategy for financing his violent bids for taking and retaining power was becoming less effective.

The shady financing of Piérola's political campaigns in the 1880s and early 1890s relied on self-serving followers and speculators expecting handsome rewards once the caliph was reinstalled. This is clearly exemplified by Piérola's "loan" from Grace in 1884 described earlier and his continued shady relationship with Dreyfus. Piérola's critics, in particular González Prada and Clorinda Matto de Turner,[82] unceasingly denounced these venal private connections and irregular financing that led to abuse of the public interest.

The immediate culprit was of course Auguste Dreyfus, Piérola's old guano partner based in Paris. The caliph received sustenance from Dreyfus under "humiliating conditions" during Piérola's exile in 1882–1883. Piérola's services for Dreyfus were then reduced to testifying in favor of Dreyfus's financial claims against Peru and its creditors in international suits. Despite Piérola's dictatorial measures in 1880 that had illegally granted Dreyfus recognition of all his questionable claims,[83] the French businessman continued to battle his case in European courts with the political support of his former lawyer, Jules Grévy, then president of the French Republic. However, in 1887 both Dreyfus and Grévy fell from grace: the French president was forced to resign due to a major scandal involving his son-in-law and political protégé, Daniel Wilson, who was implicated, among other accusa-

---

82. Clorinda Matto de Turner, "En el Perú: narraciones históricas," in *Boreales, miniaturas y porcelanas* (Buenos Aires: Imprenta de Juan A. Alsina, 1902), 11–64. Electronic version edited by Thomas Ward, http://www.evergreen.loyola.edu/~TWARD/MUJERES/MATTO/HISTORICAS/Peru1.html.

83. "Día llegará en que el país sepa si esos laudos, que son hoy una amenaza formidable suspendida sobre el porvenir financiero del Perú, fueron redactados por Ud. o por el abogado de Mr. Ford [Dreyfus's manager in Lima]." Guillermo Billinghurst to Nicolás de Piérola, Tacna, April 17, 1899, Archivo Piérola, vol. 3, BNP.

tions leveled by the French press and public opinion, in the illegal sale of military decorations in partnership with well-known French generals and a former war minister.[84]

The Peruvian press quickly associated the Grévy-Wilson scandal with official "pressure" exerted on French courts in favor of the Dreyfus's claims that Piérola consistently supported. In reaction to these revelations, Piérola ordered his faithful Peruvian lawyer, Manuel Pablo Olaechea (who also acted as legal counsel to Dreyfus in Lima), to file a libel suit against the editor of *El Nacional*. This legal move was criticized as part and parcel of Piérola's prior and subsequent attempts to silence the press.[85] The court declared the request for trial inadmissible. Close to death in 1895, Dreyfus wrote a dramatic letter to Piérola after he regained presidential power. Recalling their twenty-five-year–long friendship, Dreyfus proclaimed with heart and soul to have been to Piérola "everything a being in this world can be to another." Invoking the sake of his second wife and daughters, Dreyfus entrusted to Piérola the task of giving the ultimate solution to the Frenchman's financial claims against Peru. The lion's share of Dreyfus's capital and labor of many years was tied to the pending claims, which was the cause of his serious financial problems in the last ten years. He also entrusted Piérola and lawyer Olaechea to cleanse his "trampled" memory in Peru, making sure that two or three newspapers, and "someone who would take care of the required details," restore his name for posterity.[86] Dreyfus had also recommended in an earlier, even more blatantly commanding letter that, now that Piérola was in power, an ironclad agreement with the French government should guarantee the payment of Dreyfus's claims and deter future Peruvian governments from altering such agreement.[87] These were among the last letters between Dreyfus and Piérola demonstrating the

84. Jean Garrigues, *Les scandales de la République de Panama à Elf* (Paris: Éditions Robert Laffont, 2004), 17–25.

85. Piérola to Olaechea, Milagro, November 28, 1887, in "Expediente . . . sobre denuncia de un libelo en el periódico 'El Nacional,'" Archivo Piérola, vol. 3, BNP. The trial was started in Lima on December 10, 1887 against editor Pedro Lira, allegedly held responsible for the contents of the column, "Crónica Exterior, Francia, Correspondencia para El Nacional," signed by "Grotius," *El Nacional,* vol. 22, no. 6017, November 25, 1887. See also another libel suit filed by Piérola's sons, Isaías and Amadeo, against the editor of *La Funda* in December 1897 that led to the imprisonment of a journalist.

86. Auguste Dreyfus to Nicolás de Piérola, Paris, December 27, 1895, Archivo Piérola, vol. 3, BNP.

87. Dreyfus to Piérola, Paris, May 3, 1895; and L. de Dreyfus to Piérola, Pontchartrain, Seine & Oise, July 18, 1895, Archivo Piérola, vol. 3, BNP.

twisted relationship between the corruptor businessman and the corruptee politician.

Piérola's private correspondence also reveals other sources of funds for his political adventures and conspiracies. Many of these debts incurred with political followers and other individuals were never paid or recognized. In some cases, the only proof of debt was the irate insistence of the creditor. In 1897, Augusto Barrenechea claimed that he had waited long enough to hear even a word from Piérola concerning the repayment of money without interest given on many occasions to Piérola, his son Isaías, and a person not mentioned for reasons of "delicacy."[88] In 1903, Piérola recognized a debt of 12,400 soles to the heirs of José Araníbar, a key financial official who in 1880–1881 had supplied funds to the caliph's wife, Jesús Iturbide de Piérola, to cover "urgent expenses" resulting from the "political struggle."[89] Likewise, in 1901 and 1902 Piérola was pressed to settle the payment of old debts owed to the brothers of deceased José Francisco Canevaro (who, like Grace, had been an important arms supplier to Piérola's dictatorship in 1880), as well as to the widow of Andrés Malatesta.[90]

The most revealing indictment of Piérola's intermingled personal and public financial responsibilities and abuses comes from the correspondence with his former close political collaborator and vice president, Guillermo Billinghurst. Piqued by Piérola's political treachery, the wealthy Billinghurst wrote condemnatory letters that were read and mentioned by González Prada.[91] In the original letters, Billinghurst revealed that he had contributed towards the costs of Piérola's insurrection of 1894–1895 with up to £8,700 (including a payment of £2,000 to Piérola's associate Pedro A. del Solar). He also revealed that a Spanish financier named Oliván made contributions including $2,000 given to Piérola's old political sidekick, Juan Martín Echenique, for the purchase of a ship. Citing a letter from Piérola asking Oliván for a new loan with the promise to "compensate you out of taxes (*gravámenes*)," Billinghurst requested that Piérola provide clear account-

88. Barrenechea to Piérola, Lima, June 3, 1897, Archivo Piérola, vol. 3, BNP.

89. "Reconocimiento de deuda," Lima, November 3, 1903, Archivo Piérola, vol. 1, BNP.

90. R[afael] Canevaro to Piérola, Lima, August 3, 1901: Personal "credits" totaling £2,300 supplied to Piérola. The Canevaro brothers also claimed from the government an unpaid balance of £43,140 for weapons sold in 1880, a debt that was settled only in 1912 (see Basadre, *Historia* 12:152–53); and "Declaración de Nicolás de Piérola," Lima, October 21, 1902: Original debt of 2,500 soles owed to Malatesta dating from 1887, Archivo Piérola, vol. 5, BNP.

91. González Prada, "Figuras y figurones," in *Obras,* vol. 1, part 2, 355; "La retirada de Billinghurst," *Propaganda y ataque,* in *Obras,* vol. 2, part 2, 108.

ing of how these sums were used and whether the expenses were in violation of civil and even criminal law.[92]

Piérola replied with caution, attributing Billinghurst's attacks to a passionate outburst, and promising to repay debts incurred during his private insurrectionary activities through fiscal measures that Piérola himself would soon announce in a speech to Congress.[93] Billinghurst seized the opportunity to write back a scalding fourteen-page letter unmasking Piérola's obviously insincere and illegal promises of repayment. Billinghurst added that in 1894–1895, Echenique and Piérola's lover, Madame Garreaud, had placed a total of £6,000 in clandestine and irregular bond issues in Valparaíso and Lima to finance the revolution, a sum that once in power Piérola ordered repaid without legislative authorization. This was part of a barrage of accusations about dishonesty and insincerity spanning the old caudillo's entire political career, including his second presidential term Billinghurst described as plagued by "a few opportunists (*logreros*) that dispose of fiscal funds as if they were personal assets."[94]

During his second term (1895–1899), Piérola engaged in a series of pseudo-reforms with the political intent of adapting to the modernizing socioeconomic bases of power retention. Catering to the financial and economic interests that supported his government, Piérola and a collaborative Congress introduced several measures such as the establishment of a private collection agency (Sociedad Recaudadora de Impuestos) that retained as much as a 25-percent share of the total revenue collected, after deducting 15 percent for costs incurred, and often provided cash advances to the government. This practice, together with a much-reviled monopoly tax on salt as well as contracts for constructing a road to the central jungle (vía del Pichis), were criticized by González Prada as venues of graft and harmful intrigues (*gatuperios*) arranged with Civilista allies.[95] The radical critic also attacked new legislation for reforms of the nation's currency, banking system, and insurance industry. Strong new connections to the fast-growing financial elite allowed Piérola not only political advantages but also personal participation in speculative real estate and stock deals that provided a considerable income even after he left office. José Payán, a Cuban émigré and

92. Billinghurst to Piérola, Tacna, April 1, 1899, Archivo Piérola, vol. 3, BNP.

93. Piérola to Billinghurst, draft, Lima, April 7, 1899, Archivo Piérola, vol. 3, BNP.

94. Billinghurst to Piérola, Tacna, April 17, 1899, pp. 12-14, and 8, Archivo Piérola, vol. 3, BNP: "En el fondo . . . hay algo más que una farsa; y el tiempo se encargará de descubrirlo. No soy yo el llamado a arrojar lodo sobre su rostro."

95. González Prada, "El momento político" (1903), *Propaganda y ataque,* in *Obras,* vol. 2, part 4, 167.

central figure in Peruvian financial spheres, was Piérola's close friend and advisor on financial policy.[96]

During his presidency, Piérola also established a French military mission to "professionalize" the army. These measures translated primarily into reducing the army to half its size and cleanse it from Cacerista personnel. Military resistance and conspiracy against Piérola's government were thus substantially reduced. However, this more obedient and institutionalized military proved fateful in the containment of future Pierolista insurrectionary adventures. Likewise, the heralded electoral reform to prevent abuses that often resulted in the fraudulent election of incumbent party's candidate, failed to guarantee Piérola's subsequent reelection after his Civilista allies captured the new electoral machinery.

Despite these changes, in 1897 Piérola tried to launch a new "orgy" of fabulous foreign loans and road and railway construction to the jungle region; similar strategies had proven advantageous for profiteers in the guano age. Government offices and posts were created for friends, huge official commissions were paid to cronies, newspapers were bought to make them servile or closed if journalists failed to behave, charges of public sector fraud ignored, fiscal and accounting requirements disregarded, and laws misconstrued or not enforced.[97] All of this was engineered to fulfill Piérola's desire to remain in power at whatever cost, including the abandonment of loyal supporters and collaborators. This became obvious when Billinghurst, expecting Piérola's unconditional support for a presidential bid that would keep the Demócratas in power, was frustrated in his aspirations. Billinghurst's recalcitrant anti-Civilista stand contradicted Piérola's opportunistic new friendship with Candamo and his party. Acting as plenipotentiary in ultimately failed negotiations with Chile over Tacna and Arica, Billinghurst refused to subordinate his policy to that of the foreign affairs minister and prime minister, Civilista Enrique de la Riva Agüero. Subsequent political intrigues shifted Piérola's support toward the compromise "fusion" presidential candidate Eduardo López de Romaña, a fellow proclerical politician from Arequipa and former minister.[98]

96. Irving B. Dudley to John Sherman, Lima, May 2, 1898, no. 119, Despatches 1826–1906, roll 58, USNA.

97. Billinghurst to Piérola, Tacna, April 17, 1899, p. 7, Archivo Piérola, vol. 3, BNP, referring to the ill-conceived contract with Joseph-Herz harmful to the country's credit standing. See also González Prada, *Figuras y figurones,* in *Obras,* vol. 1, part 2, 364.

98. Dudley to Sherman, Lima, May 4, 1898, no. 126, Despatches 1826–1906, roll 58, USNA.

In response, Billinghurst attacked Piérola's inflated vanity and political duplicity as the source of his misguided political failings: "Political hypocrisy is one thousand times more disastrous than religious hypocrisy, and you . . . have the former to a degree that no one that does not know you intimately could imagine."[99] Piérola had used Billinghurst, promising that Billinghurst would succeed him as president, and then reneged on his promise. The Demócratas represented a means for Piérola to seize power, a feat that had cost "so much spilling of blood, the loss of so many millions, and the stagnation of material progress in Peru."[100] However, as González Prada justly noted, Billinghurst bore direct responsibility for this tradition of political violence that cost so much to the country's public and institutions. The division of the Demócratas undermined its political advantage owed to the "corruption and dictatorial character of the [Cacerista] Military Party on the one side, and the alleged aristocratic composition of the Civil Party on the other."[101] The election of López de Romaña, however, eventually allowed the Civilistas to displace Piérola's party and influence. By 1902, electoral obstacles challenged the ambitions of the Demócratas.[102]

Piérola and his inner circle did not cease to resist and criticize those in power after 1899, but he did not succeed in obtaining another term as president. His party declined, but not without attempting to cause serious damage to the recovery of the country's institutional stability. A policy of abstaining from (refusing to participate in) successive elections as a form of protest causing instability, as well as endless insurrectionist conspiracies compounded the growing isolation of the aging caudillo. Between 1900 and 1908, however, Piérola served as nominal manager or board member of several companies, which allowed him to enrich himself with the support of some of Lima's biggest financiers. This seems to have been a consolation prize to prevent Piérola from carrying out damaging political interventions and insurrection. The real estate and savings company La Colmena, established in 1900, promised to open up a new major street in downtown Lima, build luxury buildings financed by local savings, and sell the new properties to the public. Piérola was the firm's president and several of Lima's most prominent financiers were members of its board of directors.

99. Billinghurst to Piérola, Tacna, April 17, 1899, p. 4, Archivo Piérola, vol. 3, BNP.
100. Billinghurst to Piérola, Tacna, April 17, 1899, p. 7, Archivo Piérola, vol. 3, BNP.
101. Dudley to John Hay, Lima, March 1899, no. 223, Despatches 1826–1906, roll 59, USNA.
102. Dudley to Hay, Lima, September 16, 1902, no. 656, and September 26, 1902, no. 660, Despatches 1826–1906, roll 62, USNA.

They all expected high speculative profits. The municipality of Lima offered La Colmena the necessary permits to engage in construction that
would substantially transform an important part of the city.[103] Likewise,
Azufrera Sechura was a stock company that aimed to attract large-scale capital to develop and market sulfur products. However, by 1908–1909, both
enterprises went bankrupt due to speculative excesses exposed by a recession. A judge even ordered the imprisonment of the president and directors
of these companies, Piérola and his associates, for "wrongful bankruptcy,"
which affected a host of local savings account holders and investors.[104] The
economic sinecures awarded by the elite to Piérola had ended. A new wave
of insurrectionary ardor stirred Piérola and his followers.

On April 28, 1908, a perplexed French businessman, Raoul de Saint-
Seine, manager of the important Empresa Muelle y Dársena and representative of the Société Générale, visited the French chargé d'affaires in Lima,
Pierre Merlou, bearing a sensational revelation. The day before former president Piérola had met with M. Saint-Seine and, after explaining the political situation as one of growing discontent against the Civilistas' efforts to
elect their presidential candidate, bluntly requested £5,000 to finance a revolution scheduled to occur before the upcoming elections. The plan was for
Piérola's Demócratas to control Lima, while taking advantage of diver-
sionary provincial insurrections led by radical Liberal ally Augusto Durand.
M. Merlou immediately telegraphed and wrote a detailed letter to his superiors in Paris informing them of the situation, his thoughts on the issue,
and the course he took on advising the hesitant Saint-Seine.[105] Despite considering Piérola a great and upright popular leader and "ami sincère de
France,"[106] like most French diplomats of the time, Merlou strongly tried
to dissuade Saint-Seine of providing the requested donation to Piérola.

According to Merlou, things had changed and conditions were no longer
favorable for Pierolista insurrections. The big foreign corporations such as
the Cerro de Pasco Mining Company, Peruvian Corporation, Grace, Dun-

103. "Documentos referentes a 'La Colmena,' Sociedad Anónima de Construc-
ciones y Ahorros," Archivo Piérola, vol. 8, BNP.
104. González Prada, "La Azufrera Sechura" (originally in *Los Parias,* no. 46, January 1909), *Prosa menuda,* in *Obras,* vol. 2, part 2, 375–78.
105. Telegram by Merlou, Lima, April 28, 1908: "M. Piérola a demandé a M. St. Seine
5,000 livres sterling pour faire révolution. J'ai énergiquement conseillé refus"; Merlou to
M.A.E., Lima, April 28, 1908, no. 51, CPC-NS, Pérou, vol. 1, ff. 67–73, AMAE.
106. Merlou to M.A.E., April 28, 1908, no. 51; Merlou to M.A.E. Pichon, Lima,
February 1, 1908, no. 10, CPC-NS, Pérou, vol. 1, ff. 72, 61, AMAE.

can Fox, Graham Rowe, Lockett, and others would sternly oppose an insurrection that would disturb Peru's painfully rebuilt international credit standing. Civilista leader José Pardo and the party's candidate, chief of cabinet and Minister of Finance Augusto B. Leguía, had expanded opportunities to foreign capital investment. In addition, military officers now had good salaries and retirement benefits, and thus could not be easily swayed to participate in insurrection. Moreover, Piérola no longer enjoyed the support of wealthy backers; Merlou had been informed by reliable sources that Piérola's group had attempted to raise £10,000 through a bond issue that failed. According to Merlou, given that some people estimated that at least £400,000 were necessary to organize a revolution, failure to raise a paltry £10,000 was damning evidence of dwindling support for the Pierolistas. Saint-Seine eventually agreed with Merlou but, considering that Peru was a place where "the most implausible things sometimes become realities," he continued to ask Merlou whether it would not be prudent to pay a sort of insurance premium and offer Piérola an "advance" on La Colmena and Azufrera Sechura stock, which was mostly owned by the caliph's friends.[107] Merlou retorted that the stock of the latter was worthless and that of the former was much depreciated. Not only would it be difficult to keep such an arrangement secret with so many stockholders involved, convincing the public that a loan on such companies' stock was not a direct subsidy for the insurrection would be nearly impossible. Ultimately, Saint-Seine was told, the French legation would be unable to adequately defend him against all the reprisals and dangers he would be subjected to if he financed Piérola's revolution in any way.[108]

Durand's insurrection did take place on May 1, 1908, in Huánuco and other provinces, but Piérola's concerted action in Lima did not. Repression was effective; Durand was arrested, although he soon managed to escape to continue nurturing conspiracies.[109] Merlou's views had been correct. Even Grace & Company had become more cautious in dealing with Piérola since the late 1890s, in part due to unfulfilled financial agreements with the Peruvian Corporation, among other conflicts that Piérola had with foreign interests during his presidency.[110] By the early twentieth century, the country

107. Merlou to M.A.E., Lima, April 28, 1908, no. 51, CPC-NS, Pérou, vol. 1, f. 72v, AMAE.

108. Ibid., f. 73.

109. Basadre, *Historia* 11:166–68.

110. M. P. Grace to L. H. Sherman, November 9, 1898, box 69, no. 31, p. 477, WRGP: "I have hardly ever written a letter to President Piérola that has not been turned

had been partly modernized and institutionalized. Piérola's violent and corrupt legacy had consequently grown weaker.[111] To revamp the means for gaining and retaining corrupt power, that is, to reinvent the caliph's strategies of graft, a new type of leader had to appear. The one politician that showed such promise was Augusto B. Leguía, in many ways a disciple of Piérola.

Leguía and the Civilistas

The heirs of the political organization founded by Manuel Pardo in the 1860s were able to defeat Piérola in the long run. In the early twentieth century, the Civilistas were led by a new generation of men such as Manuel Candamo and José Pardo who helped the nation achieve an important degree of institutional modernization. However, they have since been relentlessly criticized for being part of a wealthy and retrograde elite, a small group of "polite people" (*gente decente*) encompassing urban and rural property owners, professionals, and allied provincial bosses or *gamonales*. Analysts, diplomats, and historians have described and discussed this sociopolitical conglomerate, avowedly ruling the country as an "oligarchy," since at least the late 1870s.[112]

---

down by [Dr. Emilio del] Solar [the Graces' legal advisor in Lima] and Eyre. . . I believe we could have approached Piérola years ago and made a friend of him but Mr. John Eyre and Dr. Solar were always opposed to it, and, as they were in the spot, we left the final decision in their hands." See also draft letter, M. P. Grace to Piérola, November 1, 1898, ibid., pp. 478–83, in which Grace complains about the government's unfulfilled commitments with the Peruvian Corporation.

111. This assessment coincides with that of Ulloa, *Nicolás de Piérola,* 421: "error notorio de concepto sobre la situación del país."

112. José Andrés Torres Paz, *La oligarquía y la crisis: disertación leída en la Sociedad "Jurídica–Literaria" en sesión del 29 de agosto de 1877* (Lima: Imprenta del Teatro, 1877), iii, 20. Following the cues of Leguía's informants and ideologues, U.S. diplomats referred to the Partido Civil as the "oligarchy" or "aristocratic party" since at least 1910. William Penn Cresson to S.S., Lima, March 12, 1910, no. 333, 823.00/74. A U.S. ambassador in the 1920s referred to the Civilistas as the "reactionary, ultra-conservative faction of Peru, corresponding to the group of large landowners. . . They are anti-foreign, anti-industrial and wish Peru to be solely an agricultural country without development outside of their own haciendas, with the country administered entirely for their own benefit." Miles Poindexter to S.S., Lima, April 2, 1925, no. 360, 823.00/49. U.S. Despatches 1910–1930, microcopy M746, rolls 2 and 5 respectively, USNA.

In his old quest against the Civilistas, Piérola received important support from radical mobs that chanted, "Down with the ring! White people die!" Civilistas have been also accused of using the power of money to buy voters, rig elections, control the electoral system, distort and suborn the rule of law, and marginalize popular leaders.[113] The Civilistas formed "the party of the intelligent and well-to-do; but unfortunately has always been attacked as aristocratic, and destitute of proper sympathy for the masses of the people."[114] However, compared to Piérola's administrations, Civilista governments enjoyed markedly lower levels of corruption until the rise of Leguía and the unfortunate meddling of military "protectors" of the elite's political interests.

During the transitional administration of López de Romaña (1899–1903), a few incidents of blatant corruption were made public. Perhaps the most important and well-documented case involved the president's close friend and minister of finance, the *arequipeño* businessman Mariano A. Belaúnde, also a political friend of Piérola and the strongest link between López de Romaña and the Demócrata former president. Officially acting as minister of finance in 1899, Belaúnde used his own firm's bills of exchange to transfer official funds for up to 500,000 francs to Europe for the purpose of purchasing weapons for the Peruvian army. Belaúnde's European correspondents did not accept his bills, thus triggering a major political and financial scandal. The procedure used by Belaúnde was not only irregular, but it illegally combined private and public interests. Belaúnde was accused of "reckless misappropriation" (*malversación por imprudencia temeraria*). He was arrested and his remaining wealth confiscated in the midst of a long judicial process ending only in 1904. About three thousand people organized a public protest to demand that the president ensure Belaúnde's imprisonment, and because of Belaúnde's connection with Piérola, they also demonstrated outside the headquarters of La Colmena, where several were wounded by police sabers.[115]

113. Basadre, *Historia* 9:193; González Prada defined the Civilistas as simple businessmen disguised as politicians, in "Los partidos y la Unión Nacional" (1898), in *Horas de lucha,* 202.

114. Dudley to Hay, Lima, March 1899, no. 223, Despatches 1826–1906, roll 59, USNA.

115. Basadre, *Historia* 11:30–37. See also Ramiro Gil de Uribarri to M.E., Lima, October 5, 1900, no. 85, leg. H-1678, AGMAE; *El Comercio,* no. 24201, October 1, 1900, 1; and Beauclerk to Lansdowne, Lima, July 5, 1902, no. 9, confidential, FO

A growing rift between Piérola and López de Romaña was intensified by the rewards and concessions granted to General Cáceres in exile and his military followers in Peru. López de Romaña officially entrusted Cáceres with purchasing weapons in France for the Peruvian army; it was "practically certain" that part of the funds thus made available to Cáceres served "as a bribe to Cáceres in order that he could remain quietly in easy exile."[116] According to a French diplomat who recalled the "exactions" during Cáceres's former regime, López de Romaña had imprudently surrounded himself with Caceristas to whom he entrusted important military posts as a means to oppose Piérola.[117] Cáceres returned to Peru to play an important political role in the disputed elections of 1903 that were reportedly rife with "incalculable frauds" and vote buying by the Civilistas in Lima and the provinces.[118] Civilista Manuel Candamo was elected after a strategic alliance with the militaristic Cacerista Constitutional party.[119] In 1905, Civilista José Pardo, who was elected president in controversial elections following Candamo's sudden death, rewarded Cáceres for his support with a plush plenipotentiary diplomatic representation in Rome.[120]

Malfunctioning electoral institutions in Peru were the source of much of the political conflict and allegations of political corruption that favored the candidates of the parties that controlled the electoral machine. The electoral reform law of 1902 under the presidency of López de Romaña modified the composition of the Junta Electoral Nacional, the board regulating all electoral matters that were formerly under congressional control. In 1901, the Demócratas still had a majority in the Chamber of Deputies; the abuses committed by the electoral board's head at the time, Carlos de Piérola, the

---

61/434, ff. 61–63v, esp. 61v–62, NAUK. From the latter: "[U]ndoubtedly a great deal of the money was embezzled by Señor Belaúnde, ex-Minister of Finance who has been in prison for the last two years for that offence."

116. Beauclerk to Lansdowne, July 5, 1902, no. 9, FO 61/134, ff. 61–61v, NAUK.

117. Eognes to M.A.E. Delcasse, Lima, April 10, 1903, no. 8, CPC-NS, Pérou, vol. 1, ff. 45–46v, AMAE.

118. Eognes to M.A.E. Delcasse, Lima, June 23, 1903, no. 10, CPC-NS, Pérou, vol. 1, ff. 47–47v, AMAE. On comparatively similar problems in the rest of Latin America at the time, see Eduardo Posada-Carbó, "Electoral Juggling: A Contemporary History of Corruption of Suffrage in Latin America, 1830–1930," *Journal of Latin American Studies* 32 (2000): 611–44.

119. Basadre, *Historia* 11: 118.

120. Beauclerk to Lansdowne, Lima, September 14, 1905, no. 43, FO 61/443, n.p., NAUK.

former president's brother, were conspicuous.[121] Under the new rules, the executive branch appointed a majority of electoral board members as well as board members representing the judiciary. Bickering over representation on the board and its decisions characterized practically all elections of the twentieth century. In the early part of the century, the Civilistas, Billinghurst, and Leguía were accused of electoral transgressions, especially in 1903, 1904, 1908, and 1912 that, together with the electoral abstention strategy stubbornly practiced by Piérola and his Demócratas, effectively prevented Piérola's reelection.[122]

The visceral animosity among the few families and groups engaged in political struggle produced spectacular assassination plots and aggression against individuals, such as attacks by bitter Piérolas against haughty Pardos, mob attacks against respectable homes, bloody duels of honor, and even the boycott of a Durand wedding by discriminating Civilista families. Petty personal or group interests, a French diplomat concluded, prevailed over the larger public interest.[123] Candamo and Pardo developed, however, a common financial strategy engineered by long-term finance minister and later prime minister, Augusto B. Leguía, who served in both administrations. Under the banner of "order and progress," these two administrations were constrained by fiscal and budgetary limitations, as well as the international financial panic of 1907 that effectively curbed expansive public expenditures conducive to foreign indebtedness and administrative graft. The economic recovery of the country intensified, especially under Pardo. Fewer instances of corruption were denounced in Congress.[124] Increasingly, however, Leguía pressed for new taxes on alcohol, sugar, and matches to increase revenues and justify expansionary public spending, mainly in

121. Gil de Uribarri to M.E., Lima, August 8, 1901, no. 75, leg. H-1679, AGMAE: "abusos de la Junta Electoral presidida por Carlos Piérola."

122. Basadre, *Historia* 11:66–67; Dudley to Hay, Lima, September 16, 1902, no. 656, Despatches 1826–1906, roll 62, USNA.

123. On the duel between Enrique Pardo and Gonzalo Ortiz de Zevallos, and the marriage of Juan Durand (brother of Augusto Durand) and a daughter of Dr. Flores, physician of elite Civilista families that refused to attend the wedding, see, respectively, Fréderic Clément-Simon to M.A.E. Pichon, Lima, February 4, 1909, no. 12; and March 10, 1909, no. 18, CPC-NS, Pérou, vol. 2, ff. 11–13v, 22–23v, AMAE.

124. Early in 1907, charges of misappropriation of public funds and lands against the prefecto of Puno prompted the Chamber of Deputies to request explanations from interior minister, Agustín Tovar, who shortly thereafter was forced to resign. Basadre, *Historia* 11:161.

the areas of defense and railway construction, allegedly warranted by the country's natural wealth and international security needs. Consequently, foreign debt began to slowly increase.

Leguía's expansionary policies caused friction with the fiscally austere Civilista leadership and the political opposition. Railroad construction legislation passed in 1904 stimulated an ambitious project for an expensive railroad connecting the central highlands to a port on the river Ucayali at the threshold of the Amazonian jungle. In the congress, Civilistas and Demócratas alike opposed this financially irresponsible and ill-conceived project. A proposal for a foreign loan of £3 million by the Deutsche Bank, promoted by Minister Leguía to finance the Ucayali and four other railway projects, was rejected in Congress in 1906.[125] However, in April 1907 a controversial contract to finance the Ucayali railway construction by phases was signed by Peruvian officials and U.S. entrepreneur Alfred W. McCune, a manager and partner of the Cerro de Pasco Mining Company backed by legendary financiers Morgan, Vanderbilt, Frick, and Hearst. McCune (whose namesake son left an indigenous child dead in a drunken incident in the mining town of Morococha and avoided prison in 1906 by paying bribes, according to a journalistic piece by González Prada)[126] was unable to start construction due to the 1907 financial panic that temporarily postponed further debate on the subject. The eventual division between the pro-Leguía and the "Bloque" faction of the Civilista party had its origin in these profound disagreements over financial and administrative matters rather than in Leguía's discontent with the way the Civilista political bosses treated him, a treatment allegedly resembling that of an estate owner toward his "provincial" manager or majordomo.[127]

Like Piérola, Leguía endeavored to cater to foreign interests who could offer him effective power bases. However, whereas Piérola elicited favorable comments by French and Spanish agents, Leguía was admired by British and other European and, especially, U.S. businessmen and diplomats. Considered a self-made man, although he was a scion of an old landholding family in the northern province of Lambayeque, Leguía had considerable experience in business management and spoke excellent English;

125. Dudley to Elihu Root, Lima, March 24, 1906, no. 1257, and August 3, 1906, no. 1275, Despatches 1826–1906, roll 66, USNA.

126. González Prada, "Necesidad de Tarifa" (originally in *Los Parias,* no. 27, August 1906), *Prosa menuda* (1941), in *Obras,* vol. 2, part 4, 317–20.

127. For the opinion that Leguía, born in a northern province, was humiliated by Lima's elite as a "mayordomo capaz," see Basadre, *Historia* 12:138.

together with a certain charm, strong will, and a speculative mogul's ambition, he reportedly captivated many foreigners. Before becoming a successful politician, Leguía had managed sugar estates, and worked for the U.S. export-import firm, Charles Prevost & Company, and the New York Life Insurance Company. Leguía's business and political contacts in New York and Washington proved invaluable during his political career; a contemporary of the legendary robber barons, Leguía was nurtured in the cultural climate of expanding international monopolies and trusts. He admired Porfirio Díaz, a "brilliant figure . . . to whom the social and economic reorganization [of Mexico] is entirely owed."[128] Through Leguía's marriage, and those of his three daughters, Leguía was related closely to important landowning aristocratic families. His three sons, Augusto, José, and Juan, teenagers in 1909, studied abroad under the supervision of relatives, friends, and Peruvian diplomats in active service.[129]

Under the modernizing conditions of early twentieth-century Peru, Leguía fit better than Piérola the role of a power broker willing to deliver or allow corrupt rewards, favor foreign interests, and break the rules in order to achieve and maintain power. Having guaranteed his election to the presidency as Pardo's official successor in 1908, Leguía envisioned a so-called conciliatory policy of *ubicaciones* or allotted congressional seats offered to the Pierolistas to neutralize the Civilista faction opposed to his policies in Congress. However, Leguía soon learned rude political lessons from the insurrectionary Demócratas and their allies the Liberales. The coup of May 1, 1908, engineered by the elderly Piérola and Durand, and, especially, the insurrectionary adventure of May 29, 1909, led by Piérola's brother Carlos and sons Isaías and Amadeo and supported by Orestes Ferro and Enrique Llosa, almost cost Leguía the presidency and his life. These events injected a new tone to Leguía's personal resolve to pursue and assert authoritarian goals during his first administration.[130] The subsequent repression and hardening

128. Leguía to Jacinto S. García, Lima, October 29, 1909, letterbook, no. 3, p. 335, Archivo Leguía, BNP.

129. Letters by Leguía concerning the education of Leguía's son Augusto in Paris and Switzerland, and José in the United States: to Ernesto Ayulo, Lima, November 2, 1908; Teresa O. de Prevost, Lima, January 29, 1909; and Eduardo Higginson, Consul General of Peru in New York, Lima, July 31, 1909, letterbooks, no. 1, p. 165, no. 2, p. 51, and, no. 3, pp. 56–57, respectively, Archivo Leguía, BNP.

130. After May 29, 1909, Leguía resolved to oppose the "quebrantos que viene sufriendo el Perú con los reiterados movimientos subversivos [de] unos cuantos logreros afanados en adueñarse del poder" (Leguía to Ernesto F. Ayulo, Lima, July 31, 1909);

of his regime delineated a formal and informal political and economic strategy that characterized not only the remaining years of his first administration (1908–1912) but also his eleven-year dictatorship (1919–1930).

President Leguía expanded the economic and financial projects he had introduced when he was prime minister under Pardo. He encountered a renewed and fierce Civilista congressional opposition unwilling to approve expansionist public expenditures that could lead to large budgetary deficits. Civilistas were also keenly opposed to Leguía's pragmatic foreign policy conducted by Minister Melitón Porras who, in order to allow time for a costly military build-up, proposed substantial land concessions and intermediation by the United States during negotiations of simultaneous border disputes that almost led to war with several of Peru's neighbors.[131] With a zealous combative style, Leguía pushed for his foreign policy, ambitious military and naval spending program, and a coalition of U.S. and local interests bent on constructing the grandiose and poorly engineered Ucayali railroad project.[132] Actually in 1911–1912, the Ucayali railway concession was the main issue of dispute between the Civilista "Bloque" opposition in Congress and Leguía who stubbornly continued to defend it "owing far from disinterested motives."[133] This serious conflict drove Leguía to intervene illegally in congressional elections and rules to allow his cronies to capture a majority in Congress in 1912.

Based initially on his extensive family relationships and devoid of organized party following and reliable political alliances, Leguía built instead a maverick political support network among opportunistic middle class and nouveau riche politicians who demanded rewards linked to shady public works, misappropriations of public funds, public sector procurement con-

---

"viendo que de un acto de mi voluntad dependía la suerte del país, redoblé mis energías y resolvíme a la vía crucis [sic] que me esperaba dando por hecho el sacrificio de mi persona" (Leguía to Eduardo S. Leguía, Lima, August 26, 1909); "[M]i espíritu decidido, hoy, más que nunca, a sostener el orden cueste lo que costare" (Leguía to Lt. Col. Pedro T. Salmón, prefecto of Cusco, September 2, 1909), letterbook, no. 3, pp. 71–72, 143–44, 168–69, Archivo Leguía, BNP.

131. Cresson to S.S., Lima, 12 March 1910, no. 333, 823.00/74, f. 5; and Leslie Combs to S.S., Lima, August 1, 1910, no. 382, 823.00/81, pp. 1–2, Despatches 1910–1930, roll 2, USNA.

132. Jean Guillemin to M.A.E. Pichon, Lima, December 29, 1910, no. 114, CPC-NS, Pérou, no. 2, ff. 143–46; Baron de Vaux a M.A.E. Poincaré, Lima, June 27, 1912, no. 57, CPC-NS, Pérou, vol. 3, ff. 29–30v, AMAE.

133. Lucien Jerome to E. Grey, Lima, April 9, 1911, no. 48, FO 371/1206, f. 82, NAUK.

tracts, and government posts, among other types of graft. Several of his relatives and close friends were appointed to important ministry posts and led the Leguiísta congressional faction, including Eulogio Romero, Enrique Oyanguren, Enrique C. Basadre, Germán Leguía y Martínez, and Roberto Leguía. One of Leguía's closest, yet most corrupt, collaborators and a key promoter of the Ucayali railroad, Minister of Public Works Julio Ego-Aguirre (1909–1911), had a long-standing business and professional relation, as a lawyer and partner, with Julio C. Arana, the largest landowner and rubber baron of the Putumayo region in the Amazonian province of Loreto. During Leguía's first administration, the local and international press denounced Arana and his overseers for exploiting, enslaving, and causing the death of thousands of Amazonian Indians on his extensive rubber properties. Ego-Aguirre and Loreto's prefecto, Francisco Alayza Paz Soldán, also a friend of Leguía, treated regional boss Arana with leniency and helped him surmount the scandal that was ultimately settled after several diplomatic and official investigations that cleared Arana from any direct responsibility.[134] Leguía accepted Arana's argument that such charges were the product of blackmailing by enemies.[135] The government-financed *Peru Today,* an English language publication that hired U.S. journalists in Lima as part of Leguía's innovative strategy to influence foreign public opinion, contributed to international propaganda on the government's biased Putumayo policy.[136]

Leguía's personal correspondence during his first administration revealed an incessant flow of requests for official posts and favors from a wide array of individuals recommending their relatives or favorites. Some of these bold

134. Ascensión Martínez Riaza, "Política regional y gobierno de la amazonía peruana," *Histórica* 23 (1999): 393–462; Basadre, *Historia* 12:182–88; Conversation between Sir E. Grey and Peruvian chargé d'affaires reported to Mr. Des Graz, Foreign Office, London, July 23, 1912, FO 371/1452, n.p., NAUK: "He wished to tell me very confidentially that, among the members of the Commission now appointed by the Peruvian Government, there was a man who had been Minister of Fomento, and who was lawyer and adviser to the Aranas. It was he who, as member of the Government, had induced the President to send, in all good faith, instructions to deny the original articles in *Truth.* The name of this man was Julio Ego Aguirre ... [his influence] could not be good."

135. Leguía to Abel Alarco, Lima, November 23, 1909, letterbook, no. 3, pp. 427–28, Archivo Leguía, BNP: "Yo tenía noticia del grave rumor que sobre supuestos crímenes cometidos por esa Casa [de Julio Arana], en la región del Putumayo circuló en Londres y me complace saber, ahora, por su información que sólo se trataba de un 'chantage' que espero quede bien acreditado."

136. Antonio Plá to M.E., Lima, September 10, 1912, no. 63, leg. H-1679, AGMAE.

requests were granted, rejected, or put on hold according to Leguía's changing political needs: Leguía's relatives (uncle Bernardino Salcedo and brother
Eduardo S. Leguía), and political friends (former judge Jorge Polar of Arequipa, Juan Antonio Trelles of Abancay, and Víctor Larco Herrera of Trujillo) were promptly satisfied or promised prompt satisfaction; Alejandro
Garland who requested a post for his son was invited to write on finances in
the government-run *El Diario;* the request of Mariano Ignacio Prado
Ugarteche, Civilista boss and the eldest son of the former and disgraced president Prado, on behalf of a Sr. Pérez, was politely postponed.[137]

General Andrés Cáceres, at the time well rewarded by Leguía as Peruvian diplomatic minister in Rome and later Berlin, maintained a very
friendly correspondence with his benefactor who speedily granted the promotion of the general's nephew, Ignacio Dianderas, to the subprefecto governorship of Jauja.[138] The influence General Cáceres still held in the Peruvian military provided Leguía the necessary confidence to proceed with his
increasingly aggressive policies against the opposition without having to
fear military coups.[139] In fact, according to a French diplomat, despite
Leguía's generous attitude toward Anglo-French interests, one of the president's main defects was "the patronage of General Cáceres who symbol-
izes cynical corruption and the absence of any moral sense."[140]

In fact, Leguía complied with military demands to increase defense expenditures that fed illegal commissions and graft involving officers and
foreign suppliers. In 1909, Minister of War Pedro Muñiz, a member of the
Cacerista Constitucionales, prevailed in keeping the Mauser as the army's
official rifle against proposals to replace them with the Japanese Arizaka.
Several French torpedo boats and submarines were also purchased following the advice of the French naval mission hired to organize the Peruvian
navy. Some of these purchases were questioned in Congress because of irregularities and lack of legislative authorization that contributed to unnec-

137. Letters written by Leguía between 1908 and 1909 in letterbooks nos. 1–4,
Archivo Leguía, BNP.

138. Leguía to Cáceres, Lima, January 8, 1909, and December 2, 1909, letterbook,
no. 1, pp. 497, 311, Archivo Leguía, BNP.

139. Combs to S.S., Lima, December 22, 1910, no. 452, 823.00/91, Despatches
1910–1930, roll 2, USNA, following a confidential conversation between President
Leguía and Combs on December 17 in which Leguía expressed confidence on continued military support and loyalty.

140. Merlou to M.A.E. Pichon, Lima, June 1, 1908, no. 69, CPC-NS, Pérou, vol. 2,
f. 92, AMAE.

essary growth in the foreign debt, according to Civilista minority deputies José Matías Manzanilla and Luis Miró Quesada. The acquisition of an out-dated and overpriced French battleship, the *Dupuy de Lôme,* also triggered serious charges against Leguía. The purchase in 1912 of eight submarines—pending congressional approval of treasury short-term notes totaling $862,500—from the U.S. Electric Boat Company, a naval supplier accus-tomed to paying "local commissions" (a euphemism for bribery) to obtain sales, was canceled by Leguía's successor who found the acquisition too costly. In fact, irregular budgetary transfers and overspending inflated deficits in the defense, interior (secret police), and public works ministries, while other sectors such as education were neglected. In particular, the ir-regular financing of the secret police (headed by Enrique Iza, who was no-torious for his use of excessive force) was denounced as a pernicious inno-vation of Leguía's first administration. (After Leguía's first term, this and other accusations led to the formation of a congressional commission in charge of investigating several of the Leguía government's measures and procedures. However, this commission was comprised of a Leguiísta ma-jority, and after several dilatory tactics, failed to carry out its mission.)[141]

The growing opposition never ceased to worry Leguía: His correspon-dence reflects efforts to handle political sedition, including the secret sur-veillance of suspects and of provincial authorities accused of a maverick type of corruption, that is, corruption not directed or sanctioned by the Leguía administration.[142] Leguía was growing more and more unpopu-

141. *El Comercio,* no. 33492, October 5, 1912, 1–2, and no. 33501, October 12, 1912, 1; *La Prensa,* no. 4828, October 4, 1912, 1, and no. 4847, October 15, 1912, 1; Peru, Congreso, *Diario de debates de las sesiones del Congreso: legislatura ordinaria y extraordinaria de 1912* (Lima, 1912), 85–98, 8th session, October 4, 1912; Basadre, *Historia* 12:86–87, 90, 147–48; C. K. Chester (Electric Boat Co.) to H. Clay Howard (U.S. minister at Lima), Lima, February 4, 1913, Despatches 1910–1930, roll 11, USNA; and United States, Congress, Senate, Special Committee to Investigate the Munitions Industry, *Munitions Industry: Hearings . . . Seventy-Third Congress Pur-suant to S. Res. 206, a Resolution to Make Certain Investigations Concerning the Man-ufacture and Sale of Arms and Other War Munitions,* part 1 (September 4, 5, and 6, 1934: Electric Boat Co.) (Washington, DC: Government Printing Office, 1934), 86, 116–17.

142. Leguía to Guillermo Holder Freire, Lima, January 20, 1912, accused of pock-eting funds of police fines and pro-Navy donations; José F. Crousillat, March 13, 1912, suspected of harboring bandits; M. García Bedoya, November 14, 1908, concerning the "corruptelas que ha hallado U. en la institución de la policía" of Chiclayo; Coronel José Manuel Vivanco, December 12, 1908, in reference to the "venalidades de las autori-dades" of Huancané; and Lino Velarde, December 16, 1908, in charge of secret vigi-

lar.[143] This state of affairs coincided with the following observations of a British diplomat in 1911:

> Peru is at present time in one of those phases, common enough[,] unhappily[,] in Spanish American Republics, when the central government is weak, which permits every petty authority to act in high handed manner, and which is apt to lead to most unfortunate situations. The motive in most cases is what is known in the United States as "graft" and these small officials hope to extract "graft" or blackmail from their victims knowing full well that they need fear very little from the powers above them. From many sources [we have learned of] demands for sums of money to make things run smoothly, demands sometimes, [it] is to be regretted, which have been complied with and which give encouragement to further extortion.[144]

To assert his authority in the last two years of his presidency, Leguía used outrageous measures to subvert electoral rules and congressional procedures. His regime came to rely increasingly on police supervision and spying.[145] Attempts to influence the Junta Electoral Nacional culminated in an executive decree, tantamount to a coup d'état, closing down the junta just before the congressional elections of 1911. This action combined with mob violence under the command of secret police agents, and the fraudulent installation of new members of the congress, yielded Leguía majority control of the legislature.[146] The Civilistas were now a congressional minority. Shortly before this move, Leguía had raised military salaries.[147] These po-

---

lance in Arequipa. Letterbooks, no. 4, pp. 83, 179; and, no. 1, pp. 253, 369, 379, respectively, Archivo Leguía, BNP.

143. Julián María Arroyo to M.E., Lima, April 30, 1911, no. 48, leg. H-1679, AGMAE: "[E]l descontento contra el Presidente es general pues toda persona de orden y respeto se ve perseguida si no hace lo que el Presidente quiere." Combs to S.S., Lima, November 2, 1910, no. 425, 823.00/84, Despatches 1910–1930, roll 2, USNA: "The unpopularity of the administration of Mr. Leguía increases."

144. Jerome to Grey, Lima, April 9, 1911, no. 48, FO 371/1206, ff. 89–89v, NAUK.

145. Jerome to Grey, Lima, July 1, 1911, no. 93, FO 371/1206, f. 116, NAUK. The government uncovered contraband in weapons implicating the sons of the Belgian minister in Lima. Julián María Arroyo to M.E., Lima, June 3, 1911, no. 58, leg. H-1679, AGMAE.

146. Jerome to Grey, Lima, May 22, 1911, no. 73, FO 371/1206, ff. 102–12, NAUK; Henry Clay Howard to S.S., Lima, May 22, 1911, no. 6, 823.00/97, and July 17, 1911, no. 27, 823.00/99, Despatches 1910–1930, roll 2, USNA; Basadre, *Historia* 12:113–17.

147. Cresson to S.S., Lima, April 8, 1911, no. 492, 823.00/94, Despatches 1910–1930, roll 2, USNA.

litical procedures undermining electoral, legislative, and military institutions enabled Leguía to consolidate a support group for which institutionalized graft was the main reward. This corrupt network would aid Leguía in his subsequent bids for power.

The presidential elections of 1912 allowed Leguía another opportunity to delay his departure from power and deliver yet another devastating blow to his former Civilista party. The Civilistas were confident that their candidate, Antero Aspíllaga, would easily win the elections. Suddenly a menacing candidate rushed onto the scene: The former Pierolista Guillermo Billinghurst gained popular support via classic populist demagoguery. Balloting was disrupted by violent mobs supporting Billinghurst. The presidential selection then fell to Congress where Leguía's majority struck a deal with Billinghurst to have Roberto Leguía, the lame-duck president's brother, and crony Miguel Echenique installed as first and second vice presidents, respectively. Soon, however, the irascible new president denounced the catastrophic state of the national finances he had inherited and flatly refused to engage in the deals that Leguía had initiated and expected Billinghurst to continue. The public debt amounted to 82 million soles and major cuts in expenditures were necessary.[148]

This serious disagreement between Billinghurst and Leguía had many ramifications. It initially led, after some initial hesitation, to the cancellation of several railway and irrigation projects and weapons contracts to which Leguía was deeply committed. These included the Ucayali railroad, which was awaiting completion of foreign loan deals through, mainly, the National City Bank and other U.S. financiers, and the purchase of submarines from the Electric Boat Company. Billinghurst was consequently seen by U.S. diplomats as anti-American, who preferred to deal with Anglo-French concerns.[149] Leguía himself went into exile after a mob attacked his residence in which the former president and a handful of friends defended themselves with revolvers. Billinghurst governed with a dictatorial style supported by the Comité de Salud Pública, reminiscent of Jacobin radicalism, that was linked to an urban public works bureau headed by the graft-prone militant Lauro A. Curletti. Billinghurst proceeded to expropriate a private water supply company, the Empresa del Agua de Lima, and ad-

148. *El Comercio,* no. 33488, October 3, 1912, 1.

149. Memoranda, Albert W. Bryan (Division of Latin American Affairs) to Mr. Bingham, Washington, DC, February 5, 1914, pp. 3–4, and Bryan to Mr. Long, February 12, 1914, 823.00/123, p. 1, and Bryan to Bingham, February 14, 1914, 823.00/127, pp. 6–9, Despatches 1910–130, roll 2, USNA.

vocated arming the people. He also had to deal with corruption in his own administration: A member of his cabinet was asked to resign when it was found that he profited from the sale of coal to the navy.[150]

Early in 1914, Billinghurst was planning to close Congress to rid his administration of its Leguiísta majority. Perennial conspirator Augusto Durand was planning an uprising supported by the increasingly disgruntled military. Serious disagreements between the president and Colonel Oscar R. Benavides ended with the latter's resignation as military chief of staff. All of these ominous developments culminated in a military-civilian coup, instigated by Durand, but executed by Benavides and close friends and junior officers Jorge and Manuel Prado Ugarteche, who participated in the storming of the presidential palace. The coup resulted in the assassination of the minister of war, General Enrique Varela, and the ousting of Billinghurst on February 4, 1914.[151] In a manifesto written shortly after his overthrow, Billinghurst denounced a conspiracy of "logreros políticos" personally interested in the shady Ucayali and Huacho railroad projects that were deemed sources of public fund embezzlement.[152] According to U.S. diplomatic sources, Durand, who owned extensive coca-producing land in Huánuco province, was among the supporters of the Ucayali railroad passing through the province.[153]

After the coup, Colonel Benavides took central stage. As Benavides was one of the first graduates of French military instruction initiated in 1895, it was clear that the military reform, which was aimed at keeping the military out of politics, had failed.[154] The Prado Ugarteche brothers (Mariano Igna-

150. Henry Clay Howard to S.S., Lima, August 3, 1913, no. 228, and Comité de Salud Pública enclosures, 823.00/111; Bryan to Bingham, February 5, 1914, 3, Despatches 1910–1930, roll 2, USNA; Basadre, *Historia* 12:230, 258–61.

151. Benton McMillin to S.S., Lima, April 1, 1914, no. 42, 823.00/154, pp. 5–8, 14–15, Despatches 1910–1930, roll 2, USNA; U.S. Department of State, *Papers Relating to the Foreign Relations of the United States, 1914* (Washington, DC: Government Printing Office, 1922), 1061–67.

152. Basadre, *Historia* 12:289–90.

153. Augusto Durand, deputy from Huánuco, and a very wealthy man who "practically controls the coca supply in Peru," was deeply interested in the Ucayali railroad as it was projected to pass through his land in Huánuco province. Memoranda of Bryan to Bingham, February 5, 1914, p. 1, and Bryan to Mr. Long, February 12, 1914, p. 1, Despatches 1910–1930, roll 2, USNA.

154. Already by 1909, "la politique qui n'avait perdu pied dans l'armée, y a ressuis plus d'importance et tels petits lieutenants ignorants et mal notés annoncent . . . a nos instructeurs que le Président de la République leur a positivement promis des postes de capitaine dans le régiments que les intéressés ont désignés eux mêmes." Frédéric

cio, Javier, Jorge, and Manuel), leaders of a rising faction within the Civilistas, supported Benavides as provisional president. In protest, González Prada resigned from his post as head of the National Library, a post he had held since 1911. He proceeded to attack Benavides for his militarism, or *corporalismo sudamericano,* which threatened another round of degrading servitude, favoritism, and fiscal embezzlement. Risking retaliation, González Prada denounced Benavides's surprising new fortune, which allowed the Benavides family to simultaneously settle substantial mortgages on several properties, insinuating that it proceeded from Civilista sources and the misuse of public funds. (In these his waning years, González Prada found himself, despite his long anticorruption crusade, defending Leguía against his critics.)[155]

In the early years of World War I, the Benavides provisional administration was prevented by international financial strains from indulging in major increases in foreign indebtedness or extravagant expenditures. However, increased military spending under his presidency was suspected of having rewarded "not so correct services."[156] Benavides also placed relatives in lucrative public posts; his brother, Interior (Gobierno) Minister Víctor R. Benavides, improperly speculated with short-term government debt through proxies.[157] Javier Prado Ugarteche, an intimate ally of Benavides, was directly involved in the covert sale of thousands of late-model Mauser rifles offered to the Spanish government "at a price more advantageous than that asked by the manufacturing house itself." Prado had personally recommended the agent for the transaction, Manuel Valladares, to the head of the Spanish diplomatic mission in Lima.[158] (Coincidentally, Benavides had been attached for several months in 1910 to the Mauser factory in Germany.)[159] Prado's elder brother and wealthy head of the Prado Ugarteche

Clément-Simon to M.A.E. Pichon, Lima, March 10, 1909, no. 18, CPC-NS, Pérou, vol. 2, ff. 23v–24, AMAE.

155. González Prada, *Bajo el oprobio* (1915), in *Sobre el militarismo,* 51–52, 65–66; and "Los milagros de un gobierno provisorio" (originally in *La Lucha,* June 6, 1914), *Prosa menuda* (1941) in *Obras,* vol. 2, part 4, 401–402.

156. Andrés López to M.E., Lima, July 30, 1915, no. 42, leg. H-1680, AGMAE.

157. López to M.E., Lima, June 15, 1915, no. 32, leg. H-1680, AGMAE.

158. López to M.E., Lima, February 14, 1916, no. 10, leg. H-1680, AGMAE. The U.S. diplomatic mission in Lima also conducted an investigation to clarify a "rumor" concerning the sale of 15,000 rifles to be shipped to Cuba. McMillin to S.S., Lima, April 4, 1916, 823.24/3, Despatches 1910–1930, roll 11, USNA.

159. "Brief biography of the provisional president of Peru," William Handley, Callao, June 12, 1914, 823.00/191, p. 2, Despatches 1910–1930, roll 2, USNA.

clan, Mariano Ignacio, had been also described as an unscrupulous businessman and politician with dubious morals.[160]

The early phase of a trial to clarify the assassination of General Varela during the 1914 coup was deemed vitiated due to procedural irregularities. At the end of Benavides's unpopular presidency, he was met by groups of demonstrators who shouted "thief" and "assassin."[161] José Pardo, elected in 1915 to his second presidential term, rewarded Benavides with a military diplomatic post in Europe.

Pardo governed the country with his customary fiscal conservatism. The usual electoral disputes and manipulations resulted in a growing opposition incensed by the assassination of Rafael Grau, a Leguiísta. Grau's family and the political opposition held the administration responsible for his death. The political ambitions of Javier Prado, supported by his brothers and a sizable group of Civilistas, led to a de facto division within the Civilista party that weakened Pardo's position. In addition, the controversial taxation issue involving the Brea y Pariñas oil fields haunted the executive and legislature throughout the Pardo administration. In the middle of World War I, British and U.S. agents pressed for an international court settlement of a dispute over the hitherto ridiculously low taxes paid by the London & Pacific Petroleum Company, a subsidiary of the U.S. Standard Oil Corporation. Critics later blamed the Pardo administration and Civilista majority in Congress for caving in to these demands. Pardo's regime unnecessarily delayed severance of diplomatic ties with Germany even after the United States entered the war in 1917. The opposition exploited this misguided foreign policy by conservative Enrique de la Riva Agüero.

Meanwhile, Leguía conspired from exile. After his departure from Peru in 1912, Leguía settled in London where he conducted his personal business alongside a long-distance political campaign aimed at returning to power. At his residence, 28 Holland Park, Leguía received political advice from his collaborator and former minister Julio Ego-Aguirre. For most of 1917, the British Home Office had Leguía under surveillance in case he violated the Foreign Enlistment Act by hiring British citizens to overthrow the Peruvian government. No such offense was detected. However, detailed information on Leguía's movements, contacts, and copious personal corre-

---

160. Clément-Simon to M.A.E. Pichon, Lima, June 5, 1909, CPC-NS, Pérou, vol. 2, ff. 55–60, esp. 58, AMAE. See also Felipe Portocarrero Suárez, *El imperio Prado: 1890–1970* (Lima: Centro de Investigación de la Universidad del Pacífico, 1995), 54–69.

161. López to M.E., Lima, August 30, 1915, no. 45, leg. H-1680, AGMAE.

spondence with political and military supporters in Peru, including photographic copies and translations of intercepted letters, was delivered to the Foreign Office.[162]

Thanks to this extraordinary source, it is safe to assert that Leguía was indeed planning his political comeback relying heavily on active-duty and former military officers in Peru. The most decided and engaged in the practical planning of simultaneous rebellions of troops in strategic Peruvian cities were Colonels César Gonzales, Pedro A. Ríos, and Francisco La Rosa, who, among many other officers, loathed Pardo's policy of armed forces cutbacks. In his letters, Leguía actively incited Victor Larco Herrera and other congressional candidates to join this "movimiento reaccionario" against Pardo. Lawyer José Manuel García was put in charge of the political organization and financing of the movement and press propaganda. García received funds in Lima from Leguía's eldest son, Augusto Leguía Swayne, who managed the family's sugar and cotton export firm. García's political negotiations included contacts with General Cáceres who, shunned by the Civilistas upon his return to Peru in 1915, had pledged (but was unable to deliver) support of his military party for the insurrection. Likewise, Carlos de Piérola, the opposition leader of the almost extinct Demócrata party, expressed support for Leguía's cause and leadership.[163]

Leguía's insurrectionary cause inherited the ideological and political tradition of the old anti-Civilista movements that had vowed to radically change Peru's "feudal state." One of Leguía's co-conspirators, in recounting a confidential conversation with Piérola, vividly expressed ambitious political goals that Leguía would later put to practice in his own way:

> We need a man who will lead a bloody reaction which will destroy everything that at present exists. Everything must be renewed. The ex-

---

162. Reports on "Impending revolution in Peru" by Metropolitan Police, Criminal Investigation Department, New Scotland Yard (T. McNamara, inspector), June 17 and July 6 and 20, 1917, FO 371/2991, ff. 146–149, NAUK, including details on Leguía's commercial activities, several contracts with the British government for the supply of sugar, purchases of racehorses in Newmarket, and lawyer Julio Ego-Aguirre "the ex-President's political secretary and [who] was a minister. . . [H]e is now in this country as an exile."

163. On analysis of possibilities of insurrection by followers of Leguía and Javier Prado: photographic negatives of letters by Leguía to Víctor Larco Herrera and Colonel César Gonzales; letter to Leguía by officer Pedro A. Ríos; police reports of Leguía's movements in London, FO 371/2991, ff. 1–53, 147–50; and E. Rennie to A. J. Balfour, Lima, June 18, 1917, no. 42, FO 371/2990, ff. 367–72, NAUK.

ecutive, legislative, and judicial powers. The universities, the army and all the institutions and their men must be reorganized and, as a complement, this group of men, whose existence is dangerous for the republic, must be destroyed.[164]

This correspondent was encouraged by the growing discontent among those who had abandoned Leguía's "hearth" to knock at the doors of powerful men of the "Pardista civilization" with the expectation of satiating their "eternal appetite for political predominance." These "furious and disillusioned victims," well known to Leguía, were returning to their former camp to beg for revenge. A new party should be formed among these and other political actors. Another political friend suggested that Leguía should follow the example of Billinghurst in raising expectations of the have-nots by "concrete hopes of personal benefit" such as offering Peruvian consulate posts abroad. This same Machiavellian character also proposed to entrust Julio Ego-Aguirre with the task of launching a fake electoral campaign to deceive Pardo in allowing Leguía's return to Peru.[165] However, Colonel Gonzales warned Leguía that the growing support was not sufficient in Peru where "moral decay" was great and scant reliance could be placed on those supporters and political advisors who lacked "political honesty":

> The same men whom you know with the same vices, possibly even more corrupt, compose this [new] political organization. They expect nothing from actions which might be called energetic and honourable, but prefer intrigue from which they generally gain more profit than by showing their hand.[166]

Several correspondents in this period asked Leguía for money for expenses or for support after losing their posts or congressional bids.[167] Thus, a diplo-

164. Translation of an unsigned letter to Leguía, Lima, January 28, 1917, FO 371/2991, f. 49, NAUK.
165. Translation of N. Jauly Jauly to Leguía, Callao, June 14, 1917, FO 371/2991, ff. 153–54, NAUK.
166. Translation of César Gonzales to Leguía, Lima, May 2, 1917, FO 371/2991, f. 27, NAUK.
167. Translation of Francisco La Rosa to Leguía, Lima, April 7, 1917; Anselmo Huapaya to Leguía, Lima, September 24, 1917, reporting that his resources were exhausted after losing Puno's senatorial elections and consequently being granted a pension by Leguía's son; Alejandro Llontoj Pincett to Leguía, Chiclayo, October 24, 1917. FO 371/2991, ff. 75–75v, 235–36, 274, respectively, NAUK.

mat closely following Peruvian politics at the time considered most of Leguía's supporters who urged Pardo's ousting to be a group of "disappointed self-seekers."[168]

Leguía's political strategy evolved into a covert plan to return to Peru, supported by the new political party in formation, to demand a provisional government and the convocation of a National Convention bolstered by a military uprising.[169] The premature rebellion of the garrison of Ancón in August 1918 was linked to Cáceres's military networks in support of Leguía.[170] Conditions for Leguía's return coincided with the launching of his campaign for the 1919 presidential elections in which he triumphed. But his electoral victory was not sufficient for the would-be dictator. Just before his inauguration, and arguing that he had uncovered a conspiracy to prevent him from taking office (a charge for which foreign witnesses found no evidence), Leguía led a "clever" coup with ample military support that ignominiously ended Pardo's fairly honest (and the last Civilista) administration.[171] This maneuver marked the dawn of a new era of dictatorship and graft.

Scandals of the Leguía Oncenio

Leguía began his second term (1919–1930, eleven years, or the "Oncenio") without institutionalized opposition. Faithful to his original plan, Leguía also interfered in the installation of Congress and called instead for a con-

---

168. H. J. (Division of Latin American Affairs) to Mr. Stabler, Washington, DC, March 16, 1918, 823.00/233, Despatches 1910–1930, roll 2, USNA. Apparently, Leguía's intercepted correspondence while living in London had also been read in Washington.

169. Leguía to Melitón Porras, London, September 11, 1917, FO 371/2991, ff. 220–22, NAUK: Leguía explained that if his new party was allowed to grow in Peru, "we would demand, not a presidential election, but the organization of a provisional government, and the convocation of a National Convention. But if, as is almost certain, the government should be hostile[,] . . . the employment of any means conducive to the fulfillment of the national will, becomes justifiable[, that is,] . . . overthrow force by force."

170. Conde de Galarza to M.E., Lima, September 8, 1918, no. 75, leg. H-1680, AG-MAE; Basadre, *Historia* 12:402.

171. U.S. Department of State, *Papers Relating to the Foreign Relations of the United States, 1919* (Washington, DC: Government Printing Office, 1934), 2:720–26, esp. telegram 823.00/295, McMillin to Acting S.S., Lima, July 10, 1919, 726; Handley to S.S., Lima, July 8, 1919, no. 749, 823.00/280, and McMillin to S.S., Lima, July 30, 1919, no. 371, 823.00/296, Despatches 1910–1930, roll 2, USNA.

stitutional assembly to reform the old constitution of 1860. The former
Demócrata congressman and minister under Billinghurst, Mariano H.
Cornejo, was the legal architect of the constitutional "reform" supporting a
dictatorial regime euphemistically referred to as the "Patria Nueva."[172] In
these endeavors, the opportunistic Prado brothers also collaborated with
Leguía for a while. The resulting constitution of 1920 was a major historical setback for the painfully built, albeit faulty institutions and norms that
regulated Peruvian republican democracy and political coexistence.[173]

Under Leguía's new regime, political opponents were obliterated.
Claiming to be fighting recurrent conspiracies, Leguía destroyed the
Civilista leadership through imprisonment on San Lorenzo Island, deportation, and mob attacks of homes and newspaper buildings.[174] Devastating
aggression against other political groups followed. Expenditures for the secret police increased significantly to facilitate a system of widespread
espionage. One particularly dreaded head of the secret police, "doctor"
Bernardo Fernández Oliva, was accused of torturing political prisoners.[175]
The severe repression unleashed against all political opponents by Leguía's
interior minister, Germán Leguía y Martínez, guaranteed political stability.
The drastic punitive measures dictated by Leguía's cousin caused serious
conflicts between the executive and judiciary, uproar among local business
owners and bankers, and concerns over the abuse of basic civil rights in the
international community. The legal requirement of habeas corpus was ig-

172. Jaime de Ojeda to M.E., Lima, April 5, November 20, 1920, and March 18,
1921, nos. 36, 116, and 25, leg. H-1680, AGMAE: "Poco prestigio moral de Mariano H.
Cornejo," who was rewarded with a Peruvian diplomatic post in France. See also
Basadre, *Historia* 13:29, 38.

173. Conde de Galarza to M.E., Lima, August 6, 1919, no. 37, leg. H-1680, AGMAE:
Galarza criticizes efforts to "desarticular y desconectar las normas que la rutina, la tradi-
ción y la poca cultura política han aceptado como cosas deficientes, malas añejas y hasta
retrógradas, pero en las cuales, padres e hijos, buenos y malos políticos, instruidos e ignorantes, demócratas y aristócratas, han vivido soportándolas durante 60 años."

174. Telegram, Lima, September 11, 1919, 823.00/302; William W. Smith to S.S,
Lima, September 16, 1919, no. 383, 823.00/323, Despatches 1910–1930, roll 3, USNA.

175. For the month of September 1924 alone, spending on secret police amounted
to Lp. 16,809 (Peruvian pounds). "General conditions prevailing in Peru," p. 16–17,
Miles Poindexter to S.S., Lima, October 18, 1924, no. 294, Despatches 1910–1930, roll
4, USNA. "Don Armando Vargas Machuca denuncia a Fernández Oliva, Rufino
Martínez de haberlo torturado," *El Comercio,* no. 45186, September 4, 1930, 4–5; "Una
visita al antiguo local de la comisaría de Ate," *El Comercio,* no. 45208, September 15,
1930, 5. See also charges by Víctor M. Avendaño against Prefecto Lino La Barrera
Higueras and José Rada y Gamio, *El Comercio,* no. 45204, September 20, 1930, 3.

nored and private property threatened by a politically motivated and retroactive confiscation decree.[176] Independent newspapers were closed or constantly under threat of closing, and free speech in the universities was drastically curtailed. A well-oiled propaganda machine, including *La Prensa* (expropriated from exiled Augusto Durand in 1921) and the English-language *West Coast Leader* (formerly *Peru To-Day*), praised the administration's "achievements" and confounded domestic and international public opinion.

Once political checks were dismantled, Leguía indulged freely in his cherished policy of financing, through massive foreign indebtedness, huge new public works projects rife with graft. The defunct Ucayali railroad plan was replaced by a new craze for urbanization, irrigation projects, and highway construction. Increasing support from U.S. bank loans resulted in the monopoly of urban and sanitation works by the Foundation Company, control of highway and port construction by Snare & Company, and all government irrigation projects (including the large Pampas Imperial in Cañete and Olmos in Lambayeque where Leguía held substantial economic and family interests) in the charge of Charles W. Sutton. U.S. loans and the privileges and monopolies granted to U.S. companies and entrepreneurs raised concerns among other foreign companies and governments about "insatiable Yankee greed."[177]

The lavish Peruvian independence centennial celebration brought large-scale overspending and waste of public funds despite export price declines in 1921. New public buildings and patriotic monuments were erected. To win support in the international community, Leguía presented the Spanish embassy with a building worth 45,000 Peruvian pounds (Lp.), hired U.S. professionals as public administrators, and established Spanish police and U.S. naval missions.[178] Likewise, important concessions were granted to

176. Jaime de Ojeda to M.E., Lima, December 27, 1919, no. 84, and January 3, 1919, no. 3, leg. H-1680, AGMAE; U.S. Department of State, *Papers Relating to the Foreign Relations of the United States, 1920* (Washington, DC: Government Printing Office, 1936), 3:360–67: "Peruvian Confiscation Act of December 26, 1919[:] . . . its annulment at the suggestion of the United States"; William E. Gonzales to S.S., Lima, April 6, 1921, no. 610, 823.00/386, Despatches 1910–1930, roll 3, USNA.

177. Ojeda to M.E., Lima, December 15, 1921, no. 82, leg. H-1680, AGMAE.

178. Ojeda to M.E., Lima, November 30, 1922, no. 87, leg. H-1680, AGMAE: "[E]l gobierno derroche en perpetuas fiestas; descubra monumentos y lápidas a personjes de cuyos méritos no tenemos nociones muy precisas; regale a España una casa que cuesta 45,000 libras"; "Appointment of a naval mission from the United States to Peru," in U.S. Department of State, *Papers Relating to Foreign Relations, 1920,* 3:367–69.

the Peruvian Corporation, London & Pacific Petroleum Company, and the British Marconi Wireless Company for the monopoly on local mail and telegraph services. Nearly all these agreements and contracts with foreign concerns had negative outcomes. The Marconi contract was the subject of a congressional investigation for inefficiency and alleged corruption, owing, according to a foreign informant, to the difficulty of relying on native employees who "consider public service a permanent sinecure and an opportunity for 'graft.'"[179] The Spanish police mission initially improved the professional standing of the Peruvian police, but inevitably clashed with corrupt authorities, such as Lima's prefecto Octavio Casanave.[180]

Disorder and immorality were evident from the beginning of the new regime.[181] Graft was noticed at every administrative level; the bad example was set by ministers and other high-level public servants who arrived in office without personal wealth and, after a few years, boasted fortunes. Among the most corrupt were Julio Ego-Aguirre, minister of public works, and later minister of foreign affairs and prime minister; Alberto Salomón, minister of foreign affairs[182]; and Pedro José Rada y Gamio, prime minister.[183] Doctor Lauro A. Curletti, minister of public works in 1923, was forced to resign only when he exaggerated his own presidential ambitions despite having been previously allowed to use his office for "flagrant misappropriations" of public funds.[184] A confidential biographical report of the U.S. diplomatic service on Alejandrino Maguiña, minister of justice and education and prime minister in 1926, explained that his principal motive for taking part in governmental politics was "to make money." In fact, Maguiña resigned after he

179. F. A. Sterling to S.S, Lima, September 19, 1922, no. 878, "General conditions prevailing in Peru," 823.00/425, pp. 16–17, Despatches 1910–1930, roll 4, USNA; Ojeda to M.E., Lima, February 1, 1923, no. 17, leg. H-1680, AGMAE.

180. De la Bâtie to M.A.E., Lima, September 29, 1923, no. 41, CPC-NS, Pérou, vol. 6, ff. 167v–68, AMAE. Casanave did not have a "bonne réputation," as he became wealthy while in office, and then transferred funds to Argentina after his resignation.

181. Jaime de Ojeda to M.E., Lima, December 15, 1919, no. 82, leg. H-1680, AGMAE: Ojeda notes "desorden y la inmoralidad reinantes en la pseudo administración de Justicia y, al parecer, en todos los organismos de la república."

182. Salomón submitted inflated accounts for refurbishing works at the ministry's headquarters at the Torre Tagle palace. De la Bâtie to M.A.E., Lima, September 29, 1923, no. 41, CPC-NS, Pérou, vol. 6, ff. 168–70, AMAE.

183. Rada y Gamio was involved in the embezzlement of private and public funds: Manuel Acal y Marín to M.E., Barranco-Lima, March 31, 1930, no. 33, leg. H-2603 bis, AGMAE.

184. Sterling to S.S., Lima, March 8, 1923, no. 951, 823.00/432, Despatches 1910–1930, roll 4, USNA.

repeatedly ignored congressional requests to present clear accounts of his disbursements for the building of primary schools since 1923. He was included among "the group of intelligent but frequently unscrupulous politicians of middle-class extraction whom the President has brought into Government." Likewise, "ambitious and cold-blooded" Celestino Manchego Muñoz commanded a "strong following of self-seekers."[185]

Leguía's close relatives and cronies were at the pinnacle of the graft chain: president of the new Banco de Reserva Eulogio Romero, his son-in-law Pedro Larrañaga, and close associate Miguel Echenique who benefited from the construction boom as contractors (Cia. de Autovías y Pavimentos) and privileged partners of the cement-producing monopoly (Cia. Portland Peruana). The American economist William W. Cumberland was a privileged witness of the widespread corruption of Leguía's administration and inner circle. At Leguía's request, Cumberland, a staff member of the U.S. Department of State, was appointed chief administrator of the Peruvian customs and budget office in 1921, and director of the first central bank, the Banco de Reserva del Peru, in 1922.[186] Cumberland soon discovered that fiscal expenditures were approximately double the amount of revenues, thus causing pressure for currency devaluation, and that commerce statistics were inadequate and outdated. By the second half of 1922, the "gross extravagance" of fiscal spending, through "special credits" and misappropriations, had led to unmanageable deficits in almost all ministries.[187]

Years later, Cumberland told historians that in the customs administration, "graft was rampant; very few people paid duties in accordance to what the tariffs called for—it was a matter of bargaining with the Peruvian officials."[188] A discharged customs official who had been caught participating in graft even challenged Cumberland to a duel. Moreover, Cumberland could not avoid government interference in managing the central bank. Leguía had appointed his relative Eulogio Romero, "a most astute and most

185. "Yearly report on general conditions in Peru for 1926," pp. 75, 81, Pierre de L. Boal to S.S., Lima, November 16, 1927, no. 855; and Miles Poindexter to S.S., Lima, December 22, 1926, no. 636-G, 823.00/527 (823.002/105), Despatches 1910–1930, rolls 7 and 8, respectively, USNA.

186. U.S. Department of State, *Papers Relating to the Foreign Relations of the United States, 1921* (Washington, DC: Government Printing Office, 1936), 2:656–62.

187. F. A. Sterling to S.S., Lima, November 7, 1922, no. 904, 823.00/427, "General Conditions," pp. 5–6, Despatches 1910–1930, roll 4, USNA.

188. "The Reminiscences of William Wilson Cumberland," typescript of interviews by Wendell H. Link, April–May 1951, 125, Oral History Research Project, Columbia University, New York.

unscrupulous politician," as president of the bank between 1922 and 1925. To satisfy the government's need for funds, Romero concocted and executed an illegal scheme to reduce the silver content of Peruvian coins. Consequently, Cumberland resigned as the bank's director in 1923, and later charged that Leguía "allowed all his associates to graft to their hearts content. . . [H]e wrecked the finances of Peru just as thoroughly as if he had, himself, been a grafter."[189]

Lack of fiscal resources forced payment of schoolteachers' meager salaries with *vales* or vouchers. It became customary to exchange these vales for cash through the political mediation of congressmen who charged a 25-percent "commission." Feeling challenged by Cumberland, some offered him a cut in the corrupt scheme. According to Cumberland, "this was one of the major sources of graft in Peru and one of the principal motivations for men wanting to be a Senator or Representative. Each collected a substantial part of the salaries of the schoolteachers in his district."[190]

Among Leguía's sons, the youngest, Juan Leguía Swayne, exceeded all other close associates in charging illegal "commissions" and bribes for a variety of official deals, especially with respect to contracting foreign loans and purchase of naval military equipment and war airplanes. President Leguía rewarded military and naval officers to an unprecedented level, corrupting the armed forces to the core. After the coup of July 4, 1919, several military officers were promoted. Old General Cáceres, influential supporter of Leguía's dictatorial quest, was glorified and promoted to the ultimate, rarified rank of marshal. In clandestine statements, disaffected officers denounced the use of military promotions by "unscrupulous politicians."[191] The political exploitation of the military remained a major problem in the professional development of the armed forces thereafter.

The most important foreign affairs issue of the time, the negotiation of the Tacna-Arica question with Chile, was based on a policy of rearmament, which implied enhanced military expenditures. Leguía's initiative to purchase the new weapons of the time, submarines and warplanes, had made him popular among military and nationalistic supporters. However, the con-

189. Ibid., 127, 129, 132.
190. Ibid., 135.
191. Statement by seventeen army officers in 1921, quoted in introduction to *The Politics of Antipolitics: The Military in Latin America,* ed. Brian Loveman and Thomas A. Davies (Lincoln: University of Nebraska Press, 1989), 4, from Víctor Villanueva, *El Ejército peruano: del caudillaje anárquico al militarismo reformista* (Lima: Editorial Juan Mejía Baca, 1973), 177.

tracts for the purchase of these weapons were mired in corruption. Juan Leguía—holding the rank of colonel and the official post of chief inspector of naval and military aviation—was directly involved in brokering deals with the Electric Boat Company and the Curtiss planes manufacturer. Juan Leguía traveled frequently to the United States where he made spectacular allegations against the French and German military advisors in Peru and in favor of U.S. naval and military missions. The old French military mission in Peru was ending amid scandal and accusations of insubordination, procurement irregularities, and graft. In the meantime, Peruvian politicians praised U.S. naval and aviation advisors.[192] U.S. diplomats acknowledged the role that Juan Leguía played in securing U.S. naval and military purchases and cooperation in competition with other foreign interests.[193]

In 1928, the British ambassador to Peru reported serious irregularities in the sale of navy destroyers and war materiel to Peru worth £5 million. The deal involved the head of the Peruvian army at the time, General Wilhelm von Faupel, who "caviled at many matters of detail, and was not above suspicion from a venal point of view," and had recurrent quarrels with Juan Leguía. Moreover, (former U.S. Navy commander) Captain Charles G. Davy, the acting chief of the U.S. naval mission, negotiated personally a "commission" or bribe initially set at 2.5 percent, that was eventually reduced to 1.5 percent of the total purchase value.[194] Additionally, top commanders and President Leguía himself acknowledged the widespread misappropriation of coal, arms, and materiel for private gain by military officers.[195]

One fundamental pillar of Leguía's dictatorial and corrupt abuses was the unfaltering and at times truly misguided support by U.S. banks, corporations, and even diplomats. Almost blind admiration for Leguía led some U.S. diplomats to argue that, under Peru's state of civilization, his "progressive, if autocratic" regime was perhaps the best option.[196] The friendship and support of these diplomats went as far as to declare Leguía one of

192. William Gonzales to S.S., Lima, February 24, 1921, no. 588, 823.20/1; Telegram to American Embassy in Lima, Washington, DC, April 26, 1923, 823.20/2a; Miles Poindexter to S.S., Lima, October 15, 1924, no. 291, 823.20/12; Despatches 1910–1930, roll 11, USNA.

193. "General conditions prevailing in Peru," 8, Mathew Hanna to S.S., Lima, April 2, 1928, no. 917-G, U.S. Despatches, roll 7, USNA.

194. Lord H. Hervey to Austen Chamberlain, Lima, July 19, 1928, no. 63, FO 371/12788, ff. 282–84, NAUK.

195. Cumberland, "Reminiscences," 138–39, 147–48.

196. F. A. Sterling to S.S., Lima, November 29, 1921, no. 745, 823.00/411, Despatches 1910–1930, roll 4, USNA.

the most notable men of the Western Hemisphere, a "giant of the Pacific" worthy of a Nobel Prize.[197] In fact, William Gonzales, a former ambassador to Peru favorable to Leguía, was accused by a bitter exiled Peruvian of acting as a paid propaganda agent of the dictator in New York.[198]

Despite signs of growing anti-American sentiments in Peru, U.S. diplomatic endorsement of key schemes of financial and foreign affairs sustained Leguía in power throughout his eleven-year regime. The settlement of border disputes with Chile and Colombia through treaties brokered by U.S. diplomats consolidated Leguía's international standing; however, domestic opposition to these international arrangements—most notably former political ally Senator Julio C. Arana who sought private compensation for land in the Putumayo rubber territory ceded to Colombia, as well as military discontent with the surrendering of Arica to Chile—caused Leguía some ultimately serious internal political problems.[199] U.S. diplomats also urged the granting of loans to Leguía's corrupt regime, arguing that it was beneficial for U.S. business interests in Peru. Mounting evidence of widespread corruption plaguing Leguía's administration was either dismissed or justified.[200] The painful consequence of misguided official sympathies toward Leguía's corrupt and dictatorial regime was the failure of ill-advised and clearly mismanaged loans, financed through bond issues in the U.S. capital market involving thousands of small investors. In effect, corruption finally discouraged truly honest investors from doing business in Peru.

197. Speeches by Ambassador Miles Poindexter at the "National Club," Washington, DC, "En torno a las declaraciones del Embajador norteamericano Mr. Miles Poindexter," *La Prensa,* September 11, 1927, enclosure, no. 1 to Embassy's Despatch, no. 815-G, Lima, September 17, 1927, Despatches 1910–1930, roll 6, USNA; and by Ambassador Alexander Moore in Lima, June 17, 1929, cited in Basadre, *Historia* 12:369–70.

198. Julio Chávez Cabello, "Refutación al señor Manuel de Freyre Santander, ministro y defensor de la dictadura leguiísta," Buenos Aires, December 1924, enclosed with Williamson (Division of Latin American Affairs) to White, memorandum, Washington, DC, February 5, 1925, Despatches 1910–1930, roll 5, USNA.

199. Miles Poindexter to S.S., Lima, June 18, 1924, no. 210, 823.00/457; October 18, 1924, no. 294; and "Conditions prevailing in Peru," 6–7, May 3, 1926, no. 527-G, Despatches 1910–1930, rolls 4 and 5, USNA.

200. "A policy to hold graft and the abuse of political position down to such an extent as is consistent with keeping his partisans satisfied. There is no doubt that the President finds himself obliged to wink at a great deal in order to attain the important ends for which he is working," in "Yearly report on general conditions in Peru for 1926," 56, Pierre de L. Boal to S.S., Lima, November 16, 1927, no. 855, Despatches 1910–1930, roll 7, USNA.

As with other Latin American dictators, Leguía's most serious difficulties in prolonging his regime involved his ambitions for continued reelection. In 1923, Leguía's intentions clashed with the presidential ambitions of his own stalwart cousin Germán "El Tigre" Leguía y Martínez who publicly denounced the corrosive implications of reelection, vowing to correct "inveterate vices" and fight the anti-democratic monopoly of power encouraged mainly by those who "thrive at its shadow."[201] Despite the autocratic power exercised by "El Tigre" during his three years as interior minister, apparently he did not follow the example of other high-level officials who accumulated ill-gotten fortunes.[202] Fearing growing and opportunistic support for his cousin's quixotic cause, President Leguía imprisoned and later deported him.

Other more worthy critics bravely and steadfastly opposed Leguía's abuses and subsequent reelection campaigns. The legendary González Prada had died before the inauguration of Leguía's second term in 1919. Manuel Vicente Villarán, Víctor Andrés Belaúnde, and several radical leaders of a growing movement among university students and workers carried on in his footsteps. Villarán resigned as rector of the beleaguered national university to continue a clandestine opposition. He published several widely distributed handbills and pamphlets in which he established the connections among institutional destruction and abuse, massive corruption, and the political needs of Leguía's regime:

[T]he manifestations of arbitrary and despotic violence go hand in hand with the frame of immorality. . . . Today one can notice here and there obscure stains of venalities [*concusiones*] and peculations, the gains of which are exhibited without restraint. The plague spreads day by day under the protection of tolerance. There is little hope that the government would want to engage sanitary practices. The clean-up of each contagious source would entail the loss of God knows how many of its necessary adhesions. These policies of force injure with one hand and corrupt with the other. They gain services and praise through either ill treatment or handouts. Fear of abuses mingles with the hope of perquisites.[203]

201. Germán Leguía y Martínez, "Manifiesto programa," enclosure to dispatch, no. 63, Lima, August 27, 1923, Despatches 1910–1930, roll 4, USNA.

202. Ojeda to M.E., Lima, August 20, 1923, no. 88, leg. H-1680, AGMAE.

203. Manuel Vicente Villarán, "La reelección," August 1, 1924, enclosure, no. 1 of Miles Pointdexter to S.S., Lima, August 11, 1924, no. 429, 823.00/467, Despatches 1910–1930, roll 4, USNA.

A reelection campaign in 1929, justified by a prior constitutional amendment, combined with a deteriorating international and domestic economic situation, sealed Leguía's political fate. During the last months of the Oncenio, the government-controlled press published spectacular reports on violent plots to assassinate the president. Similar alarms and revelations were used recurrently as propaganda ploys to justify internal repression. This time Leguía's popularity was at its lowest and few believed that the press reports were accurate. Much-needed foreign loans to refinance the huge public debt and purchase military equipment were either cancelled or reduced at the source due to the Great Depression. Leguía reacted angrily at what he considered a betrayal by U.S. financiers. One U.S. military advisor in Peru attempted to call the attention of Washington officials to the unwillingness of New York bankers to grant new loans to the Peruvian government for the purchase of military planes.[204] On August 22, 1930 a military revolt in Arequipa led by Lieutenant Colonel Luis M. Sánchez Cerro, a former beneficiary of the regime's rewards and promotions, triggered Leguía's fall. Three days later, in the context of growing instability and disorder, Leguía was forced to resign in favor of a military junta in Lima. Aboard a navy ship off the coast of Lima, the ailing former dictator made a feeble attempt to reclaim the presidency but was instead imprisoned, along with his detested son Juan, ironically on the dreaded island of San Lorenzo where Leguía had sent countless political prisoners. Father and son were later prosecuted for the worst corruption charges thus far leveled at a Peruvian president and his family and cronies.

Inept Sanctions

The new military regime led by Sánchez Cerro vowed to punish the defunct administration's corruption by raising moral standards of public office as a central tenet of its claim to power.[205] A special court was created on August 31, 1930 to investigate, prosecute, and punish crimes related to public of-

204. Captain H. B. Grow (Inspección General de Aeronáutica, Ministerio de Marina y Aviación) to George Akerson (Assistant to the President, White House), Lima, December 24, 1929, Despatches 1910–1930, roll 11, USNA.

205. "El manifiesto que dio en Arequipa el Comandante Sánchez Cerro," *El Comercio,* no. 45174, August 28, 1930, 4: "Vamos a moralizar primero y a normalizar después la vida institucional y económica del Estado. . . Acabaremos para siempre con los peculados, las concesiones exclusivistas, las malversaciones y las rapiñas encubiertas, porque la principal causa de nuestra actual crisis económica reside en la falta de pureza en la Administración y de honradez en el manejo de los fondos fiscales."

fice abuses, government contracts, and "illicit enrichment" by the former regime's leaders and associates. This Tribunal de Sanción Nacional encouraged ordinary citizens to submit charges and evidence on illegal activities by civil servants.[206] However, just 11 percent of an approximate total of 664 formal accusations received were actually processed by the special tribunal. Out of the 75 accusations that led to trials, most were submitted by government offices, 41 cases received sentences of not guilty, 16 were dismissed due to lack of sufficient evidence, and only approximately 10 resulted in convictions and confiscation of ill-gotten property as civil reparation.[207] (After these spectacular trials and publicity, most corrupt former authorities were quietly exonerated, lightly punished, or actually handed a clean bill of innocence).

Moreover, lack of compliance with standard legal procedures of presumption of innocence and retroactivity, military interference, and charges of unconstitutionality leveled against the special court, together with an evident inability to deal with the sheer immensity of such trials, seriously impaired the Tribunal's sentences. Based on such legal arguments, some authors have condoned or pitied Leguía's fate after his downfall. They have doubted Leguía's direct involvement in rampant corruption, and charged that the Tribunal was politically motivated to exercise revenge.[208] This opinion coincides in part with contemporary foreign journalistic accounts that claimed Leguía was guilty only of political ambition rather than graft, despite the fact that it would have been difficult for him to ignore that "his sons, relatives, and many friends were receiving millions of dollars in commissions and gains on foreign loans and public works contracted."[209] These arguments resonated in Leguía's posthumous, putative self-defense in which he argued he was not responsible for the corruption of others during his administration.[210]

206. "Se crea un Tribunal de Sanción Nacional. Todos podrán hacer denuncias previamente comprobadas," *El Comercio,* no. 45181, September 1, 1930 (afternoon edition), 1.

207. Felipe Portocarrero Suárez and Luis Camacho, "Impulsos moralizadores: el caso del Tribunal de Sanción Nacional 1930–1931," in *El pacto infame: estudios sobre la corrupción en el Perú,* ed. Felipe Portocarrero Suárez (Lima: Red de Ciencias Sociales, 2005), 35–73.

208. Luis Alberto Sánchez, *Leguía: el dictador* (Lima: Editora Pachacútec, 1993), 137; Basadre, *Historia* 13:392–94.

209. Lawrence Dennis, "¿Qué derribó a Leguía? La responsabilidad de los banqueros norteamericanos en los males del Perú" (translated article from the *New Republic*), *El Comercio,* no. 45211, September 17, 1930, 14.

210. Augusto B. Leguía, *El Oncenio y la Lima actual: memorias completas del Presidente Leguía* (Lima: Imprenta J.C.L., 1936).

Despite the ineptitude of the Tribunal de Sanción Nacional, the information it produced is valuable for tracing mechanisms of corruption and
their consequences during the late Oncenio. The director (undersecretary)
of the interior, José B. Ugarte, charged that approximately 105 million soles
had been misused during the 1920–1929 period: public funds earmarked for
the secret police were given instead to supportive political groups and to
cover Leguía's electoral expenses, and under the label of "reserved expenses," substantial supplementary wages were paid to politicians. Ugarte
concluded that such practices were at the root of the unmanageable expansion of the domestic and foreign debt.[211] It became clear that Leguía's modernizing élan was based on public works that could not justify the expo-
nential increase in public debt because corruption and incompetence had
elevated costs to as much as double their real value.[212]

At the end of the tribunal's activities in April 1931, the relatively few
proven convictions were concentrated on Leguía and his inner circle of family and cronies. These convictions were mere samples of widespread legal
transgressions mainly in public contracting, monopoly concessions, commissions, foreign loans, public works, fraudulent sale of land to the state,
and even protection of opium sales and gambling.[213] A more detailed analysis of the original documents of the Tribunal throws a clearer light on the
Oncenio corruption scandals. Corruption had infiltrated almost all aspects
of the public sector and private business life: In many provinces Indian
peasants charged that local gamonales or landholding bosses had colluded
with prefectos, subprefectos and other civil servants to expropriate land and
abuse workers for private gain in the enforcement of the law of *conscrip-
ción vial,* or state-sponsored recruitment of obligatory labor services to
build roads. Towns and cities were rife with the misappropriation of municipal taxes and graft that sheltered unscrupulous urban contractors. The
administration of public education and the building of schools also suffered
from the abuse of corrupt officials.[214]

211. "El Director de Gobierno amplía su denuncia contra los señores Leguía,
Huamán de los Heros, Salazar y Rubio," *El Comercio,* no. 45296, November 1, 1930,15.
212. Dennis, "¿Qué derribó a Leguía?"
213. Portocarrero and Camacho, "Impulsos moralizadores," 45–46; Basadre, *Historia* 13:391–92.
214. "Vecinos de Caraz acusan a Carlos Leguía, sobrino carnal de A. B. Leguía por
abuso de autoridad y apropiación de tierras," Caraz, September 5, 1930, Tribunal de Sanción Nacional, leg. 10, exp. 232, AGN. Speech by Lima's mayor, Luis Antonio Eguiguren, *El Comercio,* no. 45180, September 1, 1930, 1. "El presidente de la Asociación

One particular accusation, which was disregarded by the Tribunal, contained serious revelations that were partially corroborated in other trials and convictions. The accuser, Fernando Bontá Chávez, was a former civil servant in the Leguía administration who censored telegrams and wrote government propaganda. He cited and promised to present documentary evidence; his denunciation was made public in local newspapers.[215] Bontá denounced the illegal actions of several Peruvians and foreigners who collaborated with Leguía in a covert system of misappropriation of funds that were invested in foreign stock markets and used in the dictator's reelection campaigns. A major source of misappropriated funds originated from the collusion of the public works administration and monopoly contractor firm, the Foundation Company. Additionally, political collaborators benefited personally from this illegal collusion and graft: ministers and top politicians (Benjamín Huamán de los Heros, Mariano N. Barbosa, Alfredo Mendiola, Celestino Manchego Muñoz), high-ranking bureaucrats (Carlos Aramburu Salinas, Luis A. Guevara), mid-ranking officers who collected a 4-percent fee to expedite payments and permits, and private investors in the fraud-ridden Foundation Company. Most public employees, including Foundation Company staff, were obliged to work for Leguía's reelection campaigns.[216]

According to Bontá, Leguía further financed his political campaigns through an elaborate scheme linking his own private business managed by

---

Nacional de Normalistas denuncia . . . las irregularidades habidas en el ramo de la enseñanza," *El Comercio,* no. 45220, September 21, 1930, 1.

215. "Denuncia al Tribunal Nacional: Fernando Bontá Chávez," *El Comercio,* no. 45225, September 24, 1930, 2. Bontá was questioned as a reliable witness by one of the accused, Luis Guevara, since Bontá had been denounced for receiving illicit payments for his well-known former collaboration with the Leguía administration. *El Comercio,* no. 45226, September 25, 1930, 13. Bontá argued that he had been fired, persecuted, and forced into exile since 1926 for his previous attempts to fight the abuses he was denouncing. In recent times, Bontá's testimony might have been considered that of a "colaborador eficaz" or special witness collaborating with the prosecution in exchange for a reduced sentence or pardon.

216. "Denuncia hecha por Fernando Bontá Chávez, ciudadano, contra D. Augusto B. Leguía, Benjamín Huamán y otros por defraudación al Estado en la Bolsa de Valores a través de corredores ingleses," Lima, September 23, 1930, Tribunal de Sanción Nacional, leg. 10, exp. 225, f. 183, AGN. For a similar charge accepted by the tribunal against Leguía, Huamán, and others, see "Denuncia hecha por Ramón Venegas, Auditor General de Tráfico y Rodaje contra Augusto B. Leguía, Benjamín Huamán de los Heros, César Ugarte, y otros por delitos de malversación y defraudación de fondos de rodaje," Lima, October 11, 1930, Tribunal de Sanción Nacional, leg. 10, exp. 228, f. 19, AGN.

agents who were paid from public funds, including his British personal secretary, C. R. H. Shoobridge, and the American C. N. Griffis, Leguía's former secretary and editor-in-chief of the *West Coast Leader,* the English-language publication at the service of the dictator's political interests and designs to misinform international public opinion. Using his secretaries as decoys and the services of British brokers John Coward and H. Baum, who were stationed in Lima with a state-of-the-art stock quote and telegraph service, also paid by the Peruvian government, Leguía invested misappropriated public funds in the London and New York stock markets. Leguía's passion for racehorses, as well as his financial losses in high-risk cotton futures, might also contribute to explain the laundering and ultimate loss of his wealth gained through corruption.[217]

Enduring Legacies

The revelations arising from the investigations of the Tribunal de Sanción Nacional, and their publicity in local and foreign newspapers, provided U.S. senators with key information used in January 1932 during congressional hearings on several foreign bond issues totaling $106 million in 1927 and 1928 brokered by New York bankers. These loans were in default since April 1931 as a result of overborrowing, spending in costly and unproductive public works, economic downturn in Peru aggravated by the Great Depression, and the political turmoil that followed Leguía's overthrow. Fearing confidential information at the disposal of the senators (particularly Senator Hiram Johnson), the heads of J. W. Seligman & Company, Frederick Strauss and Henry Breck, revealed that in order to facilitate loan approval in Peru they had in effect paid commissions ranging from 0.5 to 0.75 percent of the total face value of the Peruvian loans' bond issues, amounting to $415,000, to no other than Juan Leguía, the son of the deposed dictator. In fact, a close analysis of Juan's checking account at Seligman & Company revealed that he had received deposits for approximately $1 million.[218]

217. "Claim [for £469,741] of Messrs. Kearsley and Cunningham [Liverpool] against Mr. A. B. Leguía," August 8, 1928, FO 371/13508, NAUK; Alfonso Quiroz, *Domestic and Foreign Finance in Modern Peru, 1850–1950: Financing Visions of Development* (Pittsburgh, PA: Macmillan and University of Pittsburgh Press, 1993), 103.

218. U.S. Senate, Committee on Finance, *Sale of Foreign Bonds or Securities in the United States: Hearings,* part 3, 8–15, January 1932 (Washington, DC: Government Printing Office, 1932), 1276–81; "La investigación de los empréstitos peruanos," *El Comercio,* no. 46172, February 20, 1932, 1.

In justifying this questionable action, the bankers stated that the business had been brought to them with those conditions through American intermediaries at F. J. Lisman & Company, and that initially they did not know the identity of the beneficiary. They admitted that they hired former U.S. diplomats to facilitate local approval of the loans. Under further questioning, they also revealed that they had opened a regular checking account in Juan Leguía's name where they deposited the amounts of the "commissions." During several trips to New York, Juan Leguía withdrew money from this account or wrote checks for hotel and other expenses. According to the bankers, Juan Leguía lived a grand life, spending up to $200,000 or $300,000 a year over several years. Moreover, the bankers were forced to admit that, although Juan Leguía's commission was rather steep, the contracting of such loans in Latin American countries such as Costa Rica and Colombia generally involved the payment of a "commission" negotiated with domestic officials promising government approval.[219]

In 1934 at a special U.S. Senate committee hearing on munitions businesses suspected of profiting from foreign wars and arms races, the president and vice president of the Electric Boat Company, Henry Carse and Lawrence Spear, respectively, were questioned. Electric Boat had participated in negotiations on selling submarines to the Leguía government in 1912, 1919, and throughout the rest of the Oncenio. Money for submarine purchases was obtained through an increase in the foreign debt and through domestic bond issues. Part of the dictator's popularity during his political career had been based on his aura as a modernizer vying to introduce the innovative amphibious weapon to stimulate the ongoing arms race with Chile. Electric Boat counted on the services of a Peruvian naval officer, Commander Luis Aubry (in and out of active duty during the period in question), who promoted the sale of submarines, received a 3-percent sales commission, and brokered illegal "local commissions" paid to three key officials in Peru. Between 1924 and 1926, the Peruvian navy acquired four Electric Boat submarines built in Groton, Connecticut, costing a total of $5.8 million. The executives of Electric Boat authorized Aubry to pay Peruvian officials a "commission" of $15,000 per submarine. In 1927–1929, another, ultimately frustrated deal to sell two more submarines valued at

---

219. U.S. Senate, Commitee on Finance, *Sale of Foreign Bonds,* 1283–86, 1296, 1298, 1309; "Noticias cablegráficas: nuevas sensacionales declaraciones . . . Lawrence Dennis, ex-diplomático y financiero y Oliver C. Townsend. . . La actuación de Mr. [S. A.] Maginnis," *El Comercio,* no. 46101, January 12, 1932, 11–12.

$2.5 million, included a promise by Electric Boat to pay Juan Leguía a bribe of $20,000 per boat, apart from the customary commission to Aubry and $10,000 more per boat to two other corrupt officials. The Senate committee members, particularly Senator Bennett C. Clark, obtained these blunt confessions in part through referencing and exhibiting the firm's compromising internal correspondence. When asked if he considered graft and bribery a basis of their business in South America, Spear argued that what Americans called a bribe was not considered so in South America where it was a general practice, an "old Spanish custom" to "grease the ways" and "take care of their friends through government business."[220]

All these revelations and investigations caused more public scandal in Peru but failed to produce the effective institutional reform necessary to curb ingrained corruption in politics and business.[221] Such a pervasive presence was exacerbated by Leguía's dictatorial regime in ways similar to those established by President Alberto Fujimori in the 1990s. Anticorruption efforts and moralizing impulses came up very short in achieving effective legal mechanisms to prevent future proliferation of graft.

To recapitulate, postwar recovery and modernization, particularly in the 1880s and 1890s, contained many of the same mechanisms of corruption that had peaked in the 1870s. Initially, scarce fiscal resources and foreign loans constrained the growth of inherited modes of corruption. Graft and perks benefiting a military clique were prominent, although bribery for the approval of the strategic financial settlement with foreign creditors in 1889, was particularly important for a few years. By the time Piérola was back in control of the presidency in 1895, shifts in economic and institutional structures sustained a few checks to the old caudillo style of graft and political patronage. The military was restructured and professionalized (the upper ranks bought off with financial rewards and diplomatic posts abroad). Economic interests expected clearer property rights, stability, and lower transaction costs. Budget expenditures and public works were limited (except during Leguía's first term, curbed in its excesses by Civilista congressional opposition), and the political and electoral systems reshuffled. Such mild yet noteworthy constraints to rampant corruption remained in place throughout the 1899–1919 period, although with some important interruptions by, on the one hand, Piérola's declining movement and his would-be

220. U.S. Senate, Special Committee, *Munitions Industry Hearings* (1934), part 1, 85, 92–94, 100, 116–17, 119, 126, 135–36; Basadre, *Historia* 13:284.
221. See *El Comercio*, January 9, 1932, 12, 13, 18, 21, and 23.

political heirs, Leguía and Billinghurst, and on the other, Colonel Benavides's coup of 1914.

In a context of weakened popular party structures, patronage continued to gather the support ambitious political leaders needed for gaining and retaining power. With limited fiscal resources and low civil service salaries, politicians allowed and even encouraged corruption at high and low administrative levels to complement political rewards and favors. This pattern of political corruption stubbornly persisted into the twentieth century, but the evolution of elections, an increasingly popular mechanism to legitimate governments, complicated matters for corrupt patronage networks. Competition for control of the electoral system through capture of electoral boards, fraud, vote buying, violence, and ultimately dictatorial measures, left an imprint on popular perceptions of corruption and lowered the "tolerance threshold" for the same. The financing of political parties and their campaigns depended less on foreign rent-seeking and risky contributors such as Dreyfus and more on domestic and foreign business interested in an environment of political stability for local direct investment. The press achieved a higher level of freedom despite frustrated attempts to control and manipulate it under Piérola, the first Leguía administration, Billinghurst, and General Benavides. The latter, protecting the political and economic interests of the Civilistas, contributed to military involvement in politics and injured the Civilistas' claims of electoral legitimacy.

All of these advances (albeit somewhat modest) were radically reversed during the Leguía Oncenio. Unbridled corruption and presidential intervention permeated all key institutions and the media. Constitutional checks and balances were destroyed. Foreign debt mismanagement, bribery in civil and military procurement, and graft in huge public works returned as the principal modes of corruption causing increasing deficits and costs to the public. The estimated annual average of corruption costs in the 1920s amounted to six times that of the 1910–1919 period, and fifteen times that of 1900–1909 (see Table A.5). In terms of corruption costs as a percentage of government expenditure, whereas the annual average for 1900–1909 was 25 percent, and that of 1910–1919, 28 percent, the 1920–1929 period reached a staggering 72 percent. As a percentage of GDP, corruption costs increased to 3.8 percent, compared to 1 and 1.1 percent, respectively, in the previous two decades (see Table A.6). Leguía's Oncenio was clearly the most corrupt of the modernization age, competing with corruption levels later achieved by the regimes of the 1970s, 1980s, and 1990s.

Leguía's rigging of yet another reelection bid in 1930 surpassed the limits of public tolerance, which led to a military uprising as a solution to rampant corruption. The military regime, which imposed a court of sanctions for corrupt officials to legitimize the new regime and attract popular support, bungled the legal proceedings due to their unconstitutional nature. A new era of popular and populist political actors had begun. Newer mechanisms of graft soon emerged to blend in with the older path dependence of corruption.

Chapter 5

Venal Dictators and Covert Pacts, 1931–1962

In 1930, the historian Jorge Basadre (1903–1980) witnessed the crumbling of Leguía's corrupt regime. The unsustainable modernization triggered by the Oncenio's financial extravagance opened the floodgates to a serious political and social crisis. The crisis was aggravated by economic depression and the emergence of new, popular actors.[1] Basadre had been imprisoned two times during Leguía's authoritarian regime, first in 1923 for his leftist inclinations and again in August 1930, unfairly accused of plotting against the dictator. After the fall of Leguía, the university professor and librarian engaged more openly in political activity. He joined a group of moderates bent on introducing urgently necessary democratic and electoral reforms to rebuild the country's institutional framework thoroughly undermined during the Oncenio.

Basadre asserted that Leguía had destroyed the traditional political parties.[2] After the fall of Leguía, two new political adversaries seized the moment: the "revolutionary" militaristic movement led by Lieutenant Colonel Luis Sánchez Cerro, and the new radical APRA (American Popular Revolutionary Alliance) led by Víctor Raúl Haya de la Torre. Basadre strongly

---

1. "The extravagance of and the corrupt practices under Leguía had reached . . . a point that no country, and Peru least of all, could stand in view of the ruling depression." Confidential memorandum, "The situation in Peru" by Herbert Apfel (South American representative of Hanover Bank, New York), enclosure of dispatch from W. S. Culbertson to S.S., Santiago de Chile, December 23, 1930, no. 716, 823.00/618, box 5693, Record Group (hereafter RG) 59, USNA.

2. Jorge Basadre (University of San Marcos, Lima) to Council on Foreign Relations, "Letter from Peru: The Recent Election in Retrospect," n.d., received by U.S. Department of State, Historical Adviser, March 10, 1932, 823.00/852, box 5696, RG 59, USNA.

disagreed with the undemocratic positions of both populist groups, which led Peru to the brink of civil war. Moreover, both political forces engaged in corruption to achieve their political goals.

The hotly contested presidential elections of 1931 resulted in Sánchez Cerro's triumph, soon followed by the closing of San Marcos University, Basadre's main employer. The historian traveled abroad and did not return to the country until 1935 when the university was allowed to reopen. Thereafter, and throughout his long academic and civil servant career, Basadre experienced repeated frustration of his efforts at institutional and educational reform. He faced opposition and sabotage by corrupt interests who exercised shrewd ways to profit from shifting political circumstances. Basadre also witnessed successive dictatorships and electoral processes replete with scandalous frauds and secret pacts benefiting a clique of corrupt politicians. This period was one of mounting demographic and social problems that challenged effective modernization. Despite cynical claims of administrative honesty, corruption persisted as a proven means to bolster political continuity and delay urgent reforms.

Populist Colonel versus APRA

Sánchez Cerro declared his intention of cleaning up public administration and eradicating corrupt practices prevalent during Leguía's regime. Sánchez Cerro backed his oath of "moralization" by imprisoning and confiscating the property of some very visible figureheads of the defunct regime, including former president Leguía and his son Juan. The Tribunal de Sanción Nacional—the ad hoc court established immediately after the military coup that transformed Sánchez Cerro into a popular hero—presented devastating accusations of "illicit enrichment" against Leguía and his former ministers. According to the British chargé d'affaires in Lima, these charges would "make Peru ridiculous throughout the world but they were true nevertheless."[3] In the meantime, important administrative reforms recommended to the Peru-

---

3. Verbal communication by Gurney reported in dispatch by Fred Morris Dearing to S.S., Lima, January 10, 1931, no. 397, 823.00/625, pp. 2–3, box 5693, RG59, USNA. On Sánchez Cerro's quest against "corrupt and inefficient politics," see Steve Stein, *Populism in Peru: The Emergence of the Masses and Social Control* (Madison: University of Wisconsin Press, 1980), 87–89.

vian government in 1931—similar to those effective at curbing corruption in Chile since 1925—by U.S. economist Edwin Kemmerer, who was hired as a consultant by the new regime in Lima, were largely disregarded.[4]

The aging and sick Leguía remained imprisoned until just before his death in a military hospital in February 1932. Sánchez Cerro's strict determination to punish Leguía was perceived as either a vindictive personal crusade that exacerbated political divisiveness or as a principled stance against corruption.[5] However, the legal proceedings of the Tribunal de Sanción proved inefficient and unconstitutional. The administration of property confiscated from those accused of corruption was wasteful if not outright venal. A "[g]ood deal of graft and malpractices" was involved in dealing with several of the accused who had taken refuge in foreign embassies. Examples were former Leguiísta high-level supporters Jesús Salazar, Sebastián Lorente, and Foción Mariátegui, who apparently paid bribes to avoid imprisonment or obtain exoneration.[6]

Despite his popularity among average Peruvians, and the endorsement received from the most conservative members of the elite, Sánchez Cerro still lacked an organized party to support, formalize, and prolong his inflated presidential ambitions. He was convinced that the presidency was his just reward for ousting Leguía, but he faced strong opposition among fellow military officers. An increasing number of uprisings of army and navy units threatened generalized anarchy. Sánchez Cerro resigned his position of chief of the military junta to keep his presidential options open in the coming elections. Ambitious officers such as Lieutenant Colonel "Zorro" Gustavo Jiménez eagerly contested the political space opened by the crisis. In March 1931, David Samanez Ocampo, a politician of old Pierolista leanings from the southern region, received the support of Jiménez to lead a provisional government. The short administration of Samanez Ocampo decreed a major expansion of the electorate and allowed an electoral board to

---

4. Paul W. Drake, *The Money Doctor in the Andes: The Kemmerer Missions, 1923–1933* (Durham, NC: Duke University Press, 1989), chapters 3, 6; Alfonso W. Quiroz, *Domestic and Foreign Finance in Modern Peru, 1850-1950: Financing Visions of Development* (London and Pittsburgh, PA: Macmillan and University of Pittsburgh Press, 1993), 178–79.

5. Fred Morris Dearing to S.S., Lima, March 31, 1932, 823.00/867, pp. 3–5, box 5696, RG 59, USNA.

6. Dearing to S.S., Lima, January 10, 1931, 823.00/625, p. 3, box 5693, RG 59, USNA.

implement presidential elections and those of the constituent congress in October 1931.[7]

During his short dictatorship prior to the 1931 elections, Sánchez Cerro gave "employment to his entire family and probably his collaborators did likewise."[8] Diplomatic observers believed that graft under the military junta was almost as bad as under Leguía. They cited the case of the suspicious moratorium granted to the failing Banco del Perú y Londres. They also noted that Colonel Ernesto Montagne, minister of foreign affairs, and other members of the cabinet had moved to luxurious homes and considerably improved their lifestyle without earning a commensurate official salary.[9]

Sánchez Cerro intimate political circle included his unscrupulous brother, Pablo Ernesto, a medical student who was appointed director of the public health office. Another brother, J. Hortensio, also secured a government job. Pablo Ernesto was suspected of controlling the racket formerly exploited by Juan Leguía for the sale of opium mainly to Chinese residents in Lima.[10] Pablo Ernesto was considered the "go-between" connection with gambling, drug, prostitution, and other organized crime interests who contributed money to further his brother's political ambitions.[11] Before the 1931 elections, Pablo Ernesto prepared for the arrival of his brother from abroad with the launching of a well-financed electoral campaign. Questionable contributions and aid from wealthy supporters such as the mine owner Lizandro Proaño sustained Pablo Ernesto's lavish accommodations in Lima's exclusive Hotel Bolívar.[12] Among the candidate's most notorious advisors and collaborators were Francisco R. Lanatta, a lawyer of questionable reputation with ministerial ambitions, and fascist Luis A. Flores. A new party, the Unión Revolucionaria (UR), was formed to support Sánchez Cerro's candidacy.

In the meantime, the other major contestant in the 1931 elections, politician and former student leader Haya de la Torre, also prepared his arrival in Lima after years of exile and political campaigns abroad. A well-established

7. Basadre, *Historia* 14:56–67; Stein, *Populism,* 96–98, 119–21.

8. Apfel, "Situation in Peru," 2.

9. Dearing to S.S., Lima, January 10, 1931, 823.00/625, p. 3, box 5693, RG 59, USNA.

10. Dearing to S.S., Lima, May 3, 1933, "Public sale of opium in Peru," no. 2799, 823.114/Narcotics/62, box 5709, RG 59, USNA.

11. Dearing to S.S., Lima, May 23, 1931, no. 737, 823.00/695, p. 2, box 5694, RG 59, USNA.

12. Dearing to S.S., Lima, May 20, 1931, no. 725, 823.00/693, p. 2, box 5694, RG 59, USNA.

opposition leader throughout the Oncenio, Haya had founded APRA, a fledgling movement of radical-populist, interventionist, and anti-imperialist inclinations, in Mexico. Haya's educated and disciplinarian collaborators in Peru had been organizing this rapidly growing party since 1930, under the tactically modified name of Peruvian Aprista Party (PAP), on the basis of massive appeals to organized labor and the lower middle and professional classes.[13] Years of struggle against dictatorship had produced an APRA leadership ready to use any means, including violence and clandestine or illegal actions, to achieve the ultimate goal of seizing power.

Apristas also claimed to be dedicated to the fight against government corruption as well as the corrupting influence of the wealthy. They vowed to establish an efficient, technocratic, and interventionist state against domestic and foreign privileges.[14] They accused Sánchez Cerro of receiving support and funds from the most conservative anti-Aprista members of the elite. The most noticeable among them were the Miró Quesada clan, owners of *El Comercio,* the most important and influential local newspaper. APRA, however, received support from prominent Leguiístas eager to defeat their nemesis Sánchez Cerro. Two significant Leguiísta leaders headed the party's strategic secretariats of finance and politics.[15] Moreover, U.S. diplomats reported that an important donor to APRA's cause in 1931 was Carlos Fernández Bácula, a former diplomat "suspected of being an agent [in the] . . . clandestine traffic of narcotics." Fernández Bácula confided to a member of the U.S. Embassy that he had contributed handsomely to Haya's campaign.[16]

As in comparable cases in other Latin American countries, the struggle to secure and monopolize the political opportunities opened up by the crisis of the early 1930s in Peru resulted in the clash of competing ideologies from the far right and left. This strife to capitalize on the "populist moment" featured charismatic leaders promising to save the country. After a bitter and

13. Víctor Villanueva, *El APRA en busca del poder* (Lima: Editorial Horizonte, 1975); "The Petty-Bourgeois Ideology of the Peruvian Aprista Party," *Latin American Perspectives* 4 (1977): 57–76; Peter Klarén, *Modernization, Dislocation, and Aprismo: Origins of the Peruvian Aprista Party, 1870–1932* (Austin: University of Texas Press, 1973), 146–49.

14. Harry Kantor, *The Ideology and Program of the Peruvian Aprista Movement* (New York: Octagon Books, 1966 [1953]), 61; Klarén, *Peru,* 273.

15. Basadre, *Historia* 14:155; Stein, *Populism,* 113; Víctor Villanueva, *El militarismo en el Perú* (Lima: Imprenta Scheuch, 1962).

16. Dearing to S.S., Lima, October 16, 1931, no. 1132, 823.00/767, box 695, RG 59, USNA.

massive campaign, Sánchez Cerro clearly won the elections that, according to Basadre and other impartial observers, were considered uncommonly clean.[17] However the Apristas, in the tradition of the old Pierolistas, claimed there had been "Sancho-Civilista" electoral fraud and swiftly moved to exert pressure through violent insurrectionary action.[18]

Once in power, the Sánchez-Cerristas and their conservative allies implemented a widespread change of government personnel, further alienating the opposition.[19] They had also obtained a majority in the constituent congress: Even Pablo Ernesto, the president's incompetent brother and "petty grafter," gained a congressional seat representing the province of Piura.[20] Sánchez Cerro then proceeded to repress the Apristas and the military officers and enlisted men who supported APRA's insurrectionary actions. APRA's elected congressional representatives were detained and deported. A retaliatory, failed assassination attempt on the life of Sánchez Cerro, carried out by a teenage Aprista in March 1932, was followed by massive repression of APRA and the imprisonment of Haya. A few days later, an APRA-inspired mutiny aboard two navy ships stationed in the harbor of Callao on May 7 was defeated. Approximately one thousand persons were killed in the northern city of Trujillo following a violent and bloody Aprista uprising led by Haya's brother Agustín. Several unarmed military officers, soldiers, and policemen imprisoned by the Apristas were assassinated. Army troops retook the city and massacred Aprista militants and followers. Hundreds of Apristas received death sentences during a speedy court martial, although a few were spared after paying bribes to people in charge of carrying out the executions.[21]

17. Basadre, "Letter from Peru: Recent Election in Retrospect," 4; Dearing to S.S., Lima, December 18, 1931, 823.00/811, p. 1, box 5696, RG 59, USNA; *Historia* 14:166–70.

18. Dearing to S.S., dispatches nos. 1200, 1303–4, 1322, Lima, December 5, 6, and 11, 1932, 823.00/800, 801, and 805, box 5696, RG 59, USNA.

19. Dearing to S.S., Lima, December 18, 1921, 823.00/811, p. 4, box 5696, RG 59, USNA.

20. Memorandum by Burdett, May 4, 1933, enclosure 1 in Dearing to S.S., Lima, May 4, 1933, no. 2803, 823.00/976, box 5697, RG 59, USNA; Basadre, *Historia* 14:8–9.

21. William C. Burdett to S.S., Lima, May 18, 1933, no. 2830, 823.00/986, box 5697, RG 59, USNA; Acal y Marin to M.E., Lima, July 14, and August 1, 1932, nos. 129 and 147, leg. R-338, exp. 4, AGMAE; Daniel Masterson, *Militarism and Politics in Latin America: Peru from Sánchez Cerro to Sendero Luminoso* (Westport, CT: Greenwood Press, 1991), 48–51; Klarén, *Modernization,* 137–41. APRA persisted in its then open armed struggle against the Sánchez Cerro regime. With APRA's promise of support, Lt. Col. Jiménez led an uprising from Cajamarca in March 1933 with the aim of

As a result of the bullet wounds in the chest, which almost killed him, Sánchez Cerro spent a month in the hospital. In his absence, a most scandalous case of corruption surfaced, involving the president's most trusted and closest political collaborator, Lanatta, who was prime minister and minister of finance. Such was the gravity of the accusations of dishonesty and graft against Lanatta that Sánchez Cerro interrupted his recovery to personally oversee the resignation of his minister in early April.[22] However, Lanatta retained a seat in the constituent congress where he was rehabilitated with the help of the Sánchez-Cerrista majority. Lanatta thus avoided being formally charged with the crimes of corruption in office cited in the minority findings of a special congressional investigation commission.[23] The public became nevertheless fully aware of Lanatta's guilt. In consequence, Sánchez Cerro's claims of probity lost even more credibility.[24]

The extent of Lanatta's graft is revealed in the confidential correspondence of U.S. businessmen and diplomats. Immediately after the assassination attempt against Sánchez Cerro, Lanatta endeavored to dominate the scene. He intensified his harassment of major foreign enterprises for purposes of graft and attempted graft. He was known as an unscrupulous lawyer who two decades before had been a junior attorney of the Cerro de Pasco Copper Corporation. Everybody seemed to know about his corrupt activities and certain interest groups wanted him in a high-level political post so that "questionable maneuvers could be carried out."[25]

At least ten serious instances of graft involving Lanatta and his assistant Sr. Botto were reported to the U.S. Embassy. First, was the delay of negotiations with the Cerro de Pasco and Frederick Snare corporations for the construction of the new Callao port facilities with the expectation of receiving 20,000 soles as "a slight consideration in his favor." Lanatta also asked for a high-paying position in port administration for the president's

---

taking Trujillo and seeing the entire northern region rise in revolt; his campaign failed and Jiménez killed himself before being taken prisoner. Basadre, *Historia* 14:246–51; Antonio Jaén to M.E., Lima, April 7, 1933, no. 35, leg. R-338, exp. 4, AGMAE.

22. Dearing to S.S., Lima, April 11, 1932, no. 1688, confidential, 823.002/185, pp. 1–2, box 5706, RG 59, USNA: "Lanatta has proven so venal and is such a millstone about the neck of public administration that the President has been forced to chop him."

23. Basadre, *Historia* 14:202, 210–11; "Venality of Dr. F. R. Lanatta," Dearing to S.S., Lima, April 14, 1932, no. 1706, 823.002/189, pp.2–3, box 5706, RG 59, USNA.

24. Burdett to S.S., Lima, August 5, 1932, no. 1981, 823.002/199, pp. 2–3; and Dearing to S.S., Lima, April 14, 1932, no. 1706, 823.002/189, box 5706, RG 59, USNA.

25. Dearing to S.S., Lima, April 11, 1932, no. 1692, 823.002/186, box 5706, RG 59, USNA.

brother.[26] Other incidents included a kickback proposal to settle a 70,000 soles debt owed to the International Petroleum Company for fuel supplied to the Peruvian Navy, and the manipulation of customs *vales* for 60,000 soles assigned to the navy (apparently the latter schemes were brought to the attention of Sánchez Cerro); the extortion of several Chinese merchants for 10,000 soles; the appropriation of 15,000 soles for subsidies to the University of San Marcos; an unknown amount collected from Grace and Company; and an attempt to get a 30,000 soles bribe from H. J. Gildred and Company, the contractor for construction of the Palace of Justice.[27] Lanatta's customary illegal "commission" ranged between 45 and 60 percent; in total he could have hoarded around one million soles through this type of brazen graft.[28] A few years later, Lanatta was also involved in the illegal introduction into the United States of cocaine samples intended for distribution among large chemical companies.[29]

As early as February 1932, the U.S. ambassador, who was wary of Sánchez Cerro's unstable temperament and attitude toward foreign corporations, wrote that his regime "had become rotten at the core" and he had "surrounded himself by the least principled and most hot-headed members of his following."[30] These men replaced the Civilista figures of Sánchez Cerro's first brief administration, except for the minister of the navy, Alfredo Benavides Correa, brother-in-law of General Benavides.[31] Former president Benavides, Sánchez Cerro's mentor and supporter, was rewarded with an ambassadorship in Madrid and later London and restoration of un-

26. Garret Ackerson to S.S., Lima, April 18, 1932, no. 1713, 823.1561/42, box 5711, RG 59, USNA.

27. Dispatch by Julian D. Smith (Assistant Commercial Attaché), Lima, April 8, 1932, no. 41, pp. 2–3, enclosed in 823.002/186, box 5706; and Dearing to S.S., Lima, April 6, 1932, no. 1671, 823.002/184, box 5706, RG 59, USNA, regarding memorandum of interview with Lanatta by Eduardo Pombo, general manager of the International Petroleum Company.

28. Dearing to S.S., Lima, April 14, 1932, no. 1706, 823.002/189, pp. 3–4, and enclosure 1 (Julian D. Smith, Lima, April 15, 1932, no. 48, 1), box 5706, RG 59, USNA.

29. U.S. Department of State, Washington, DC, March 4, 1937, 823.114/Narcotics/127, box 5709, RG59, USNA.

30. Dearing to S.S., Lima, February 12, 1932, no. 1534, 823.00/843, pp. 2–4, box 5696, RG 59, USNA. For similar views on Sánchez Cerro's "carácter impulsivo," "violento y nada respetuoso" that impaired his ability to deal with various individuals and groups, see Acal y Marin to M.E., Lima, November 25 and December 25, 1932, nos. 217 and 235, leg. R-338, exp. 4, AGMAE.

31. Joaquín Carrillo de Albornoz to M.A.E., Lima, February 1, 1932, no. 29, leg. R-338, exp. 4, AGMAE.

paid salaries accumulated during his exile imposed by the Leguía regime. Moreover, Benavides had rallied support among his military friends for Sánchez Cerro's election.[32] The new members of the cabinet, all elected congressmen, included Luis A. Flores (interior minister, aided by the corrupt and bloodthirsty police director Ricardo Guzmán Marquina), Carlos Sayán Alvarez (minister of justice), the corrupt Francisco Lanatta, and Gerardo Balbuena, a "clever and unprincipled lawyer-politician."[33] Lt. Col. Guzmán Marquina was considered by some as the "cruelest and most venal feature" of the Sánchez Cerro administration. Guzmán Marquina was penniless before the 1931 election, but only a few months after he was wealthy and living in extravagant style. He allegedly enriched himself through bribery in government contracts and collecting large sums in return for not carrying out death sentences imposed on Aprista insurrectionists in Trujillo and Cajamarca.[34]

The increasing "acts of corruption and absurd mismanagement in public office" had alienated most of Sánchez Cerro's more respectable collaborators.[35] However, the conservative and xenophobic Antonio Miró Quesada continued to support the president's harmful policies. A close friend of the owner of *El Comercio,* the aging former Civilista congressman José Matías Manzanilla, tarnished his fairly clean reputation by obsequiously proposing in Congress to promote Sánchez Cerro to the rank of general. This political backing by Manzanilla later earned him appointment as minister of foreign affairs and prime minister.[36]

Growing financial pressure forced a delay of several months in payment of civil servants and army personnel. This was a dangerous situation since the regime relied on a steady cash flow to maintain itself in power. A temporary but irresponsible solution was to raid the Central Reserve Bank. Likewise, Colonel Rodrigo Zárate, member of the diplomatic commission of the constituent congress, pressed foreign diplomats to spend more to en-

---

32. Benavides to Sánchez Cerro, Nice, October 9, 1930, in Pedro Ugarteche, *Sánchez Cerro: papeles y recuerdos de un presidente del Perú* (Lima: Editora Universitaria, 1969), 1:232–36.

33. Dearing to S.S., Lima, September 4, 1933, no. 3006, 823.00/1027, p. 2, box 5697, RG 59, USNA.

34. Burdett to S.S., Lima, May 18, 1933, no. 2830, 823.00/986, pp. 2–3, box 5697, RG 59, USNA.

35. Burdett to S.S., Lima, June 1, 1932, no. 1835, 823.00/894, p. 2, box 5696, RG 59, USNA.

36. Dearing to S.S., Lima, December 27, 1932, no. 2465, 823.00/946, box 5697, RG 59, USNA.

tertain ministers, congressmen, and the president to facilitate negotiations with foreign interests: Accordingly obeisance and gifts to Sánchez-Cerrista authorities were strongly expected from foreign representatives.[37] However, formal public contracts were often violated and public revenues were "diverted for private purposes."[38]

The regime's troubles continued to grow compounded by controversial, incompetent, and illegal official decisions and actions. A border dispute with Colombia in the Leticia (formerly Putumayo) region threatened to escalate into a full-blown war. Sánchez Cerro was determined to undo the international settlement signed with Colombia during the Leguía administration. With the backing of *El Comercio* and foreign affairs minister Manzanilla, the bellicose president decided to follow a path to war. However, he was confronted with the pathetic lack of preparation and financial problems plaguing the armed forces. To boost his war-mongering campaign, Sánchez Cerro appointed his old mentor, General Benavides, at the time ambassador in London, to the post of general chief of national defense, a new post superior to those of the war and navy ministers.[39]

Moreover, the regime negotiated a secret "guano-for-arms" pact with Japan in response to the unwillingness of the United States to sell arms to Peru under circumstances of impending war with Colombia. This very costly and clearly unconstitutional deal, first carried out by the Okura Trading Company, also supposedly entailed the surrender of Peruvian sovereignty to a guano island for exploitation by Japanese interests. Covert shipments of thousands of rifles from Japan to Peru were reported by Colombian and U.S. diplomats. This improvised effort to supply weapons to the Peruvian army also implied the allowance of large-scale smuggling of Japanese goods and probably also opium through strategically located guano islands. This scandal exploded in Peru only after Sánchez Cerro's demise.[40]

37. Dearing to S.S., Lima, October 8, 1932, no. 2206, 823.00/930, p. 3, box 5696, RG 59, USNA.

38. Dearing to S.S., Lima, April 7, 1933, no. 2748, 823.00/960, p. 4, box 5697, RG 59, USNA.

39. Antonio Jaén to M.E., Lima, April 20, 1933, no. 43, leg. R-338, exp. 4, AGMAE. With the appointment to the Jefatura de la Defensa Nacional, Benavides was promoted to the rank of division general. Masterson, *Militarism*, 51–52.

40. Jeffrey Caffery to S.S., "Leticia incident: reported exchange of rifles and guano between Japan and Peru," Bogota, November 17, 1932, no. 898, 823.0141/20; Dearing to S.S., "[6,000 tons of] guano exports to Japan [in the *Hakutaku Maru* from the Ballestas islands]," Lima, December 9, 1932, no. 2425, 823.0141/19; Dearing to S.S., "Guano contract with Okura Trading Co.," Lima, December 6, 1933, no. 3175, 823.0141/21;

The ill-conceived and perilous war plans ended abruptly in the early afternoon of April 30, 1933 when the president's motorcade was about to leave the site of a military parade. A seventeen-year-old Aprista pauper approached the president and discharged several pistol bullets, resulting in the death of Sánchez Cerro. A few hours later, an emergency session of Congress voted by overwhelming majority to appoint General Benavides as president for the remaining term of the deceased Sánchez Cerro. The measure, however, contradicted the new 1933 constitution, which prohibited active-duty military officers from serving as president. Fearing ensuing disorder, martial law was imposed. Benavides included in his first cabinet the radical Sánchez-Cerristas Luis A. Flores, minister of the navy, and Pablo Ernesto Sánchez Cerro, minister of public works. This was clearly a measure to appease angry UR party members who had contemplated a rampage to assassinate Haya de la Torre and other Apristas in prison. This plan was thwarted through an initiative taken by foreign diplomats.[41] From that moment on Benavides proved deft at negotiating an exit to the dangerous situation bordering on civil and foreign war by making use of legal and authoritarian, as well as corrupt means.

Restoration under Benavides

In his brief acceptance speech, President Benavides declared that, not being a politician, he expected the collaboration of all Peruvians. This statement was interpreted as a promise for a much needed general political amnesty that would benefit mainly the Apristas.[42] Benavides had the necessary "skills" for a negotiated yet conservative solution to the political crisis, as he was considered "astute, shrewd, cruel, and unprincipled."[43] The

---

Dearing to S.S., "Japan, lease of the island of 'Asia'," Lima, January 18, 1934, no. 3221, 823.0141/22; Louis G. Dreyfus to S.S., Lima, September 28, 1934, no. 3611, 823.0141/31: "Ignacio Brandariz in a letter to *El Comercio* gives history of guano contract with Japanese firm Okura Co.," box 5707, RG 59, USNA; Dreyfus to S.S., Lima, February 1, 1934, no. 3253, 823.00/1071, p. 4, box 5697, RG 59, USNA: "*La Tribuna* reports a sale of guano by the Sánchez Cerro government to the firm Okura and Company at no more than one third of its true value, with resulting loss of 690,000 soles to Peru."

41. Jaén to M.E., Lima, May 27, 1933, no. 53, leg. R-338, exp. 4, AGMAE.

42. Dearing to S.S., Lima, May 1, 1933, no. 2797, 823.00/975, p. 3, box 5697, RG 59, USNA.

43. Dearing to S.S., Lima, May 4, 1933, no. 2803, 823.00/976, p. 4, box 5697, RG 59, USNA.

president started by terminating government funds provided by the former regime to UR party offices and spy rings.[44] Benavides then upheld a military court decision acquitting, for lack of evidence and confessions exacted under torture, a group of twenty Apristas accused of involvement in the assassination of Sánchez Cerro. Consequently, the three Sánchez-Cerrista ministers in Benavides's first cabinet resigned.[45]

Facing limited political support and a venal UR majority in Congress, Benavides endeavored to divide the UR and control the political right. In November 1933, a campaign was launched in the Chamber of Deputies against the UR majority on account of the mishandling of 4 million soles allocated for the chamber's expenses.[46] Benavides's main enemy was UR leader Luis Flores who conspired to organize a fascist legion after the Italian model with the collaboration of sympathetic government officials and members of the business elite.[47] Flores's sidekick, the hated and corrupt Guzmán Marquina, was removed from the political scene by appointing him "air attaché" in France, although soon after Guzmán Marquina ran for a congressional post.[48] By offering diplomatic posts to several members of the Miró Quesada family, the powerful influence of *El Comercio* was also temporarily bought off and curbed.[49] Carefully and with the support of a majority in the armed forces, Benavides defused the possibility of war with Colombia through means of a peaceful diplomatic settlement in 1934.[50]

While pursuing such perilous political course, Benavides received initial advice and assistance from his old friend Jorge Prado Ugarteche, who was appointed prime minister in June 1933. Prado became the spearhead of a policy of conciliation aimed at "buying" the cooperation of APRA. In sharp contrast to Sánchez Cerro's counterproductive war of extermination against

44. Jaén to M.E., Lima, July 6, 1933, no. 64, leg. R-338, exp. 4, AGMAE.

45. Burdett to S.S., Lima, June 23, 1933, no. 2884, 823.00/999, box 5697, RG 59, USNA.

46. Acal y Marin to M.E., Lima, November 13, 1933, no. 128, leg. R-338, exp. 4, AGMAE.

47. Burdett to S.S., Lima, June 26, 1933, no. 2887, 823.00/1000, box 5697, RG 59, USNA.

48. Burdett to S.S., Lima, May 18, 1933, no. 2830, 823.00/986, p. 1, box 5697, RG 59, USNA.

49. "500,000 soles anuales reciben del fisco los Miró Quesada: herencias de la pasada tiranía," *La Sanción,* October 18, 1933, enclosure, no. 1, Dearing to S.S., Lima, October 21, 1933, no. 3095, 823.00/1040, RG 59, USNA.

50. Burdett to S.S., Lima, June 8, 1933, no. 2863, 823.00/993, box 5697, RG 59, USNA.

APRA, Prado envisioned and put in practice a policy of cooptation that proved partially successful. He was the first of several subsequent right-wing politicians to realize that the venal foundation of Peruvian politics could also ensnare APRA leaders.[51] Temporary conciliation arrived only after negotiations that included talks with APRA leader Haya de la Torre. By July 1933, political prisoners, except Haya, had been released, and Juan Leguía had been allowed to leave the country.[52] Although APRA remained an illegal party, Haya's release on August 9 was granted with the understanding that he would moderate his party's political actions, and after leaving prison, Haya visited Benavides.[53] The regime proceeded to restore constitutional guarantees. Eventually, under the official motto of "peace, order, and work," the Peruvian economy began to recover thanks to improving world market demand and prices for cotton and other exports, expansion of the country's agricultural land base, private and public financing reforms, rising industrial output, and public works and road construction policies that provided thousands of jobs.[54]

Despite these significant achievements, the Benavides regime was unable to build or co-opt organized political support. Political opposition from the left and right continued to threaten the survival of the regime, especially with the approaching presidential elections of October 1936. The various political groups viewed the government as a temporary phenomenon, but General Benavides envisioned the end of his restorative mission only with a satisfactory transfer of power to his handpicked candidate, Jorge Prado. The unsatisfied ambitions of the APRA, UR, and other party leaders threatened the political stability that underpinned economic recovery. These leaders soon conspired to overthrow Benavides by violent means. As early as

51. Víctor Villanueva, "The Military in Peruvian Politics, 1919–1945," in *The Politics of Antipolitics: The Military in Latin America,* ed. Brian Loveman and Thomas Davies (Lincoln: University of Nebraska, 1989), 126–35, esp. 130.

52. Burdett to S.S., Lima, July 17, 1933, no. 2921, 823.00/1008, box 5697, RG 59, USNA.

53. Jaén to M.E., Lima, August 17, 1933, no. 84, and Acal y Marin to M.E., Lima, November 13, 1933, leg. R-338, exp. 4, AGMAE.

54. *Progresos del Perú 1933–1939 durante el gobierno del Presidente de la República General Oscar R. Benavides* (Buenos Aires: Editorial Guillermo Kraft, 1945), 9–10; "Peru in 1938: another year of peace and plenty," *West Coast Leader* 27, no. 1404 (January 10, 1939): 5; Orazio Ciccarelli, "Fascism and Politics in Peru during the Benavides Regime, 1933–39: The Italian Perspective," *Hispanic American Historical Review* 70, no. 3 (1990): 405–32, esp. 411–12; Quiroz, *Domestic and Foreign Finance,* 83–85.

November 1933, Jorge Prado was forced to resign as prime minister due to mounting political pressure, print media campaigns, and reactionary opposition to his conciliatory policy and support of constitutional rights.[55]

Prado was replaced by the archconservative intellectual José de la Riva Agüero, who was focused on responding harshly to APRA-led strikes and conspiracies. Such activities were on the upswing in the northern region where APRA exercised strong political influence, and among pro-APRA military officers of medium and lower ranks. Despite these blatant threats, Haya continued to meet with Benavides.[56] This characteristic behavior of Haya has been interpreted as an opportunistic attempt to negotiate his access to power hidden from his party's constituency and general public opinion.[57] As the Aprista leader later confided to American social scientist and historian Frank Tannenbaum during an interview in Lima, Benavides offered Haya significant personal and political enticements, including a 25-percent congressional representation for APRA, providing that Haya collaborated with the general's electoral plans.[58]

Obviously, Benavides could not trust Haya's intentions when under pressure from other more radical Aprista leaders. In fact, the APRA leadership was deeply involved in destabilizing the Benavides regime before the 1936 presidential elections. On May 15, 1935, a nineteen-year-old Aprista assassinated the conservative and influential leader Antonio Miró Quesada and his wife María Laos de Miró Quesada. This action resulted in serious political problems for Benavides. A new cabinet composed entirely by military officers was established two days after the murder. The extreme right increased its pressure on the politically weakening regime. The Miró Quesada family, *El Comercio,* and the UR attacked Benavides for his refusal to use a military tribunal to prosecute the assassin.[59]

In May 1936, the APRA leadership in exile plotted to arm Aprista militants and launch an insurrection in the southern region of the country under

55. Acal y Marin to M.E., Lima, November 27, 1933, no. 135, leg. R-338, exp. 4, AGMAE.

56. "Política interior del Perú," n.d. (ca. November 1934), leg. R-347, exp. 12, AGMAE.

57. Thomas Davies and Víctor Villanueva, eds., *Secretos electorales del APRA: correspondencia y documentos de 1939* (Lima: Editorial Horizonte, 1982), 14.

58. Dreyfus to S.S., Lima, September 8, 1938, no. 639, 823.00/1315, box 5699, USNA.

59. Luis Avilés y Tíscar to M.E., Lima, May 17, 1935, no. 82; Luis Guillén Gil, Lima, November 7, 1935, no. 166, leg. R-847, exp. 12; Dreyfus to S.S., Lima, May 17, 1935, no. 3966, 823.00/1155, box 5698, RG 59, USNA.

the command of Julio Cárdenas. The plan involved courting Colonel David Toro—the Bolivian leftist president who disliked the Benavides regime—to provide money and arms to APRA militants at various locations on the Peru–Bolivia border. In exchange, Aprista leader Manuel Seoane promised Toro that, after the downfall of Benavides, Peru would not oppose the Chilean concession of a Bolivian outlet to the Pacific Ocean through former Peruvian territory. This part of the deal between Toro and APRA was a violation of the 1883 Peru–Chile peace treaty of Ancón. The APRA-Bolivia plot suffered crucial delays due to lack of funds: the Aprista bonds for a "social action" loan of $1 million did not find sufficient or major investors apart from certain foreign political figures such as Lázaro Cárdenas. The scandalous conspiracy ultimately failed as a result of forceful diplomatic pressures by the Benavides government. A later plot hatched by the next Bolivian president, Germán Busch, to provide arms to APRA-backed conspirators was also discovered by spies and defeated by Benavides's agents who arrested the Peruvian ringleaders in La Paz.[60]

As the electoral campaign advanced, APRA was described as an illegal international organization, and thus was proscribed in Peru. Unable to field its own candidate, APRA supported Lima's former mayor, Luis Antonio Eguiguren, presidential candidate for the left-leaning Frente Democrático alliance and formerly Sánchez Cerro's close collaborator. The right went to the polls in utter disunity. The profascist UR was led by Flores and José Quesada. Jorge Prado had tried to negotiate APRA's support, but the party's leadership in exile rejected Prado's approach. For Prado, the possibilities of electoral success at the head of a Frente Nacional alliance dwindled.[61] Under these disadvantageous circumstances and as the votes were being counted, Benavides, with the help of a subservient Congress, declared the elections invalid because the tally was clearly in Eguiguren's favor. Congress then dissolved itself, and Benavides was left in control of the country until new elections were held in 1939. Flores was exiled to Mexico.[62] Op-

---

60. Thomas Davies and Víctor Villanueva, eds., *300 documentos para la historia del APRA: correspondencia aprista de 1935 a 1939* (Lima: Editorial Horizonte, 1978), 11–14, 16–19, doc. 28–37 (from the archives of Aprista leader Col. César E. Prado); Masterson, *Militarism,* 55–56; "Los famosos bonos del empréstito aprista," *La Prensa,* enclosure to Luis Avilés's dispatch to M.E., Lima, April 5, 1936, no. 39, leg. R-847, exp. 11, AGMAE.

61. Gonzalo Portocarrero Maisch, "La oligarquía frente a la reivindicación democrática (las opciones de la derecha en las elecciones de 1936)," *Apuntes* 12 (1982): 61–73.

62. Klarén, *Peru,* 281–82; Masterson, *Militarism,* 56.

position to these actions by various economic and political groups increased, further undermining Benavides's government.

The APRA leadership launched a campaign to discredit the Benavides regime at both the international and domestic levels. Aprista authors accused Benavides of siding with Mussolini and the fascist movement.[63] These accusations have been proven unfounded by recent historical research based on Italian diplomatic correspondence of the time. Benavides was actually an ideological moderate who emphasized a political position of "neither communism nor fascism."[64] For practical reasons, Benavides participated in financial arrangements with the Italian community in Peru. He also purchased Italian infantry and air force materiel, trained Peruvian pilots in Italy, allowed the Italian Caproni airplane factory to be established in Lima, and contracted an Italian police mission whose espionage efforts caused major problems for APRA. But these actions did not make him into a fascist. According to a fascist Italian ambassador, Peru was not fertile ground for fascism in 1937, and Benavides would never embrace the fascist ideology due to his cultural background and "old liberal democratic" leanings.[65]

However, APRA's politically motivated charges of corruption against the Benavides regime struck a chord in the growing public perception about continuing irregularities in public administration. In September 1934, the misappropriation of one million soles from the Compañía Administradora del Guano's profits was denounced publicly in an open letter signed by the company's former manager, the Sánchez-Cerrista Adolfo Lainez Lozada.[66] Illegal guano sales to Japan continued to raise suspicions among U.S. authorities as late as March 1938, when director of the Federal Bureau of Investigation, J. Edgar Hoover, communicated to the secretary of state that an informant, a former Peruvian vice consul at Yokohama, alleged that guano continued to be exchanged for Japanese arms.[67] Likewise, an Aprista handbill denounced graft and misuse of public funds in the administration's secret contracting of 300 million soles in domestic loans for public works

63. Portocarrero Maisch, "Oligarquía," 61–73.

64. Ciccarelli, "Fascism and Politics," 419–21, 429.

65. Ibid., 416–17, 421.

66. Confidential memorandum by U.S. Vice Consul Arthur B. Jukes, Callao, September 27, 1934, "Annual balance statement of the Compañía Administradora del Guano," 823.0141/32, box 5707, RG 59, USNA.

67. Hoover to S.S., Washington, DC, March 11, 1938, 823.00/1300, box 5699, RG 59, USNA. The Peruvian former diplomat was identified as Héctor Paulet Wilquet, who also reported that the Peruvian consul in Hong Kong at the time was engaged in the illegal sale of Peruvian passports to Chinese nationals for $1,500 each.

projects. These illegal financial maneuvers allegedly explained the luxurious homes of the interior minister, General Antonio Rodríguez, and the former minister of public works, Colonel Federico Recabarren. The leaflet stated furthermore that Benavides's arrangements to ensure that a "friendly" candidate would succeed him were motivated by his desire to prevent investigation into these financial irregularities at the end of his administration.[68] This serious charge was not confirmed by other sources.

Other more reliable pieces of evidence exist in connection to administrative corruption during the Benavides regime. In a complaint signed by residents of Satipo, Benavides's first minister of public works, the venal Sánchez-Cerrista Arturo Chávez Cabello, was publicly accused of diverting public subsidies destined for the jungle colony.[69] Likewise, amid growing tension between the executive and the legislature, the minister of finance, Benjamín Roca, was forced to resign in December 1934. Roca was accused of refusing to dismiss a manager of the Caja de Depósitos y Consignaciones (tax collection agency), which had been denounced in the newspapers and Congress for being plagued by misappropriation of funds, incompetent employees, and lost deposits.[70]

Moreover, in February 1937, the district attorney (*fiscal*) of Lima's Superior Court of Justice, Julio Villegas, opened a Pandora's box after successfully prosecuting a case of graft in the Interior Ministry. The guilty employee was discharged from his post, but soon thereafter, a private citizen, José Carlos Bernales, published an open letter addressed to Villegas in which he denounced serious irregularities in the government's mortgage bank, Banco Central Hipotecario. Villegas answered with another open letter in local newspapers announcing that he would begin investigating the case. He also revealed that he had received anonymous reports of corruption and various forms of maladministration in key governmental offices including the Presidential Secretariat, Ministry of Finance, and the military general staff (Estado Mayor). Immediately judges of the Supreme Court reprimanded Villegas for his candid but inappropriate disclosures.[71] Ru-

68. Dreyfus to S.S., Lima, June 7, 1939, no. 1051, 823.00/1365, box 5699, RG 59, USNA.

69. *La Sanción* 20, no. 945 (September 27, 1933): 2.

70. Dearing to S.S., Lima, December 17, 1934, no. 3743, 823.002/270, box 5706; Dearing to S.S., Lima, December 20, 1934, no. 3748, 823.00/1131, box 5698, RG 59, USNA.

71. Dreyfus to S.S., Lima, March 2, 1937, no. 4999, 823.00/1266, box 5698, RG 59, USNA; "Sobre una reciente actuación del fiscal doctor Villegas," *El Comercio,* March 2, 1937.

mors soon began to circulate concerning the widespread level of public graft. A U.S. diplomat described the situation as follows:

> One of the topics of increasing volume of conversation at the club and in political circles is the amount of graft which is believed to exist in public office. Concrete cases are cited from time to time. The government does nothing about the matter except on rare occasion to dismiss subordinate employees accused of graft.[72]

Two presidential decrees theoretically aimed at curbing corruption were issued on August 9, 1937, bearing the signatures of Benavides and General Rodríguez. The first decree—based on penal code articles 333, 343, and 353 against breach of duties in public office such as soliciting or receiving illegal payments for public services rendered (*concusión*), perversion or maladministration of justice for private gain (*prevaricato*), and bribery (*cohecho*)—stated that public employees who did not denounce such violations would be dismissed from their posts and prosecuted under the law. The second decree established that public employees may not participate or act as agents in contracts in which a public agency was a party.[73]

These legal measures were rarely enforced while bribing and corruption remained customary in official business. In this regard, a case involving a U.S. company is revealing. In February 1939, the president of Contract Sales Inc., a marketing consortium of U.S. manufacturers of furniture, wrote a letter to the U.S. secretary of state complaining that European firms in Peru enjoyed diplomatic support that placed U.S. companies at a disadvantage since they did not enjoy the same "latitude" from their diplomatic representatives. The U.S. ambassador in Lima, Laurence Steinhardt, took offense at such complaint and proceeded to report in detail on the illegal dealings that the Contract Sales agent in Lima, Hans von Dreyhausen, had been involved in since April 1938. The Peruvian government had customarily purchased furniture from the London-based Maple and Company and Waring and Gillow. Determined to displace the British competitors through techniques of "high-pressure salesmanship," von Dreyhausen informed

72. Dreyfus to S.S., Lima, August 18, 1937, no. 5294, 823.00/1282, box 5698, RG 59, USNA.

73. "Castigando el delito contra los deberes de funciones," and "Los empleados públicos no podrán contraer contratos con el Estado o corporaciones oficiales," *El Comercio,* August 12, 1937.

Steinhardt that a "commission of some kind" had been part of an "arrangement" between Maple and Company and the Peruvian ambassador to Great Britain, Mrs. Benavides's brother, for an order of $100,000. Moreover, von Dreyhausen offered Gustavo Berckemeyer, President Benavides's personal agent and financial advisor, an illegal commission of 25,000 soles if he could convince the president to place an order with Contract Sales. This transaction failed because the president refused the offer. However, von Dreyhausen did succeed in guaranteeing an order of $300,000 for the decoration and furnishing of the new Palace of Justice by arranging to pay a "strict reciprocity financing" commission of more than 10 percent to the chief architect and engineer, Juvenal Monge.[74] Ambassador Steinhardt concluded that the "latitude" demanded by Contract Sales from U.S. diplomats in Peru "appears to be of a character which no self-respecting individual—whether engaged in private business or representing a government—would indulge in." In the absence of international law prohibiting the bribery of foreign officials, U.S. businesspeople had the same "rights" as the Europeans, including "the right to offer commissions to public officials," as von Dreyhausen had done to secure contracts "behind the scenes."[75]

Despite the achievements of the Benavides administration toward political stabilization and economic recovery, several factors contributed to the survival of corrupt practices in the 1933–1939 period. Benavides had weak political support beyond his military institutional base. Even this apparently solid constituency seriously faltered in February 1939, as evidenced by the coup led by trusted General Rodríguez and backed by both APRA and UR. The coup failed, Rodríguez was killed in the attempt, and more than forty military conspirators received stiff prison sentences. However, this violent development forced Benavides to follow the 1939 electoral calendar.[76] This time Benavides supported Manuel Prado, Jorge's younger brother, former president of the Central Reserve Bank and facilitator of the regime's interventionist policies concerning national monetary reserves. With mounting criticism against Benavides for opening the door to Aprista electoral backing of the official candidate, Prado was expected to win the elections in

74. Laurence A. Steinhardt to S.S., Lima, March 4, 1939, no. 902, 823.157/6, box 4353; and Robert E. Greenwood (president, Contract Sales Inc.) to Sumner Welles, New York, March 10, 1939, 823.157/7, box 5711, RG 59, USNA.

75. Steinhardt to S.S., Lima, March 15, 1939, no. 196, 823.157/8, box 5711, RG 59, USNA.

76. Davies and Villanueva, *Secretos electorales,* 11, and *300 documentos,* 8; Masterson, *Militarism,* 58–59.

October 1939.[77] Yet numerous negotiations on the eve of the elections combined several opportunistic possibilities of political alliances such as a previously inconceivable pact between Flores and Haya to back UR-supported candidate José Quesada.[78] Given the disorientation of Aprista voters combined with a dose of electoral fraud, Prado won the presidential elections practically by default. The restricted, rigged, and fraudulent elections of 1936 and 1939 under Benavides planted the seed of similar subsequent electoral processes, especially in 1950, 1956, and 1962 that sanctioned undemocratic political outcomes and the continuity of corrupt public administration.

Under growing criticism from all flanks, especially the virulent rightist attack by the Miró Quesada family,[79] Benavides sought to guarantee essential support from his rather fickle and corruptible constituencies that included the military and public bureaucracies, the Prado Ugarteche clan, and a few other elite groups. There is little doubt that Benavides's government permitted corrupt practices among his fellow military and political appointees under the guise of expansive public works that offered badly needed jobs in the midst of recession. Likewise his electoral manipulations remained a model of fraud and dishonest political deal-making. However, unlike previous periods of unbound corruption, during the Benavides regime certain cosmetic efforts were exerted to "moderate" corruption. Therefore, Benavides's restoration can also be interpreted as a "normalization" of high levels of inherited and persistent corruption.

Unprincipled War Politics

At the time President Manuel Prado Ugarteche took office in December 1939 in the midst of World War II, Jorge Basadre had achieved prominence as professor and librarian at the University of San Marcos. His stature as an independent and progressive intellectual was widely recognized among the political and intellectual elites. He returned to Peru in 1935 after studying and lecturing in the United States, Germany, and Spain, and had witnessed the rise of fascism in Europe. Under the stern gaze of President Benavides, Basadre delivered an inaugural speech at the Congress of Americanists held

77. Dreyfus to S.S., Lima, June 16, 1939, no. 1068, 823.00/1372, box 5699, RG 59, USNA.

78. Ibid., 14; Klarén, *Peru,* 281.

79. Steinhardt to S.S., Lima, January 12 and February 2, 1939, nos. 827 and 862, 823.00/1329 and 1335, box 5699, RG 59, USNA.

in Lima in 1939. Also in 1939, his first general history of the Peruvian Republic was published. A few years later, Prado appointed Basadre to an important yet difficult position, director of the National Library, entrusted with rebuilding the library after a disastrous fire. This and subsequent experiences as a civil servant allowed Basadre an insider's view of the entrenched and customary corruption in the country's national government bureaucracy and administrative decision making.

The war significantly altered the political landscape in Peru. The official support that Prado had received to become president prevented a broad-based political following. He had to rely instead on the military, his political cronies, and a banking and business community infiltrated by pro-Axis interests. Prado faced serious political opposition from the profascist UR and the antifascist APRA. As the war progressed, pressure increased to force Prado to compete with APRA for Allied sympathies. After rejecting an early offer by Prado for the formation of a "coalition cabinet" in early 1940, Haya launched an intense campaign to destabilize his government. Part of Haya's strategy was to prey on the regime's weaknesses. In several meetings Haya had with U.S. diplomats and FBI agents, he accused Prado and his ministers of protecting Axis interests, allegedly part of Haya's political and intelligence information provided to agents of Allied governments. The APRA leadership now catered to international antifascism with the expectation of enjoying the favor of various foreign governments, but especially the United States, in pressing Prado to restore civil liberties and freedom of expression.[80] This was a blatant invitation to foreign intervention in Peruvian internal affairs, supposedly justified by growing totalitarian dangers. Like Getúlio Vargas in Brazil, but unlike Juan Perón in Argentina, the populist Haya de la Torre threw his lot to the Allied camp motivated by political convenience in advancing APRA's quest for power in Peru. Prado responded by increased collaboration with the Allies, especially by early 1942, just after the United States entered the war. Prado also bribed or enticed several Communist Party and Aprista leaders to defect and join his camp, while at the same time engaged in a relentless repression campaign to curb APRA's activities.[81]

80. R. Henry Norweb to S.S., Lima, January 3, 1942, no. 2512, 823.00/1500; George H. Butler to S.S., Lima, January 9, 1942, no. 2559, 823.00/1501; Norweb to S.S., Lima, March 10, 1942, no. 3057, 823.00/1515, box 4346, RG 59, USNA; Masterson, *Militarism*, 68–69.

81. A former Aprista secretary of propaganda and defector who joined the Prado camp, Julio Marcial Rossi, and his son were assassinated, according to police informa-

The international war situation also provided a changed environment for customary corruption. Growing demand for agricultural goods and other raw materials by German, Italian, and Japanese concerns provided incentives to Peruvian exporters, merchants, and venal authorities despite Allied blacklisting of pro-Axis business concerns. Allied intelligence reported on supply networks to Axis powers allowed or protected by bribed Peruvian authorities. Zealous surveillance was applied to the production and commercialization of locally produced drugs (mainly cocaine and opium), cotton, petroleum products, and other strategic exports.

On the basis of FBI intelligence gathering in Peru, J. Edgar Hoover informed the U.S. Department of State in October 1941 that the Peruvian government was selling fuel oil to the Japanese from reserve stocks at almost double its normal price; there were also growing concerns over the cultivation and purchase of cotton by Japanese companies. A few months later, Hoover also provided confidential information about a cocaine trafficking ring formed by Argentine and Peruvian pro-Axis agents.[82] Minister of Finance David Dasso informed U.S. diplomatic officials in 1941 that around 1,000 kilos of cocaine had been legally exported to Germany and Italy via the Lufthansa airline through Bolivia and Brazil; likewise, U.S. Department of State officials estimated that 1,200 kilos of cocaine had been smuggled out of Peru to Germany and Italy through Argentina.[83] Other suspicious destinations of the drug were Switzerland and Spain.[84]

Cocaine production in excess of legal export and domestic market demand was being funneled to the black market. In 1943, several drug traf-

---

tion, by Aprista killers. George Butler to S.S., Lima, April 6, 1942, no. 3290, 823.00/ 1520, box 4346, and Hoover to Adolf Berle (assistant secretary of state), Washington, DC, August 31, 1943, 823.00/1567, box 4347, RG 59, USNA.

82. Hoover to Berle, Washington, DC, October 29, 1941, 823.00/1479, box 4346, and January 19, 1942, 823.114/244, box 4351, RG 59, USNA. Some authors are skeptical about the quality of U.S. intelligence gathering (Office of Naval Intelligence, FBI, Office of Strategic Services) in Peru during the war, specifically regarding Japanese economic activities there. Daniel Masterson and Sayaka Funada-Classen, *The Japanese in Latin America* (Chicago: University of Illinois Press, 2004), 117, 154. The intelligence information cited in this study has been corroborated by, or contrasted as much as possible with other sources.

83. J. F. McGurk to S.S., Lima, April 25, 1941, no. 1063, 823.114/220 and 223–25, 248, box 4351, RG 59, USNA.

84. Jefferson Patterson to S.S., Lima, September 16, 1942, no. 4905, 823.114/283; U.S. Legation to S.S., Bern, April 28, 1942, no. 2402, 823.114/275, box 4351, RG 59, USNA.

ficking rings were discovered and eliminated in Peru.[85] The most notorious involved transactions between Axis buyers and smugglers Héctor Pizarro and "Chino" Morales. The investigation of the case revealed that the undersecretary of the interior ministry (director de gobierno), César Cárdenas García, had received a bribe of 5,000 soles per month, and Lima's prefecto another of 2,000 soles per month, for leaving the smuggling activities unmolested.[86]

Other high-level officials in the Prado government were also suspected of war profiteering. In September 1942, the interior minister, Guillermo Garrido Lecca, was publicly denounced, and later removed from office, for speculating in rice and exporting large quantities and thus contributing to domestic shortages of this basic staple.[87] Likewise, Minister of Finance David Dasso, a close collaborator of U.S. diplomats in commercial and economic matters, suffered a heart attack shortly after being denounced in the Peruvian Congress for facilitating excess profits benefiting his family's lumber import company (thanks to lower tariffs on lumber that he had personally negotiated in a trade agreement with the United States) as well as obtaining personal income from a government coal and iron development program.[88]

These scandals, rising inflation, price controls, and higher local taxes fueled public opinion against the suspected concentration of wealth by the "Imperio Prado" during the war years.[89] U.S. diplomats observed a marked deterioration in the regime's position due to

85. Case of Carlos Mindreau: Julian Greenup to S.S., Lima, October 1 and 7, 1943, nos. 7994 and 8044, 823.114/312 and 313, box 4351, RG 59, USNA.

86. Hoover to Berle, Washington, DC, October 5, 1943, 823.114/314, box 4351, RG 59, USNA. According to the "confidential reliable" source, the investigation was carried out by the police Intendant Rouillon and only the interior minister, Ricardo La Fuente, was informed about the scandalous corruption of his staff.

87. Hoover to Berle, Washington, DC, September 5, 1942, 823.00/1581, and Memorandum from J. F. Melby to Keith, Bonsal, and Duggan, Division of American Republics, Department of State, Washington, DC, October 26, 1942, 823.00/1603, box 4347, RG 59, USNA.

88. Hoover to Berle, Washington, DC, August 1, 1942, 823.00/334, box 4350, and Patterson to S.S., Lima, July 3, 1942, no. 4199, 823.00/1350, box 4347, RG 59, USNA.

89. APRA underground publications consistently accused the regime of corruption schemes such as complicity in the smuggling of Japanese silk (*La Tribuna*, January 10, 1941, enclosure in Hoover to Berle, Washington, DC, February 10, 1941, 823.00/1445), and the Prados' enrichment through "peculados con las subsistencias que ampara el mercado negro"; Incahuasi, *Carta abierta al ciudadano* (Lima, 1944), quoted in Felipe Portocarrero Suárez, *Imperio Prado, 1890–1970* (Lima: Centro de Investigación de la

gossip concerning the economic activities of President Prado and the group which surrounds him and on which he depends. The allegation is increasingly made in all groups that the Prado coterie is step by step acquiring all available sources of wealth in the country. . . Against these charges no effective defense has ever been advanced.[90]

Prado opted for fortifying his castle internally and externally. Despite serious doubts on the part of U.S. Department of State officials concerning his regime's commitment to the Allies, by March 1942, Prado had achieved important diplomatic gains, described as a change "from a hesitant and indecisive policy to a definitely pro-democratic approach of cooperation with the United States."[91] Peru participated in the Rio Conference, which endorsed the democratic defense of the hemisphere, broke diplomatic relations with the Axis powers, and reached a settlement with Ecuador over the border conflict of 1941. The favorable outcome of this brief war between the two nations helped consolidate Prado's national standing and strengthen his military support. The armed forces reaffirmed their professional commitment to national defense. Through a special defense budget financed by secretive domestic loans, Prado provided generous rewards in the form of military promotions and higher pay to guarantee political support by the armed forces. Moreover, social security and large public works programs, also financed mainly by domestic loans, continued as part of the fiscal policy inherited from Benavides.[92] Nevertheless, corruption, deficits, and inflationary policies began to spiral out of control. These interrelated problems would continue to afflict the Peruvian economy for most of the rest of the twentieth century.

The regime's measures of economic sanctions and expulsion applied against Axis nationals in Peru included serious cases of civil servant corruption. Japanese and German funds were frozen, the Banco Italiano was suspended and forced to change its name, imports were not delivered to a

---

Universidad del Pacífico, 1995), 119. APRA's partisan motives reduce the factual certainty of most of these accusations.

90. Melby to Keith, Bonsal, and Duggan, Washington, DC, October 26, 1942, 823.00/1603, box 4347, RG 59, USNA.

91. Memorandum, Melby to Woodward and Bonsal, Washington, DC, March 31, 1942, attached to 823.00/1519, box 4346. Compare with anti-Prado and pro-APRA appraisal in Toop to Melby, January 13, 1942, 823.00/1512, box 4346, RG 59, USNA.

92. Norweb to S.S., Lima, March 14, 1942, no. 3103, 823.00/1519, box 4346, RG 59, USNA; Masterson, *Militarism*, 70, 73.

"proclaimed list" of firms, and laws 9586 and 9592 were enacted to suppress Axis commercial, banking, agricultural, and industrial operations in Peru.[93] The government enforced these measures following the recommendations of U.S. officials. More than 1,800 Japanese male nationals, including teachers and members of local Japanese associations, were forcibly deported to the United States.[94] Japanese schools, associations, businesses, and properties were closed and their assets expropriated. All of these measures were preceded by mob violence against Japanese people and property, in particular the rampages of May 1940.[95]

Several high-level officials collected bribes from Japanese and German nationals attempting to avoid deportation or illegally appropriated confiscated property of people who had been deported.[96] Hoover reported that the police investigation division chief, Moisés Mier y Terán, along with the interior undersecretary (director), César Cárdenas García, were indicted in connection to large-scale graft and other serious irregularities perpetrated during the deportation of Axis nationals in February 1943. Mier, a key agent in the repression of Apristas, had been promoted by the president's unscrupulous pro-German cousin, Manuel Ugarteche Jiménez. Despite the charges against him, Mier continued to work for the investigation division in the interior provinces.[97] Another scheme carried out by high-level officials of the Ministry of Foreign Affairs involved selling Peruvian citizenship papers for thousands of soles to Japanese people about to be deported.[98]

With growing problems in restraining corruption, political opposition, and declining finances, the Prado administration prepared for the elections

93. Patterson to S.S., Lima, July 3, 1942, no. 4199, 823.00/1350, box 4347, RG 59, USNA.

94. Patterson to S.S., Lima, May 14, 1942, no. 3695, 823.00/1535, box 4346, RG 59, USNA.

95. Armando Villanueva and Guillermo Thorndike, *La gran persecución (1932–1956)* (Lima: Correo-Epensa, 2004), 178.

96. See Masterson and Funada-Classen, *Japanese,* 162–65; John K. Emmerson, *The Japanese Thread: A Life in U.S. Foreign Service* (New York: Holt, Rinehart and Winston, 1978), 126–29; and C. Harvey Gardiner, *Pawns in a Triangle of Hate: The Peruvian Japanese and the United States* (Seattle: University of Washington Press, 1981), 104–5.

97. Hoover to Berle, Washington, DC, June 25, 1943, 823.00/1650, box 4347, RG 59; ONI, Lima, October 2 and December 11, 1942, intelligence cards nos. 27608C-0.15 and 27605–0.15, box 353, RG 226, USNA; Klarén, *Peru,* 283.

98. Intercepted letter (photostatic copy), Fernando de Cossío (Banco Popular) to Javier de Cossío, Lima, May 16, 1943, 823.012/42, box 4350, RG 59, USNA. Among the corrupt diplomatic agents involved in the case was a Dr. Balarezo, director de extranjería, and top aide to the prime minister.

scheduled for June 1945. Aprista publications continued their attacks, but now they openly appealed to young military officers to take action against what Apristas considered to be a thoroughly corrupt government.[99] Just prior to the elections, the Revolutionary Committee of Army Officers (CROE), led by pro-APRA Major Víctor Villanueva, who criticized political influence peddling and corruption within the military, began to worry Peruvian authorities and U.S. intelligence officers.[100]

Prado toyed with the idea of reelection, but sensing the likelihood of failure, finally opted to provide support to General Eloy Ureta, a hero of the 1941 war with Ecuador. This electoral move favoring the continuation of the elite–military partnership formula of governance upset the elderly Marshal Oscar Benavides who had returned to Peru from his diplomatic missions with the expectation that Prado would reciprocate the electoral favor of 1939. In January 1945, Benavides published a manifesto urging the candidacy of an honest civilian candidate and unity among the armed forces, an obvious political rebuff to both Prado and Ureta. This move by the savvy Benavides divided Prado's rightist camp and favored leftist tendencies supported by APRA.[101]

APRA negotiated with the Frente Democrático Nacional (FDN) coalition, whose candidate was José Luis Bustamante y Rivero, considered in his native Arequipa as "too honest and too lacking in political character" to govern Peru.[102] Marshal Benavides opposed Ureta, asserting that a civilian president in Peru was a necessity. Benavides's stand benefited Bustamante and his Aprista allies. However, last-minute talks between APRA leaders and UR supporters of Ureta threatened the leftist alliance with the FDN. The alliance was also jeopardized by APRA's exacting demands on the FDN concerning APRA shares of parliamentary candidates.

---

99. Patterson to S.S., Lima, January 22, 1944, no. 8858, 823.00/1753, box 4347, and Edward G. Trueblood to S.S., Lima, January 11, 1945, no. 2353, 823.00/1-1145, box 5292, RG 59, USNA, analyzing the political position of *La Tribuna.*

100. On the insurgent Comité Revolucionario de Oficiales del Ejército (CROE), see Hoover to Frederick B. Lyon (Division of Foreign Activity Correlation, U.S. Department of State), Washington, DC, May 22, 1945, 823.00/5-2245, box 5293, RG 59, USNA. See also Masterson, *Militarism,* 76–78.

101. Trueblood to S.S., Lima, January 9, 1945, no. 2353, 823.00/1-945, and June 21, 1945, no. 3510, 823.00/6-2148, box 5292, RG 59, USNA; Marqués de Aycinea to M.E., Lima, February 10, 1945, no. 30, leg. R-1656, exp. 3, AGMAE.

102. Vice Consul Jack Dwyre to Ambassador John White, Arequipa, February 28, 1945, enclosure of Trueblood to Milton Wells, Lima, February 27, 1945, 823.00/2-2745, box 5292, RG 59, USNA.

These electoral maneuvers were considered "a series of double-crosses, breath-taking even for Peruvian politics," and reminiscent of the electoral intrigues of 1939.[103] This persistent pattern of unprincipled electoral opportunism that effectively undermined democracy to benefit a few politicians was part of the high transaction costs in a political culture plagued with distrust and corruption. In the end, Bustamante was elected president by a wide margin over Ureta thanks in large part to Aprista votes. The sudden death of Marshal Benavides in early July 1945 when the votes were being counted deprived Bustamante's FDN of an important ally to moderate Aprista rising political expectations.[104] The APRA's leadership and rank and file were now poised to "co-govern" as a means to seizing more power through all available means.

Transition on the Tightrope

Immediately after his inauguration, Bustamante issued several decrees intended to "clean the house" inherited from the previous administration. The new measures were aimed at scrutinizing state finances, eliminating sinecures and superfluous jobs, and ousting dishonest civil servants.[105] His first cabinet, dubbed the *gobierno moralizador,* was formed by young professionals. The politically independent Basadre was appointed minister of education, a post from which he battled graft among the ministry's high-level officials. Although with limited experience for such a post, Basadre maintained that "at least we were honest."[106] One of his first acts was to call for an in-depth investigation of the suspicious fire that destroyed the National Library, a disaster that had not yet been fully investigated.[107]

To assume his new ministerial position, Basadre left the directorship of the National Library, a post for which he had been appointed immediately after the fire of May 1943. In charge of a campaign to restore the library,

103. J. C. White to S.S., Lima, June 2, 1945, no. 3398, 823.00/6-245, and enclosure 1, "secret memorandum" by Trueblood, box 5292, RG 59, USNA.
104. Secret dispatch, Lima, July 6, 1945, no. 3573, 823.00/7-645, box 5292, RG 59, USNA.
105. William D. Pawley to S.S., Lima, August 7, 1945, no. 83, 823.00/8-745, box 5292, RG 59, USNA, citing local newspapers.
106. Jorge Basadre, *La vida y la historia* (Lima: Industrial Gráfica, 1981), 697, n. 5.
107. Pawley to S.S., 823.00/8-745, op. cit. The investigation concluded that the fire was mainly due to gross administrative negligence.

Basadre had conflicts with the company contracted by the Ministry of Public Works to construct the library's new building: Costs kept on rising without regard to budgetary and technical requirements. At the helm of the Ministry of Education, Basadre also discovered a costly scheme to defraud the state of approximately 40 percent of the value of a sizable number of school desks manufactured by a contractor in collusion with a high-level official. Basadre pressed charges and submitted the case to an indifferent court. The accused corrupt official countered by relying on political influence to avoid prosecution and initiating a legal suit against Basadre for defamation. This episode and political pressure exerted by APRA forced Basadre's resignation. He concluded from this experience that the government bureaucrats in Peru assumed that illicit enrichment through graft was a normal activity.[108]

Aprista publications had unceasingly criticized and insulted Basadre for his political independence, calling him "a coward and a sycophant who has sacrificed the integrity of his views for a sinecure."[109] APRA pressed for the control of several key ministries, including the Ministry of Education, to advance its political goals. Basadre and other ministers became favorite targets in APRA's strategy to embarrass, obstruct, and destabilize Bustamante's regime. Basadre served as minister for only three months, after which he returned to direct the National Library.

Bustamante and his prime minister, Rafael Belaúnde, had initially offered APRA two ministries, but Aprista leaders wanted more. They demanded at least four portfolios, including the strategic ones of foreign affairs, finance, public works, and education.[110] From the start, the initial electoral alliance did not translate into collaboration in government. APRA had won more than 50 percent of all congressional seats. In control of the legislature, the vertically organized "people's party" checked Bustamante's legislation initiatives and disputed his executive authority. The first act of this "independent" Congress was to vote a widespread amnesty law that

108. Case of the "carpeta apócrifa": Basadre, *La vida y la historia,* 711–12; Jorge Basadre and Pablo Macera, *Conversaciones* (Lima: Mosca Azul, 1974), 114; Alfonso W. Quiroz, "Basadre y su análisis de la corrupción en el Perú," in *Homenaje a Jorge Basadre: el hombre, su obra y su tiempo,* ed. Scarlett O'Phelan and Mónica Ricketts (Lima: Instituto Riva Agüero, 2004), 163–65.

109. Trueblood to S.S., Lima, January 11, 1945, no. 2380, 823.00/1-1145, box 5292, RG 59, USNA.

110. José Luis Bustamante y Rivero, *Tres años de la lucha por la democracia en* el Perú (Buenos Aires: Chiesino, 1949), 28–29; Confidential dispatch, Lima, August 17, 1945, no. 124, 823.00/8-1745, box 5293, RG 59, USNA.

mainly benefited Aprista members imprisoned for acts of violence. Following a strict hierarchical discipline, the Aprista congressmen endeavored to legislate based on the party's agenda. All elected Aprista senators and deputies had to submit a blank letter of resignation to the party's chief. By Aprista initiative, several congressional investigative commissions were formed, avowedly to prosecute corruption but actually to meddle in the affairs of the executive branch. An APRA-sponsored law of municipal elections facilitated the party's control of many local municipalities that competed with the national government's taxation prerogatives. This was a risky and dangerous strategy of political opposition that exacerbated civil strife.[111]

Serious differences between Bustamante and his prime minister over how to handle the increasingly violent Aprista demonstrations resulted in Belaúnde's resignation. In January 1946, Bustamante tried to appease the Apristas by granting them three strategic cabinet posts: finance, public works, and agriculture. APRA's enhanced influence in economic policy translated in the growth of the state bureaucracy to a total of 44,700 employees, 160 percent more than under Benavides and 60 percent more than under Prado.[112] Many of the new state jobs created went to Aprista members. This expansionary budget policy clashed with the deteriorating economic situation, inflation, and depleted foreign exchange reserves already observed by the end of the previous administration. For Apristas, among others, the drive for social reform justified the increase in public expenses, although this benefited mainly the state bureaucracy itself.

Likewise, the policy of foreign exchange and import controls inherited from the Prado regime—measures allegedly necessary to increase foreign exchange reserves and avoid capital flight—really benefited the holders of exchange and import licenses. These permits allowed privileged monopolistic advantages and were generally obtained through influence or bribes ("fees" and "presents").[113] In the meantime, exchange controls dampened

---

111. Bustamante, *Tres años*, 32–33, 42, 44–45.

112. Federico Prieto Celi, *El deportado: biografía de Eudocio Ravines* (Lima: Editorial Andina, 1979), 119.

113. Gonzalo Portocarrero Maisch, *De Bustamante a Odría: el fracaso del Frente Democrático Nacional 1945–1950* (Lima: Mosca Azul, 1983), 104–6, citing Pawley to S.S., Lima, October 18, 1945, in U.S. Department of State, *Foreign Relations of the United States: Diplomatic Papers, 1945* (Washington, DC: Government Printing Office, 1969), 9:1355–59. The exchange and import controls were initiated by the Prado administration in January 1945 and continued throughout the Bustamante administration under both Pradista and Aprista influence.

incentives to export and consequently export quantum values stagnated and export earnings declined. Led by Pedro Beltrán, exporters voiced their discontent. Food staple shortages fueled popular unrest. Price controls made things even worse. The critical shortage of foreign exchange intensified the need for foreign stabilization loans that were thwarted by the thorny issue of previous and prolonged default. Despite frantic official efforts, foreign debt negotiations continued to fail, adding to the difficulties of the beleaguered Bustamante regime.[114] Aprista influence in economic policy, combined with these inherited misguided policies, proved disastrous.

Regardless of the worsening economic and social situation, the Aprista ambition for supreme power justified not only unsound economic policies, but also irregular and illegal practices by Aprista members. One early strategic action advantageous to APRA's clandestine operations was to disband the police investigation division and introduce a general "reorganization" of the police forces through pressure from Aprista legislators.[115] APRA members were also named prefectos and subprefectos of key provinces. Moreover, aided by a biased municipal electoral law passed in Congress, Aprista politicians abusively controlled "transitory juntas" that misappropriated municipal funds, a "true peculation."[116] Anonymous confidential informants of the U.S. military attaché reported that APRA had illegally appropriated sizable funds through their handling of the national finances, patronage in public works, and control of import licenses. These funds were allegedly being transferred by a trusted Aprista confidant to the United States and Europe for party operations in case of difficulties in Peru. Although the U.S. ambassador considered this information exaggerated, other

114. See Pawley to S.S., Lima, February 19, 1946, no. 1026, 823.51/2-1946, in U.S. Department of State, *Foreign Relations of the United States, 1946* (Washington, DC: Government Printing Office, 1969), 11:1251–55, and Cooper to S.S., Lima, December 12, 1946, telegram, 823.51/12-1246, in U.S. Department of State, *Foreign Relations, 1946*, 11:1258–59. Haya, trying to further ingratiate himself with U.S. officials, told the U.S. ambassador that withholding loans would contribute to bringing about a satisfactory arrangement of Peru's external debt payments. Prentice Cooper to S.S., Lima, November 11, 1946, telegram 1165-A, 823.51/11-1146, box 5321, RG 59, USNA; Manuel Acal to M.A.E., Lima, February 11, 1946, no. 25, and Pedro García Conde ío M.A.E., Lima, May 9, 1947, no. 65, leg. R-1754, exp. 4 and 5, AGMAE.

115. Major Jay Reist to Trueblood, Lima, September 6, 1946, enclosure to Pawley to S.S., Lima, September 10, 1945, no. 241, 823.00/9-1045, box 5292, RG 59, USNA; Bustamante, *Tres años*, 108.

116. Bustamante, *Tres años*, 44–45, 338; Pedro García Conde to M.A.E., Lima, March 12, 1948, no. 38, leg. R-2315, exp. 1, AGMAE.

officials believed that the report coincided with independent information on "growth of widespread graft in Peru." Several names and examples were quoted as evidence.[117]

For strategic purposes of maintaining their good footing with U.S. officials and interests, APRA leaders supported Bustamante's hasty ad referendum contract to grant perpetual oil exploration rights to the International Petroleum Company (IPC), a Canadian subsidiary of Standard Oil of New Jersey, in the northern Sechura desert. This pro-IPC stance gained APRA influential friends in Washington. However, serious opposition to this contract was raised by conservatives and communists alike. They argued not only that the contract should have followed the enactment of general petroleum exploitation legislation, but also that Aprista politicians were unduly involved in the project for their own economic gain. The contract was not approved in Congress, as the conservative Alianza Nacional, led by Beltrán, supported the abstention of opposition congressmen in the July 1947 opening sessions of Congress. This action forced a lengthy congressional recess.[118]

One of the most active opponents to the Sechura contract was Francisco Graña Garland, president of the board of the daily newspaper *La Prensa* and influential businessman. On February 7, 1947, Graña was shot to death as he left the building of one of his enterprises by several men who then fled

117. "Haya de la Torre and the Apra Party," memorandum by U.S. Military Attaché, Lima, October 24, 1946, enclosure to Cooper to S.S., Lima, November 6, 1946, no. 660, 823.00/11-646, box 5292, RG 59, USNA; Dearborn to Wells and Trueblood, office memorandum, Washington, DC, December 11, 1946, box 5292, RG 59, USNA. The carrier of these illegal funds was identified as Antenor Fernando Soler; the tunnels and irrigation contractor, Sindicato Peruano Americano, S.A., was managed by Carrillo Roca.

118. Hoover to Lyon, Washington DC, June 18, 1946, 823.00/1846, box 5292. In a conversation with a U.S. diplomat, Haya talked about "foreign capital investment in Peru protected by the Government" in oblique reference to the Sechura contract. American Embassy to S.S., Lima, January 31, 1947, no. 1103, 823.00/1-3147, box 4352. In another interview with U.S. diplomat Maurice Broderick, Haya denounced the opposition to the Sechura contract as a deliberate anti-American and communist tactic, and that he would like to re-establish the liaison with the "FBI boys" who had left Peru. In Cooper to S.S., Lima, November 3, 1947, no. 2124, 823.00/11-347. The U.S. Department of State's Latin American affairs staff concluded: "Since APRA is now also strongly in favor of collaboration with the U.S., APRA legislators have advocated encouragement to U.S. capital, oil development concessions to U.S. companies (Sechura contract with International Petroleum) and an earnest effort to settle Peru's external debt." Owen (NWC) to Daniels (ARA), Washington, DC, July 12, 1948, 823.00/7-1248, box 5293, RG 59, USNA. See also Bustamante, *Tres años,* 102–3.

in a green Buick. Despite the utter disorganization of the investigative police who ultimately bungled the case, the owner of the automobile, Manuel López Obeso, was identified, and Aprista congressman Alfredo Tello, the party's secretary of defense in charge of strong-arm squads, formally charged.[119] APRA denied involvement in the assassination and instead communicated through several channels its own wild theories that pointed to other culprits.[120] In effect, Graña's assassination transformed the political scene and undermined APRA's political position; its leaders were forced to call for a "strategic withdrawal" and the resignation of the three Aprista cabinet members. Bustamante openly broke with APRA and blundered into forming an all-military cabinet aimed at stabilizing the volatile situation. (This over-reliance on the armed forces opened the doors to costly military intervention.)

APRA did not cease to conspire and campaign among junior officers and interfere in the military promotion process. The CROE and other illegal military organizations prepared for a climate of insurrection encouraged both by Aprista leaders on the one hand, and reactionary sectors on the other.[121] In an interview with U.S. diplomats in August 1948, Haya announced that

119. Cooper to S.S., Lima, January 9, 1947, no. 962, 823.00/1-947, March 31, 1947, no. 1389, 823.00/3-3147, box 4352, and June 16, 1947, no. 1701, 823.00/6-1647, box 4352; S.S. to American Embassy, Washington, DC, September 18, 1947, 823.00/7-2347 (enclosing declarations of a Japanese citizen made in Japan acknowledging that he had left a Mauser gun in the care of López Obeso when he left Peru in 1942), box 5293, RG 59, USNA; Bustamante, *Tres años,* 108–12. Apristas Tello and Héctor Pretell were convicted of the crime and were imprisoned for several years. Many questions surrounding this key political assassination have remained unresolved for decades. *Caretas,* no. 1447, January 9, 1997, 42-43, 89; Prieto, *El deportado,* 148–50.

120. Haya communicated to U.S. diplomats that Graña's assassination was the result of illegal dealings in narcotics or was engineered by Eudocio Ravines. Other Apristas blamed Moisés Mier y Terán or defended political crimes as laudable under certain conditions (e.g., article by Víctor Graciano Mayta, senator for Junín, in *La Tribuna,* May 10, 1948). Donnelly to S.S., Lima, February 3, 1947, no. 1108, 823.00/2-347, box 4352; Cooper to S.S., Lima, November 3, 1947, no. 2124, 823.00/11-347, box 5293; Lambert to S.S., Lima, May 21, 1948, no. 395, 823.00/5-2148, box 5293, RG 59, USNA.

121. On the clandestine activities of the CROE led by pro-APRA Major Villanueva and the Logia Mariscal La Mar headed by pro-UR Lieutenant Colonel Alfonso Llosa (who staged a failed garrison uprising in Juliaca, Puno, in July 1948), see Hoover to Lyon, Washington, DC, November 1, 1945, 823.00/11-145, and November 28, 1945, 823.00/11-2845, box 5293; memorandum by Owen (NWCA) to Mills, Woodward, and Daniels, Washington, DC, August 11, 1948, 823.03/8-1048, box 5321, and October 28, 1948, 823.00/10-248, box 5293, RG 59, USNA. See also Masterson, *Militarism,* 93–94, 105–6.

plans were proceeding for what he envisioned as a "bloodless" military ouster of President Bustamante.[122] Likewise, Haya told the Spanish ambassador that the oppression of oligarchies would cease at any moment.[123] The high military command became concerned about the approaching Aprista revolution.

In April 1948, a large quantity of weapons feared to have been destined to revolutionaries was found aboard the Peruvian Navy warship BAP *Callao,* returning from repairs at a New York shipyard. Involvement of Aprista navy officers was suspected. Haya had been in New York in early 1948 when the ship was still in port. Moreover, he was invited to dine on board the *Callao* by the ship's commanding officers.[124] According to witnesses, drug trafficking ringleader Eduardo Balarezo, who was closely linked to Haya's brother Senator Edmundo Haya, had hosted Víctor Raúl at his house in Long Island. Balarezo was suspected of supplying arms, munitions, and funds to APRA. He boarded the *Callao* carrying expensive contraband artifacts intercepted at the port of Callao by customs officials who were bribed. APRA's connection with Balarezo's illegal trade was exposed in U.S. and Peruvian newspapers in 1949–1950. A Federal Bureau of Narcotics investigation in New York revealed Balarezo's cocaine smuggling operation in the United States and his suspected links to Haya's party.[125]

122. Pierrot to S.S., Lima, August 14, 1948, no. 444, 823.00/8-1448, box 5293, RG 59, USNA.

123. Fernando Castiella to M.A.E., Lima, October 19, 1948, no. 158, leg. R-2315, exp. 1, AGMAE.

124. Weekly political report, Lima, April 29, 1948, no. 319, 823.00/4-2948, box 5293, RG 59, USNA. The Aprista officers were Commander Alberto del Castillo and Captain Alejandro Bastante.

125. Harold Tittman to Department of State, Lima, February 7, 1950, no. 184, 723.00/2-750, and February 10, 1950, 723.00/2-1050, box 3297, RG 59, USNA; *Última Hora,* no. 19, February 3, 1950; *El Comercio,* no. 58221, February 9, 1950, 5, 9; *New York Times,* August 20, 1949, 1, 26; Bustamante, *Tres años,* 182. Despite compelling yet polemical evidence (including photos of Balarezo with Haya), historian Paul Gootenberg hastily dismissed the Balarezo-Haya link as mere "fabrications," citing Glenn Dorn's interpretation, which was detailed and sympathetic toward Haya, and U.S. Department of State top officials' realpolitik intervention on his behalf. See Gootenberg, "Birth of the Narcs: The First *Illicit* Cocaine Flows in the Americas" (2004), 9, http://catedras.ucol.mx/transformac/PDF/NARCSu.pdf, and "Between Coca and Cocaine: A Century or More of U.S.–Peruvian Drug Paradoxes 1860–1980," *Hispanic American Historical Review* 83, no. 1 (2003): 137–50, esp. 140–41; and Dorn, "'The American Presumption of Fair Play': Víctor Raúl Haya de la Torre and the Federal Bureau of Narcotics," *The Historian* 65, no. 5 (2003): 1083–1101.

After an aborted attempt in February 1948, the much awaited Aprista uprising took place on October 3, 1948, which involved the actions of navy officers and sailors in Callao, air force pilots at the Las Palmas base, and civilians in Lima on October 3, 1948. The insurrectionists controlled several battleships, the navy school and arsenal, and the garrison of Real Felipe, but failed to secure strategic army and air bases. In Lima, a mob attacked the central telephone exchange and disrupted the city's telephone communication. Because of the identity of the naval leadership of the insurrection, and the coordinated action with armed militants, there was no doubt that Aprista radicals had engineered the uprising. They had been consistently encouraged to take these decisive actions, although the party's leadership might have gotten cold feet at the last moment.[126] The Aprista insurrection lost momentum and was crushed by the army. The party's main leaders hid or sought asylum in several embassies.

Bustamante remained extremely dependent on the action of the army's former chief of staff and interior minister, General Manuel Odría, who since May 1947 had been actively pressing for outlawing APRA and a free hand in domestic security matters.[127] Odría was a decided anti-APRA champion with strong support among high-ranking military officers committed to destroying the people's party and its pernicious influence within the armed forces. Bustamante ousted Odría from the cabinet in June 1948, but was unable to halt his conspiracy. Only a few weeks after the Aprista insurrection, Odría launched a carefully planned, textbook-style military coup on October 28, 1948 in Arequipa, very similar to that staged in 1930 by Sánchez Cerro. The most important regiments in the provinces and Lima supported Odría's bid to oust Bustamante, who was forced to go into exile.[128] The military dictatorship inaugurated by Odría opened a new chapter in the history of public sector corruption, which deeply embraced the military establishment now in complete charge of the government and its resources.

126. Bustamante, *Tres años,* 178–85; American Embassy, Lima, October 4, 1948, no. 801, 823.00/10-448, box 5293, RG 59, USNA; Castiella to M.A.E., Lima, October 19, 1948, no. 158, leg. R-2315, exp. 1; Víctor Villanueva, *La sublevación aprista del 48* (Lima: Milla Batres, 1973); Klarén, *Perú,* 296–98; Masterson, *Militarism,* 111–12, 117–19.

127. Ralph Ackerman to S.S., Lima, May 19, 1947, no. 1595, 823.00/5-1947, box 5293, RG 59, USNA.

128. Tittman to S.S., Lima, November 4, 1948, no. 919, 823.00/11-448; Memorandum, Owen to Mills, Washington, DC, October 28, 1948, 823.00/10-2848, box 5293, RG 59, USNA; Castiella to M.A.E., Lima, October 30, 1948, no. 172, leg. R-2315, exp. 1, AGMAE.

General Odría's Reward

Following the past examples of Cáceres, Benavides, and Sánchez Cerro, once again a military leader rose to "restore" and "rescue" Peruvian politics from extreme instability and internal conflict. Odría gave his coup the oxymoronic title of the "restoration revolution." His dictatorial movement could succeed in maintaining itself in power only if, as a politician of the time had warned, "it had the ability to resolve economic problems . . . or iron fist to repress and open hand to bribe."[129] Initially key anti-APRA members of the agro-export and business elite supported Odría's restoration movement that promised new presidential elections in 1950.[130] The Central Bank president, Pedro Beltrán, provided economic policy expertise for a strong shift toward liberal economic principles that stamped out exchange, trade, and price controls to allow economic recovery and encouraged foreign investment. According to Beltrán, these interventionist controls "had resulted in corruption, needless government intervention in private industry, and had achieved precisely the opposite effects from those desired."[131]

Some have argued from an unorthodox economic perspective that this initial alliance expressed a partisan transaction between the agro-export "oligarchy," seeking to maximize its foreign exchange earnings, and Odría's military dictatorship.[132] However, as the promised elections of 1950 approached, Beltrán and an important sector of the economic elite organized in the Alianza Nacional coalition quarreled openly with Odría and his military entourage. Their principal differences concerned fundamental economic and political matters in which electoral fraud and graft-laden, deficit-prone public spending were central.[133] Odría proceeded to suppress elite

129. Rafael Belaúnde, "Apostasía democrática del gobierno peruano," *Bohemia* (1948): 57, enclosure to memorandum from Pawley to Armour, Washington, DC, January 19, 1948, 823.00/1-1948, box 5293, RG 59, USNA.

130. According to press reports, among those who greeted Odría on his arrival in Lima after the coup in Arequipa, the prominent names of Beltrán, Gildemeister, Aspíllaga, Pardo, Prado, Miró Quesada, Aramburú, Chopitea, and Ochoa were listed: Harold Tittman to S.S., Lima, November 17, 1948, no. 970, 823.00/11-1748, and Tittman to Paul Daniels (ARA), Lima, March 31, 1949, 823.00/3-3149, box 5294, RG 59, USNA.

131. Memorandum of conversation on stabilization loan for Peru between Beltrán and officers of the U.S. Department of State, Washington, DC, July 11, 1953, 823.5151/ 7-1149, box 5321, RG 59, USNA.

132. David Collier, *Squatters and Oligarchs: Authoritarian Rule and Policy Change in Peru* (Baltimore: Johns Hopkins University Press, 1976), 57; Thorp and Bertram, *Peru,* 255–56; Portocarrero, *De Bustamante a Odría,* 188–91.

133. Beltrán, and his associate Eudocio Ravines, campaigned against the "rotten

opposition and rig the 1950 elections, arguably the most fraudulent in Peruvian history. These actions allowed Odría to govern until 1956 with an overwhelming majority of subservient senators and deputies such as Héctor Boza, Claudio Fernández Concha, Antonio Graña Garland, Enrique Miró Quesada, and Julio de la Piedra.[134] Similar to past dictatorships, political parties were torn asunder leaving behind a small collection of opportunistic individuals and groups with an "almost absolute lack of serious doctrinal principles."[135]

Odría's inner circle was characterized as a radically "nationalistic" group, according to confidential diplomatic reports and sources.[136] High-ranking military officers controlled practically all ministerial posts. Among his close civilian advisors, until the last years of Odría's government, was Benavides's former minister of public works, Héctor Boza. In this transformed political scene, the regime delivered increasingly more power and resources to military institutions and the officer cadre. The salaries of military officers were raised by up to 25 percent and the military defense budget increased by 45 percent during the first year of Odría's regime alone.[137] Among the armed forces, several factions disputed the power zealously guarded by Odría as the top caudillo. There was, for example, the pro-UR faction formed by the volatile Colonel Alfonso Llosa, who was financially compensated with public funds for his insurrectionary actions against Bustamante as well as appointed minister of public works in 1948; Marshal Ureta who, like UR leader Flores himself, was rewarded with an ambassadorship in Europe; and old Sánchez-Cerrista General Ernesto Montagne, a longtime beneficiary of military perks. This faction was soon eradicated for its increasing political ambition and defiant electoral bid in 1950. Another faction included the

---

borough system" of the electoral statute and in favor of constitutional democratic conditions for the 1950 elections in *La Prensa* and *Última Hora.* Castiella to M.A.E., Lima, April 21, 1950, no. 150, leg. R-2441, exp. 18, AGMAE; Tittman to Department of State (hereafter DS), Lima, January 16, 1950, box 3297, RG 59, USNA.

134. Electoral fraud in July 1950 was described as "*un catálogo de picaresca electoral, por lo demás bastante burda como para no engañar mas que a los previamente dispuestos a aceptar el engaño.*" Fernando Castiella to M.A.E., Lima, July 14, 1950, no. 345, and Angel Sanz Briz to M.A.E., Lima, August 25, 1950, no. 423, leg. R-2441, exp. 18, AGMAE.

135. Castiella to M.A.E., Lima, May 12, 1950, no. 176, leg. R-2441, exp. 18, AGMAE.

136. Tittman to S.S., Lima, November 11, 1948, no. 952, 823.00/11-1148, box 5293, RG 59, USNA.

137. Klarén, *Peru,* 300; Masterson, *Militarism,* 131.

pro-American Admiral Roque Saldías. However, General Zenón Noriega, Odría's sidekick and beneficiary of the public funds at his disposal, espoused Peronist views. Noriega was radically opposed to elite influence during a historical period in which Perón's political influence, antithetical to economic liberalism, was increasing in Latin America.[138]

Odría also sought support among the growing migrant population arriving from the countryside to Lima and other cities by offering increased social welfare spending and allowing illegal seizures of unused plots of land by shantytown residents. Expensive irrigation and road construction projects, including a road to Odría's native Tarma, were accelerated in early 1951.[139] The growing budget deficit pressed for currency devaluation and forced an increase in the public sector's foreign debt, recently restructured in 1952 after almost two decades of default.[140] All of these economic miscalculations had at their origin a deliberate policy of corrupt patronage among military and civilian supporters of the regime. A diplomat commented on Odría's patronage networks: "[T]he pattern is the familiar one in Latin America—that of a strong able leader surrounded by a group who benefit from and are loyal to the 'patron.'"[141] The increasing patronage needs of the military-dominated regime clashed with the liberal policies advocated by Beltrán and the budgetary restraint advised by a special economic commission headed by a former U.S. Department of Commerce undersecretary, Julius Klein.[142]

Despite his populist tendencies, Odría continued to depend on stabilization loans and increasing military aid and equipment from the United States. Several of his most trusted officers traveled to Washington to negotiate

138. Castiella to M.A.E., Lima, May 12, 1950, no. 176, and Angel Sanz to M.A.E., Lima, September 21, 1950, no. 460, leg. R-2441, exp. 18, AGMAE; A. Ogden Pierrot to Tittman, Lima, March 29, 1950, 723.00/3950, box 3297, RG 59, USNA.

139. *El Comercio,* March 17, 1951, clipping in Castiella to M.A.E., Lima, March 30, 1951, no. 194, leg. R-2826, exp. 26, AGMAE. The estimated costs were 1.2 billion soles for road building and 2 billion soles for irrigation. Interest in carrying out these costly projects date to late 1949 when they were considered already "grandiose" by financial advisor Julius Klein. Robert Phillips to DS, Lima, December 22, 1949, 823.154/12-2249, box 5301, RG 59, USNA.

140. Quiroz, *Domestic and Foreign Finance,* 185.

141. Carl Breuer to DS, Lima, May 9, 1955, no. 548, 723.00/5-955, box 3010, RG 59, USNA.

142. Robert Phillips to DS, Lima, December 22, 1949, no. 1176, 823.154/12-2249, box 5301; Tittman to Edward Miller, Lima, May 1, 1950, 723.00/5-150, box 3297, RG 59, USNA.

loans and the purchase of jet planes, submarines, tanks, and other military equipment on credit.[143] Odría constantly used his alleged support for liberal economic policies and continental military collaboration against communism as principal playing cards in his approach to the relations between Peru and the United States. In several key diplomatic issues, however, the Odría administration clearly contradicted U.S. foreign policy of maintaining a peaceful and stable "backyard" in Latin America in the middle of the Cold War.[144] These instances of friction included bartering Argentine wheat with the arch anti-American Perón to ameliorate food shortages, continued border disputes with Ecuador, an increasingly nationalistic maritime policy,[145] and the highly publicized case of Haya's asylum in the Colombian Embassy in Lima, an incident of important international repercussions that brought Peru and Colombia once again to the verge of war.[146]

In trying to elude Odría's heavy repression and persecution, Haya sought asylum inside the Colombian embassy in January 1949. By refusing to grant Haya safe conduct to exit the country, Odría exacerbated international opposition to the criminal and drug trafficking charges leveled by the Peruvian government against Haya's right to asylum. The wrangling over Haya increased tensions between Peru and Colombia leading to the submission of the case to the International Court of Justice at The Hague. Despite the concern of U.S. law enforcement officials regarding increased cocaine

143. Elliott (Munitions Division) to Barber (Inter-American Affairs, hereafter IAA), Washington, DC, November 16, 1949, 823.248/10-2349, in U.S. Department of State, *Foreign Relations of the United States, 1949* (Washington, DC: Government Printing Office, 1975), vol. 2; Olmsted (U.S. Department of Defense) to Martin (Mutual Security Affairs), Washington, DC, August 11, 1952, 723.5 MSP/9-1152; and memorandum of conversation, Roque Saldías (Peruvian rear admiral), Berckemeyer, Cabot, and McGinnis, Washington, November 2, 1953, 823.00/11-253, in U.S. Department of State, *Foreign Relations of the United States, 1952–1954* (Washington, DC: Government Printing Office, 1983), 4:1502–3. See also U.S. Department of State, *Foreign Relations of the United States, 1955–1957* (Washington, DC: Government Printing Office, 1987), 7:1029–55.

144. Mann (IAA) to Krieg (North and West Coast Affairs, NWCA), Washington, DC, November 24, 1950, 723.00/11-2450, in U.S. Department of State, *Foreign Relations of the United Stated, 1950* (Washington, DC: Government Printing Office, 1976), 2:994–96 (original in box 3297, RG 59, USNA).

145. Memorandum by Edgar McGinnis (NWCA), Washington, DC, February 23, 1949, 623.3531/2-2849, in U.S. Department of State, *Foreign Relations, 1949*, 2:764–66.

146. Memorandum by Mills to Miller, Washington, DC, December 20, 1949, 823.00/12-2049, in U.S. Department of State, *Foreign Relations, 1949*, 2:773–75.

smuggling from Peru[147]—an activity widely publicized due to the Balarezo drug trafficking case tried in New York—the official U.S. diplomatic position was that there was no definitive evidence connecting Balarezo's financing of the Aprista uprising of October 3, 1948.[148] Haya's connection with Balarezo had surfaced prominently in U.S. Federal Bureau of Narcotics correspondence (letters from Garland Williams, New York narcotics commissioner, to his chief Harry J. Anslinger) as well as in the proceedings of the Balarezo case.[149] The New York prosecutor Joseph Martin pursued the political ramifications of the narcotics case only to a limited extent (as did New York district attorney Robert Morgenthau in a 1991 money laundering case involving the highest Aprista leader and former Peruvian president, Alan García). Department of State officials—pressed by influential people in the United States who considered Haya a hero of democracy threatened by a brutal dictatorial government—opted to allow Haya off the hook in the name of continental stability and peaceful inter-American relations. Haya remained confined in the Colombian embassy until 1954 when he was finally allowed to leave the country after bilateral negotiations between Peru and Colombia.[150]

Evidence of specific cases of corruption during the Odría regime surfaced only rarely before 1956. It was a time of repressive conditions, constant danger of deportation, limited freedom of the press, and an obsequious legislature. However, growing concerns of the illicit enrichment of Odría and his ministers and inner circle circulated behind the scenes among the political opposition and diplomats. One diplomatic dispatch affirmed that "Odría has acquired at least three homes as gifts from calculating adherents

147. Memorandum of conversation between Fernando Berckemeyer (Peruvian ambassador), Harry J. Anslinger (Commissioner of Narcotics), Carlos Gibson, and George Morlock, Washington, DC, May 2, 1949, 823.114/5-249, box 5321, RG 59, USNA.

148. Tittman to DS, Lima, February 7, 1950, no. 184, 723.00/2-750, and February 10, 1950, no. 208, 723.00/2-1050. Memorandum of conversation between Berckemeyer and Lobenstein (NWCA), Washington, DC, April 7, 1950, 723.00/4-750, box 3297, RG 59; "U.S. refutes story in narcotic case," *New York Times,* August 25, 1949, 19.

149. Memorandum from Lobenstine to Krieg, Barber and Jamison, Washington, DC, April 13, 1950, 723.00/4-1350, and Lobenstine to U.S. Embassy in Lima, Washington, DC, April 19, 1950, 723.00/4-1950, box 3297, RG 59, USNA; *El Comercio,* no. 58221, February 9, 1950, 3–4, no. 57889, August 23, 1949, 3, 7, no. 57893, August 25, 1949, 3, and no. 58131, December 25, 1949, 5.

150. Atwood (South American Affairs) to Holland (IAA), Washington, DC, May 13, 1954, 723.00/5-1354, in U.S. Department of State, *Foreign Relations, 1952–1954,* 4:1514–16.

and is reported to have acquired other forms of wealth. . . [That he] would be willing to leave such rewarding and lofty position seems most improbable."[151] These elements of illicit personal gain, later duly proven through incriminating property deeds, were used as principal arguments to request a formal congressional investigation in the post-Odría legislature of 1956.

Moreover, a domestic abuse incident in Washington, DC, involving complaints filed with police by a U.S. citizen married to Captain Antonio Ipinza Vargas, a close aide of Odría, raised well-grounded suspicions of shady financial connections. Ipinza had been Odría's aide since the time the general was interior minister in 1947–1948. Confidential sources in Lima confirmed that Ipinza was an "unscrupulous man" who had used his official position to enrich himself and extort money from Chinese and Japanese subjects. Ipinza remained close to Odría during and after the coup of 1948, and in 1952 obtained a business visa from the U.S. embassy at the request of the Peruvian government. In Washington, DC, Ipinza bought properties for the then phenomenal sums of $55,000 and $265,000, leading to the conclusion that "he may be carrying out some private financial transactions for the President."[152] In 1958, following the end of Odría's regime, Ipinza was elected deputy and later was involved in a failed plot to oust the Peruvian president at that time. In this plot, Ipinza was associated with other corrupt Odriístas who had enriched themselves through a shoddy arms production concern (Fábrica de Armas Los Andes) and official sale contracts with Odría's ministry of war.[153]

By early 1954, the worsening monetary and economic situation underscored Odría's declining political position. The national currency was further depreciated and new stabilization loans were contracted to offset govern-

151. Breuer to DS, Lima, May 9, 1955, no. 548, 723.00/5-955, box 3010, RG 59, USNA.

152. Sandy Pringle to Robert Dorr, Lima, June 17, 1952, 723.521/6-1752; Dorr to Bennet, Washington, DC, July 11, 1952, 723.521/7-1152, box 3303, RG 59, USNA. The FBI had also communicated to the Department of State about another complaint of a woman who accused Ipinza of chasing her 15-year-old daughter. Despite these legal transgressions, Ipinza was granted another official visa in December 1952.

153. Robert Sayre to DS, Lima, March 7, 1958, no. 662, 723.00/3-758, box 3011, RG 59, USNA. Ipinza's fellow plotters included Senator Wilson Sologuren, and his brothers Wilfredo and Alberto Sologuren, a former air force captain and manager of the Los Andes arms factory, respectively. Two official contracts granted to the factory in 1951–1955 involved the government paying 5.4 million soles or $350,000 for the manufacture of submachine guns that were rejected for technical defects. Other conspirators included former deputy Clemente Revilla, Lieutenant Colonel Alejandro Izaguirre, air force Commander Julio César Cornejo, and Captain Atilio Copelo Fernández.

ment overspending, expansion of bank credit (generated by the government's domestic borrowing), and the external trade deficit.[154] In August 1954, the politically ambitious minister of war, General Noriega, and a group of army officers launched a failed coup against Odría with Perón's suspected blessing. Having lost faith in his close political and military associate, Odría confided to U.S. Ambassador Harold Tittman that he had allowed Noriega to use his official position as minister of war and official funds at his disposal to further his own political aims, "although this action was obviously improper since he should have resigned before starting a political campaign."[155]

With the general elections scheduled for July 1956 approaching, Odría was attacked from various sides, particularly over his regime's administrative abuses and misappropriations. In December 1954, history professor and former diplomat Raúl Porras Barrenechea publicly criticized the regime's unjustifiable delay in the reconstruction of sizable sections of the city of Cusco after the earthquake of 1951.[156] (In 1956, Porras spearheaded a motion in the Senate to investigate Odría's administrative transgressions and corruption.) The regime's internal security and election laws were a clear threat to clean democratic elections and the welfare of formal political parties. The overwhelming control that Odría exerted over his unconstitutional congress was evident in the following tally: of a total 47 senators, 41 were Odriístas, and of a total 156 deputies, 146 were also Odriístas. In *La Prensa*, Beltrán continued to criticize Odría's inflationary policies, waste of government funds in "sumptuous" public works, inadequate housing policies, and undemocratic impositions.[157]

The abusive interior minister, Alejandro Esparza Zañartu, became the target of a negative public relations campaign that ended in his resignation in late 1955 in the midst of large-scale strikes.[158] In a printed message to the nation in 1955 aptly summarizing the ills generated by Odría's dictatorship, the exiled former president Bustamante wrote that

---

154. Monthly summary, January 25, 1954, 723.00/1-2554, box 3299, RG 59, USNA.

155. Tittman to W. Tapley Bennet (OSA), Lima, August 13, 1954, 723.00/8-1354, box 3299, RG 59, USNA. On Noriega's coup, see Masterson, *Militarism,* 144–45.

156. U.S. attaché (Department of the Air Force) to D. S. Peruvian desk officer, Lima, December 16, 1954, 723.00 (W)/12-1654, box 3300, RG 59, USNA.

157. Breuer to D. S., Lima, July 15, 1955, no. 30, 723.00/7-1555, box 3010, RG 59, USNA.

158. Antonio Grullón to M.A.E., Lima, December 26, 1955, no. 1681, leg. R-3814, exp. 11, AGMAE.

the country has descended many degrees in the level of social ethics. . . . [C]ases of illicit enrichment are notorious among the regime's high [-level officials]. . . Great fortunes have been improvised in the shadow of political position and influence. This dirt has splashed the military institutions.[159]

According to Bustamante, the Odría administration had a system of "commissions," "shares," and "premiums" for granting public works contracts and conduct other official business. Through this traffic of "favors," political support was bartered for illegal profit: politicians became brokers and brokers became politicians. They had no social justice concerns or interest in reform. People in power needed to guarantee advantageous electoral results at the end of the dictatorship to protect themselves from future prosecution.[160]

Precisely under the appalling circumstances described by Bustamante, a new frenzy of political negotiations preceded the elections of 1956. Odría had the intention of rigging the elections in his favor but was forced to negotiate his exit from government due to mounting military conspiracies. The uprising of the Iquitos military garrison led by General Marcial Merino contributed to denunciations of Odría's false electoral promises. Odría overreacted by ordering the imprisonment of leading right-wing civilians, among them Beltrán, who was erroneously linked to Merino's revolt. Odría now played a crooked electoral game. Surprisingly, the dictator held political negotiations with Ramiro Prialé, a leader of the illegal APRA who was recently released from prison. Odría favored the candidacy of lawyer Hernando Lavalle, initially courted as well by APRA leaders. Lavalle was, however, ultimately rejected by voters mainly because he was Odría's candidate. Former president Manuel Prado arrived from Paris to bargain the promise of amnesty, political coexistence (*convivencia*), and future congressional posts to APRA in exchange for Aprista electoral support. Prado also promised Odría and his ministers immunity against future charges of corruption and unconstitutional acts.[161]

This dishonest pact, sealed just a few hours before the elections, ensured Prado's triumph despite strong support obtained by architect Fernando Belaúnde Terry. Supported by a young and popular movement that fought to

159. José Bustamante y Rivero, *Mensaje al Perú* (Lima: N.p., 1955), 3, in leg. R-3814, exp. 11, AGMAE.

160. Bustamante, *Mensaje al Perú*, 3–8.

161. Memorandum, Sircusa to Holland, Washington, DC, June 15, 1956, 723.00/6-1556, RG 59, USNA; Carlos Miró Quesada, *Radiografía de la política peruana* (Lima: Editora Páginas Peruanas, 1959), 203–205; Klarén, *Peru,* 307.

obtain his inclusion in the electoral process, Belaúnde proclaimed the urgent need for social and institutional reforms that opportunistic leaders had practically abandoned.[162] Belaúnde's fresh political stance was devoid of the stain of unprincipled and suspicious political pacts. Tragically, Prado's regime further delayed crucial reforms under the influence of political cronies, corrupt members of his own party, and compromises that limited the efficiency and direction of his second administration.

Forgive and Forget

One of the first pieces of legislation approved in Congress and enacted by the Prado administration shortly after its inauguration in July 28, 1956, was a general political amnesty embodied in law 12654. This law not only benefited APRA members but also protected Odría and his entourage from prosecution. However, the congressional opposition led by the novel Christian Democratic Party (PDC) and the Belaundista movement, pressed for the investigation and sanction of the Odría regime's flagrant constitutional infringements and administrative irregularities. Invoking existing laws penalizing transgression of public sector functions and the 1933 Constitution, on August 14, 1956, a special commission was formed in the Senate to investigate constitutional violations during the Odría regime and determine culpability.[163] Likewise, in the Chamber of Deputies and under the initiative of PDC Deputy Héctor Cornejo Chávez, several motions where presented to investigate Odría's secret police, administrative irregularities, tax evasion, and illicit enrichment.[164]

A constitutional debate ensued in the Senate during the month of September. This important controversy had repercussions on the reinforcement of curbs to constitutional transgressions and corrupt practices under existing legislation. The commission in charge of investigating Odría's consti-

---

162. Timberlake to S.S., Lima, June 10, 1956, telegram, no. 737, 723.00/6-956, RG 59, USNA.

163. Motion presented by senators Raúl Porras Barrenechea, Alejandro Barco López, and Miguel Monteza, August 14, 1956, in Peru, Senado, *Diario de los debates del Senado* (Lima: Talleres del Senado, 1956), 2:189.

164. Peru, Cámara de Diputados, *Diario de los debates de la Cámara de Diputados* (Lima: P. L. Villanueva, 1956), 5th session, August 20, 1956, 1:293–94; *El Comercio,* August 21, 1956, no. 62,873, 2, 4, 6; *La Prensa,* August 21, 1956; Antonio Gullón to M.A.E., Lima, August 21, 1956, no. 1100, leg. R-4454, exp. 8, AGMAE; U.S. Air Force attaché confidential report, Lima, September 1956, weekly report, no. 36, 723.00 (W)/9-756, box 3012, RG 59, USNA.

tutional violations was split, resulting in a majority and a minority report. The majority report defended by four senators (three Pradistas and one "independent") was a legalistic argument against investigating past constitutional violations based on two premises. First, existing legislation did not specify which measures could be typified as unconstitutional, which in turn prevented the judicial branch from establishing the same. Second, the general policy of political amnesty recently decreed in law 12654 had to be upheld. In sustaining this view, Senator Víctor Arévalo argued that amendments to the existing constitution were necessary to resolve legal loopholes and gaps in language, and that the charges of constitutional violation against Odría were extemporaneous because they could be filed only against current rather than former officials.[165]

The minority report was a rebuttal of the majority text that obviously did not comply with the initial senatorial mandate to investigate constitutional transgressions. Christian Democrat senator Mario Polar sustained the minority's view by enumerating some of the most serious constitutional violations committed by Odría and his former interior minister Esparza Zañartu, who was outrageously rewarded with a diplomatic post abroad. Among the numerous violations cited, constitutional rights had been suppressed for eight years, which clearly violated the legislation on the "state of siege" that contemplated the suspension of certain rights only to defend the constitutional order. Articles 8 and 31 of the constitution had been violated, as Odría was illegally exempt from paying taxes on his personal real estate transactions. The minority report then analyzed the specific legal mechanisms through which clear culpability could be established according to existing legislation. Polar did not agree with the thesis of a legal loophole preventing an investigation. He cited articles 20 and 179 of the constitution that specifically stated the political, civil, and criminal responsibilities of public officials, as well as articles 19 to 22 of the 1878 law, which established that the Senate had the mandate to decide whether a former president could be prosecuted after the Chamber of Deputies had formally brought charges.[166] Another opposition-party senator observed that the minority report did not ask for an investigation into the illegal enrichment of congressmen and former government officials, including "gifts" of houses, plots of land, and jewels by companies in compensation for public sector contracts,

165. Peru, Senado, *Diario,* session September 11, 1956, 2:189–91, 199–209; *El Comercio,* no. 62,918, September 12, 1956, 4.

166. Peru, Senado, *Diario,* session of September 11, 1956, 2:191–99.

or an estimated $10 million that Odría had stashed in U.S. bank accounts (according to a June 1954 issue of *Visión*, a biweekly Spanish-language magazine printed in New York by Time Inc. for Latin American markets). The senator stated that those were tasks for the Chamber of Deputies. The minority report asked only for the investigation of constitutional violations that would themselves represent at least a moral sanction and a wake-up call for correcting any legal or constitutional loopholes or imprecise language so that such infractions could be prosecuted.[167]

In support of his position, Polar cited legal experts that advocated "government of law and not of men" and Max Weber's thesis of limited government to insist on the need to uphold constitutional law against the mockery of it by the majority report favorable to allowing Odría's impunity. Polar charged that the majority report was akin to Pontius Pilate's action of washing his hands. Polar concluded that, with impunity and consigning such wrongdoing to oblivion, it would be impossible to implement a radical change in methods and systems. This would contradict what Peruvian voters had chosen in the recent elections, that is, a democratic constitutional order. The Senate's president, historian Raúl Porras, expressed similar positions against *continuismo*. This political continuity arranged between groups such as Prado's Movimiento Democrático Peruano (MDP) and Odría's Partido Restaurador (PR), was a mechanism that undermined basic institutions.[168]

Unfortunately, the reformist efforts of the minority were defeated in the Senate. On September 20, 1956, the majority report was approved in the Senate by a vote of 30 to 13.[169] Pradista politicians had consistently denied the existence of a pre-election pact between Prado and Odría. Yet the public was convinced that such a secret pact existed because the Pradistas refused to investigate the former dictator. This was a predictable outcome. According to a foreign official, President Prado had "suggested to various congressmen that if they attempt[ed] to prosecute Odría, he would help to pave the way for a Junta government."[170] That day a negative precedent for

167. Intervention of Senator Barco López in Peru, Senado, *Diario*, 26th session, September 20, 1956, 2:243–44. Detailed information provided by Deputy Cornejo Chávez on Odría's foreign bank deposits, also in Peru, Diputados, *Diario*, 22nd session, September 13, 1956, 1:520.

168. Peru, Senado, *Diario*, session of September 11, 1956, 2:210–21, 224–35.

169. *El Comercio*, no. 62934, September 21, 1956, 4, 9.

170. U.S. Air Force attaché, Lima, September 1956, weekly report, no. 37, 723.00 (W)/9-1456, box 3012, RG 59, USNA.

granting immunity to constitutional violators was established out of political convenience. The crucial aspect of instituting and respecting constitutional rules in order to curb corruption—a notion preeminent in the elaboration and enforcement of the U.S. constitution—was ignored by the representatives of the political majority in Peru. This neglect reaffirmed the political practice of allowing and providing incentives for political corruption.

The debate in the Chamber of Deputies lasted longer than that in the Senate at the dogged insistence of PDC deputies headed by Cornejo Chávez. On August 20, the PDC deputies submitted a request to investigate fiscal irregularities during the previous regime and demanded relevant information from the ministries of finance, public works, navy, and agriculture. The suspected irregularities cited as examples of corruption included tax waivers on imported cars owned by Odría and others; the true financial origins of the residences donated to or purchased by Odría while in office in Lima, Monterrico, San Bartolo, Paracas, and other parts of the country; a house donated to former minister Zenón Noriega; accounts and assets of the charity and welfare office Asistencia Social formerly headed by Odría's wife; and the handling of funds to transport fuel for Peruvian Navy ships.[171] Many other specific requests for congressional investigation were filed in the following weeks. Suspected illegal and corrupt transactions and misappropriations during the Odría regime were numerous.[172]

The issue that unleashed the most heated debates was a request to investigate the origin of Odría's properties that had been purchased, transferred, and taxes waived during his regime. In his quest for uncovering and punishing "corruption and immorality," Cornejo Chávez proved with legal documents that Odría had received those properties as donations and had evaded corresponding taxes.[173] Moreover, Odría's donors included public sector contractors such as the U.S. company Anderson and Clayton, which was in charge of an irrigation project in Pampa de los Castillos for which it received 50 percent of affected land in spite of protests by the local com-

171. Peru, Diputados, *Diario,* 5th session, August 20, 1956, 1:293–94.

172. A sample of the enterprises and activities involved in accusations of corruption and requests for investigation of administrative irregularities during the Odría regime in the 1956 Congress follows: land distribution in Río Quiroz irrigation project; Santa, Vapores, and Vivienda corporations; irrigation La Esperanza; Empresa Petrolera Fiscal; foreign loans; contracts by Ministry of War; and Choclococha Lake dam (Montgomery Company). *El Comercio,* no. 62867, August 18, 1956, 4, no. 62894, September 1, 1956, 4, no. 62918, September 13, 1956, 15, no. 62975, October 12, 1956, 4, no. 63015, November 1, 1956, 20, and no. 63058, November 20, 1956, 4.

173. Peru, Diputados, *Diario,* 22nd session, September 13, 1956, 1:516–23.

munity.[174] On September 14, Javier Ortiz de Zevallos, leader of the Pradista MDP, stated that his party would vote against such an investigation to remain faithful to the unity and amnesty goals it had embraced. Odriísta PR party members and Pradista deputies attacked the Christian Democrats for their proximity to the failed Bustamante regime, lack of Christian spirit for failing to support pardons, and the waste of legislative time on issues that did not directly pertain to the constructive action of enacting laws for the present.[175] Among the Restaurador deputies who steadfastly defended Odría were Víctor Freundt Rosell (whose brother, Alberto, benefited from illegal tax waivers on imported cars),[176] Manuel Montesinos, Héctor Castañeda (Odría's former secretary and military officer), Pedro Chávez Riva, and Antonio Ipinza Vargas (Odría's former aide and suspected financial agent in Washington, DC). Nevertheless, the PDC request for information on Odría's tax payments on properties acquired during his regime was granted.[177]

On December 11, Cornejo Chávez denounced the inordinate delay and factual errors made by the Ministry of Finance in providing the requested information. Cornejo Chávez considered these developments the expression of the current government's policy of *borrón y cuenta nueva,* that is, forgiving or dismissing past corruption in order to proceed with a supposed "fresh start."[178] The debate continued until early January 1957.[179] The Pradista deputies insisted that Odría could not be charged in the Senate or the courts due to lack of specificity in the constitution and their party's commitment to amnesty. Ortiz de Zevallos reaffirmed his party's position and denied once again support for a bipartisan pact favorable to the alleged *continuismo* practiced by the Prado administration. Some independent (mainly

174. Peru, Diputados, *Diario,* 3rd session of 2nd extraordinary legislature, December 27, 1956, 1:89; "Debate sobre nombramiento de una comisión," *El Comercio,* no. 63131, December 28, 1956, 4, 9.

175. "Nuevo y acre debate sobre las casas de Odría," *La Prensa,* September 15, 1956; Gullón to M.A.E., Lima, September 15, 1956, no. 1240, leg. R-4454, exp. 8, AG-MAE. The U.S. Air Force attaché also opined that "the congressional term is now half over and so much time has been spent in wrangling over what should be done about the past administration that progress has been seriously impeded." Lima, September 1956, weekly report, no. 39, 723.00(W)/9-2856, box 3012, RG 59, USNA.

176. "Cartas del diputado doctor Héctor Cornejo Chávez," *El Comercio,* no. 63161, January 12, 1957, 5, 6.

177. U.S. Air Force attaché, Lima, September 1956, weekly report, no. 38, 723.00(W)/9-2056, box 3012, RG 59, USNA.

178. Peru, Diputados, *Diario,* 8th session of 1st extraordinary legislature, December 11, 1956, 1:390–91.

179. *El Comercio,* December 28, 1956, no. 63131, 4, 9.

Aprista) deputies agreed with this legal argument.[180] Like in the Senate, the repeated requests to open a congressional investigation on Odría's scandalous transgressions were denied in the Chamber of Deputies by a vote of 91 to 39.[181] Only a couple of the other ongoing investigations continued to have repercussions in coming years, most conspicuously the inquiry into military supply contracts of the 1950–1955 period that made a scapegoat of Francisco Mendoza, a corrupt businessman who had ties with the disgraced General Zenón Noriega and used extensive bribes to obtain sales contracts of overpriced, defective, and obsolete materiel.[182] However, practically all of these investigations effectively disappeared and did not result in sanctions meted out by the judiciary.

The impunity allowed to the past dictatorial regime also encouraged serious corruption among Prado's high-level ministry officials and congressmen. The venality of Pradista politicians and civil servants was observed first hand by the honest and politically independent Jorge Basadre who was appointed, for a second time, minister of education by president Prado. Basadre held that post between July 1956 and October 1958 when he resigned, reportedly due to health reasons. However, Basadre later revealed that his resignation had other causes. During his second tenure as minister of education, Basadre endeavored to carry out a comprehensive study of the real situation of Peruvian education and, on that basis, propose to Congress a general law on public education. These constructive efforts were subject to overwhelming difficulties in Congress. Basadre's serious differences with some Pradista senators and deputies continued and intensified over the issue of building several schools.[183] The growing Peruvian population at the time was already outstripping the limited educational system. Basadre's aim was to introduce urgent educational reforms. Sadly, a number of cor-

180. Aprista deputy Carlos Malpica criticized the position of his own party members and sided with Cornejo Chávez's request for investigating the former regime's "peculados." This was the start of a long career as a leftist anticorruption politician. Peru, Diputados, *Diario,* 3rd session of 2nd extraordinary legislature, December 27, 1956, 1:130.

181. *El Comercio,* no. 63152, January 8, 1957, 4, 9.

182. "Denúnciase malos manejos en licitaciones del ramo de guerra entre 1950 y 1955," *El Comercio,* November 16, 1958, 4, 9.

183. Basadre, *Introducción a las bases,* 1:29, n. 2; Basadre and Macera, *Conversaciones,* 114, 124; Basadre, *Materiales para otra morada: ensayos sobre temas de educación y cultura* (Lima: La Universidad, 1960); Quiroz, "Basadre y su análisis de la corrupción," 165.

rupt congressmen had other priorities that once again derailed efforts toward reform. Delays of necessary reforms due to partisan interests during the second Prado regime had costly consequences for Peruvian society and economy in subsequent decades.

Minister Basadre was pressured by top leaders of the MDP to approve demands by the building contractor RIMSA. This company had a dispute with the Ministry of Education over a substantial increase in costs charged by RIMSA for building two large schools (Colegio Hipólito Unánue and Unidad Escolar de Huaraz) whose original construction plans had been modified to comply with new requirements. Technical experts asserted that those changes did not justify the exorbitant cost increase.[184] During these negotiations, MDP leaders exerted their political influence over Basadre. As the minister had a close relationship with officials at the U.S. Embassy, he confided that he was forced to hide in a tiny inconspicuous office at the ministry to avoid incessant importuning, influence, and demands by political appointees. He also told U.S. diplomats that the three main politicians pressuring him were no other than Carlos Ledgard Jiménez (president of the Chamber of Deputies and MDP chief), Javier Ortiz the Zevallos (leader of the MDP congressional bloc), and Max Peña Prado, an influential relative of the president.[185]

Basadre wrote a memorandum to President Prado in June 1958 stating his conditions for remaining in the cabinet. The minister required an overall administrative housecleaning that would eliminate peculation agents and illegal access by civil servants and others to public sector payments and public works contracting and financing. Basadre also urged enactment of a law against illegal enrichment, and proposed constitutional reforms to limit uncontrolled budgetary expenses and undue interference of congressmen and other officials in the functions of government outside their jurisdiction. According to a U.S. diplomat, Basadre's memo caused considerable uproar because it proposed to eliminate political graft and favoritism. Unfortunately, Basadre was a "voice in the wilderness."[186]

184. "Movieron influencias en el caso RIMSA," *La Prensa,* January 22, 1959; Gullón to M.A.E., Lima, January 22, 1959, no. 43, leg. R-5530, exp. 29, AGMAE.

185. Robert Sayre to DS, Lima, January 22, 1959, no. 698, 723.00/1-2259, box 3011, RG 59, USNA.

186. Sayre to DS, Lima, June 20, 1958, no. 960, 723.00(W)/6-1058, box 3013, RG 59, USNA. See also Basadre's memorandum published in *Presente: Revista Semanal Peruana,* no. 55 (June 21, 1958): 7–9.

The Prado regime was experiencing great political and financial difficulties in mid-1958, dubbed a "crise de régime."[187] Prado's reliance on a small and venal group of MDP politicians, and the damaging alliance with Apristas and Odriístas brought increased criticism to his administration. An attempted coup led by several lieutenant colonels, aided by corrupt Odriísta Deputy Ipinza and Senator Sologuren who enjoyed parliamentarian immunity, was foiled in March 1958. Sologuren reacted by insulting the interior minister, Jorge Fernández Stoll, who satisfied his honor in a duel, which was forbidden yet still fashionable.[188]

Budget deficits increased in 1957 and 1958.[189] The Peruvian currency was depreciated by 30 percent. A supporter of expanding the money supply, the minister of finance Augusto Thorndike, was dropped from the cabinet in June 1958 due to his well-known graft operations. According to *El Comercio,* Thorndike had sold 170 tax waivers on imports to dealers of European automobiles.[190] Likewise, another scandal involving tax waivers on imported cars granted to twenty-two senators and sixty-seven deputies, was exposed by *La Prensa* in September 1958 and exploited by the opposition.[191]

The most damaging scandal for the Prado regime developed as a result of signing a 200-million-soles contract with the International Standard Electric Corporation of New York for the modernization of the Peruvian government's teletype network (*teletipos*), without previous public tender, on December 24, 1958. The local press and Deputy Cornejo Chávez in Congress charged that this obscure deal included a "margin" of 60 million soles or 30 percent of the total contracted sum. The equipment's real price was considerably lower than the price quoted in the contract, with the price differential allegedly channeled to corrupt officials. The MDP's leader, Ledgard Jiménez, Interior Minister Carlos Carrillo Smith, and several leg-

187. Ambassador Theodore Achilles to D.S., Lima, May 21, 1958, no. 889, 723.00/5-2158; May 23, 1958, no. 883, 723.00/5-2358; and telegram to S.S., Lima, May 27, 1958, no. 1067, 723.00/5-2758, box 3011, RG 59, USNA.

188. Sayre to D.S., Lima, March 7, 1958, no. 662, 723.00/3-758, box 3011, and March 11, 1958, no. 675, 723.00 (W)/3-1158, box 3012, RG 59, USNA

189. J. M. Ramírez Gastón, *Política económica y financiera: Manuel Prado, sus gobiernos de 1939–45 y 1956–62. Apuntes para la historia económica* (Lima: Editorial La Confianza, 1969), 114–15.

190. Sayre to D.S., Lima, June 10, 1958, no. 960, 723.00 (W)/6-1058, box 3013, RG 59, USNA.

191. *El Comercio,* no. 64,263, September 5, 1958, 4, 12, and no. 64,265, September 6, 1958, 2; Sayre to D.S., Lima, September 3, 1958, no. 206, 723.00/9-358, box 3011, RG 59, USNA.

islators were held responsible for promoting and allowing corrupt transactions. The political fallout over this case included the resignation of Carrillo from the ministry and the stepping down of Ledgard as chief of the MDP. The contract was rescinded. Basadre chose this opportunity to publicly announce that his resignation as minister of education had been due to political pressure exerted in the RIMSA case.[192] In analyzing these corruption scandals, a U.S. diplomat concluded that although "graft is an ever present problem in Peru, it appears that in these cases persons close to the Prado administration may have over-reached themselves."[193]

Postponed Reforms

"Perhaps the greatest single unfavorable factor," wrote U.S. Ambassador Theodore Achilles in recounting the deteriorating socioeconomic and political situation in Peru, "is overpopulation in the sierra, on too small, too infertile holdings per family."[194] Urgent reforms and more efficient governance were necessary to prevent masses of poor Indians from emerging on the wrong side of the Iron Curtain. Fernando Belaúnde and Pedro Beltrán were the most conspicuous critics of the Prado administration. Both emphasized the need of housing and land reform, as well as the "moralization" of civil service. Both had presidential ambitions for the 1962 elections. As early as January 1957, through a highly publicized radio address, Belaúnde denounced the covert pact among the Pradistas, Odriístas, and Apristas as the main reason why the Prado regime had accomplished so little. Moreover, Belaúnde underscored a comprehensive set of reforms to truly transform the country. A published rebuttal by MDP Deputy Eduardo Watson prompted Belaúnde to cite his injured honor and gentlemanly valor as reasons for demanding a duel with sabers that was sensationalized by the press.[195]

192. Sayre to D.S., Lima, January 22, 1959, no. 698, 723.00/1-2259, box 3011, RG 59, USNA; Gullón to M.A.E., Lima, January 22, 1959, no. 43, leg. R-5530, exp. 20, AG-MAE; *La Prensa,* January 22, 1959; *El Comercio,* no. 64525, January 27, 1959, 3, 10, no. 64527, January 28, 1959, 3, 5, and no. 64540, February 4, 1959, 4, 12. See also recollection by owner of the newspaper *El Pueblo* (Callao), in Enrique León Velarde, *¿El Chino y yo jodimos al Perú? Confesiones de Enrique León Velarde* (Lima: N.p., 2000), 83.

193. Sayre to D.S., Lima, January 22, 1959, no. 6958, 723.00/1-2259, p. 2, box 3011, RG 59, USNA.

194. Achilles to D.S., Lima, June 5, 1958, no. 950, 273.00/6-558, box 3011, USNA.

195. The inexperienced duelers received only superficial cuts. The Spanish ambassador considered the duel old-fashioned and extraneous to major issues, while the U.S.

Beltrán's criticism was unleashed in May 1958 through editorials and reports of corruption scandals that were widely publicized in his newspaper *La Prensa*. This journalistic display angered President Prado and MDP congressmen.[196] In October 1958, Beltrán wrote a cogent political proposal in which he argued for radical changes in political norms and behavior, "moralization" and efficiency in all public sector activities, a technocratic agrarian reform, a housing program to address mushrooming city slums, easier credit, and tax reform. From a liberal perspective, Beltrán believed that the state was growing at the expense of citizens and cited the scandalous tax waivers on imported cars granted to congressmen as an example of how politicians think only about themselves and not about those they govern. According to Beltrán, the majority of Peruvians wished for a widespread rollback of corruption in executive, judicial, educational, and university matters. They aspired for an end to abuses, illegal enrichment of civil servants, favoritism, and dishonest administration. Such "public sector moralization," Beltrán asserted, would be the basis for a spiritual renaissance to support faith in the future.[197]

The prolonged political crisis came to a head in March 1959. Prado's prime minister and finance minister, Luis Gallo Porras, attempted to introduce urgent economic and tax measures to address currency devaluation. The MDP old guard faction opposed these measures and, as a consequence, was forced out of the party's leadership. Surprisingly, in July 1959, Beltrán was called on to act as prime minister and finance minister, posts he accepted to carry out an economic stabilization and recovery program. An increase in mineral and fishmeal exports contributed to an improvement in the economic situation, and fiscal deficits were significantly reduced in 1960–1961. However, Beltrán succumbed to the extant realpolitik, becoming deeply involved in the Prado-APRA covert pact, which cost him dearly in terms of his presidential aspirations. (Already in August 1957, newspapers reported that Eudocio Ravines, Beltrán's close political associate, had visited the Miraflores home of his old foe Haya de la Torre from where they

---

attaché found it to be contradictory to democratic principles and perhaps a liability for Belaúnde's political career. Gullón to M.A.E., Lima, January 16, 1957, no. 76, and January 18, 1957, leg. R-4353, exp. 19, AGMAE; U.S. Air Force attaché, Lima, January 1957, weekly reports nos. 3 and 4, 723.00(W)/1-1757 and/1-2457, box 3012, RG 59, USNA.

196. Achilles to S.S., Lima, May 27, 1958, telegram, no. 1067, and dispatch, no. 910, 723.00/5-2758, box 3011, RG 59, USNA.

197. *La Prensa: 7 Días del Perú y el Mundo*, October 5, 1958, 1, 3–4, 10; Gullón to M.A.E., Lima, October 6, 1958, no. 868, R-5030, exp. 25, AGMAE.

emerged reconciled on the bases of shared anti-communism, acceptance of foreign investment, and support for agrarian reform).[198]

The bulk of Beltrán's earlier political reform program did not materialize despite periodic reaffirmations of the same in *La Prensa* and the grandiose announcement of a 1.7-billion sol program for agrarian and housing reform in April 1961.[199] Beltrán reinforced his approach to APRA by appointing a pro-APRA minister of public works, Jorge Grieve.[200] The opposition on the right and the left continued to attack the covert pacts supporting the Prado regime.

El Comercio, faithful to its anti-Aprista editorial line, was relentless in its exposure of the convivencia deals between APRA and the Prado government. In June 1957, the sensational story was reported that a Peruvian Aprista priest, José Luis Arteta Yábar, was involved in forging 300 million soles in Caracas. The Venezuelan police implicated Arteta in the intent to supply forged currency to the APRA party for "revolutionary purposes." The priest, with approval of Pradista authorities, acted as cultural attaché in the Peruvian embassy in Caracas.[201] *El Comercio* intensified its anti-convivencia campaign in 1961 and 1962. A series of articles revealed a number of APRA's corrupt activities, including illegal benefits from links with the Federación de Choferes, a transport union that had been granted tax waivers on imported cars and buses; subsidies provided by the Interior Ministry to the Aprista newspaper *La Tribuna;* a smuggling operation moving weapons from Colombia; and several other allegations of bribery, misappropriation, and favoritism implicating Aprista and Pradista authorities.[202]

As a result of investigations by a U.S. congressional subcommittee, it was also found that Pradista authorities had been involved in the diversion and misappropriation of 60 percent of U.S. foreign aid funds destined for building roads and providing food relief.[203] A proposal to investigate Bel-

198. Henry Dearborn to D.S., Lima, August 7, 1957, no. 120, 723.00/8-757, box 3011, RG 59, USNA.

199. "Texto de la exposición del premier: Tierra para los que la trabajan y techo para los que lo necesitan," *Revista: La Prensa,* April 26, 1961.

200. Alfonso Marqués de Merry del Val to M.A.E., Lima, April 27, 1961, no. 204, leg. R-6518, exp. 14.

201. *El Comercio,* no. 63429, June 2, 1957, 3, no. 63430, June 3, 1957, 3, no. 63438-9, 7 June, 1957, 5, 1, and no. 63449, June 13, 1957, 5.

202. *El Comercio,* no. 66053, May 16, 1961, 4, 18, no. 66285, September 20, 1961, 4, no. 66289, September 22, 1961, 2, no. 66494, January 14, 1962, 2. Article series under the title "Cuentas y cuentos de la convivencia."

203. *El Comercio,* no. 65956, May 23, 1961, 1, and no. 65958, May 24, 1961, 1.

trán's connection to suspected illegal deals by urban development companies Mutual Perú and Urbanizadora Repartición was blocked by Pradista and
Aprista deputies in Congress.[204] Christian Democrat congressmen petitioned
for Beltrán's resignation. Just before the June 1962 elections, the Beltrán cabinet was under intense fire as its economic program floundered.[205]

The inability of the convivencia establishment to successfully address
or ameliorate some of the country's urgent problems also resulted in the
growth of the radical left. APRA lost a large number of its young members
to pro-guerrilla groups APRA Rebelde and Movimiento de Izquierda Revolucionaria (MIR). Less than two years after the Cuban revolution, a well-
organized pro-Cuba lobby had emerged, which exploited the weaknesses of
the convivencia regime, notably the ardently debated Brea y Pariñas issue
over the disputed ownership of northern oilfields held by the International
Petroleum Company, a subsidiary of Standard Oil of New Jersey.

In November 1960, a raid on the offices of the Cuban embassy carried
out by anti-Castro Cuban exiles exposed secret documents signed by the
Cuban ambassador in Peru, Luis Ricardo Alonso. The seized documents implicated a vast network of Peruvian leftist politicians, congressmen, journalists, student leaders, and activists as paid agents of the Cuban government. On January 4, 1961, additional Peruvian intelligence information was
presented in a stormy session of the Senate by the minister of government
and police, Ricardo Elías Aparicio, and the minister of war, Alejandro
Cuadra Ravines, who named those who had received stipends and monthly
payments by the Cuban government through the Cuban embassy to carry
out political campaigns against the Peruvian government. Among the paid
leftist political operators the most conspicuous anti-IPC campaigners were
prominent. Despite ideological excuses and justifications in the name of social justice and anti-imperialism, this type of corruption within the legal left
was widespread from the beginning of its influence on national high politics.[206] Moreover, in 1961–1962 urban guerrilla actions and bank robberies

204. *El Comercio*, no. 65706, November 8, 1960, 1, 6, and no. 65714, November
12, 1960, 1.

205. *El Comercio*, May 31, 1962.

206. Adalberto Pinelo, *The Multinational Corporation as a Force in Latin American Politics: A Case Study of the International Petroleum Company in Peru* (New York:
Praeger, 1973), 83–84; Peru, Cámara de Senadores, *Diario de los debates del Senado,
1960* (Lima: Imprenta Torres Aguirre, 1965), 1:157–220, 1a. legislación extraordinaria
de 1960, 6a. sesión extraordinaria, January 4, 1961; and Román Oyarzun to M.A.E.,
Havana, February 25, 1969, leg. R-10,671, exp. 12, AGMAE. For a partisan denial of

were launched by the Frente de Izquierda Revolucionaria (FIR) in support of land seizures encouraged by Trotskyist leader Hugo Blanco in the La Convención valley of Cusco.[207]

Failure of reform also had an impact among military officers educated in the newly upgraded Centro de Altos Estudios Militares (CAEM). Anti-insurgency strategy was combined with military "reformist" policies for developing the country under the growing influence of leftist nationalist ideologies derived from Nasserism.[208] It is precisely from these new tendencies that new political opportunities and roles were envisioned by a faction of high-level military commanders. This new political stance among military officers, a substantial variation of Odría's venal caudillo nationalism, laid the foundations for the "institutional" military coups of 1962 and 1968.

Just prior to the June 1962 elections, the Belaundista opposition denounced electoral fraud perpetrated by the parties in power. Belaúnde's party, Acción Popular (AP), claimed that as many as 200,000 voter registrations were fraudulent. Already the major political leaders of the convivencia were negotiating electoral alliances and under-the-table pacts. The National Electoral Jury (Jurado Nacional de Elecciones, JNE) was integrated mostly by Pradistas. A few days before the elections, judicial inquiries confirmed the falsification of illegally obtained voter rosters in APRA and MDP party offices. APRA was not sanctioned for these illegal practices. The high command of the armed forces, traditionally anti-Aprista, conducted independent investigations. The military found that 40 percent of the voter registrations they investigated were not correct or fraudulent and publicly asserted, with a deliberately neutral language, that a "will" to commit electoral fraud existed. This was an ominous warning sign directed at APRA's electoral pretensions. U.S. embassy officials believed

---

the charges against leftist politicians and sympathizers who received "revolutionary" payments for exerting political influence on Peruvian institutions—a reliable list of bribed leftist politicians and agents, cross-checked with the above three sources, that includes Alberto Ruiz Eldredge, Benito Montesinos, Héctor Béjar; journalists Francisco Igartúa, Ismael Frías, Francisco Moncloa; and deputies Alfonso Benavides Correa, Carlos Malpica, Efraín Ruiz Caro, and Germán Tito Gutiérrez, among many others—see José A. Fernández Salvatecci, *Los militares en el Perú: de libertadores a genocidas* (Lima: N.p., 1994), 105.

207. American Embassy to S.S., Lima, May 8, 1962, telegram, no. 858, 723.00/5-862, box 1554, RG 59, USNA.

208. C. E. Bartch to D.S., Lima, July 18, 1960, no. 24, 723.00/7-1860, box 1553, RG 59, USNA; Marqués de Merry to M.A.E., Lima, August 1, 1962, leg. R-6750, exp. 14, AGMAE.

that fraud had occurred, but its scale was interpreted as not large enough to influence the elections.[209] The electoral board disregarded complaints of fraud and proceeded with the elections. With support from Prado and Beltrán, Aprista leader Haya received slightly more votes than Belaúnde. Odría, at the head of his newly formed party, the Unión Nacional Odriísta (UNO), placed third. Haya's 32.9% electoral victory was not enough to satisfy the legal requirement of two-thirds of the votes to be declared president. The task of selecting the new president was now in the hands of the newly elected Congress.[210]

In this tense political situation, the military command called for annulment of the elections. The tension increased when Belaunde's followers threatened to rebel and appealed for military intervention. In a last-minute move, Haya renounced his presidential ambitions in favor of his former archenemy Odría. But it was too late. On July 18, 1962, a military junta headed by General Ricardo Pérez Godoy ousted and arrested President Prado. The elections were annulled. The military junta promised new elections for the following year. When the exiled Prado arrived in his beloved Paris to ask for diplomatic immunity, as he had done before in 1948, the French authorities informed him that there was a legal limit on the value of jewels and precious metals that his family could bring into France.[211] The elections of 1963 raised hopes for the prompt establishment of a cleaner and more honest democratic order without venal dictators, unprincipled politicians, and covert pacts.

To conclude, the economic and constitutional rebuilding after the damaging Leguía administration was riddled with political conflict and civil strife framed by the difficult international context of the 1930s and 1940s. These conflicts served to obscure official corruption and at times the ruthless abuse of power, as well as for radical and violent transgressions by a

209. Bartch to D.S., Lima, June 7, 1962, no. 721, 723.00/6-762, box 1554, RG 59, USNA.

210. Arnold Payne, *The Peruvian Coup D'Etat of 1962: The Overthrow of Manuel Prado* (Washington, DC: Institute for the Comparative Study of Political Systems, 1968), 41–45; Marqués de Merry to M.A.E, Lima, June 6, 1962; July 9, 1962, no. 418, leg. R-6750, exp. 14, AGMAE; Francisco García Belaúnde, *Así se hizo el fraude* (Lima: Acción Popular, 1963), 13–15; W. Obelson, *Funerales del APRA y el fraude electoral* (Lima: Librería Universo, 1962), 10, 24–25; César Martín, *Dichos y hechos de la política peruana: una descripción auténtica, sobria y condensada de los dos procesos electorales y las dos juntas militares* (Lima: Tipografía Santa Rosa, 1963).

211. Biens et ressortissants péruviens en France, November 9, 1962, no. 26, Série B "Amérique," 1952–1963, Pérou, AMAE.

new populist movement unfettered by legal and ethical restraints to its ultimate goal of attaining power.

Older and persistent modes of corruption mingled with newer forms arising from shifts in financial, economic, and institutional conditions and policies. Military graft in arms procurement increased in importance at a time when the political role of the armed forces was paramount (during the regimes of Colonel Sánchez Cerro, General Benavides, and General Odría), and international border conflicts led to military build-ups. Public debt mismanagement shifted from a focus on foreign debt (long-term default and consequences originating in the 1920s) to domestic loans that involved local banks and economic cliques during the Benavides and first Prado regimes. Bribery and graft in public works and services remained a constant, although with a tendency to increase during the Odría and second Prado regimes.

A change in policy related to exchange controls and import licenses, part of a spreading protectionist wave in Latin America known as "import substitution industrialization," opened the flood gates for favoritism, graft, and abuse during the two Prado and Bustamante regimes in the 1940s and 1950s. (These "novel" interventionist devices of corruption continued to make their mark in the second half of the century.) Inflation and deficits resulted, and lost revenue due to contraband ballooned. Losses due to early drug trafficking and forgone foreign investment were relatively low. Increasing reliance on foreign debt and aid, and its concomitant mismanagement, followed the restructuring and resumed service on the defaulted foreign debt by 1952.

In comparative terms, estimated average corruption costs per year remained high but stable in the 1930s. These costs doubled in current figures (not controlled for inflation) in the 1940s, and doubled again in the 1950s (see Table A.5). However, as percentages of government expenditures, the levels of corruption costs increased from 31 percent per year in the 1930s, to 42 percent in the 1940s, and 46 percent in the 1950s. As percentages of GDP, the progression in the levels of estimated corruption costs was 3.1, 3.3, and 3.6 percent, respectively, for each of the three decades (compare in Table A.6). This constant and gradual growth of corruption costs is perhaps why Basadre considered graft at the time as ubiquitous and structural.

As the contentious political sphere played a crucial role in the years 1931–1962, electoral disputes, rigging, and fraud conditioned government legitimacy, or lack thereof. When dictatorial solutions had run their course, elections were called and political cliques behind the scenes established covert pacts. The results of these pacts and alliances were at times so scandalous that they triggered widespread outcries about the hopelessness of expecting politicians to work for the common good. In the meantime, urgent policy and institutional reforms were neglected despite mounting social and economic problems. The press increasingly reported on pacts hidden from the public eye, the privileges they generated, and the scandals that ensued. Press coverage and congressional opposition, particularly in the 1950s, exposed scandals and made public the pardon of former corrupt leaders—a classic formula of *borrón y cuenta nueva* (clean slate) that generated profound popular skepticism toward the political establishment. Once again a military solution, this time to preclude alleged corruption in elections, was considered an option in the midst of considerable apathy. These weak foundations for the return of democracy in the 1960s limited Peruvian institutions' ability to curb corruption and preclude renewed military intervention.

Fig 14. Polemical ad hoc court, established in August 1930 by the military regime of Lieutenant Colonel Luis M. Sánchez Cerro, to punish former officials accused of corruption just after the fall of Leguía: "The extension, tribunal of sanction" by Raúl Vizcarra. *Variedades* vol. 28, no. 1209 (1931), 1.

Courtesy of Biblioteca Central, Universidad Católica, Lima.

Fig 15. Intentions of President José Luis Bustamante y Rivero (1945–48). Despite his personal honesty and attempts to cleanse his administration of graft, the ill-fated Bustamante failed in his moralizing quest undermined by APRA, the military, and the right: "As in Hamlet's Denmark 'there is something rotten smelling' in Peru" by Geo. *Suácate*, vol. 1, no. 7 (1945), 1.

Courtesy of Biblioteca Nacional del Perú, Lima.

Fig 16. Military dictator General Manuel A. Odría (left), and sidekick General Zenón Noriega (right), 1954. Odría (1948–56) gained power by staging a coup against Bustamante, enriched himself during his eight-year dictatorship, and allowed the abuse of power and public funds by subaltern officials.

Fig 17. President (right, in suit) Odría enjoying a carnival party, ca. 1956. In stark contrast with his stern military pose, Odría was known to engage in extravagant celebrations among elite circles, cronies, and fellow military.

Fig 18. Congressional corruption, exemplified by perks and fraud in tax-exonerated automobile importation during the second administration of President Manuel Prado (1956–62): "Latest Model 1958" by Víctor Marcos "Vimar." *Rochabús*, año 1, no. 49 (1958), center fold 8-9.

Courtesy of Biblioteca Nacional del Perú, Lima.

Fig 19. *Teletipos* equipment scandal. It originated from a 200-million soles contract with the International Standard Electric Corporation of New York and compromised Minister of Government Carlos Carrillo Smith. In the cartoon Carrillo tries to avoid being tarnished: "Shady deal (*negociado*) of telegraphs," by Pablo Marcos "Marcos." *Rochabús*, año 2, no. 73 (1959), 2.

Fig 20. President Manuel Prado unconcerned about corruption scandals. Prado washes his hands, a symbolic depiction of his attitude toward the scandals that plagued his second administration: "At last something clean in this regime!" by Pablo Marcos "Marcos." *Rochabús*, año 2, no. 76 (1959), 1.

Fig 21. President General Juan Velasco Alvarado (1968–75), surrounded by fellow military in power in 1969. Through the dismantling of constitutional and congressional curbs, and the control of mass media, the "revolutionary" military regime engaged in bureaucratic waste and mismanagement that camouflaged widespread administrative corruption.

Archivo Revista *Caretas.*

Fig 22. Military card game: coup or steal? In the middle of strikes, repression, and persistent military perks and corruption, President Francisco Morales Bermúdez (1975–80) and Prime Minister Pedro Richter Prada are depicted playing a fateful game: "Card playing is the rage" by Carlos Tovar "Carlín." *Monos y Monadas*, año 74, no. 134 (1979), 3.

Courtesy of Biblioteca Nacional del Perú, Lima.

Fig 23. Assault on the banks. In 1987 President Alan García (1985–1990) adds to the public suspicions of foul play with his attempt to nationalize the banking system: "Hands up! This is an expropriation, nationalization, democratization, Apristization, etc.," by Eduardo Rodríguez "Heduardo." *La historia según Heduardo* (Lima: Empresa Editora Caretas, 1990), n.p.

Archivo Revista *Caretas.*

Fig 24. Former President Alan García defending himself against accusations of corruption in 1991. Serious charges against him derived from evidence originated in New York, Italy, and congressional investigations. García was exonerated by a combination of shrewd legal defense, human rights allegations backed by the Inter-American Commission on Human Rights, and technicalities of legal procedure.

Archivo Revista *Caretas.*

Fig 25. Vladimiro Montesinos, real chief of the national intelligence service (SIN) under President Alberto Fujimori (1990–2000), counting bribe money before military and civilian witnesses. Still of covertly taped video: *Vladivideo* no. 1778–79, November 6, 1999.

From *State of Fear*, a Skylight Pictures film, www.skylightpictures.com.

Fig 26. TV interview of Vladimiro Montesinos and President Alberto Fujimori. Held at the SIN's infamous conference hall (*salita*), 1999. The close political and corrupt association between Fujimori and Montesinos is amply demonstrated.

Archivo Revista *Caretas*.

Fig 27. President Fujimori facing a long list of corruption-related charges accumulated during his long regime (1990–2000): "Heduardo in his ink: And you think we will be relentless with corruption?" by Eduardo Rodríguez "Heduardo." *Caretas*, no. 1562 (1999), 13.

Fig 28. Press conference by President Fujimori and various government officials on August 21, 2000. It was staged to divert attention away from the mounting scandal of thousands of Kalashnikov rifles bought in Jordan by Montesinos to supply the subversive FARC of Colombia.

Photo by Oscar Medrano. Archivo Revista *Caretas*.

Fig 29. Vladimiro Montesinos, General Nicolás Hermoza, politician Víctor Joy Way, and other unnamed prisoners behind bars convicted of diverse crimes of corruption: "Carlincaturas: Frankly I don't see what's good with that Paniagua." Under the interim administration of President Valentín Paniagua (2000–1; deceased October 16, 2006), hundreds of corrupt officials of the former Fujimori regime were arrested and prosecuted. *La República*, October 18, 2006, año 25, no. 9057, p. 10.

Chapter 6

Assaults on Democracy, 1963–1989

As of this writing, former congressman Héctor Vargas Haya still lived in the same small house he and his family have occupied for many years in a non-affluent district of Lima. There were no signs of extravagant wealth in his daily life. Since the 1960s he has been intimately engaged in investigating notorious cases of corruption in public administration. Among his credentials Vargas Haya can boast serving honestly as an elected deputy for close to twenty years and as president of the Chamber of Deputies in 1988–1989. After over ten years of bitter dissent with the corrupt leadership of his own party, he officially renounced his life-long Aprista militancy in 2000. He has consistently denounced graft in its various forms, calling for an urgent constitutional reform to rebuild institutions in obvious decline for decades. In a recent newspaper interview, he claimed that in Peru "to be honest is like being a leper."[1]

The retired politician can be justified for having a pessimistic view concerning corruption and its connection to institutional weaknesses. During his lifetime, several times hopes of achieving real government reform were frustrated and wasted due in large part to corrupt interests. Like Basadre, the historian and civil servant, Vargas Haya, the politician and legislator, witnessed from inside the political system of his time. He has authored important books that document in detail evolving modes of high-level corruption during the two Belaúnde administrations (1963–1968 and 1980–1985), the "revolutionary" military dictatorship (1968–1980), the first pres-

1. "Héctor Vargas Haya, ex parlamentario," interview by José Gabriel Chueca, *Perú.21,* no. 1248, January 19, 2006, 16–17; Héctor Vargas Haya, *Hacia la reforma del Estado: camino a la segunda república* (Lima: Edigrama, 2001), 17–21.

idential period of APRA's leader Alan García Pérez (1985–1990), and the Alberto Fujimori regime (1990–2000). In the historical account that follows, the solitary public voice of Vargas Haya is compared and contrasted with other exceptional sources to depict a particularly difficult struggle in which key democratic advances—under the pressure of a growing and impoverished population—were assaulted by corrupt politicians and military chieftains alike.

Belaúnde's Promises Dashed

The nationalist reformist candidate Fernando Belaúnde, supported by the alliance of Acción Popular (AP) and the Christian Democrats, was elected president of Peru in June 1963. These elections were regulated and closely monitored by the military junta that governed Peru in 1962–1963. Several leaders of the high military command favored Belaúnde and sympathized with his technocratic ideology. The junta had justified its seizure of power based on the alleged fraud of the annulled 1962 elections and their desire for a "truly democratic republic." To contain illegal land invasions in Cusco, the military government implemented, with loans from the U.S. Agency for International Development (USAID), a pilot agrarian reform in the valley of La Convención with some encouraging yet limited results. The junta had also backed its technocratic aspirations with the creation of the National Planning Institute (INP), a centralizing organism for development strategies. These measures favored center-left political and bureaucratic tendencies coinciding with military opposition to APRA's bid for power.

Various factions in the military junta expressed themselves in the months prior to the 1963 elections. The junta's most visible spokesman, General Ricardo Pérez Godoy, together with the interior minister, General Juan Bossio, embodied a personalist authoritarian tendency similar to that of previous military dictators. Pérez Godoy and Bossio sought public recognition through attempts to nullify the controversial 1922 settlement that granted surface rights in the La Brea y Pariñas oilfields to the International Petroleum Company (IPC). This unilateral solution to the problem was part of the nationalist dogmas developed since 1959 by leftist ideologues and filtered into the "reformist" interventionist strategies of the Center for Advanced Military Studies (CAEM). This radical approach was opposed by General Nicolás Lindley and two other junta members. These "moderates" prevailed over Godoy and Bossio, forcing their resignation, and fulfilling the promise of holding elections without further unconstitutional interventions. Lindley was later rewarded by Belaúnde with an ambassadorship in Madrid.[2]

Prior to officially assuming his post, President-elect Belaúnde held an important private meeting with U.S. Ambassador John Wesley Jones. Regarding relations with the United States, Belaúnde foresaw one issue that he considered a "time bomb" if it was not solved promptly: the La Brea y Pariñas question. This problem had been inherited from past administrations and its solution was urgent and long overdue. Belaúnde then revealed that his party's position on the issue was similar to that of the military: the 1922 award to the IPC was "null and void" since the IPC arguably owed Peru a large sum in back taxes. For political reasons concerning the opposition Belaúnde expected in Congress, it was imperative that some kind of arrangement, not necessarily in cash, be negotiated between the company and the Peruvian executive branch. Jones replied that Belaúnde's position with regard to the 1922 award would not help negotiations with the IPC and U.S. financial circles.[3] A few days later Celso Pastor, brother-in-law and close advisor to Belaúnde, declared to a surprised U.S. diplomatic official that Belaúnde's most pressing problem was to consolidate his authority over the military.[4]

Despite a clean democratic provenance, Belaúnde's political reliance on the military to defeat APRA's candidate Haya de la Torre was perhaps the most important liability that would eventually doom his administration. When asked by a foreign journalist what he thought about the proper role of the armed forces in national affairs, Belaúnde answered that cooperation between civilians and the military was necessary and that the armed forces were schools for indigenous recruits.[5] This temporizing attitude towards the military was understandable, according to a U.S. diplomat "in view of the debt he owes the Armed Forces for his election in 1963."[6] The revamping of Peruvian constitutional democracy, radical reforms, and "moralizing"

2. Adalberto Pinelo, *The Multinational Corporation as a Force in Latin American Politics: A Case Study of the International Petroleum Company in Peru* (New York: Praeger, 1973), 74–77, 95; Daniel Masterson, *Militarism and Politics in Latin America: Peru from Sánchez Cerro to Sendero Luminoso* (Westport, CT: Greenwood Press, 1991), 189, 192; Bartch to D.S., Lima, July 25, 1963, no. A-464, box 4012, RG 59, USNA.

3. Jones to D.S., Lima, June 22, 1963, no. A-954, box 4014, RG 59, USNA.

4. Bartch to D.S., Lima, July 3, 1963, no. A-6, box 4013, RG 59, USNA.

5. Interview by John Hightower (Associated Press), in Cutter to D.S., Lima, November 18, 1963, no. A-392, box 4014, RG 59, USNA.

6. James Haahr to D.S., Lima, November 16, 1963, no. A-384, box 4012, RG 59, USNA.

practices promised by Belaúnde paradoxically relied to an important extent on the old perilous game of enticing and rewarding the military to side with one political faction against another. This strategic mistake mirrored one previously made by Bustamante under circumstances of Aprista insurrectionary pressure in 1948. In the long run, the implicit understanding between Belaúnde and the military backfired without containing the sinuous and destabilizing trajectory of APRA, a party that in the past had itself attempted on several occasions to penetrate and influence military officers. The initial military support given to Belaúnde also granted the Apristas a historical justification to sternly oppose his regime and its urgently necessary reform program. APRA formed an unprincipled reactionary coalition with Odría's UNO party (Unión Nacional Odriísta) to control the Congress and counteract Belaúnde's initial popularity. In his first presidential address, Belaúnde had promised to promptly resolve the La Brea y Pariñas issue. In a preemptive attempt to gain the initiative as well as votes for the approaching municipal elections, the APRA-UNO congressional bloc passed a bill on October 31 in both chambers declaring the 1922 award null "for having violated pertinent legal requirements."[7]

Belaúnde's ambitious reform program thus became the prey of both congressional and military pressures. On the same day of Belaúnde's inauguration, a renewed and more serious wave of land invasions spread in the countryside. This time the promise of agrarian reform through expropriations with compensation encouraged illegal land occupations by tenants and landless peasants. Leftist infiltration in the Acción Popular party, government institutions, and armed forces was also a concern. While dealing with the land invasions and expropriating a few estates by decree, Belaúnde submitted his agrarian reform project to Congress as early as August 1963, where it was stalled for eight months. When the agrarian reform law was finally approved, it had been watered down to fit APRA-UNO interests and emasculate its effectiveness. With growing concern over the negative fiscal and inflationary effects of Belaúnde's expensive reform and public works programs, Apristas and Odriístas also tenaciously opposed the president's pet project to build the Carretera Marginal de la Selva, a north–south highway traversing more than 1,000 kilometers of the high jungle region.[8]

7. Siracusa to D.S., Lima, November 9, 1963, no. A-367, box 4012, RG 59, USNA; see also Masterson, *Militarism,* 196–98, 206.

8. Klarén, *Peru,* 327; Masterson, *Militarism,* 207–209; Marqués de Merry to M.A.E., Lima, August 10 and 20, October 7 and 21, 1963, nos. 516, 533, 618, and 674, leg. R-7254, exp. 2, AGMAE.

Although Christian Democrats were put in charge of key posts in the Ministry of Agriculture and the Agrarian Reform Institute, Cornejo and his party resented the final outcome of the agrarian reform law, as well as the subsequent lower priority given to the original radical reform program on which the AP-PDC alliance was based. Congressional opposition was also eroding this alliance.[9] Likewise, several of Belaúnde's earlier ministers were censured by the APRA-UNO coalition in Congress. Weary of congressional obstructionism, Belaúnde considered an unconstitutional referendum to back the executive's initiatives while relying more on military ministers to occupy key cabinet posts. Military officers were also given important posts as national planners and directors of public works. With the spread of armed guerrilla activity in 1965, the military pressed and obtained from Belaúnde a free hand in dealing with domestic insurrectionary movements. In 1967, the military also succeeded in securing the purchase of Mirage Vs, expensive and sophisticated French warplanes. This purchase brought tensions with the U.S. government, as it was attempting to limit supersonic aircraft proliferation in the region with future sales of U.S.-made F-5s.[10]

Belaúnde's decision making was further limited by a small group of intimate advisors and friends, the "Carlistas," so-called because several among them were named Carlos, including wealthy industrialist Carlos Ferrero, and businessmen and relatives Carlos Velarde and Carlos Muñoz. The members of this privileged and conservative clique, more interested in expanding personal assets than in public service, benefited from governmental favors and contracts through administrative irregularities. Among the most conspicuous Carlistas were Manuel Ulloa, considered by foreign observers as self-seeking and unscrupulous, and Carlos Muñoz, Belaúnde's cousin by marriage, head of a company of customs brokers as well as government-appointed board member of the National Health and Welfare Fund.[11] Among the AP rank-and-file, the Carlistas were opposed by the *ter-*

9. Cutter to D.S., Lima, September 29, 1963, no. A-258, box 4013, RG 59, USNA; Angel Sanz Briz to M.A.E., Lima, May 8, 1965, no. 716, leg. R-7834, exp. 4, AGMAE.

10. Sanz to M.A.E., Lima, October 6, 1964, no. 819, leg. R-7509, exp. 12, AGMAE; Masterson, *Militarism*, 205, 215, 221; memorandum of conversation at White House, November 8, 1967, President Lyndon Johnson, Assistant Secretary of State Covey Oliver, William Bowdler, and Ambassador J. Wesley Jones, no. 19701, box 2423, RG 59, USNA. See also François Le Roy, "Mirages Over the Andes: Peru, France, the United States, and Military Jet Procurement in the 1960s," *Pacific Historical Review* 71, no. 2 (2002): 269–300.

11. T. G. Belcher to Lima Embassy, Washington, DC, November 18, 1963, telegram, no. 391, box 4014; Jones to D.S., Lima, February 1, 1967, no. A-431, box 2419, RG 59, USNA.

mocéfalo or hot-head faction led by the doctrinaire Edgardo Seoane, an ardent advocate of administrative rectitude and supporter of the AP's original nationalist reformist ideology.

Belaúnde's weakening and dependent political position hindered vigorous action to curb and repulse the ever more obvious graft among his administrators and the military establishment. According to a foreign political analyst, "AP leaders feel that patronage is a natural reward of political control."[12] This network of *amiguismo,* or cronyism, had traditionally permeated the executive, which was heavily concentrated in Lima despite efforts at decentralization. This bureaucracy exerted an elitist, tutelary, or guided democracy breeding red tape and inefficiency.[13] The Belaúnde administration was no exception to this pattern, but brought to it specific manifestations.

The first signs of corruption in the Belaúnde administration included favoritism, graft, and kickbacks in government contracts. One such case was that of a minister of development and public works, Sixto Gutiérrez, and other high officials bribed by an Italian consortium eager to secure a public works contract. With rare support from the APRA-UNO coalition in Congress in early 1966, the government had canceled a previous contract with an Anglo-German firm for a development project in Huancavelica province's Mantaro valley. The project's contract was then granted to the Italian contractor, which had tendered the lowest bid by 15 percent. However, the project took longer to be finished and the cost rose to $237 million, almost 140 percent more than what the first contractor had budgeted. When Gutiérrez stepped down as minister, he retained a senatorial seat but was ousted from the AP in 1967 for "straying from the party line" in obvious reference to his corrupt behavior as minister.[14]

Another early and little publicized indication of graft was uncovered by the first congressional investigative commission in which the young deputy Vargas Haya participated in 1963–1965. The investigation centered on the deals between the National Fund for Economic Development (FNDE) and a French-Peruvian company, Socimpex, in charge of financing electrification projects. With the complicity of FNDE officials, Socimpex had over-

12. E.V. Siracusa to D.S., Lima, May 28, 1967, no. 686, box 2420, RG 59, USNA.
13. Jack Hopkins, *The Government Executive of Modern Peru* (Gainsville: University of Florida Press, 1967), 1–2, 107, 116–19.
14. Jones to S.S., Lima, March 13, 1968, no. A-514, box 2421, RG 59, USNA; Richard Goodsell, *American Corporations and Peruvian Politics* (Cambridge, MA: Harvard University Press, 1974), 99.

billed interest charges to the Peruvian government totaling more than $10 million. A Peruvian lawyer and representative of the financing company tried to buy Vargas Haya's favors to "improve" the investigation, offering him a paid trip to "visit" the company's main supplier, Schneider Electric, in Paris. Vargas Haya immediately pressed charges against the briber. The congressional commission proceeded to report its scathing findings that led to the cancellation of the contract with Socimpex and reimbursement of the amount over-billed. Several officials and businessmen were prosecuted, but soon the judicial case was dropped without imposing effective sanctions.[15] Likewise, the discovery of a large quantity of contraband carried by Peruvian Navy ships in 1962–1965 was hushed up with the dismissal of several petty officers. These apparently isolated incidents generated only marginal publicity, although they were the early manifestations of widespread graft at the higher and lower levels of the government and military institutions, a scandal ready to explode under the appropriate political and economic circumstances.

According to well-informed and insightful reports, Belaúnde's government was initially considered one of the cleanest administrations in the country's history by "Peruvians, many of whom tend to be cynically tolerant of the widespread corruption which has traditionally pervaded the Peruvian government from top to bottom."[16] Belaúnde's early popularity owed much to the image he projected as an incorruptible president requiring high levels of integrity from his ministers and officials. However, after the regime's first three years the fiscal situation showed alarming signs of mismanagement arising from enormously higher public expenditures without a corresponding increase in revenues. The promised tax reform to increase direct taxation and diminish reliance on indirect taxes, as well as the urgent creation of new indirect taxes, was effectively opposed by the APRA-UNO coalition in Congress. Foreign aid and loans were limited and even stalled as a result of the intensified IPC dispute and the Mirage purchases. Higher fiscal deficits were met with monetary expansion, leading to inflation and devaluation of the Peruvian sol in November 1967.[17] The Belaúnde administration's prestige plummeted. Rumors that the state was failing to collect badly needed revenue funds as a result of widespread smug-

15. Personal communication by Vargas Haya, San Miguel-Lima, May 7, 2003.

16. Jones to S.S., Lima, March 13, 1968, no. A-514, box 2421, RG 59, USNA.

17. Pedro Pablo Kuczynski, *Peruvian Democracy Under Economic Stress: An Account of the Belaúnde Administration, 1963–1968* (Princeton, NJ: Princeton University Press, 1977); Thorp and Bertram, *Peru,* 289–90; Klarén, *Peru,* 332–33.

gling aided by government officials, snowballed in early 1968 to capture critical public attention.

The Contraband Frenzy

In February 1968, Lima newspapers displayed front page stories of a sensational illegal landing of a four-engine plane belonging to the Peruvian air cargo carrier Rutas Internacionales Peruanas S.A. (Ripsa). The press reported in December 1967 that the plane had been seen unloading cargo at a clandestine desert strip close to the Pan-American highway 160 miles south of Lima. This was just one of many illegal landings detected.[18] Information on Ripsa's illegal activities were apparently provided to the newspaper *El Comercio* by domestic textile interests who were losing money due to the growing contraband.[19] Soon thereafter several other cases were denounced in the press and Congress. These contraband scandals damaged the image of the Belaúnde regime and the armed forces. A multipartisan congressional commission led by Aprista Deputy Vargas Haya was formed to investigate the contraband, which involved government officials, civilian businessmen, and customs police. Apart from revealing reports from the fiscal police, the commission soon received more than 500 pages of charges and complaints by private citizens and anonymous whistle-blowers.[20] The scale and nature of contraband networks with official protection was larger and more serious than previously suspected.

The contraband scandal intensified when Senator Cornejo Chávez cited a July 1965 official report,[21] quoted previously by the Aprista newspaper

18. Jones to D.S., Lima, February 28, 1968, no. A-471, box 2423, RG 59, USNA.

19. Reference to complaints against contraband and private investigations on the matter by textile industrialists headed by Manuel Cillóniz, president of the textile committee of the Sociedad Nacional de Industrias (SNI), and Gonzalo Raffo, president of the SNI, in Héctor Vargas Haya, *Contrabando* (Lima: Offset Peruana, 1976), 165; and Siracusa to S.S., Lima, May 15, 1968, no. 638, box 2420, RG 59, USNA.

20. The commission was formed in early March 1968 and consisted of its president Vargas Haya, Rafael Cubas Vinatea (PDC), Ramón Ponce de León (APRA), Jaime Serruto Flores (AP), Oscar Guzmán Marquina (UNO), Hugo Carrillo (UNO), and Mario Villarán (independent leftist). For a list of accusations and complaints, see "Denuncias," file 4, exp. GR-08, Cámara de Diputados: Comisión Investigadora del Contrabando de 1968 (hereafter CIC), Fondo Histórico del Archivo General del Congreso del Perú (hereafter AGCP).

21. "Intervenciones Dr. Cornejo Chávez," Senate session, March 8, 1968, Oficio, no. 020-967, file, no. 39, exp. PD-8, CIC, AGCP.

La Tribuna as early as 1966, revealing that several former Navy officers had participated in extensive smuggling aboard Peruvian Navy ships. Cornejo's remarks prompted the Navy minister, Vice Admiral Raúl Delgado, to appear before the Senate admitting to contraband issues in the Navy and promising to court-martial those responsible for contraband found in the BAP *Callao*'s cargo in 1965. That year an unexpected reshuffling of the cabinet deprived Admiral Florencio Texeira of the Navy ministerial post. Since his appointment as minister in 1963, Texeira had signed contracts with private business concerns to lease the *Callao* to import merchandise intended for contraband. The vessel, commanded by navy personnel, was engaged in several such irregular journeys while Minister Texeira was able to protect contraband imports. However, as a new minister was taking office in September 1965, the *Callao* was placed under strict surveillance. Contraband merchandise valued at 10.9 million soles (and costing 44 million soles in import tax evasion)—destined for the Navy, Army, and Air Force department stores (*bazares*)—remained unclaimed at port warehouses. With sufficient documentation in hand, the congressional commission found that Texeira was directly responsible for this case of contraband. Another similar case involving the BAP *Chimbote* in 1964 was also investigated by the congressional commission, which found adequate evidence to charge a former interior minister and a general director of the Republican Guard, later tried in a military court and found guilty of the lesser charge of fraud. Texeira was formally charged, found guilty, and served prison time, despite attempts by other high-level navy officers to have the case dismissed.[22] This was a truly unprecedented sanction in a long history of de facto immunity enjoyed by corrupt public officials.

The contraband scandal and related investigations spun off in various directions in March through May of 1968. Deputy Napoleón Martínez had to defend himself from evidence in an official report that indicated he had abused his official diplomatic and tax-exemption privileges. Martínez had established an arrangement with a businessman, Sigmund Markewitz, to import Mercedes Benz cars purchased at a discount as well as without paying taxes to later sell them at a huge profit in Peru. In his defense, the deputy asserted that he had imported only nine instead of twelve cars under his

22. Vargas Haya, *Contrabando,* 211–30; Jones to S.S., Lima, March 11 and 13, 1968, nos. 3932 and A-514, box 2421, RG 59, USNA; "80 bultos Guardia Republicana" and "Bazar de la Guardia Republicana," files nos. 2 and 2-A, exp. GR-9, CIC, AGCP; Domingo García Rada, *Memorias de un juez* (Lima: Editorial Andina, 1978), 272–73.

name, that there were many other similar cases of fraud, and that a foreign country was conspiring against him, a classic illustration of the dictum "patriotism is the last resort of the scoundrel."[23] He was eventually deprived of his congressional immunity, prosecuted, and found guilty in 1969.[24] Another smuggler of imported car parts and other merchandise investigated by the commission, Isaías Wolfenson, eluded arrest due to official protection acquired through bribery and personal connections with police authorities.[25]

The widely publicized Ripsa scandal impacted squarely on President Belaúnde's inner circle. The congressional commission presented serious charges against executives of a customs broker company, Consorcio Aduanero, managed by José Carlos Quiñones Muñoz, and headed by his uncle Carlos Muñoz, the conspicuous Carlista adviser to Belaúnde. Quiñones had bribed investigations police (PIP) officers to secure the dispatch of contraband merchandise at customs and collected bribe money for Muñoz.[26] Muñoz was suspended from the AP in disgrace. Several other relatives of the president and former ministers and AP members were also suspected of corruption, including secretary of the presidency Alvaro Llona and former finance minister Sandro Mariátegui.[27] Llona had placed AP member Víctor Guillén as customs surveyor at the Jorge Chávez International Airport. Thanks to the abuse of that position and the illegal income it produced, Guillén soon acquired houses, commercial buildings, and even shares of Muñoz's customs broker company. Guillén helped Quiñones to obtain extremely low tax assessments via declaration of undervalued imports handled for several companies (Continental Motors, Nadir, Hiltra, Globoimport) connected to a group of businessmen involved in other cases of contraband. Guillén confessed to police investigators his corrupt deals with Quiñones and the way bribes were distributed: 30 percent went to the general director of customs, José Chaparro Melgar, 20 percent to the airport customs director, 20 percent to Guillén, and 30 percent to other customs per-

23. Jones to S.S., Lima, May 5, 1968, no. 4922, box 2421. See also Jones to S.S., Lima, March 11, 1968, nos. 3932 and 3991, box 2421, RG 59, USNA.

24. García Rada, *Memorias,* 271–72.

25. "Oficios recibidos," Lima, November 19, 1968, file, no. 30, ff. 93–95, 110–11, and file 39, exp. PD-8; "Síntesis de las investigaciones efectuadas para la localización de Isaías Wolfenson," in file "Documentos caso Isaías Wolfenson Hleap," exp. GR-08, CIC, AGCP.

26. Jones to S.S., Lima, March 16, 1968, no. 4039, box 2421, RG 59, USNA.

27. "Preguntas efectuadas al Dr. Hernán Zapata," Lima, March 22, 1968, file, no. 33 (Sandro Mariátegui), exp. PD-8, CIC, AGCP.

sonnel.[28] Revelations of the Ripsa affair resulted in dismissal of the highly placed PIP director Javier Campos Montoya, who was charged with protecting contraband in exchange for bribes. In response to an article in *Caretas* magazine on his opulent lifestyle, Montoya told the press that he had won the lottery twice in 1958 and had been lucky with race track bets.[29] Montoya and Chaparro were formally indicted, taken to court, and found guilty of receiving bribes and abusing their posts.

The fiscal police also submitted to the congressional investigators detailed evidence of a contraband network comprising a majority of Lima's postal customs officers in collusion with local businessmen to undervalue sundry imports, forge documents, and evade import taxes. The accused included twenty postal customs employees, including chief administrator Luis Porras Tizón and treasurer Alberto Núñez Alarco, and an astounding array of owners and managers of well-known businesses such as Chicolandia, Hogar S.A., Otecsa, and Casa Fernández Hermanos, among many others.[30] In addition to the postal customs employees of Lima, dozens more were also fired from jobs as customs officers at the port of Callao and the international airport.[31] The entire customs administration was apparently thoroughly rotten.

In March 1968, *La Prensa* reported that twenty-nine imported packages, whose contents were labeled as parachute fabric and addressed to the army high command, contained instead rich fabrics destined for women's apparel. The interior minister, Vice Admiral Luis Ponce, asserted that such false press reports caused harm to the country. Ponce also told an U.S. embassy official that he thought the ongoing contraband scandal was being manipulated by APRA to discredit the administration and the armed forces.[32] At this crucial point, Belaúnde appointed General Francisco Morales Bermúdez as minister of finance not only to deal with the fiscal crisis but

28. "Manifestación del Sr. Víctor Guillén Acosta," Lima, April 7, 1968, unnumbered file, exp. GR-08, CIC, AGCP.

29. Jones to S.S., Lima, March 20, 1968, no. 4091, box 2421, RG 59, USNA.

30. "Atestado policial, no. 12 DIE: Por delitos de defraudación de rentas de aduana, corrupción de funcionarios y contra la fe pública cometidos por los empleados . . . y los comerciantes," Lima, March 31, 1968, file, no. 14 (Documentos sobre Aduana Postal), ff. 313–17, leg. PD-04, CIC, AGCP.

31. "Resolución suprema, no. 75-HC/DA," signed by Belaúnde and Morales Bermúdez, Lima, April 26, 1968, Oficio, no. 974-P, file "leyes," exp. PD-04, CIC, AGCP.

32. Jones to S.S., Lima, March 18, 1968, no. 4072, box 2421, RG 59, USNA; Vargas Haya, *Contrabando,* 140.

also to manage the executive branch's own customs and contraband inquiry. To discourage further investigation of the army's involvement in contraband scandals, War Minister Julio Doig, in presence of the army commander-in-chief General Juan Velasco Alvarado and chief of staff Roberto Dianderas, held a press conference to affirm that the army was not involved in the "parachutes" contraband. Doig also remarked that maneuvers of the extreme left sought to link the armed forces with contraband to discredit them.[33]

Unexpectedly, General Morales Bermúdez provided important assistance to the congressional commission. Fiscal police investigators had seized the correspondence of an import company, Novelty Supply, and its Panamanian associate, Peikard S.A., suspected of being engaged in extensive contraband. Morales Bermúdez surrendered the incriminating correspondence to the congressional commission.[34] To the general's and the commissioners' amazement, these letters, dated from December 1965 to January 1968, provided evidence of illegal business operations and implicated senior military officers in cover-ups and in facilitating contraband in exchange for favors and bribes. The main authors of these letters, businessmen José Trajtman and Sam Kardonsky, revealed their elaborate strategies to ensure protection and collusion from military and police officers through a web of personal contacts and intermediaries with privileged insider information. They discussed the convenience of granting "commissions" or bribes to one or another officer. The officers in question competed with each other for bribes, complained about inadequate bribes, and accepted "gifts" of imported washing machines and other appliances.[35]

The heart of these contraband operations was the merchandise imported under the cover of the military and police department stores or bazaars. All the military and police forces had been granted the privilege of importing a certain amount of tax-exempt merchandise for exclusive sale to military and police personnel. However, these bazaars had only a limited line of credit guaranteed by the central government. Several companies such as Novelty Supply offered much more private credit, which considerably enhanced the importing capability of the bazaars. Additionally, these companies obtained from bazaar managers and supervising generals and ministers huge quanti-

33. Jones to S.S., Lima, March 25, 1968, no. 4163, box 2421, RG 59, USNA; Vargas Haya, *Contrabando,* 137–43.

34. Vargas Haya, *Contrabando,* 67–70.

35. A selection of these letters are published in Vargas Haya, *Contrabando,* 76–100. See also Baella Tuesta, *El poder invisible* (Lima: Editorial Andina, 1977), 57–58.

ties of tax-exempt merchandise for sale to civilians. This illegal operation netted large profits to such firms in exchange for bribes to all the commanding officers involved.[36]

Among the most notorious of the senior military officers involved in the contraband scheme exploited by Trajtman and Kardonsky were Vice Admiral Ponce (future interior minister), General Italo Arbulú (former armed forces chief of staff), General Diógenes Montenegro, Colonels Ernesto Sánchez, Héctor Ríos, Clodomiro Rosas, and Lieutenant Colonels Tomás Carnero and Julio Portugal, among others. Instead of making these names public, the congressional commission forwarded the list of the military and police personnel mentioned in the letters to respective ministries for internal investigation. The ministries basically dismissed the charges and declared the suspects "innocent." A report received and signed by General Velasco Alvarado and forwarded to the congressional commissioners exonerated all suspected army officers implicated by the letters for "lack of proof."[37]

As a result of the congressional investigation of 1968, more than 300 people, including government officials and private businessmen, were prosecuted in Peruvian civil courts after the abrupt suspension of the commission's activities in October of that year.[38] Most of the accused military officers were prosecuted by military courts, and most of them were acquitted. According to a U.S. diplomatic source at the time, the scandal had shaken public confidence in Belaúnde and tarnished the prestige of the armed forces, causing strains within the military with great significance for domestic politics: "There can be no doubt that smuggling of luxury and other goods into Peru had become a massive, well organized business by the end of 1967, evidently operating with the knowledge and connivance of high civilian and military officials of the Peruvian government."[39]

In his 1976 book titled *Contrabando,* Vargas Haya developed estimates of the total cost of contraband and forgone tax revenue for the 1963–1967

36. Vargas Haya, *Contrabando,* 71–72.

37. General Alejandro Sánchez Salazar, Inspector General del Ejército, to General Juan Velasco Alvarado, Comandante General del Ejército, Lima, April 11, 1968, report no. 003-KI, in file 37 ("Informe de los ministerios [en] relación Trajman"), exp. PD-08, CIC, AGCP.

38. "Relación y estado de los procesos penales por delitos de contrabando, defraudación de rentas de aduana y peculado," signed by Ricardo Tirado, Procurador General de la República de Asuntos Especiales y Penales, Lima, July 11, 1968, file no. 30, exp. PD-8, CIC, AGCP. See also letters in Vargas Haya, *Contrabando,* esp. 77–78, 81–84, 90, and 98–99.

39. Siracusa to D.S., Lima, May 15, 1968, no. A-638, box 2420, RG 59, USNA.

period. To the declared value of taxable imports (47 billion soles), Vargas Haya added the estimated value of contraband and undervalued imports (70 billion soles), for a total of 117 billion soles. By applying an average tax rate of 70 percent to this total, import tax revenue should have totaled about 82 billion soles (16.4 billion per year). Given that actual import tax revenue totaled 23 billion soles, forgone revenue came to 59 billion soles (average 11.8 billion soles or $440 million per year).[40] Had the government collected even a third of this forgone income, the average annual trade deficit of 3 billion soles may have been eliminated.

Vargas Haya's estimates were based on a high average tax rate as well as a high average evasion rate. The same author developed different estimates in 1968. Thus, approximately 68 percent of customs duties went uncollected in 1967 alone due to contraband, undervaluation, and exemptions. Based on data obtained during the congressional investigations, he estimated import tax evasion rates of 45 percent for 1966, 32 percent in 1965, 24 percent in 1964, and 18 percent in 1963, for an average 37 percent per annum in 1963 through 1967.[41] Based on a more realistic average taxation rate of 50 percent and an evasion rate of 37 percent, the forgone tax revenue due to contraband and evasion would have amounted to 14 billion soles (or an average 2.8 billion soles/$104 million per year), almost enough to just cover the average annual deficit for the period. Consequently, according to these revised estimates, the cost of contraband activities facilitated by corruption during the Belaúnde regime was equivalent to approximately 14 to 15 percent of national government revenue for the 1963–1967 period.[42]

By April 1968, the political pressure on the members of the congressional investigating commission was enormous as rumors circulated that high-ranking individuals implicated in the contraband scandal may have included close relatives of Belaúnde, top military officers, and congressional leaders of various parties.[43] The investigating commission's members and their families were threatened by anonymous phone callers and suffered annoying inquiries

40. Vargas Haya, *Contrabando,* 159–62.

41. Jones to S.S., Lima, April 1, 1968, no. 4296, box 2421, RG 59, USNA.

42. Based on Banco Central de Reserva, *Cuentas Nacionales,* and tables 12, 14, and 18, in Pedro Pablo Kuczynski, *Democracia bajo presión económica: el primer gobierno de Belaúnde* (Lima: Mosca Azul, 1980), 102, 112, 232–34, n. 25. This author emphasizes the political damage caused by the contraband scandal, but dismisses its alleged magnitude and economic impact. He cites instead an estimate that suggests the cost of contraband during the years 1963–1967 was insignificant.

43. Jones to S.S., Lima, April 10, 1968, no. 4356, box 2421, RG 59, USNA.

by other authorities. *El Comercio* claimed for the prompt release of the names of high-ranking individuals involved in the scandal.[44] The military authorities escalated the pressure particularly against Christian Democrat Rafael Cubas Vinatea, a leading member of the investigating commission.

At this crucial moment, General Doig surprisingly announced in an oblique press statement that the military high command was dropping its traditional veto on Haya de la Torre's presidential possibilities. This unleashed the speculation that a deal was being made between the military and APRA to halt the contraband investigations and avoid revealing the names of implicated military officers. Vargas Haya denied the existence of such a deal and asserted that the congressional investigation would continue undeterred.[45] However, as a disciplined member of the APRA party many of the political decisions were beyond his control since they were taken by Haya de la Torre and the party secretary, Armando Villanueva del Campo. The PDC and Cornejo Chávez in the Senate warned the congressional investigators about their apparent sidestepping and denounced a "political deal" being forged to quash the contraband investigations; Cubas Vinatea resigned as a member of the contraband commission.[46] It appears that APRA was being forced to back down in the midst of growing concern about a military coup. By mid-May, the contraband investigations seemed to have diminished considerably, with further measures against government officials considered very unlikely.[47]

The contraband scandal aggravated the political crisis of the regime and the parties and factions supporting it. Finance Minister Morales Bermúdez resigned in May, stating that "party political considerations" had dangerously delayed a solution to the fiscal and economic crisis. In Congress, APRA had opposed an increase in gasoline taxes, a crucial part of Morales Bermúdez's fiscal recovery program. The military leaders had also quietly withdrawn their support for Morales Bermúdez because of the role he played in the contraband investigations.[48] The divided Christian Democrats

44. Jones to S.S., Lima, April 17 and 18, 1968, nos. 4562 and 4579, box 2421, RG 59, USNA.

45. Jones to S.S., Lima, April 23, 1968, no. 4674, box 2422, RG 59, USNA; Vargas Haya, *Contrabando,* 145–49.

46. Jones to S.S., Lima, April 29, 1968, no. 4773, box 2421, box 2421, RG 59, USNA; Baella Tuesta, *Poder invisible,* 58.

47. Siracusa to S.S., Lima, May 17, 1968, no. 5108, box 2421, RG 59, USNA.

48. Siracusa to S.S., Lima, May 22 and 23, 1968, nos. 5200 and 5201, box 2421, RG 59, USNA.

broke their alliance with AP over issues of policy principles. Even the
APRA–UNO coalition disintegrated. Finally, AP itself split in two following a clash regarding the IPC between the termocéfalo faction headed by
Edgardo Seoane and the pro-regime majority. However, Belaúnde had
found in "Carlista" Ulloa, appointed minister of finance and prime minister, a valuable political aide for striking a temporary deal with APRA to
solve some of the fiscal problems. Under these extremely critical political
circumstances, it was in APRA's interest to shore up Belaúnde temporarily
until the 1969 elections that were guaranteed to give Haya a long-awaited
victory.[49]

The contraband scandal had subsided, but left in its wake a profound dissatisfaction and lack of public confidence in the regime. Belaúnde's government had hoped that burying the affair would put an end to its public hu-
miliation.[50] However, another scandal, this time related to oil and the IPC
broke out. IPC executives had approached Belaúnde and expressed the desire to reach a final agreement on the La Brea y Pariñas problem. Previous
disputes were quickly negotiated so as to score badly needed political points
for Belaúnde. It appeared as if the issue that arose several decades earlier,
largely because of corruption in previous regimes, was about to be resolved.
A contract would sanction the surrender of La Brea y Pariñas surface and
subsurface rights to the Peruvian state. The contract was signed in a hurry
by Fernando Espinosa, general manager of the IPC, and Carlos Loret de
Mola for the state-run Empresa Petrolera Fiscal (EPF). However, weeks
later Loret de Mola announced in a televised broadcast what would become
the final crisis of the beleaguered Belaúnde regime. The EPF president reported a page in the original contract was missing (the infamous page
eleven), on which he had signed and stipulated in his own handwriting the
basis for the price of the oil EPF would sell to the IPC for refining.

Some have questioned whether such a page ever existed or the likelihood
of accidental loss, while others blame Loret de Mola's political motivations,
ambitions, irresponsibility, or naiveté as the cause of the scandal.[51] One

49. Kuczynski, *Democracia bajo presión,* 293; Masterson, *Militarism,* 223.

50. "Asunto golpe de Estado en el Perú," information note to M.A.E., October 3,
1968, no. 54, leg. R-10,671, exp. 11, AGMAE: "El escándalo ocasionado hace algunos
meses por el descubrimiento de una amplísima defraudación al Fisco por contrabando
dejó a la vista la corrupción imperante en altas esferas gubernamentales y militares. El
gobierno, en definitiva, echó tierra al asunto, sin que nadie se considere satisfecho por
la detención de algunas altas personalidades, incluso algunas de la intimidad del Presidente, cuyo prestigio sufrió, aunque su integridad personal quedara a salvo."

51. Pinelo, *Multinational Corporation,* 139–44; Kuczynski, *Democracia bajo presión,* 286–93; García Rada, *Memorias,* 309–10.

thing was certain: past corruption scandals and the distrust they had generated weighed heavily on public perceptions at the time.[52] The uproar about the "disappearance" of page eleven and accusations of abject surrender or "entreguismo" to the IPC were, according to all evidence, part of a partisan campaign that accused the Belaúnde regime of treasonous corruption. The charge was in all particulars unfounded but it had immense political repercussions. A group of military conspirators took full advantage of the scandal to publicly justify and execute a coup that brought drastic changes to the political, social, and economic makeup of the country and its institutions.

Military "Revolution"

As tanks besieged the presidential palace at the onset of the coup to oust Belaúnde on October 3, 1968, special military detachments occupied Congress. A few days later army troops sequestered and sacked the congressional contraband commission's offices and documents.[53] These developments had a devastating impact on Deputy Vargas Haya, who was deprived of his congressional seat and access to documentary evidence to finalize ongoing contraband investigations. His party, APRA, was also denied a sure victory in the 1969 elections that were never held.

Vargas Haya decided to risk writing a book to document the findings of the contraband commission and publish damning evidence against the military. In April 1970, secret police agents broke into the premises of the plant where the book was being printed to confiscate and subsequently destroy the book's entire first edition. Vargas Haya claimed that this attack on freedom of expression was ordered by General Velasco. Years later these assertions were confirmed in statements to reporters by a former interior minister. The book's second edition was released only in 1976 when Velasco was no longer president.[54]

The military officers who engineered the coup intended to remain in power for a long time. This was not an ordinary "bridge coup," serving as a

---

52. Manuel Alabart to M.A.E., Lima, October 8, 1968, no. 1044, leg. R-10,671, exp. 11, AGMAE. "La devaluación del sol primero, el escándalo del contrabando luego, las dificultades económicas, finalmente las irregularidades y ligerezas cometidas con ocasión del contrato del petróleo con la I.P.C., habían acorralado prácticamente al Presidente."

53. Norman Gall, "Peru: The Master is Dead," *Dissent* 18 (1971): 281–20, esp. 309; Baella Tuesta, *Poder invisible,* 57.

54. Vargas Haya, *Contrabando,* 25–34; *Defraudadores y contrabandistas* (Lima: Nueva Educación, 1980), 71–80; *Perú: 184 años de corrupción e impunidad* (Lima: Editorial Rocío, 2005), 300–8; Baella Tuesta, *Poder invisible,* 55–61.

transitional government from one civilian, or constitutionally mandated, regime to the next. Velasco and his close advisors said there were four main causes of military intervention against democracy: the imperatives of defending national "dignity" injured by the IPC and the "page-eleven" scandal, introducing socioeconomic structural reforms, halting the dangerous deterioration of civilian political conditions that opened the gates to APRA's electoral victory as well as communist insurrection, and reversing the "moral degradation" of the country.[55] Conventional accounts of the historical role of the 1968 military regime have underscored these official arguments.[56]

In contrast, Vargas Haya consistently argued that the coup leaders had two major objectives: to bury forever evidence of the military and Velasco's personal involvement in the contraband scandal, and to frustrate once more APRA's access to power.[57] Vargas Haya provided some telling, although necessarily partial, evidence to back this contention. His partisan support of the dogged Aprista opposition to the military regime, as well as the existence of other more likely institutional and ideological causes of the 1968 coup, can be pointed out as arguments against Vargas Haya's explanation. However, diverse independent sources indicate that corruption and patronage did have a prominent place among the causes and consequences of the coup and of the political foundations of the "revolutionary" regime. Vargas Haya and others have argued that the IPC and page-eleven affair was just a pretext for destroying Peruvian democracy. Moreover, political analysts agree that the tough "nationalist" stance against the IPC was used by Velasco and his faction to consolidate their control of the regime and displace other more moderate military factions.[58]

55. Velasco's speech at the Air Force Academy, printed in *El Peruano,* November 29, 1968, mentioned in Jones to S.S., Lima, November 29, 1968, no. 8666, box 2418, RG 59, USNA. In conversation between a U.S. embassy officer and Enrique León Velaŕde, close advisor and crony of Velasco, Velarde cited the following as the main reasons for the coup: economic and financial mismanagement, moral decay, unsatisfactory and scandalous IPC settlement, disintegration of parties opening the way for APRA victory, fear of eventual communist takeover, and structural reforms that might take ten years to implement. Jones to S.S., Lima, October 9, 1968, no. 7811, box 2423, RG 59, USNA. See also report on meeting of Velasco and U.S. Ambassador Jones, in Jones to S.S., Lima, November 6, 1968, no. 8336, box 2421, RG 59, USNA.

56. See Luis Pásara, "El docenio militar," in *Historia del Perú,* ed. Juan Mejía Baca (Lima: Editorial Juan Mejía Baca, 1980), vol. 12: 325–433; Henry Pease, *El ocaso del poder oligárquico: lucha política en la escena oficial* (Lima: Desco, 1977); and Dirk Kruijt, *Revolution by decree: Peru, 1968–1975* (Amsterdam: Thela, 1994).

57. Vargas Haya, *Defraudadores,* 57–58; *Contrabando,* 153–57.

58. Vargas Haya, *Perú: 184 años,* 289; *Defraudadores,* 26; George Philip, *The Rise and Fall of the Peruvian Military Radicals, 1968–1976* (London: Athlone Press, 1978), 88–91.

An early "moralization" campaign in 1968 was used to discredit democratic institutions and former civilian officials of the Belaúnde administration. Velasco and his radical followers launched a harsh attack against the alleged incompetence, illegal enrichment, and embezzlement of deposed officials who also allegedly allowed unfair enrichment of foreign interests. They were branded "bad" Peruvians who had betrayed their country.[59] Although no ad hoc tribunal to impose sanctions was formed, as happened during the Sánchez Cerro dictatorship of 1930–1931, the military government assumed legislative and even judicial powers to denounce, charge, and prosecute several former ministers for graft related to the IPC scandal, among other charges.[60] Velasco also leveled threats against former congressmen to deal with what he termed the "parliamentary scandal" of misused public funds.[61] The interior minister, General Armando Artola, charged that serious irregularities had been detected in Congress and at the Junta de Asistencia Nacional under the leadership of Belaúnde's sister. These charges were not fully proven or were found to be baseless.[62]

A special commission was established in early 1969 to investigate alleged illegal transfers of $17 million in IPC repatriated profits allowed by the Central Bank and the Finance Ministry after the 1968 coup. This commission, led by Vice Admiral Enrique Carbonel Crespo and comprised of radical civilian advisors, dismissed the Central Reserve Bank's top managers and terminated its independence. In this way, Velasco neutralized journalistic attacks against the integrity of his "tough" IPC policy, forced the resignation and subsequent prosecution of the moderate finance minister, General Angel Valdivia, and strengthened the regime's control key financial institutions.[63] The head of the Carbonel commission, a former navy intelligence chief directly involved in the navy's contraband scandal, was a close friend and collaborator of Velasco. Unlike other vulnerable navy of-

59. Velasco speech, *El Peruano,* November 29, 1968.

60. The former ministers arrested and prosecuted over the IPC scandal included Carriquiry, Hercelles, Ulloa, Arias Stella, Calmell, and Hoyos Osores. Jones to S.S., Lima, October 8, 1968, no. 7765, box 2421; and October 21, 1968, no. 8040, box 2422, RG 59, USNA. Other former ministers and officials facing other charges included Carlos Velarde, Sandro Mariátegui, Fernando Schwalb, Enrique Tola, Octavio Mongrut, José Navarro Grau, Luis Vier, Augusto Semsch Terry, Pedro Pablo Kuczynski, and Carlos Rodríguez Pastor.

61. Meeting of Velasco and Spanish Ambassador Manuel Alabart, Alabart to M.A.E., Lima, October 22, 1968, no. 1085, leg. R-10,671, exp. 11, AGMAE.

62. Jones to S.S., Lima, October 21, 1968, no. 8048, box 2421; and October 24, 1968, no. 8108, box 2422, RG 59, USNA.

63. Jones to S.S., Lima, March 20, 1969, no. 1988, April 10, 1969, no. 2550, and May 1, 1969, no. 3127, box 2422, RG 59, USNA.

ficers involved in the scandal and later purged for political expediency, Carbonel was spared and later promoted to chair the Joint Chiefs of Staff. Thus, the army with Velasco at the helm dominated the navy as well as the air force whose customary order of promotions was manipulated by Velasco on behalf of his cousin, Lieutenant Colonel Eduardo Camino Velasco, and other officers supportive of the dictator.[64]

The consolidation of Velasco's faction in power brought about the emergence of the leftist "Earthquake" generation of colonels and generals bent on implementing radical structural reforms. The most conspicuous among them were the energy and mines minister, General Jorge Fernández Maldonado, and the head of the vertical corporatist organization SINAMOS, General Leonidas Rodríguez Figueroa, among others. These radical ministers appointed, as their closest paid advisors and high-ranking officials, several leftist civilians who had been prominent in the long political and legal campaign against the IPC. Some of these advisors had risen to unprecedented political influence by infiltrating the military academy and the CAEM, and orchestrating fanatical "nationalist" campaigns in support of Velasco's confiscatory IPC policy. This group of advisors included Alberto Ruiz Eldredge, Alfonso Benavides Correa, Germán Tito Gutiérrez, Guillermo García Montúfar, Efraín Ruiz Caro, Augusto Zimmerman (nephew of polemic former senator Alfonso Montesinos), and former guerrilla leader Héctor Béjar, among many others.[65]

Leading members of these privileged leftist advisors, including former congressmen and public figures, had received illegal funds from the Cuban government since 1961 to subvert Peruvian democracy and its institutions and organize political campaigns such as the La Brea y Pariñas–IPC crusade. Many received monthly stipends of thousands of soles. Although obscured by ideological "revolutionary" justification, foreign payments to Peruvian officials and influential people constituted flagrant cases of corruption at the cost of national interests. According to the Spanish chargé d'affaires in Havana, influential journalists such as Francisco Igartúa, Francisco Moncloa, and Ismael Frías, among others, may also have received

---

64. Philip, *Military Radicals,* 84–85, 91–92; Gall, "Peru: The Master Is Dead," 309; Vargas Haya, *Defraudadores,* 107–108; Jones to S.S., Lima, November 4, 1968, no. 8259, box 2421.

65. Jones to S.S., Lima, October 21, 1968, no. 8048, box 2421; March 3, 1969, nos. 1356, 1357, 1358, 1359, 1360, 1362, box 2419, RG 59, USNA; Pinelo, *Multinational Corporation,* 95; Vargas Haya, *Defraudadores,* 120–21.

Cuban money. These journalists contributed to various deceptions propagated in pro-Velasco media campaigns.[66]

The leftist advisors and journalists formed a network of associates who, along with the military leaders, distributed jobs and favors among their ideological followers and friends. Some senior leftist advisors and confidants advocated intimate collaboration with the Soviet Union. One of these influential advisors, who controlled two government newspapers, was paid (at least $5,000 in 1971) by the KGB to influence government decisions and public opinion. The KGB counted on nine such strategic and confidential contacts in 1972, many enticed by gifts, money, and trips to the Soviet Union. The Peruvian intelligence service, the Servicio Nacional de Inteligencia (SIN), also formally cooperated with its Soviet counterpart, which was eager to neutralize U.S. espionage networks.[67] The apparent successes of Soviet and Cuban covert influence, propaganda, and disinformation were countered by competing CIA operations in Peru.

Captain Vladimiro Montesinos, nephew of Alfonso Montesinos and cousin of the intellectual and financially troubled Augusto Zimmerman, chief of the National Information Office (ONI), also had access to favors distributed by the leftist network.[68] However, Vladimiro Montesinos worked for U.S. intelligence. His contacts with the U.S. embassy in Lima and his role as a confidential informant have been confirmed by documentary evidence. For this reason, as well as for traveling to Washington, DC, as a guest of the U.S. government without Peruvian official authorization, he was ar-

---

66. Ramón Oyarzun (encargado de negocios, Embajada de España en La Habana) to M.A.E., Havana, February 25, 1969, leg. R-10,671, exp. 12, AGMAE. "[A]djunto remito a V.E. una relación de ciudadanos peruanos a quienes el gobierno de Cuba pudiera haber subvencionado en años pasados [desde 1961], para llevar a cabo en su país campañas políticas y actividades subversivas." See also Pinelo, *Multinational Corporation,* 83–84, 94, citing correspondence of Cuban Ambassador Luis Ricardo Alonso Fernández, raided by anti-Castro Cubans in Lima, and passed on to Peruvian authorities; and Peru, Cámara de Senadores, *Diario de los Debates,* session January 4, 1961.

67. Christopher Andrew and Vasili Mitrokhin, *The World Was Going Our Way: The KGB and the Battle for the Third World* (New York: Basic Books, 2005), 62–63, citing Mitrokhin Archive documents K-22, 42, 21, 188, and 233. Although the recruited senior advisor's name appears in Mitrokhin's notes (classified documents held by the U.K. Secret Intelligence Service or M16), no such name has been printed in this eye-opening publication due to classification constraints negotiated with a Whitehall (U.K. government offices) "interdepartmental working group."

68. Jones to S.S., Lima, March 3, 1969, no. 1362, box 2419; Belcher to D.S., Lima, November 7, 1969, no. A-405, box 2421, RG 59, USNA; Vargas Haya, *Defraudadores,* 335–36; Baella Tuesta, *Poder invisible,* 257–59, 261–63.

rested in 1977. He was described as a CIA agent who collected information from among the leftist advisory entourage of key generals, ministers, and former intelligence chiefs Edgardo Mercado Jarrín, Enrique Gallegos Venero, and Fernández Maldonado.[69]

Among nonleftist networks of civilians, prominent conservatives such as Beltrán and the Miró Quesadas lent initial support to the military regime's nationalist policies.[70] However, these and other conservative politicians and businessmen were soon alarmed by the regime's turn to the left. However, one particular group of influential friends, the so-called Altecos,[71] remained faithful to the Velasco regime almost until the end. The most conspicuous member of this group was wealthy politician and playboy Enrique León Velarde, a close friend to Velasco. León Velarde had crucial patronage relationships with civilian interest groups and was instrumental in the appointment (*dedocracia*) of mayors in Lima's key district municipalities. The selection of mayors, in which León Velarde exercised his influence in favor of close friends and Velasco's Alteco "social cronies," represented a "throwback to corrupt practices which characterized local government of pre-Belaúnde era."[72]

León Velarde, a real estate and finance mogul and owner of purebred horses, offered Velasco access to the local glitterati at parties in private mansions and yachts. He was an important political advisor of populist inclinations who was appointed Interior Ministry undersecretary in 1971. From this strategic position, León Velarde solved many problems for his cronies and friends through his direct access to Velasco. In his candid and scintillating

69. Dean to S.S., Lima, April 7, 1977, no. 2813, unclassified U.S. Department of State (USDS) copy in Peru Documentation Project (PDP), box 1, file Montesinos trip to D.C., National Security Archive, Gellman Library, George Washington University (hereafter NSA); José A. Fernández Salvatecci, *La revolución peruana: yo acuso* (Lima: Editorial El Siglo, 1978), 193–96; Sally Bowen and Jane Holligan, *El espía imperfecto: la telaraña siniestra de Vladimiro Montesinos* (Lima: Peisa, 2003), 56–58.

70. Philip, *Military Radicals*, 86–87; Vargas Haya, *Defraudadores*, 49–50.

71. Name given to Velasco's socialites who participated in gatherings often extending beyond lunch into the late hours of the night, derived from "almuerzo, te y comida" (al-te-co). On the bond connecting participants of this festive custom, a U.S. diplomat wrote: "As President Velasco enjoys lavish parties and relaxation early into the morning hours among jovial drinking companions, social relationship between Velasco and [Miguel Angel] Testino is a close one." Jones to S.S., Lima, March 3, 1969, no. 1364, box 2419, RG 59, USNA.

72. E.W. Clark to D.S., Lima, December 17, 1969, no. A-466, box 2423, RG 59, USNA.

memoirs, León Velarde recounts the special favors and inside gossip of the Velasco years. Without appearing to be aware of the political, institutional, social, and moral distortions introduced by Velasco's "revolution," León Velarde painted an apologetic yet telling picture of the damaging legacy of military dictatorship for institutional curbs to rampant corruption.[73]

Among those favored by Velasco, his Aprista brother-in-law Luis Gonzales Posada was placed on the payroll of several state enterprises and acted as director of the mismanaged social welfare fund (seguro social).[74] All these patronage networks provided temporary political support, in exchange for favors and collusion in corrupt arrangements, to a regime that was never really able to rally and organize a mass political following. This organic failure eventually eroded the regime's hold on power in the midst of generalized institutional decay.[75]

Patronage and corruption during the military regime benefited from radical institutional change that demolished the weak foundations of political democracy in Peru. This transformation has had a lasting legacy. The new rules and practices introduced by the military between 1968 and 1979, together with new state enterprises, ministries, and organizations, bred over-

73. Enrique León Velarde, *¿El Chino y yo jodimos al Perú?: confesiones de Enrique León Velarde* (Lima: N.p., 2000), 68, 182, 193, 200–2, 211. In Jones to S.S., Lima, October 9, 1968, no. 7811, box 2423, and March 3, 1969, no. 1363, box 2419, RG 59, USNA, 38-year-old León Velarde, also director of the Jockey Club and mayor of the slum district of San Martín de Porras, is described as "rakish, agile and interesting," displaying unusual frankness, and as a "ruthless, ambitious political opportunist [who is] . . . personally attractive in a raffish manner who despite his personal amorality has many friends. His interest in the poor appears to be based largely upon his desire for political power base."

74. Philip, *Military Radicals,* 152; Vargas Haya, *Defraudadores,* 358, and *Perú: 184 años,* 295. Also, a "relative of President Velasco's wife, occupying 'a high position' in the administration, was exposed as, allegedly, a CIA agent." Andrew and Mitrokhin, *World Was Going,* 64.

75. On the conundrum of insufficient political participation, divisiveness among supporters (in conditions of uncertainty, opting for personal enrichment while in office), and entrepreneurial apathy and opportunism that challenged the radical military dictatorship, see Philip, *Military Radicals,* 167; Gall, "Master Is Dead," 311–12; Peter Cleaves and Martin Scurrah, *Agriculture, Bureaucracy, and Military Government in Peru* (Ithaca, NY: Cornell University Press, 1980), 44, 49; Bernardo Sorj, "Public Enterprises and the Question of the State Bourgeoisie, 1969–1976," in *Military Reformism and Social Classes: The Peruvian Experience, 1968–80,* ed. D. Booth and B. Sorj (New York: St. Martin's Press, 1983), 72–93, esp. 87–89; and Anthony Ferner, "The Industrialists and the Peruvian Development Model," in *Military Reformism,* ed. Booth and Sorj, 40–71, esp. 66.

all inefficiency and abuse that hid or protected corruption.[76] Among the multitude of these institutional deformations, just a few provide telling and crucial examples.

The organization of the state was restructured through a series of decree-laws (*decretos leyes*) and "organic" laws that enhanced centralization, executive power, and the personal power of Velasco and his successor Morales Bermúdez. The presidential committee of advisors (COAP) became a strategic decision-making organ. It had power to legislate but lacked the ability to centralize implementation, which was subject to often contradictory and inconsistent interpretations of vastly autonomous and capricious ministers.[77] The reorganization of the judiciary through the illegal and unconstitutional Organic Law of Judicial Power (decree 18060) in effect deprived the country of a truly independent judicial system, since judges were appointed and subject to confirmation by the executive branch. The lawyers who contributed to this damaging act against judicial autonomy were the well-known leftist legal advisors Ruiz Eldredge, Benavides Correa, Alfonso Montesinos, and Christian Democrat Cornejo Chávez, all of whom received compensation, such as ambassadorships or profitable government posts at home. The triggering of this judicial demolition was the arrest of a Supreme Court judge who, making use of his diplomatic passport, had tried to smuggle diamonds into the United States: The military government used Judge Félix Portocarrero's shameful affair to charge the Supreme Court with corrupt practices.[78] Other experienced and honest judges were thus dismissed and replaced by mediocre and often corrupt magistrates. Foreign observers concluded that the rule of law had in effect been abolished. Mistrust of the judiciary increased and became a more or less permanent feature of public opinion.[79]

76. Vargas Haya, *Defraudadores,* 260–62, 267–71.

77. Jones to S.S., Lima, April 3, 1969, no. 2377, box 2421; Hughes (Director of Intelligence) to S.S., Washington, DC, August 11, 1969, RAR-3, box 2421, RG 59, USNA; Ernest H. Preeg, *The Evolution of a Revolution: Peru and Its Relations with the United States, 1968–1980* (Washington, DC: NPA Committee on Changing International Realities, 1981), 9.

78. Jones to S.S., Lima, May 6, 1969, no. 3231, box 2418, RG 59, USNA.

79. Belcher to S.S., Lima, December 24, 1969, no. 8073, box 2422; and F. V. Ortiz to D.S., Lima, December 31, 1969, no. A-481, box 2421, RG 59, USNA; García Rada, *Memorias,* 250, 259–62, 323–40; Luis Pásara, *Jueces, justicia y poder en el Perú* (Lima: Centro de Estudios de Derecho y Sociedad, 1982), 27; prologue by Alfonso Baella Tuesta to Gonzalo Ortiz de Zevallos's *Entreguismo: los contratos petroleros de 1974* (Lima: Grafiser, 1978), xxix.

The most conspicuous case of economic bungling was the inept administration of the fishing industry by corrupt state officials that led to overfishing, expropriation, and the demolition of entrepreneurial capacity in this key productive sector. Moreover, the resources of the fishing sector administered by Pescaperu were used to promote reactionary political patronage at the expense of workers and consumers.[80] As a result, Peruvians had significantly less fish to eat and the once buoyant fishmeal export industry was seriously impaired. Likewise, the 1969 agrarian reform, much praised in certain quarters for vertically redistributing land more equitably, contributed to a decline in agricultural productivity that reduced strategic agro-exports and enhanced dependency on food imports without solving the problems of the vast majority of agricultural sector workers (smallholders and landless peasants comprised 85 percent of the agrarian labor force). Abuses and graft in implementing the reform and managing the newly formed agricultural cooperatives were not uncommon. The inclusion of large agro-exporting complexes in the expropriation scheme bankrupted native capitalists such as the Prado and Aspíllaga groups that represented business concerns of diversified portfolios beyond export agriculture.[81] This development was hailed as the successful twilight of the "oligarchy," a much manipulated term obscuring the significance of interest groups, vested interests, and corruption networks that exercised decisive influence in modern Peruvian history.

Most state enterprises such as Petroperu, Mineroperu, EPSA, Pescaperu, Sedapal, and CPT were inefficient. As part of a vicious cycle of poor administrative and payment practices, these enterprises consistently accumulated financial losses, which the government financed through credit expan-

80. Carlos Malpica, *Anchovetas y tiburones* (Lima: Editora Runamarka, 1976), 7, 34–36; Vargas Haya, *Defraudadores,* 274–78. Inept handling of the ecology, which was destroyed by overfishing, is exemplified by the appointment of the inexperienced Vice Admiral Luis Ponce as chief of the Instituto del Mar. Ponce, as former interior minister under Belaúnde, had tried to hush up the 1968 contraband scandal. Jones to D.S., Lima, January 17, 1969, no. A-24, box 2419, RG 59, USNA. See also Sorj, "Public Enterprises," 87.

81. Vargas Haya, *Defraudadores,* 178–89; Philip, *Military Radicals,* 132–33; José Luis Rénique, *La batalla por Puno: conflicto agrario y nación en los Andes peruanos* (Lima: Instituto de Estudios Peruanos / Sur / Cepes, 2004), 171; A. Eugene Havens, Susana Lastarria-Cornhiel, and Gerardo Otero, "Class Struggle and the Agrarian Reform Process," in *Military Reformism,* ed. D. Booth and B. Sorj (New York: St. Martin's Press, 1983), 14–39, esp. 34; Charlotte Burenius, *Testimonio de un fracaso: Huando, habla el sindicalista Zózimo Torres* (Lima: Instituto de Estudios Peruanos, 2001).

sion and foreign borrowing. Deficit financing at the state enterprise level, however, offered excellent cover for civil servants' personal gains at the expense of the majority of citizens and taxpayers.[82] The monstrous growth in foreign debt was in part due to inefficient administration coupled with graft. The military's flawed oil policy was also criticized by a few individuals who, after raising the charges of surrendering national oil resources to Japanese and other foreign concerns, were persecuted and deported.[83]

The initial ideological and repressive control exercised over the press became absolute with the expropriation of all means of mass communication in 1974. Perhaps more than ever before, salaried journalists, dependent on the state for their income, sold their pens and consciences. They engaged in defamation of the political opposition and psychosocial campaigns to manipulate public opinion. The few independently minded journalists and media outlet owners were deported if they stepped over the line.[84] Most importantly, the watchdog role of a free press against injustice, abuse, and corruption disappeared.

Under the distorted institutional conditions imposed by the military regime, the uncovering of corruption scandals was also limited by dictatorial control of the judiciary and the means of mass communication. In the absence of the legislative power, congressional investigations into blatant cases of public sector graft were impossible. Moreover, a general attitude of partisan collusion prevented potential whistle-blowers from unveiling corruption. Fear of retribution and repression silenced many voices. Political and economic culture had changed so dramatically, and incentives and disincentives were so distorted, that authorities patently had conceptual difficulties in recognizing their own corruption. Further research focused on public administration from 1968 through 1980 will undoubtedly uncover abysmal new depths in the history of corruption in Peru. Nevertheless, there are some well-documented cases of corruption scandals during the military

82. Daniel Schydlowsky and Juan Wicht, *Anatomía de un fracaso económico: Perú, 1968–1978* (Lima: Centro de Investigación de la Universidad del Pacífico, 1979), 8, 51; Arturo Salazar Larraín, *La herencia de Velasco, 1968–1975: el pueblo quedó atrás* (Lima: Desa, 1977), 21, 174; Alfredo Ferrand Inurritegui and Arturo Salazar Larraín, *La década perdida* (Lima: Sociedad de Industrias, 1980), 39; Alfred H. Saulniers, *Public Enterprises in Peru: Public Sector Growth and Reform* (Boulder, CO: Westview Press, 1988), 169, 196–97.

83. Ortiz de Zevallos, *Entreguismo,* 53, 79.

84. The case of Enrique Zileri and *Caretas:* Jones to S.S., May 26 and June 19, 1969, nos. 3842 and 4541, box 2423, RG 59, USNA.

regime that can be cited as proof of the underlying general state of unconstrained corruption.

Through interviews with former military officers, a specialist in Peruvian military studies learned that the extended use and abuse of power had the effect of substantially increasing corruption among the armed forces and its institutions.[85] One of the most guarded and secret privileges of the military, the purchase of weapons and materiel abroad, allowed substantial kickbacks that enriched a few officers and commanders. The official report regarding the apparently advantageous purchase of Soviet military equipment and tanks at low-interest, long-term financing, was never published.[86] Likewise, military officers enjoyed perquisites such as the use of cars with chauffeurs and free gasoline, which annoyed average civilians. The stricter protectionist policies adopted by the military government did not reduce contraband. On the contrary, the smuggling of prohibited imports, such as automobiles, appliances, and color TVs, patently increased.[87]

In October 1974, a huge embezzlement scandal involving EPSA, the state enterprise in charge of domestic market food retailing, erupted in the controlled press. More than a hundred employees were implicated and arrested and the minister of commerce, Luis Barandiarán, was forced to resign. This form of graft touched a chord among average Peruvians because it affected basic food staples, and thus survival of the impoverished population. The scandal also forced the resignation and subsequent imprisonment of the minister of agriculture, General Enrique Valdez Angulo. Charges were later reduced and eventually dropped due to difficulties experienced by prosecutors in ascertaining EPSA's irregularities separate from the overall interventionist, deficit-generating, and debt-financing system.[88]

The most conspicuous case of corruption involving a senior military officer was that of General Javier Tantaleán Vanini, who ran the state fisheries enterprise, Pescaperu. Funds earmarked for the enterprise were spent on

85. Masterson, *Militarism,* 265–66. See also Philip, *Military Radicals,* 152.

86. Philip, *Military Radicals,* 266; Vargas Haya, *Defraudadores,* 259–61; Julio Velarde and Martha Rodríguez, *Impacto macro económico de los gastos militares en el Perú, 1960–1987* (Lima: Centro de Investigación de la Universidad del Pacífico / Apep, 1989), 165–67.

87. Vargas Haya, *Defraudadores,* 92–94; Belcher to D.S., Lima, August 14, 1972, no. A-295, box 2542, RG 59, USNA.

88. Philip, *Military Radicals,* 140, citing articles in *Oiga* and *Nueva Crónica;* Vargas Haya, *Defraudadores,* 179, 337; Cleaves and Scurrah, *Agriculture, Bureaucracy, and Military Government,* 191, 210–16, citing *Nueva Crónica* (October 17, 1974), *El Comercio* (October 19, 1974), and *El Peruano* (November 14–15, 1971).

travel in private jets, soccer teams, and luxuries. Pescaperu deficits were virtually ignored, since it was known that the state would cover the deficits through generating new debt. Toward the end of the Velasco presidency, Tantaleán and other corrupt military officers and ministers had privileged access to the president. This reactionary group, known as La Misión, had displaced the Altecos as Velasco's inner circle, in part due to a temporary but serious disagreement between León Velarde and Velasco. In the meantime, Tantaleán, related to Velasco through the Gonzales Posada political family, was considered to be Velasco's most likely successor. La Misión supported the physically and mentally declining Velasco with the expectation of taking advantage of their closing window of opportunity for self-enrichment through graft.[89]

When Velasco was finally ousted from power by General Morales Bermúdez in 1975, Tantaleán and other Velasquistas, including León Velarde and several other Altecos, were imprisoned and their bank accounts and property embargoed. The isolation of these rightwing men and their wealth was carried out by the new administration mainly to curb nearly unmanageable corruption in its crucial early days.[90]

Morales Bermúdez then proceeded to undermine leftist groups in the midst of a truly difficult political and economic situation. Like Velasco, the new military president tried and failed to establish a political support base until it became obvious that he needed a constitutional exit strategy. Morales Bermúdez opted to implement a well-planned transitional schedule (*cronograma*) lasting three years to accomplish the transfer of power to civilians and the return of the military to their barracks. Social unrest, although harshly repressed, gave way to promised elections for a Constituent Assembly in 1978, as well as general elections after the completion of the new constitution.

However, in the 1975–1979 period, Morales Bermúdez enjoyed authoritarian powers similar to those exercised by Velasco. In fact, deportations of politicians, celebrities, and journalists of the left and right increased. Media censorship, public sector dysfunction, and economic inefficiency continued with little modification. The deteriorating economic situation fueled by increasing budget deficits and foreign debt was addressed through controversial economic stabilization policies and debt refinancing. Public

89. Philip, *Military Radicals,* 152–53; Alfonso Baella Tuesta, *El miserable* (Lima: Editorial Andina, 1978), 25–29.

90. Vargas Haya, *Defraudadores,* 336–37; León Velarde, *El Chino,* 213, 221, 237.

deficits declined to single-digit percentages. A revamped policy for encouraging "nontraditional" manufactures exports, especially textiles, had some initial positive results thanks to tax and financial incentives and subsidies in the form of the Certex (Certificados de Reintegro Tributario a las Exportaciones), which soon became mechanisms for graft by fake exporters.[91]

The military regime made clear that the Constituent Assembly should incorporate the "achievements" of the "revolution." An implicit agreement was established between Morales Bermúdez and the resuscitated political parties, mainly APRA and the Partido Popular Cristiano (PPC), which formed the majority in the new assembly. As long as each step of the transition was accomplished, the cronograma would not be altered. Morales Bermúdez expended great effort in mending the longtime feud between the military and APRA. To its ultimate political advantage, Belaúnde's AP steered clear from this onerous compromise with the military regime by not participating in the elections for the Constituent Assembly.

With the expectation of winning the 1980 presidential elections, the Aprista and PPC assembly members designed a constitution with serious flaws. In an attempt to solve impasses between the executive and legislative branches made obvious in past democratic regimes, the 1979 charter strengthened the executive branch and weakened the legislature. An example was providing the executive with the right to issue special decrees in economic and financial matters. Next, the president could suspend constitutional rights for renewable sixty-day periods in cases of emergency. Likewise, the president was given the authority to nominate Supreme Court and superior court judges from a pool selected by a council headed by the attorney general. The constitution itself could be amended only with great difficulty.[92] These constitutional flaws and their exploitation by civilian presidents contributed to undermining crucial checks to corruption in the 1980s and beyond.

Among other damaging legacies of the military regime, the appalling neglect of provincial and countryside infrastructure development and security allowed the Maoist subversive threat of Shining Path (Sendero Luminoso) to become established and grow. Additionally, the explosive growth

91. Preeg, *Evolution,* 2, 20–21, 26; Daniel Schydlowsky, "The Tragedy of Lost Opportunity in Peru," in *Latin American Political Economy: Financial Crisis and Political Change,* ed. Jonathan Hartlyn and Samuel Morley (Boulder, CO: Westview Press, 1986), 217–42, esp. 226, 228–29.

92. James D. Rudolph, *Peru: The Evolution of a Crisis* (Westport, CT: Praeger, 1992), 78–79; Vargas Haya, *Hacia la reforma del Estado,* 117–20; Preeg, *Evolution,* 28.

of cocaine production and smuggling in the Andean area in the 1970s posed intractable problems for law enforcement, the criminal justice system, and the rule of law. Since at least the mid-1970s, wealthy and powerful drug cartels had infiltrated and bribed investigative police authorities. The military regime's last interior minister, General Fernando Velit, was later implicated in the illegal release from prison of the drug trafficker and financier Carlos Langberg. The same drug lord sought political insurance during the transition by contributing to the campaign of Armando Villanueva, APRA's unsuccessful presidential candidate.[93]

Belaúnde, elected president for the second time in 1980, faced escalating terrorism and drug trafficking, as well as exaggerated state economic intervention, a $10 billion foreign debt, and other adverse conditions for the revival of democratic institutions. Additionally, the new Belaúnde administration had to confront the recurring dilemma of how to deal with the military and its pressing demands for retaining privileges, resources, and immunities under the newly restored civilian democracy.

Benign Neglect

The democratic order inaugurated in July 1980 had the initial enthusiastic support of a large proportion of Peruvian citizens. Belaúnde was elected by a respectable majority of the vote, and his party, Acción Popular, which was allied to the PPC, secured a supportive majority in Congress. Belaúnde promised a democratic renewal coupled with ambitious public projects despite the serious problems of an uncertain transition threatened by opposing vested interests, economic and institutional legacies, and growing subversive and drug-trafficking activities.[94]

93. Gustavo Gorriti, *The Shining Path: A History of the Millenarian War in Peru* (Chapel Hill: University of North Carolina Press, 1999), 40, 265, n. 4. See also Gorriti's most recent chronicle of his journalistic investigation into the Langberg case: *La calavera en negro: el traficante que quiso gobernar un país* (Lima: Editorial Planeta, 2006), 131–48; and Jordan to S.S., Lima, June 8, 1984, no. 6674, unclassified USDS document, in Drug Policy Collection (hereafter DPC), box 6, NSA.

94. Sandra Woy-Hazelton and William Hazelton, "Sustaining Democracy in Peru: Dealing with Parliamentary and Revolutionary Changes," in *Liberalization and Redemocratization in Latin America,* ed. George Lopez and Michael Stohl (Westport, CT: Greenwood Press, 1987), 105–35, esp. 106–10; "Latin American Review," July 3, 1981, unclassified CIA copy, in DPC, box 7, NSA.

At the onset of his regime, Belaúnde did not engage in a "moralization" campaign, nor did he inventory the adverse financial, social, and institutional conditions of government he had inherited. On the contrary, the new regime was quick to appease the still influential military, declaring that it had no intention of seeking restitution or retribution. Furthermore, Belaúnde established a pragmatic agreement with General Rafael Hoyos Rubio, the most senior military officer with organic links to Morales Bermúdez's regime. The armed forces were guaranteed autonomy in professional internal matters, and immunity for any past offenses and misdeeds, in exchange for confining themselves to the purely military sphere.[95] This modus vivendi pact with the military had serious political and economic consequences in the coming years. After a border skirmish with Ecuador in early 1981 and the sale of used jetfighters to Argentina during the 1982 Falklands-Malvinas conflict, the military was granted the go-ahead to acquire a fleet of modern Mirage 2000 jetfighters for $870 million, financed at a high interest rate; this expense clashed with the liberal economic policy program attempted by the new regime.[96]

Under the liberal slogan "to work and allow others to work" (*trabajar y dejar trabajar*), Belaúnde was aided by a technocrat team dubbed the "Dynamo," headed by Manuel Ulloa, the controversial prime minister and minister of finance. At the helm of this highly trained group of professional economists, who were educated abroad and with experience in foreign corporations and international agencies, Ulloa launched a haphazard effort at liberalizing trade, privatizing state enterprises, and promoting foreign investment. Newspapers were returned to their former owners, and a few state enterprises were privatized (e.g., Cementos Lima). Belaúnde allowed the Dynamo group freedom of action, while concentrating instead on designing and publicizing expensive and uneconomic public projects that ultimately contradicted deficit-cutting policies. A faction within the AP led by Javier Alva Orlandini also pressed for more public spending.[97] Continued reliance on foreign debt and its refinancing mechanisms actually increased the foreign debt.

95. Masterson, *Militarism,* 269–70; Preeg, *Evolution,* 29.

96. Rudolph, *Peru,* 83; Masterson, *Militarism,* 270.

97. The Majes irrigation project, for example, although initiated by the previous military regime, ultimately cost more than its projected returns. Rudolph, *Peru,* 81–83. See also Francisco Durand, *Riqueza económica y pobreza política: reflexiones sobre las elites del poder en un país inestable* (Lima: Fondo Editorial Universidad Católica, 2003), 204–5, 209; Carol Wise, *Reinventando el Estado: estrategia económica y cambio institucional en el Perú* (Lima: Universidad del Pacífico, 2003), 169–70.

Ulloa's liberal economic agenda was sternly opposed by entrenched interests in the manufacturing sector that were dependent on state protection, and the managerial staff of state enterprises. Opposition to dismantling of inherited statist and protectionist systems, and glaring inconsistencies and irregularities in the implementation of certain key measures, led to a truncated and ultimately ineffective economic liberalization.[98] Leftist and Aprista congressmen and politicians, including Vargas Haya, also protested what they considered to be pro-foreign and elitist policies reminiscent of the "submissiveness" or "entreguismo" of Belaúnde's first administration. Furthermore, the Dynamo team generated executive decrees that circumvented legislative debate. Congress not only lost importance but deteriorated from within as deputies and senators pursued private businesses aided by their congressional influence.[99]

The Belaúnde regime's honeymoon was over by the end of 1982. Several factors contributed to the catastrophic erosion of Belaúnde's political support. The international recession and financial contraction of 1982–1983 contributed to the declining prices of major Peruvian exports and a drastic decline of the country's terms of trade and balance of payments. The reduction in fiscal revenues produced a widening deficit and galloping inflation. In 1983, the gross domestic product declined by 13 percent and annual inflation reached 130 percent. The foreign debt increased by 40 percent for a total of $14 billion. To make matters even worse, a series of climatic disasters destroyed infrastructure, causing damages estimated at $1 billion.[100]

In the meantime, the Shining Path escalated its violent attacks and assassinations. The subversive organization's growth was unchecked in this early crucial period due, to a large extent, to the inefficiency and corruption of investigative police units led by corrupt generals, among them the notorious Eduardo Ipinze and José Jorge, who were linked to the drug trafficking cartel of Reynaldo Rodríguez López (a.k.a., "El Padrino").[101] In a misguided effort to confront growing terrorism and subversion, Belaúnde made

98. Schydlowsky, "Tragedy of Lost Opportunity," 217–18, 232–36; and Cynthia McClintock, "Comment on Chapter 9/Daniel Schydlowsky," in *Latin American Political Economy,* ed. Hartlyn and Morley, 360–66; Rudolph, *Peru,* 83–84.

99. Héctor Vargas Haya, *Democracia o farsa* (Lima: Atlántida, 1984), 38, 164; Wise, *Reinventando el Estado,* 175, 198.

100. Ortiz to S.S., Lima, July 12, 1983, no. 7909, unclassified USDS document; "Peru: President's Belaúnde's prospects," Directorate of Intelligence, unclassified CIA copy, in DPC, box 7, NSA.

101. Gorriti, *Shining Path,* 40, 114. Confirming this solid journalistic assessment, a

the fateful decision of suspending constitutional guarantees and allowing the military to have absolute control of several central Andean provinces in so-called "emergency zones." Instead of pacifying the region, the military exacerbated violence and engaged in human rights abuses. By 1984, military control had expanded to other regions, including the coca-producing Upper Huallaga Valley that had been penetrated by Shining Path rebels who offered coca growers protection against U.S.-sponsored coca eradication and drug interdiction operations. Thus, basic civil rights were curtailed for approximately 60 percent of the Peruvian population.[102]

Threats posed by the Shining Path and the growing *narcotráfico* undermined already weakened democratic institutions and the rule of law.[103] Political parties were exposed to the influence of drug lords who sought political leverage. In the early 1980s, Carlos Langberg, the drug trafficker who had help finance APRA's electoral campaign in 1980, continued to be closely associated with the opposition party.[104]

One of the core institutions that suffered the most from the insurgent and drug trafficking onslaught was the judiciary. Already undermined in its autonomy and integrity during the military regime, the 1979 constitution allowed the executive to exert influence on the court system through the nomination of judges. Scandalous cases of judicial inefficiency, miscarriage of justice, and bribing of judges contributed to the precipitous fall in prestige of the judiciary. The increasing number of prisoners awaiting trial and the perception that judges were partial to, afraid of, or bribed

---

U.S. official in charge of submitting the bi-annual budget for coca control and reduction in Upper Huallaga (CORAH) wrote: "Although the PIP [Peruvian Investigative Police] continues to play an important role, its effectiveness as an anti-narcotics force has been undermined by growing corruption." Jordan to S.S., Lima, April 23, 1984, no. 4664, unclassified USDS copy, in DPC, box 7, NSA.

102. Philip Mauceri, "The Transition to 'Democracy' and the Failures of Institution Building," in *The Peruvian Labyrinth: Polity, Society, and Economy,* ed. Maxwell Cameron and Philip Mauceri (University Park: Pennsylvania State University Press, 1997), 13–36, esp. 33–34; Rudolph, *Peru,* 91; Jordan to S.S., Lima, November 29, 1984, no. 13882, and February 1, 1985, no. 1265, unclassified USDS copies, in DPC, box 7 and box 31, NSA; Carlos Iván Degregori and Carlos Rivera Paz, *Perú, 1980–1993. Fuerzas Armadas, subversión y democracia: redefinición del papel militar en un contexto de violencia subversiva y colapso del régimen democrático* (Lima: Instituto de Estudios Peruanos, 1994), 9–11.

103. Cameron and Mauceri, eds., *Peruvian Labyrinth,* 3–5.

104. Francisco Durand, *Business and Politics in Peru: The State and the National Bourgeoisie* (Boulder, CO: Westview Press, 1994), 117.

by detained rebels and traffickers exacerbated cynicism about the judicial establishment.[105]

In 1980, the wealthy drug trafficker, Guillermo Cárdenas Dávila, a.k.a. "Mosca Loca," astounded everyone with the alleged bold pledge to repay Peru's foreign debt if his illegal activities were left undisturbed. In 1981, Mosca Loca was in detention awaiting sentencing in the trial brought against him and his associates before the Supreme Court. Five Supreme Court judges, including César Barrós Conti, found insufficient evidence to convict the obviously guilty drug lord, and ordered his immediate release and the dismissal of all charges. Public outcry and a rebuttal from the attorney general's office (Ministerio Público) forced the judges in the case to reverse their decision, which was, according to the same judges, taken without looking at the principal evidence that had been "inadvertently" excluded from their consideration. Mosca Loca was ultimately condemned to twenty years in prison.[106] While serving his prison sentence, Mosca Loca was able to pay corrupt jail administrators for living accommodations and luxuries denied to other prisoners. At one point, Mosca Loca shared a cell with Shining Path ideologue Antonio Díaz Martínez. In 1984, Mosca Loca was killed in a prison revolt triggered by severe overcrowding and overall appalling living conditions.

Prison and corrections administration was the responsibility of the justice minister. Belaúnde bestowed this key ministerial post to his PPC allies. A notable lawyer and PPC leader, Enrique Elías Laroza, was appointed minister of justice in 1981–1982. During his one-year tenure as minister, Elías Laroza signed important contracts for the construction and equipment of new "state-of-the-art" prisons with the Spanish company Guvarte. The deal was part of a credit assistance agreement between the Peruvian and Spanish governments. The high cost of $55 million for the new prisons and their alleged inadequacies raised suspicions of foul play and graft. Incompetence, graft, and the ensuing investigation process further delayed solutions to the dismal conditions in the state prisons. The comptroller general, Miguel Angel Cussianovich, filed charges against Elías Laroza and his close collaborators for misappropriation of public funds. The case was eventually dropped as Elías Laroza acquired congressional immunity after he was

105. Manuel Angel del Pomar Cárdenas, *Autonomía e idoneidad en el poder judicial: fundamentos para una acusación constitucional* (Lima: Editorial Justicia y Derecho, 1986), 11–12.

106. Pomar, *Autonomía e idoneidad,* 46, 76–108; Jordan to S.S., Lima, June 8, 1984, no. 6674, unclassified USDS document, in DPC, box 6, NSA.

elected deputy in 1985. In his defense, Elías Laroza claimed that the charges were motivated by a political conspiracy against him from the left and a sector of AP politicians with vested interests.[107]

Vargas Haya participated in several congressional commissions that were established to investigate alleged cases of administrative corruption after the end of the Belaúnde regime. Several constitutional violation charges resulted from these investigations. Aprista and leftist congressmen and politicians especially targeted the measures, law decrees, and public contracts implemented and promoted by two finance ministers, Manuel Ulloa and Carlos Rodríguez Pastor, and the energy and mines minister, Pedro Pablo Kuczynski. Some of these charges had a clear political bias in line with "nationalist" positions typical of the Velasco regime. However, other charges arose from genuine scandals involving egregious conflicts of interest. Ulloa, for example, was a businessman with interests in a number of industries, including the media (the newspaper *Expreso* and TV channel 5). Moreover, Ulloa's resignation in December 1982 came just after the Vollmer scandal that triggered a congressional investigation and political pressure. Ulloa had been partial to a Venezuelan business conglomerate, the Vollmer group, in the sale of Irrigadora Chimbote S.A., of which he had been a shareholding member of its board of directors.[108]

The failed 1982 state-sponsored rescue of a private bank, Bancoper, which was in serious financial difficulties for making loans to enterprises of a major shareholder, the Bertello group, resulted in using up to $30 million from the Banco Central de Reserva and Banco de la Nación to repay private-sector foreign debts. This irregular procedure unleashed congressional charges ("acusación constitucional") in 1985 based on the majority report of a congressional investigating committee.[109] Another charge was delivered against

107. Enrique Elías Laroza, *La conspiración Guvarte: las pruebas de la inquisición* (Lima: N.p., 1985), 8, 434–38; Miguel González del Río v. Peru, U.N. document, Human Rights Committee, 46th session, Communication, no. 263/1987, U.N. document CCPR/C/46/D263/1987 (1992), University of Minnesota, Human Rights Library, http://www1.umn.edu/humanrts/undocs/html/dec263.htm; Vargas Haya, *Perú: 184 años*, 312–13.

108. Vargas Haya, *Democracia o farsa*, 16, 167; Carlos Malpica, *Petróleo y corrupción: la ley Kuczynski* (Lima: Escena Contemporánea, 1985), 22–23; Durand, *Riqueza política*, 209; Woy-Hazelton and Hazelton, "Sustaining Democracy," 115.

109. Perú, Cámara de Diputados, Comisión Especial Dictaminadora sobre la Acusación Constitucional en el Caso Bancoper, Registro, no. 1653–Dic/87, "Dictamen de la Comisión Especial sobre acusación constitucional a . . . Manuel Ulloa, Carlos Rodríguez Pastor y . . . Juan Klingerberger," typescript copy. Vargas Haya, *Perú: 184 años*, 315–16; Durand, *Riqueza económica*, 219.

two other former ministers of the Belaúnde regime for accepting a $42-million debt (raised later to $73 million) generated by losses resulting from the lease and subsequent "purchase" of two useless cargo ships, the *Mantaro* and the *Pachitea,* arranged in 1981 with an Italian company by the general manager of the Peruvian Steam Corporation (CPV), Sandro Arbulú Doig, and other CPV officials.[110] Both charges did not move forward due to congressional and judicial stumbling blocks associated with the political principle of a "fresh start" applied during the succeeding administration headed by Alan García. But perhaps the most scandalous case of abuse involved the fraudulent use of Certex fiscal incentives allowed by officials in the Ministry of Finance and in customs administration. Unscrupulous exporters, among them the owners of Confecciones Carolina, received Certex cash payments for the shipment of containers with fake or nonexistent "nontraditional" exports or, in its "carrousel" mode, for "exporting" and "importing" the same product to and from a neighboring country. These and other abuses contributed to disputes with the United States over bilateral trade in textile products.[111]

In the end, the major casualty of the mismanagement, graft, and incompetence of the Belaúnde regime's benign neglect was liberal democracy itself. It was dubbed a "delegative" democracy or democracy with an asterisk.[112] Declining confidence in democratic institutions camouflaged a generalizing proclivity toward corruption in all quarters of public administration and daily life. Economic problems exacerbated this tendency. The growing perception of the inadequacy of liberal democracy to solve urgent problems raised the stakes in favor of the populist, state-interventionist positions embraced by the young Aprista candidate Alan García Pérez who promised honesty and urgent measures to overcome the crisis.[113]

Alan García's Means

García's inauguration in July 1985 was received with great expectations. It was the first time in its tortuous history that the old APRA party held unri-

110. Vargas Haya, *Perú: 184 años,* 311.

111. Vargas Haya, *Democracia o farsa,* 191–96, 201, 205; Vargas Haya, *Perú: 184 años,* 313–15; Durand, *Riqueza económica,* 208–209; "Meeting with Arq. Fernando Belaúnde Terry," Buenos Aires, December 10, 1983, unclassified USDS copy, in DPC, box 7, NSA.

112. Mauceri, "Transition," 30; Cynthia McClintock and Abraham Lowenthal, foreword in *Peruvian Labyrinth,* eds. Cameron and Mauceri, xii.

113. Héctor Vargas Haya, *Frustración democrática y corrupción en el Perú* (Lima: Editorial Milla Batres, 1994), 24.

valed executive power and a clear majority in Congress. The expected rewards for so many years of political struggle warmed the hearts of young and old Apristas: This was the long-awaited opportunity to solve Peru's problems according to the sectarian motto, "Only APRA will save Peru." The thirty-six-year-old García relied heavily on the old radical populist school rather than the retreating moderate stance.[114] With the support of the aging party leader Armando Villanueva, García displaced contending factions that emerged after Haya's death in 1979, to consolidate partisan authority and become APRA's secretary general and presidential candidate in 1984.

Displaced Apristas soon criticized what they saw as the growing ideological and moral distance separating García from the revered patriarch Haya. They also denounced García's inability to overcome "bribery and graft" in his newly inaugurated government.[115] Vargas Haya, an elected deputy for APRA in 1985 and president of the Chamber of Deputies in 1988, disagreed with the "procedures" of his party's leadership in several areas, particularly with what he perceived as pardoning the previous administration's corruption.[116] It took several years for Vargas Haya to publicly denounce his party's ills and finally quit his long-lasting Aprista militancy. Growing disappointment with the García administration within APRA and among those who voted for him grew after the government's first year. Dissatisfaction became ever more widespread after García's second year in power.

García managed initially to retain both massive support as well as collaboration from influential elite groups through personal charisma and secretive political and economic transactions. His core economic policy was developed by a small group of left-leaning, "heterodox" economic strategists. It soon became apparent that García intended to manipulate economic management to obtain political results. His interventionist policies were reminiscent of the Bustamante and Velasco regimes as they favored price, import, and foreign exchange controls, all principal sources of abusive discretionary power, favoritism, and graft. Additionally, García raised wages, launched an ambitious employment program, and vowed to reduce military spending.[117]

114. Carol Graham, *Peru's APRA: Parties, Politics, and the Elusive Quest for Democracy* (Boulder, CO: Lynne Rienner, 1992), 102.

115. Roberto Okura in prologue to César Vásquez Bazán, *La propuesta olvidada* (Lima: Okura Editores, 1987), xv, xvii; Vargas Haya, *Frustración democrática*, 79–89.

116. Vargas Haya, *Frustración* democrática, 10, 28, 130–37.

117. Graham, *Peru's APRA*, 110.

Dangers of populist intervention did not faze major economic interests who had reached a pact or *concertación* with the García administration to reactivate the economy through expansion of domestic supply. Policies that reduced underutilized industrial capacity and allowed privileged access to foreign exchange at a lower subsidized rate (Mercado Único de Cambio or dollar MUC) were especially beneficial to a dozen or so elite domestic groups, whose leaders came to be known as the "twelve apostles" for their commitment to García. The most important among them had discreetly yet generously contributed to García's presidential campaign.[118]

García's economic and financial strategy also rested on the controversial early decision to limit interest payments on foreign debt to 10 percent of Peru's total export earnings. The international political implications of this bold announcement placed Peru, a country with urgent needs for foreign financing and investment, in an awkward situation with the international financial establishment. This vulnerability eventually had negative consequences for Peruvian finances and reserves. For a while, however, García emerged as a valiant defender of a small country besieged by big international banking institutions. The contradictory economic artifice concocted by García and his advisors and allies worked for only two years. It started to collapse after García announced his decision to nationalize all private banks and insurance companies in July 1987. This decision was a truly monumental blunder that alienated his capitalist friends, several of whom were owners of the country's major banks, and most of the middle class. Despite serious efforts by the executive to implement the nationalization, growing opposition and legal hurdles defeated García's plan.

Regarding the police and military, García's early measures targeted "moralization" and respect for human rights. The populist president's reaction to the appalling corruption of the various branches of the police at the end of the Belaúnde regime achieved modest gains. He forced the dismissal or retirement of corrupt officials and authorities and reorganized the Civil, Republican, and Investigative Police forces. In early 1986, they were renamed, respectively, General, Security, and Technical Police departments, and all were placed under the umbrella of the National Police. In particular, the investigative Technical Police, thoroughly corrupted during the previous administration, experienced improvement in dealing with drug-related felonies.[119]

---

118. Schydlowsky, "Tragedy of Lost Opportunity," 237; Durand, *Business and Politics,* 119, 136–41; Vargas Haya, *Frustración democrática,* 68–71.

119. Watson to S.S., Lima, April 29, 1987, no. 4919, unclassified USDS copy, in DPC, box 7, NSA; Rudolph, *Peru,* 122.

García envisioned relying more heavily on the police forces under the authority of his interior minister, while limiting the inflated power of the military in matters of weapons procurement spending and terrorist repression. Several generals were held responsible for civilian massacres in the emergency zones and forced to retire. García sent mixed messages to the military regarding antiterrorist efforts, and created a single Ministry of Defense that absorbed the three armed forces ministries. Although the change was mainly bureaucratic and cosmetic, it was considered undesirable meddling in military affairs by many senior officers who warned of a military coup.[120] But perhaps his most controversial decision concerning the military involved cutting back the purchase of twenty-six Mirage 2000 jet fighter planes contracted by the Belaúnde administration with the French state-run companies Marcel Dessault and Snecma Thomson. García and his advisers argued that reducing the purchase to twelve planes would save the Peruvian government a considerable sum that could be used for other more urgent needs. However, the secretive negotiations and final settlement of the matter left lingering doubts.[121]

The mass media had a benign attitude toward García during his early years in office. Newspaper, radio, and TV owners had privileged access to official rate MUC dollars to import goods and pay for services abroad. Moreover, García had the support of key media owners such as his close friend and official advisor Héctor Delgado Parker, co-owner of the most important TV network. The influential *Caretas* magazine and the leftist *La República* newspaper sympathized with García. Other newspapers tied to influential economic groups avoided troubling the young president in expectation of successful concertación deals. It is not surprising that few corruption scandals surfaced before 1987. Only a dogged opposition deputy, Fernando Olivera, raised questions about the origins of the president-elect's income and property just before his inauguration. Olivera proposed a congressional investigation that was rejected by the APRA majority in the Chamber of Deputies.[122]

The first signs and perceptions of growing corruption appeared as a result of the increasing takeover of civil service posts and institutions by Aprista militants and sympathizers. Technical competence and merit took

120. Directorate of Intelligence, "Insurgency Review," June 1987, unclassified CIA copy, in DPC, box 7, NSA; Degregori and Paz, *Peru, 1980–1993,* 11–12.

121. Pedro Cateriano, *El caso García* (Lima: Ausonia, 1994), 75–76; Carlos Malpica, *Pájaros de alto vuelo: Alan García, el BCCI y los Mirage* (Lima: Editorial Minerva, 1993), x.

122. Cateriano, *Caso García,* 9.

second place to party patronage. Key bureaucracies such as the Central Reserve Bank (BCR), taxation department (DGC), and social security (IPSS) were controlled by Apristas suspected of widespread graft.[123] Close friends of García and his party, such as businessman Alfredo Zanatti, had access to dollars at an undervalued exchange rate for their own private businesses. Similar issues brought down the Collor de Mello regime in Brazil.

The justice system continued its seemingly unstoppable decline. García's administration imposed the selection of several judges from among his own party. Urgently needed resources were not forthcoming; thus, conditions of incompetent judges, extremely low salaries, and dangerous case backlog, 80 percent of which involved people being held in prison, were unchanged or exacerbated. Many drug traffickers operated with virtual impunity via bribing judges, while judges in Lima and the provinces were afraid to convict terrorists for fear of reprisals.[124] In explaining the insights gained by the USAID program officers on judicial reform in Peru since 1987, a U.S. official listed the inadequate budget as "probably the single most important cause of the system's failure because it leads to corruption of judicial personnel who depend on under-the-table payments from attorneys and clients for economic survival."[125]

One of the scandals that rocked the García administration derived from appalling living conditions in state prisons. Imprisoned Shining Path militants, a majority of whom were awaiting trial, had made several prisons strongholds of resistance, propaganda, and recruitment. On the eve of the International Socialist Conference held in Lima in June 1986, during which García intended to play a stellar role, Shining Path prisoners coordinated uprisings in three prisons in Lima. García ordered the high command of the armed forces to take charge, a military action that left about three hundred prisoners dead, a large number of them executed on site after surrendering.[126] When the magnitude of the massacre was known a few days later,

---

123. Francisco Durand, "Dinámica política de la corrupción y participación empresarial," in *El pacto infame: estudios sobre la corrupción en el Peru,* ed. Felipe Portocarrero (Lima: Red de Ciencias Sociales, 2005), 287–330, esp. 301, 304; Vargas Haya, *Frustración democrática,* 46; and Graham, *Peru's APRA,* 124; Malpica, *Pajaros de alto vuelo,* viii.

124. Rudolph, *Peru,* 121–22.

125. M. Jacobsen, "Overview of Peruvian Justices System and Summary of AID Justice Sector Reform," July 1, 1991, unclassified USDS copy, in DPC, box 6, NSA.

126. Rolando Ames, et al., *Informe al Congreso sobre los sucesos de los penales* (Lima: Talleres Gráficos Ocisa, 1988).

demands for an inquiry into human rights abuses multiplied inside and outside the country. García backpedaled from his initial defiance and blamed the weak Republican Guard, instead of the military or his civilian leadership, for what he termed "excesses" in repressing the uprisings. On this occasion, García demonstrated his true colors, by avoiding his responsibilities. His reputation had been damaged, and his image began to erode.[127]

Corruption scandals began to surface after the failed nationalization of the banks in 1987, which convinced an important sector of the elite and mass media to oppose García's inconsistencies, policy contradictions, and betrayals. Dionisio Romero, one of the richest and most influential bankers in Peru, declared on TV (channel 5) that he had contributed exclusively to the financing of Alan García's presidential campaign.[128] The irregular deposits of dwindling BCR reserves in the troubled Bank of Credit and Commerce International (BCCI), which was guilty of laundering money and other illegal practices at a global level, caught the attention of the growing opposition. The suspicious role played by the government in possible cover-up of weapons trafficking with connections to General Manuel Noriega of Panama (case of the Danish vessel *Pía Vesta*) and Interior Minister Agustín Mantilla (Peruvian ship *Sabogal,* Polish vessel *Zuznica*), García's former secretary and right-hand man, who was accused of harboring paramilitary commandos, led to sundry inquiries and speculation.[129] The disastrous economic performance that led to four-digit inflation rates and a 14-percent decline of GDP increased pressure against the regime and the party in power. Failed or inefficient public works such as the costly electric train, which had been heralded as the solution to Lima's transportation problems, and the irrigation project Chavimochic in the northern region, became symbols of graft.

The failure of García's agricultural policy of price controls and food import restrictions had several dire consequences. A black market for food products developed; speculation and other manipulations caused great hardship for low-income consumers. And of course, public sector officials were intimately involved in numerous scandals. For instance, the minister of agriculture, Remigio Morales Bermúdez, was forced to resign in mid-

127. Jordan to S.S., Lima, June 20 and 28, 1986, nos. 7217 and 7533; Whitehead to embassies, Washington, DC, June 28, 1986, no. 205132, unclassified USDS copies, in Bigwood Collection (BC), box 2, NSA; Cateriano, *Caso García,* 68–69.

128. "Dionisio Romero: 'Sí financiamos campaña de Alan,'" *La República,* August 14, 1987, 15–19; August 12, 1987, 5.

129. Cateriano, *Caso García,* 153–54.

1988 after a shipment of imported meat was discovered rotten on arrival allegedly due to bureaucratic mismanagement and graft.[130] In addition, many agricultural producers shifted their efforts from food to coca production. Thus, the García administration's unfortunate agricultural policy also contributed to increased drug production and trafficking.

The regime's commitment to coca eradication and trafficking interdiction, in collaboration with programs of the U.S. Justice Department's Drug Enforcement Administration (DEA) that rubberstamped U.S. congressional certification for aid, was undermined by leftist political opposition and rebel activities in the Upper Huallaga Valley. The military response to insurgent attacks on the antidrug police base of Santa Lucía (near Uchiza, San Martín province), under the command of Brigadier General Alberto Arciniega, was to protect coca growers and traffickers as a means to counteract the influence of Shining Path as well as for personal gain.[131] A report by the U.S. Defense Intelligence Agency (DIA) stated in September 1989 that the "Peruvian military is now involved with drug traffickers while trying to eradicate the insurgency."[132]

However, the most important revelations and discoveries of mismanagement and corruption took place after García left office in July 1990. A number of complicated allegations and charges leading to congressional investigations, sanctions, and trials threw light on the García administration's wide range of corrupt activities. They started in congressional investigations. García, with the unfailing support of his political and legal advisors and collaborators, defended himself with energetic displays of legal and oratorical prowess. A new breed of anticorruption politician—Deputies Fernando Olivera, Lourdes Flores, and Pedro Cateriano, among others—joined forces to deprive García of his congressional immunity as a first step to have him face trial.

The principal charges against García in 1991 included illicit enrichment as a public official resulting from undeclared income of dubious origin, and probable illegal gains from direct involvement in the Mirage and BCCI cases. Later charges included demanding and receiving bribes from the Ital-

130. Graham, *Peru's APRA,* 110; Vargas Haya, *Perú: 184 años,* 328–29.

131. Rudolph, *Peru,* 123–25; U.S. Embassy to S.S., Lima, November 6, 1986, no. 13,248; and Watson to S.S., Lima, April 30, 1987, no. 5016, unclassified USDS copies, in DPC, boxes 7 and 36, NSA.

132. Joint Staff to various, Washington, DC, September 27, 1989, unclassified U.S. Department of Defense (USDD) copies, in DPC, box 7; see also Quainton to S.S., Lima, January 22, 1990, no. 1008, unclassified USDS copies, in DPC, box 7, NSA.

ian state agency that financed the construction of Lima's electric train system. Former senior officials, including Mantilla, García's last minister of the interior, faced charges. The most damning evidence came from initially unconnected investigations in the United States and Italy, and fallout from congressional and judicial inquiries in the 1990s. Despite evident procedural mistakes that ultimately derailed the prosecution's case against García, and the corrupt political and institutional context of the Fujimori regime, important lessons were learned that would be useful in establishing modern anticorruption procedures of the Peruvian political and legal systems.

García's oratorical and demagogic skills made him a charismatic popular leader. But he was far from being a good leader. Vargas Haya considered that García was driven mainly by "immediate personal benefit with the end of conquering power."[133] García's notorious egocentric, autocratic, and sectarian tendencies undermined rather than reinforced public sector institutions in dire need of overhauling. Many analysts have focused on the negative consequences of García's populist and authoritarian traits, while neglecting the widespread corruption that such a political leadership style engendered.[134] The history of the legal cases against him between 1990 and 2001 illustrates a pattern of manipulation and exploitation of judicial incompetence and corruption as a means to regain power, which García managed to do in 2006.

Frustrated Prosecution

On August 16, 1990, during one of the first sessions of the new legislature, a multiparty motion was approved in the Chamber of Deputies to create a special committee dedicated to investigating García's foreign and domestic financial transactions during his tenure. Public dissatisfaction with García's regime supported the legislative move toward investigating the former president and senator-for-life. If the inquiry produced evidence to demonstrate reasonable doubt of García's administrative honesty, the former president could lose his congressional immunity and face trial for "illicit enrichment." The congressional decision to allow the special committee to investigate

133. Vargas Haya, *Frustración democrática,* 22.

134. John Crabtree, *Peru under García: An Opportunity Lost* (Pittsburgh, PA: University of Pittsburgh Press, 1992), 212, 214–15, and postscript to Spanish translation, and *Alan García en el poder: Perú, 1985–1990* (Lima: Peisa, 2005), 328–29; Carlos Reyna, *La anunciación de Fujimori: Alan García, 1985–1990* (Lima: Desco, 2000).

García's finances appeared as a mere formality since an ongoing APRA-Fujimori understanding could have easily derailed any effective congressional action against García. A concurrent effort to charge García of human rights violations in connection with the 1986 prison massacres was thwarted by Aprista and Fujimorista deputies.

The inquiry into García's suspicious income was led by a determined elected deputy, Fernando Olivera, who represented a new party, the Independent Moralizing Front (FIM), which had competed in the 1990 elections under the banner of anticorruption. The committee was also integrated by three other able and promising lawyers and members of the minority opposition: Lourdes Flores, Pedro Cateriano, and Fausto Alvarado. The Olivera committee, as it was called, had a limited mandate: find credible evidence to present to the Chamber of Deputies on which to decide whether to file formal charges against García.

With little time to build a case, the Olivera committee opted to seek evidence of suspicious income that could become grounds for a charge of illegal enrichment. This approach, however, had a glaring weakness: Even if the committee members could prove a sizable disproportion between García's official income and his declared assets, additional evidence was necessary to convince a congressional audience or jury of corruption-related crimes while serving as president.

García's complete income tax returns and other official financial records were difficult to obtain because senior officials in the new Fujimori administration were not helpful. However, the committee collected data by examining witnesses and hiring two private detective agencies, Kroll of New York and Larc of Miami. In addition, investigations into the Mirage case revealed that far from being an advantageous transaction for the Peruvian state as García had claimed, the government had lost approximately $300 million in potential income. According to the original contracts, if the French government approved, Peru could have resold the fourteen unwanted aircraft at a profit made possible by the interim increase in market price. Thus, a third party, acting on behalf of a Middle Eastern country, could have bribed Peruvian officials to benefit from the resale transaction that the government declined to carry out. The Olivera committee obtained evidence that meetings between García and legendary arms dealer Abderraman El Assir had taken place, which García denied.[135] Meanwhile, representatives of President François Mitterrand's government declared that there were no irregularities in the Peruvian purchase.

---

135. Cateriano, *Caso García*, 76–78, 205–9; Malpica, *Pájaros de alto vuelo*, 11–12.

In the meantime, the Kroll and Larc agencies produced, independently from each other, evidence of possible bank accounts under García's name or that of his wife in the United States during the 1980s. García, legally represented by an Aprista lawyer and former congressman and mayor of Lima, Jorge del Castillo, had retained the services of the influential and expensive law firm Arnold & Porter of Washington, DC, to counteract the Olivera committee's investigations in the United States.[136] The inquiries of Kroll and Larc were limited by several factors. The Olivera committee had difficulties paying for the services provided by Kroll and Larc, as it lacked official financial support for expenses. Moreover, Arnold & Porter, on behalf of García, filed formal complaints against both agencies for business irregularities. The complaint filed in Florida resulted in minor fines imposed on Larc's investigator and owner, Ralph García, a circumstance that APRA and its supporters exploited in the Peruvian media to discredit the findings of the Olivera committee.

When the investigation was about to flounder, additional evidence emerged from an unexpected direction. While in the United States trying to salvage the evidence delivered by Kroll and Larc, and appealing to U.S. authorities to allow disclosure of García's financial holdings in that country, the Olivera committee members also followed the lead of García's BCCI connections. They met with the staff of the U.S. congressional committee headed by Senator John Kerry charged with investigating the BCCI's international money laundering and weapons trafficking, among other matters. In July 1991, British and U.S. authorities issued court orders for the closing of BCCI branches in fourteen countries and seizure of company records. In Washington, DC, the Olivera committee members were informed that Robert Morgenthau, district attorney of New York City, was investigating the case.

A few weeks later, the *New York Times* and other media sources published reports of suspected illegal transactions between the Peruvian government under García and the BCCI. On August 1, 1991, Morgenthau reported in a newscast aired in Peru that the two highest officials of the Peruvian Central Reserve Bank (BCR) in 1985–1986, president Leonel Figueroa and manager Héctor Neyra, had received bribes totaling $3 million in two off-shore accounts for arranging the deposit of BCR reserves for up to $250 million in the BCCI Panamanian branch. Morgenthau revealed the accounts' code names and affirmed that García knew and approved of these risky transactions. Independent information also confirmed that García and his close ad-

---

136. Cateriano, *Caso García,* 98–99.

visors had met with senior BCCI executives presumably to seal the deal. Morgenthau's information derived from examination of captured BCCI documents and, more importantly, from indicted witnesses who opted to collaborate with the prosecution in exchange for reduced sentences or acquittal. Morgenthau advised the Olivera committee that trades with such witnesses were the only way to obtain legally admissible evidence in such cases. In Peru, legal procedures for obtaining testimony from indicted or indictable witnesses in exchange for protection and plea bargains (*colaboración eficaz*) were only introduced years later.

With all the information thus collected, the Olivera committee submitted its report to the Peruvian Chamber of Deputies. Public opinion was overwhelmingly favorable to prosecuting García, Figueroa, and Neyra (the latter two had fled the country). Additional information requested from the U.S. Treasury Department yielded evidence that García's wife, as well as several close collaborators, such as Morales Bermúdez, Zanatti, and Gonzales Po-sada, had declared large sums of dollars in cash to U.S. customs. Then, in October 1991 a majority of deputies and senators resolved to suspend García's immunity and prosecute him for illicit enrichment.[137] Peru's first penal court quickly dismissed the case against García for lack of evidence and imprecision of criminal charges. The judges responsible for this controversial decision had been appointed during the García regime or had strong links with APRA.

On April 5, 1992, the Fujimori self-coup supported by the military demolished any constitutionally based legal appeals of the court decision on the García case. Military officers were dispatched to arrest the former president and other political leaders. García allegedly evaded prison or worse by hiding for three days at a construction site near his home. Then, after several months in hiding, García sought asylum in a traditional Aprista haven, the Colombian embassy. Colombian President César Gaviria personally arranged for a military aircraft to remove García from Peru in June 1992. The Fujimori regime simply allowed García's departure without recourse to deportation procedures. García spent the next eight years living in Bogotá and Paris where he reportedly acquired prime real estate properties.

137. Peru, Congreso de la República, Cámara de Diputados, "Informe final de la comisión investigadora sobre las operaciones y adquisiciones de inmuebles en el Perú y el extranjero, vinculadas con el patrimonio personal del Sr. Alan García Pérez, durante el ejercicio de su actividad como funcionario público," March–May 1991, esp. ff. 251075–77; "Acusación constitucional: Dictamen de la comisión especial encargada de la denuncia contra el doctor Alan García Pérez," September 23, 1991, in AGCR; and Cateriano, *Caso García,* 168–69.

Prosecutors initiated proceedings against García in absentia in a special criminal court in September 1992; the case (file 21-92) incorporated all evidence provided by the Olivera committee.[138]

Additional crucial evidence against García was obtained in November 1993 when an Italian prosecutor, Vittorio Paraggio, arrived in Lima to share and corroborate investigation results. Paraggio was investigating corruption of Italy's former president Bettino Craxi and his minister of foreign affairs Giulio Andreotti. A special Italian witness, Sergio Siragusa, head of Tralima—an agency connected to the Italian foreign aid department in charge of financing the construction of Lima's electric train system, so eagerly promoted by García—provided incriminating testimony through the Italian plea bargaining procedure. Siragusa asserted that García had personally requested "commissions" (similar to those of "Bettino," according to García's quoted words) for facilitating the construction project. Siragusa attested that he had personally delivered cash as well as made deposits to an account (280762361-2952733) in the Barclays Bank of Grand Cayman, belonging to García's crony Alfredo Zanatti, for a total amount of about seven million dollars. This novel evidence was the basis for a new case opened in 1995 (01-95) that incorporated and superseded the previous one (21-92). The ad hoc, public, and justice ministry prosecutors agreed on the charges against García: conspiracy to defraud (*colusión ilegal*), influence peddling (*negociación incompatible*), bribe taking (*cohecho pasivo*), and illicit enrichment.[139] A court order was distributed to appropriate foreign government agencies for the arrest of García on contempt of court charges (*reo contumaz*).

Del Castillo, García's legal counsel, and del Castillo's successor, Aprista lawyer Judith de la Matta, grounded García's defense on a complaint filed with the Inter-American Commission on Human Rights (CIDH) of the Organization of American States, then headed by former Colombian president Gaviria. The CIDH decision issued in 1995 was completely favorable to García and recommended the dismissal of the charges for reasons of polit-

138. Peru, Corte Suprema de Justicia, Sala Penal Especial, Expediente Asuntos Varios (A.V.) 21-92, acusado: Alan Gabriel García Pérez, agraviado: el Estado, delito: enriquecimiento ilícito, cuadernos A -Z23, Archivo de la Corte Suprema de Justicia (hereafter ACSJ).

139. Peru, Corte Suprema de Justicia, Sala Penal Especial, Exp. A.V. 01-95, 10 anexos, acusado: Alan Gabriel García Pérez, agraviado: el Estado, delito: colusión ilegal, negociación incompatible, cohecho pasivo y enriquecimiento ilícito, ACSJ. See also Peru, Congreso Constituyente Democrático (CCD), "Informe: Comisión Investigadora de los contratos del Tren Eléctrico de Lima (CITEL)," November 1994, AGCR.

ically motivated restrictions to the exercise of García's human rights. After the fall of Fujimori, the special criminal court in charge of case 01-95, in contemplating the CIDH decision endorsed by then-minister of justice, Diego García Sayán, approved dismissal of the charges due to statutory limitations of the alleged crimes. This controversial decision was appealed to no avail by ad hoc prosecutor Jorge Melo-Vega Layseca. Because García was no longer facing prosecution, he was able to launch his candidacy for president in the April 2001 elections.

Scandals involving members of García's inner circle continued to surface. Aprista leader and congressman Agustín Mantilla, García's former interior minister, was caught in video recordings (1830 and 1831, March 13, 2000) receiving $30,000 from Vladimiro Montesinos to finance APRA's sagging electoral campaign and render credibility to the electoral farce of 2000.[140] The congressional investigation and judicial prosecution of Mantilla's case revealed dealings, as interior minister and vice minister in the 1985–1990 period, with Israeli arms trafficker Zvi Sudit and his associates; the latter avoided prison sentences upon providing testimony against both Montesinos and Mantilla.

Two companies incorporated in the British Virgin Islands belonging to Mantilla and his brother, Jorge Luis Mantilla, moved more than six million dollars at the Miami branch of the Union Bank of Switzerland (UBS). These accounts had been opened in 1990 with deposits from accounts of the Israeli Discount Bank, Sudit's preferred bank.[141] According to the Mantilla brothers, the money in their secret accounts derived from unsubstantiated foreign donations for APRA's campaigns in Peru. Most transfers made from Mantilla's USB accounts used the "swift" mode that protected the recipient's identity. The foreign funds were channeled into Peru through a series of accounts in Peruvian banks under the names of numerous relatives and associates. After five years in prison, Mantilla was released in 2005. Throughout the trial and his imprisonment, Mantilla did not admit to creating or par-

140. "Reunión de Agustín Mantilla con Vladimiro Montesinos," March 13, 2000, official congressional transcription of videos nos. 1830 and 1831, in Peru, Congreso, *En la sala de la corrupción: videos y audios de Vladimiro Montesinos (1998–2000)*, ed. Antonio Zapata (Lima: Fondo Editorial del Congreso del Peru, 2004), 4:2203–11.

141. Peru, Congreso de la República, Comisión Investigadora de los casos de corrupción de la década de 1990 (Comisión Herrera), "Informe: cuentas bancarias de Agustín Mantilla en el Union Switzerland Bank (UBS)," and "Informe: Agustín Mantilla y su vínculo con el autodenominado Comando Democrático Rodrigo Franco," July 2003, AGCR; and press clippings from *La República, Comercio,* and *Correo,* 2001 to 2006.

ticipating in a covert network funneling money to García and APRA. Finally, in September 2006 in a publicly broadcast video clip, Mantilla said that he had "followed orders."[142]

García asserted that he was not involved in the corrupt activities of Mantilla, Zanatti, Figueroa, and Neyra. During his exile in Colombia, García wrote a fictionalized account of his recent political adventures titled *The World of Machiavelli*.[143] García consistently argued that the various charges against him were politically motivated, and equally consistently, mounted a detailed and spirited defense based on technicalities, including transgressions of his human and political rights, inappropriate retroactive application, and statutory limits of the alleged crimes he had committed. Other Aprista experts offered detailed legal refutations against the charges that they described as violations of the constitution and/or motivated by revenge.[144] These legal defense arguments are remarkably similar to the arguments used by viceroys and colonial officials when confronting their alleged "enemies" and "partisan" accusers in the *juicios de residencia.*

Corruption Patterns Endure

The APRA party demonstrated that its legendary internal discipline, savvy lawyers, and international connections could be used for unjust and institutionally destructive objectives. Furthermore, Fujimori's unconstitutional regime after 1992 indirectly aided García's legal case through its interference with a clumsily handled prosecution that resulted in dismissal of the cases against the exiled president. In brief, García and his associates benefited from continued deterioration of the Peruvian legal system influenced and corrupted further by the forces behind the Fujimori regime.

To recap: It is fair to say that assaults on democracy in the 1960s through the 1980s underscored the weak institutional bases, incomplete reforms, and mounting social problems inherited from the 1950s. Despite the will to

142. "Agustín Mantilla reaparece," broadcast by TV program "La ventana indiscreta," September 4, 2006, http://www.youtube.com, based on a home video filmed in Lima, July 29, 2006, released by TV program Cuarto Poder, September 3, 2006; *La República,* September 4, 2006.

143. Alan García, *El mundo de Maquiavelo* (Lima: Mosca Azul, 1994).

144. Alan García, *La defensa de Alan García* (Lima: N.p., 1991); Humberto Carranza Valdivieso, *El asesinato jurídico de Alan García (5 de abril de 1992)* (Lima: Centro de Estudios Tierno Galván, 2000), 17, 289–90.

proceed with honest reform, the first Belaúnde administration got trapped in a political quagmire that ultimately brought about its downfall. Belaúnde and his party were subject to growing military influence and procurement graft, which was allowed or ignored due to past political favors owed to the armed forces high command. A recalcitrant congressional opposition headed by APRA, vying to succeed in the next presidential elections, undermined the regime with the stalling of urgent reforms and policy measures. Reactive foreign interests, increasing inflation, and a growing deficit and foreign debt compounded the crisis. Belaúnde also faced high-level corruption within his own ranks, who were involved in contraband schemes, along with private businessmen and military officers. The contraband scandal obliterated the dwindling prestige of the regime and resulted in heavy corruption costs in the form of lost public sector revenue and official bribes.

Congressional investigations of widespread contraband were cut short in 1968 by a military coup that razed the weak democratic advances of recent decades. For twelve years the constitution, institutions, public policy, the economy, and the media were subject to military intervention and control. Congress was closed down, and judicial and local government authorities appointed and confirmed by the military. Government was carried out mainly through executive decrees. In this institutional setting, corruption and inefficiency remained unchecked, and the two were often difficult to separate. Growing deficits accruing from failing state-run enterprises were covered by new foreign loans. A transitional scheme was then put into practice to put elected officials back in power in 1981.

However, devices of corruption inherited from the military regime—such as the abuse of export subsidies, exchange controls, and preferential dollar rates—continued throughout the 1980s. Lost government revenue and other costs of corruption continued to be serious under the second Belaúnde regime and the first García administration. (Similar scandals in other Latin American nations, under new democratic governments in the 1980s and early 1990s, brought down regimes and led to indictments and even prison terms. These cases included the diversion of public resources to secret party and presidential coffers by Carlos Andrés Pérez and Jaime Lusinchi of Venezuela, and bribery schemes benefiting Fernando Collor de Mello of Brazil.)[145]

145. Walter Little and Antonio Herrera, "Political Corruption in Venezuela," in *Political Corruption in Europe and Latin America,* ed. Walter Little and Eduardo Posada-Carbó (London: Macmillan, 1996), 267–85.

Increasing foreign debt also brought with it mismanagement and irregular and illegal use of the country's public credit, foreign aid, and reserves. Military procurement and public works contracts continued to be used as mechanisms of graft. Since the late 1970s and, particularly, in the 1980s, drug trafficking problems associated mainly with increased production and smuggling of cocaine, seriously corroded law enforcement and judicial institutions. The illegal financing of politicians and political parties and campaigns through narco-dollars was also common in Peru during this period, as it was in other Latin American countries, such as the electoral campaign of Colombian President Ernesto Samper in the early 1990s. Indirect costs of forgone foreign investment increased when foreign direct and portfolio investment became more available in the 1970s and 1980s, but institutional instability and corruption hampered investor confidence and incentives.

Overall costs of corruption increased consistently in the 1960–1989 period, reaching an estimated annual average of about one billion dollars in the 1980s (Table A.5). However, in comparative terms, the highest levels of estimated corruption took place in the 1970s, at 42 percent of government expenditures and 4.9 percent of GDP. Compare these to 31 percent of expenditures and 3.7 percent of GDP in the 1960s, and 35 percent of expenditures and 3.9 percent of GDP in the 1980s (Table A.6). Consequently, the military "revolutionary" regime can be considered the most corrupt of the period, followed by the first administration of Alan García (Table A.7).

While the indictment and prosecution of former president Alan García was bungled and ultimately derailed for technical reasons, important lessons were learned concerning the exposure, investigation, and legal proceedings for prosecuting corruption. Likewise, public perceptions, tolerance, and reaction gathered experience to eventually deal with the immense wave of corruption that grew during the "infamous decade" of the predatory Fujimori-Montesinos regime.

Chapter 7

Corruption and Conspiracies, 1990–2000

The complexities of Peruvian society and politics have simultaneously fascinated and repulsed the famed writer Mario Vargas Llosa (b. 1936). In his earlier novels of autobiographical and historical inspiration, he depicted the corrupt environment of military life, dictatorship, and prostitution in the Peru of his youth.[1] In the late 1980s, at the height of his literary career, Vargas Llosa led civic and political movements opposed to state interventionism affecting institutions and markets. His passage through the labyrinth of Peruvian power struggles in search of modernizing institutional and economic reform was swift but significant. His reformist quest was soon derailed by powerful corrupt interests. Vargas Llosa followed in the steps of those who fought corruption in the past and, in the process, uncovered evidence useful to our understanding of its persistent and costly burden.

With the zeal of a new convert, Vargas Llosa embraced orthodox, free-market political and economic liberalism after a tortuous break with the leftist positions he had espoused since the 1950s.[2] A decided reaction against

---

1. Mario Vargas Llosa, *La ciudad y los perros* (Barcelona: Seix Barral, 1963); *La casa verde* (Barcelona: Seix Barral, 1966); *Conversación en la Catedral* (Barcelona: Seix Barral, 1969).

2. Vargas Llosa was a somewhat removed supporter of the Peruvian Communist Party while studying at the Universidad de San Marcos during the military dictatorship of General Manuel Odría. Vargas Llosa defended the Cuban revolution and initially supported the Peruvian revolution led by the military in the 1970s. His departure from leftist politics was gradual following the 1968 Soviet invasion of Czechoslovakia, and especially the 1971 "Padilla affair," the forced public recanting of Cuban poet Heberto Padilla. Vargas Llosa, *Contra viento y marea (1962–1982)* (Barcelona: Seix Barral, 1983),

President Alan García's mistaken attempt to expropriate private banks in 1987 catapulted Vargas Llosa to a meteoric rise in the Peruvian political arena as leader of the Libertad movement and Democratic Front (FREDEMO) coalition. On a platform of thorough economic restructuring, Vargas Llosa ran as the absolute favorite in the 1990 presidential campaign. He campaigned under difficult conditions of growing subversion and terrorism, political opportunism among his allies, and dirty tricks of his opponents. Vargas Llosa won the first round of elections in April just ahead of maverick candidate Alberto Fujimori Fujimori (b. 1938), who had appeared as a serious contender only a few weeks prior to election day.[3] Without a true party organization behind him, Fujimori nevertheless won the second round of elections in June benefiting from Aprista and leftist votes.

Just after the elections, most analysts believed that the Peruvian electorate and their populist leaders had rejected "elitist" Vargas Llosa and favored instead a compromise candidate. Fujimori appeared to be a popular reformer usurping part of Vargas Llosa's political agenda but promising not to implement radical economic adjustment.[4] Soon after he assumed power, however, it became clear to many that Fujimori's promises and improvised government plans were part of a demagogic ploy to gain power and seek unchecked executive dominance. Covert assistance to Fujimori during his miraculous electoral ascent, brokered by the rising influence of Vladimiro Montesinos Torres (b. 1945) in the national intelligence service (SIN), became public knowledge only a couple of years after the 1990 elections.

Based on pioneering journalistic revelations, in 1992–1993 Vargas Llosa and his son Alvaro publicized the illegal means that brought Fujimori to the presidency. Thanks to pre-electoral political affinities with the Aprista leadership, Fujimori obtained significant political favors that included precious state-owned media exposure through a nationwide TV program he conducted in the late 1980s. Moreover, facing sure electoral defeat of their own candidate, APRA leaders bolstered Fujimori's presidential campaign by

---

30–35, 75–76, 138–39, 160–73, and 225–30. On Vargas Llosa's early leftist affiliations and sympathy toward the Cuban revolution, see U.S. embassy to D.S., Lima, March 12, 1966, no. A-80, box 2573, RG 59, USNA.

3. Under the 1980 Peruvian Constitution, framed mainly by APRA and PPC legislators, a presidential candidate needed at least 50 percent of the vote to avoid a runoff election.

4. Mario Vargas Llosa, *El pez en el agua: memorias* (Barcelona: Seix Barral, 1993); "A Fish Out of the Water," *Granta* 36 (1991): 15–75.

providing illicit support at a critical electoral moment.[5] In fact, between the months of April and June 1990, departing President García ordered the intelligence service headed by army General Edwin Díaz to support Fujimori's campaign with privileged logistical and polling information.[6] Very few believed Vargas Llosa at the time. Quite the opposite, public opinion was largely hostile to Vargas Llosa for opposing Fujimori's increasingly authoritarian regime.

The illegal operations that influenced the 1990 electoral process, the beginning of a systematic pattern of violation of laws and corruption, were widely acknowledged only after the fall of Fujimori and Montesinos. The emergence of a unique body of evidence since September 2000 corroborated previous, often unreported claims of profound corruption among the highest Peruvian authorities throughout the 1990s. Vargas Llosa and other determined journalists and opposition leaders, had been correct in their assessments and denunciations. Irrefutable proof showed that illegal maneuvers contributed not only to Vargas Llosa's electoral defeat, but also to Fujimori's victory in all the elections of the decade.

Thanks to evidence from audiovisual, judicial, and special witnesses' sources implicating approximately 1,600 individuals in complex networks of corruption, it is now possible to portray in detail the systemic graft inherited and amplified by Fujimori and his partner Montesinos. This extraordinary evidence is at the core of a necessary reinterpretation of the historical role of corruption, both as a consequence of weakened institutions and as an active factor undermining further the regulatory bases of Peruvian political, social, and economic life. Illegal association, authoritarian conspiracy, and concealed networks interacted to emasculate formal institutions and the rule of law so as to enrich and sustain another small, corrupt group at the top.

5. Vargas Llosa, *Pez en el agua,* 534; Álvaro Vargas Llosa, *La contenta barbarie: el fin de la democracia en el Perú y la futura revolución liberal como esperanza de la América Latina* (Barcelona: Editorial Planeta, 1993), 24–25; and Catherine M. Conaghan, *Fujimori's Peru: Deception in the Public Sphere* (Pittsburgh, PA: University of Pittsburgh Press, 2005), 16–17.

6. Jeff Daeschner, *La guerra del fin de la democracia: Mario Vargas Llosa versus Alberto Fujimori* (Lima: Peru Reporting, 1993), 193–96, 268, based on interviews with García's political advisor, Hugo Otero, who collaborated with Fujimori's campaign, and information from *Caretas* (1990–1991). See also Álvaro Vargas Llosa, *La contenta barbarie,* 25; Francisco Loayza Galván, *Montesinos: el rostro oscuro del poder en el Perú* (Lima: N.p., 2001), 11.

Revamping Corruption

Since 1988 a group of military officers, inspired by the old militaristic tradition of "patriotic" intervention at critical political junctures, had devised a secret plan to stage a coup against the regime of President García. At the time, public opinion was expected to tolerate such a coup because many people were disenchanted with the corrupt APRA administration. This plan did not materialize but was embraced and modified by the unscrupulous spymaster Montesinos, a former army officer with influential connections for developing corrupt networks. The original conspiracy's blueprint contemplated neoliberal economic policies enforced by unconstrained authoritarian rule hidden behind a semblance of electoral democracy.[7]

Montesinos met Fujimori while performing the SIN-assigned, illegal undercover task of assisting Fujimori's 1990 electoral campaign. The candidate relied heavily on Montesinos to "solve" serious tax evasion and other legal issues that threatened to ruin Fujimori's reputation and presidential campaign.[8] According to confidential information gathered by U.S. diplomatic officials, Montesinos' agents placed a bomb to scare an outspoken congressman who had uncovered part of Fujimori's dark secrets.[9]

7. Dictatorial military plans revealed by inside sources (León Dormido group) to magazine *Oiga* in 1993. The blueprint was initially authored by General José Valdivia in the late 1980s, according to Gustavo Gorriti, *La República,* no. 7205, September 22, 2001, 7; Vargas Llosa, *La contenta barbarie,* 24; "Plan verde" analyzed in Raúl A. Wiener F., *Bandido Fujimori: el reeleccionista,* 2nd ed. (Lima: WWW Editores, 2001), 31–35; Maxwell Cameron, "Endogenous Regime Breakdown: The Vladivideo and the Fall of Peru's Fujimori," in *The Fujimori Legacy: The Rise of Electoral Authoritarianism in Peru,* ed. Julio Carrión (University Park: Pennsylvania State University Press, 2006), 268–93, esp. 274.

8. Revealing details of Montesinos's intelligence, strategic, and judicial "aid" to Fujimori (through the assistant attorney general for criminal cases, Pedro Méndez Jurado, and Attorney General Hugo Denegri, appointed during the García administration), as well as sundry information on Montesinos's checkered trajectory, provided by cross-referenced confidential sources (including Francisco Loayza) to U.S. diplomats, in U.S. Embassy (Mack) to S.S., Lima, October 14, 1994, no. 9601, unclassified USDS copy, in PDP, box 1, file SIN unit bio, no. 20, NSA.

9. Montesinos was linked to a May 1990 bombing near the home of FIM opposition congressman Fernando Olivera, who had accused Fujimori of income tax evasion during the 1990 presidential campaign. The confidential source told a U.S. embassy political officer "about an 'inculpatory' three-way conversation [the informer] had with then-presidential candidate Fujimori (after the first round of the election) and Vladimiro Montesinos . . . in late May or early June 1990. . . Montesinos told an astonished Fujimori 'not to worry,' that he had taken care of Olivera. 'We have given him a little bomb'

Montesinos had focused his conspiratorial schemes on the venal Fujimori to gain privileged access to supreme executive power. Montesinos was armed with dictatorial plans, deep knowledge of military and judicial corruption codes, CIA links, and connections with drug traffickers. With these assets, Montesinos contributed invaluably to Fujimori's electoral victory, including the alleged brokering of a $1-million donation from Pablo Escobar, the chief of the Medellín drug cartel.[10] From these seedy origins, corruption spread in almost all directions during Fujimori's "infamous decade."

Like Vargas Llosa, Vladimiro Montesinos Torres was born to an established middle-class family in Arequipa, the second largest city, of Peru. Moreover, both young men received a military education in Lima.[11] The parallels stop there. While Vargas Llosa denounced in his first novel the cruel and dehumanizing character of the Peruvian military culture, young Montesinos mastered its secrets during his studies at the Chorrillos Military School. At age nineteen, Cadet Montesinos was trained for a month at the U.S. Army School of the Americas (SOA) in Panama in early 1965, just prior to the SOA graduation of another former student of the Chorrillos Military School, the future Panamanian dictator Manuel Antonio Noriega.[12] From the initial connections and favors that Montesinos nurtured during his military career, especially among his infantry regiment friends, he built a network of conspiring cronies that would eventually gain commanding control of the armed forces and other key government positions in the 1990s.

The military coup of 1968 opened up opportunities for aspiring espionage agents. Since the early 1970s, Montesinos, a young ambitious infantry cap-

---

(le hemos metido una bombita)." Alvin Adams to S.S., Lima, August 22, 1994, no. 7691, 1, 3–4, unclassified USDS copy, in PDP, box 1, file SIN unit bio, no. 18 (duplicate in DPC, box 36), NSA. See also Caretas, *Montesinos: la historia completa,* ed. Domingo Tamariz Lúcar (Lima: Caretas, 2001), 30–31; Luis Jochamowitz, *Vladimiro: vida y tiempo de un corruptor* (Lima: El Comercio, 2002), 1:55–58.

10. Roberto Escobar Gaviria, *Mi hermano Pablo* (Bogotá: Quintero Editores, 2000), 8–11, 135–46. These uncorroborated claims against "Montecristo" and Fujimori raised by Escobar's brother, through the pen of investigative reporter Juan Carlos Giraldo, are still under investigation. See also Loayza, *Montesinos,* 197; *Revista Cambio* (Bogotá), November 12–20, 2000; *El País Internacional,* no. 1654, November 12, 2000.

11. Vargas Llosa entered Lima's Leoncio Prado military school in 1950 at age fourteen. Vargas Llosa, *Pez en el agua,* and *Ciudad y los perros.* Montesinos studied first in the military boarding school of Arequipa and then was accepted in 1961, at age sixteen, to the Escuela Militar de Chorrillos in Lima, where he graduated as an infantry officer in 1966. Jochamowitz, *Vladimiro,* 1:73–78.

12. Jochamowitz, *Vladimiro,* 1:129; Sally Bowen and Jane Holligan, *El espía imperfecto: la telaraña siniestra de Valdimiro Montesinos* (Lima: Peisa, 2003), 29–30.

tain, managed to position himself successively as personal secretary or junior assistant to three important military and former intelligence chiefs: foreign minister and prime minister, Edgardo Mercado Jarrín (1973–1974); minister of agriculture, Enrique Gallegos Venero (1974–1975); and two other prime ministers, Jorge Fernández Maldonado (1976), and Guillermo Arbulú Galiani (July–August 1976). As President Juan Velasco's health deteriorated, Montesinos plotted on behalf of his bosses.[13]

Montesinos also gathered abundant confidential information that he shared with the U.S. embassy and CIA agents in Lima. The U.S. embassy nurtured Montesinos as an important contact among military officers with leadership potential.[14] However, General Francisco Morales Bermúdez ousted Velasco in August 1975 and prevailed over the leftist faction of Gallegos and Fernández Maldonado. Consequently, Montesinos lost his mentors and bases of influence. He was forced out of Lima's corridors of power and reassigned to a distant military post in the middle of a northern desert. Without official permission, and using a forged military clearance, Montesinos abandoned his post to travel to the United States in 1976 sponsored by a U.S. government foreign leader visitors' grant.[15] At his return, Montesinos was accused of traveling without permission, spying, and insubordination. He was tried by a military court, expelled from the army, and confined to a military prison for almost two years in 1976–1978.

During his imprisonment, Montesinos studied law and, a few months af-

---

13. Robert Dean to S.S., April 4, 1977, no. 2686, unclassified USDS copy, in PDP, box 1, file Montesinos trip to DC, NSA. See also biographical and confidential information on corruption and narcotics allegations against Montesinos, in Anthony Quainton to S.S., Lima, January 7, 1992, no. 228, unclassified USDS copy, PDP, box 1, file SIN unit bio, no. 8, NSA.

14. Ambassador Dean reported that Montesinos was "a valued Embassy contact, a relationship that was quite open and known to his superiors. (In fact, I mentioned the relationship to Fernández Maldonado). . . [Montesinos had a] recognized competence and usefulness to his superiors." Dean to S.S., Lima, April 4, 1977, no. 2686, 1, unclassified USDS copy, in PDP, box 1, file Montesinos trip to DC, NSA.

15. The U.S. international visitor leader grant allowed Montesinos to have official and academic meetings in the United States between September 5 and September 21, 1976. Among the academics and officials he chose to meet were Alfred Stepan (Yale), Albert Fishlow (UC Berkeley), Luigi Eunadi (Department of State), and Abraham Lowenthal (Council of Foreign Relations). Dean believed that "the formal permission matter was but a pretext to cashier Montesinos who was in fact purged for political/personal reasons and that Arbulú at least acquiesced." Dean to S.S., Lima, April 4, 1977, no. 2686, 2–3, and April 7, 1977, no. 2813, unclassified USDS copy, in PDP, box 1, file Montesinos trip to DC, NSA.

ter his release, he graduated as a lawyer in record time. He then started a new career as a defense attorney catering to drug traffickers, including Evaristo Porras Ardila, a Medellín cartel drug lord, in 1978. Montesinos had contacts in the judicial system and the know-how to "solve" his cases through bribery, blackmail, and pressure. During the "lost decade" of the 1980s, Peru was governed by democratically elected governments that did little to revamp a crumbling, overwhelmed judiciary. Like most public institutions, the justice system was swamped by a constant inflow of new cases and lack of resources. In these circumstances, Montesinos contributed to further undermine the judicial system while simultaneously increasing his income.

A desire for revenge against the military faction that jailed him and engineered the democratic transition drove Montesinos to challenge the top military leadership in the early 1980s. Montesinos collaborated as a strategist with his cousin, Augusto Zimmerman, the disgraced former press secretary of dictator Velasco. Zimmerman's sensationalist magazine *Kausáchum* specialized in revealing embarrassing military intelligence secrets and documents, insulting generals, and generalized mudslinging. Montesinos bragged that he had thoroughly penetrated military intelligence. The military moved to prosecute him once again as a traitor and instigator of complicated plots that included bomb threats. Finally, a full public disclosure of his past forced Montesinos to flee the country in 1983.[16] He lived in Argentina until 1985, and upon his return the military high command banned him from entering any military installation or office. Among Montesinos's many enemies among the military and its intelligence apparatus was former major José Fernández Salvatecci, who had consistently accused Montesinos of traitorous activities, including espionage on behalf of the CIA.[17] The well-known disreputable past of Montesinos haunted him throughout his rise to covert influence and power.

Montesinos's fame in certain circles grew in the late 1980s as a result of his defense of drug traffickers in two important cases. In 1985, a drug case, dubbed by the press "Villa Coca," involved a large cocaine trafficking ring in collusion with police. The captured drug lord, Reynaldo Rodríguez López, "El Padrino," implicated seventy-two people in the case, among them sev-

---

16. "Pieza clave de una investigación militar: el ex capitán Vladimiro Montesinos," *Caretas,* no. 765, September 12, 1983, 10-17, 72.

17. Jochamowitz, *Vladimiro,* 1:193–203; 139–42; José Antonio Fernández Salvatecci, *La revolución peruana: yo acuso* (Lima: Ediciones El Siglo, 1978), 193–96.

eral high-level officials of the Peruvian Investigative Police (PIP), as well as military officers, politicians, and show business celebrities.[18] Montesinos coordinated the defense of the accused police officers and, with the help of Attorney General Hugo Denegri, defeated the prosecution's case against his clients in 1988.[19]

The second case involved defense of the infantry general, José Valdivia, accused of human rights violations for ordering punitive action against the inhabitants of the Andean town of Cayara, Ayacucho, which left twenty-eight peasants dead in May 1988. This time the assassination of witnesses and threats to the prosecutor, ultimately removed from the case, led to another "legal" victory by Montesinos and exoneration of the culprit.[20] Montesinos earned a reputation for successfully defending military and police officers against diverse charges. This penchant for upholding impunity for the military gained him renewed access to and praise from the officers who replaced his enemies after they retired from the army high command. The military ban against Montesinos was lifted. In 1989, he approached the SIN chief, Edwin Díaz, with confidential judicial documents on suspects accused of terrorism. Through such means, Montesinos obtained a coveted prominent post in the intelligence community.

Montesinos became Fujimori's trusted advisor and the de facto head of SIN since July 1990. The formal chiefs of the intelligence service became mere figureheads. Montesinos's covert power was beyond oversight or control. From this unofficial position, Montesinos exercised undue influence and decision making as the invisible power behind the Peruvian presidency. Montesinos exploited institutional loopholes aided by a president in a vulnerable political position and willing to undermine constitutional rules to reactivate a tradition of unchecked executive power. Fujimori lacked a coherent political party and his followers did not have a majority in Congress. Moreover, Montesinos also fueled Fujimori's insecurity by alarming him about alleged plots to oust him from power and kill him.

Increasing narcotics-related corruption at the highest levels of the police forces provided the opportunity for the Fujimori-Montesinos duo to swiftly reshuffle top police echelons immediately after Fujimori took office in July

18. "El Padrino cambió la coca por los pasaportes," *Perú.21,* no. 249, April 26, 2003, 3. PIP General José Jorge Zárate was expelled from the force and imprisoned.

19. Gustavo Gorriti, "Fujimori's Svengali, Vladimiro Montesinos: The Betrayal of Peruvian Democracy," *Covert Action* 49 (1994): 4–12, 54–59, esp. 10.

20. Gorriti, "Fujimori's Svengali," 10–11.

1990. In his inaugural speech, Fujimori launched a "moralizing" campaign against inherited corruption in an early show of his demagogic take-charge style. A total of 135 senior police officers, including many capable and honest people, were retired or transferred. A few days before, the cunning Montesinos had met with U.S. diplomatic officers to leak damaging "intelligence" information on drug trafficking involvement of high-level police officers and the entourage of the former Aprista minister of the interior, Agustín Mantilla.[21] Not surprisingly, the vacant police command posts were then assigned to military officers in a strategic reversal of the prominence the police had achieved during the Aprista regime in the fight against drugs and subversion. With this assertive move, the antinarcotics and antiterrorist programs, recipients of sizable U.S. drug interdiction aid, came under full military control.

These were the opening salvos of a behind-the-scene tug of war affecting the professional institutionalization of the police and military. The ultimate practical aim was to expurgate pro-APRA officers as well as institutional career commanders and enemies of Montesinos who might oppose new corruption strategies. One by one, generals and admirals were reassigned or retired and replaced by new commanders instrumental to the Montesinos-Fujimori scheme. Acting as the national security linchpin, Montesinos had convinced Fujimori of coup threats posed by commanders that he advised the president to sack. As early as August 1990, some newspapers reminded their readers of Montesinos's ties with drug traffickers. Prominent retired generals protested before U.S. army intelligence officials that, because of the undue influence Montesinos exerted over Fujimori, the national intelligence service was in fact running the Peruvian government and state.[22]

The new military chiefs included the most corrupt and inept generals and admirals. These men provided the underground power bases sought by Fujimori and Montesinos to consolidate their regime. General Jorge Torres

21. U.S. Embassy (Dion) to S.S., Lima, June 19, 1990, no. 9127, unclassified USDS copy, in DPC, box 36, file SIN unit bio; Quainton to S.S., Lima, July 28, 1990, no. 11147, and August 9, 1990, no. 11756, unclassified USDS copies, PDP, box 2, file SIN unit bio, NSA.

22. Confidential declarations by retired generals Edgardo Mercado Jarrín, Luis Cisneros Vizquerra, and Sinecio Jarama Dávila, in U.S. Army Intelligence Threat Analysis Center (USAITAC), "Counterintelligence Periodic Summary," Pentagon, Washington, DC, October 23, 1990, no. 395616, unclassified U.S. Army Intelligence and Security Command (USAISC) copy, in BC, box 1, file Montesinos, NSA.

Aciego became minister of defense in July 1990. Vice Admiral Luis Montes Lecaros replaced Admiral Alfonso Panizo as chief of the Joint Command. General José Valdivia (Montesinos's client in the human rights case of 1988) replaced dissenting General Jaime Salinas Sedó as commander of the strategic Second Military Region based in Lima. Infantry Colonel Alberto Pinto Cárdenas, a personal friend of Montesinos, was placed as head of army intelligence. In December 1991, General Nicolás Hermoza Ríos was appointed commander-in-chief of the army above other generals in line for promotion. With this last appointment, Montesinos rounded up his informal network within the military high command, thus undermining time-honored military promotion rules.[23] Acting as an unofficial liaison between Fujimori and the military command, Montesinos advanced the bases for the 1992 coup. In this process, military efficiency and respect for the constitution deteriorated throughout the 1990s.[24]

These strategic changes in the leadership of the military and police forces would not have been possible without the prior manipulation of the judicial system and attorney general office to guarantee immunity from prosecution to military allies. Montesinos developed an integrated system of corrupt judges, prosecutors, prison officials, and police officers. Montesinos continued to perfect this system between July 1990 and April 1992 to effectively provide virtual impunity and favors to a growing network of military and civilian allies. Likewise, Montesinos manipulated the corrupt judicial apparatus to punish and intimidate independent media reporting. A USAID-sponsored evaluation by Peruvian legal scholars concluded in September 1991 that under the pressures of large-scale corruption, drug trafficking, and terrorism, the crisis of the judicial system was a breeding ground for human rights violations.[25]

Montesinos used his unique sources of information to renew his con-

23. Fernando Rospigliosi, *Montesinos y las Fuerzas Armadas: cómo controló durante una década las instituciones militares* (Lima: Instituto de Estudios Peruanos, 2000), 26–30; Martín Paredes Oporto, "El lado verde de la corrupción," *Quehacer* 144 (2003): 10–20; Wiener, *Bandido Fujimori,* 41–43.

24. Fernando Rospigliosi, "Controversias: la grave situación de las FF.AA.," and "Controversias: politización total," in *Caretas,* no. 1374, August 3, 1995, 17, and no. 1552, January 28, 1999, 23.

25. Gorriti, "Fujimori's Svengali," 8; libel suit against Enrique Zileri, director of the weekly *Caretas,* in June–August 1991, for reporting on Montesinos's growing informal power, Caretas, *Montesinos,* 28–29; "Evaluation of the Peruvian Judicial System," coordinated by Lorenzo Zolezzi, in USAID copy, in DPC, box 6, file Peru evaluation of Peruvian judicial system AID/AOJ project, NSA.

nections with the CIA and to undermine the DEA's antidrug efforts in Peru.[26] In April–September 1991, Montesinos assumed control of the joint U.S.–Peruvian antidrug efforts that received U.S. aid of approximately $35 million in 1991 and $40 million in 1992. A SIN "anti-drug" division was formed, but did little to prosecute drug traffickers since it was used mainly for covert purposes, including political assassinations, as in the case of Barrios Altos, and telephone surveillance (*chuponeo*) of important opposition leaders such as Vargas Llosa.[27]

A top U.S. diplomat, sympathetic to Fujimori's apparent technocratic efficiency in antiterrorist actions and drug interdiction during his first year in power, noted "the prevalent problem of internal government corruption," and that despite police reshuffling, "corruption and inefficiency within the Peruvian National Police ranks are still very real concerns." In the Upper Huallaga Valley, "the triple plagues of drugs, terrorism, and corruption are everywhere."[28] An influential U.S. congressional group, including Senators Edward Kennedy and John Kerry, worried about meeting requirements for certification to receive additional antidrug assistance, wrote to President George H. Bush expressing concern for the "egregious" human rights conditions in Peru underscored by four years of undiminished "disappearances" by security forces.[29]

Montesinos generously rewarded those who supported him. The illegal diversion of official defense and intelligence funds, bribes and illegal commissions in military materiel acquisition, and levies on drug trafficking activities in military-controlled zones of the jungle, were the main means of payment for the corrupt military command and Fujimori's political entourage. Using such sources, Montesinos also reinforced the undercover and illegal operations directed by the SIN. An investigative congressional commission working before the 1992 coup advanced revealing information on the drug-related corruption at military bases in the jungle and antidrug

26. Gorriti, "Fujimori's Svengali," 54–55.

27. On November 3, 1991, military commandos linked to Montesinos stormed a chicken barbecue fund-raiser in a popular sector of downtown Lima (Barrios Altos) and executed fifteen people suspected of being terrorist sympathizers. Opposition leaders who were subjected to illegal telephone surveillance included Mario Vargas Llosa, Fernando Belaúnde, Javier Diez Canseco, and Agustín Mantilla. Caretas, *Montesinos*, 24–25, 44–46.

28. Quainton to S.S., Lima, April 27, 1991, no. 5610, and July 31, 1991, no. 10219, unclassified USDS copies, in DPC, box 7, file Peru Santa Lucía Base, NSA.

29. Congressmen to President Bush, Washington, DC, July 23, 1991, unclassified USDS copy, in DPC, box 6, file Peru certification, NSA.

institutions under Montesinos's new management.[30] However, the coup interrupted this commission's investigation, as the bulk of its reports and documents also "disappeared."

Civilian-Military Dictatorship

From the start of Fujimori's regime, the evolving intelligence and military shadow networks worked toward overthrowing the constitutional, congressional, and judiciary checks encumbering authoritarian control of the state. Such a coup was ideologically justified to achieve the unfettered "dirty" obliteration of terrorism. However, in the international context of the early 1990s, absolute dictatorship and outright suppression of freedom of expression and the press were no longer viable.[31] The emerging authoritarian stances had adapted to these international circumstances. Meanwhile, the government supported implementation of seemingly orthodox economic policies, while simultaneously facilitating the corruption that fed informal mechanisms sustaining continuous authoritarian rule. Corruption was a means to achieve and consolidate power as well as a reason to continue in power. This distorted principle has been labeled the "immoral economy" of Fujimorismo.[32]

Internationally, Fujimori managed early on to obtain strong support from the International Monetary Fund (IMF) after a swift mending of fences, brokered by economist Hernando de Soto through his international contacts, over the issue of unpaid foreign debt inherited from the García administration. A drastic adjustment package that achieved a degree of inflation control was implemented in August 1990 by Fujimori's first finance minister, Juan Carlos Hurtado Miller. Surprisingly, there was practically no popular reaction to the economic package, in part due to the decline in inflation and the ongoing struggle against terrorism that inhibited popular protest activities. Domestically, Fujimori and Montesinos relied on media disinforma-

30. Interview with former deputy from Cusco, Julio Castro Gómez, Lima, April 7, 2003.

31. Based on assessment by Cynthia McClintock and Fabián Vallas, *The United States and Peru: Cooperation at a Cost* (New York: Routledge, 2003), chapter 5; Peter H. Smith, *Talons of Eagles: Dynamics of U.S.–Latin American Relations,* 2nd ed. (New York: Oxford University Press, 2000); Conaghan, *Fujimori's Peru,* chapter 1.

32. Catherine Conaghan, "The Immoral Economy of Fujimorismo," in *The Fujimori Legacy: The Rise of Electoral Authoritarianism in Peru,* ed. Julio Carrión (University Park: Pennsylvania State University Press, 2006), 102–25, esp. 103.

tion and manipulation (*psicosocial*) campaigns that fueled conservative public opinion, while an explosion of opinion polls indicated support of a "strong" government.[33]

Fujimori's popular appeal was further boosted by his clientelistic "social" programs of free food and medicine distribution, and politically motivated public works such as the building of schools. Under his direct control and execution, these programs were financed through the irregular administration of foreign (mainly Japanese) donations and monthly clandestine fund transfers from the SIN as early as 1991.[34]

The ideological road toward the 1992 coup was built on key political and legislative campaigns spearheaded by Fujimori. In 1991, Fujimori went on the attack and called the judiciary headquarters the "injustice palace," and Congress was described as a lobby of drug trafficking. Fujimori cajoled FREDEMO and APRA members of Congress to approve extraordinary executive powers to issue decrees on economic reforms and privatizations, labor issues, and the war against terrorism. A state of domestic emergency was invoked to supersede Congress: Law 25327 was approved in June 1991 allowing Fujimori expanded powers to propose legislation in the above areas for a period of 150 days. In November, just before the period was to expire, the executive issued an avalanche of 126 legislative decrees inspired by Finance Minister Carlos Boloña working closely with Montesinos. Many of these decrees clearly transgressed the legal limits allowed by Congress. The executive had usurped the right to make decisions on—sans any congressional deliberation—the privatization of key state enterprises (decree 674), public sector reform, foreign financing, labor rights, public health, private education, and security measures curtailing civil rights and traditional status of universities as sanctuaries. Boloña's personal interests and enterprises benefited greatly from these decrees.[35]

The government decrees went beyond the pale and unleashed strong congressional opposition in matters of domestic security and intelligence. De-

33. Julio F. Carrión, "Public Opinion, Market Refoms, and Democracy in Fujimori's Peru," in *Fujimori Legacy,* 126–49.

34. "Ex edecanes revelan que retiraban dinero del SIN para el dictador" (testimony of retired army colonels Enrique Burga and Guillermo Ponce de León before the Townsend Commission, September 29, 2001), *La República,* September 12, 2003.

35. U.S. Embassy (Charles Brayshaw) to S.S., Lima, November 23, 1991, no. 16510, unclassified USDS copy, in DPC, box 7, file Peru Santa Lucía Base, NSA; US-AITAC, "Counterintelligence Periodic Summary," Pentagon, Washington, DC, January 17, 1992, no. 3482, unclassified USAISC copy, in PDP, box 2, file SIN, NSA; Wiener, *Bandido Fujimori,* 79–83.

cree 643 established the National Defense System (SDN) led by a council (CND) headed by the president and comprised of the minister of defense, joint command chief, commander generals, head of the SIN, the finance and interior ministers, and the prime minister. In addition, decree 746 integrated all intelligence units of the armed forces and police under the National Intelligence System (SINA). Congress rejected several of these decrees as blatant violations of civil rights. Fujimori entered into a collision course with the Congress, accusing legislators of obstructing "national interests."[36]

Newspaper articles in *Expreso* and *La República* since February 1992 further undermined the reputations of the judicial and penal systems; scores of rebel prisoners were allegedly being released based on existing law that permitted the reduction of prison terms. The Supreme Court also dropped illegal enrichment and terrorism charges against, respectively, Alan García and Shining Path leader Abimael Guzmán. Public opinion associated the obvious corruption in the judiciary to the appointment of judges during the García regime.[37] Death threats and assassinations complemented the attack on the constitutional order existing before April 5, 1992.

Montesinos and two military officers planned the coup at army headquarters. In the late evening of Sunday, April 5, a taped message by Fujimori was aired on TV, General Valdivia, commander of the Lima military region, and military intelligence chief Alberto Pinto Cárdenas staged a military show of force. To prevent a countercoup, the commanders of the country's other military regions had been ordered to attend urgent meetings in Lima at the same time the coup was taking place.[38]

The coup closed down Congress indefinitely and all judiciary offices for more than 20 days. The headquarters of the most important media outlets were occupied for almost two days. Several journalists, politicians, and labor leaders were detained or kidnapped by the military. The archives of the judicial palace and the attorney general containing confidential information were seized and removed to a secret location from which they never resurfaced. The opposition cried foul and asserted that the coup was a direct consequence of the compromising revelations by Fujimori's wife,

36. USAITAC, "Counterintelligence Periodic Summary," 17 January 1992, no. 3482; Wiener, *Bandido Fujimori,* 84–92.
37. Quainton to S.S., Lima, April 23, 1992, no. 6024, unclassified USDS copy, in BC, box 1, file 1992 coup, NSA; and Conaghan, *Fujimori's Peru,* 32.
38. A. Vargas Llosa, *Contenta barbarie,* 14–17; Gorriti, "Fujimori's Svengali," 57; Wiener, *Bandido Fujimori,* 92–93.

Susana Higuchi, who accused her in-laws of administrative irregularities and corruption.[39]

An immediate international outcry resulted in the suspension of most of the foreign aid on which Peru depended. International economic sanctions against the Fujimori dictatorship were not imposed because U.S. officials and others believed that such actions would jeopardize the war against terrorism in Peru. Sanctions proposed by members of the Organization of American States (OEA) were avoided through a last-minute compromise that was brokered in part by the U.S. ambassador in Lima in conversations with Finance Minister Boloña, who did not resign and thus lent with his international prestige decisive support to the coup.[40] Fujimori promised to call elections for a constituent assembly. The road toward the "institutionalization" of the coup and government by decree was now open.[41] Vargas Llosa, however, held firm in his journalistic attacks against Fujimori and the "self-coup."

Violence escalated soon after the coup. Terrorist acts multiplied against strategic targets (e.g., TV channel 2 in June, Calle Tarata in Miraflores in July where twenty-two people were killed and many more injured). The regime used harsh methods to halt terrorism including the mass execution of prisoners (Canto Grande in May) and the "disappearance" of innocent university students (La Cantuta in July, carried out by the SIN's death squad "Grupo Colina"). Luckily for Fujimori and Montesinos, the principal Shining Path leader Abimael Guzmán was captured in September 1992 by the police intelligence unit GEIN-DINCOTE led by General Ketín Vidal, who was stubbornly independent of Montesinos's network.[42] Thereafter, threats by the Shining Path considerably diminished.

---

39. Quainton to S.S., Lima, April 9, 1992, no. 5223, confidential, unclassified USDS copy, in BC, box 1, file 1992 coup; secret CIA report, April 13, 1992, unclassified CIA copy, in BC, box 2, file 1992 attempted coup, NSA.

40. Quainton to S.S., Lima, April 27, 1992, no. 6224, unclassified USDS copy, in BC, box 1, file miscellaneous; U.S. Embassy (Quainton, drafted by intelligence officer Gebigler), Lima, May 12, 1992, no. 6955, unclassified USDS copy, in BC, box 2, file different people's reaction on Fujimori's coup, NSA.

41. Conaghan, *Fujimori's Peru*, 40–41, and "Immoral Economy," 109; see also U.S. Congress, House of Representatives, Committee on Foreign Affairs, *Peru: U.S. Priorities and Policies. Hearing before the Subcommittee on Western Hemisphere Affairs of the Committee on Foreign Affairs, House of Representatives, One Hundred Third Congress, First Session, March 10, 1993* (Washington, DC: Government Printing Office, 1993), 2–5, 12–13, 16.

42. The Grupo Especial de Inteligencia (GEIN), an elite division of the Peruvian

The process of adapting institutions and economic policy to goals of unchecked autocratic presidentialism received a boost with the 1992 coup. Independent judges and prosecutors were sacked and the judiciary restructured, downsized, and tailored to the political needs of Fujimori and Montesinos. Corrupt judge Luis Serpa Segura was appointed chief justice of the Supreme Court and the venal magistrate Blanca Nélida Colán was designated attorney general. Criminal acts carried out by civil servants were not prosecuted and impunity guaranteed. Unconstitutional "faceless" courts and judges conducted summary trials and delivered tough sentences against terrorism suspects, many of whom were innocent.

In public opinion polls, the so-called judicial reform had support ratings of 95 percent. Talk of revamping the bases of the criminal justice system from Roman law precepts to those of the U.S. system led Ambassador Anthony Quainton to consider Fujimori's attack on the judiciary as a major opportunity to influence reforms that he believed would serve U.S. interests.[43] Although the coup had negative effects for bilateral cooperation in areas emphasized by U.S. foreign policy—mainly "democracy, development, and drugs," Quainton concluded that "Peru is heading in a direction which is consistent with our long-term interests."[44]

Montesinos and the army command continued to purge constitutionalist, honest, and dissident officers accused of conspiring against Fujimori. General Jaime Salinas Sedó and others who were implicated in a coup attempt aimed at restoring the constitution and opposing the November 1992 electoral fraud were imprisoned. A military judge, General Alberto Arciniega Huby, who blamed Montesinos for destroying the independence of military justice and the country's institutions as a whole, was accused of defamation of character and sent into forced retirement in January 1993. In May 1993, General Rodolfo Robles Espinoza was forced to retire and go into exile for

---

Police Dirección Nacional Contra el Terrorismo (DINCOTE), infiltrated Shining Path militants, recruited informants, and focused almost exclusively on capturing rebel leaders. The GEIN did not share its intelligence information with other intelligence agencies. After several breakthroughs, GEIN's efforts paid off and proved more efficient than those of SIN and military strategies characterized by human rights abuses. Rospigliosi, *Montesinos,* 138–42.

43. Quainton to S.S., Lima, August 26, 1992, no. 11368, unclassified USDS copy, in BC, box 2, file 1992 attempted coup, NSA.

44. Quainton to S.S., Lima, July 10, 1992, no. 9596, unclassified USDS copy, in BC, box 2, file Fujimori before the coup, NSA.

publicly denouncing the existence of the Grupo Colina death squad that was responsible for the Barrios Altos and La Cantuta massacres under the orders and protection of Montesinos and army commander-in-chief General Hermoza.[45]

The re-establishment of the legislature in the form of a constituent assembly resulted from international pressure. However, the limited autonomy and fundamental weakness of the new legislature was intentional. Instead of Peru's customary two chambers and 240 members, the new Congreso Constituyente Democrático (CCD, 1992–1995) was unicameral, comprised of only eighty members from a single national electoral district. Fujimori's attack on political parties as corrupt oligarchies contributed to the perceived irrelevance of formal politics. Fujimori's own representatives in the CCD were elected not for their merits but simply as followers of the populist leader. A slight pro-Fujimori CCD majority surrendered important legislative prerogatives to the executive. After the new constitution was completed in August 1993 and it was approved by a small margin via referendum, the constitution was opposed by the national association of mayors, among other organizations concerned about excessive centralization of public sector functions.[46]

The 1993 constitution, coupled with ad hoc executive laws, further enfeebled the institutional framework, human rights protections, and anticorruption barriers. With the connivance of ministers and corrupt officials, approximately 250 unconstitutional decrees were put into effect between April 5, 1992, and November 20, 2000.[47] Armed with these ad hoc institutional

45. The aborted coup of November 1992 reflected "uneasiness among army officers regarding what they consider presidential interference in military affairs . . . [and] the role being played . . . by former army captain Montesinos," according to retired army General Luis Cisneros Vizquerra, writing in *Expreso* on November 29–30, 1992 as reported in U.S. Embassy (Palmer) to S.S., Lima, December 7, 1992, no. 15647, unclassified USDS copy, in BC, box 1, file Montesinos, NSA. On the Salinas case, U.S. Embassy (Skol) to S.S., Caracas, November 20, 1992, unclassified USDS copy, in BC, box 1, file miscellaneous, NSA; and Jaime Salinas Sedó, *Desde el Real Felipe: en defensa de la democracia* (Lima: Mosca Azul, 1997), cited by Conaghan, *Fujimori's Peru*, 55. On Arciniega Huby, U.S. Embassy to S.S., Lima, January 5, 1993, no. 88, unclassified USDS copy, in PDP, box 1, file Montesinos, NSA. For an insider informant on the internecine struggles within the military in the early 1990s, see U.S. Embassy (Brayshaw) to S.S., Lima, May 17, 1993, no. 5589, unclassified USDS copy, in PDP, box 2, file SIN unit bio, NSA.

46. Conaghan, *Fujimori's Peru*, 49, 53, 59–63.

47. According to the commission headed by Minister of Justice García Sayán to in-

weapons, the Fujimori regime lasted until November 2000, through fraudulent elections, including those in 1992–1993, 1995 (first reelection), and
2000 (second reelection).

Fujimori's unchecked autocratic rule by decree and populist outreach
was contested by a few outspoken opponents and journalistic campaigns
that encountered insurmountable obstacles after the 1992 coup. The regime's
initial vulnerable spots were invariably tied to human rights violations and
the role played by Montesinos, who did not show his face in public. The
print media occasionally questioned the invisible Montesinos's political influence and involvement in atrocities and drug trafficking–related matters.
The country's television networks and other influential media unquestion-
ably backed the regime. Fujimorista legislators and judicial authorities defended and protected Montesinos. In an interview, Fujimori rejected drug
trafficking allegations against Montesinos by implicitly acknowledging his
advisor's links with the CIA.[48]

The judicial investigations of the La Cantuta and Barrios Altos massacres,
prompted by reporting by courageous journalists and eyewitness accounts,
ended up in military court, in which a few scapegoats were sentenced to 20-
year prison terms. However, following his 1995 reelection, on June 15, Fujimori signed a comprehensive "amnesty law," approved the day before the
CCD ended, that pardoned all officers condemned for human rights crimes
since 1982. Protests in the press, Congress, and even among normally ac-
quiescent yet poorly paid judges raged. U.S. Ambassador Alvin Adams advised Washington to express disappointment to the Peruvian ambassador,
congressional president Jaime Yoshiyama, and Montesinos himself.[49]

---

vestigate irregular legislation under Fujimori. "Dieron leyes para convertir al Estado en
un botín de Fujimori y Montesinos," *La República,* no. 7133, July 12, 2001, 8. Among
the ministers who collaborated with this legislation, the following have been indicted by
Congress: Jorge Camet, Víctor Joy Way, Jorge Baca Campodónico, and Efraín Golden-
berg as former finance ministers; Tomás Castillo, César Sauceda, Julio Salazar, and Carlos Bergamino as former defense ministers; and Juan Briones and José Villanueva as
former interior ministers. *La República,* no. 7742, March 13, 2003, 9.

48. U.S. Embassy (Hamilton) to U.S. Information Agency, Lima, November 17,
1992, unclassified USDS copy, in PDP, box 2, file SIN unit bio (and duplicate in BC,
box 1, file Montesinos), NSA.

49. U.S. Embassy (Adams) to S.S., Lima, June 15, 1995, no. 5676, unclassified
USDS copy, in PDP, box 2, file SIN, NSA. See also Adams to S.S., Lima, June 30, 1995,
no. 6089, and November 7, 1995, no. 10405, unclassified USDS copy, in BC, box 1, file
Montesinos, NSA.

Unbeknownst to the public, Ecuadoran troops had occupied a small portion of Peruvian boundary territory in January 1995. This was an embarrassing military defeat for the Peruvian inept army commanders that led to a frantic diplomatic effort to reach a peaceful settlement in the middle of the reelection campaign.[50]

Other scandals surfaced. In 1997, the assassination of Mariela Barreto and the alleged torture of Leonor La Rosa, both female military intelligence officers, and electronic eavesdropping and wiretapping linked to the SIN, captured public opinion. In December, Fujimori's regime was stunned by the bold action of hostage taking by the MRTA at the Japanese ambassador's residence in Lima. After a standoff of several weeks, special security forces stormed the residence and killed all the hostage takers.

Paradoxically, the eighth international anticorruption conference was held in Lima in September 1997. With characteristic cynicism, Fujimori, accompanied by OEA President César Gaviria, Attorney General Blanca Nélida Colán, and Comptroller Víctor Caso Lay, along with other Fujimorista dignitaries, opened the event. Some Peruvian journalists were quick to note the irony in the conference's host country being the worst example of public sector administration in existence. A long list of cases screamed for investigation that was systematically denied by the appropriate governmental authorities, including Attorney General Colán. These cases included the burning issue of the origins of Montesinos's income, the denunciations by Susan Higuchi concerning the Fujimori family's nongovernmental organizations (NGOs), the plunder of the military and police pension fund, and embezzlement in the state-owned insurance company Popular y Porvenir, among others.[51]

During the last three years of the Fujimori regime, 1998 to 2000, the regime's decline, linked to economic problems and the Montesinos liability factor, and a rising political and civic opposition, are better analyzed through the evidence of secret recordings by the SIN and cases by state prosecutors grounded on such evidence. Political developments in the 1990s concealed the consolidation and growth of covert, informal networks of disproportionate influence and power fueled by graft and abuse.

50. Fernando Rospigliosi, "Controversias: los intereses políticos y el conflicto," and "Controversias: el costo de la farsa," *Caretas,* no. 1349, February 9, 1995, 15, and no. 1351, February 23, 1995, 31.

51. Silvia Rojas, "Blanca Nélida Colán: una fiscal y varios delitos," and Julio Panduro, "El mal ejemplo del gobierno peruano," *La República,* September 8, 1997.

Networks of Corruption

Montesinos and Fujimori customarily celebrated special occasions in the company of their intimate friends and cronies in a shroud of secrecy. Reporters were absolutely excluded from those events, symbolic indicators of the corrupt liaisons between supreme power and its collaborators. Those meetings were recorded only by intelligence photographs and videotapes. For Montesinos's fifty-third birthday on May 20, 1998, there was plenty to celebrate in the gloomy rooms and corridors of the SIN. The regime was securely in power, the corrupt machine was working with few problems, and the way was being paved for Fujimori's second reelection. The awkwardly festive gathering was attended by a select group of members of Congress, ministers, military and police generals, judges, the attorney general, and businessmen. This and other secret celebrations paraded a representative cross-section of the vast corruption networks and branches in the 1990s.[52]

The corruption networks of the 1990s had at their center the alliance between Fujimori and Montesinos. Fujimori mainly dealt with politics and acted as a populist media showboat; Montesinos negotiated secretly with the military command and raised illegal funds amid multiple other intelligence tasks from his spymaster compound. By the latter part of Fujimori's regime, Montesinos had liaisons with nearly all branches of the corrupt structure that controlled power, manipulated public information, sabotaged the opposition, and set the example for the public sector lower ranks and society in general. The size, scope, and membership of that corrupt web were astounding (see Figure 7.1). The strategic areas of the public sector had been infiltrated. A large group of the Peruvian political and economic elite was involved. Executives of major domestic and foreign corporations also interacted with the corrupt web. Even media moguls and celebrities were bribed to provide support for the regime's campaigns and abuses. Never before in Peruvian history had it been possible to obtain such a clear and detailed x-ray depicting the clandestine workings of corruption.

52. "Un cumpleaños a lo grande," *El Comercio,* no. 83932, August 8, 2001, a8, and http://www.agenciaperu.com/investigacion/2001/AGO/VLADICUMPLE.HTM. See also "Montesinos y Fujimori celebraron cuando crisis arreciaba en el Perú" and *vladifotos* of the exclusive party, held on July 23, 2000, for the sixty-second anniversary of the Peruvian Air Force (FAP) gathering, among corrupt generals and congressmen, the soon-to-be reappointed minister Carlos Boloña, Julio Favre (vice president and future president of the Confederation of Peruvian Entrepreneurial Institutions, CONFIEP), Mendel Winter (owner of TV channel 2), and Moisés Wolfenson (owner of "mutt press" newspapers), *El Comercio,* no. 8393, August 13, 2001, a6, and http://www.agenciaperu.com/investigacion/2001/AGO/VLADIFAP.HTM.

Figure 7.1 Branches, networks, and links of corruption, 1990–2000.

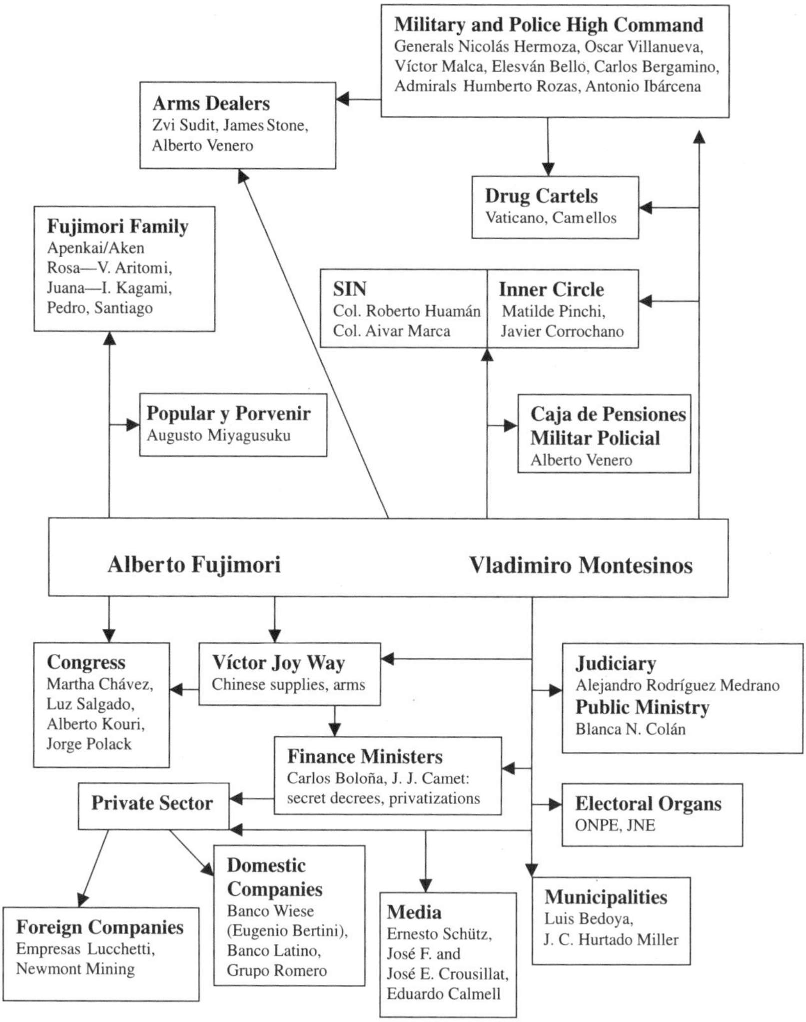

Military and Police High Command
Generals Nicolás Hermoza, Oscar Villanueva,
Víctor Malca, Elesván Bello, Carlos Bergamino,
Admirals Humberto Rozas, Antonio Ibárcena

Arms Dealers
Zvi Sudit, James Stone,
Alberto Venero

Fujimori Family
Apenkai/Aken
Rosa—V. Aritomi,
Juana—I. Kagami,
Pedro, Santiago

Drug Cartels
Vaticano, Camellos

SIN
Col. Roberto Huamán
Col. Aivar Marca

Inner Circle
Matilde Pinchi,
Javier Corrochano

Popular y Porvenir
Augusto Miyagusuku

**Caja de Pensiones
Militar Policial**
Alberto Venero

Alberto Fujimori   **Vladimiro Montesinos**

Congress
Martha Chávez,
Luz Salgado,
Alberto Kouri,
Jorge Polack

Víctor Joy Way
Chinese supplies, arms

Judiciary
Alejandro Rodríguez Medrano
Public Ministry
Blanca N. Colán

Finance Ministers
Carlos Boloña, J. J. Camet:
secret decrees, privatizations

Private Sector

Electoral Organs
ONPE, JNE

**Domestic
Companies**
Banco Wiese
(Eugenio Bertini),
Banco Latino,
Grupo Romero

Media
Ernesto Schütz,
José F. and
José E. Crousillat,
Eduardo Calmell

Municipalities
Luis Bedoya,
J. C. Hurtado Miller

Foreign Companies
Empresas Lucchetti,
Newmont Mining

Sources: Evidence published by *La República, El Comercio,* and Peruvian Congress.

Fujimori had an inner core of family members who aided in managing private and family interests and businesses revolving around the corruption of his post. Víctor Aritomi Shinto, married to Fujimori's sister Rosa, was appointed Peruvian ambassador to Japan in 1991, a key post held until the very last days of the regime. With the aid of Japanese officials, Fujimori and Aritomi skillfully played the card of their Japanese nationality that could eventually award them protection and impunity. Among several illegal operations, Aritomi used his diplomatic immunity to regularly transport Fujimori's illicit income to Japan in amounts manageable to launder without leaving obvious traces. Moreover, Fujimori's personal secretary made bank transfers to Aritomi from illegal funds received by Fujimori in Peru. Aritomi also solicited donations and humanitarian relief funds that were channeled to the Fujimori clan.[53]

Shortly before his swearing-in as president in 1990, Fujimori received a $12.5 million Japanese "donation" intended for meetings the needs of poor children. However, as with so many other Japanese donations, Fujimori and his relatives mismanaged those funds as a political slush fund from a bank account in Japan.[54] Video evidence shows Fujimori handling "social aid" resources in cash disbursements without keeping appropriate legal accounts.[55] Since 1990, the president's siblings Rosa, Pedro, and Juana Fujimori formed and managed in Peru the NGOs APENKAI and AKEN, which were notorious for their lax accounting practices and improper usage of storage areas in public customs buildings. The Fujimoris' NGOs served to funnel an estimated $100 million worth of donations coming from Japan and local illegal sources into the family's coffers[56] (only about 10 percent of donations reached their intended recipients).[57]

53. "Un millón de dólares envió Fujimori a su cuñado Víctor Aritomi en Japón," *La República,* no. 7127, July 6, 2001, 2; "Las cuentas de Fujimori," *La República,* no. 7128, July 7, 2001, 18. Aritomi also facilitated Fujimori's escape to Japan, along with large quantities of incriminating evidence, in November 2000, according to the case prepared by prosecutor José Luis Lecaros. "Enjuician a Fujimori por extraer 'vladivideos' comprometedores," *La República,* no. 7797, May 7, 2003, 9.

54. The account in the Bank of Tokyo was in the name of the foundation Peru No Kodomo No Kikin, but its movements were ordered by Fujimori himself. "Fiscalía halla en Japón cuenta que dirigía Fujimori," *El Comercio,* no. 83901, July 8, 2001, a4.

55. *La República,* September 2, 2003, commenting on two videos shown on the TV program "Cuarto Poder," América Televisión, in which Fujimori is seen handing an envelope full of cash to Vidal Bautista Carrasco, director of the national program of food aid, PRONAA, and an executive of APENKAI.

56. Research by Primera Fiscalía Anticorrupción and Fiscal de la Nación Nelly Calderón, "Implican a hermanos de Fujimori en red familiar para sacar dinero del Estado," *La República,* no. 7793, May 3, 2003, 10, and "Fujimori usaba ONG Apenkai para desviar donaciones japonesas," *La República,* no. 7148, July 27, 2001, 15. APENKAI's storage manager was the brother of Carmen Higaonna, customs superintendent and later comptroller general. "Apenkai tenía sus almacenes en el depósito de Aduanas," *El Comercio,* no. 83980, September 25, 2001, a7; "Apenkai enriqueció a Fujimori," *La República,* no. 7723, April 13, 2003, 18.

57. According to Ministerio Público sources cited in "Sólo repartían 10% de donaciones," *El Comercio,* no. 83912, July 19, 2001, a8.

Just before the 1992 coup, Susana Higuchi, Fujimori's estranged wife, denounced the illegal appropriation of Japanese donations by Fujimori's family entourage and specifically her in-laws Rosa and Santiago. Fujimori publicly declared that his wife was mentally unstable and kept her as a virtual prisoner at the presidential palace. Fujimori's children dismissed their mother's statements and sided with their father. The four children received elite college educations in the United States financed with $460,000 delivered in cash in New York and Boston through irregular means.[58]

Moreover, in 1998, Juana Fujimori and her husband Isidro Kagami Jiraku sold overvalued real estate to a company established in the British Virgin Islands. That company was used to launder corruption proceeds by one of Montesinos's top agents, Enrique Benavides Morales.[59] Aritomi and his wife Rosa Fujimori had sizeable, unexplained balances in local and foreign bank accounts.[60] Fujimori's favorite brother, Santiago, headed the administration and local distribution of presidential assets and donations until his fall from Montesinos's grace in 1996.

Apart from the straightforward graft involving his inner family circle, Fujimori also established close partnerships in the abuse of power with key executives and politicians who guaranteed confidentiality and trust. Augusto Miyagusuku Miagui collaborated actively with Fujimori's NGOs as treasurer and legal representative between 1991 and 1997. Miyagusuku was also the chair of the board of directors of the mostly state-owned insurance company Popular y Porvenir from where he also administered AKEN. Miyagusuku colluded with Fujimori in fraudulent insurance schemes involving the insurance policies that Popular y Porvenir sold to public sector bureaucracies, including the army. Approximately twenty former company directors and officials and five high-ranking military officers participated in the insurance collusion. As a result of irregular management that diverted the company's income into private hands, Popular y Porvenir lost its market share, and was saved from bankruptcy only through an irregular privatization process.[61]

---

58. "Triangularon dinero del SIN para Keiko, Hiro y Sachie," *La República*, no. 7795, May 5, 2003, 8; "La dama del contenedor," *La Revista de la República*, no. 7810, May 11, 2003, 7–10.

59. "Así blanquearon su botín Alberto Fujimori y familia," *La República*, no. 7769, April 9, 2003, 8–9.

60. "Recurría a desvío de fondos y donaciones," *La República*, no. 7745, March 16, 2003, 9. As in Aritomi's case, these are findings of local and international financial investigations considered by a congressional investigative commission, headed by Mauricio Mulder, as grounds for an indictment against Fujimori for "enriquecimiento ilícito y peculado."

61. Congreso del Perú, Comisión Investigadora de Delitos Económicos y Financieros

Víctor Joy Way was perhaps Fujimori's most intimate political crony, who served as minister of industry in 1991, and then as congressman, prime minister, and finally, as finance minister in 1999. Joy Way, invariably dressed in elegant designer suits, amassed a fortune of at least $22 million, which was eventually sequestered in Swiss and Luxembourg banks, and owned luxurious homes in Peru, thanks to blatantly corrupt deals allowed and partnered by Fujimori.[62]

Between 1990 and 1998, Fujimori, in collaboration with Joy Way, implemented several decrees following a cholera outbreak to favor emergency medicine imports. With the collaboration of three consecutive corrupt health ministers, public sector health-related agencies were used as façades to purchase at inflated prices, tax-exempt Chinese tractors, planes, generic medicines, and surgical and laboratory instruments and supplies in contravention of legal procedures. Joy Way, the owner of several import companies that sold the Chinese merchandise to the state, skimmed off hefty margins in these irregular transactions. Of these operations, which totaled $312 million, the state lost approximately $190 million to graft and mismanagement.[63] Moreover, a large portion of these Chinese goods, officially purchased for several ministries, ended up being appropriated by Fujimori's offices, the presidential ministry created just after the 1992 coup, and the palace guard administration (Casa Militar), for Fujimori's direct political use. In his many trips to the interior provinces, the populist president personally distributed these medicines and tractors, especially during the electoral campaigns of 1993 and 1995.[64]

1990–2001, *Informe final,* ed. Oscar Ugarteche (Lima: Impresora Peruana, 2003), 23–27; "Denuncian penalmente a Miyagusuku y 21 ex directivos de Popular y Porvenir," *La República,* no. 7295, December 21, 2001, 13.

62. Joy Way's career as a civil servant began in the 1970s. In 1986, while working for a private financial firm with privileged insider information, he speculated with Peruvian debt bonds. In the late 1980s, Joy Way acted as Peruvian sales representative of diverse Chinese products. Already in 1988, Joy Way was involved in a scandal of irregular sales of Chinese medicines to the Peruvian Social Security Institute (IPSS). "Víctor Joy Way: antecendentes de una fortuna en Suiza," http://www.agenciaperu.com/actualidad/2001/ABR/JOYWAY.HTM.

63. "Se invirtieron más de 28 millones de dólares en medicinas chinas," *El Comercio,* no. 83926, August 2, 2001, a2, based on Public Ministry documents. "Fiscal Calderón acusa a Fujimori por irregular compra de medicinas chinas," *La República,* no. 7775, April 15, 2003, 10; "Abren nuevo proceso a Fujimori y Joy Way," *La República,* no. 7800, May 10, 2003, 28.

64. "Acusan a Fujimori por compras irregulares de US$ 300 millones," http://

Aided by his inner circle of family and friends, Fujimori drained the Peruvian government's treasury of approximately $400 million through the illegal abuse of power during his administrations. Only a small amount of the total has been recovered. According to post-Fujimori financial and judicial authorities, part of these illegal funds can be indirectly traced to bank accounts in Japan and Europe. However, unlike Joy Way's and Montesinos's confirmed secret accounts abroad, international investigators have not yet identified accounts that are directly linked to the former president. Financial investigators have concluded that Fujimori's legally documented income received between 1990 and 2000, totaling more or less $1 million, represents only 0.3 per cent of the total estimated income he received in the same period. Therefore, approximately $372 million remain unaccounted for, and hard evidence shows that this income proceeded from illegal diversion of public funds and corrupt commissions.[65] The main sources of Fujimori's illicit funds were the misappropriation of foreign donations by his family-run NGOs ($90 million), Chinese import deals with Joy Way ($80 million), commissions from several partners including Miyagusuku ($50 million), secret subsidies from the SIN ($62 million), and a politically motivated "contingency fund" accumulated mainly from the milking of the military and police pension fund, illegal commissions from arms purchases, and privatization funds ($122 million). The two latter sources implied a close collaboration with Montesinos and the military chiefs. Beyond personal greed, the main motivation for this disproportionate graft was to retain power with enough funds to bribe and run fraudulent electoral and media campaigns.[66]

---

www.elcomercioperu.com.pe/noticias/html/2003–03–20/politi7097.html; "Ordenan captura de tres ex ministros de Salud por millonaria compra fraudulenta de medicinas chinas en mal estado." Additionally, Joy Way was involved in the sale of Peruvian citizenship certificates to Chinese citizens. In 2000, Joy Way was the major intermediary in bribing several members of Congress and the press. In 2001, Joy Way was accused in a congressional resolution of "patrocinio ilegal, enriquecimiento ilícito, omisión de declaraciones y defraudación tributaria." "Congreso aprobó acusar a Víctor Joy Way por cuatro delitos graves," *El Comercio,* no. 83947, August 23, 2001, a3.

65. Financial investigation by Superintendencia Nacional de Banca y Seguros, Attorney General Nelly Calderón, and Judge José Luis Lecaros. "Desbalance patrimonial de Fujimori alcanza los US$ 371 millones," *La República,* no. 7745, March 16, 2003, 8. See also no. 7780, 14, no. 7792, 10, and "Denuncian a Fujimori por desbalance patrimonial de US$ 372 mlls.," *Cadena Peruana de Noticias,* October 31, 2001, http://www.cpnradio.com.pe/html/2001/10/31/1/351.htm.

66. Evidence surfaced from innumerable judicial and congressional proceedings, witnesses, and financial analyses. See, for example, "Fujimori pedía plata a Montesinos

If Fujimori was supported by an inner core of family and friends who participated in the spoils of corruption, Montesinos's inner core consisted mainly of intelligence officers and administrators based at the SIN, as well as compromised financial agents, arms dealers, and lawyers in charge of facilitating the flow of illegal funds in and out of the country. Some members of Montesinos's immediate family were only partially involved as nominal holders of some of his bank accounts in Peru. But from his intelligence headquarters, Montesinos's corrupting influence spread to many sectors. The more political dissent there was against Fujimori's regime,[67] the more Montesinos extended his reach in two interrelated activities: the illegal appropriation of public funds through various schemes, and the bribing of public officials, private sector entrepreneurs, and media personalities. The illegal appropriation of funds was the means to obtain support and connivance for retaining political control. Following conspicuous and scandalous cases of bribery allows the identification of the various tentacles and branches of these corrupt networks. The depth and scope of these networks are truly startling.

Héctor Chumpitaz was the captain of the Peruvian soccer team during the 1970s, perhaps the team's most successful period ever. In the middle of the frenzy of recruiting political support for Fujimori and allies, the soccer hero received bribes of $10,000 a month (totaling $30,000) directly from Montesinos to run for alderman in the failed slate of Lima's mayoral candidate Juan Carlos Hurtado Miller in 1998.[68] Montesinos financed the campaign of Hurtado Miller—Fujimori loyalist and former finance minister—by spending an estimated $261,300. Montesinos also provided Hurtado

---

para su campaña reeleccionista" [Townsend Congressional Commission], *La República,* no. 7197, September 14, 2001, 4; "Dieron leyes para convertir al Estado en un botín de Fujimori" [judicial commission headed by García Sayán], *La República,* no. 7133, July 12, 2001, 8; and "Ex ministro Jorge Camet implica a Fujimori en compra de armamento" [testimony before prosecutor José Ugaz], *La República,* no. 7109, June 18, 2001, 2–3.

67. "Actividad del SIN fue asegurar la reelección de Fujimori," *El Comercio,* no. 83941, August 17, 2001, a6, based on legal testimony by Montesinos. "El SIN gastó millonaria suma del tesoro público para sobornos," *El Comercio,* no. 83960, September 5, 2001, a1, based on anticorruption court reports.

68. "No temo dar la cara," *La República,* no. 7127, July 6, 2001, 16; "El partido más difícil del gran capitán Héctor Chumpitaz," *El Comercio,* no. 84003, October 18, 2001, a11; "Chumpitaz: faltan piezas," *Caretas,* no. 1769, April 24, 2003, 42–43. Anticorruption judge Magalli Báscones condemned Chumpitaz to house arrest, a penalty he endured for more than a year before facing trial in 2004; he was given a suspended sentenced of four years.

Miller with strategic support against a key opposition candidate, Alberto Andrade, a potentially dangerous rival in the approaching presidential elections of 2000.[69] Another candidate who ruined his political career as well as the political legacy of his father was Luis Bedoya de Vivanco, the former mayor and candidate for mayor of Miraflores, one of Lima's middle-class districts. Bedoya was taped receiving $25,000 from Montesinos, and accepting media access and sensitive intelligence information from the same to use in a ploy against Andrade's brother, Fernando, who was running for reelection as mayor of Miraflores.[70]

Montesinos's bribe coffers seemed bottomless. He paid monthly bribe money to Fujimori himself and, following Fujimori's instructions, to several of his ministers at various times. Montesinos even paid for tailored suits for a prime minister who reportedly had no taste in clothes.[71] Moreover, the power and corrupting influence exerted by Montesinos in the judiciary became almost absolute after 1992. Judges of the Supreme Court and lower and provincial courts formed a secretive web that granted decisions and

69. "Montesinos le pagó la campaña electoral a Hurtado Miller" and "Montesinos y Borobio asesoraron la campaña de Vamos Vecino" include still frames and text excerpts of incriminating video and sound recordings at the SIN, in *La República,* no. 7126, July 5, 2001, 10–11. For full transcripts, see audio tapes labeled "Entrega de fondos a Hurtado Miller," August 2 and 11, 1988, audio tapes 1183–1184 and 1188–1189, in Perú, Congreso, *En la sala de la corrupción: videos y audios de Vladimiro Montesinos (1998–2000),* ed. and notes Antonio Zapata (Lima: Fondo Editorial del Congreso del Perú, 2004), 3:1483–1686, esp. 1646–1647, http://www.geocities.com/agenciaperu/vladi_borobio_hurtadomiller1188.htm.

70. "Luis Bedoya de Vivanco también será juzgado por asociación ilícita," *La República,* no. 7749, March 20, 2003, 15; "Campaña de Bedoya se planificó en el SIN," *La República,* no. 7750, March 21, 2003, 16. See transcripts of Montesinos's videos ("vladivideos") by Departamento de Transcripciones, Congreso de la República, videos 1568 and 1569 (June 12, 1999), and 1577 and 1578 (June 17, 1999), http://www.agenciaperu.com/archivo/vladivideos/vladivideos.htm; "Reunión Doctor, Bedoya, Reátegui," June 12 and July 5, 1999, videos nos. 1568–1569, 1601–1602, in Perú, Congreso, *En la sala de la corrupción,* 3:1965–2048, esp. 2019.

71. According to testimonies before judge Saúl Peña on June 27, 2001, the ministers who received bribes from Montesinos were Alberto Bustamante (justice and chief of cabinet, $10,000 monthly), Alberto Pandolfi (transport and chief of cabinet, $5,000 to $10,000 monthly), Belisario Casas (agriculture, $3,000 monthly), and Federico Salas (education and chief of cabinet, $30,000 monthly). "Montesinos declara que pagó a cuatro ministros de Estado," *El Comercio,* no. 83915, July 22, 2001, a2. Bustamante, Pandolfi, and Salas were also charged with constitutional violations and other crimes, together with fifteen other former ministers, by a congressional commission in September 2001.

judgments in favor of private and political interests protected by Montesinos. The main ally of Montesinos in the Supreme Court was Judge Alejandro Rodríguez Medrano, who called judges to press them for favorable decisions sought by Montesinos.[72] In one particularly shameful case, Montesinos handed the president of the Supreme Court a draft resolution on an appeal to allow Fujimori to run for president for a third time despite constitutional impediments. The judge and the entire Supreme Court constitutional division met with Montesinos at the SIN to actually discuss such a resolution, which they later approved.[73]

Since its pseudo-reform in 1992, the entire justice system was plagued with institutional "innovations" that served as incentives for mediocre and corrupt judges and as punishment for honest judges. Approximately fifty judges of superior and provincial courts collaborated in Montesinos's judicial network.[74] In perhaps the most corrupt case in the administration of Peruvian justice, the attorney general (fiscal de la Nación) and head of the executive branch's prosecuting and legal defense ministry (Ministerio Público), Blanca Nélida Colán, dismissed several formal indictments against Montesinos. With the $10,000 a month that Montesinos paid Colán during her long tenure (1992–2001), she was able to live in luxury.[75]

Bribery of electoral authorities to carry out fraud was particularly shocking. In December 1999, the head of the electoral processing office (ONPE), José Portillo, and approximately forty associates linked to members of Congress Absalón Vásquez and María Jesús Espinoza, forged thousands of signatures necessary for the registration of Fujimori's renamed political movement, Peru 2000. The fraud was exposed by investigative reports published

---

72. "El brazo del 'Doc' era Rodríguez Medrano," *Peru.21,* no. 15, January 23, 2003, 7.

73. In a congressional hearing, the former head of the Supreme Court, Luis Serpa, admitted Montesinos's gross interference in the administration of justice and his own and his colleagues' scandalous acquiescence. "Ex vocales supremos admiten interferencia de Montesinos," *El Comercio,* no. 83981, September 26, 2001, a6. See also bribery and partiality of judge of the Supreme Court's Sala Superior de Delitos Tributarios, "Cayó Orestes Castellares, otro ex vocal supremo montesinista," *La República,* no. 7753, March 24, 2003, and no. 7754, March 25, 2003, 10.

74. "Fueron suspendidos 42 magistrados en 60 días," *El Comercio,* no. 83925, August 1, 2001, a2; "Denuncian penalmente a 12 ex magistrados," *La República,* no. 7292, December 18, 2001, 7.

75. In January 2003, Colán was condemned to ten years in prison. "Encarcelan a Colán Maguiño por sus vínculos con el Doc," *El Comercio,* no. 83919, July 26, 2001, a2. Miguel Aljovín was another former attorney general who was bribed to dismiss charges against Montesinos. See *El Comercio,* no. 83910, July 17, 2001, a2.

in *El Comercio.* Confidential voting records from previous elections were used for the falsification. In addition, a sophisticated apparatus for massive telephone spying that provided information directly to Montesinos was placed at ONPE headquarters. Portillo, as well as the head of the electoral legal office (JNE), Alipio Montes de Oca, visited Montesinos at the SIN on a regular basis.[76] The JNE invariably rejected all legal complaints against Fujimori's unconstitutional reelection maneuvers.

Pro-government members of Congress charged steep prices to further de-institutionalize the bruised legislative power. The pro-Fujimori majority in Congress, especially during the legislature of 1995–2000, had systematically surrendered congressional legislative and oversight rights. This allowed Fujimori and Montesinos to exert unchecked power over other key institutions, such as the judiciary and electoral tribunals, and remain unpunished for their crimes and transgressions. Not a single motion to open urgent human rights or corruption investigations was approved in a Congress dominated by pro-Fujimori forces. The degree of servile behavior observed among many members of Congress can only be explained by taking into account the massive distribution of bribe money in their midst.

Key elected congressional representatives received financial support for their electoral campaigns as well as monthly payments of between $10,000 and $20,000. Moreover, Montesinos organized meetings at the SIN to dictate directives and coordinate strategies with these representatives; one such meeting in 2000 brought together almost all Fujimori's supporters in Congress, or 54 out of the 120 members elected in 1995.[77] These representa-

---

76. "La danza del millón de firmas: ordenan la captura de 37 personas," *El Comercio,* no. 83919, July 26, 2001, a2; "La falsificación de firmas se hizo con actas digitalizadas," *El Comercio,* no. 83946, August 22, 2001, a2; "Portillo y Cavassa montaron gigantesco equipo de 'chuponeo,'" *La República,* no. 7289, December 15, 2001, 2–3; "Vi a Portillo en la época en que se preparaba segunda vuelta electoral," *El Comercio,* no. 83910, July 17, 2001, a2.

77. "Asesor y fujimoristas sometieron el Congreso," *El Comercio,* no. 83915, July 22, 2001, a4, based on testimony before Judge Saúl Peña on July 13, 2001. Among the most conspicuous were Víctor Joy Way, Carmen Lozada, Luz Salgado, Martha Chávez, and Martha Hildebrandt. See also transcripts of video, "Parlamentarios Cambio 90" meeting with Montesinos at the SIN in April 1998, http://www.elcomercio.com.pe/ece-spe/html/montesinos/video806_807.html. In this meeting, the following members of Congress were present: Carlos Blanco, Jorge Trelles, Alfredo Quispe, Eduardo Pando, Miguel Velit, Ricardo Marcenaro, Adolfo Amorín, Oscar Medelius, Jorge Ruiz Dávila, Luz Salgado, Víctor Joy Way, Carmen Lozada, Daniel Espichán, Edith Mellado, and Gilberto Siura. Ministers Alberto Pandolfi Arbulú and Rafael Urrelo were also present.

tives plotted ways to uphold the regime and destroy the opposition. They discussed various ways of undermining democracy to remain in power and derive personal benefit. Montesinos acted as the intermediary with these legislators. They reciprocated by defending Montesinos every time he was denounced in Congress for his illegal activities.[78] They also actively participated actively in the illegal procedures that Montesinos used to recruit members of the opposition to achieve a majority in Congress.[79]

Several elected members of the opposition in Congress were also bribed by Montesinos to switch party allegiance on key issues, provide confidential information about opposition parties, or secretly support the pro-Fujimori group in votes. This type of bribery had occurred since at least 1992, but it was stepped up after the 2000 election because Fujimori's group did not win a majority. The bribed representatives had secret meetings with Montesinos at the SIN to arrange payments; some received their money directly from Montesinos's hands. Each turncoat (*tránsfuga*) had his or her own price. Perhaps the most shameless was Alberto Kouri, who received $60,000 to change his party allegiance just after the 2000 elections.[80]

Investigations into the illegal activities of another congressional turncoat, Jorge Polack, proved quite revealing of the deals between Montesinos and the media aimed at manipulating public opinion. Polack—the wealthy owner of a radio broadcasting company, Radio Libertad, a valuable instrument in his own election campaign—had been elected to Congress in 2000 as a member of the opposition party Solidaridad Nacional. From Montesino, Polack received $500,000, the highest turncoat bribe of all. Moreover, in August 2000, Polack's radio network was paid $118,000 to broadcast political ads by three companies under the control of Montesinos and

---

78. Guillermo González Arica, ed., *Los escaños de Montesinos* (Lima: Fimart, 2001).

79. "Formalizan acusación por 'reclutar' tránsfugas," *El Comercio,* no. 83924, July 31, 2001, a7.

80. "Alberto Kouri es culpable del delito de cohecho propio," *El Comercio,* no. 83973, September 18, 2001, a8; "Piden otros cinco años de cárcel para Alberto Kouri," *La República,* no. 7810, May 20, 2003, 10. Kouri was sentenced to a jail term of six years. Apart from Kouri, the long list of bribed turncoats of the 2000 legislature included Jorge D'Acunha ($10,000), Milagros Huamán Lu ($30,000), Guido Pennano ($35,000), José Luna ($7,000), Waldo Ríos ($10,000), Juan Carlos Mendoza ($10,000), Gregorio Ticona ($41,000), José Elías ($40,000), Luis Cáceres ($20,000), Roger Cáceres ($20,000), Mario Gonzáles ($20,000), and Ruby Rodríguez ($50,000). "Fujimori me exigía seguir con el reclutamiento de congresistas," *El Comercio,* no. 83914, July 21, 2001, a10; "Huamán Lu recibió US$ 30 mil," *La República,* no. 7775, April 15, 2003, 11.

his financial agents. Polack also collaborated with one of Montesinos's confidential agents in charge of telephone surveillance equipment.[81] Polack, however, was just the tip of the corrupt media iceberg.

Due to their strategic roles, media network moguls were the highest paid by Montesinos.[82] The corrupt spymaster consciously targeted TV broadcasting as the most influential means of communication as print media was accessible by only a fraction of the population. Media outlets were not directly censored nor controlled by the government. This deceptive "freedom" of expression and the press was the cover for unceasing and well orchestrated media campaigns supportive of Fujimori's "electoral authoritarian" regime. Bribery of media moguls and celebrities (many of whom enthusiastically offered their services) in exchange for political support and launching defamation campaigns against the opposition was one of the regime's most pernicious forms of corruption.[83]

The most egregious participants in media corruption were José Francisco and José Enrique Crousillat, father and son, owners of TV América Televisión, channel 4. This TV station offered propaganda by reality show host Laura Bozzo and news anchor Nicolás Lúcar for a price. Starting as early as 1997, the Crousillats sold their editorial content to Montesinos for approximately $600,000 a month. Montesinos arranged the illegal refinanc-

81. Unlike Kouri, who was captured in a famous video, Polack has been accused by the protected witness Matilde Pinchi before Judge José Lecaros of receiving $490,000 at the SIN. Polack remained free and continued to collaborate with the imprisoned Montesinos in 2003. "Polack recibió $490 mil," *Peru.21,* no. 253, April 30, 2003, 7; "Pinchi Pinchi: 'Polack compró equipos de chuponeo pare el SIN,'" *La República,* no. 7790, April 30, 2003, 11; "Sintonía tránsfuga," *Caretas,* no. 1771, May 8, 2003, 17–19; "Oscar López Meneses revela sus conexiones con Montesinos," *La República,* no. 7747, March 18, 2003, 18–19; "En 1999 exculparon a López de tenencia ilegal de armas," *El Comercio,* no. 83936, August 12, 2001, a10. López was the son-in-law of former general and defense minister Víctor Malca.

82. John McMillan and Pablo Zoido, "How to Subvert Democracy: Montesinos in Peru," CESifo Working Paper, no. 1173 (2004), and *Journal of Economic Perspectives* 18, no. 4 (2004): 69–92.

83. Under Peruvian law, the charges for these crimes include "asociación ilícita (para delinquir), tráfico de influencias, y peculado en agravio del Estado." For access to official transcripts of videos involving corruption and the media, see http://www.rcp.net.pe/contenidos/prensa-corrupcion. See also Fernando Rospigliosi, "Controversias: Libertad de empresa, no de información," and "Controversias: Un gobierno impresentable," in *Caretas,* no. 1566, May 6, 1999, 16, and no. 1610, March 16, 2000, 16; Ernesto Toledo Brückmann, *¿¡Hasta cuándo!?: la prensa peruana y el fin del fujimorato* (Lima: Editorial San Marcos, 2001), chapter 2.

ing of the Crousillats' \$7-million debt owed to the local Banco Wiese, with the help of his friend Eugenio Bertini, a senior manager at the bank. Montesinos guaranteed Bertini a payment of \$6 million to the Crousillats through the shady Caja de Pensiones Militar Policial-Banco de Comercio, which was under Montesinos's financial control. The Crousillats amassed personal fortunes of approximately \$5 million in real estate and in offshore accounts in the Caribbean and Panama.[84]

The Crousillats and Bozzo were also the most enthusiastic participants in the so-called "escuelita del SIN," a series of briefing sessions held by Montesinos and military strategists to instruct them on the appropriate political line to follow. Incredibly, owners of the country's other major TV broadcast outlets also participated in those sessions: Ernesto Schütz (president of the board of Panamericana Televisión, channel 5), Samuel and Mendel Winter (owners of Frecuencia Latina, channel 2), and Julio Vera Abad (owner of Televisión Andina, channel 9).[85]

Montesinos referred to this group of corrupt media moguls as the "team." Video footage recorded in 1999 showed Schütz bargaining with Montesinos over \$12 million for selling his editorial content and attacking the opposition. Schütz had to settle for \$1.5 million a month for a total of \$9 million plus free money laundering advice from the expert Montesinos.[86] The Win-

---

84. Excerpts from transcripts of vladivideo, no. 1607, July 19, 1999, in "'El canal [4] se ha jugado por el Gobierno, el presidente y la reelección,' dice ex asesor: fue en el SIN en una reunión con Crousillat y Eugenio Bertini," *El Comercio*, no. 83903, July 19, 2001, a3; "Los hechos y delitos por los que son procesados," *El Comercio*, no. 84052, December 6, 2001, a3. Full transcript, "Reunión Dr., Crousillat, Sr. Wo, Sr. Bresani," July 19, 1999, video, no. 1607, in Perú, Congreso, *En la sala de la corrupción*, 1:223–51, esp. 237–38. The Peruvian state had difficulties seizing the Crousillats' properties and accounts while they remained fugitives; they were imprisoned and extradited from Argentina to face trial in June and September 2006; they were convicted and sentenced to eight years in prison. "Los prófugos Crousillat gastaron US\$ 5 millones en propiedades," *La República*, no. 7802, May 12, 2003, 8, based on information provided by an anonymous protected informant, "colaborador 018." See also Fernando Rospigliosi, *El arte del engaño: las relaciones entre los militares y la prensa* (Lima: Tarea, 2000), 103–4, 109–14, 124–25.

85. "Los Winter hunden más a Laura y a los Crousillat," *Peru.21*, no. 272, May 19, 2003, 3.

86. "Schütz: 'Tengo necesidad de 12 millones de dólares.' Empresario solicita dinero al ex asesor en cuotas de 1.7 millones de dólares porque 'Panamericana es un canalazo.'" *El Comercio*, no. 83989, October 4, 2001, pa4, a2. Schütz tried to escape in October 2001, but was detained in Buenos Aires on his way to Switzerland. Advised by Montesinos, between April and September 2000, Schütz transferred a total of \$1.5

ter brothers received less for the sale of their content, but had good reasons to be very grateful. The Winters were able to own channel 2 in 1996 thanks to the prosecution of the channel's majority shareholder, Baruch Ivcher, who had been forced into exile and stripped of his Peruvian citizenship after withdrawing his support for Fujimori and airing revealing reports on torture and telephone spying by the military.[87] Genaro Delgado Parker, a major shareholder in channel 13, who had chronic legal troubles, promised Montesinos that he would fire independent journalist César Hildebrandt in exchange for a favorable judgment concerning a stock ownership dispute.[88]

Among the elaborate financial schemes that were used to disguise the bribery of media moguls, the one devised by the owners of Cable Canal de Noticias (CCN), channel 10, was perhaps the most baroque. CCN was owned by Manuel Ulloa van Peborgh, son of a corrupt finance minister who served in the early 1980s, and Eduardo Calmell del Solar, a former congressman. Both were also co-owners of the rabidly pro-Fujimori newspapers *Expreso* and *Extra,* although Ulloa held a two-thirds majority of the stock. The two partners and Montesinos found a third person, a former stockholder of CCN, to arrange the fictitious sale of CCN stock to the Ministry of Defense for $2 million to pay off Ulloa and Calmell. Additionally, Ulloa and Calmell shared $1.75 million received from Montesinos as a reward for the pro-Fujimori editorial content of *Expreso.*[89]

The dregs of the print media, known collectively as the *prensa chicha* (mutt press), served the poor and uneducated. The owners and editors of

million to the Miami branch of the Crédit Lyonnais. "Detectan millonaria transferencia de Schütz Landázuri a cuenta en EEUU," *La República,* no. 7801, May 11, 2003, 16–17.

87. Wiener, *Bandido Fujimori,* 383–88; Rospigliosi, *Arte del engaño,* 89–91.

88. See official congressional transcripts of vladivideos nos. 1459–60, and 1487–88, meetings between Genaro Delgado Parker with Montesinos and Joy Way, April 7 and 21, 1999, http://www.elcomercioperu.com.pe/ecespe/html/montesinos/video1459delgado _joy.html and http://www.elcomercioperu.com.pe/ecespe/html/montesinos/video_ Genaro.html. See also "Reunión Joy-Way, Genaro Delgado Parker," April 4, 1999, videos nos. 1364–65, in Perú, Congreso, *En la sala de la corrupción,* 1:377–403, 405–69. See also Rospigliosi, *El arte del engaño,* 85–88, 120–21.

89. Official transcripts of vladivideos nos. 1778–79 and audio 1780, meeting "Montesinos, Calmell, Vicente, Gral. Delgado," November 6, 1999, in Perú, Congreso, *En la sala de la corrupción,* 1:581–631; and "Montesinos pagó 2 millones de dólares en efectivo por Canal 10: utilizó a Vicente Silva Checa para que 'compre' acciones a Manuel Ulloa y Calmell del Solar sirvió de testigo," *La República,* no. 7129, July 8, 2001, 20–27; "Calmell del Solar admitió que se había producido el pago," *El Comercio,* no. 83901, July 8, 2001, 10; "Calmell: Ulloa van Peborgh recibió US$ 350,000 por apoyo a Fujimori," *Correo,* no. 8306, April 29, 2003, 9; "Pagando Pato," *Caretas,* no. 1772, May 15, 2003, 24.

these "rags" displayed great imagination for bizarre insults, misinformation, and manipulation. The most successful at this brand of journalism and its particular "psicosocial" campaigns were the brothers Alex and Moisés Wolfenson (the latter a pro-Fujimori congressman elected in 2000), editors of *El Chino*. Other chicha press owners, Rubén Gamarra (*La Yuca*) and José Olaya (*El Tío*), received between $200,000 and $600,000 in 1999. A journalist close to the SIN, Augusto Bresani, worked with Montesinos and the publicist Daniel Borobio to transmit both headlines and money to the editors of chicha newspapers. Smear campaigns targeted prominent journalists uncovering the regime's underbelly. Most surprisingly, Bresani not only received money from Montesinos but also, since 1997, from important private corporations bent on providing support to Fujimori and his dirty campaigns. Key foreign companies and national business groups were among the principal contributors to the mutt press.[90] In March and April 1998, the prensa chicha launched a virulent campaign against journalists, particularly those publishing reports on the malfeasance of military and intelligence officers in *La República,* including Fernando Rospigliosi, Ángel Páez, and Edmundo Cruz. Complemented by death threats and accusations of treason, the manipulation of the yellow press amounted to an ex post facto censorship that was extremely threatening to honest journalists.[91]

Private Sector Corruption

Corrupt networking in the 1990s clearly also had strategic branches in the private sector. Bribery funds had to be raised wherever possible. Private sector interests provided the Montesinos-Fujimori machinery with an important source of illegal funds to corrupt and dominate the Peruvian structure of power. These private interests actively sought special favors and protection, opposed effective reforms, and participated in covert corruption

---

90. "Firma Lucchetti pagaba prensa chicha de Bresani," *Perú.21,* no. 279, May 26, 2003, 3; "Gremco y Alicorp [Grupo Romero] dieron también plata a Bresani," *Perú.21,* no. 280, May 27, 2003, 5, "Empresa Daewoo daba también plata a Bresani," *Perú.21,* no. 282, May 29, 2003, 6. These private companies paid approximately 200 invoices of an average $30,000 each for "*asesoramiento periodístico*" to Bresani & Asociados (exp., no. 036, 1er. Juzgado Especial Anticorrupción). "Bresani presentó 200 facturas de empresas," *Perú.21,* no. 281, May 28, 2001, 7.

91. Ambassador Dennis Jett to S.S., Lima, April 30, 1998, no. 2803, unclassified USDS copy, in BC, box 2, NSA.

networks. Once again, important private economic interests provided support to a regime promising to maintain the status quo. However, in the 1990s the domestic private sector was hit hard by international competition. The drastic liberalization and privatization of the economy under an increasingly authoritarian regime initially was of interest only to risk-taking foreign investors. Thus, foreign companies also competed for official favors.

Liberal reform under Fujimori-Montesinos did not result in straightforward market rules. Key sectors of the liberalized economy were now being brokered by corrupt authorities. Some domestic and foreign companies accepted the crooked rules and played them to their advantage. Macroeconomic results seemed advantageous at first to all sides. Privatization funds contributed to the mirage. Most of these funds were not allocated in ways to buttress the economic system, but rather were diverted to bribes and superfluous activities to consolidate political control. In the end, increasing economic problems that originated in part from the corrupt management of the economy and lack of fiscal controls, exacerbated conflicts within and among domestic and foreign interests.[92] Corrupt economic reforms had unintended consequences. Another historical opportunity to achieve badly needed economic reform was distorted and ultimately wasted.

Dionisio Romero was undoubtedly the richest man in Peru in the 1990s. The economic group that he led, already a mature empire since the late 1970s, encompassed banking (Banco de Crédito del Perú, BCP, the largest domestic bank) and agro-industrial enterprises (ALICORP), among other key investments in the domestic market. Romero had shown himself to be an entrepreneurial wizard at adaptation and transformation of his group's assets with a "little help" from the state. His group successfully survived the agrarian reform of the 1970s by speculating with agrarian expropriation bonds to enter and dominate the protected industrial and banking sectors. In the 1980s, Romero also benefited from investment, exchange, and tax incentives delivered by President García, while BCP management diversified its financial assets to include offshore activities at a time of increasing in-

---

92. Lack of honest financial control allowed a pyramid scheme through an informal financial institution, the Latin American Business Counseling Center (CLAE), which attracted thousands of depositors offering abnormally high yields on savings. Government agencies shut it down in April 1993, but could not start the liquidation until several months later. Carlos Manrique, who headed the CLAE, allegedly paid Montesinos, through lawyer Javier Corrochano, $1 million for a favorable judicial decision in his case. Alvin Adams to S.S., September 20, 1994, no. 8695, unclassified USDS copy, in BC, box 1, file Montesinos, NSA; Caretas, *Montesinos,* 47.

flux of drug-related dollars. In due time, however, Romero and other bankers successfully thwarted the expropriation of the private banking system announced unexpectedly in 1987 by the populist García.[93] During the Fujimori regime, Romero offered full political support to a government that granted his group special favors as well as an authoritarian-style general stability. Based on existing historical evidence, the real scope of the connections between the most powerful domestic group in Peru and corrupt networks in power in the 1990s can only be partially surmised.

Romero and Montesinos held secret meetings at which high-level military, police, and navy commanders were present, but rarely participated.[94] From the recordings of such meetings, the mutual respect of Montesinos and Romero is obvious. Romero promised Montesinos that he would deliver political statements favorable to Fujimori's reelection in a journalistic interview published soon after one of their meetings. Moreover, in the midst of the hostile restructuring of property, policy, and assets in the 1990s, Romero was involved in several debt collection cases, for which his bank obtained Montesinos's assistance in obtaining favorable decisions via corrupt judges. One such case involved the shipping company Hayduk, whose owners denounced a drug trafficking scheme; the firm was then confiscated and absorbed into the Romero group, which was a major creditor of Hayduk.[95]

Romero was definitely not alone among leading domestic entrepreneurs and financiers who established covert illegal agreements with Montesinos and Fujimori. In 1994–1997, a high-level manager of the BCP, Jorge Peschiera, was intimately involved in using insider information to purchase depreciated Peruvian foreign debt bonds. Successive presidents of the Peruvian confederation of entrepreneurs, CONFIEP, supported Fujimori under very suspicious circumstances. Bertini, the senior manager of another important domestic bank, Banco Wiese (BW), as mentioned earlier, was a

93. Enrique Vásquez, *Estrategias del poder: grupos económicos en el Perú* (Lima: CIUP, 2000), chapter 4.

94. "Reunión del señor Vladimiro Montesinos Torres con Dionisio Romero Seminario, el General EP César Saucedo Sánchez, General PNP Fernando Dianderas Ottone, Almirante Antonio Ibárcena Amico, General EP José Villanueva Ruesta y General EP Elesván Bello Vásquez," June 14, 1999 (broadcast February 16, 2001), congressional transcription of videos nos. 1574–75, in Perú, Congreso, *En la sala de la corrupción,* 1:143–83.

95. "Reunión Dr. [Montesinos], Dionisio Romero," June 22, 1999, video, no. 1583, in Perú, Congreso, *Sala de corrupción,* 1:185–222; Manuel Dammert, *Fujimori-Montesinos: el Estado mafioso; el poder imagocrático en las sociedades globalizadas* (Lima: Ediciones El Virrey, 2001), 165.

childhood friend of Montesinos. The two men exchanged favors: Montesinos "solved" legal issues and delayed government financial charges against the BW; Bertini agreed to help finance and launder illegal funds to finance corrupt media moguls. Bertini also advised Montesinos on ways of moving his "hot" money abroad and hiding his and his partners' domestic accounts that may come under public scrutiny.[96]

Government rescue operations benefiting BW and several other local banks, including the Banco Latino, exposed a scheme of misappropriated state funds and ad hoc modification of banking regulations (Bank Law of 1996) that expressly prohibited government assistance to failing banks. According to official accounts, in the 1998–2000 period these rescue operations, totaling between $935 million and $1.145 billion in public funds, benefited private sector interests linked to Montesinos and finance ministers Jorge Baca Campodónico (1998) and Joy Way (1999).[97] In part, these public "rescue" funds originated in the hasty liquidation of the state-owned development banking institutions. The BW was experiencing serious problems in 1998; disregarding warnings by the official banking regulatory agency (Superintendencia de Banca y Seguros, SBS), the bank's management opted to enter in a merger scheme with a local bank held by Italian-French interests, the Banco de Lima Sudameris. Despite the BW's extremely weak financial situation, the merger proceeded in June 1999 with the active support of the finance ministry. The ministry provided $251 million ($55 million in cash and $196 million in financial guarantees) to buttress the BW's depreciated assets. This rescue operation meant a diversion of public funds made possible by a suspiciously timed emergency decree (Decreto de Urgencia No. 034–99) of June 25, 1999.[98]

Banco Latino was the flagship of the Picasso economic group, led by Jorge Picasso Salinas, with investments in vineyards and wineries, mining, and stock brokerage firms. By 1996, Banco Latino had over-specialized in

96. "Reunión Dr. [Montesinos]-Bertini," video, no. 1788, November 11, 1999, official congressional transcription (2000), http://www.elcomercio.com.pe/EcEspe/html/montesinos/Video1788b.html; "Reunión Dr. [Montesinos] Crousillat. Sr. Wo. Sr. Bertini," video, no. 1607, July 19, 1999, http://www.elcomercio.com.pe/EcEspe/html/montesinos/video1607b.html; "Encuentran responsable a Bertini," *Perú.21,* no. 274, May 21, 2003, vol. 1, 7; "El ex banquero bloqueó US$ 32 mllns. de la mafia," *Perú.21,* no. 248, April 25, 2003, 8.

97. Perú, Congreso, Comisión Delitos Económicos, *Informe final,* 59–60; Dammert, *Estado mafioso,* 186.

98. Perú, Congreso, Comisión Delitos Económicos, *Informe final,* 67–68; Dammert, *Estado mafioso,* 186–87.

granting credit to the Picasso group companies, which in turn "bought" highly depreciated assets from the bank. This group's irregular self-financing scheme patently violated banking regulations and put its clients' deposits at risk. The banking regulator SBS signaled a red light that the bank's shareholders did not heed. Minister of Finance Jorge Baca Campodónico then instructed the Banco de la Nación and development fund COFIDE, both state institutions, to assist Banco Latino. COFIDE thus became an 86-percent majority stockholder in the faltering Banco Latino. Thereafter, COFIDE took control of the bank and continued to inject cash infusions for a total loss of approximately $436 million. The Banco Latino was liquidated at the state's expense and only then absorbed by another bank in 2000.[99] Other rescued or liquidated banks (Banco Nuevo Mundo, NBK, Banex, Banco República, Orion, Daewoo, Serbanco, and Finsur) accounted for additional losses of between $248 and $521 million in unrecoverable public funds.

A number of foreign companies also dealt with Montesinos to obtain judicial and other official favors through bribes paid to top public officials. The complicated and corrupt legal structure of property rights attracted only the most committed multinational managers who were willing to use public administrative corruption for their own advantage. This is not a new problem; foreign companies engaged in corrupt practices with government officials in Latin America have a long history. This pattern has only recently been partly curbed by stiff regulations in the United States and Europe against the bribing of foreign officials. However, as demonstrated by recent journalistic studies, prosecution and effective punishment of those foreign companies in their own countries is extremely difficult due to the deep pockets and the battalion of corporate lawyers that many multinationals can wield.[100]

Clear evidence has surfaced implicating three foreign companies in bribery and tax evasion deals. Each of these companies defended interests worth hundreds of millions of dollars of investment in Peru. The Chilean

99. Perú, Congreso, Comisión Delitos Económicos, *Informe final,* 61–66; "Baca Campodónico malversó fondos públicos," *La República,* no. 7826, June 5, 2003, 27; "Otro ex ministro al banquillo. Baca Campodónico inhabilitado por 7 años," *La Gaceta. Semanario del Congreso de la República,* no. 290, May 25, 2003, 4–5; Dammert, *Estado mafioso,* 185–86.

100. Andrés Oppenheimer, *Ojos vendados. Estados Unidos y el negocio de la corrupción en América Latina* (Buenos Aires: Editorial Sudamericana, 2001); Neil Jacoby, Peter Nehemkis, and Richard Eells, *Bribery and Extortion in World Business: A Study of Corporate Political Payments Abroad* (New York: Macmillan, 1977).

Empresas Lucchetti competed in Lima's food processing industry, the U.S. Newmont Mining fought for the ownership of the rich Yanacocha gold-mining site in Cajamarca, and the Canadian Barrick Gold endeavored to save millions in a tax evasion scheme involving gold mines in Ancash.

In 1998, Lucchetti was engaged in a serious legal dispute with Lima's mayor and Fujimori's main political opponent, Alberto Andrade. The issue concerned Andrade's belated opposition to the building of a sophisticated noodle factory valued at $150 million (under contract with the J. J. Camet construction company, which was linked to Fujimori's former finance minister Jorge Camet) in the ecologically sensitive marshes of Villa (Chorrillos, Lima). However, other local and foreign companies had built plants in the same protected area. The president of the Chilean mother company, Andrónico Luksic, one of the richest men in Latin America, traveled to Lima to meet with Montesinos at the SIN. In secretly recorded meetings, Luksic and other Lucchetti executives openly discussed the issue with Montesinos who promised to help them obtain a favorable judicial decision. Soon after, Lucchetti was granted the right to continue operations of the noodle factory. Witnesses confirm that Lucchetti paid Montesinos $2 million as a political campaign contribution in exchange for judicial favors. This case had serious repercussions in bilateral government relations since it was uncovered; the Lucchetti factory closed in January 2003.[101]

The richest gold mine in South America, Yanacocha is an open pit mine of ninety-seven square miles near the city of Cajamarca. By 1992, the exploration and early development of the mine was carried out mainly by the Peruvian Minas Buenaventura (Grupo Benavides), 32.3 percent shareholder; Denver-based Newmont Mining Corporation, 38 percent shareholder; and the French state-run company, Bureau de Recherches Geo-

101. "Lucchetti también pagó a Montesinos," *La República,* no. 7148, July 27, 2001, 30, based on witness statements before anticorruption judge Jorge Barreto. "Funcionarios de firma Lucchetti sí delinquieron," *Perú.21,* no. 295, June 11, 2003, 7, according to anticorruption prosecutor's report. "Diálogo con chileno [Gonzalo Menéndez, president of Lucchetti Peru] [en] oficina," January 8, 1998, video, no. 864, and "Diálogo Dr. [Montesinos]-Lucchetti," February 10, 1998, audio nos. 858–61, transcriptions in Perú, Congreso, *En la sala de la corrupción,* vol. 1, 5–86; and http://www.agenciaperu.com/actualidad/2001/MAR/TRANS_ LUCHETTI.HTM. See also Mario Vargas Llosa, "Piedra de Toque," *Caretas,* nos. 1682, August 9, 2001, 40-41, no. 1683, August 16, 2001, 82-85; and no. 1756, January 23, 2003, 32-34. Luksic met with Montesinos on March 6, 1998, and in 2000. Videos nos. 856–57, Perú, Congreso, *En la sala de la corrupción,* 1:87–141; "Wagner: cierre de Lucchetti afectó relaciones Perú–Chile," *Correo,* no. 8234, February 17, 2003, 6.

logiques et Minières (BRGM), with a 24.7-percent stake. The World Bank's International Finance Corporation also participated as a minority partner with a 5-percent stake. In 1994, the mine's first year of fabulously profitable operations, the French state privatized BRGM and Normandy Mining Ltd. took control of the BRGM's assets. Newmont, one of the largest gold mining companies in the world, and Buenaventura claimed as original partners that they had the contractual legal right to the BRGM's 24.7 percent.[102]

The ensuing lawsuit, which jeopardized an investment of approximately $500 million, reached the Peruvian Supreme Court in 1998. The trial became a focal point of opposite escalating pressures from the governments of the United States and France on President Fujimori. Peter Romero, the U.S. undersecretary for Latin American affairs, pressed the issue in meetings with Fujimori and calls to Montesinos. The U.S. ambassador in Lima, John Hamilton, also met with Montesinos on the same subject.[103] Consequently, Montesinos summoned the Supreme Court judge, Jaime Beltrán, to his office where he had a revealing meeting recorded for posterity. Montesinos told Beltrán that Peruvian national interests were at stake and that the judicial matter was no longer a private matter between mining companies. There was no other option: The trial had to be settled in favor of U.S. interests because, as the international referee, the United States could urge the Ecuadoran government to promptly sign a crucial treaty with Peru. Montesinos also promised Beltrán a promotion. The next day, Judge Beltrán's vote tipped the balance for a decision favorable to Newmont-Buenaventura.[104] (Coincidentally, in December 1998, Judge Beltrán bought a beach house well beyond his means.) Eventually, Newmont settled the financial issue with Normandy for $80 million. However, French businessman Patrick Maugein, advisor to French President Chirac, as well as special anticorruption witnesses, declared in 2002 that Newmont-Buenaventura had paid up to $4 million to Montesinos in 1998.[105]

102. "Yanacocha: un cerro de oro y un juicio de órdago," *Caretas,* no. 1400, February 8, 1996, 18–19, 65.
103. "Peter Romero hizo lobby con Montesinos a favor de minera," *La República,* no. 7813, May 23, 2003, 8.
104. See official judicial transcription of vladivideo, no. 892, "Reunión Dr. Montesinos- Sr. [Judge Jaime] Beltrán," May 19, 1998, in Perú, Congreso, *En la sala de la corrupción,* 2:1093–123; and http://www.agenciaperu.com/actualidad/2001/ENE/FRANCIA.HTM.
105. See also Jean Montaldo, *Main basse sur l'or de la France* (Paris: Albin Michel, 1998); Jean-Claude Gawsewitch, *Yanacocha: comment déposséder l'Etat française d'un*

The tax evasion scheme of the Canadian company Barrick Gold Corporation was possible due to the fiscal mismanagement characteristic of the corrupt Fujimori regime. Thanks to a legal loophole (the 1996 Supreme Decree 124-4-EF) designed to extend special favors to mergers and privatizations, Barrick simulated the merger of two of its own subsidiary companies to obtain tax deductions amounting to $141 million owed to the Peruvian government plus $51 million in interest for the 1996–2003 period.[106] This case, however, apparently did not involve bribing tax or finance authorities. Nevertheless, Barrick's tax issue was part of the larger issue of corrupt economic policy management, including crooked privatization and banking rescue schemes executed by key finance ministers linked to private and foreign interests. Under such circumstances of corruption, several other foreign-controlled companies also abused or defrauded tax and other financial arrangements with the Peruvian state.[107] During the 1990s, institutional deterioration caused by systematic corruption prevented the inflow of an estimated $10 billion of foreign investment, since many foreign enterprises perceive almost mandatory payment of bribes as an excessively costly and high-risk tax.[108]

Carlos Boloña was a promising economist, educated at top Peruvian and foreign universities. Before becoming Fujimori's second finance minister in February 1991, Boloña was a successful private entrepreneur, co-owner of a private university, and holder of several foreign franchises in Peru. In the early 1990s, Boloña's liberal views degenerated into authoritarian economic and political ambition.[109] He collaborated actively with Fujimori and

---

milliard de dollars sans que personne ne dise rien (Neuilly-sur-Seine: Lafon, 2003); and "Peru: The Curse of Peruvian Gold," PBS Frontline/World, October 2005, http://www.pbs.org/frontlineworld/stories/peru404/thestory.html.

106. "Minera Barrick intentó eludir pago de US$ 141 millones en impuestos," *La República,* May 17, 2003, vol. 22, no. 7807, 16–17, based on SUNAT tax agency information; Alberto Quimper Herrera, "El caso minera Barrick," *La República,* no. 7826, June 5, 2003, 21.

107. "Denuncian a Boloña y asesores por fraude de . . . 244 millones. En complicidad con Edelnor y Luz del Sur, según informe fiscal," *La República,* no. 7808, May 18, 2003, 34. See also Congreso, Comisión Delitos Económicos, *Informe final,* 30–39.

108. Transparency International's estimate. Shang-Jin Wei, "Impact of Corruption on Levels of International Investment," in *El Estado y la sociedad civil en la lucha contra la corrupción* (Lima: Ministerio Público, 1999), 51–67, proceedings of the 8th International Anticorruption Conference, Lima, September 1997.

109. A biographical profile depicted Boloña as follows: "The high profile Minister of Economics and Finance who is implementing what is probably the most thorough-

Montesinos to implement a radical yet devious economic transformation in Peru. On the surface, the advance of inflation control and structural transformation, including the restructuring of tax collection, tariffs and customs, and finances, and the privatization of state companies and services, helped liberalize constrained domestic markets.[110] However, under Boloña's tenure, twenty-nine illegal and unconstitutional secret decrees were signed to allocate funds at the political whim of the president. A few private companies (including Boloña's own), foreign companies, and military groups benefited from these "secret decrees" that evaded legal requirements and congressional oversight of an important part of public funds and expenditures. During his second tenure, under orders by Fujimori in September 2000, Boloña signed the last secret decree that paid a covert farewell compensation of $15 million to the disgraced Vladimiro Montesinos.[111]

These secret decrees were used many times as special favors and politically motivated rewards. During Boloña's first tenure as finance minister, the self-coup of 1992 took place in part to permit even more authoritarian economic measures and the misappropriation of public and privatization

---

going economic and structural reform program in Latin American history, he is an exceptionally capable professional with graduate degrees from the University of Iowa and Oxford University. Activist and outgoing, he is involved in a whole range of issues of importance to the USG—economic restructuring, narcotics control and human rights. He is accessible to Embassy officers and frank in discussing his complicated relationship with President Fujimori." U.S. Embassy (Quainton) to S.S., July 10, 1991, no. 9181, p. 3357, unclassified USDS copy, in BC, box 1, file Montesinos, NSA.

110. Efraín Gonzales de Olarte, *El neoliberalismo a la peruana: economía política del ajuste estructural, 1990–1997* (Lima: Instituto de Estudios Peruanos, 1998), 121–22; Carlos Boloña, "The Viability of Alberto Fujimori's Economic Strategy," in *The Peruvian Economy and Structural Adjustment: Past, Present, Future,* ed. E. Gonzales de Olarte (Miami: University of Miami North-South Center Press, 1996), 183–264; Carol Graham, "Introduction: Democracy in Crisis and the International Response," in *Peru in Crisis: Dictatorship or Democracy?,* ed. Joseph Tulchin and Gary Bland (Boulder, CO: Lynne Rienner, 1994), 1–21; Drago Kisic, "Privatizaciones, inversiones y sostenibilidad de la economía peruana," in *El Perú de Fujimori: 1990–1998,* ed. John Crabtree and Jim Thomas (Lima: Centro de Investigación de la Universidad del Pacífico / Instituto de Estudios Peruanos, 2000), 75–113.

111. Between February 1991 and January 1993, "Boloña admite que firmó diez decretos secretos para dar bonificaciones a FF.AA.," *El Comercio,* no. 83870, June 7, 2001, a5. In 2001, the commission headed by Minister García Sayán and other constitutional experts reported that 250 unconstitutional decrees and laws were enacted under Fujimori. "Comisión detecta hasta 250 normas inconstitucionales," *El Comercio,* no. 83905, July 12, 2001, a4; "Jalilie admite haber recibido llamadas de Montesinos para acelerar los desembolsos," *Liberación,* no. 589, June 27, 2001, 18.

funds. Remaining as finance minister, Boloña granted an economic imprimatur to the unconstitutional regime. In 2000, Montesinos planned another coup to place Boloña as the new civilian face for the decaying authoritarian regime. Financial and economic mismanagement considerably increased transaction costs, and the government relied mainly on failing foreign investment, privatization funds, and primary exports. However, these policies engineered and implemented by Boloña had widespread support in the domestic private sector and among existing foreign investors.

Engineer Jorge Camet also had a strong business background before becoming finance minister in January 1993, at the end of Boloña's first tenure. Camet continued the financial administration of the corrupted "neoliberal" model initiated by Hurtado Miller and Boloña. However, Camet continued as finance minister to June 1998, one of the longest tenures for a finance minister in twentieth-century Peru. Conflict of interest was very apparent in the way that Camet's family enterprise, J. J. Camet Contratistas Generales (JJC), expanded during his tenure as minister. From a medium-sized construction company, JJC became one of Peru's four largest contractors thanks to receipt of important public sector projects.[112] However, the issues that brought major legal problems to Camet after the fall of Fujimori were the "secret" or "silent" purchase of Peruvian foreign debt bonds between 1994 and 1996, and the misappropriation and misallocation of privatization funds made possible by Camet's signing of thirteen urgent "secret decrees."

With increasing privatization funds, IMF credits, and negotiated lower interest as part of the Brady Plan, Peruvian government officials set out to purchase Peruvian debt bonds of the 1980s at the devalued market prices of the 1990s. This transaction was generally considered irregular and unacceptable by international financiers. Nevertheless, a number of foreign financial institutions, including J. P. Morgan, Chase, ING, Merrill Lynch, and Citibank, among others, eventually participated. As originally conceived by Boloña in 1992, the transaction should have taken only six months, and the Peruvian government through the broker J. P. Morgan, should have paid only 10 to 15 percent of the bonds' face value. The transaction was delayed and implemented by Finance Minister Camet in consultation with several local private and foreign bankers (including executives of the BCP and Swiss Bank).[113] The operation extended over three years and included a

112. Congreso, Comisión Delitos Económicos, *Informe final,* 88–90.

113. "Camet admite 'compra silenciosa' de papeles de la deuda externa," *La República,* no. 7757, March 28, 2003, 8.

clumsily negotiated debt owed to Russia. The "secret" transactions obviously turned into a game of insider information in which the Peruvian state invested $1 billion to purchase the bonds at 35 to 50 percent of face value. Thus, a group of approximately twenty-five big private domestic and foreign bankers ended up sharing the projected foreign debt savings of the Peruvian government.[114]

Regardless of whether the privatization schemes were clean or not,[115] the Fujimori-Montesinos regime was responsible for diverting the privatization funds away from growth-promoting areas. The privatization funds were mainly used for military expenses endorsed by Camet. Privatization funds for $992 million accounted for more than half of the total defense procurement budget of $1.885 billion in the 1990s. All in all, approximately 78 percent of the total privatization income of $4.359 billion received by the government between 1992 and 2000 was diverted in foreign debt deals, weapons purchases, and politically related expenditures.[116] The most scandalous and corrupt aspect of this use of privatization funds was the purchase of used planes and other depreciated military equipment from foreign governments at the time of the border disputes with Ecuador in the 1995–1998 period. Camet, Fujimori, Montesinos, seventeen other former ministers (including Alberto Pandolfi, Alberto Bustamante, Federico Salas, Víctor Joy Way, and Efraín Goldenberg), the comptroller general Víctor Caso Lay, and high-ranking military associates participated in this scheme, an important part of the military graft machine at the center of public and private corruption in the 1990s.[117]

114. Dammert, *Estado mafioso,* 165–83.

115. Serious indictments against the most important privatization deals in the 1990s were presented by leftist and heterodox economists unhappy with the liberal economic model. Irregularities were noted in the privatization of Petroperu (partial), Aeroperu, Siderperu, Electro Lima, Sol Gas, Hierroperu, Pescaperu, and Corporación Peruana de Vapores, among others. However, in most of these cases there is no "smoking gun" since the public officials (Jaime Yoshiyama, Daniel Hokama Tokashiki, Jorge González Izquierdo, and Alberto Pandolfi) who were in charge of implementing many of these privatizations, although linked to corrupt networks, did not leave behind recordings or other evidence of corrupt transactions. See Congreso, Comisión Delitos Económicos, *Informe final,* chapter 1; Dammert, *Estado mafioso,* part 2, chapters 3–5; Raúl Wiener, *La venta sucia: la privatización de Petroperú como fraude a la nación* (Lima: N.p., 1996), 30–35.

116. Humberto Campodónico, "Como se robaron la plata de la privatización," *La República,* no. 7743, March 14, 2003, 12, based on COPRI's statistics; "Investigarán mal uso de US$ 2 mil millones de la privatización," *La República,* no. 7768, April 8, 2003, 10; "Se esfumaron fondos de la privatización," *La Gaceta,* no. 216, December 23, 2001, 2.

117. "Por traición a la patria acusan a Fujimori, Pandolfi y Camet: mediante decre-

Military Graft

Montesinos devised and adapted to the Peruvian power structure a complex, informal, and covert mechanism of illegal income and expenditure that fed the principal supports of Fujimori's regime. The working details of this machinery explain the diverse and at times surprising sources of graft and illegal slush funds. Under the weakened institutions created by the 1992 coup and reorganization of the military command, Montesinos mounted a corrupt engine centered at the SIN with several branches, especially among military and police institutions and respective high commands.

The use and abuse of confidential information produced power and money for Montesinos and his allies. Enhancing the reach and the budget of the centralized intelligence system under his command was the means to expanding and maintaining Fujimori's bases of support. The SIN's top technical operator, army colonel Roberto Huamán, was in charge of recording secret meetings and telephone conversations with political friends and foes. Huamán remained loyal to Montesinos until the end.[118] Montesinos's personal security force was in charge of police colonel Manuel Aivar Marca and a host of other officers, some of them linked to the murderous Grupo Colina and large-scale signature forgeries in the electoral process. Montesinos's legal advisory team was headed by Javier Corrochano and included Pedro Huertas and Grace Riggs, among others.[119] The administrative management of Montesinos's complex web was, in part, operated by two women: Matilde Pinchi Pinchi, his entrepreneurial partner and aide in money laundering scams and sundry illegal operations, and María Arce Guerrero, a secretary who delivered bribe money to recipients.[120] The SIN's

---

tos de urgencia se gastaron US$ 1,885 millones en 'compras de material bélico,'" *La República,* no. 7810, May 20, 2003, 7; "Fiscal denuncia a Fujimori, Caso Lay, Camet y Baca," *Correo,* no. 8342, June 4, 2003, 10. In his defense, Camet indicated that Fujimori bore the principal responsibility for illegal weapons purchases. "Ex ministro Jorge Camet implica a Fujimori en compra de armamento" [testimony before special prosecutor José Ugaz], *La República,* no. 7109, June 18, 2001, 2.

118. "La enorme y ponzoñosa telaraña de la corrupción," in "Alias el Doc," special section of *El Comercio,* no. 83888, June 25, 2001, a6–a7; "Abogados de mafia montesinista coaccionan a testigos claves para ocultar la verdad en casos de espionaje telefónico con fines políticos," *La República,* no. 3701, December 27, 2001, 8.

119. "748 implicados y 67 prófugos por el caso Fujimori-Montesinos," special report in *La República,* no. 7162, August 10, 2001, 16; "Detienen y encarcelan a ex conviviente de Montesinos," *El Comercio,* no. 83934, August 10, 2001, a10.

120. "Pinchi Pinchi: la prima donna," *Caretas,* no. 1705, January 24, 2002, 45–47.

cashier, José Villalobos, managed the illegal "acciones reservadas" funds. Two formal heads of the SIN, Army General Julio Salazar Monroe (1991–1998) and Rear Admiral Humberto Rozas (1998–2000), were simply figureheads who followed orders from Montesinos and Fujimori. However, the vulnerable underbelly of Montesinos's organization, because of the sensitive information it kept, was his closest associates. Most of the damning evidence later presented in court against him originated from this inner core, especially from protected witnesses Pinchi, Corrochano, Salazar, Rozas, and Villalobos.[121]

The Montesinos family—his sisters, brothers-in-law, nephews, wife, and daughter—whose names on accounts, bonds, and the like served to hide his personal fortune, provided only passive assistance, and had little to do with the machine's overall administration.[122] Likewise, his mistress, Jacqueline Beltrán, received expensive gifts and favors but had little or no operational role to play.

The income generated by the vast and varied sources tapped by Montesinos's web required sophisticated financial management and laundering. Several financial advisors offered their services for these illegal operations. The most important financial agents or *testaferros* (figureheads) were also partners in large-scale weapons and materiel purchases from which Montesinos, Fujimori, and top military and police commanders obtained hefty illegal commissions. There were three main groups or companies that brokered the purchase of arms and equipment: W21 Intertechnique led by Alberto Venero and Luis Duthurburu, which participated in arms deals worth $473 million; the "Jewish group" of Zvi Sudit, James Stone, and partners (Sutex/SEP International), $248 million; and Chinese interests represented by Joy Way, $120 million.[123] The irregularities in the contracting of these

121. "Sólo 16 integrantes de la mafia lograron acogerse a colaboración eficaz," *La República,* no. 7780, April 20, 2003, 16; "Beltrán y Pinchi Pinchi pico a pico," *El Comercio,* no. 84506, March 5, 2001, a1, a3; "Ex jefes del SIN afirman que Fujimori les ordenó entregar dinero a Montesinos" [statements in court proceedings of Bedoya-Montesinos case], *Correo,* no. 8252, March 7, 2003, 10.

122. "Detienen a hermana mayor y cuñado de Montesinos y a ocho de sus socios," *La República,* no. 7160, August 8, 2001, 2.

123. Congreso, Comisión Delitos Económicos, *Informe final,* 86; Dammert, *Estado mafioso,* 205–207. Other implicated partners of W21 Intertechnique included Moshe Rothschild, Claus Corpancho, Enrique Benavides, and Gerald Kruger; partners of Sutex/SEP included Ilan Weil Levy, Rony Lerner, Isaac Veroslavsky, and Jorge Carulla (Ghiss Iberica); Joy Way dealt with Chinese companies CAMC and CATIC represented in Peru by Liu Jun Li.

major purchases implied low-quality equipment that endangered soldiers' lives as well as their missions. The most scandalous case was the purchase of used Belarussian MiG-29 and Sukhoi-25 war planes (brokered by W21 Intertechnique), some of which fell from the air and crashed during training flights.

The discovery of secret bank accounts in Switzerland and elsewhere by Peruvian and international authorities and protected witnesses' confessions have helped to uncover the workings of an international financial network of money laundering closely linked to illegal commissions in the purchase of military equipment. The main groups of arms brokers and agents charged 15 percent to cover their own commissions and costs in each deal, and "paid" an additional customary 15-percent "commission" per deal directly to Montesinos who shared it with his principal military and political partners.[124] Thus, these irregular purchases of military equipment resulted in a more than 30-percent loss to the Peruvian state. The illegally appropriated funds by Montesinos and partners were transferred to bank accounts in the United States, Luxemburg, Moscow, Israel, and the Caribbean, with the aid of the same arms dealers turned financial agents.

Constant transfers among international accounts were used as a device for money laundering. Eventually, Montesinos placed a large portion of these illegal funds in Swiss bank accounts through the expensive services of weapons and financial agents. These financial services also included opening accounts and transferring funds to several other military partners in arms deals, including army chief of staff Nicolás Hermoza, and even delivering cash to Fujimori's children studying in Boston.[125] The Swiss bank accounts connected to Montesinos and his agents and partners, totaling $114 million, were seized by Swiss authorities in 2000–2001. Montesinos-related bank accounts located abroad totaled more than $246 million.[126]

124. "Don dinero: Zvi Sudit, el judío que hizo rico a Montesinos," *Domingo: La Revista de La República,* no. 259, May 18, 2003, 12–15; "Traición en la familia," *Domingo: La Revista de La República,* no. 262, June 8, 2003, 16–19; "'Grupo judío' mintió a jueces anticorrupción," *La República,* no. 7831, June 10, 2003, 16–17.

125. "Uruguayo Isaac Veroslavsky manejaba las cuentas de Fujmori y Montesinos," *La República,* no. 7809, May 19, 2003, 9; "Triangularon dinero del SIN para Keiko, Hiro y Sachie," *La República,* no. 7795, May 5, 2003, 8.

126. "Un 40% de los fondos en Suiza está a nombre de Montesinos. Fiscal [Cornelia] Cova sigue congelando más cuentas del ex asesor," *El Comercio,* no. 83890, June 27, 2001, a4; "Montesinos cobró un millón de dólares de comisión por compra de armas a Israel," *Liberación,* no. 589, June 27, 2001, 10; "Conclusiones de la Comisión Waisman. Fueron detectados más de $246 millones de Montesinos. Se ha logrado blo-

Weapons financial agents Venero and Duthurburu also participated in the embezzlement of the military and police pension fund, resulting in $500 million in losses between 1992 and 1999. The Caja de Pensiones Militar Policial (CPMP) centralized the pension funds of approximately 100,000 active and retired military personnel. This operation was an important source of funds for the Montesinos corruption network. It consisted mainly of appropriating cash through the faked sales of real estate to the pension fund. In 1992, the CPMP was reorganized to meet the needs of cash-hungry Montesinos and his agents. Montesinos, in collusion with high-level military authorities in charge of the CPMP, changed the conservative financial strategy of the pension fund. The CPMP then began to participate in risky real estate and credit operations devised and executed by Venero, Duthurburu, Juan Valencia Rosas, and associates. These agents and partners created twelve enterprises in Peru and ten in Panama to manage and launder illegal proceeds and help Montesinos transfer funds in and out of the country.[127]

The CPMP thus purchased overvalued buildings, hotels, empty lots, and other properties from private sector owners who paid 10-percent transaction "commissions" in cash. Half of this bribe was handed directly to Montesinos by Venero and the rest was divided among Venero's partners and other authorities. Another source for an earlier period, 1992, indicated that the distribution of graft in the CPMP was as follows: 25 percent for Montesinos, 25 percent for the minister of defense (General Víctor Malca), 25 percent distributed among the generals and admirals of the CPMP's board of directors, and 25 percent for Venero and his partners. From this operation, Montesinos obtained more than $20 million. Consequently, the CPMP's

---

quear $166 millones [de cuentas bancarias en Gran Caimán, Suiza y Estados Unidos]," *El Comercio,* no. 83879, June 16, 2001, a6. Montesinos's agents opened accounts with deposits of $40 million from front companies (Delmar Service, Cross International, Ranger Limited) in the Bahamas; accounts in the United States (Swiss Bank Corporation, Bank of New York) amounted to $50 million; in Gran Cayman, $33 million; Panama, $13 million; Mexico, $2.3 million; and Bolivia, $210,000. The ten accounts in Switzerland to which transfers were made from other places were in the following banks: UBS AG Lugano, Bank Leu Zurich, Canadian Imperial Bank, Fibi Bank, and Bank Leumi. *Liberación,* no. 587, June 25, 2001, 11.

127. "Condenan a 5 años de prisión a testaferro de Montesinos. Luis Duthurburu se había acogido a beneficios de colaboración eficaz," *La República,* no. 7805, May 15, 2003, 24; "Cobraba coima de 50% a empresarios. Montesinos montó red para dilapidar fondos de la Caja Militar, según testaferro Juan Valencia," *La República,* no. 7148, July 27, 2001, 18–19.

liquidity plummeted from $124 million in 1991 to only $5 million in 1999. Additionally, risky real estate assets increased from $32 million to $217 million, clients' debt increased from $67 million to $479 million, and the institution's liabilities rose from $282 million to $670 million.[128]

Previously existing patterns of military corruption were modified.[129] Montesinos effectively centralized not only the national intelligence network, previously segmented in various military and police forces, but also the income from graft in the armed forces. Montesinos positioned himself as a privileged rentier benefiting from military income shared in agreed patterns and percentages with the high military command, defense ministers, and Fujimori himself. Each major appointment in the armed forces and the ministries of defense and internal security was closely supervised and approved by Montesinos. This influence was facilitated by the contacts, family, and friends he cultivated in the military among members of his infantry officers' graduation class.[130] He made sure that the appointed individuals would play his game and follow the informal rules he had established in graft extraction and distribution. However, growing unrest among unfairly displaced officers was detected by U.S. diplomats since April 1993. A few dangerous military opponents were dealt with swiftly and ruthlessly. The humiliating defeat in the limited war with Ecuador in January–February 1995 added to the military's growing loss of prestige.[131]

128. "Malca manejó fondo de contingencia," according to reports by anticorruption judge José Luis Lecaros and Attorney General Nelly Calderón, *La República,* no. 7822, June 1, 2003, 41; "Mafia pretende retomar control de hoteles de la Caja Militar," *La República,* no. 7133, July 12, 2001, 4; "Por corrupción Caja Militar perdió más de US$500 millones," October 25, 2001, http://www.agenciaperu.com/economia/2001/oct/caja1.HTM.

129. The U.S. embassy in Lima had confidential information on military corruption in the form of diverting weapons purchases to third countries. "Kickbacks for foreign arms purchases and a pattern of involvement in illegal third-country transfers to pariah regimes has fueled chronic military corruption." According to a lengthy interview with U.S. embassy officials, a knowledgeable informant (whose name was excised in the declassification process) "denied knowledge of wide-scale narcotics-related corruption in the [Peruvian] Navy. The BAP *Eten* incident was an exception. But he said diverting high tech weaponry was a major source of profits. The Nicaraguan Contras had been a prime customer with Oliver North as a go-between." Cable U.S. Embassy (Quainton) to S.S., Lima, December 19, 1990, no. 19117, pp. 2, 6, originally "secret," unclassified USDS copy, in DPC, box 36, SIN unit bio, NSA.

130. Jimmy Torres and Fernando Rospigliosi, "El '97 viene la promoción de Vladimiro," *Caretas,* no. 1430, September 5, 1996, 10–13, 92.

131. "EE.UU. supo en 1993 de malestar en FF.AA.," press report on disclosure of

According to protected witnesses, Montesinos demanded 25 percent of the total graft commission (customarily 15 percent of the total transaction value) in the purchase of materiel and equipment, arguing that the SIN had exceptionally urgent operational costs that had to be covered confidentially. In the case of the police forces that were supplied by SEP International dealers, after deducting Montesinos's share, the remaining 75 percent of the total graft commission was shared with a similar justification as follows: 25 percent for the interior minister, 17 percent for the director of the General Administration Office (OGA) of the Interior Ministry, 17 percent for the director of the Peruvian National Police (PNP), and 16 percent for the PNP director of logistics.[132]

Thus, a close partnership in graft and political alliance was established between Montesinos and successive generals in charge of military and police institutions and ministries. The list of corrupt partners included more than thirty army, air force, and police generals and navy admirals. Several corrupt top generals considerably increased their wealth by being successively appointed ministers of either defense or interior, or both, as well as commanders of a major branch of the armed forces. An episode related by beleaguered former finance minister Jorge Camet, in his statements to special prosecutor José Ugaz in 2001, helped unravel the connections among the military command, defense and interior ministers, Montesinos, and Fujimori. On June 12, 1997, Camet was summoned by the defense minister, Army General César Saucedo Sánchez, to an urgent meeting at the army's central headquarters, also known as the "Pentagonito" (little Pentagon), with the chiefs of the three armed forces: General Nicolás Hermoza (army), Admiral Antonio Ibárcena Amico (navy), and General Elesván Bello Vásquez (air force).

At the meeting with Camet, the military chiefs demanded more weapons purchases despite the recent upsurge in arms expenditures financed through

---

U.S. embassy document, "Peru: Army Attitudes (002-01)," April 20, 1993, NSA, in *El Comercio,* no. 83903, July 10, 2001, a5. In May 1993, the third highest ranking general, Rodolfo Robles, accused the commander general Nicolás Hermoza and Montesinos of being responsible for Grupo Colina's operations. To avoid threats and reprisals, Robles had to seek asylum in the U.S. embassy; in 1996, he was kidnapped by intelligence agents. In 1997, an army intelligence agent, Leonor La Rosa, was tortured for allegedly informing the press about dirty campaigns against journalists; another agent, Mariela Barreto, was murdered. Rospigliosi, *Montesinos,* 218, 256–57, 160–63.

132. "Todos recibían una 'comisión,'" based on confessions by General Oscar Villanueva. *La República,* no. 7836, June 15, 2003, 16.

secret decrees. Arguing that a renewed escalation of Ecuador's military buildup required more spending, they asked Camet to comply with their demands for a total of $425 million. Camet particularly objected to the purchase of six Russian war planes demanded by the air force commander since only a year before, the purchase of thirty-six Belarussian MiG-29s and SU-25s had been financed with scandalous results. To Camet's surprise, Fujimori eventually approved the overvalued purchase of three Russian Mig-29s through Sutex/SEP International. The government paid $42 million instead of the standard price of $30 million for each aircraft. On July 4, 1998, one of Montesinos's secret cameras taped him, together with the military commanders and other officers, toasting with wine glasses the signing of the purchase contract for the warplanes.[133] Why were they so happy?

Montesinos and the army commanders had just concluded another transaction linking them in a corrupt alliance that had existed since at least 1992 when the head spy imposed several complementary agreements between the military and Fujimori. High-level corruption had its goals and logic beyond dispersed individual benefits. The rock-bottom cause and objective of Peruvian corruption in the 1990s was political. At the SIN's headquarters in May 1992, Fujimori and Montesinos agreed on the formation of a "contingency fund" destined to finance reelection campaigns that would preserve the Fujimori-Montesinos regime. The slush fund was to be formed with a quarter of all illicit commissions charged by military and police authorities in the purchase of weapons and materiel as well as commissions from CPMP transactions and an undetermined portion of privatization funds. Montesinos implemented Fujimori's proposal by bringing together Defense Minister General Víctor Malca and the armed forces commanders at the time: Nicolás Hermoza, Alfredo Arnaiz, and José Nadal. Initially, Montesinos and Malca took charge of managing this illegal contingency fund, which accumulated more than $200 million in accounts abroad managed by Montesinos and his agents by the late 1990s. Apart from their own shares, General Malca and successive defense ministers, all of them army generals, were promised lengthy tenures in their posts.[134] Obviously, the

133. "Ex ministro Jorge Camet implica a Fujimori en compra de armamento," *La República,* no. 7109, June 18, 2001, 2–3; "Se tiraron 42 [sic: 36] millones de dólares con tres MIG-29. Ex ministro de Economía Jorge Camet señala a Elesván Bello como responsable de operación," *El Comercio,* no. 84038, November 22, 2001, a6.

134. This important thesis was sustained by both Judge José Luis Lecaros and Attorney General Nelly Calderón in the state's case accusing Fujimori and his ministers of illicit association. "Malca manejó fondo de contingencia," *La República,* no. 7822, June

bigger the military expenditure, the heftier the income from graft.[135] Malca, appointed ambassador to Mexico in 1996–1997, accumulated a personal fortune of approximately $14 million in several bank accounts in Peru, New York, and Grand Cayman.[136]

As part of the 1992 deal, the military and police forces delivered illegal funds to the SIN totaling between $63 and $74 million in the1992–2000 period. This transfer enhanced the SIN's official budget by approximately 260 to 300 percent. However, the military and police institutions were compensated for these funds surrendered to the SIN. Montesinos devised a mechanism customarily used thereafter by which the armed and police institutions, together with the SIN, would deliver special budget increase requests to the finance minister (Boloña at the time, later Camet and others) for a "special execution regime" (*"regimen de ejecución especial"*) or "emergency zone component" (*"componente de zona de emergencia"*). These requests for special funds, approved through secret decrees, were justified for reinforcing the national intelligence system in the face of an emergency situation created by terrorism and drug trafficking. Once granted, the military and police institutions would also transfer a portion of these special funds to the SIN.[137]

1, 2003, 41. Anticorruption Judge Cecilia Polack accused several military former heads of illicit association and misappropriation of funds, including Rozas, Bello, Ibárcena, and ten other generals, including Augusto Patiño, Ricardo Sotero, Carlos Indacochea, Abraham Cano, Juan Yanki, Rubén Wong, Luis Herrera, Percy Araníbar, Luis Cubas, and Víctor García, among other high-ranking officers. "Grupo de militares se benefició con dinero del Estado," *El Comercio*, no. 84589, May 27, 2003, a8.

135. Only two major internal crises in the civilian-military regime almost foundered the tripartite alliance in graft and politics among president, spymaster, and military commander. General Hermoza, army commander-in-chief between December 1991 and August 1998, ordered tanks to parade in the streets of Lima in April 1993 to protest against the advancing congressional investigation in the La Cantuta case. Fujimori acquiesced to military pressure and influence in his regime. Several years later, in December 1997, the first anniversary of the storming of the Japanese ambassador's residence and the taking of hostages by MRTA terrorists, Hermoza tried to repair his tattered image (since the Tiwinza debacle in the Cenepa jungle during the Ecuadoran conflict of 1995) by claiming a stellar role in the hostage rescue operation Chavín de Huantar. Fujimori, heading toward a reelection campaign, claimed the leading role in the operation, along with Montesinos. The ensuing tug of war between Fujimori and Hermoza initially humiliated Fujimori, but Hermoza's hawkish opposition to the peace agreements with Ecuador in August 1998 led to his replacement by General Saucedo as army commander. Rospigliosi, *Montesinos,* chapter 6; Wiener, *Bandido Fujimori,* 430–38.

136. "El Arca de Malca," *Caretas*, no. 1651, December 28, 2000, 22–24.

137. "Fuerzas Armadas dieron al SIN $63 millones sin sustento legal. Juzgado an-

All subsequent defense and interior ministers and military commanders-in-chief engaged in various transactions that resulted in their obvious enrichment. One important example is that of Ministry of the Interior officials. Between 1997 and 2000, that ministry agreed to thirty-two secret contracts with dealers Sudit and Lerner for the supply of uniforms, vehicles, and other equipment. These contracts stipulated the graft commissions: 16 percent of the entire purchase value went to Montesinos and 4 percent to ministry authorities.[138] With bribe funds, the interior minister and former defense minister, General Saucedo, opened an offshore bank account in the Dutch Antilles held by a front company Sanford Overseas Corporation under the general's daughters' names.[139] Also, General Oscar Villanueva Vidal, former head of the army's financial office (OEE) and the Interior Ministry's general management office (OGA), who earned only 5,700 soles ($1,600) a month, was able to manage five front companies (along with partners such as Venero and Kruger who were linked to Montesinos's financial management). Villanueva Vidal was a close collaborator of ministers Hermoza, Saucedo, and José Villanueva Ruesta, and owned three houses valued at a total $750,000. Before committing suicide in September 2002, Villanueva Vidal delivered informative confessions to a prosecuting judge.[140]

One of the last military purchases of the Fujimori regime involved 100 aging and overvalued thoroughbred horses in January 2000; documents reported an open bidding process that never took place. Both the minister of defense at the time, General Carlos Bergamino, and army commander-in-chief, General Villanueva Ruesta, rubberstamped the fraud. Villanueva

---

ticorrupción dice que dinero se utilizó para los sobornos entre otras cosas," according to inquiry report by anticorruption Judge Saúl Peña Farfán, *El Comercio,* no. 83960, September 5, 2001, a3; "Villalobos Candela: VMT recibió . . . millones de FFAA," and "Ex jefes del SIN afirman que Fujimori les ordenó entregar dinero a Montesinos," *Correo,* no. 8252, March 7, 2003, 10.

138. "Denuncian mafia en el Ministerio del Interior," *Peru.21,* no. 273, May 20, 2003, 6. The article reported on charge by attorney Jorge Luis Cortés, based on protected witness's (*colaboración eficaz*) surrender of thirty-two secret contracts to the Sixth Special Court headed by Judge Saúl Peña.

139. "Colaborador eficaz revela cuenta millonaria de general Saucedo," *La República,* no. 7816, May 26, 2003, 25. Petitioned by Peruvian judges, Dutch authorities revealed information about the account in the EBNA Bank; the account was opened through the Banco Interamericanao de Finanzas del Perú.

140. "Las empresas fantasma del tesorero del Ejército," *Correo,* no. 7742, October 12, 2001, 6–7; "Montesinos manejaba a su antojo licitaciones en sector de Interior," *La República,* no. 7836, June 15, 2003, 16.

Ruesta, also a former minister of defense and of the interior (1997–1999), owned illegally acquired assets worth more than $1 million. Bergamino's last corrupt act was to facilitate, in collaboration with Minister Boloña, the $15-million farewell compensation for Montesinos.[141] However, the misappropriation of public funds was not the only major source of illegal income for Montesinos and his military partners. Other means of raising illegal funds for personal gain, power, and political goals involved the growing scourge of drug trafficking.

Collusion with Drug Kingpins

Montesinos and the military also colluded with drug traffickers. These daring activities ultimately proved very damaging for the international and domestic prestige of the military and intelligence establishments and ultimately contributed to the regime's downfall.

Under the economic and sociopolitical impact of drug trafficking since the 1980s, Montesinos and the military sought to dominate antidrug policy and enforcement. The objective implied the displacement and transformation of police agencies customarily in charge of repressing the drug trade in Peru, as well as penetrating the national police with corrupt agents.[142] The strategy evolved from the military's experience in dealing with the dual problem of drug trafficking and terrorism in the late 1980s.[143] Advised by

141. "100 caballos pura sangre viejos compró mafia del Ejército," *La República,* no. 7753, March 24, 2003, 10; "Comienza proceso a Villanueva Ruesta," *La República,* no. 7754, March 25, 2003, 10; "[Former finance vice minister Alfredo] Jaililie admite haber recibido llamadas de Montesinos para acelerar desembolsos," *Liberación,* no. 589, June 27, 2001, 18.

142. In 1992, Fujimori placed the armed forces in charge of antidrug operations in several key regions. Police antidrug efforts were divided. The OFECOD (Oficina Ejecutiva de Control de Drogas) was in charge of traffickers' seized properties. In 1993, Montesinos created a special SIN antidrug division that paralleled the police DINANDRO (Dirección Nacional Antidrogas), which in turn shared responsibilities with a new division of small scale drug offenses, DIVANDRO (División Antidrogas). Dammert, *Estado mafioso,* 300–301. For general context, see Julio Cotler, *Drogas y política en el Perú: la conexión norteamericana* (Lima: Instituto de Estudios Peruanos, 1999).

143. A biographical report on army General Alberto Arciniega by U.S. Ambassador Quainton remarked: "Formerly commander of the eighth emergency military/political zone comprising all of the Upper Huallaga Valley (UPV) and the San Martín and Huanuco Departments (April–December 1989). . . He achieved prominence in Peru and notoriety in U.S. drug trafficking circles for his policy of tolerating drug trafficking while

Montesinos and two military ministers in 1990, Fujimori reorganized the Ministry of the Interior, which was under suspicion of narcotics corruption, as a first step toward military control of both antinarcotics and antiterrorism operations.[144] This move was complemented by undermining the specialized courts prosecuting drug-related crimes, and replacing them with regular courts presided over by corrupt judges and prosecutors working closely with Montesinos within the judicial system.[145]

Enhanced control by the military and intelligence agencies over the administration of drug interdiction efforts was justified to prevent alliance between drug traffickers and terrorists. A step toward solving the drug problem in isolated jungle regions where Shining Path and MRTA rebels were active was to first destroy the terrorist threat.[146] However, the unorthodox militarization of antidrug efforts led to informal "rewards" received by military commanders from quotas imposed on drug traffickers.[147]

---

fighting the Sendero Luminoso and MRTA in the UHV." Cable U.S. Embassy (Quainton) to S.S., Lima, July 10, 1991, no. 9181, p. 3356, unclassified USDS copy, in BC, box 1, file Montesinos, NSA.

144. "Outgoing police officials tell us that the military wants all of the graft instead of just half of it. . . It is inevitable that our anti-narcotics program will be slowed temporarily as new relationships are formed." Report by Quainton, "Fujimori reorganizes the police," U.S. Embassy to S.S., Lima, August 9, 1990, no. 11756, pp. 6, 7, unclassified USDS copy, in DPC, box 36 (duplicate in box 2), file SIN unit bio, NSA. Police corruption at the U.S.-backed Santa Lucía Base was confirmed by U.S. officials who reported witnesses among the police personnel "sick of the corruption and the tainted image which everyone at SLB suffers as a result." Report by Quainton, "Police corruption at the Santa Lucía Base: some bad news and some good news," U.S. Embassy to S.S., Lima, May 30, 1991, no. 7133, pp. 1–2, unclassified USDS copy, in DPC, box 31, file Peru Santa Lucía Base; and report by Quainton, "Peru's Huallaga Valley: Where Coca is King (Part I)," U.S. Embassy to S.S., Lima, April 27, 1991, no. 5610, unclassified USDS copy, in DPC, box 7, file Peru Santa Lucía Base, NSA.

145. The U.S.-backed antidrug court presided over by Judge Inés Villa was replaced by a chamber presided over by the corrupt Alejandro Rodríguez Medrano, supported by Attorney General Blanca Nélida Colán and antidrug prosecutors Flor María Mayta and Julia Eguía. "Superfiscal del SIN tras las rejas," *La República*, no. 7836, June 18, 2003, 13; Rospigliosi, *Montesinos*, 203.

146. Sewall H. Menzel, *Fire in the Andes: U.S. Foreign Policy and Cocaine Politics in Bolivia and Peru* (Lanham, MD: University Press of America, 1996), 212.

147. "A further factor working to undermine the anti-drug policy in Peru was the element of corruption which played upon the endemic overall poverty of the Peruvian people and the low salaries of the government's officials and security forces. This became a serious issue as they came into contact with narco-traffickers . . . [who] could always afford to invest . . . millions of dollars as part of the cost of doing business to bribe or otherwise buy sufficient government officials, police and military personnel who might otherwise inhibit trafficking operations." Menzel, *Fire in the Andes*, 204.

Moreover, the tension created between Montesinos's military allies and specialized police agencies also involved the opposing strategies of two U.S. agencies acting in Peru: the CIA and the Drug Enforcement Administration (DEA).[148] This tension preceded the friction between Montesinos and the U.S. drug czar Barry McCaffrey during his visits to Peru in 1996 and 1998. Montesinos appeared unannounced in meetings attended by McCaffrey and other Peruvian officials. Following the meetings, edited videos portraying an apparent endorsement of Montesinos by McCaffrey, were released to the press. As a result of this bold game, Montesinos enhanced his stature as a potentially dangerous liability in the eyes of certain U.S. officials. A serious charge was that Montesinos and the military used U.S. antidrug aid monies to perpetrate human rights violations instead.[149]

Montesinos's past involvement in defending drug traffickers and providing intelligence information to the CIA was instrumental in laying the foundations of a perverse antidrug system that was firmly established after the 1992 coup. Executive decrees gave exclusive command of antidrug operations in key regions to the army, drug control operations in airports to the Peruvian Air Force, and drug control operations in the ports to the Peruvian Navy. The system had contradictory goals. On the one hand, Mon-

148. The DEA mainly followed Washington's policy of supply-side antidrug strategy in Peru as a source country. Menzel, *Fire in the Andes,* ix, 215–16, criticizes this rigid approach as self-defeating in the long term. The CIA had mainly an antiterrorist, better-Montesinos-than-Sendero approach. See also U.S. Congress, House of Representatives, *The Situation in Peru and the Future of the War on Drugs: Joint Hearing before the Subcommittee on Western Hemisphere Affairs and Task Force on International Narcotics Control, 102nd Congress, 7 May 1992* (Washington, DC: Government Printing Office, 1992).

149. Fernando Rospigliosi, "El Zar y Rasputín," in *Caretas,* no. 1437, October 24, 1996, 27; "Montesinos: Crimen y Fastidio," *Caretas,* no. 1517, May 21, 1993, 12-14; Terry Allen, "CIA and Drugs, Our Man in Peru," *CovertAction Quarterly,* December 1996, no. 59, in Robert Carlson (USDS) to Henry Bisharat (Lima), Washington, DC, December 17, 1996, in BC, box 1, file U.S.–Peru counternarcotics programs, NSA. McCaffrey's difficult position and dilemma of the impossibility of avoiding Montesinos, despite the latter's tainted reputation and dirty tricks during both of McCaffrey's visits in 1996 and 1998, and the one planned for 1999, are depicted in three USDS cables: "[Retired Peruvian] General [Rodolfo] Robles visits Department of State," S.S. to U.S. Embassy-Lima, Washington, DC, March 12, 1997, no. 45270, p. 3; "ONDCP Director speaks and Montesinos reacts," U.S. Embassy (Dennis Jett) to S.S., Lima, May 15, 1998, no. 3152, pp. 1–6; "D/ONDCP visit—The Montesinos factor," U.S. Embassy (Hodges) to S.S., Lima, July 22, 1999, no. 4555, pp. 1–4, unclassified USDS copies, in DPC, box 36, NSA; "Ayuda antidrogas sirvió para violar DD. HH. en el Perú," *El Comercio,* no. 83906, July 13, 2001, a2.

tesinos had the necessary domestic and international support to take control of the drug interdiction operations that, under his command, were deemed "effective" by specialists. On the other hand, the military–SIN apparatus allowed drug trafficking activities to continue by milking them.[150]

A growing public exposure of drug-related scandals, together with glaring issues of human rights violations, undermined the political space available to Montesinos and the military to play with domestic and international support. A congressional working group obtained confessions and statements by soldier witnesses denouncing corrupt deals between military authorities and narco-traffickers. Under adverse conditions, the working group's congressmen uncovered the payment of quotas to the military for allowing drug transport, and aid by officers to imprisoned drug lords. The press reported in detail these cases of corruption in the armed forces and police. This pattern clearly surfaced in the scandal triggered by drug traffickers' statements in open court.[151]

Demetrio Chávez Peñaherrera, a.k.a. "Vaticano," operated from an air strip in Campanilla, the Upper Huallaga Valley region, as a supplier of cocaine paste to Colombian cartels in the early 1990s. Vaticano's operations comprised 280 light aircraft flights between Peru and Colombia in 1991–

150. In 1996, a U.S. officer thought that Montesinos's "role in counter-narcotics related legislation has proven key in breaking major trafficking rings. Likewise, there is a general recognition that since assuming his position as national intelligence guru, Montesinos has enhanced the effectiveness of the SIN and the Peruvian national intelligence apparatus." U.S. Embassy (Mack) to S.S., Lima, September 6, 1996, no. 7710, p. 6, unclassified USDS copy, in DPC, box 36, NSA.

151. Interview with former congressman Julio Castro Gómez (1985–1995), Lima, April 7, 2003; Congreso Constituyente Democrático, Comisión de Fiscalización, GTEIN, "Informe final del Grupo de Trabajo de Estudio de Investigación del Narcotráfico [GTEIN]," coord. Julio Castro Gómez (typescript, 1995), in Papeles de Comisiones Especiales, AGCP. This congressional group began its work in February 1993; a previous subcommission created in 1990 to investigate drug trafficking activities was closed, together with the entire Congress, after the April 1992 coup, and its records disappeared. Confidential witnesses included subteniente EP Guillermo Guerra, suboficial EP Francisco Palomino, and captain EP Gilmar Valdiviezo, who accused top officers of colluding with narco-traffickers. Commanding officers involved included Generals Nicolás Hermoza, Eduardo Bellido (commander-in-chief of Frente Huallaga), and Colonels Eduardo Morán and Oscar Bernuy, among many others. Several military officers were prosecuted as scapegoats by the military courts, and were soon released or given light sentences. GTEIN, "Informe final," 72–78, and appendices. GTEIN also uncovered irregularities in the protection, release, or escape of major narco-traffickers "Mosquito," "Ministro," and "Vaticano." GETEIN, "Informe final," 84–102. See also Evaristo Castillo Aste, *La conjuntura de los corruptos: narcotráfico* (Lima: Editorial Brasa, 2001), 28–33.

1993. He publicly attested at his trial that he had delivered $50,000 a month to Montesinos and the zone military commanders for turning a blind eye to the flights. When the quota was increased to $100,000, Vaticano refused to pay and escaped to Colombia. He was arrested in Bogotá on January 1994 and extradited to Peru, where he was accused of collaborating with terrorists, and was held isolated and subjected to torture in a military prison. Because of lack of evidence of terrorist connections, the case was transferred to a civilian court. In these public proceedings, Vaticano declared that he had bribed Montesinos and military authorities and that, occasionally, he received radio messages warning of imminent antidrug raids.[152]

In January 1995, a shipment of 3,342 kilos of pure cocaine was seized in the northern city of Piura before being loaded on a ship bound for Mexico. This was one of the biggest drug seizures to date in Peru. The seized drug arrived in the city in a caravan of trucks that remained unsearched all the way from an estate owned by the López Paredes brothers near the jungle town of Juanjuí and the military bases of Bellavista, Upper Huallaga Valley. This antidrug operation and subsequent major seizures were carried out by police agents alerted by the DEA. The López Paredes brothers led the

152. "Acusación: la denuncia de Vaticano, el silencio de Vladimiro," *Caretas,* no. 1428, August 22, 1996, 14-20, 88-89. Information on Montesinos's links with narcotraffickers was known by U.S. diplomats in Lima since late 1990. U.S. Embassy (Quainton) to S.S., Lima, December 19, 1990, no. 19117, secret, pp. 1–8, unclassified USDS copy, in DPC, box 36, file SIN unit bio, NSA. However, another secret report on the subject of "Intelligence chief Montesinos accused of protecting drug traffickers" by U.S. diplomat James Mack in Lima refuted "with the information available to us" the charges made by jailed trafficker Vaticano. According to passages of the report, originally excised and later reinserted by a Department of State review panel, "The effort to arrest 'Vaticano' and dismantle his operations relied on extensive cooperation among U.S. law enforcement and intelligence agencies, the Peruvian drug police and intelligence service, and Colombian law enforcement elements. The investigation also revealed corruption by three Peruvian officials. . . Montesinos has been a close collaborator with US on counternarcotics matters." Mack concluded that Montesinos had no protection deals with Vaticano and downplayed the Peruvian sensationalist press reports and "conspiracy-minded Peruvians." U.S. Embassy (Mack) to S.S., Lima, September 6, 1996, no. 7710, pp. 1, 3, 4, 6, unclassified USDS copy, in DPC, box 36, NSA. A follow-up report by Mack, "Drug trafficker 'Vaticano' and retired army general convicted on drug trafficking" reported on the civil court conviction of Jaime Ríos, commander of the Upper Huallaga front in 1991, together with two other army commanders, for "allowing 'Vaticano' to operate . . . in exchange for payments to army officials in the area." U.S. Embassy (Mack) to S.S., Lima, October 18, 1996, no. 9024, pp. 417–418, in BC, box 1, file Montesinos, NSA. Another fugitive commander of the Upper Huallaga front, Eduardo Bellido Mora, blamed instead former General Hermoza and Montesinos. "Hermoza y Montesinos desprestigiaron a las FFAA," *Correo,* no. 8347, June 9, 2003, 10.

Los Norteños cartel with contacts among high-level officers in the Ministry of Interior and the military command. Members of the Los Norteños cartel captured in Peru and Mexico denounced bribe soliciting by Javier Corrochano, a close Montesinos associate.[153]

Corrochano and others close to Montesinos also had contacts with the cocaine producer group, Los Camellos, linked to the Tijuana cartel and led by the Panamanian Boris Foguel and Peruvian race car driver Bruno Chiappe. By 1999, Los Camellos had integrated the drug's production and commercialization: raw material in the jungle of Ayacucho, cocaine processing in Chincha, and drugs shipped along with noncontraband textile and biological products from the port of Callao. Likewise, the Cachique Rivera family of the Oxapampa region in central Peru, produced cocaine paste and paid military authorities in the area $15,000 per flight loaded with cocaine paste. The Cachique Rivera operations averaged at least ten flights a month.[154]

Among the most embarrassing incidents involving corrupt military and intelligence authorities was the discovery in May 1996 in Lima of 174 kilograms of cocaine aboard a Peruvian Air Force DC-8 jet, a plane earmarked for the president's use, about to take off for Europe. Drugs were also found in two Peruvian navy ships: 162 kilograms of cocaine in the BAP *Matarani* and 62 kilograms in the BAP *Ilo.* Based on judicial investigations and statements by protected witnesses, these operations were directed by Montesinos. He ordered the use of military vessels, planes, and helicopters, in close coordination with Los Camellos and other local traffickers linked to the Tijuana and Medellín cartels, to export drugs to Mexico, Spain, Portugal, Italy, Bulgaria, and Russia.[155]

These are the most important cases among many arrangements between narco-traffickers and the military-police-Montesinos "antidrug" establishment. The drug-related scandals reported by the press were emphatically denied by Peruvian officials closing ranks in defense of Montesinos. These scandals added to growing suspicions of the military and intelligence clique

---

153. Dammert, *Estado mafioso,* 307–17; "Dos testaferros de Montesinos negociaron con cártel mexicano," *El Comercio,* no. 83902, July 9, 2001, a1, a8.

154. "Montesinos habrá exportado droga a Europa en productos hidrobiológicos y textiles," *Correo,* no. 8338, May 31, 2003, 10; Dammert, *Estado mafioso,* 309–10.

155. Documents and statements accepted as proof by special judge Magalli Báscones to open trial for drug trafficking to Montesinos and accomplices in May 2003. "Procesan por drogas a Montesinos," *La República,* no. 7817, May 27, 2003, 27; "Montesinos representaba en el Perú al cartel de Tijuana de México," *La República,* no. 7818, May 28, 2003, 25; "Montesinos habría sido dueño de droga incautada en narcoavión y en narcobuques," *Correo,* no. 8336, May 28, 2003, 9.

around Fujimori. In 1998, with illegal funds pointing to drug-related origins, Montesinos's undercover apparatus purchased 10,000 used AK-47 Kalashnikov automatic rifles from the Jordanian army through the arms dealer Sarkis Soghanalian.[156] Although the guns were reported to be for the Peruvian army, the "apparatus" intended to sell them at a huge profit to the Colombian FARC guerrillas. The political objectives of this operation remained obscure when the FARC arms scandal blew up in Montesinos's face in August 2000.[157] This was the beginning of the final phase of the corrupt regime.

A Cinematic Downfall

The crumbling of the Fujimori-Montesinos-military clique that captured the principal institutions of the Peruvian state during the "infamous decade" of the 1990s came about as a result of successive crises and scandals unleashed in several key areas.[158] The exposure of corrupt scandals was central to the

156. "Montesinos negoció 1,000 misiles antiaéreos SAM-7 para la FARC," *La República,* no. 8058, January 23, 2004, 3. Lebanese dealer Soghanalian met with Montesinos two times in Lima to negotiate a $78 million purchase that included 50,000 AK-47 rifles at $70 each, and 1,000 SAM–7 missiles at $300 each. In the end, the transaction was limited to $700,000 for 10,000 Kalashnikov rifles, according to a 2001 official transcription of statements by Soghanalian in the United States before prosecutor José Ugaz, validated by Attorney General John Ashcroft. Prosecutor Ronald Gamarra speculated about CIA involvement in the operation. "Montesinos se burla de la justicia," *La República,* no. 8056, January 21, 2004, 5, and *El Comercio,* no. 84828, January 21, 2004, a1.

157. A possible link between drug trafficking funds and the secretive purchase of AK-47 rifles from Jordan is revealed in a statement by Carmen Delgado, an informant and antinarcotics agent working for British intelligence in Peru. Since 1991, Delgado followed a narcotics and weapons smuggling case implicating Montesinos and General Hermoza. Delgado asserted that she discovered in 1998 links among Montesinos, Hermoza, agents and brothers José Luis and Luis Frank Aybar Cancho, and dealer Soghanalian. This operation was nicknamed Mochila (Backpack) and later renamed Plan Siberia. This intelligence information was shared with U.S. embassy officials in Lima. "Declaración testimonial de Carmen Guadalupe Delgado Méndez," before the provincial prosecutor for Lima, Antenor Córdova Díaz, Judge Celinda Segura Salas, and defense lawyers, Lima, November 28, 2000, unclassified USDS copy, in DPC, NSA. See also "Prueban que Montesinos compró fusiles a Jordania para las FARC," *La República,* no. 7810, May 20, 2003, 16–17, based on ruling, no. 10-2003 by Judge Jorge Chávez Cortina, Fiscalía de la Nación. "Luis Frank Aybar confirma vínculo de su hermano con traficante de armas," *La República,* no. 7774, April 14, 2003, 10; and "Freddy Castillo, el operador secreto de Montesinos," *La República,* no. 7826, June 5, 2003.

158. César Robles Ascurra, *El ocaso de la década infame: el comienzo del fin del fujimorismo* (Lima: N.p., 2000), 23–27; Toledo Brückmann, *¡¿Hasta Cuándo?!,* chs. 1, 4.

downfall of the regime. Corruption seems to be tolerated, even in countries with weak institutions, only up to a certain degree. The anger unleashed by the feeling of betrayal among previously manipulated masses of people is dangerously unpredictable. The classic Latin American case in this sense is that of the fall of Porfirio Díaz and the Mexican Revolution in 1910.

The beleaguered political opposition to Fujimori grew as scandals of corruption and violations of human rights escalated. Corruption scandals revolving around Fujimori's unconstitutional third election as president opened a final wound that ended the regime. Interests supporting corrupt regimes acting in authoritarian environments seek reelection in a vain attempt to protect and extend corrupt favors and gains. Since 1996, Fujimori and Montesinos endeavored to force through all means a legal dispensation for Fujimori's third presidential candidacy. Resistance to this ploy in Congress and the Constitutional Tribunal was crushed in 1997. Judges and congressmen were bought, and media owners were bribed or punished in order to achieve the reelection goal.

The regime-controlled judiciary and legislature rejected a 1998 effort by democratic groups and student demonstrations toward a national referendum on the legality of Fujimori's reelection. Information on Montesinos's sizable accounts in a local bank was reported by a TV journalist in 1999; Attorney General Miguel Aljovín cited legalistic reasons for failing to investigate Montesinos's financial records. In February 2000, a huge fraud implicating top election officials in the forgery of a million signatures endorsing Fujimori's party was discovered and fully reported by a major newspaper; this major scandal triggered violent protests when the first round of elections took place in April 2000. Predictably, Fujimori won, although his followers in Congress did not obtain a majority. International observers certified more than one hundred incidents of electoral fraud. The opposition candidate receiving the most votes, Alejandro Toledo, did not accept the election results and called for civic resistance and protest. Toledo decided not to participate in the run-off elections held in May 2000 in the midst of protest and repression. A group of elected opposition party members of Congress shifted allegiance, providing Fujimori's party a slim majority in Congress. On July 28, angry crowds disrupted the ceremony of Fujimori's swearing-in as president.[159]

After this electoral storm, the regime seemed to have momentarily gained the upper hand. However, a series of devastating blows quickly ended the

159. "Cronología de la crisis política," in Wiener, *Bandido Fujimori,* 511–30; Hugo Neira, *El mal peruano 1990–2001* (Lima: Sidea, 2001), 22–25.

regime. In August 2000, Montesinos made a major blunder in his reaction to Colombian and Peruvian sources reporting contraband shipments from Jordan via Peru, facilitated by the Peruvian military, to supply arms to the FARC guerrillas. In an attempt to revamp their tarnished image, Fujimori and Montesinos appeared together in a TV broadcast during which they reported the successful dismantling of a criminal network smuggling rifles from Jordan to Colombia. The ploy backfired after Jordanian, Colombian, and U.S. authorities refuted Montesinos's version: In 1998, Jordan made what appeared to be a legal weapons sale to Peruvian authorities.[160]

Then, on September 14, 2000, another media bombshell exploded. A local cable TV station aired a secretly recorded video of Montesinos's own making in which an elected opposition congressman, Alberto Kouri, was shown accepting $15,000 in cash from Montesinos himself in exchange for turncoat support in Congress.[161] On September 16, Fujimori announced that there would be new elections and that SIN functions had been suspended. A bit later, Montesinos left the country for Panama in Dionisio Romero's jet after receiving the previously mentioned farewell present of $15 million authorized by Fujimori, General Bergamino, and Boloña.[162]

Unique incriminating videotaped evidence seized in one of Montesinos's apartments by ad hoc prosecutors was surrendered to judicial and congressional authorities. An ad hoc prosecuting judge, José Ugaz, was named by Fujimori himself. Ugaz denounced secret bank accounts belonging to Montesinos and partners in several foreign countries. Fujimori tried to fire Ugaz, but was unable to do so. It was too late for him to successfully manipulate the groundswell reaction demanding investigation and prosecution.

160. Jochamowitz, *Vladimiro,* 1:22–23; Neira, *El mal peruano,* 27–30; Vargas Llosa, "Piedra de toque: la herencia maldita," *Caretas,* no. 1639, October 5, 2000, 31-32, 76.

161. Years later it was confirmed that Montesinos's trusted assistant at the SIN, Matilde Pinchi, through unsophisticated intermediaries (her chauffeur Moisés Reyes and his friend German Barrera, a.k.a. "Patriota"), spirited several compromising video copies out of the SIN and offered them to several opposition politicians in a bizarre marketing operation. Barrera finally sold the video for $100,000 to FIM members headed by Fernando Olivera and Luis Iberico and financed by capitalist Francisco Palacios. Pinchi became an important protected informant in the conviction of Montesinos for multiple crimes. "Historia secreta del video que cambió al país," *La República,* no. 8417, January 16, 2005, 2–7.

162. Secret Oficio, no. 11296 MD-H/3 soliciting 69.6 million soles for a "Plan de operaciones . . . a fin de neutralizar cualquier acción que parta de elementos de la FARC." Minister of Defense General Carlos Bergamino to Minister of Economy Carlos Boloña, San Borja, Lima, August 25, 2000, http://www.agenciaperu.com/investigacion/2001/MAY/BERGAMINODOC1.HTM.

The drama, however, was not over. In October, only a month after his departure, Montesinos returned to Peru. Fujimori faked a major search effort to apprehend his former ally. Montesinos escaped again, this time in a private yacht to the Galapagos, Costa Rica, and eventually Venezuela. Major changes were forced on the military and the police. Fujimori took with him incriminating video evidence when he boarded a plane for Brunei and Japan, allegedly to participate in an international meeting. On November 20, 2000, Fujimori sent a fax addressed to the Peruvian Congress resigning the presidency.

Culmination of a Cycle

A transitional government was formed, headed by opposition leader Valentín Paniagua, who was selected to serve as interim president by the Congress. After a diplomatic and political tug-of-war with the corrupt spymaster's shield, Venezuelan President Hugo Chávez, Montesinos was apprehended in June 2001 and immediately extradited to Peru to face numerous charges and prison time. After much commotion and trauma, the country was left with the task of evaluating the costs of corruption during the "infamous decade," rebuilding damaged institutions, establishing special courts to prosecute corruption, and introducing institutional devices for controlling systematic corruption. Most importantly, anticorruption efforts and denunciations received an unprecedented boost. The media awakened, civil society was informed and heard from, and a new generation of anticorruption leaders, journalists, and judges of diverse political backgrounds emerged. Legislators reclaiming oversight rights and special judges reassessing the autonomy of the judiciary contributed to institutional renovation. Lourdes Flores, Fernando Olivera, Anel Townsend, Ernesto Herrera, Fernando Rospigliosi, Gustavo Gorriti, José Ugaz, and Nelly Calderón enhanced and complemented the anticorruption revelations of Vargas Llosa and others, in perhaps a qualitative break with the past that still awaits a definitive consolidation.

In conclusion, the Fujimori-Montesinos administration reached new heights of boundless graft, the most recent in a long history of structural, systemic corruption. This authoritarian regime, although similar to that of Leguía (based on strong military underpinnings reminiscent of the Benavides, Odría, or Velasco dictatorships), had to maintain a semblance of democracy to legitimate itself in the new international context of the 1990s. With the ideological excuse of advancing the struggle against terrorist insurgents and drug trafficking, a secret police and military apparatus was formed to capture and manipulate the state and perpetrate human rights abuses. At the center of covert mechanisms of political control, repression, manipulation, and corruption, was the national intelligence service, headed by spymaster Montesinos, the president's notorious "advisor." The SIN's hoarding of secret slush funds from military procurement graft, misappropriation of pension funds, drug trafficking levies, and the brokering of foreign and domestic lobbies, among many other mechanisms of corruption, were useful in financing influence peddling and bribery at practically all levels of the establishment.

Starting with the presidency, the political and electoral campaigns, as well as the social and infrastructural programs that legitimated and kept Fujimori in power, were financed in part by the Montesinos-directed secret funds. Fujimori also relied on his own network of family and cronies to divert funds from foreign aid, corrupt businessmen, and political associates. In the history of Peru, there have been several classic examples of the dual partnership in corrupt government and abuse of power, starting with Viceroy Amat and his advisor Salas, Gamarra-Gutiérrez de La Fuente, Echenique-Torrico, Balta-Piérola, Piérola-Dreyfus, Leguía-Ego-Aguirre, Odría-Noriega, Velasco-Tantaleán, and García-Mantilla, among others. However, the Fujimori-Montesinos duo probably surpassed them all in terms of breadth and depth of corruption.

Tentacles of the Fujimori-Montesinos apparatus spread to capture influence and control in Congress by paying illegal salaries to and bribing both Fujimorista and opposition congressmen. The judiciary also came under the spell of corruption through illegal payments and bribes to judges, as did the electoral board, municipal governments, and the police and armed forces. Orthodox economic and financial management, supposedly one of the regime's accomplishments, was plagued with opaqueness and "secret" decrees that allowed mismanagement, favoritism, and corruption in privatizations, foreign debt operations, and domestic bank rescues. An important historical opportunity for a true and more equitable economic restructuring was mostly wasted. Significantly, media moguls also received illegal payments to influence public opinion, orchestrate ideological campaigns, and support Fujimori's policies.

The annual average costs of corruption during the Fujimori regime are estimated at between $1.4 and $2 billion (see Tables A.1 and A.5). Forgone foreign investment accounted for a huge portion of indirect costs of corruption as Peru clearly became a risky and costly investment destination due to the high transaction costs of corruption. Moreover, estimated comparative levels of corruption reached the highest combined indices of the twentieth century, 50 percent of government expenditures (surpassed only by the Leguía regime at 72 percent) and 4.5 percent of GDP (slightly lower than the 4.9 percent recorded for the military regime of the 1970s). Perhaps the claim that the Fujimori-Montesinos regime has been the most corrupt in Peruvian history (at least during the twentieth century) holds some truth. However, corruption in the 1990s was just part of a long, structural history of unchecked corruption that has made the exaggerations of the 1920s, 1970s, and 1990s possible.

The public's tolerance and perception of political and administrative corruption have had, however, certain limits even under authoritarian regimes with covert control of the media. As in the case of Leguía, the approaching end of Fujimori's presidency was accelerated by ambitions of being reelected for a third time. Strenuous efforts to guarantee Fujimori's reelection and a majority in the new Congress proved to be too much. Thanks to unprecedented evidence, made possible by new surveillance technology used and abused by Montesinos, the few remaining independent media outlets simply had to show embarrassing and incriminating video footage to unleash the avalanche of revelations that followed. Overwhelmingly negative public opinion and media investigations produced the fall from grace of both Montesinos and Fujimori. A new era had begun in which the growing realization of the need to curb and efficiently prosecute corruption might finally advance the necessary and elusive institutional reforms conducive to genuine economic and social development.

Epilogue

Anticorruption Uncertainties

The new millennium began in Peru with the most comprehensive anticorruption overhaul in modern history. Seldom before had public sector institutions been subjected to internal and external scrutiny directed at punishing and preventing bureaucratic corruption. Media coverage of anticorruption investigations had an unprecedented impact on the public's awareness of the harmful effects of unchecked graft. These sweeping departures from the rampant corruption of only a few months ago were encouraging. However, judging from past anticorruption efforts, the struggle lying ahead was enormous in scope and complexity. The sustainability of the anticorruption fight was fraught with seemingly insurmountable challenges and uncertainties.

The spectacular fall of the Fujimori-Montesinos regime—prompted by extraordinary videotaped evidence on illicit schemes for retaining power in the midst of rising civic-democratic opposition—contributed to momentous changes in public attitudes toward systematic corruption. The new authorities put in place during the interim regime of Valentín Paniagua (November 2000–July 2001) and the elected administration of Alejandro Toledo (2001–2006), with all their obvious faults and contradictions, managed to implement fragile advances in the fight against customary impunity and endemic corruption.

For their anticorruption efforts these officials received ample domestic and foreign support. That support began to fade with the uncovering of fresh corruption scandals that by all accounts were less significant than the unrestrained graft schemes of the 1990s. Increasing and (sometimes) demagogic complaints about high salaries paid to senior government officials and elected representatives, some of obviously mediocre abilities, contributed to the lower incidence in corruption. Despite ongoing reforms, the public's mistrust of public officials and institutions and polls indicating high levels of perceived corruption persisted. Only efficient and honest administration, especially in providing common public sector services, over a long period of time can erase the legacy of many decades of corruption from collective memory. Institutional reforms must be applied consistently and systematically.

Since the year 2000, there have been important gains in the struggle against corruption. Unlike the unconstitutional framework of the Tribunal de Sanción Nacional established in 1930 to punish corruption under Leguía, legal measures adopted since late 2000 to prosecute corruption-related crimes were carefully grounded in strict constitutional bases of the separation of powers. Recent international models of innovative and effective investigative and prosecution procedures—such as the *mani pulite* (clean hands) campaign of Italian magistrates against corruption and organized crime—inspired Peruvian legal authorities to implement a new anticorruption system.[1]

As early as November 2000, the specially appointed anticorruption public prosecutor, José Ugaz, proposed two legislation projects aimed at resolving serious dysfunctions between the executive's attorney general's prosecuting ministry (Ministerio Público) and the nation's judiciary. Based on the Italian model, and, indirectly, the U.S. justice system, Ugaz argued for a law that would facilitate the gathering of incriminating "efficacious" information by offering the witness a reduced sentence and protection (similar to the plea bargain and witness protection program). He also favored a system of a few, eventually only four, special anticorruption prosecutors.[2] These legal initiatives were soon approved by Congress as part of an anticorruption package agreed upon by Ugaz and Justice Minister García Sayán.[3]

Congress independently developed its own investigations through several special commissions headed by, among others, lawmakers David Wais-

1. For a legal synthesis of U.S. and European legal procedures in the prevention and prosecution of corruption that are being used as examples in different areas of the world, including Peru, see Luis H. Contreras Alfaro, *Corrupción y principio de oportunidad: alternativas en materia de prevención y castigo a la respuesta penal tradicional* (Salamanca: Ratio Legis, 2005), part I.

2. "Misión imposible," *Caretas,* no. 1644, November 9, 2000, 14–16; and "La lucha contra la corrupción," *Caretas,* no. 1645, November 16, 2000, 22–24, 83. Under extreme pressure, Fujimori appointed independent prosecutor Ugaz and attorney general Calderón just a few days before he fled and tendered his resignation via fax. The first appointed anticorruption procurators were Ugaz, César Azabache, Luis Vargas, and Ronald Gamarra.

3. "Nueva ley anticorrupción," *Caretas,* no. 1650, December 21, 2000, 14–15.

man and Anel Townsend. Based on these investigations, the congressional commissions formulated charges and cases and evidence was passed on to anticorruption prosecutors and judges. The judicial system followed suit in July 2001 with the appointment of six special anticorruption judges who carried out their own investigations and initiated the complex and overwhelming task of judging and sentencing the large number of people accused of corruption.[4] In response to allegations that the new anticorruption legal measures were unconstitutional, the Constitutional Tribunal delivered a decision stating that the measures met constitutional requirements.[5]

From the huge amount of evidence contained in approximately 2,300 videos, analyzed and transcribed by the congressional commissions, and 700 additional videos under judicial scrutiny, plus other domestic and financial records and information from special witnesses, as of July 2003, approximately 1,250 individuals had been prosecuted and more than $225 million in secret bank accounts were confiscated while $1 billion more were in the process of being recovered.[6] Information from witness collaborators Matilde Pinchi and Alberto Venero, among others, reinforced the prosecutors' cases against Montesinos and his military and civilian associates.[7] From September 2002 to the end of 2007, Montesinos was brought to trial many times on more than fifty charges (Peruvian law does not allow multiple charges in a single trial). So far he has been found guilty on more than ten counts, including the one tied to the Kalashnikov/FARC case that ended in September 2006. As of July 2007, Montesinos has received prison terms totaling more than thirty years.[8] Meanwhile, the prosecution of Fujimori on charges of human rights violations, corruption, and criminal conspiracy be-

---

4. *El Comercio,* no. 83897, July 3, 2001, a6; "Los vladijueces," *Caretas,* no. 1678, July 12, 2001, 10–14. The first appointed anticorruption judges were Magalli Báscones, Jimena Cayo, Jorge Barreto, David Loli, Victoria Sánchez, and Saúl Peña Farfán; other prosecution judges (*vocals*) included José Luis Lecaros, Inés Villa Bonilla, Roberto Barandiarán, Inés Tello, and Marco Lizárraga.

5. *El Comercio,* no. 89627, July 4, 2003, a3; *La República,* no. 8065, January 30, 2004, vol. 23, 5.

6. *Peru.21,* no. 156, January 23, 2003, 9.

7. In February 2002, Pinchi was pardoned for eleven charges of criminal conspiracy, and received a suspended sentence of only four years in prison. *La República,* no. 7792, May 2, 2003, 3. Venero testified against more than 200 members of Montesinos corrupt networks. *Correo,* no. 8340, June 2, 2003, 9.

8. *Caretas,* no. 1855, December 30, 2005, 44–45; Coletta Youngers, Eileen Rosin, and Lucien O. Chauvin, "Drug Paradoxes: The U.S. Government and Peru's Vladimiro Montesinos," *Drug War Monitor* 3 (July 2004): 1–18, esp. 2.

gan in December 2007 after a long but ultimately successful legal battle to extradite him from Japan and Chile where he had taken refuge to evade Peruvian justice.

The complicated process of prosecuting and sentencing former officials has not been a smooth one. Anticorruption prosecutors and judges have worked with extremely limited resources,[9] and have been subjected to slander and political pressure.[10] In 2003, a congressional oversight commission (*comisión de fiscalización*), headed by APRA's Mauricio Mulder and the independent Jorge Mufarech, threatened to prosecute Ugaz and derail the anticorruption system.[11] Many suspects—approximately 125 counted as of 2003—had fled the country before the anticorruption system was in place; extradition procedures continue for some few, while others remain as fugitives at large. Many convicted defendants have already been released from prison as a result of reduced sentences approved by lenient judges. According to Supreme Court Judge Hugo Sivina, a number of corrupt judges remain within the judiciary.[12] All things considered, however, the Peruvian justice system has thus far demonstrated independence and efficiency despite limited resources and enormous political and administrative pressures.

The partial reform of the judiciary needs to be intensified from within to prevent executive branch interference. The endemic weaknesses of the judiciary were exacerbated during the military regimes of the 1970s, and reached critical levels during the rampant corruption of the 1980s and 1990s. This historical problem demands to be addressed through a comprehensive judicial overhaul. Important first steps have been taken to strengthen the anticorruption system. Newly revamped oversight mechanisms within the judicial system, such as the Oficina de Control de la Magistratura, have been useful in removing incompetent judges. These efforts must continue and become firmly institutionalized. Political allegiances among high-court judges, continued under-funding, overwhelming case backlogs, and recent attempts to "reform" the system for political ends, continue to threaten the system's overhaul.

9. *Correo,* no. 7729, September 29, 2001, 6. The four prosecutors had only thirty-five assistants, and their initial budget amounted to only $120,000, which Congress took months to approve.

10. *La República,* no. 7819, May 29, 2003, 16–17; *Peru.21,* no. 258, May 5, 2003; *Caretas,* no. 1718, April 25, 2002, no. 1718, 22–23.

11. *La República,* no. 7762, April 2, 2003, 5; *Peru.21,* no. 251, April 28, 2003, 8–9.

12. "Sivina: sigue red de corrupción en PJ," *La República,* no. 7849, June 28, 2003, 7. Also, see *El Comercio,* no. 84627, July 4, 2003, a3.

Sanctions against people guilty of corruption in the past were not sufficient to curb systemic corruption. The reconstruction of institutions during the transition since 2000 also implied the restructuring of ingrained formal and informal structures of incentives and disincentives for graft. This is a truly major challenge. Thus far, results have been encouraging albeit limited. The Comptroller General (Contraloría General), a traditional yet weak audit and oversight institution (which, in the Chilean case, had a fundamental role in curbing administrative corruption since the mid-1920s) that had achieved little by 2003, despite a newly installed corruption intelligence unit, was reasserting itself in 2006 and 2007.[13] The anticorruption czar's office, among other new mechanisms, has been practically useless, while the recently created anticorruption police, among others, has had better results. Transparency in budgetary transactions and hiring in public sector institutions has improved markedly through specific legislation (laws 2780 and 27482) that encourage the establishment of official websites for information dissemination and the publication of civil servants' income tax returns. However, public opinion polls of the overall transparency of the state continued to rate it low because of general mistrust of government officials and issues of limited effective transparency.

The media or "fourth power" has made major contributions to uncovering corruption and informing the public of same. The role of the media is essential in maintaining public vigilance of graft and corruption. However, corrupt political and business interests continue to threaten the independence of major TV networks and newspapers in Peru. The legal settlement of pending issues regarding ownership and control over major networks was complicated by the prosecution of media moguls charged with corruption. The government's temporary assignment of Panamericana Televisión to the politically connected Genaro Delgado Parker was legally challenged by Ernesto Schütz's counselors. This affair developed into a scandal involving conflicting verdicts by corrupt judges.[14]

Considerable progress has occurred in the sentencing of corrupt generals, admirals, and other senior military and police officers and the subsequent reorganization of the armed forces and the police. Since the early nineteenth

13. Eduardo Morón, "Transparencia presupuestal: haciendo visible la corrupción," in *El pacto infame,* ed. Felipe Portocarrero (Lima: Universidad del Pacífico, 2005), 147–76; *El Comercio,* no. 84626, July 3, 2003, a4.

14. *El Comercio,* no. 84635, July 12, 2003, a4, a19, and no. 84639, July 16, 2003, a3; *Correo,* no. 8381, July 13, 2003, 3–4.

century, the military comprised a patronage system in which officers were rewarded for corrupt practices—justified and protected in the name of patriotism—and launched numerous political interventions harmful to the constitutional order. Particularly intense corruption in military organizations occurred under authoritarian caudillos, especially during the Gamarra, Echenique, Balta, and Cáceres regimes of the nineteenth century. Professionalization reforms by the early twentieth century seemed to have reduced officers' expectations of enrichment through corruption. Under Leguía's dictatorial regime of the 1920s, however, military corruption increased again as officers were informally rewarded with undeserved promotions and graft in military spending for their political support. With the dictatorial precedents of Sánchez Cerro and Benavides in the 1930s, Odría's eight-year dictatorship in the early 1950s and the twelve-year military "revolutionary" regime of the 1970s enhanced militaristic entitlements over public funds and civic freedoms. The Fujimori-Montesinos military graft was the most recent in a long line of authoritarian regimes breeding systematic corruption.

Thanks to the sacking and prosecution of the officers who collaborated with Fujimori and Montesinos, and the restructuring of the military hierarchy, a new generation of military and police officers has emerged under improved public oversight of military spending and purchasing contracts. The legal foundations for the respect of military professional and judicial autonomy were restructured by mid-2001 through the initiative of Defense Minister Walter Ledesma, a retired army general.[15] Personnel cutbacks and reclassification resulted in a 40-percent decline in active-duty numbers (245,294 to 147,228). By year-end 2001, a total of 485 senior officers (including 23 army generals, 2 admirals, and 23 air force generals) had been cashiered or retired by a special commission comprised of retired generals and admirals and the ministers of war and interior.[16] The police in particular were overhauled, with specific emphasis on demilitarization and curbing corruption. The civilian interior minister, Fernando Rospigliosi, fired or retired a total of 618 police officers, including 21 generals and 244 colonels.[17] However, the immense pressure exerted by corrupt interests linked to drug trafficking continues to threaten military and police integrity.

15. "Las FF.AA. están haciendo su rediseño," *El Comercio,* July 6, 2001, a5.

16. *La República,* no. 7301, July 27, 2001, 1–3, and no. 7302, July 28, 2001, 3.

17. *La República,* no 7290, December 16, 2001, no. 7292, December 18, 2001, and no. 7297, December 23, 2001, 12; Elisabeth Acha and Javier Diez Canseco, eds., *Patios interiores de la vida policial: ética, cultura civil y reorganización de la Policía Nacional* (Lima: Fondo Editorial del Congreso del Perú, 2004), 154–69; and Carlos Basombrío

For historical reasons, professional, efficient, and honest civil servants are hard to find in Peru. Since colonial times, unpaid or poorly paid officers benefited from corruption to supplement earnings, often with the implicit or explicit complicity of the highest political leadership. According to the rules of demand and supply, it is rational to pay more for better-trained civil servants, thereby avoiding in part the unpredictable and much more damaging costs of systemic corruption. Under President Toledo, some state-run enterprise managers and congressmen earned more than during the Fujimori era, but under improved fiscal control (*fiscalización*), institutional transparency, and revenue collection. However, other civil servants such as judges and teachers continued to be grossly underpaid. Such inequalities, and the popular perception that in a poor country civil servants should be paid very little, have been used as arguments in relentless opposition and criticism.[18]

Members of the Peruvian Congress, most of them truly unprepared for their complex responsibilities, were especially targeted. The prestige of the legislative body was seriously undermined by cases of petty corruption and political squabbling affecting mainly representatives of the loose government coalition of small parties.[19] However, extremely important investigations by congressional committees contributed to the underpinnings of necessary anticorruption reforms. Paradoxically, despite positive investigative outcomes, Congress as a whole was criticized for not legislating efficiently on other real and pressing problems. The media had been saturated with seemingly endless coverage of investigative commissions and subcommissions dealing with past and present corruption. The overall legislative tasks to regulate honest and efficient governance are still in need of extensive and far-reaching reforms.

Incessant exposés of petty corruption, nepotism, and personal scandals involving the family and inner circle of President Toledo escalated to a crescendo in January 2004 causing serious damage to his government. An audio recording (dated in late 2001) of Toledo's intimate advisor, intelligence agency (renamed CNI) former chief César Almeyda, negotiating with one of Montesinos's former agents seeking legal leniency was sensational-

---

and Fernando Rospigliosi, *La seguridad y sus instituciones en el Perú a inicios del siglo XXI: reformas democráticas o neomilitarismo* (Lima: Instituto de Estudios Peruanos, 2006), chapter 1.

18. "Burocracia dorada también vive el privilegio de los altos sueldos," *La República*, no. 8309, March 4, 2004, 3.

19. "Expulsan [del P.P.] a [Víctor] Valdez y amonestan a Anel [Townsend], [Jorge] Mufarech y Jaimes," *Peru.21*, no. 258, May 5, 2003, 4.

ized by the media. Almeyda, also linked to mismanagement in other state agencies such as Petroperu, was accused of extortion and prosecuted although the charges were later dropped because of reasonable doubts regarding the audio evidence.[20] The prestige of Toledo's close ally and Minister of Justice Fernando Olivera was another casualty of the scandal due to unproven insinuations by the media. Coincidentally, Vice President Raúl Diez Canseco resigned upon acknowledging influence peddling. Toledo's approval rating plummeted to only 7 percent. There were grounds for expecting the return of rampant corruption, although these were not the exclusive province of Toledo and his group's mistakes, false promises, and sleazy secrets.[21] Two APRA regional party leaders, Miguel Angel Mufarech (Lima) and Freddy Ghilardi (Ancash), were also involved in serious graft schemes.[22]

Despite its relative economic policy management success, the Toledo regime ended in disrepute. All the major candidates who participated in the April–May 2006 presidential and congressional elections declared their commitment to fight corruption. Former president Alan García was elected after a populist campaign catering to disillusioned and alarmed voters facing a radical alternative, especially in the interior provinces.[23]

Former presidents with corruption baggage who returned from exile and stepped into recycled positions of power in the past included Echenique, Piérola, Leguía, and Prado. García had been accused of serious corrupt practices, but acquitted thanks to legal technicalities (e.g., statute of limitations) and the procedural aberrations of a court system plagued by corruption in the 1990s. Just a few months after his second inauguration, President García and his party began to disassemble some of the important advances obtained against systemic anticorruption. Civil servant salaries have been cut based on the argument of disproportion with the extensive poverty of Peruvian population, and many fear that political motivations inspired steps toward judiciary and police "reforms." However, public scrutiny remained high throughout 2007 and posed important obstacles to

20. *El Comercio,* no. 84635, July 12, 2003, a7; *El Comercio,* no. 84838, January 31, 2004, a1; *La República,* no. 8098, March 3, 2004.

21. Gustavo Gorriti, "El cartero va a Palacio: carta sin sobre a Toledo," *Peru.21,* June 22, 2003, 6.

22. *El Comercio,* no. 84635, July 12, 2003, a6; *Domingo: Revista de la República,* no. 267, July 13, 2003, 14–15.

23. Cynthia McClintock, "An Unlikely Comeback in Peru," *Journal of Democracy* 17, no. 4 (2006): 95–109.

the reckless mismanagement, policies, and partisan spoils characteristic of García's first administration in the 1980s.

García's own party was in dire need of a structural overhaul and cleansing to perform as a trustworthy political organization within a restored party system. (Opposition parties of the center-right also needed to create a functional alliance that can avoid corrupting financial interests and build confidence among the poor.)

Peru is currently at a crossroads in which anticorruption gains can be made permanent or swept away once more by powerful vested interests. Peru's fragile institutional framework and party system continues to allow executive prerogatives and improper ad hoc laws that weaken democratic debate and oversight, although under Toledo such devices were limited. The Peruvian Congress continues to function as a unicameral legislature under the current, seriously flawed 1993 constitution. Corrupt interests continue to lobby for impunity and cosmetic reforms that can obscure illegal gains for a select few.

True institutional reform would imply simultaneous revamping of the constitutional rules of the legislative, judicial, executive, and private systems. Lukewarm initiatives in Congress for constitutional reforms have been mostly disregarded. A thorough constitutional reform is necessary to guarantee effective independence of the three branches of government, checks and balances, decentralization, and the eradication of informal forces that are opposed to formal institutions regulating modern social interactions. Due to the historical impact of corruption, any constitutional reforms in Peru should have at their center mechanisms to curb corruption.

Such reforms should include a law establishing general regulatory principles of political financing, campaign donations, and formal party organization frameworks (in Peru political parties are not required to submit thorough financial reports for public scrutiny). A comprehensive judicial reform should aim to modernize, simplify, and lower the costs of prosecution, and contemplate a degree of citizen oversight of judges. Another lingering issue that requires urgent action is the thorough restructuring of the public education system, beset by teachers' low salaries and politically motivated strikes. Only a truly informed, educated citizenry can defeat the recalcitrant "culture" of corruption. Young Peruvians have the right to be taught the value of institutions and the damage caused by corruption.

As discussed in this study, much of what we know about the hows and whys of corruption in the past derives from the struggles of anticorruption reformers. Such reformers have become more numerous in recent times, and may soon reach a critical mass. From these and other judicial, congressional, fiscal, journalistic, and diplomatic sources, it is possible to ascertain that anticorruption efforts in the past have failed in large measure because of partisan or vested interests' opposition to reform. Extensive reform projects contradicted institutional conditions that allowed systematic corrupt gain. By taking advantage of fragile institutions and their further weakening through informal networks, corruption "trickles" down from the highest-level officials to the middle and lower ranks of the state bureaucracy. Institutional fragility has bred corruption. In the case of Peru, corruption has been a systematic phenomenon, not an anecdotal or periodic occurrence. If export bonanza is coupled with unchecked authoritarian rule, the incentives for corruption increased. Privileges and protection generally sought by domestic and foreign private companies from the state generated abuse. Corruption has assumed multiple forms and new ones are constantly being invented and reinvented. It is arguably one of the main causes of Peruvian underdevelopment.

Thus, the history of Peru has been in part the history of successive cycles of corruption followed by very short anticorruption reform periods that are brought to an end by antireformist vested interests. According to the calculations and estimates shown in the Appendix to this study, these successive waves of corruption may have involved in the long term (1820 to 2000) the direct and indirect loss, diversion, or misallocation of funds equivalent to an average of 30 to 40 percent of government expenditures, and 3 to 4 percent of gross domestic product. These huge losses due to corruption would represent 40 to 50 percent of the country's developmental possibilities in the long run (if we consider that for development to occur, sustained growth of 5 to 8 percent of GDP must be achieved). The unquantifiable institutional costs of corruption have been enormous as well. There has been no historical period or cycle of little or no corruption; all the cycles surveyed were characterized by moderately high, high, and very high indicators of corruption.

The periods in which corruption achieved high or very high levels of corruption coincided with the most authoritarian regimes: late viceregal (1800–1820), early caudillo (1822–1839), the decade of debt consolidation (1850s), late guano (1869–1872), postwar militarism (1885–1895), Leguía's Oncenio (1920s), the Military Docenio (1968–1980), and the Fujimorato (1990s).

These major cycles represented both the continuity of systematic corruption under patrimonial, executive-led structures as well as changes in modes of graft in diverse economic and technological contexts. Other occasional, often short-lived changes derived from changing public attitudes toward the unbearable weight of corruption in people's lives.

Variations in the intensity of corruption depended, therefore, on two main factors: the opportunistic adaptations of corrupt interests and networking mechanisms to economic, technological, and institutional transformations; and the varying strengths of anticorruption efforts at establishing institutional barriers to rampant corruption. Ultimately, corruption will persist unless it is systematically curbed over time. In the long run, what makes a major difference for developmental change is the collective understanding of why corruption matters and how and why constant efforts to eliminate and reduce it are necessary.

The historical persistence of systemic corruption was intimately tied to an institutional and political tradition of patrimonial and centralizing executive power undermining necessary checks and balances. From viceregal and caudillo patronage, to authoritarian military and civilian-military dictatorships, unchecked presidentialism through government by decree, guided democracy, and electoral authoritarian establishments, there has been a continuum of institutional and informal incentives to corrupt gains. Necessary reform has consistently been a casualty of "pragmatic" politics as usual and "clean slate" impunity.

Rampant corruption has had a significant, and at times decisive, impact on Peruvian history and development. The study of the historical role of corruption is part of a necessary reevaluation and uncovering of the informal and hidden forces shaping human social evolution. Corruption has been a systemic fixture since the earliest formation of a modern state in Peru through unofficial viceregal patronage networks opposing reform, to military caudillo cliques undermining domestic and foreign credit and economic policies. It proceeded with the wasteful use of guano revenues for colossal public works, crony modernization that imposed corrupt levies on developmental efforts, radical populist and military organizations bent on achieving and maintaining power at any cost and, ultimately, the undercover corrupt manipulation of national institutions and democratic aspirations. To achieve overall development, Peru and other developing societies must contain and radically minimize, through homegrown collective means, the economic and institutional burdens caused by systematic corruption. The harmful effects of unrestrained graft should never be underestimated.

Appendix

Estimates of Historical Costs of Corruption in Peru

This is an exercise at estimating the costs of corruption throughout Peruvian modern history. Many of the methodological issues implied herein are still being debated among specialists.

The costs of corruption can be conceptualized in two ways: (1) the monetary value of funds that did not reach the intended public or developmental objective because they were diverted by corrupt interests (diverted direct and indirect costs), and (2) the damage caused to key institutions that facilitate stability and investment (institutional costs). The first calculation is quantitative, while the second is primarily qualitative. Since corruption is assumed to be a cost of public administration, this analysis does not include calculation of benefits. Most funds diverted or redirected by corrupt practices tend to exit the country as a way of protecting or laundering them. Some illegal funds remain in the local economy, but are misallocated or used in consumption of luxury goods, thus contributing to economic distortions and underdevelopment.

Various methodological options are initially considered for estimating diverted and institutional costs associated with administrative and political corruption. This discussion is followed by a model that is specifically adjusted to the available information, to measure corruption costs relative to public funds and national income, that is, as percentages or ratios of total government expenditures and gross domestic product (GDP). The next step is to preliminarily apply such a model to quantify detected corruption during the Fujimori-Montesinos regime (1990–2000). The same model is then applied to quantify corruption during the 1850s, encompassing the public financial scandals of the consolidation and conversion of the domestic debt and the manumission of slaves. After these two trial calculations, uniform

435

estimates of direct and indirect costs of corruption are aggregated by decades and major types of corruption for the nineteenth and twentieth centuries, and measured in relation to government expenditures and GDP.

Using data obtained from contemporary overall estimates, published works, budgetary accounting, evidence collected for prosecution of civil servants charged with corruption, congressional investigations, diplomatic correspondence, and other historical sources, this exercise will finally proceed to derive comparative levels of estimated corruption costs under various administrations.

Methodological Debate

Until recently, corruption in less-developed and bureaucratized countries was ignored, underestimated, or assumed to have positive dimensions by most social scientists. Corruption was sometimes considered to be inherent to underdevelopment or certain cultural traits. The absence of reliable databases quantifying corruption obstructed analyses based on often contradictory theories on corruption. There was no adequate methodological and theoretical framework to systematically study corruption until the publication of new works by economists in the mid-1990s.[1] Thereafter, a growing consensus has evolved on the intrinsically negative impact of corruption for investment and, consequently, economic growth. Succinctly put, higher levels of corruption correspond to lower investment and growth. However, corruption also has an impact on several other aspects, including institutional stability and the allocation of public resources in education, for example.[2] Instead of performing as "grease," corruption actually acts as "gravel" in the machinery of public sector institutions.

Recent efforts at measuring this wide array of corruption costs have centered on the elaboration of a corruption perceptions index (CPI), based on

1. Paolo Mauro, "Corruption and Growth," *Quarterly Journal of Economics* 110 (1995): 681–712; Alberto Ades and Rafael Di Tella, "The New Economics of Corruption: A Survey and Some New Results," in *Combating Corruption in Latin America,* ed. Joseph Tulchin and Ralph Espach (Washington, DC: Woodrow Wilson Center Press, 2000), 15–52.

2. Paolo Mauro, "The Effects of Corruption on Growth, Investment, and Government Expenditures: A Cross-Country Analysis," in *Corruption and the Global Economy,* ed. Kimberly Ann Elliot (Washington, DC: Institute for International Economics, 1997), 83–108; "Corruption and the Composition of Government Expenditure," *Journal of Public Economics* 69 (1998): 263–79.

specialized surveys worldwide carried out by nongovernmental organizations such as Transparency International. Every year, countries are classified according to high to low public perceptions of corruption. On the basis of these perception indices, several socioeconomic variables can be correlated to indicate relevant dependent and independent linkages associated with corruption.[3] The growing use of these indices, however, has generated polemics over their degree of subjectivity. Perceptions of corruption change dramatically due to external factors such as current media coverage, scandals, and politics. Also, comparisons with past regimes using such indices are not possible.

Economic historians have quantified the incidence of key words, such as "corruption" and "fraud," after digitizing the text of major newspapers over a period of 160 years to develop historical indices of corruption via press coverage.[4] Apart from obvious variations in linguistic and conceptual fashions over time, this type of index is not applicable in historical periods during which the press was controlled or censored.

A new set of studies has generated more reliable, concrete data by focusing on funds diverted from their intended or planned objectives in public sector facilities or bureaucracies (e.g., hospitals).[5] Unfortunately, there is no single or unified statistical source available to quantify these real costs of corruption since such transactions are typically covert and performed precisely in ways to avoid leaving traces in official records. With due care in the use of historical sources it is possible, however, to adapt the hard data approach to the evaluation, estimation, and calculation of corruption as diverted costs from national budget expenditures and, consequently, measure it relative to, and as a percentage or ratio of government expenses and GDP. To these budgetary diversions, one can then add opportunity costs (indirect costs) of corruption in terms of domestic and foreign investment and other types of revenue and income diminished or forgone by the impact of corruption.

---

3. For up-to-date calculations and debates over corruption perception indices, see Charles Sampford, Arthur Shacklock, and Carmel Connors, *Measuring Corruption* (Aldershot, Hampshire, England: Ashgate, 2006), esp. chapters 5 and 7.

4. Edward Glaeser and Claudia Goldin, "Corruption and Reform: Introduction," and Mathew Gentzkow, Glaeser, and Goldin, "The Rise of the Fourth Estate: How Newspapers Became Informative and Why It Mattered," in *Corruption and Reform: Lessons from America's Economic History,* ed. E. Glaeser and C. Goldin (Chicago: University of Chicago Press, 2006), 3–22, esp. 15, and 187–230.

5. Rafael Di Tella and William Savedoff, *Diagnosis Corruption: Fraud in Latin America's Public Hospitals* (Washington, DC: Inter-American Development Bank, 2001).

From this brief methodological debate, one can conclude that there is a difference between cycles of corruption evaluated on the bases of public perceptions and media coverage, and cycles of corruption estimated on the bases of real values diverted from public funds. Although these two types of cycles are interconnected and influence each other, the former is more volatile and visible, whereas the latter is more structurally based and intimately linked to economic and institutional oscillations and variations. While we have occasionally used perceptions by average citizens and media outlets in the narrative of certain chapters, in the following model design and application, the hard data approach is used despite its current limitations. Conclusions throughout the book also reflect the quantitative conclusions of this model and its results.

Model

For the Peruvian case, there are basic historical statistics that measure and estimate, using projections and extrapolations, the GDP and government expenditures for the 1820–2000 period.[6] I have also estimated diverted funds due to corruption for the decades and government administrations of the nineteenth and twentieth centuries. Thus, it is theoretically possible to express these varying costs of corruption as percentages of government expenditures and GDP. In this way, decades and administrations can be classified as periods of high, medium, or low corruption. The development of more precise historical statistical series and estimates of corruption costs may eventually enhance the rigor of this model.

6. Bruno Seminario and Arlette Beltrán, *Crecimiento económico en el Perú: 1896–1995* (Lima: Centro de Investigación de la Universidad del Pacífico, 1998); Felipe Portocarrero S., Arlette Beltrán, and Alex Zimmerman, *Inversiones públicas en el Perú (1900–1968): una aproximación cuantitativa* (Lima: Centro de Investigación de la Universidad del Pacífico, 1998); B. R. Mitchell, *Internacional Historical Statistics: The Americas, 1750–1993,* 4th ed. (London: Macmillan, 1998); Oxford Latin American Economic History Data Base (Latin American Centre, Oxford University), http://oxlad.qeh.ox.ac.uk; Shane J. Hunt, "Growth and Guano in Nineteenth-Century Peru," Discussion Paper, no. 34 (Princeton, NJ: Woodrow Wilson School, Princeton University, 1973), and "Price and Quantum Estimates of Peruvian Exports, 1830–1962," Discussion Paper, no. 33 (Princeton, NJ: Woodrow Wilson School, Princeton University, 1973); Ernesto Yepes del Castillo, *Peru 1820–1920: un siglo de desarrollo capitalista* (Lima: Instituto de Estudios Peruanos, 1972).

Regarding institutional costs, it is assumed that institutional damage varies according to modes of corruption and historical period. Qualitative information added to the quantitative estimates allows the identification of key institutional costs that left significant legacies. In this regard, contemporary evaluations of the institutional consequences of corruption and lost development opportunities are helpful. In the next section, these procedures of measuring diverted funds and institutional costs of corruption are applied to the specific case of the Fujimori-Montesinos "década infame."

Infamous Decade (1990–2000)

Was President Alberto Fujimori's administration the most corrupt in the history of Peru? At first sight it might appear to be, considering the ample coverage of generalized and systematic corruption involving a bewildering array of institutions and private and public persons. The nation's public administration was clearly captured by a group of corrupt military and civilian cronies.

According to some historians, the level of corruption during the 1990s definitely surpassed that of all other governments in modern history,[7] perhaps comparable only with that of the colonial period when corrupt mechanisms were inherent to the system of power and wealth generation. When aided by informal rules, authoritarian governance, judicial impunity, and lack of transparency, corruption becomes generalized and widely accepted as intrinsic to the institutional system.

Table A.1 attempts to quantify the most notable confirmed cases of diverted funds by corrupt means on the basis of congressional, judicial, and fiscal investigations since the end of the Fujimori regime (as of July 2007). (For detailed discussion of specific corruption schemes, see Chapter 7.) In the elaboration of this table, care has been taken to avoid double counting.

Apart from the most notorious corruption scandals associated with Fujimori, Montesinos, and the armed forces, huge indirect costs resulted from forgone foreign investment (opportunity cost of investment) due to corruption. Higher levels of domestic and foreign investment were thus prevented with losses in domestic output, employment, and education. In general, the 1990s was a period of lost historical opportunities to efficiently reform the

---

7. Among others, Nelson Manrique's views in "¿Es usted honesto?" *Caretas,* no. 1649, December 14, 2000, 40–42.

Table A.1 Major direct and indirect costs of corruption, Peru, 1990–1999 ($ millions)

Institution/person	Amount	Concept/origin	Source
Direct Costs			
1. Presidency: Fujimori	400	Apenkai/Aken: 90	a, b, c
		Contingency fund: 120	
		Minister Joy Way: 80	
		SIN transfers: 60	
		Popular y Porvenir scam: 50	
2. Secret Service:			
Montesinos	450	SIN diversions: 150	c, d,e
		Drug trafficking: 200	
		Other: 100	
3. Interior and Defense			
Ministries	146	Transfer to SIN: 146	
4. Military Pension Fund	200	Transfer to SIN: 100	d
		Figureheads: 100	
5. Armed Forces	216	Illegal commissions	c
6. Minister Joy Way	80	Irregular purchases from China: 80	a, b, c, d
7. Miyagusuku			
and partners	50	Popular y Porvenir scam: 50	a
8. Foreign debt	500	Irregular operations	a, c, d
9. Privatizations	1,400	Misappropriation, bribes, favors	
		(*decretos secretos*)	a, c, d, f
10. Bank bail-outs	1,145	Wiese: 250	a, b, f
		Latino: 490	
		NBK: 198	
		Nuevo Mundo, others: 207	
Indirect costs			
11. Foreign investment			
forgone	10,000	Opportunity cost (1,000 per year)	c, g
Total costs (1990–1999)	**14,087**		
Annual average costs	**1,409**		

Sources: (a) Peru, Congreso, Comisión Investigadora, *Informe final* (2003); (b) Dammert, *Estado mafioso;* (c) *La República* (2001–2003); (d) *El Comercio* (2001–2003); (e) *Correo* (2003); (f) *La Gaceta* (2003); (g) based on revision of estimates by Transparency International.[8]

state-interventionist system without sacrificing more equitable income distribution and orthodox economic policies. Other institutional costs included serious damage to the military, police, and intelligence institutions; legislature and judiciary branches; education; and, most importantly, to the constitutional framework and rule of law.

8. Several issues of newspapers *El Comercio* (2001–2003), *Correo* (2003), and *La Gaceta* (2003), including reports by Transparency Internacional on estimated foreign

According to the estimates in Table A.1 and without adding other forms of corruption, the average cost of corruption in the 1990s reached $1.4 billion per annum, an amount equivalent to 34 percent of annual government spending, and 3.1 percent of average annual GDP. Other previous calculations have underestimated total costs of corruption by not taking into account indirect investment costs.[9]

Another Lost Decade (1850–1860)

A similar calculation as the one for the 1990s is possible thanks to ample fiscal, judicial, and journalistic information generated by the public finance scandals of the consolidation and conversion of the domestic debt (1850–1854) and the manumission of slaves with compensation to slave owners (1855–1857). Table A.2 shows diverted amounts and respective percentages of the total operations of consolidation, conversion, and manumission, as well as the estimated indirect cost of forgone investment due to corruption.

Assuming that total government expenses during the 1850s amounted to approximately $8 million annually,[10] then, according to Table A.2, the annual cost of corruption in public credit operations and management, without considering other forms of corruption, reached approximately 48 percent of annual government expenditures, a somewhat larger proportion than that of the 1990s. Now, estimating the annual productive value on the basis of the $11.6 million annual export value, annual GDP at current prices amounted to $116 million (assuming that exports represented 10 percent of GDP).[11] Accordingly, the estimated annual direct and indirect costs of corruption in public credit operations and related forgone investment in this decade was equivalent to 4 percent of GDP, also slightly higher than that calculated for the 1990s.

---

investment lost due to corruption, esp. "Transparencia Internacional analiza sobornos a políticos y funcionarios," *La República,* June 28, 2001, and "Perú pierde US$ 2,333 millones de inversión extranjera al año por casos de corrupción," June 18, 2001, in "Círculo internacional: Libertad & Paz," sapiens.ya.com/alecia/circulointernacional.htm.

9. Iniciativa Nacional Anticorrupción, *Un Perú sin corrupción: condiciones, lineamientos y recomendaciones para la lucha contra la corrupción* (Lima: INA / Ministerio de Justicia, 2001), 3–4; Gabriel Ortiz de Zevallos and Pierina Pollarolo, eds., *Estrategias anticorrupción en el Perú* (Lima: Instituto Apoyo, 2002), 20–26.

10. Hunt, "Growth and Guano," table 9, 73–74.

11. Based on estimate for 1876–1877 by Hunt, "Growth and Guano," table 14, 95.

Table A.2 Direct costs of corruption in public debt operations and indirect investment costs, Peru, 1850–1859 (millions of pesos = millions of dollars)

Concept	Amount	Percentage of total operation	Sources
1. Consolidation (vales impeached)	12	50	a, b, c
2. Conversion (commissions, favors)	3	30	c, d
3. Manumission (overvaluation of slaves)	4	50	e
4. Indirect investment costs (opportunity costs)	20		f
Total costs (1850–1859)	**39**		
Annual average costs	**3.9**		

Sources: (a) Junta de Examen Fiscal, *Informes* (1857); (b) Comisión Especial de Crédito Público, *Informe* (1856); (c) *El Peruano,* March 31, October 31, and November 4, 1857; (d) Alfredo Leubel, *El Perú en 1860 o sea anuario nacional;* (e) Márquez, *Orjía financiera;* (f) based on figures of lagging mining and portfolio investment in Hunt, "Growth and Guano," 46–48.

Historical Comparisons

Aggregate and overall estimates of the total costs of corruption in its most important forms need, however, to be elaborated on the basis of uniform categories applicable to all periods considered. To approximate this general quantification, one must rely on discrete estimates for specific periods using contemporary, incomplete, or sporadic information and calculations (subject to some degree of over- or under-estimation). The next step is to complete the estimates for all periods (when data are insufficient, via extrapolation), and then relate these estimated figures to statistical series on national budgets and production so as to establish relevant ratios and comparisons over time. A similar exercise was carried out for the colonial period in Tables 1.1 and 1.2.

In Table A.3, estimates of corruption costs are shown for direct and indirect costs of various modes of corruption, during the decades of the nineteenth century, under five general categories relevant to existing institutional characteristics and available sources: irregularities and mismanagement of foreign and domestic public debt and its service; caudillo and military graft associated with misappropriations and illegal commissions in the procurement of arms and equipment; bribery in public contracts for commercial purposes and public works or other general procurement; indirect loss of revenue due to contraband; and indirect loss of foreign and domestic investment due to the general climate of bribery and corruption.

The first general mode of corruption encompasses irregularities in the management of the public debt that resulted in a critical erosion of the coun-

Table A.3 Estimates of direct and indirect costs of corruption per decade, Peru, 1820–1899 (millions of pesos and soles)

Decade	I Foreign and domestic debt handling	II Caudillo and military graft	III Bribery in public contracts	IV Indirect lost revenue to contraband	V Indirect forgone investment	Total	Annual Average
1820–1829	4	3	2	8	10	27	2.7
1830–1839	2	2	1	5	12	22	2.2
1840–1849	3	2	3	4	13	25	2.5
1850–1859	19	4	3	4	20	50	5
1860–1869*	20	10	19	4	30	83	8.3
1870–1879	25	20	25	3	35	108	10.8
1880–1889	3	8	6	2	10*	29	2.9
1890–1899	3	12	15	2	15	47	4.7

* One peso = 8 reales = US$1. In 1863, Peru adopted the sol of 10 reales; 1 sol = US$0.925.
Sources: Same as Table A.2; Chapters 2–4; Basadre, *Historia* 1:220–23, 8:252–53, 9:155–64; Flores Galindo, *Aristocracia y plebe,* 222–24; Quiroz, *Deuda defraudada,* 30–36; Palacios, *Deuda anglo-peruana,* 15; Mathew, "First Anglo-Peruvian Debt," 83, 96–98, "Foreign Contractors," 604–7; and *House of Gibbs,* 102–8, 230–31; Marichal, *Century of Debt,* 21; Gamarra, *Epistolario,* 165, 172; Despatches 1826–1906, rolls 5 and 11, USNA; 5-17/1846, 1849, 1851, and 5-14A/1858, AMRE; Palacios, "Un empresario peruano," 14–18; Bonilla, *Guano y burguesía,* 95–98; Dreyfus Frères, *Texto del contrato,* 16–17; U.S. Congress, *Investigación acerca venta,* 3, appendix B; Colección Pardo, D2-52/3398, AGN; Stewart, *Henry Meiggs,* 51–52; Márquez, *Orjía financiera,* 66–67; Witt, "Diaries," vol. 7, 8–9, 122, 149, 244, 263, 343; Rougemont, *Una pájina,* 49; box 58, no. 155, p. 292, box 59, no. 159, 146–48, box 71, no. 10, p. 425, WRGP; Billinghurst to Piérola, April 1 and 17, 1889, Archivo Piérola, vol. 3, BNP.

try's international credit and financial development. Losses incurred due to the mishandling of foreign loans and domestic debts since the birth of the fledging republic in the 1820s have been discussed. Estimates in this category start with an approximate 40-percent loss of the first foreign loans and the interested depreciation of domestic debts for unpaid salaries (see Chapter 2). Similar criteria to those of Table A.2 are used to estimate the direct costs of the corrupt mishandling of the public credit throughout the century's decades. This mode of corruption appeared as an "innovation" with independence, and has had a long history thereafter. It has been a preferred high-level, extremely costly means to hide, recycle, or launder corrupt gains at the expense of the general citizenry, and is closely linked to the cycles of foreign indebtedness.

The second category or mode of corruption prominent throughout the nineteenth century—caudillo-type corrupt patronage and misappropriations for personal or political purposes and graft among military officers (often connected to the purchase of weapons and equipment and procurement contracts)—had deep roots in the colonial period but developed new ramifications as the political sphere, military technology, and modern warfare evolved, and domestic and international wars occurred. The calculations per decade for this type of corruption cost are based on flagrant expropriations and interested plunder by caudillo networks as well as documented irregularities—such as bribes, "commissions," and "advances"—in the purchase contracts of warships, rifles, and other ordnance.

The third mode of corruption, bribery in official contracts for the commercialization of guano abroad, public works (especially railway and dock construction), and other public procurement transactions, became a prominent fixture and symbol of corruption throughout the nineteenth century. Monopoly rights of the state were exploited initially by executive branch officials for corrupt gain. Later, legislative and judiciary officials also had an important role due to constitutional issues and litigation, the solution of which depended on bribery (*cohecho, concusión, prevaricato*) of congressmen and judges. All these illegal transactions increased transaction costs considerably. To estimate the amounts involved in bribes in exchange for the approval or extension of public contracts, costs are calculated as a percentage of the total official cost of the project under contract. In the case of Meiggs, for example, bribes paid amounted to approximately 10 percent of the total railway construction costs. The cost of bribes was an important component of the total official costs since contractors added the amount paid in bribes to the final operating costs, thus shifting the real cost of bribes to the public. Other important cases of bribery in public procurement included the early guano, Dreyfus, and Grace contracts.

The fourth and fifth types of corruption costs estimated in Table A.3 are indirect costs. Since colonial times, contraband contributed to the loss of trade and silver tax revenue at a rate of 20 percent of the amounts involved in smuggling. Corruption and bribery of local authorities allowed such forgone revenue. In the early republican period, such rates continued as contraband increased with clandestine exports of untaxed silver and imports of foreign goods. Figures of unregistered bullion in British ships in the 1820s and 1830s provide the basis for the calculation of lost revenues due to contraband. With more liberal trade legislation since the 1850s, revenue losses due to contraband tended to decline but did not disappear (while other corruption costs increased).

Foregone foreign and domestic investment, the fifth category of costs, is counted as contraction in the willingness to invest in a country of high, cumbersome, and capricious transaction costs and structural instability fueled by bribery and corruption. Such conditions benefited mainly investors willing to pay bribes with the expectation of monopoly and windfall profits. This forgone investment is only a portion of the total investment lost due to other adverse policy and institutional conditions. Lost investment due to corruption can be calculated only in general and very approximate terms as a percentage of reduction in the amount of direct and portfolio investment per period.

Table A.4 now integrates the estimates of aggregate corruption costs in a comparative perspective, using ratios of annual average corruption costs over government expenses and GDP figures per decade. These estimates are quite revealing.

Although the largest estimated actual costs of corruption corresponded to the 1860s and 1870s, increased government expenditures and production in these decades contributed to relatively lower (but still high) levels of corruption measured as percentages of expenditures and GDP. The highest levels, due to fiscal penury and depressed production caused by war and caudillo depredations, were achieved in the 1820s, 1830s, and 1880s, whereas the 1850s and 1890s had very high levels as percentages of expenditures and less so as percentages of GDP. Throughout these eighty years, however, an annual average of almost 57 percent of expenditures and 4.3 percent of

Table A.4 Comparative estimated costs and levels of corruption, Peru, 1820–1899 (annual averages per decade in millions of current pesos/soles)

	I	II	III	IV	V	VI
	Estimated	Government	Cost of	Level of	Level of	
Decade	GDP	expenditure	corruption	expenditure	GDP	
Exports	(a)	(b, d)	(b, c)	(e)	IV/III %	IV/II %
1820–1829	4.4	44	2	2.7	135	6.1
1830–1839	5.1	51	2.8	2.2	79	4.3
1840–1849	6	60	6	2.5	42	4.2
1850–1859	11.6	116	8	5	63	4.3
1860–1869	24	240	26	8.3	32	3.5
1870–1879	22	236	53	10.8	20	4.6
1880–1889	5.8	58	7.1	2.9	41	5
1890–1899	20.2	210	10.1	4.7	47	2.2

Notes: GDP is assumed to be equal to approximately exports times 10 (based on Hunt's estimate for 1876–1877, and Seminario and Beltrán for 1896–1899). Currency before 1863 is pesos, and for 1863 and after is soles (see also Table A.3).
Sources: (a) Mitchell, *International Historical Statistics* (1998): 442, 444, 447; (b) Shane Hunt, *Guano and Growth* (1973): 73–74, 95; (c) Yepes, *Perú* (1972): 42–44, 131; (d) Seminario and Beltrán, *Crecimiento económico* (1998): 174; (e) same as for Table A.3.

GDP were very high overall levels that seriously undermined long-term economic development. These levels are not greatly different from those of the late colonial period, although the opportunity cost of foreign investment, historically relevant only by the nineteenth century, can bias the comparison between colonial- and republican-era levels of corruption.

Similar methods to those used in Tables A.3 and A.4 are applied for the twentieth century in Tables A.5 and A.6. Differences in the modes of estimated corruption costs concern the old military caudillo misappropriation subsumed in systematic military corruption. Presidential graft, clearly present, especially in the 1920s and 1990s, replaces the former caudillo category. Corrupt mishandling of debt management continues to cause damage in the 1920s, 1970s, 1980s, and 1990s. Although the Peruvian foreign debt remained in default throughout the 1930s and 1940s, reliance on domestic loans (up to $66 million in the 1930s) and raids on reserves provided op-

Table A.5 Estimates of corruption costs per decade, Peru, 1900–1999 (annual average per decade in millions of current dollars)

Decade	I Irregular public debt management	II Presidential and military graft	III Bribery in public procurement and services	IV Indirect loss to contraband and trafficking	V Indirect forgone investment	Total annual average
1900–1909	0.1	0.5	0.5	0.7	0.4	2.2
1910–1919	0.3	1	1	1	1.7	5
1920–1929	2.1	5	9	7	8	31.1
1930–1939	1	3	5.5	3	4	16.5
1940–1949	2	4	10	8	5	29
1950–1959	2.9	18	25	12	10	67.9
1960–1969	8.6	15	20	105	30	178.6
1970–1979	98	30	60	190	240	618
1980–1989	150	60	100	400	300	1,010
1900–1999	165	120	153	600	1,000	2,038

Sources: Table A.1; Chapters 2–4; Oxford Latin American Economic History Database (foreign debt and foreign direct investment serve as basis for calculations); Thorp and Bertram, *Peru,* 339, table A.2.2; Marichal, *Century of Debt,* 213, 255; U.S. Senate, *Sale of Foreign Bonds* (1932), part 3, 1276–81, and *Munitions Industry: Hearing* (1934), part 1, 85–86, 100, 116–17, 135–36; Hervey to Chamberlain, Lima, July 19, 1928, no. 63, FO 371/12788, ff. 282–84, NAUK; Cumberland, "Reminiscences," 135, 138–39; Dearing to S.S., April 14, 1932, 823.002/189, 3–4, box 5706; Steinhardt to S.S., March 4, 1939, 823.157/6, box 4353, and March 15, 1939, box 5711; Hoover to Berel, October 5, 1943, 823.114/314, box 4351; Pringle to Dorr, June 17, 1952, 723.521/6–1752, box 3303; Sayre to D.S., March 7, 1958, 723.00/3-758, box 3011, RG 59, USNA; Basadre, *La vida y la historia,* 711–12; Masterson, *Militarism,* 131, 265–70; Peru, Senado, *Diario,* 26th session, September 20, 1956, 2:243–44; Peru, Diputados, *Diario,* 5th session, August 20, 1956, 1:293–94; *El Comercio,* November 16, 1958, January 4, 9, and 27, 1959; Goodsell, *American Corporations,* 99; Vargas Haya, *Contrabando,* 159–62, *Defraudadores,* 92–94, 179, 337, *Democracia o farsa,* 191–205, and *Perú: 184 años,* 311–16; Philip, *Military Radicals,* 140; Rudolph, *Peru,* 81–83; Caterino, *Caso García,* 235–40.

Table A.6 Comparative estimated costs and levels of corruption, Peru,
1900–1999 (annual averages per decade in millions of current dollars)

Decade	I GDP (a, b)	II Government expenditure (a, b)	III Cost of corruption (c)	IV Level of expenditure III/II %	V Level of GDP III/I %
1900–1909	230	8.9	2.2	25	1
1910–1919	445	17.8	5	28	1.1
1920–1929	809	43.2	31.1	72	3.8
1930–1939	539	36.4	16.5	31	3.1
1940–1949	866	69.2	29	42	3.3
1950–1959	1,883	149	67.9	46	3.6
1960–1969	4,863	571	178.6	31	3.7
1970–1979	12,540	1,464	618	42	4.9
1980–1989	25,303	2,889	1,010	35	3.9
1990–1999	45,624	4,090	2,038	50	4.5

Sources: (a) Oxford Latin American Economic History Database, compared and corrected for inflation using (b) Seminario and Beltrán, *Crecimiento económico* (1998), tables V.1 and X.2, 174–77 and 259–62; (c) same as Table A.1.

portunities for corruption and mismanagement. With an increasing and underpaid bureaucracy, bribery, inefficiencies, and irregularities in general administration and public procurement contracts tended to increase. The old problem of lost revenue to contraband escalated with the inception of protectionist, interventionist regimes in the 1940s through the 1980s, whereas corruption-related drug trafficking costs, the modern version of old contraband, increased exponentially since the 1970s through the 1990s. With the expanding international supply of investment funds since the 1950s, opportunity costs of foreign investment due to corruption increased as systematic corruption structurally tied to interventionist regimes and distorted orthodox economic policies contributed to higher bribery-related transaction costs (a kind of illicit tax on investment).

After calculating the costs of corruption for the decades of the nineteenth and twentieth centuries, comparisons of the costs of corruption by government administrations are possible, as shown in Table A.7.

General Trends and Cycles

From the information in Table A.7, the following general trends can be observed: (1) the periods for which the levels of diverted and indirect costs of corruption were equivalent to more than 30 percent of the annual budget,

Table A.7 Costs of corruption as percentage of public expenditures and GDP and related institutional costs, by administration, Peru, 1810–2000

Government/administration	% Public expenditures	% GDP	Institutional costs and conditions
1. Late colonial (1810–1820)	41	4	Failure of reform, decline of intendant system, viceroy's patrimonial power regained, rise of military, contraband
2. Early independence (1821–1829)	139	6.1	Weakened property rights, collapse of public credit, caudillo plunder and rule of force
3. Gamarra/La Fuente (1829–1933, 1839–1841)	80	4.7	Antigrowth trade policies, emergency finance, caudillo patronage, instability
4. 1st Castilla (1845–1851)	41	4.1	Exclusive guano contracts, centralism and maturation of caudillo networks
5. Echenique (1851–1855)	65	5	Damaged credit and financial bases, reliance on guano advances, civil war
6. 2nd Castilla, Pezet, 1st M. I. Prado (1855–1868)	33	3.5	Defeat of anticorruption measures, foreign meddling, increasingly venal legislature and judiciary
7. Diez Canseco, Balta/Piérola (1868–1872)	24	5	Deficits, chronic indebtedness, onerous public works, dysfunctional transportation and development planning (Meiggs, Muelle y Dársena, Dreyfus)
8. Manuel Pardo, 2nd M. I. Prado (1872–1879)	18	3.5	Ultimately failed management of inherited crisis, weakened defense system, state intervention
9. 1st Piérola, Iglesias (1879–1881, 1882–1885)	70	5.5	Rampant disregard of law, wartime plunder, defensive incapacity, foreign dominance
10. Cáceres, Morales Bermúdez, Borgoño (1886–1895)	47	4	Politicized militaristic control, favored foreign speculation (Grace Contract)
11. 2nd Piérola (1895–1899)	40	2.2	Venal alliance with money cliques, faulty electoral laws
12. Civilistas (1899–1908)	25	1	Increasingly biased income distribution, control of electoral bodies, bought military support

Table A.7 Continued

Government/administration	% Public expenditures	% GDP	Institutional costs and conditions
13. 1st Leguía (1909–1912)	30	2	Breakdown of political consensus, military build-up and patronage, greater debt, secret surveillance, electoral meddling
14. Billinghurst, 1st Benavides, 2nd José Pardo (1913–1919)	25	1	Return of political instability, crisis, "professional" military intervention
15. Leguía's Oncenio (1919–1930)	72	3.8	Indebtedness, dictatorship, breakdown of checks and balances and political system, opposition debilitated, widespread espionage, media censorship, propaganda, political use of military
16. Sánchez Cerro (1931–1933)	34	3.5	Instability, systematic repression, nepotism, antiforeigner prowar stance, military favoritism, devalued currency
17. 2nd Benavides (1933–1939)	30	2.6	Dictatorial, nepotistic economic clique, hand-picked successor, electoral manipulation
18. 1st Manuel Prado (1939–1945)	43	3.4	Guided democracy, distorted policies, deficits, inflation, internal loan abuse, military rewards, first illegal drug rings
19. Bustamante (1945–1948)	41	3.2	Uncontained populist interventionism, political obstruction and infiltration, bloated bureaucracy, price controls, inflation, reliance on military, instability
20. Odría's Ochenio (1948–1956)	47	3.7	Dictatorship, increased public spending, military budget, and foreign debt, rigged elections, abuses and repression, constitutional violations and infringement
21. 2nd Manuel Prado (1956–1962)	45	3.5	Neglect and stalling of urgent reforms, unprincipled political pacts, deficits, growing leftist influence, electoral manipulation
19. 1st Belaúnde (1963–1968)	30	3.4	Favors owed to military, legislative conflict with recalcitrant

(*continued*)

Table A.7 Continued

Government/administration	% Public expenditures	% GDP	Institutional costs and conditions
			opposition, stalled reform, contraband, deficit, inflation, conflicts with foreign capital and aid
20. Military "revolution" (1968–1980)	43	5	Dictatorship, eroded judiciary, decrees, deficit finance, indebtedness, favoritism, unorthodox economic and financial policy, inefficient state enterprises, contraband, media control, leftist penetration, narco-trafficking
21. 2nd Belaúnde (1981–1985)	33	3.8	Neglect, unreformed state structure, insurgent terrorism, foreign debt reliance military autonomy, limited rights, fiscal deficits, inflation, favored bank rescues
22. 1st Alan García (1985–1990)	37	4	Unorthodox policies, instability, hyperinflation, economic-political crisis, rising narco-terrorism, black markets, rising case backlog and weak judiciary
23. Fujimori/Montesinos (1990–2000)	50	4.5	Predatory capture of state institutions, presidentialism, covert abuses, distorted economic reforms, damage to armed forces, legislature, judiciary, elections, the media, and rule of law

Sources: Same as Tables 1.2, A.1 to A.6; Chapters 1–7.

and between 4 and 6 percent of GDP, can be classified as periods of very high corruption; (2) periods for which corruption levels were equivalent to between 20 and 29 percent of the budget and 2.1 and 3.9 percent of GDP should be considered periods of high corruption; (3) periods for which corruption was equivalent to less than 20 percent of the budget and 1 to 2 percent of GDP can be labeled periods of moderate corruption. In this historical survey and estimation exercise, periods of low or very low corruption were not detected.

Departing from the late colonial period when it is assumed that levels of corruption were very high, subsequent cycles of corruption during postindependence republican history can be described as follows: very high levels in the 1820s and 1830s; return to very high levels in the 1850s, early 1870s, and 1880s; moderate levels between the late 1890s and the 1910s; a stiff increase to very high levels in the 1920s; moderate to high levels again in the 1930s and 1940s; and a steady increase to higher levels in the 1950s, 1960s, and 1970s, reaching very high levels in the late 1980s and 1990s.

Conclusion

At an estimated average annual level of around 30 to 40 percent of budget expenditures, and 3 to 4 percent of GDP in the long term (years 1820 to 2000), the costs of corruption for Peruvian economic and social development throughout its republican history have been structurally and consistently high or very high despite cyclical variations. Considering that achieving self-sustained growth requires an average annual rate of GDP growth of 5 to 8 percent in the long run, Peru lost or misallocated through systematic, uncontrolled corruption an equivalent of approximately 40 to 50 percent of its developmental possibilities.

Bibliography

Archival Sources

Archives du Ministère des Affaires Étrangères, Paris (AMAE): Affaires Diverses Politiques; Correspondance Politique, Pérou, Pérou Supplément; Correspondance Politique et Commerciale, Nouvelle Série, Pérou; Série B Amérique, Pérou.

Archivo de la Corte Suprema de Justicia, Sala Penal Especial (ACSJ): Expedientes Asuntos Varios 21–92 and 01–95.

Archivo General del Congreso de la República del Perú, Lima (AGCP): Cámara de Diputados; Senado; Papeles de Comisiones Especiales.

Archivo General de Indias, Sevilla (AGI): Gobierno, Audiencia de Lima; Indiferente General; Escribanía; Diversos, Archivo Abascal.

Archivo General de la Nación, Lima (AGN): Libros Manuscritos Republicanos; Causas Civiles y Criminales; Colección Manuel Pardo; Colección Santa María; Corte Superior de Justicia de Lima; Tribunal de Sanción Nacional.

Archivo General del Ministerio de Asuntos Exteriores, Madrid (AGMAE): Correspondencia, Embajadas y Legaciones, Perú; Política, Política Exterior e Interior, Perú.

Archivo General y Documentación, Ministerio de Relaciones Exteriores del Perú, Lima (AMRE): Embajada del Perú en Francia; Embajada del Perú en Gran Bretaña.

Archivo Histórico Militar, Lima (AHM): Correspondencia General; Colección Julián Heras.

Archivo Histórico Nacional, Madrid (AHN): Consejos Suprimidos, Consejo de Indias; Estado.

Archivo Histórico Riva Agüero, Lima (AHRA): Colección Mendiburu; Colección Plácido Jiménez.

Biblioteca Nacional del Perú, Lima (BNP): Manuscritos, Archivo Leguía; Archivo Paz Soldán; Archivo Piérola.

Biblioteca Nacional de Madrid (BNM): Manuscritos.

Biblioteca del Palacio Real, Madrid (BPR): Manuscritos.

Columbia University, Butler Library, New York: Rare Books and Manuscripts, W. R. Grace and Company Papers (WRGP); Oral History Research Project (OHRP).

Library of Congress, Washington, DC (LOC): Rare Books and Special Collections.

National Archives of the United Kingdom, Kew (NAUK): Foreign Office (F.O. 61, 371).

National Security Archive, Gellman Library, Georgetown University, Washington, DC (NSA): Bigwood Collection (BC), Drug Policy Collection (DPC), Peru Documentation Project (PDP).

Real Academia de la Historia, Madrid (RAH): Colección Mata Linares.

Servicio Histórico Militar, Madrid (SHM).

U.S. National Archives and Records Administration, Washington, DC (USNA): General Records of the Department of State, Record Group 59, Diplomatic Correspondence; Despatches from United States Ministers to Peru, 1826–1906, microcopy T52; Records of the Department of State Relating to Internal Affairs of Peru, microcopy M746; Records of the Office of Strategic Services, Record Group 226.

Published Sources

Abascal, José Fernando de. *Memoria de gobierno.* Edited by Vicente Rodríguez Casado and J. A. Calderón Quijano. 2 vols. Seville: Escuela de Estudios Hispano-Americanos, 1944.

Acevedo y Criado, Ismael. "La institución del Registro de la Propiedad Inmueble en el Perú, sus antecedentes legales y formas más urgentes." *Revista de la Facultad de Derecho y Ciencias Políticas* (1959): 95–182.

Acha, Elisabeth, and Javier Diez Canseco, eds. *Patios interiores de la vida policial: ética, cultura civil y reorganización de la Policía Nacional.* Lima: Fondo Editorial del Congreso del Perú, 2004.

Acosta, Antonio. "Estado, clases y Real Hacienda en los inicios de la conquista del Perú." *Revista de Indias* 66, no. 236 (2006): 57–86.

Ades, Alberto, and Rafael Di Tella. "The New Economics of Corruption: A Survey and Some New Results." In *Combating Corruption in Latin America.* Edited by Joseph Tulchin and Ralph Espach, 15–52. Washington, DC: Woodrow Wilson Center Press, 2000.

Adorno, Rolena. *Guamán Poma: Writing and Resistance in Colonial Peru.* 2nd ed. Austin: University of Texas Press, 2000.

Alatas, Syed Hussein. *Corruption: Its Nature, Causes, and Functions.* Aldershot, Hampshire, England: Avebury, 1990.

Albornoz de López, Teresa. *La visita de Joaquín Mosquera y Figueroa a la Real Audiencia de Caracas (1804–1809): conflictos internos y corrupción en la administración de justicia.* Caracas: Academia Nacional de Historia, 1987.

Alsedo y Herrera, Dionisio de. *Memorial informativo, que pusieron en las reales manos del rey nuestro señor (que Dios guarde) el Tribunal de Consulado de la ciudad de los Reyes, y la Junta General del comercio de las provincias del Perú sobre diferentes puntos tocantes al estado de la Real hazienda, y del Comercio, justificando las causas de su descaecimiento, y pidiendo todas las providencias que conviene para restablecer en su mayor aumento el Real Patrimonio, y en su antigua comunicación, y prosperidad los comercios de España y de las Indias.* Madrid: N.p., 1726.

Alt, James, and David Dreyer Lassen. "Political and Judicial Checks on Corruption: Evidence from American State Government." Copenhagen: Economic Policy Research Unit Working Paper Series, University of Copenhagen, 2005.

Amat y Junyent, Manuel de. *Memoria de gobierno.* Edited by Vicente Rodríguez Casado and Florentino Pérez Embid. Seville: Escuela de Estudios Hispano-Americanos, 1947.

Ames, Rolando, et al. *Informe al Congreso sobre los sucesos de los penales.* Lima: Talleres Gráficos Ocisa, 1988.

Amunátegui, Manuel, et al. *Señor, los abajo firmados propietarios y comerciantes de esta ciudad y tenedores de vales de consolidación.* Lima: N.p., 1862.

Andrew, Christopher, and Vasili Mitrokhin. *The World Was Going Our Way: The KGB and the Battle for the Third World.* New York: Basic Books, 2005.

Andrien, Kenneth J. "The Sale of Juros and the Politics of Reform in the Viceroyalty of Peru, 1608–1695." *Journal of Latin American Studies* 13 (1981): 1–19.

———. "The Sale of Fiscal Offices and the Decline of Royal Authority in the Viceroyalty of Peru, 1633–1700." *Hispanic American Historical Review* 62 (1982): 49–71.

———. *Crisis and Decline: The Viceroyalty of Peru in the Seventeenth Century.* Albuquerque: University of New Mexico Press, 1985.

———. "The *Noticias Secretas de América* and the Construction of a Governing Ideology for the Spanish American Empire." *Colonial Latin American Review* 7, no. 2 (1998): 175–92.

Anna, Timothy. "Economic Causes of San Martín's Failure in Lima." *Hispanic American Historical Review* 54 (1974): 657–81.

———. "Peruvian Declaration of Independence: Freedom by Coercion." *Journal of Latin American Studies* 7 (1975): 221–48.

Anonymous. *Al gobierno, a la Convención Nacional y a la opinión pública.* Lima: Imprenta Libre, 1856.

———. *El tratado de 21 de mayo, o el protectorado anglo-francés.* Lima: J. Sánchez Silva, 1856.

———. *La acusación de D. G. Bogardus contra D. Manuel Pardo ministro de Hacienda y D. Federico Barreda ex-ministro plenipotenciario del Perú en Francia.* Paris: Imprenta Parisiense Guyot y Scribe, 1867.

———. *El señor J.M.Q. y el contrato Grace.* Lima: Imprenta Bacigalupi, 1887.

Aponte, Juan de. "Memorial que trata de la reformación del reino del Pirú." In *Colección de documentos inéditos para la historia de España,* vol. 51: 521–62. Madrid: Real Academia de la Historia, 1867.

Aragón, Ilana Lucía. "El teatro, los negocios y los amores: Micaela Villegas, 'La Perricholi.'" In *El virrey Amat y su tiempo.* Edited by Carlos Pardo-Figueroa and Joseph Dager, 353–404. Lima: Instituto Riva Agüero, Pontificia Universidad Católica, 2004.

Arellano Hoffmann, Carmen. "El intendente de Tarma Juan Ma. de Gálvez y su juicio de residencia (1791): aspectos de la corrupción en una administración serrana del Perú." *Histórica* 20, no. 1 (1996): 29–57.

Arrillaga Aldama, Luis. *Clientelismo, caciquismo, corporativismo: ensayo sobre algunas formas de particularismo social.* Pamplona: Zubillaga, 1994.

Asociación Venezolana de Derecho Tributario. *La corrupción en Venezuela.* Valencia, Venezuela: Vadell Hermanos, 1985.

Avilés, Marqués de. *Memoria del virrey del Perú marqués de Avilés.* Edited by Carlos Alberto Romero. Lima: Imprenta del Estado, 1901.

Baella Tuesta, Alfonso. *El poder invisible.* Lima: Editorial Andina, 1977.

———. *El miserable.* Lima: Editorial Andina, 1978.

Bailyn, Bernard. *The Ideological Origins of the American Revolution.* Cambridge, MA: Harvard University Press, 1992.

Balmori, Diana, Stuart Voss, and Miles Wortman. *Notable Family Networks in Latin America.* Chicago: University of Chicago Press, 1984.

Banco de la Providencia. *Exposición que hacen al público, a los tribunales, al supremo gobierno, el directorio y accionistas.* Lima: Imprenta de El Comercio, 1868.

Barriga Alvarez, Felipe (Timoleón). *El Perú y los gobiernos del general Echenique y de la revolución.* Lima: J. M. Monterola, 1855.

Barroilhet, Carlos. *Examen crítico de un opúsculo sobre el huano.* Paris: Imprenta Tipográfica de G. Kugelmann, 1860.

———. *Examen crítico de dos publicaciones del señor don Francisco Rivero.* Paris: Imprenta Tipográfica de G. Kugelmann, 1861.

Basadre, Jorge. *Materiales para otra morada: ensayos sobre temas de educación y cultura.* Lima: La Universidad, 1960.

———. *Historia de la República del Perú.* 6th ed. 16 vols. Lima: Editorial Universitaria, 1968.

———. *Introducción a las bases documentales para la historia de la República del Perú.* 2 vols. Lima: P. L. Villanueva, 1971.

———. *Sultanismo, corrupción y dependencia en el Perú republicano.* Lima: Editorial Milla Batres, 1979.

———. *La vida y la historia.* Lima: Industrial Gráfica, 1981.

———, and Pablo Macera. *Conversaciones.* Lima: Mosca Azul, 1974.

Basombrío, Carlos, and Fernando Rospigliosi. *La seguridad y sus instituciones en el Perú a inicios del siglo XXI: reformas democráticas o neomilitarismo.* Lima: Instituto de Estudios Peruanos, 2006.

Bayley, David. "The Effects of Corruption in a Developing Nation." In *Political Corruption: Readings in Comparative Analysis.* Edited by A. Heidenheimer, 521–33. New York: Holt, Rinehart, and Winston, 1970.

Blanc, Olivier. *La corruption sous la Terreur (1792–1794).* Paris: Éditions Robert Laffont, 1992.

Blanchard, Peter. "The 'Transitional Man' in Nineteenth-Century Latin America: The Case of Domingo Elías of Peru." *Bulletin of Latin American Research* 15 (1996): 157–76.

Bogardus, Guillermo. *La Compañía Nacional y Thomson Bonar y Ca., consignatarios del guano en Inglaterra y agentes financieros del Perú en Londres: dedicado al público y muy especialmente a los diputados del Congreso de la Restauración.* Lima: Imprenta Liberal, 1866.

Boloña, Carlos. "The Viability of Alberto Fujimori's Economic Strategy." In *The Peruvian Economy and Structural Adjustment: Past, Present, Future.* Edited by Efraín Gonzales de Olarte, 183–264. Miami: University of Miami North-South Center Press, 1996.

Bonilla, Heraclio. *Guano y burguesía en el Perú.* Lima: Instituto de Estudios Peruanos, 1974.

———. *Un siglo a la deriva: ensayos sobre el Perú, Bolivia y la guerra.* Lima: Instituto de Estudios Peruanos, 1980.

Bowen, Sally, and Jane Holligan. *El espía imperfecto: la telaraña siniestra de Vladimiro Montesinos.* Lima: Peisa, 2003.

Brading, David A. *The First America: The Spanish Monarchy, Creole Patriots, and the Liberal State, 1492–1867.* Cambridge: Cambridge University Press, 1991.

Brewer, John. *The Sinews of Power: War, Money, and the English State, 1688–1783.* London: Unwin and Hyman, 1989.

Brown, Kendall. *Bourbons and Brandy: Imperial Reform in Eighteenth-Century Arequipa.* Albuquerque: University of New Mexico Press, 1986.

————. "La crisis financiera peruana al comienzo del siglo XVIII, la minería de plata y la mina de azogues de Huancavelica." *Revista de Indias* 48 (1988): 349–81.

————. "The Curious Insanity of Juan de Alasta and Antonio de Ulloa's Governorship of Huancavelica." *Colonial Latin American Review* 13 (2004): 199–211.

Bullick, Lucie. *Pouvoir militaire et société au Pérou aux XIXe et XXe siècles.* Paris: Publications de la Sorbonne, 1999.

Burenius, Charlotte. *Testimonio de un fracaso: Huando, habla el sindicalista Zózimo Torres.* Lima: Instituto de Estudios Peruanos, 2001.

Burkholder, Mark A. "From Creole to Peninsular: The Transformation of the Audiencia of Lima." *Hispanic American Historical Review* 52 (1972): 395–415.

————. *Politics of a Colonial Career: José Baquíjano and the Audiencia of Lima.* 2nd ed. Wilmington, DE: Scholarly Resources, 1990.

————, and D. S. Chandler. "Creole Appointments and the Sale of Audiencia Positions in the Spanish Empire under the Early Bourbons, 1701–1750." *Journal of Latin American Studies* 4, no. 2 (1972): 187–206.

————, and D. S. Chandler. *From Impotence to Authority: The Spanish Crown and the American Audiencias, 1687–1808.* Columbia and London: University of Missouri Press, 1977.

————, and D. S. Chandler. *Biographical Dictionary of Audiencia Ministers in the Americas, 1687–1821.* Westport, CT: Greenwood Press, 1982.

————, and Lyman Johnson. *Colonial Latin America.* 5th ed. New York: Oxford University Press, 2004.

Bustamante y Rivero, José Luis. *La ideología de don Francisco García Calderón.* Paris: Desclée de Brouwer, 1946.

————. *Tres años de la lucha por la democracia en el Perú.* Buenos Aires: Chiesino, 1949.

————. *Mensaje al Perú.* Lima: N.p., 1955.

Cáceres, Andrés Avelino. *Memorias del Mariscal Andrés A. Cáceres.* 2 vols. Lima: Editorial Milla Batres, 1986.

Cameron, Maxwell. "Endogenous Regime Breakdown: The Vladivideo and the Fall of Peru's Fujimori." In *The Fujimori Legacy: The Rise of Electoral Authoritarianism in Peru.* Edited by Julio Carrión, 268–93. University Park: Pennsylvania State University Press, 2006.

Cameron, Maxwell, and Philip Mauceri, eds. *The Peruvian Labyrinth: Polity, Society, and Economy,* prologue by Cynthia McClintock and Abraham Lowenthal. University Park: Pennsylvania State University Press, 1997.

Campell, Leon G. "A Colonial Establishment: Creole Domination of the Audiencia of Lima during the Late Eighteenth Century." *Hispanic American Historical Review* 52 (1972): 1–25.

————. "The Army of Peru and the Tupac Amaru Revolt, 1780–1783." *Hispanic American Historical Review* 56 (1976): 31–57.

————. *The Military and Society in Colonial Peru, 1750–1810.* Philadelphia: American Philosophical Society, 1978.

Camprubí, Carlos. *Historia de los bancos en el Perú (1860–1879).* Lima: Editorial Lumen, 1959.

Cándido. *Adefesios.* Lima: L. Williez, 1855.

Cárdenas Sánchez, Inés. *Andrés A. Cáceres: biografía y campañas.* Lima: Editora Lima, 1979.

Caretas. *Montesinos: toda la historia.* Edited by Domingo Tamariz Lúcar. Lima: Caretas Dossier, 2001.

Caro Costas, Aída R. *El juicio de residencia a los gobernadores de Puerto Rico en el siglo XVIII.* San Juan, Puerto Rico: Instituto de Cultura Puertorriqueña, 1978.

Carranza Valdivieso, Humberto. *El asesinato jurídico de Alan García (5 de abril de 1992).* Lima: Centro de Estudios Tierno Galván, 2000.

Carrió de la Vandera, Alonso (Concolocorvo). *El lazarillo de ciegos caminantes.* Edited by Antonio Lorente Medina. Caracas and Barcelona: Biblioteca Ayacucho, 1985.

———. *Reforma del Perú.* Edited by Pablo Macera. Lima: Universidad de San Marcos, 1966.

———. *El Lazarillo: A Guide for Inexperienced Travelers between Buenos Aires and Lima.* Edited and translated by Walter D. Kline. Bloomington: Indiana University Press, 1965.

Carrión, Julio F. "Public Opinion, Market Reforms, and Democracy in Fujimori's Peru." In *The Fujimori Legacy: The Rise of Electoral Authoritarianism in Peru.* Edited by Julio Carrión, 126–49. University Park: Pennsylvania State University Press, 2006.

Casanave, E. J. *El contrato Galup-Dársena en sus relaciones con los intereses fiscales.* Lima: Tipografía Industrial, 1886.

Casós, Fernando. *Para la historia del Perú: Revolución de 1854.* Cusco: Imprenta Republicana, 1854.

———. *Romances históricos: Los hombres de bien; Los amigos de Elena.* Paris: Renée Schmitz, 1874.

Castillo Aste, Evaristo. *La conjura de los corruptos: narcotráfico.* Lima: Editorial Brasa, 2001.

Cateriano, Pedro. *El caso García.* Lima: Ausonia, 1994.

Chang-Rodríguez, Eugenio. *La literatura política de González Prada, Mariátegui y Haya de la Torre.* Mexico: Ediciones de Andrea, 1957.

Chanduví Torres, Luis. *El APRA por dentro: lo que hice, lo que vi, y lo que sé.* Lima: Copias e Impresiones, 1988.

Ciccarelli, Orazio. "Fascism and Politics in Peru during the Benavides Regime, 1933–39: The Italian Perspective." *Hispanic American Historical Review* 70, no. 3 (1990): 405–32.

Cisneros, Luis B. *Obras completas de Luis Benjamín Cisneros: mandadas publicar por el gobierno del Perú.* 3 vols. Lima: Librería e Imprenta Gil, 1939.

Clarke, William. *Peru and Its Creditors.* London: Ranken & Company, 1877.

Clayton, Lawrence A. *Grace: W. R. Grace & Co.: The Formative Years, 1850–1930.* Ottawa, IL: Jameson Books, 1985.

Cleaves, Peter, and Martin Scurrah. *Agriculture, Bureaucracy, and Military Government in Peru.* Ithaca, NY: Cornell University Press, 1980.

Cobb, Gwendolyn B. *Potosí y Huancavelica: bases económicas del Perú, 1545–1640.* La Paz: Academia Boliviana de la Historia, 1977.

Cole, Jeffrey. "Viceregal Persistence versus Indian Mobility: The Impact of Duque de la Palata's Reform Program on Alto Peru, 1681–1692." *Latin American Research Review* 19 (1984): 37–56.

Collier, David. *Squatters and Oligarchs: Authoritarian Rule and Policy Change in Peru.* Baltimore: Johns Hopkins University Press, 1976.

Comisión Especial del Crédito Público. *Informe de la Comisión Especial del Crédito Público sobre los vales consolidados y tachados.* Lima: Imprenta Félix Moreno, 1856.

Comisión Permanente de Historia del Ejército del Perú. *Cáceres: conductor nacional.* Lima: Ministerio de Guerra, 1984.

Conaghan, Catherine M. *Fujimori's Peru: Deception in the Public Sphere.* Pittsburgh: University of Pittsburgh Press, 2005.

—. "The Immoral Economy of Fujimorismo." In *The Fujimori Legacy: The Rise of Electoral Authoritarianism in Peru.* Edited by Julio Carrión, 102–25. University Park: Pennsylvania State University Press, 2006.

Contreras Alfaro, Luis H. *Corrupción y principio de oportunidad: alternativas en materia de prevención y castigo a la respuesta penal tradicional.* Salamanca: Ratio Legis, 2005.

Cook, Noble David. "The Corregidores of the Colca Valley, Peru: Imperial Administration in an Andean Region." *Anuario de Estudios Hispanoamericanos* 60, no. 2 (2003): 413–39.

Cortés, Hernán. *Letters from Mexico.* Edited and translated by Anthony Pagden. New Haven, CT: Yale Nota Bene, 2001.

Costa, Miguel. "Patronage and Bribery in Sixteenth-Century Peru: The Government of Viceroy Conde del Villar and the Visita of Licentiate Alonso Fernández de Bonilla." PhD diss., Florida International University, 2005.

Cotler, Julio. *Drogas y política en el Perú: la conexión norteamericana.* Lima: Instituto de Estudios Peruanos, 1999.

Crabtree, John. *Peru under García: An Opportunity Lost.* Pittsburgh: University of Pittsburgh Press, 1992.

—. *Alan García en el poder: Perú, 1985–1990.* Lima: Peisa, 2005.

Crahan, Margaret. "The Administration of Don Melchor de Navarra y Rocafull, Duque de la Palata: Viceroy of Peru, 1681–1689." *The Americas* 27, no. 4 (1971): 389–412.

Daeschner, Jeff. *La guerra del fin de la democracia: Mario Vargas Llosa versus Alberto Fujimori.* Lima: Peru Reporting, 1993.

Dammert, Manuel. *Fujimori-Montesinos: el Estado mafioso: el poder imagocrático en las sociedades globalizadas.* Lima: Ediciones El Virrey, 2001.

Dancuart, Emilio. *Anales de la Hacienda Pública.* 6 vols. Lima: Guillermo Stolte, 1902; Imprenta de La Revista, 1903.

Davies, Thomas, and Víctor Villanueva, eds. *300 documentos para la historia del APRA. Correspondencia aprista de 1935 a 1939.* Lima: Editorial Horizonte, 1978.

—. *Secretos electorales del APRA: correspondencia y documentos de 1939.* Lima: Editorial Horizonte, 1982.

Dawson, Frank Griffith. *The First Latin American Debt Crisis: The City of London and the 1822–25 Loan Bubble.* New Haven: Yale University Press, 1990.

Degregori, Carlos Iván, and Carlos Rivera Paz. *Perú 1980–1993. Fuerzas Armadas, subversión y democracia: redefinición del papel militar en un contexto de violencia subversiva y colapso del régimen democrático.* Lima: Instituto de Estudios Peruanos, 1994.

Delgado, Luis Humberto. *La obra de Francisco García Calderón.* Lima: American Express, 1934.

Di Tella, Rafael, and William Savedoff. "Shining Light in Dark Corners." In *Diagnosis Corruption: Fraud in Latin America's Public Hospitals.* Edited by R. Di Tella and W. Savedoff, 1–26. Washington, DC: Inter-American Development Bank, 2001.

Díaz-Briquets, Sergio, and Jorge Pérez-López. *Corruption in Cuba: Castro and Beyond.* Austin: University of Texas Press, 2006.

Díaz Herrera, José, and Ramón Tijeras. *El dinero del poder: la trama económica en la España socialista.* Madrid: Cambio 16, 1991.

Díaz Herrera, José, and Isabel Durán. *Los secretos del poder: del legado franquista al ocaso del felipismo, episodios inconfesables.* Madrid: Ediciones Temas de Hoy, 1994.

———. *Pacto de silencio (el saqueo de España II: la herencia socialista que Aznar oculta).* Madrid: Temas de Hoy, 1996.

Diez Canseco, Jesús Antonio. *Para la historia de la patria: el ferrocarril de Arequipa y el Gral. Don Pedro Diez Canseco.* Arequipa: N.p., 1921.

Dirks, Nicholas. *The Scandal of Empire: India and the Creation of Imperial Britain.* Cambridge, MA: Harvard University Press, 2006.

Doig, Alan. "Politics and the Public Sector Ethics: The Impact of Change in the United Kingdom." In *Political Corruption in Europe and America.* Edited by Walter Little and Eduardo Posada-Carbó, 173–92. London: Macmillan, 1996.

Domínguez Ortiz, Antonio. "Un virreinato en venta." *Mercurio Peruano* 49, no. 453 (1965): 43–51.

Donoso, Ricardo. *Un letrado del siglo XVII, el doctor José Perfecto Salas.* 2 vols. Buenos Aires: Universidad de Buenos Aires, 1963.

Dorn, Glenn J. "'The American Presumption of Fair Play': Víctor Raúl Haya de la Torre and the Federal Bureau of Narcotics." *The Historian* 65, no. 5 (2003): 1083–1101.

Doyle, William. *Venality: The Sale of Offices in Eighteenth-Century France.* Oxford: Clarendon Press, 1996.

———. "Changing Notions of Public Corruption, c. 1700–c. 1850." In *Corrupt Histories.* Edited by Emmanuel Krieke and William Chester Jordan, 83–95. Rochester, NY: University of Rochester Press, 2004.

Drake, Paul W. *The Money Doctor in the Andes: The Kemmerer Missions, 1923–1933.* Durham, NC: Duke University Press, 1989.

Dreyfus Frères & Cie. *Texto del contrato celebrado por el Supremo Gobierno del Perú con la casa Dreyfus Hermanos y Ca.: aclaraciones presentadas por los contratistas.* Lima: Tipografía Aurelio Alfaro, 1869.

———. *Refutación de las acciones interpuestas judicialmente por "Los Nacionales" con motivo del contrato Dreyfus; precedido de algunas consideraciones económicas, fiscales y políticas sobre dicho contrato por un antiguo contradictor de las consignaciones y los consignatarios.* Lima: Tipografía Aurelio Alfaro, 1869.

———. *Exposición que la Casa Dreyfus Hermanos y Compañía hace ante la sana opinión pública del Perú sobre su manejo de los negocios fiscales del Perú.* Lima: Imprenta La Patria, 1873.

Duffield, Alexander James. *Peru in the Guano Age: Being a Short Account of a Recent Visit to the Guano Deposits with Some Reflections on the Money They Have Produced and the Uses to Which It Has Been Applied.* London: Richard Bentely & Son, 1877.

Durand, Francisco. *Business and Politics in Peru: The State and the National Bourgeoisie.* Boulder, CO: Westview Press, 1994.

———. *Riqueza económica y pobreza política: reflexiones sobre las elites del poder en un país inestable.* Lima: Fondo Editorial Universidad Católica, 2003.

———. "Dinámica política de la corrupción y participación empresarial." In *El pacto infame: estudios sobre la corrupción en el Peru.* Edited by Felipe Portocarrero Suárez, 287–330. Lima: Red de Ciencias Sociales, 2005.

Echenique, José Rufino. *El general Echenique, presidente despojado del Perú, en su vindicación.* New York: N.p., 1855.

————. *Memorias para la historia del Perú.* Edited by Jorge Basadre and Félix Denegri Luna. Lima: Editorial Huascarán, 1952.

Eigen, Meter. *Las redes de la corrupción: la sociedad civil contra los abusos del poder.*
Barcelona: Editorial Planeta, 2004.

El Nacional. *La Excma. Corte Suprema en el juicio sobre el contrato celebrado por el
supremo poder ejecutivo con la casa de Dreyfus HH. y Ca.* Lima: Imprenta de El Nacional,1869.

El Republicano (Arequipa): Noviembre 1825–Febrero 1827. Facsimile ed. Caracas: Gobierno de Venezuela, 1975.

Elías, Domingo. *El señor don Domingo Elías a la faz de sus compatriotas.* Valparaíso,
Chile: Imprenta del Mercurio, 1853.

————. *Manifiesto de D. Domingo Elías a la Nación.* Arequipa: Imprenta Libre de Mariano Madueño, 1855.

————, ed. *Documentos que prueban el hecho del asesinato contra la persona del Consejero de Estado Domingo Elías en la noche del 12 de abril del corriente año de
1849.* Lima: Imprenta del Correo, 1849.

Elías Laroza, Enrique. *La conspiración Guvarte: las pruebas de la inquisición.* Lima:
N.p., 1985.

Emmerson, John K. *The Japanese Thread: A Life in U.S. Foreign Service.* New York:
Holt, Rinehart & Winston, 1978.

Enciclopedia Universal Ilustrada. Madrid: Espasa Calpe, 1929.

Engelsen, Juan Rolf. "Social Aspects of Agricultural Expansion in Coastal Peru, 1825–
1878." PhD diss., University of California-Los Angeles, 1977.

Ertman, Thomas. *The Birth of the Leviathan: Building States and Regimes in Medieval
and Early Modern Europe.* Cambridge: Cambridge University Press, 1997.

Escobar Gaviria, Roberto. *Mi hermano Pablo.* Bogotá: Quintero Editores, 2000.

Ferguson, Niall. *Empire: The Rise and Demise of British World Order and the Lessons
for Global Power.* New York: Basic Books, 2003.

Fernández Salvatecci, José A. *La revolución peruana: yo acuso.* Lima: Editorial El Siglo,
1978.

————. *Los militares en el Perú: de libertadores a genocidas.* Lima: N.p., 1994.

Fisher, John R. *Government and Society in Colonial Peru: The Intendant System, 1784–
1814.* London: Athlone Press, 1970.

————. "Silver Production in the Viceroyalty of Peru, 1776–1824." *Hispanic American
Historical Review* 55 (1975): 25–43.

————. *Silver Mines and Silver Miners in Colonial Peru, 1776–1824.* Liverpool: University of Liverpool, 1977.

————. "Royalism, Regionalism, and Rebellion in Colonial Peru." *Hispanic American
Historical Review* 59 (1979): 232–57.

————. *The Economic Aspects of Spanish Imperialism in America, 1492–1810.* Liverpool: Liverpool University Press, 1997.

————, ed. *Arequipa, 1796–1811: la Relación de Gobierno del intendente Salamanca.*
Lima: Seminario de Historia Rural Andina,Universidad Nacional Mayor de San Marcos, 1968.

————, Allan J. Kuethe, and Anthony McFarlane, eds. *Reform and Insurrection in
Bourbon New Granada and Peru.* Baton Rouge: Louisiana State University Press,
1990.

Flores Galindo, Alberto. *Aristocracia y plebe: Lima, 1760–1830.* Lima: Mosca Azul, 1984.

Ferner, Anthony. "The Industrialists and the Peruvian Development Model." In *Military Reformism and Social Classes: The Peruvian Experience, 1968–80.* Edited by David Booth and Bernardo Sorj, 40–71. New York: St. Martin's Press, 1983.

Ferrand Inurritegui, Alfredo, and Arturo Salazar Larraín. *La década perdida.* Lima: Sociedad de Industrias, 1980.

Gall, Norman. "Peru: The Master is Dead." *Dissent* 18 (1971): 281–320.

Gamarra, Agustín. *Epistolario del Gran Mariscal Agustín Gamarra.* Edited by Alberto Tauro. Lima: Universidad Nacional Mayor de San Marcos / P. L. Villanueva, 1952.

García, Simón. *Pequeñas observaciones que Simón García hace a parte del manifiesto del Sr. Coronel D. Rufino Echenique publicado en el Cuzco en 23 de julio de 1834.* Arequipa: Imprenta de Francisco Valdés, 1834.

García Belaúnde, Francisco. *Así se hizo el fraude.* Lima: Acción Popular, 1963.

García Calderón, Francisco. *Diccionario de la legislación peruana.* 2 vols. Lima: Imprenta del Estado por Eusebio Aranda, 1860.

———. *Estudios sobre el Banco de Crédito Hipotecario y las leyes de hipotecas.* Lima: Imprenta J. M. Noriega, 1868.

———. *Diccionario de la legislación peruana: segunda edición corregida y aumentada con las leyes y decretos dictados hasta 1877.* 2nd ed. 2 vols. Paris: Librería de Laroque, 1879.

———. *Mensaje de S. E. el Presidente Provisorio de la República Dr. D. Francisco García Calderón al Congreso Extraordinario de 1881.* Lima: Edición Oficial, 1881.

———. *Mediación de los Estados Unidos de Norte América en la Guerra del Pacífico. El Señor Cornelius A. Logan y el Dr. D. Francisco García Calderón.* Buenos Aires: Imprenta y Librería De Mayo, 1884.

———. *Memorias del cautiverio.* Lima: Librería Internacional, 1949.

García Pérez, Alan. *La defensa de Alan García.* N.p., 1991.

———. *El mundo de Maquiavelo.* Lima: Mosca Azul, 1994.

García Rada, Domingo. *Memorias de un juez.* Lima: Editorial Andina, 1978.

García Sayán, Diego, ed. *Coca, cocaína y narcotráfico: laberinto en los Andes.* Lima: Comisión Andina de Juristas, 1989.

Garcilaso de la Vega, Inca. *Comentarios reales.* Edited by César Pacheco Vélez, Alberto Tauro, and Aurelio Miró Quesada. Lima: Banco de Crédito, 1985.

———. *Comentarios reales.* Edited by Mercedes Serna. Madrid: Editorial Castalia, 2000.

Gardiner, C. Harvey. *Pawns in a Triangle of Hate: The Peruvian Japanese and the United Status.* Seattle: University of Washington Press, 1981.

Garland, Gerardo. *F. García Calderón y la casa de Schutte y Compañía: Contestación al Sr. D. Gerardo Garland.* Lima: Imprenta de El Nacional, 1875.

Garner, Richard. "Long-Term Silver Mining Trends in Spanish America." *American Historical Review* 93 (1988): 898–935.

Garrett, David. *Shadows of Empire: The Indian Nobility of Cusco, 1750–1825.* New York: Cambridge University Press, 2005.

Garrigues, Jean. *Les scandales de la République de Panama à Elf.* Paris: Éditions Robert Laffont, 2004.

Gates, Eunice Joiner. "Don José Antonio de Areche: His Own Defense." *Hispanic American Historical Review* 8 (1928): 14–42.

Gawsewitch, Jean-Claude. *Yanacocha: comment déposséder l'Etat française d'un milliard de dollars sans que personne ne dise rien.* Neuilly-sur-Seine: Lafon, 2003.

Gille, Bertrand Gille. *État sommaire des archives d'entreprises conserves aux Archives Nationales (série AQ).* Paris: Imprimerie Nationale, 1957.

Ginzburg, Carlo. *El juez y el historiador: acotaciones al margen del caso Sofri.* Madrid: Anaya, 1993.

Glaeser, Edward, and Claudia Goldin. "Corruption and Reform: Introduction." In *Corruption and Reform: Lessons from America's Economic History.* Edited by E. Glaeser and C. Goldin, 3–22. Chicago: University of Chicago Press, 2006.

Gonzales de Olarte, Efraín. *El neoliberalismo a la peruana: economía política del ajuste estructural, 1990–1997.* Lima: Instituto de Estudios Peruanos, 1998.

―――, ed. *The Peruvian Economy and Structural Adjustment: Past, Present, and Future.* Miami: University of Miami North-South Center Press, 1996.

González, José María. *Carta dirigida por el Sr. D. José María González diputado a Congreso al Sr. D. Fernando Palacios y su respuesta, en la que se revelan hechos de gran importancia en el negociado Dreyfus.* Lima: Imprenta de La Libertad, 1870.

González Arica, Guillermo, ed. *Los escaños de Montesinos.* Lima: Fimart, 2001.

González de Salcedo, Pedro. *Tratado jurídico político del contra-bando compuesto por el licenciado Pedro González Salcedo, alcalde que fue de las guardas de Castilla y juez de contra-bando de esta corte: en esta tercera y última impresión sale corregida de muchos yerros que en la segunda se había introducido, y se han añadido muchas reales cédulas que después han salido concernientes a la materia de contra-bando y también los sumarios a los capítulos de toda la obra. Con privilegio.* Madrid: Juan Muñoz, 1729.

González Jiménez, Manuel, et al. *Instituciones y corrupción en la historia.* Valladolid: Universidad de Valladolid, 1998.

González Prada, Manuel. *Páginas libres; Horas de lucha.* Caracas: Biblioteca Ayacucho, 1976.

―――. *Sobre el militarismo (antología). Bajo el oprobio.* Edited by Bruno Podestá. Lima: Editorial Horizonte, 1978.

―――. *Obras.* 3 vols., 7 parts. Lima: Ediciones Copé, 1985.

Goodsell, Richard. *American Corporations and Peruvian Politics.* Cambridge, MA: Harvard University Press, 1974.

Gootenberg, Paul. *Between Silver and Guano: Commercial Policy and the State in Post-independence Peru.* Princeton. NJ: Princeton University Press, 1989.

―――. "North–South: Trade Policy, Regionalism, and Caudillismo in Post-Independence Peru." *Journal of Latin American Studies* 23 (1991): 1–36.

―――. *Imagining Development: Economic Ideas in Peru's "Fictitious Prosperity" of Guano, 1840–1880.* Berkeley: University of California Press, 1993.

―――. "Paying for Caudillos: The Politics of Emergency Finance in Peru, 1820–1845." In *Liberals, Politics, and Power: State Formation in Nineteenth-Century Latin America.* Edited by Vincent Peloso and Barbara Tenenbaum, 134–65. Athens: University of Georgia Press, 1996.

―――. "Between Coca and Cocaine: A Century or More of U.S.–Peruvian Drug Paradoxes 1860–1980." *Hispanic American Historical Review* 83, no. 1 (2003): 137–50.

———. "Birth of the Narcs: The First *Illicit* Cocaine Flows in the Americas." 2004. http://catedras.ucol.mx/transformac/PDF/NARCSu.pdf.

Gorriti, Gustavo. "Fujimori's Svengali, Vladimiro Montesinos: The Betrayal of Peruvian Democracy." *Covert Action* 49 (1994): 4–12, 54–59.

———. *The Shining Path: A History of the Millenarian War in Peru.* Chapel Hill: University of North Carolina Press, 1999.

———. *La calavera en negro: el traficante que quiso gobernar un país.* Lima: Editorial Planeta, 2006.

Gough, Barry M. "Specie Conveyance from the West Coast of Mexico in British Ships, c. 1820–1870: An Aspect of the Pax Britannica." *Mariner's Mirror* 69 (1983): 419–33.

Goyeneche y Gamio, Juan M. de. *Los arreglos del dictador y el contrato Rosas-de Goyeneche.* Paris: A. Chaix et Cie., 1880.

Graham, Carol. *Peru's APRA: Parties, Politics, and the Elusive Quest for Democracy.* Boulder, CO: Lynne Rienner, 1992.

———. "Introduction: Democracy in Crisis and the International Response." In *Peru in Crisis: Dictatorship or Democracy?* Edited by Joseph Tulchin and Gary Bland, 1–21. Boulder, CO: Lynne Rienner, 1994.

Grahn, Lance. "An Irresoluble Dilemma: Smuggling in New Granada, 1713–1763." In *Reform and Insurrection in Bourbon New Granada and Peru.* Edited by J. Fisher, A. Kuethe, and A. McFarlane, 123–46. Baton Rouge: Louisiana State University Press, 1990.

Guamán Poma de Ayala, Felipe. *Nueva corónica y buen gobierno.* Edited by Franklin Pease. 2 vols. Caracas: Biblioteca Ayacucho, 1980.

———. *Nueva crónica y buen gobierno.* Edited by John Murra, Rolena Adorno, and Jorge Urioste. 2 vols. Mexico City: Siglo XXI, 1980; and 3 vols. Madrid: Historia 16, 1987.

Gutiérrez de La Fuente, Antonio. *Manifiesto que di en Trujillo en 1824 sobre los motivos que me obligaron a deponer a D. José de la Riva Agüero y conducta que observé en ese acontecimiento.* Lima: José M. Masías, 1829.

Gutiérrez Paredes, Ramón. *Abusos y reformas del Poder Judicial en todos sus grados.* Lima: Imprenta del Universo, 1889.

Haber, Stephen, ed. *Crony Capitalism and Economic Growth in Latin America: Theory and Evidence.* Stanford, CA: Hoover Institution Press, 2002.

Haigh, Samuel. *Sketches of Buenos Ayres, Chile, and Peru.* London: Efingham Wilson, 1831.

Hanke, Lewis. "Dos palabras on Antonio de Ulloa and the *Noticias Secretas.*" *Hispanic American Historical Review* 16 (1936): 479–514.

Harling, Philip. "Rethinking 'Old Corruption.'" *Past and Present* 147 (1995): 127–58.

———. *The Waning of "Old Corruption": The Politics of Economical Reform in Britain, 1779–1846.* Oxford: Clarendon Press, 1996.

Havens, A. Eugene, Susana Lastarria-Cornhiel, and Gerardo Otero. "Class Struggle and the Agrarian Reform Process." In *Military Reformism and Social Classes: The Peruvian Experience, 1968–80.* Edited by David Booth and Bernardo Sorj, 14–39. New York: St. Martin's Press, 1983.

Heidenheimer, Arnold, ed. *Political Corruption: Readings in Comparative Analysis.* New York: Holt, Rinehart, and Winston, 1970.

———, Michael Johnson, and Robert Levine, eds. *Political Corruption: A Handbook.* New Brunswick, NJ: Transaction Books, 1989.

————, and Michael Johnston, eds. *Political Corruption: Concepts and Contexts.* 3rd ed. New Brunswick, NJ: Transaction Publishers, 2002.

Herzog, Tamar. *Upholding Justice: Society, State, and the Penal System in Quito (1650–1750).* Ann Arbor: University of Michigan Press, 2004.

Holguín Callo, Oswaldo. *Poder, corrupción y tortura en el Perú de Felipe II: el doctor Diego de Salinas (1558–1595).* Lima: Fondo Editorial del Congreso, 2002.

Hopkins, Jack. *The Government Executive of Modern Peru.* Gainsville: University of Florida Press, 1967.

Humphreys, R.A. *Liberation in South America 1806–1827: The Career of James Paroissien.* London: Athlone Press, 1952.

————, ed. *British Consular Reports on the Trade and Politics of Latin America, 1824–1826.* London: Royal Historical Society, 1940.

Hunt, Shane. "Price and Quantum Estimates of Peruvian Exports, 1830–1962." Discussion Paper no. 33. Princeton, NJ: Woodrow Wilson School, Princeton University, 1973.

————. "Growth and Guano in Nineteenth-Century Peru." Discussion Paper no. 34. Princeton, NJ: Woodrow Wilson School, Princeton University, 1973.

Hurstfield, Joel. *Freedom, Corruption, and Government.* London: Jonathan Cape, 1973.

Iniciativa Nacional Anticorrupción. *Un Perú sin corrupción: condiciones, lineamientos y recomendaciones para la lucha contra la corrupción.* Lima: INA / Ministerio de Justicia, 2001.

Iturregui, Juan Manuel. *Reimpresión de los artículos con que se vindica Juan Manuel Iturregui en el empréstito que celebró por orden del Supremo Gobierno.* Trujillo: N.p., 1847.

Jacoby, Neil, Peter Nehemkis, and Richard Eells. *Bribery and Extortion in World Business: A Study of Corporate Political Payments Abroad.* New York: Macmillan, 1977.

James, Marquis. *Merchant Adventurer: The Story of W. R. Grace.* Wilmington, DE: SR Books, 1993.

Jiménez Sánchez, Fernando. *Detrás del escándalo politico: opinión, dinero y poder en la España del siglo XX.* Barcelona: Tusquets Editores, 1995.

Jochamowitz, Luis. *Vladimiro: vida y tiempo de un corruptor.* Lima: El Comercio, 2002.

Johansen, Elaine. *Political Corruption: Scope and Resources. An Annotated Bibliography.* New York: Garland Publishing, 1990.

Johnston, Michael. "Corruption and Democratic Consolidation." In *Corrupt Histories.* Edited by Emmanuel Krieke and William Chester Jordan, 138–64. Rochester, NY: University of Rochester Press, 2004.

Juan, Jorge, and Antonio de Ulloa. *Noticias secretas de América sobre el estado nàval, militar y político de los reinos del Perú y provincias de Quito, costas de Nueva Granada y Chile; gobierno y régimen particular de los pueblos de indios; cruel opresión y extorsiones de sus corregidores y curas; abusos escandalosos introducidos entre estos habitantes por los misioneros; causas de su origen y motivos de su continuación por el espacio de tres siglos. Escritas fielmente según las instrucciones del excelentísimo señor marqués de la Ensenada, primer secretario de Estado, y presentadas en informe secreto a S.M.C., el señor Fernando VI . . . sacadas a la luz para el verdadero conocimiento del gobierno de los españoles en la América meridional por David Barry.* 2 vols. London: R. Taylor, 1826.

————. *Secret Expedition to Peru, or, the Practical Influence of the Spanish Colonial System Upon the Character and Habits of the Colonists. Exhibited in a Private Re-*

port Read to the Secretaries of His Majesty, Ferdinand VI, King of Spain, by George J. [sic] and Anthony Ulloa. Boston: Crocker and Brewster, 1851.

———. *Popery Judged by Its Fruits: As Brought to View in the Diary of Two Distinguished Scholars and Philanthropists, John and Anthony [sic] Ulloa, during a Sojourn of Several Years in the States of Colombia and Peru.* Translated from the Spanish by a Member of the Principia Club. Edited by I. W. Wheelwright. Boston: Albert J. Wright, 1878.

———. *Discourse and Political Reflections on the Kingdoms of Peru. Their Government, Special Regimen of Their Inhabitants, and Abuses Which Have Been Introduced into One and Another, with Special Information on Why They Grew Up and Some Means to Avoid Them.* Edited by John TePaske, trans. with Besse Clement. Norman: University of Oklahoma Press, 1978.

———. *Noticias secretas de América.* Edited by Luis J. Ramos Gómez. Madrid: Historia 16, 1990.

Junta de Examen Fiscal. *Informes de la Junta de Examen Fiscal creada por resolución suprema de febrero de 1855 para revisar los expedientes relativos al reconocimiento de la deuda interna consolidada de 20 de abril de 1851, publicación oficial.* Lima: Imprenta del Estado, 1857.

Kantor, Harry. *The Ideology and Program of the Peruvian Aprista Movement.* New York: Octagon Books, 1966.

Kawata, Junichi, ed. *Comparing Political Corruption and Clientelism.* Aldershot, Hampshire, England: Ashgate, 2006.

Kenney, Charles D. *Fujimori's Coup and the Breakdown of Democracy in Latin America.* Notre Dame, IN: University of Notre Dame Press, 2004.

Kisic, Drago. "Privatizaciones, inversiones y sostenibilidad de la economía peruana." In *El Perú de Fujimori: 1990–1998.* Edited by John Crabtree and Jim Thomas, 75–113. Lima: Centro de Investigación de la Universidad del Pacífico / Instituto de Estudios Peruanos, 2000.

Klarén, Peter F. *Modernization, Dislocation, and Aprismo: Origins of the Peruvian Aprista Party, 1870–1932.* Austin: University of Texas Press, 1973.

———. *Peru: Society and Nationhood in the Andes.* New York: Oxford University Press, 2000.

Klein, Herbert S. *The American Finances of the Spanish Empire: Royal Income and Expenditures in Colonial Mexico, Peru, and Bolivia, 1680–1809.* Albuquerque: University of New Mexico Press, 1998.

Klitgaard, Robert. *Controlling Corruption.* Berkeley: University of California Press, 1988.

Krüggeler, Thomas. "El doble desafío: los artesanos del Cusco ante la crisis regional y la constitución del régimen republicano, 1824–1869." *Allpanchis* no. 38 (1988): 13–65.

Kruijt, Dirk. *Revolution by decree: Peru, 1968–1975.* Amsterdam: Thela, 1994.

Kuczynski, Pedro Pablo. *Peruvian Democracy Under Economic Stress: An Account of the Belaúnde Administration, 1963–1968.* Princeton, NJ: Princeton University Press, 1977.

———. *Democracia bajo presión económica: el primer gobierno de Belaúnde.* Lima: Mosca Azul, 1980.

Kuethe, Allan. "Guns, Subsidies, and Commercial Privilege: Some Historical Factors in the Emergence of the Cuban National Character, 1763–1815." *Cuban Studies* 16 (1986): 123–39.

————, and G. Douglas Inglis. "Absolutism and Enlightened: the establishment of the Alcabala, and Commercial Reorganization in Cuba." *Past and Present* 109 (1985): 118–43.

La Opinión Nacional. *Lo que se ve y lo que no se ve: ojeado sobre los principales actos del govierno civil (editoriales de "La Opinión Nacional").* Lima: Imprenta La Opinión Nacional, 1874.

Lambsdorff, Johann Graf. "Corruption and Rent-Seeking." *Public Choice* 113 (2002): 97–125.

Larrea y Loredo, José. *Principios que siguió el ciudadano José de Larrea y Loredo en el Ministerio de Hacienda y Sección de Negocios Eclesiásticos de que estuvo encargado.* Lima: Imprenta J. M. Concha, 1827.

Latasa, Pilar. "Negociar en red: familia, amistad y paisanaje; el virrey Superunda y sus agentes en Lima y Cádiz (1745–1761)." *Anuario de Estudios Americanos* 60, no. 2 (2003): 463–92.

Leff, Nathaniel. "Economic Development through Bureaucratic Corruption." In *Political Corruption: Readings in Comparative Analysis.* Edited by Arnold Heidenheimer, 510–20. New York: Holt, Rinehart, and Winston, 1970.

Leguía, Augusto B. *El Oncenio y la Lima actual: memorias completas del Presidente Leguía "Yo tirano, yo ladrón."* Lima: Imprenta J.C.L., 1936.

León Velarde, Enrique. *¿El Chino y yo jodimos al Perú? Confesiones de Enrique León Velarde.* Lima: N.p., 2000.

Le Roy, François. "Mirages Over the Andes: Peru, France, the United States, and Military Jet Procurement in the 1960s." *Pacific Historical Review* 71, no. 2 (2002): 269–300.

Leubel, Alfredo. *El Perú en 1860 o sea anuario nacional.* Lima: Imprenta El Comercio, 1861.

Lipset, Seymour Martin, and Gabriel Salman Lenz. "Corruption, Culture, and Markets." In *Culture Matters: How Values Shape Human Progress.* Edited by Lawrence Harrison and Samuel Huntington, 112–24. New York: Basic Books, 2000.

Little, Walter, and Antonio Herrera. "Political Corruption in Venezuela." In *Political Corruption in Europe and Latin America.* Edited by Walter Little and Eduardo Posada-Carbó, 267–85. London: Macmillan, 1996.

Loayza Galván, Francisco. *Montesinos: el rostro oscuro del poder en el Perú.* Lima: N.p., 2001.

Lohmann Villena, Guillermo. *Los ministros de la Audiencia de Lima en el reinado de los Borbones (1700–1821): esquema de un estudio sobre un núcleo dirigente.* Sevilla: Consejo Superior de Investigaciones Científicas, Escuela de Estudios Hispano-Americanos, 1974.

————. "Estudio preliminar." In *Un tríptico del Perú virreinal: el virrey Amat, el marqués de Soto Florido y la Perricholi: el drama de dos palanganas y su circunstancia.* Edited by Guillermo Lohmann Villena. Chapel Hill: University of North Carolina Department of Modern Languages, 1976.

————. *Las ideas jurídico-políticas en la rebelión de Gonzalo Pizarro: la tramoya doctrinal del levantamiento contra las Leyes Nuevas en el Perú.* Valladolid: Universidad de Valladolid, 1977.

López Aldana, Fernando, et al. *Refutación documentada de las principales falsedades y errores de hecho y de derecho que contiene el manifiesto publicado por el S. D. D. Mariano Santos Quirós contra los magistrados de la Suprema Corte de Justicia que sentenciaron en primera instancia el juicio de su pesquisa.* Lima: Imprenta de José Masías, 1831.

López Aliaga, Diego. *Breve exposición que el apoderado de la casa Thomas Lachambre y Cia. presenta a la ilustrísima Corte Superior de Justicia sobre el pleito que su parte sigue con el Sr. Dr. D. José Gregorio Paz-Soldán.* Lima: Imprenta Calle de la Rifa, 1863.

Lorandi, Ana María. *Ni ley, ni rey, ni hombre virtuoso: guerra y sociedad en el virreinato del Perú, siglos XVI y XVII.* Barcelona: Editorial Gedisa, 2002.

Loth, David. *Public Plunder: A History of Graft in America.* New York: Carrick and Evans, 1938.

Loveman, Brian, and Thomas A. Davies, eds. *The Politics of Antipolitics: The Military in Latin America.* Lincoln: University of Nebraska Press, 1989.

Machado de Chaves, Mariano. "Estado político del reino del Peru." *Revista Peruana* 4 (1880): 147–90, 351–69, 497–504.

Malamud, Carlos. *Cádiz y Saint Malo en el comercio colonial peruano, 1698–1725.* Cádiz: Diputación Provincial de Cádiz, 1986.

Malpica, Carlos. *Los dueños del Perú.* 5th ed. Lima: Peisa, 1973.

———. *Anchovetas y tiburones.* Lima: Editora Runamarka, 1976.

———. *Petróleo y corrupción: la ley Kuczynski.* Lima: Escena Contemporánea, 1985.

———. *Pájaros de alto vuelo: Alan García, el BCCI y los Mirage.* Lima: Editorial Minerva, 1993.

Manning, William, ed. *Diplomatic Correspondence of the United States Concerning the Independence of the Latin American Nations.* New York: Oxford University Press, 1925.

Marchena Fernández, Juan. "The Social World of the Military in Peru and New Granada, 1784–1810." In *Reform and Insurrection in Bourbon New Granada and Peru.* Edited by John Fisher, Allan Kuethe, and Anthony McFarlane, 54–95. Baton Rouge: Louisiana State University Press, 1990.

Marichal, Carlos. *A Century of Debt Crises in Latin America: From Independence to the Great Depression, 1820–1930.* Princeton, NJ: Princeton University Press, 1989.

Márquez, José Arnaldo. *La orjía financiera del Perú: el guano y el salitre, artículos publicados en La Libertad Electoral.* Santiago, Chile: Imprenta de La Libertad Electoral, 1888.

Martín, César. *Dichos y hechos de la política peruana: una descripción auténtica, sobria y condensada e los dos procesos electorales y las dos juntas militares.* Lima: Tipografía Santa Rosa, 1963.

Martín de Pozuelo, Eduardo, Jordi Bordas, and Santiago Tarín. *Guía de la corrupción.* Barcelona: Plaza y Janés, 1994.

Martínez Riaza, Ascensión. *"A pesar del gobierno": españoles en el Perú, 1879–1939.* Madrid: Consejo Superior de Investigaciones Científicas, 2006.

———. "Política regional y gobierno de la amazonía peruana." *Histórica* 23 (1999): 393–462.

Maso, Manuel María del (Ibrahim Clarete). *Aniversario.* Lima: A. Alfaro y Cia., 1861.

Masterson, Daniel. *Militarism and Politics in Latin America: Peru from Sánchez Cerro to Sendero Luminoso.* Westport, CT: Greenwood Press, 1991.

———, and Sayaka Funada-Classen. *The Japanese in Latin America.* Chicago: University of Illinois Press, 2004.

Mathew, W. M. "The First Anglo-Peruvian Debt and Its Settlement, 1822–49." *Journal of Latin American Studies* 2 (1970): 81–98.

―――. "Foreign Contractors and the Peruvian Government at the Outset of the Guano Trade." *Hispanic American Historical Review* 52 (1972): 598–620.

―――. "A Primitive Export Sector: Guano Production in Mid-Nineteenth-Century Peru." *Journal of Latin American Studies* 9 (1977): 35–57.

―――. *The House of Gibbs and the Peruvian Guano Monopoly.* London: Royal Historical Society, 1981.

Matto de Turner, Clorinda. "En el Perú: narraciones históricas." In *Boreales, miniaturas y porcelanas,* 11–64. Buenos Aires: Imprenta de Juan A. Alsina, 1902. Edited by Thomas Ward. http://www.evergreen.loyola.edu/~TWARD/MUJERES/MATTO/HISTORICAS/Peru1.html.

Mauceri, Philip Mauceri. "The Transition to 'Democracy' and the Failures of Institution Building." In *The Peruvian Labyrinth: Polity, Society, and Economy.* Edited by Maxwell Cameron and Philip Mauceri, 13–36. University Park: Pennsylvania State University Press, 1997.

Mauro, Paolo. "Corruption and Growth." *Quarterly Journal of Economics* 110, no. 3 (1995): 681–712.

―――. "The Effects of Corruption on Growth, Investment, and Government Expenditures: A Cross-Country Analysis." In *Corruption and the Global Economy.* Edited by Kimberly Ann Elliot, 83–108. Washington, DC: Institute for International Economics, 1997.

―――. "Corruption and the Composition of Government Expenditure." *Journal of Public Economics* 69 (1998): 263–79.

Mazzeo, Cristina A. *El comercio libre en el Perú: las estrategias de un comerciante criollo, José de Lavalle y Cortés, conde de Premio Real, 1777–1815.* Lima: Fondo Editorial Universidad Católica, 1994.

McClintock, Cynthia. "Comment on Chapter 9/Daniel Schydlowsky." In *Latin American Political Economy: Financial Crisis and Political Change.* Edited by Jonathan Hartlyn and Samuel Morley, 360–66. Boulder, CO: Westview Press, 1986.

―――. "Electoral Authoritarian Versus Partially Democratic Regimes: The Case of the Fujimori Government and the 2000 Elections." In *The Fujimori Legacy: The Rise of Electoral Authoritarianism in Peru.* Edited by Julio Carrión, 242–67. University Park: Pennsylvania State University Press, 2006.

―――. "An Unlikely Comeback in Peru." *Journal of Democracy* 17, no. 4 (2006): 95–109.

―――, and Fabián Vallas. *The United States and Peru: Cooperation at a Cost.* New York: Routledge, 2003.

McFarlane, Anthony. "Political Corruption and Reform in Bourbon Spanish America." In *Political Corruption in Europe and Latin America.* Edited by Walter Little and Eduardo Posada-Carbó, 41–63. London: Macmillan, 1996.

Mc Evoy, Carmen. *Un proyecto nacional en el siglo XIX: Manuel Pardo y su visión del Perú.* Lima: Fondo Editorial Universidad Católica, 1994.

―――. "Estampillas y votos: el rol del correo político en una campaña electoral decimonónica," *Histórica* 18, no. 1 (1994): 95-134.

McLynn, Frank. *Napoleon: A Biography.* New York: Arcade Publishing, 2002.

McMillan, John, and Pablo Zoido, "How to Subvert Democracy: Montesinos in Peru." *Journal of Economic Perspectives* 18, no. 4 (2004): 69–92.

Medina, José Toribio. *Biblioteca Hispano-Americana*. Santiago, Chile: Imprenta casa del autor, 1901.

Mendiburu, Manuel de. *Consideraciones sobre el empréstito de 1853*. London: T. F. Newell, 1853.

———. "Noticias biográficas de los generales que ha tenido la República desde 1821." *Revista Histórica* 25 (1960–1961): 160.

———. *Biografías de los generales republicanos*. Edited by Félix Denegri Luna. Lima: Academia Nacional de la Historia, 1963.

Menzel, Sewall H. *Fire in the Andes: U.S. Foreign Policy and Cocaine Politics in Bolivia and Peru*. Lanham, MD: University Press of America, 1996.

Merino, Luis. *Estudio crítico sobre las "Noticias secretas de América" y el clero colonial*. Madrid: Consejo Superior de Investigaciones Científicas, Instituto Santo Toribio de Mogrovejo, 1956.

Miller, Rory. "The Making of the Grace Contract: British Bondholders and the Peruvian Government, 1885–1890." *Journal of Latin American Studies* 8 (1976): 73–100.

———. "Foreign Capital, the State, and Political Corruption in Latin America between Independence and the Depression." In *Political Corruption in Europe and Latin America*. Edited by Walter Little and Eduardo Posada-Carbó, 65–96. London: Macmillan, 1996.

Mitchell, B. R. *Internacional Historical Statistics: The Americas 1750–1993*. 4th ed. London: Macmillan, 1998.

Miró Quesada, Carlos. *Radiografía de la política peruana*. Lima: Editorial Páginas Peruanas, 1959.

Molina Martínez, Miguel. *Antonio de Ulloa en Huancavelica*. Granada: Universidad de Granada, 1995.

Montaldo, Jean. *Main basse sur l'or de la France*. Paris: Albin Michel, 1998.

Monteagudo, Bernardo. *Memoria sobre los principios políticos que seguí en la administración del Perú y acontecimientos posteriores a mi separación*. Quito: Imprenta de Quito, 1823; and Guatemala: Beteta, 1824.

Montes de Oca, Juan Evangelista [Rafael Valdés?]. *Carta de un particular al Jeneral El-es-burro Prefecto de Lima*. Guayaquil: J. Rodríguez, 1832.

Moody-Stuart, George. *Grand Corruption: How Business Bribes Damage Developing Countries*. Oxford: Worldview, 1997.

Moreno Cebrián, Alfredo. *El corregidor de indios y la economía peruana en el siglo XVIII (los repartos forzosos de mercancías)*. Madrid: Consejo Superior de Investigaciones Científicas, Instituto Gonzalo Fernández de Oviedo, 1977.

———. *Relación y documentos de gobierno del virrey del Perú, José A. Manso de Velasco, conde de Superunda (1745–1761)*. Madrid: Consejo Superior de Investigaciones Científicas, Instituto Gonzalo Fernández de Oviedo, 1983.

———. *El virreinato del marqués de Castelfuerte 1724–1736: el primer intento borbónico por reformar el Perú*. Madrid: Editorial Catriel, 2000.

———, and Núria Sala i Vila. *El "premio" de ser virrey: los intereses públicos y privados en el Perú virreinal de Felipe V*. Madrid: Consejo Superior de Investigaciones Científicas, 2004.

Moreno Ocampo, Luis. "Corruption and Democracy: The Peruvian Case of Montesinos." *Revista: Harvard Review of Latin America* 2, no. 1 (2002): 26–29.

Morón, Eduardo. "Transparencia presupuestal: haciendo visible la corrupción." In *El pacto infame: estudios sobre la corrupción en el Perú.* Edited by Felipe Portocarrero, 147–76. Lima: Red de Ciencias Sociales, 2005.

Morris, Stephen. *Corruption and Politics in Contemporary Mexico.* Tuscaloosa: University of Alabama Press, 1991.

Moura, Francisco Ercilio, et al. *Deudas corruptas: crímenes de cuello blanco.* Lima: Plataforma Interamericana de Derechos Humanos, Democracia y Desarrollo, 2005.

Moutoukias, Zacarías. "Power, Corruption, and Commerce: The Making of the Local Administrative Structure in Seventeenth-Century Buenos Aires." *Hispanic American Historical Review* 68 (1988): 771–801.

Mücke, Ulrich. "Elections and Political Participation in Nineteenth-Century Peru: The 1871-72 Presidential Campaign." *Journal of Latin American Studies* 33 (2001): 311-46.

―――. *Political Culture in Nineteenth-Century Peru: The Rise of the Partido Civil.* Pittsburgh: University of Pittsburgh Press, 2004.

Municipalidad de Lima. *Lima justificada en el suceso del 25 de julio: impreso por orden de la ilustrísima Municipalidad.* Lima: Manuel del Río, 1822.

Muñoz Pérez, José. "Los proyectos sobre España y las Indias en el siglo XVIII: el proyectismo como género." *Revista de Estudios Políticos* no. 81 (1955): 169–95.

Neira, Hugo. *El mal peruano 1990–2001.* Lima: Sidea, 2001.

Niblo, Stephen. *Mexico in the 1940s: Modernity, Politics, and Corruption.* Wilmington, DE: Scholarly Resources, 1999.

Nieto, Alejandro. *Corrupción en la España democrática.* Barcelona: Ariel, 1997.

Noonan, John T. *Bribes: The Intellectual History of a Moral Idea.* Berkeley: University of California Press, 1984.

North, Douglass. *Structure and Change in Economic History.* New York: Norton, 1981.

―――. *Institutions, Institutional Change, and Economic Performance.* Cambridge: Cambridge University Press, 1990.

―――. *Understanding the Process of Economic Change.* Princeton, NJ: Princeton University Press, 2005.

Nye, J. S. "Corruption and Political Development: A Cost Benefit Analysis." In *Political Corruption: Readings in Comparative Analysis.* Edited by A. Heidenheimer, 564–78. New York: Holt, Rinehart, and Winston, 1970.

Obelson, W. *Funerales del APRA y el fraude electoral.* Lima: Librería Universo, 1962.

O'Leary, Cornelius. *The Elimination of Corrupt Practices in British Elections, 1868–1911.* Oxford: Clarendon Press, 1962.

Olivera Prado, Mario. *Relaciones peligrosas: legislación desinstitucionalizadora y corrupción en el Perú.* Lima: Instituto de Defensa Legal, 1999.

O'Phelan Godoy, Scarlett. *Un siglo de rebeliones anticoloniales: Perú y Bolivia 1700–1783.* Cusco: Centro Bartolomé de las Casas, 1988.

―――. *La gran rebelión en los Andes: de Túpac Amaru a Túpac Catari.* Cusco: Centro Bartolomé de las Casas/Petroperú, 1995.

―――. "Sucre en el Perú: entre Riva Agüero y Torre Tagle." In *La independencia en el Perú: de los Borbones a Bolívar.* Edited by Scarlett O'Phelan, 379–406. Lima: Instituto Riva-Agüero, Pontificia Universidad Católica, 2001.

―――. "Orden y control en el siglo XVIII: la política borbónica frente a la corrupción fiscal, comercial y administrativa." In *El pacto infame: estudios sobre la corrupción en el Perú.* Edited by Felipe Portocarrero Suárez, 13–33. Lima: Red de Ciencias Sociales, 2005.

Oppenheimer, Andrés. *Ojos vendados: Estados Unidos y el negocio de la corrupción en América Latina.* Buenos Aires: Editorial Sudamericana, 2001.

Ortiz de Zevallos, Gabriel, and Pierina Pollarolo, eds. *Estrategias anticorrupción en el Perú.* Lima: Instituto Apoyo, 2002.

Ortiz de Zevallos, Gonzalo. *Entreguismo: los contratos petroleros de 1974.* Lima: Grafiser, 1978.

Orrego, Juan Luis. "Domingo Elías y el Club Progresista: los civiles y el poder hacia 1850," *Histórica* 14, no. 2 (1990): 317–49.

Oxford Latin American Economic History Data Base. Latin American Centre: Oxford University. http://oxlad.qeh.ox.ac.uk.

Palacio Atard, Vicente. *Areche y Guirior: observaciones sobre el fracaso de una visita al Perú.* Seville: Escuela de Estudios Hispano-Americanos, 1946.

Palacios McBride, María Luisa. "Un empresario peruano del siglo XIX: Manuel de Argumaniz." B.A. thesis, Universidad Católica, 1989.

Palacios Moreyra, Carlos. *La deuda anglo peruana 1822–1890.* Lima: Studium, 1983.

Pardo, Manuel. *Los consignatarios del guano: contestación de Manuel Pardo a la denuncia de Guillermo Bogardus precedida de un estudio histórico por Evaristo San Cristóbal.* Lima: Imprenta Gloria, 1922.

Paredes Oporto, Martín. "El lado verde de la corrupción." *Quehacer* 144 (2003): 10–20.

Parrón Salas, Carmen. *De las reformas borbónicas a la república: el Consulado y el comercio marítimo de Lima, 1778–1821.* San Javier, Murcia: Academia General del Aire, 1995.

Parry, J. H. *The Sale of Public Office in the Spanish Indies under the Hapsburgs.* Berkeley: University of California Press, 1953.

Pásara, Luis. "El docenio militar." In *Historia del Perú.* Edited by Juan Mejía Baca, vol. 12: 325–433. Lima: Editorial Juan Mejía Baca, 1980.

———. *Jueces, justicia y poder en el Perú.* Lima: Centro de Estudios de Derecho y Sociedad, 1982.

Patch, Robert. "Imperial Politics and Local Economy in Colonial Central America 1670–1770." *Past and Present* no. 143 (1994): 77–107.

Payne, Arnold. *The Peruvian Coup d'état of 1962: The Overthrow of Manuel Prado.* Washington, DC: Institute for the Comparative Study of Political Systems, 1968.

Payne, Robert. *The Corrupt Society: From Ancient Greece to Present-Day America.* New York: Praeger, 1975.

Paz Soldán y Unánue, Pedro (Juan de Arona). *Diccionario de peruanismos.* Lima: Ediciones Peisa, 1974.

Pearce, Adrian J. "Huancavelica 1700–1759: Administrative Reform of the Mercury Industry in Early Bourbon Peru." *Hispanic American Historical Review* 79 (1999): 669–702.

Pease, Henry. *El ocaso del poder oligárquico: lucha política en la escena oficial.* Lima: Desco, 1977.

Pearson, Roger. *Voltaire Almighty: A Life in Pursuit of Freedom.* New York: Bloomsbury, 2005.

Peck, Linda Levy. *Court Patronage and Corruption in Early Stuart England.* Boston: Unwin Hyman, 1990.

Peralta Ruiz, Víctor. *En defensa de la autoridad: política y cultura bajo el gobierno del virrey Abascal, Perú, 1806–1816.* Madrid: Consejo Superior de Investigaciones Científicas, 2002.

———. "Un indiano en la corte de Madrid: Dionisio de Alsedo y Herrera y el *Memorial* informativo del Consulado de Lima (1725)." *Histórica* 27, no. 2 (2003): 319–55.

Pérez Briceño, Conrado. *La corrupción revolucionaria: informe sobre los principales casos de corrupción de la administración de Hugo Chávez.* Caracas: Editorial CEC, 2004.

Perú, Congreso del. Cámara de Diputados. *Informe de la Comisiones de Hacienda y Justicia de la H. Cámara de Diputados sobre el contrato celebrado por el Supremo Gobierno con la casa de Dreyfus Hermanos y Compañía de París, en 17 de agosto de 1869.* Lima: N.p., 1870.

———. Cámara de Diputados. *Diario de los debates de la Cámara de Diputados.* Lima: Imprenta de El Nacional; P. L. Villanueva, 1876–1965.

———. Cámara de Senadores. *Diario de los debates del Senado.* Lima: Imprenta de El Comercio; Talleres del Estado, 1872–1965.

———. Comisión Investigadora de Delitos Económicos y Financieros 1990–2001. *Informe final.* Edited by Oscar Ugarteche Galarza. Lima: Impresora Peruana, 2003.

———. *Diario de debates de las sesiones del Congreso: legislatura ordinaria y extraordinaria de 1912.* Lima, 1912.

———. *En la sala de la corrupción: videos y audios de Vladimiro Montesinos (1998–2000).* Edited by Antonio Zapata. 6 vols. Lima: Fondo Editorial del Congreso del Perú, 2004.

Perú, Gobierno del. *Protesta que hace el gobierno del Perú contra la conducta del Encargado de Negocios de Su Majestad Británica D. Belford Hinton Wilson y su inmotivada separación del territorio peruano, acompañada de los documentos principales sobre los motivos de queja alegados por ese funcionario.* Lima: Imprenta del Estado por Eusebio Aranda, 1842.

Pezet, Juan Antonio Pezet. "Exposición del General don Juan Antonio Pezet ex-presidente del Peru." In *La administración del General don Juan Antonio Pezet en la República del Perú.* Paris: Imprenta Parisiense Guyot y Scribe, 1867.

Philip, George. *The Rise and Fall of the Peruvian Military Radicals, 1968–1976.* London: Athlone Press, 1978.

Phelan, John Leddy. *The Kingdom of Quito in the Seventeenth Century: Bureaucratic Politics in the Spanish Empire.* Madison: University of Wisconsin Press, 1967.

Pietschmann, Horst. "Corrupción en las Indias españoles: revisión de un debate en la historiografía sobre Hispanoamérica colonial." In *Instituciones y corrupción en el historia.* Edited by Manuel González Jiménez, et al., 33–52. Valladolid: Universidad de Valladolid, 1998.

Pinelo, Adalberto. *The Multinational Corporation as a Force in Latin American Politics: A Case Study of the International Petroleum Company in Peru.* New York: Praeger, 1973.

Pocock, J. G. A. *The Machiavellian Moment: Florentine Political Thought and the Atlantic Republican Tradition.* Princeton, NJ: Princeton University Press, 1975.

Pomar, Manuel Angel del. *Autonomía e idoneidad en el Poder Judicial: fundamentos para una acusación constitucional.* Lima: Editorial Justicia y Derecho, 1986.

Porta, Donatella della, and Alberto Vannucci. *Corrupt Exchanges: Actors, Resources, and Mechanisms of Political Corruption.* Hawthorne, NY: Aldine de Gruyter, 1999.

———. "A Typology of Corrupt Networks." In *Comparing Political Corruption and*

Clientelism. Edited by J. Kawata, 23–44. Aldershot, Hampshire, England: Ashgate, 2006.

Portocarrero Maisch, Gonzalo. "La oligarquía frente a la reivindicación democrática (las opciones de la derecha en las elecciones de 1936)." *Apuntes* 12 (1982): 61–73.

———. *De Bustamante a Odría: el fracaso del Frente Democrático Nacional, 1945–1950*. Lima: Mosca Azul, 1983.

Portocarrero Suárez, Felipe. *Imperio Prado, 1890–1970*. Lima: Centro de Investigación de la Universidad del Pacífico, 1995.

———, Arlette Beltrán, and Alex Zimmerman. *Inversiones públicas en el Perú (1900–1968): una aproximación cuantitativa*. Lima: Centro de Investigación de la Universidad del Pacífico, 1998.

———, and Luis Camacho. "Impulsos moralizadores: el caso del Tribunal de Sanción Nacional 1930–1931." In *El pacto infame: estudios sobre la corrupción en el Perú*. Edited by Felipe Portocarrero Suárez, 35–73. Lima: Red de Ciencias Sociales, 2005.

Posada-Carbó, Eduardo. "Electoral Juggling: A Contemporary History of Corruption of Suffrage in Latin America, 1830–1930." *Journal of Latin American Studies* 32 (2000): 611–44.

Preeg, Ernest H. *The Evolution of a Revolution: Peru and Its Relations with the United States, 1968–1980*. Washington, DC: NPA Committee on Changing International Realities, 1981.

Prieto Celi, Federico. *El deportado: biografía de Eudocio Ravines*. Lima: Editorial Andina, 1979.

Progresos del Perú 1933–1939 durante el gobierno del Presidente de la República General Oscar R. Benavides. Buenos Aires: Editorial Guillermo Kraft, 1945.

Proctor, Robert. *Narrative of a Journey Across the Cordillera of the Andes, and of Residence in Lima and Other Parts of Peru, in the Years 1823 and 1824*. London: Thomas Davison, 1824.

Puente, José de la. *Encomienda y encomenderos en el Perú: estudio social y político de una institución colonial*. Sevilla: Diputación Provincial, 1992.

Putnam, Robert D., Robert Leonardi, and Raffaella Y. Nanetti. *Making Democracy Work: Civic Traditions in Modern Italy*. Princeton, NJ: Princeton University Press, 1993.

Quimper, José María. *Manifiesto del ex-Ministro de Hacienda y Comercio: J. M. Quimper, a la Nación*. Lima: Imprenta F. Masías e Hijo, 1881.

———. *Las propuestas de los tenedores de bonos por J.M.Q.* Lima: Imprenta de La Época, 1886.

———. *El principio de libertad*. Edited by Alberto Tauro del Pino. Lima: Ediciones Hora del Hombre, 1948.

———. *Exposición a los hombres de bien*. Lima, 1880.

Quirós y Allier, Compañía. *Exposición que Quirós y Allier hacen a los señores diputados que componen la Comisión de Hacienda*. Lima: Imprenta de J. Masías, 1849.

Quirós Salinas, Rafael. *Los Quirós: una familia criolla en la historia del Perú*. 2 vols. Lima: Propaceb, 2000.

Quiroz, Alfonso W. "Las actividades comerciales y financieras de la casa Grace y la Guerra del Pacífico." *Histórica* 7 (1983): 214–54.

———. *La deuda defraudada: consolidación de 1850 y dominio económico en el Perú*. Lima: Instituto Nacional de Cultura, 1987.

————. "Estructura económica y desarrollos regionales de la clase dominante, 1821–1850." In *Independencia y revolución (1780–1840)*, vol. 2. Edited by Alberto Flores Galindo, 201–67. Lima: Instituto Nacional de Cultura, 1987.

————. *Deudas olvidadas: instrumentos de crédito en la economía colonial peruana, 1750–1820.* Lima: Fondo Editorial Universidad Católica, 1993.

————. *Domestic and Foreign Finance in Modern Peru, 1850–1950: Financing Visions of Development.* London and Pittsburgh: Macmillan and University of Pittsburgh Press, 1993.

————. "Reassessing the Role of Credit in Late Colonial Peru: *Censos, Escrituras*, and *Imposiciones.*" *Hispanic American Historical Review* 74 (1994): 193–230.

————. "Historia de la corrupción en el Perú: ¿es factible su estudio?" In *Homenaje a Félix Denegri Luna.* Edited by Guillermo Lohmann, et al., 685–90. Lima: Fondo Editorial Universidad Católica, 2000.

————. "Implicit Costs of Empire: Bureaucratic Corruption in Nineteenth-Century Cuba." *Journal of Latin American Studies* 35 (2003): 473–511.

————. "Basadre y su análisis de la corrupción en el Perú." In *Homenaje a Jorge Basadre: el hombre, su obra y su tiempo.* Edited by Scarlett O'Phelan and Mónica Ricketts, 145–70. Lima: Instituto Riva Agüero, Pontificia Universidad Católica, 2004.

————. "Redes de alta corrupción en el Perú: poder y venalidad desde el virrey Amat a Montesinos." *Revista de Indias* 66 (2006): 237–48.

Quiroz Chueca, Francisco. "Movimiento de tierra y de piso: el terremoto de 1746, la corrupción en el Callao y los cambios borbónicos." *Investigaciones Sociales* 3: 4 (1999): 37–50.

Ramos Gómez, Luis J. "Los intentos del virrey Eslava y del presidente Araujo en 1740 para obtener préstamos del comercio del Perú desplazado a Quito y la requisa de 100,000 pesos en 1741." *Revista de Indias* 63 (2003): 649–74.

Ramos Núñez, Carlos. *Toribio Pacheco: jurista peruano del siglo XIX.* Lima: Fondo Editorial Universidad Católica, 1993.

————. *Historia del Derecho Civil peruano, siglos XIX y XX: la codificación del siglo XIX, los códigos de la Confederación y el Código Civil de 1852.* Vol. 2. Lima: Fondo Editorial Universidad Católica, 2001.

————. *Historia del Derecho Civil peruano, siglos XIX y XX: los jurisconsultos El Murciélago y Francisco García Calderón.* Vol. 3. Lima: Fondo Editorial Universidad Católica, 2002.

Ramírez Gastón, J. M. *Política económica y financiera: Manuel Prado, sus gobiernos de 1939–45 y 1956–62. Apuntes para la historia económica.* Lima: Editorial Literaria La Confianza, 1969.

Real Academia Española. *Diccionario de la Real Academia Española.* Madrid: Imprenta de Francisco del Hierro, 1729; Madrid: Herederos de Francisco del Hierro, 1737.

Real Academia de la Historia. *Colección de documentos inéditos para la historia de España.* Madrid: Real Academia de la Historia, 1867.

Rénique, José Luis. *La batalla por Puno: conflicto agrario y nación en los Andes peruanos.* Lima: Instituto de Estudios Peruanos / Sur / Cepes, 2004.

Retamozo Linares, Alberto. *Responsabilidad civil del Estado por corrupción de funcionarios públicos.* Lima: N & S Editores, 2000.

Reyna, Carlos. *La anunciación de Fujimori: Alan García, 1985–1990.* Lima: Desco, 2000.

Richardson, Jeremy J., ed. *Pressure Groups.* Oxford: Oxford University Press, 1993.

Ricketts, Mónica. "Pens, Politics, and Swords: The Struggle for Power during the Breakdown of the Spanish Empire in Peru and Spain, 1760–1830." PhD diss., Harvard University, 2007.

Riva Agüero, José. *Exposición de don José de la Riva Agüero acerca de su conducta política en el tiempo que ejerció la presidencia de la República del Perú.* London: C. Wood, 1824.

Rivadeneyra, José G. *Breves observaciones sobre los derechos de Cochet y Landreau a propósito de la gran compañía Americana destinada a explotar el Perú.* Valparaíso, Chile: N.p., 1882.

Rivero, Francisco. *Reflexiones sobre una carta del doctor Luis Mesones publicada el 13 de diciembre de 1860 en el no. 6693 del periódico Comercio de Lima.* Paris: Imprenta Tipográfica de G. Kugelmann, 1861.

Rizo-Patrón, Paul. *Linaje, dote y poder: la nobleza de Lima de 1700 a 1850.* Lima: Fondo Editorial Universidad Católica, 2000.

———. "Las emigraciones de los súbditos realistas del Perú a España durante la crisis de la independencia." In *La independencia en el Perú: de los Borbones a Bolívar.* Edited by Scarlett O'Phelan, 407–28. Lima: Instituto Riva-Agüero, Pontificia Universidad Católica, 2001.

Robles Ascurra, César. *El ocaso de la década infame: el comienzo del fin del fujimorismo.* Lima: N.p., 2000.

Robles Egea, Antonio, ed. *Política en penumbra: patronazgo y clientelismo políticos en la España contemporánea.* Madrid: Siglo Veintiuno, 1996.

Robertson, John P., and William P. Robertson. *Letters on South America.* London: J. Murray, 1843.

Rodríguez, Eduardo ("Heduardo"). *La historia según Heduardo.* Lima: Empresa Editora Caretas, 1990.

Roniger, Luis, and Ayşe Güneş-Ayata, eds. *Democracy, Clientelism, and Civil Society.* Boulder, CO: Lynne Rienner, 1994.

Rosas, Francisco. *La verdad sobre el contrato Rosas-Goyeneche y sobre los contratos Piérola-Dreyfus.* Paris: Imprenta Hispano-Americana, 1881.

Rose-Ackerman, Susan. *Corruption and Government: Causes, Consequences, and Reform.* New York: Cambridge University Press, 1999.

Rosen, Keith, and Richard Downes. *Corruption and Political Reform in Brazil: The Impact of Collor's Impeachment.* Coral Gables, FL: North-South Center Press / University of Miami, 1999.

Rospigliosi, Fernando. *Montesinos y las Fuerzas Armadas: cómo controló durante una década las instituciones militares.* Lima: Instituto de Estudios Peruanos, 2000.

———. *El arte del engaño: las relaciones entre los militares y la prensa.* Lima: Tarea, 2000.

Rougemont, Philippe de. *Una pájina de la dictadura de D. Nicolás de Piérola.* Paris: Imprenta Cosmopolita, 1883.

Rubinstein, W. D. "The End of 'Old Corruption' in Britain 1780–1860." *Past and Present* 101 (1983): 5–86.

Rudolph, James D. *Peru: The Evolution of a Crisis.* Westport, CT: Praeger, 1992.

Ruzo, Daniel. *Los consignatarios del huano y muy especialmente los titulados nacionales según su propia confesión en los contratos de préstamos y prórrogas: doc-*

umentos oficiales para la historia financiera del Perú recogidos y publicados por el Dr. D. Daniel Ruzo. Lima: Imprenta de la Sociedad, 1870.

Sáenz-Rico, Alfredo. *El virrey Amat: precisiones sobre la vida y la obra de don Manuel de Amat y de Junyent.* 2 vols. Barcelona: Museo de Historia de la Ciudad, 1967.

———. "Las acusaciones contra el virrey del Perú, marqués de Castelldosrius, y sus 'noticias reservadas' (febrero 1709)." *Boletín Americanista,* no. 28 (1978): 119–35.

Saguier, Eduardo. "La corrupción administrativa como mecanismo de acumulación y engendrador de una burguesía comercial local." *Anuario de Estudios Americanos* 46 (1989): 261–303.

Sala i Vila, Núria. *Y se armó el tole tole: tributo indígena y movimientos sociales en el virreinato del Perú, 1784–1814.* Huamanga: Instituto de Estudios Rurales José María Arguedas, 1996.

———. "La escenificación del poder: el marqués de Castelldosrius, primer virrey Borbón del Perú (1707–1710)." *Anuario de Estudios Americanos* 61, no. 1 (2004): 31–68.

Salamanca, Bartolomé. "Relación de gobierno que forma Bartolomé María de Salamanca." *Boletín de la Sociedad Geográfica de Lima* 10 (1900): 207–36, 312–37.

Salazar Larraín, Arturo. *La herencia de Velasco, 1968–1975: el pueblo quedó atrás.* Lima: Desa, 1977.

Salinas Sedó, Jaime. *Desde el Real Felipe: en defensa de la democracia.* Lima: Mosca Azul, 1997.

Sampford, Charles, Arthur Shacklock, and Carmel Connors, eds. *Measuring Corruption.* Aldershot, Hampshire, England: Ashgate, 2006.

Sánchez, Luis Alberto. *Mito y realidad de González Prada.* Lima: P. L. Villanueva, 1976.

———. *Leguía: el dictador.* Lima: Editorial Pachacútec, 1993.

Sánchez Soler, Mariano. *Villaverde: fortuna y caída de la Casa Franco.* Barcelona: Planeta, 1990.

———. *Negocios privados con dinero público: el vademécum de la corrupción de los políticos españoles.* Madrid: Foca, 2003.

Sanz, Toribio. *Guano: comunicaciones importantes del Señor Toribio Sanz, Inspector General de las consignaciones de guano con el despacho de Hacienda y Comercio, públicas por acuerdo de la H. Cámara de Diputados.* Lima: Imprenta de El Comercio, 1868.

Saulniers, Alfred H. *Public Enterprises in Peru: Public Sector Growth and Reform.* Boulder, CO: Westview Press, 1988.

Savage, James D. "Corruption and Virtue at the Constitutional Convention." *Journal of Politics* 56 (1994): 174–86.

Schulte-Bockholt, Alfredo. *The Politics of Organized Crime and the Organized Crime of Politics.* Lanham, MD: Lexington Books, 2006.

Schydlowsky, Daniel. "The Tragedy of Lost Opportunity in Peru." In *Latin American Political Economy: Financial Crisis and Political Change.* Edited by Jonathan Hartlyn and Samuel Morley, 217–42. Boulder, CO: Westview Press, 1986.

———, and Juan Wicht, *Anatomía de un fracaso económico: Perú, 1968–1978.* Lima: Centro de Investigación de la Universidad del Pacífico, 1979.

Scott, James C. *Comparative Political Corruption.* Englewood Cliffs, NJ: Prentice-Hall, 1972.

Secada, C. Alexander G. de. "Arms, Guano, and Shipping: The W. R. Grace Interests in Peru, 1865–1885." *Business History Review* 59 (1985): 597–621.

Seligson, Mitchell. "The Impact of Corruption on Regime Legitimacy: A Comparative Study of Four Latin American Countries." *Journal of Politics* 64, no. 2 (2002): 408–33.

Seminario, Bruno, and Arlette Beltrán. *Crecimiento económico en el Perú: 1896–1995.* Lima: Centro de Investigación de la Universidad del Pacífico, 1998.

Shleifer, Andrei, and Robert Vishny. *The Grabbing Hand: Government Pathologies and Their Cures.* Cambridge: Cambridge University Press, 1998.

Simpson, Lesley Byrd. "Review of *Indian Labor in the Spanish Colonies* by Ruth Kerns Barber." *Hispanic American Historical Review* 13 (1933): 363–64.

Smith, Peter H. *Talons of Eagles: Dynamics of U.S.–Latin American Relations.* 2nd ed. New York: Oxford University Press, 2000.

Solano Pérez-Lila, Francisco de. *La pasión por reformar: Antonio de Ulloa, marino y científico 1716–1795.* Sevilla: Escuela de Estudios Hispano-Americanos / Universidad de Cádiz, 1999.

Socolow, Susan. *The Bureaucrats of Buenos Aires, 1769–1810: Amor al Real Servicio.* Durham, NC: Duke University Press, 1987.

Soler Serrano, Joaquín. *Pérez Jiménez se confiesa.* Barcelona: Ediciones Dronte, 1983.

Sorj, Bernardo. "Public Enterprises and the Question of the State Bourgeoisie, 1969–1976." In *Military Reformism and Social Classes: The Peruvian Experience, 1968–80.* Edited by David Booth and Bernardo Sorj, 72–93. New York: St. Martin's Press, 1983.

S.T. *Informe [sobre el contrabando].* Lima: Imprenta de José M. Masías, 1832.

Stapenhurst, Rick, and Sahr Kpundeh. *Curbing Corruption: Toward a Model for Building National Integrity.* Washington, DC: World Bank, 1999.

Stein, Stanley. "Bureaucracy and Business in Spanish America, 1759–1804: Failure of a Bourbon Reform in Mexico and Peru." *Hispanic American Historical Review* 61 (1981): 2–28.

Stein, Steve. *Populism in Peru: The Emergence of the Masses and Social Control.* Madison: University of Wisconsin Press, 1980.

Stewart, Watt. *Henry Meiggs: Yankee Pizarro.* Durham, NC: Duke University Press, 1946.

———. *Chinese Bondage in Peru: A History of the Chinese Coolie in Peru, 1849–1874.* Westport, CT: Greenwood Press, 1951.

Suárez, Margarita. *Comercio y fraude en el Perú colonial: las estrategias mercantiles de un banquero.* Lima: Instituto de Estudios Peruanos, 1995.

———. *Desafíos transatlánticos: mercaderes, banqueros y Estado en el Perú virreinal, 1600–1700.* Lima: Fondo Editorial Universidad Católica, 2001.

Tauro del Pino, Alberto. *Enciclopedia ilustrada del Perú.* 6 vols. Lima: Peisa, 1987.

Távara, Santiago. *Administración del huano escrita con motivo de la moción del H. Diputado por Parinacochas.* Lima: Imprenta de El Comercio, 1856.

TePaske, John J., and Herbert S. Klein, with Kendall Brown. *The Royal Treasuries of the Spanish Empire in America.* Vol. 1: *Peru.* Durham, NC: Duke University Press, 1982.

TePaske, John J., and Richard Garner. "Annual Silver Data: Colonial Lower and Upper Peru, 1559–1821." 2005. http://home.comcast.net/~richardgarner05/TPfiles/PeruS .xls.

Toledo Brückmann, Ernesto. *¿¡Hasta cuándo!?: la prensa peruana y el fin del fujimorato.* Lima: Editorial San Marcos, 2001.

Torres, Andrés. *La financiación irregular del PSOE: seguido de las armas del poder.* Barcelona: Ediciones de la Tempestad, 1993.

Torres Arancivia, Eduardo. *Corte de virreyes: el entorno del poder en el Perú del siglo XVII*. Lima: Fondo Editorial Universidad Católica, 2006.

Torres Paz, José Andrés. *La oligarquía y la crisis: disertación leída en la Sociedad "Jurídica–Literaria" en sesión del 29 de agosto de 1877*. Lima: Imprenta del Teatro, 1877.

Torrico, Joaquín. *Informe del fiscal de la Corte Central Sr. Coronel Joaquín Torrico en la vista de la causa Tratado Vivanco-Pareja de 27 de enero de 1865*. Lima: Imprenta del Estado por J. E. del Campo, 1867.

———. *Manifestación documentada que eleva al soberano Congreso de 1876 el Coronel Joaquín Torrico, en su carácter de la Comisión de Delegados Fiscales del Perú en Londres*. Lima: Imprenta de La Patria, 1877.

Trazegnies, Fernando de. *La idea del derecho en el Perú republicano del siglo XIX*. Lima: Fondo Editorial Universidad Católica, 1992.

Tristán, Flora. *Peregrinaciones de una paria, 1833–1834*. Edited by Fernando Rosas. Arequipa: Ediciones El Lector, 2003.

Turiso, Jesús. *Comerciantes españoles en la Lima borbónica: anatomía de una elite de poder (1701–1761)*. Valladolid: Universidad de Valladolid, 2002.

Ugarteche, Pedro. *Sánchez Cerro: papeles y recuerdos de un presidente del Perú*. Lima: Editorial Universitaria, 1969.

Ulloa Sotomayor, Alberto. *Don Nicolás de Piérola: una época en la historia del Perú*. Lima: Minerva, 1981.

Urquiza, José Manuel. *Corrupción municipal: por qué se produce y cómo evitarla*. Córdoba: Editorial Almuzara, 2005.

U.S. Congress. *Investigación acerca de la venta hecha por el gobierno de los Estados Unidos de los monitores Oneoto y Catawba hoy Manco-Cápac y Atahualpa*. Lima: Imprenta El Nacional, 1869.

———. House of Representatives. *The Situation in Peru and the Future of the War on Drugs: Joint Hearing before the Subcommittee on Western Hemisphere Affairs and Task Force on International Narcotics Control, 102nd Congress, 7 May 1992*. Washington, DC: Government Printing Office, 1992.

———. House of Representatives. Committee on Foreign Affairs. *Peru: U.S. Priorities and Policies: Hearing before the Subcommittee on Western Hemisphere Affairs of the Committee on Foreign Affairs, House of Representatives, 103rd Congress, 1st Session, March 10, 1993*. Washington, DC: Government Printing Office, 1993.

———. Senate. Committee on Finance. *Sale of Foreign Bonds or Securities in the United States. Hearings,* part 3, January 8–15, 1932. Washington, DC: Government Printing Office, 1932.

———. Senate. Special Committee to Investigate the Munitions Industry. *Munitions Industry: Hearings . . . Seventy-Third Congress Pursuant to S. Res. 206, a Resolution to Make Certain Investigations Concerning the Manufacture and Sale of Arms and Other War Munitions,* part 1 (September 4, 5, and 6, 1934, Electric Boat Co.). Washington, DC: Government Printing Office, 1934.

U.S. Department of State. *Papers Relating to the Foreign Relations of the United States*. 1872-1931. Washington, DC: Government Printing Office, 1873–1947.

———. *Foreign Relations of the United States: Diplomatic Papers*. 1932–1945. Washington, DC: Government Printing Office, 1947–1969.

———. *Foreign Relations of the United States*. 1946-1968. Washington: Government Printing Office, 1969–2004.

Valdivia, Juan Gualberto. *Memorias sobre las revoluciones de Arequipa desde 1834 hasta 1866.* Lima: Imprenta de La Opinión Nacional, 1874.

Varela, Consuelo. *La caída de Cristóbal Colón.* Edited and transcribed by Isabel Aguirre. Madrid: Marcial Pons, 2006.

Vargas Haya, Héctor. *Contrabando.* Lima: Offset Peruana, 1976.

———. *Defraudadores y contrabandistas.* Lima: Nueva Educación, 1980.

———. *Democracia o farsa.* Lima: Atlántida, 1984.

———. *Frustración democrática y corrupción en el Perú.* Lima: Editorial Milla Batres, 1994.

———. *Hacia la reforma del Estado: camino a la segunda república.* Lima: Edigrama, 2001.

———. *Perú: 184 años de corrupción e impunidad.* Lima: Editorial Rocío, 2005.

Vargas Llosa, Álvaro. *La contenta barbarie: el fin de la democracia en el Perú y la futura revolución liberal como esperanza de la América Latina.* Barcelona: Editorial Planeta, 1993.

———. *Liberty for Latin America: How to Undo Five Hundred Years of State Opression.* New York: Farrar, Straus and Giroux, 2005.

Vargas Llosa, Mario. *La ciudad y los perros.* Barcelona: Seix Barral, 1963.

———. *La casa verde.* Barcelona: Seix Barral, 1966.

———. *Conversación en la Catedral.* Barcelona: Seix Barral, 1969.

———. *Contra viento y marea (1962–1982).* Barcelona: Seix Barral, 1983.

———. "A Fish Out of the Water." *Granta* 36 (1991): 15–75.

———. *El pez en el agua: memorias.* Barcelona: Seix Barral, 1993.

Varón, Rafael. *La ilusión del poder: apogeo y decadencia de los Pizarro en la conquista del Perú.* Lima: Instituto de Estudios Peruanos / Instituto Francés de Estudios Andinos, 1996.

Vásquez, Enrique. *Estrategias del poder: grupos económicos en el Perú.* Lima: Centro de Investigación de la Universidad del Pacífico, 2000.

Vásquez Bazán, César. *La propuesta olvidada.* Lima: Okura Editores, 1987.

Velarde, Julio, and Martha Rodríguez. *Impacto macro económico de los gastos militares en el Perú, 1960–1987.* Lima: Centro de Investigación de la Universidad del Pacífico / Apep, 1989.

Velarde, Manuel. *El General Velarde ex-ministro de Gobierno y el contrato Grace.* Lima: Imprenta de La Época, 1886.

Vidal, Francisco. "Memoria escrita en 1855, después de la Batalla de La Palma." *Fénix: Revista de la Biblioteca Nacional* 6 (1949): 595–640.

Villanueva, Armando, and Guillermo Thorndike. *La gran persecución (1932–1956).* Lima: Correo-Epensa, 2004.

Villanueva, Víctor. *El militarismo en el Perú.* Lima: Imprenta Scheuch, 1962.

———. *El Ejército peruano: del caudillaje anárquico al militarismo reformista.* Lima: Editorial Juan Mejía Baca, 1973.

———. *La sublevación aprista del 48.* Lima: Milla Batres, 1973.

———. *El APRA en busca del poder.* Lima: Editorial Horizonte, 1975.

———. "The Petty-Bourgeois Ideology of the Peruvian Aprista Party." *Latin American Perspectives* 4 (1977): 57–76.

———. "The Military in Peruvian Politics, 1919–1945." In *The Politics of Antipolitics: The Military in Latin America.* Edited by Brian Loveman and Thomas Davies. Lincoln: University of Nebraska, 1989.

Villegas, Julio. *La crisis moral.* Tésis doctoral, Facultad de Jurisprudencia, Universidad de la Libertad. Trujillo, Peru: Tipografía Olaya, 1915.

Walker, Charles. *Smoldering Ashes: Cuzco and the Creation of Republican Peru, 1780–1840.* Durham, NC: Duke University Press, 1999.

Walker, Geoffrey. *Spanish Politics and Imperial Trade, 1700–1789.* Bloomington: Indiana University Press, 1979.

Wallis, John Joseph. "The Concept of Systematic Corruption in American History." In *Corruption and Reform: Lessons from America's Economic History.* Edited by Edward Glaeser and Claudia Goldin, 23–62. Chicago: University of Chicago Press, 2006.

Waquet, Jean-Claude. *Corrruption: Ethics and Power in Florence, 1600–1700.* Cambridge, MA: Polity Press, 1991.

———. "Some Considerations on Corruption, Politics, and Society in Sixteenth and Seventeenth Century Italy." In *Political Corruption in Europe and Latin America.* Edited by Walter Little and Eduardo Posada-Carbó, 21–40. London: Macmillan, 1996.

Ward, Peter, ed. *Corruption, Development, and Inequality: Soft Touch or Hard Graft?* London: Routledge, 1989.

Wei, Shang-Jin. "Impact of Corruption on Levels of International Investment." In *El Estado y la sociedad civil en la lucha contra la corrupción,* 51-67. Lima: Ministerio Público, 1999.

Weyland, Kurt. "The Politics of Corruption in Latin America." *Journal of Democracy* 9 (1998): 108–21.

Whitaker, Arthur Preston. "Antonio de Ulloa." *Hispanic American Historical Review* 15 (1935): 155–94.

———. "Documents: Jorge Juan and Antonio de Ulloa's Prologue to Their Secret Report of 1749 on Peru." *Hispanic American Historical Review* 18 (1938): 507–13.

———. *The Huancavelica Mercury Mine: A Contribution to the History of the Bourbon Renaissance in the Spanish Empire.* Cambridge, MA: Harvard University Press, 1941.

Whitehead, Laurence. "On Presidential Graft: The Latin American Evidence." In *Corruption: Causes, Consequences, and Control.* Edited by Michael Clarke, 142–62. New York: St. Martin's Press, 1983.

———. "High-Level Political Corruption in Latin America: A 'Transitional' Phenomenon?" In *Combating Corruption in Latin America.* Edited by Joseph Tulchin and Ralph Espach, 107–29. Washington, DC: Woodrow Wilson Center Press and Johns Hopkins University Press, 2000.

Wiener F., Raúl A. *La venta sucia: la privatización de Petroperú como fraude a la nación.* Lima: N.p., 1996.

———. *Bandido Fujimori: el reeleccionista.* 2nd ed. Lima: WWW Editores, 2001.

Williams, Robert, and Alan Doig, eds. *Controlling Corruption.* Cheltenham, England, and Northampton, MA: Edward Elgar, 2000.

Wilson, Graham K. *Interest Groups.* Oxford: Basil Blackwell, 1990.

Wise, Carol. *Reinventando el Estado: estrategia económica y cambio institucional en el Perú.* Lima: Universidad del Pacífico, 2003.

Witt, Heinrich. *Diario y observaciones sobre el Perú (1824–1890).* Translated by Kika Garland de Montero, prologue by Pablo Macera. Lima: Cofide, 1987.

———. *Diario 1824–1890: un testimonio personal sobre el Perú del siglo XIX.* 2 vols. Translated by Gladys Flores-Estrada Garland. Lima: Banco Mercantil, 1992.

Witt & Schutte. *Consignatarios del guano.* Lima, 1867.

Woy-Hazelton, Sandra, and William Hazelton. "Sustaining Democracy in Peru: Dealing with Parliamentary and Revolutionary Changes." In *Liberalization and Redemocratization in Latin America.* Edited by George Lopez and Michael Stohl, 105–35. Westport, CT: Greenwood Press, 1987.

Wu, Celia. *Generals and Diplomats: Great Britain and Peru, 1820–40.* Cambridge: Centre of Latin American Studies, University of Cambridge, 1991.

Yepes del Castillo, Ernesto. *Perú 1820–1920: un siglo de desarrollo capitalista.* Lima: Instituto de Estudios Peruanos, 1972.

Youngers, Coletta, Eileen Rosin, and Lucien O. Chauvin. "Drug Paradoxes: The U.S. Government and Peru's Vladimiro Montesinos." *Drug War Monitor* 3 (July 2004): 1–18.

Zegarra, Luis Felipe. *Causas y consecuencias de la corrupción: un análisis teórico y empírico.* Lima: Centro de Investigación de la Universidad del Pacífico, 2000.

Periodicals

Caretas. Lima, 1950–2007.

Correo. Lima, 1986–2007.

El Cascabel. Lima, 1872–1873.

El Comercio. Lima, 1839–2007.

El Peruano. Lima, 1855–2007.

El Republicano. Arequipa, 1825–1827.

Fray K Bezón. Lima, 1907–1908.

Gaceta del Gobierno. Lima, 1835.

La Campana. Lima, 1867.

La Gaceta del Congreso. Lima, 2003–2007.

La República. Lima, 1982–2007.

La Sanción. Lima, 1933.

La Zamacueca Política. Lima, 1859.

Liberación. Lima, 2000-2005.

Mercurio Peruano. Lima, 1827–1840.

New York Times. New York, 1851–2007.

Perú.21. Lima, 2002–2007.

Rochabús. Lima, 1957–1958.

Suácate. Lima, 1945.

Variedades. Lima, 1908–1932.

Index